Brief Contents

Successful College Writing

SKILLS · STRATEGIES · LEARNING STYLES

6th edition

Successful College Writing

SKILLS • STRATEGIES • LEARNING STYLES

KATHLEEN T. MCWHORTER
Niagara County Community College

BEDFORD/ST. MARTIN'S
Boston • New York

For Bedford/St. Martin's

Vice President, Editorial, Macmillan Higher Education Humanities: *Edwin Hill*

Editorial Director for English and Music: *Karen S. Henry*

Publisher for Composition and Business and Technical Writing
and Developmental Writing: *Leasa Burton*

Executive Developmental Editor: *Jane Carter*

Executive Editor for Rhetorics and Business Tech Writing: *Molly Parke*

Production Editor: *Kendra LeFleur*

Senior Production Supervisor: *Jennifer Wetzel*

Marketing Manager: *Emily Rowan*

Associate Editor: *Leah Rang*

Copy Editor: *Beverly Miller*

Indexer: *Steve Cspike*

Photo Researcher: *Sheri Blaney*

Director of Rights and Permissions: *Hilary Newman*

Senior Art Director: *Anna Palchik*

Text Design: *Castle Design*

Cover Design: *Marine Miller*

Cover Art: *Shade* (acrylic on board) by Sara Hayward/Private Collection/
Bridgeman Images

Composition: *Graphic World*

Printing and Binding: *RR Donnelly*

Manufactured in the United States of America.

1   0   9   8   7   6
f   e   d   c   b   a

For information, write: Bedford/St. Martin's, 75 Arlington Street, Boston, MA 02116
(617-399-4000)

ISBN 978-1-319-08774-6 (Student Edition with Handbook)
ISBN 978-1-319-08775-3 (Student Edition without Handbook)
ISBN 978-1-4576-8437-1 (Instructor's Annotated Edition)

Acknowledgments

Other texts assume that first-year composition students already possess the basic skills they will need to succeed in college, but my own experience tells me that this is not true. That is why I wrote *Successful College Writing*. It uses a unique, highly visual, student-centered approach to teach students the reading and study skills they need while guiding them through the writing strategies and activities that form the core of composition instruction. The overwhelmingly positive response to the first five editions demonstrates that *Successful College Writing* fulfills an important need.

The sixth edition continues to meet students where they are and get them where they need to go by building on the strengths of earlier editions while recognizing changes to the first-year composition course, including increasing emphasis on assessment, common core implementation in high school and earlier, course redesign, and the placement of developing writers into first-year composition classes.

PROVEN FEATURES OF *SUCCESSFUL COLLEGE WRITING*

True to its goal of offering more coverage of essential skills, *Successful College Writing* provides abundant guidance and support for inexperienced writers along with thorough help with reading and study skills. Every chapter of *Successful College Writing* provides practical, student-oriented instruction, along with extra help for those students who need it.

PRACTICAL, STEP-BY-STEP WRITING ASSIGNMENTS

Successful College Writing provides the tools to approach writing as a flexible, multifaceted process, alleviating some of the frustration students often feel.

Part 1 begins this process by emphasizing the importance of writing to students' success in college and career, and it alerts students to the expectations their college instructors will have for them as writers. It emphasizes reading and critical thinking skills, including coverage of thinking critically about and responding to both texts and images and reading to write.

Part 2 provides detailed coverage of the writing process—from choosing and narrowing a topic and generating ideas to developing and supporting a thesis, drafting essays and paragraphs, revising, editing, and proofreading. Each chapter in Part 2 includes the following:

- plenty of skill-building exercises, many of them collaborative,
- a writing-in-progress sample essay following a student writer through the various stages of drafting and revision, and
- Essay-in-Progress activities that lead students through each step in writing an essay.

Parts 3 and 4 cover the patterns of development that students encounter most frequently in college and on the job, including a new chapter on reading and writing essays that use multiple rhetorical modes. Guided Writing Assignments in each chapter — now streamlined, with a more graphic layout — lead students step by step through the process of writing a particular type of essay, giving student writers the support they need, whether they are working in class or on their own. Instructors will also find these reimagined assignments easier to teach, as they emphasize activities for generating and evaluating ideas, developing a thesis, organizing and drafting the essay, revising, and editing.

Part 5 provides instruction for writing the research project, including information about finding useful and reliable sources, synthesizing information and ideas from sources to support the writer's ideas, and incorporating and documenting material borrowed from sources.

Part 6 covers writing in academic and business settings, from writing about literature, taking essay exams, and creating a portfolio to making presentations and writing résumés, job application letters, and business emails.

APPEALING, HELPFUL VISUALS

Because inexperienced writers are often more comfortable with images than with text, *Successful College Writing* employs a visual approach to writing instruction. Look for the following visual aids throughout the book:

- **Writing Quick Starts** jumpstart each chapter, providing engaging images for students to respond to in writing, introducing them to the main topic of the chapter.
- **Graphic Organizers** — charts that display relationships among ideas — offer tools both for analyzing readings and for planning and revising essays, and they present students with an alternative to traditional outlines.
- **Guided Writing Assignments** — now in a streamlined, step-by-step, visual format — walk students through the process of writing essays in each of the rhetorical modes.
- **Revision Flowcharts** help students systematically read and revise their own essays as well as review those of their peers.
- **Visualizing the Reading** activities give students a simple way to chart key features of the reading, with the first part of each chart done for them to provide guidance.
- Numerous **figures**, **photographs**, **boxes**, and **bulleted lists** throughout the text reinforce key points and summarize information.

IMPROVING READING SKILLS: A FIVE-PRONGED APPROACH

Recognizing that students frequently enter first-year writing courses without the active and critical reading skills they need to succeed in first-year composition and all their college courses, *Successful College Writing* supports students with a five-pronged approach to improving their reading skills that will also help students become better writers. This five-pronged approach includes:

1. **Overt reading instruction in Chapters 3 and 4**, including a Guide to Active Reading and a Guide to Responding to Text in Chapter 3, and detailed coverage of reading both text and visuals critically in Chapter 4

2. **Activities to foster critical reading** following readings in Parts 3 and 4 and in LearningCurve, Bedford/St Martin's adaptive quizzing program. (Activities on eleven core topics are available free with each new book; for more information, see p. xix.)
3. **Graphic organizers** in Parts 3 and 4 that help students recognize the structure of the essay
4. **Collaborative activities** to enhance critical reading
5. **Peer review–style activities and revision flowcharts**, which can be used for peer review, to emphasize reading/thinking critically

Over the years, my work with students has convinced me that skills taught in isolation are seldom learned well or applied, so each of the chapters on the patterns of development in Parts 3 and 4 reinforces the reading skills taught in Chapters 3 and 4. As students develop their writing skills by writing a particular type of essay, they simultaneously learn practical strategies for reading that type of essay.

ATTENTION TO STUDY SKILLS

Students need practical survival strategies that they can use not only in their writing course but also in all their college courses. Chapter 1 includes advice on such critical topics as the following:

- time management,
- assessing and managing stress,
- academic integrity, and
- working with classmates.

Chapter 26 includes practical advice on preparing for and taking essay examinations, and Chapter 27 offers practical advice on crafting and delivering a presentation.

HIGH-INTEREST READINGS

In addition to guidelines for reading different types of texts, *Successful College Writing* includes reading selections from the diverse array of texts students are likely to encounter in their personal, academic, and professional lives. Since students who enjoy what they read become more proficient readers, the selections in this text were carefully chosen not only to function as strong rhetorical models but also to interest students. Selections come from such well-known writers as Bill Bryson, Mary Roach, and Brent Staples, and address intriguing topics from animal intelligence to how our possessions define us. Compelling e-readings (available through LaunchPad; see p. xxiii) include selections such as a narrative by Nobel Prize–winning geneticist Paul Nurse in which he announces his own surprising genetic history and an animated video analyzing the contents of a favorite morning beverage.

COMPREHENSIVE COVERAGE OF RESEARCH AND DOCUMENTATION

Because finding and evaluating useful sources has become so challenging in the digital age and because of the ease with which writers can copy and paste information from sources into their own writing, *Successful College Writing* provides three full chapters (Part 5) on writing with sources, including a careful discussion of accidental plagiarism and paraphrasing without "patchwriting," supporting the writer's own ideas, and coverage of documenting sources in MLA and APA styles.

THOROUGH REFERENCE HANDBOOK

The handbook in Part 7 covers basic grammar, sentence problems, punctuation, mechanics, spelling, and ESL troublespots and includes the following:

- hand-corrected examples to make needed revisions easy to understand,
- key grammatical terms defined in the margin,
- helpful revision flowcharts and summary boxes, and
- sentence and paragraph exercises.

It also reinforces students' learning with plenty of opportunities for practice, with exercises in the text, a booklet of additional exercises (ISBN 978-1-4576-8445-6) keyed to the handbook, and supplemental practice through LearningCurve, Bedford/St. Martin's adaptive quizzing program, with activities on eleven core topics available in LaunchPad (free when packaged with the book). A collection of supplemental exercises, keyed to the handbook in the full edition of *Successful College Writing*, is also available.

A UNIQUE EMPHASIS ON LEARNING STYLES

Students learn in different ways, yet most writing texts do not take these differences in learning style into account. In this text, I focus on four learning styles that are relevant for writing:

- verbal versus spatial,
- creative versus pragmatic,
- concrete versus abstract, and
- social versus independent.

A brief questionnaire in Chapter 2 enables students to assess their learning styles. Recognizing that no one strategy works for every student, the text includes a variety of methods for generating ideas and revising an essay.

ATTENTION TO OUTCOMES

Successful College Writing helps students build proficiency in the four categories of learning that writing programs across the country use to assess student work:

- rhetorical knowledge,
- critical thinking, reading, and composing,
- processes, and
- knowledge of conventions.

For a table that correlates the Council of Writing Program Administrators (WPA) outcomes to features of *Successful College Writing,* see pages xvi–xxiii.

NEW TO THE SIXTH EDITION

The main goal of the revision — based on feedback from experienced instructors familiar with the needs of today's students — was to focus on four key areas:

1. Reading and thinking critically, including reading to write, synthesis, using
   research to support the students' own ideas, and other skills so necessary to
   writing effectively in college
2. Readability of the instructional text, so important to conveying key concepts
   that students will need to apply and practice throughout the course
3. Updated content and selections that students will find engaging and relevant,
   that reflect current practices and the kinds of readings students are likely to
   encounter in other classes, and that make good rhetorical models, including
   compelling professional selections and effective student essays
4. Online selections, tutorials, and practice that take advantage of what the Web
   can do to reinforce key concepts, reach resistant readers, and appeal to students
   with nonverbal learning styles

I address these core areas through the following new or enhanced features:

New! More writing, right from the beginning. Chapter 1 now includes a reading
selection, "The New Marshmallow Test: Students Can't Resist Multitasking," that
addresses an issue pertinent to many students' success in college. This relevant reading
selection in the first chapter provides students with the opportunity to practice reading
and responding right from the beginning.

New! Enhanced coverage of synthesis. Because synthesizing ideas is crucial to
writing effectively in college, the text now offers even more coverage of synthesis:

- Chapter 3 shows students how to synthesize a writer's ideas with their own to
  create a thoughtful response.
- Chapter 4 demonstrates how students can use synthesis to challenge and inter-
  rogate a text.
- Chapter 5 provides instruction on using synthesis as a way to discover ideas
  about a topic.
- Chapter 6 shows students how to use synthesis to generate a working thesis.
- Chapters 11 to 21 end with a box that encourages students to synthesize ideas
  across readings. These boxes include activities and essay assignment ideas to give
  students practice in this important skill.
- Chapter 22 highlights synthesis as an expectation implicit in all researched
  writing.
- Chapter 23 emphasizes the role synthesis plays in joining the conversation on a
  topic.
- Chapter 24 emphasizes the role of synthesis in writing the research project,
  including using synthesis categories or a graphic organizer to organize ideas and
  evidence and write the project.
- Chapter 26 suggests using synthesis as a study strategy.

New! Enhanced coverage of critical thinking and reading to write. Chapter 3 has been revised to focus readers' attention on reading to write, with a new Guide to Responding to Text that helps students analyze the response assignment, synthesize the writer's ideas with the student's own ideas, and analyze the reading in order to respond in writing. The chapter also includes coverage of analyzing student essays in preparation for the kind of peer-review activities common to the composition classroom. Chapter 4 has been expanded to help students learn to approach texts of all kinds with a critical eye, providing new strategies in each of the following areas:

- examining the author's use of inference,
- analyzing how the author uses evidence to support opinion,
- analyzing the author's tone and use of language, including connotation and figurative language, as well as of euphemisms and doublespeak,
- examining the assumptions and generalizations the author makes, and
- using patterns of development and synthesis to think critically about text.

New! A chapter on mixing the patterns. Because most writing, especially the writing students will be reading in college courses, uses more than one pattern of development, Part 3 now opens with a chapter that provides an overview of the patterns and shows how writers use multiple patterns to achieve their purposes with their readers. It guides students in choosing a primary pattern that best helps them achieve their purpose and convey their message, and shows them how to use secondary patterns to further develop their ideas and make them compelling for readers.

New! More visual, concise, and easy-to read format. The entire book has been edited to make instructional content easier to access and absorb, with more direct prose, more scannable lists, and more highlighting and annotating to help students glean what is important at a glance. The Guided Writing Assignments, too, have been converted into a more visual, step-by-step, graphic format, to enable students to get an overview of the entire process, and identify more readily those portions to which they need to pay particular attention.

New! Updated professional and student readings. The print book includes nineteen new professional reading selections and five new essays by student writers. The new readings deal with important contemporary issues, such as why we can't learn effectively while multitasking, why we can't resist junk food, and how the labels we're assigned come to define us. Accessible scholarly selections, such as "The Psychology of Stuff and Things" and "Dining in the Dark," as well as selections by renowned scholars such as Franz de Waal, Sherry Turkle, and Amitai Etzioni, give students practice with the kinds of readings they will be expected to tackle in college courses, with some also demonstrating effective use of sources. The five new student essays discuss topics such as a Mexican student's experience of "being double," privacy in a surveillance culture, the uses and abuses of Facebook, and the effects of file sharing on the music business.

New multimedia readings in LaunchPad (available free when packaged with the book) — one for each of the ten rhetorical modes plus one that demonstrates a mixing of modes — range from a video narrative about a surprising, if accidental, revelation to a podcast that explains why movie sound effects have become so gruesome.

New! **Updated coverage of research writing.** Revised coverage of research writing in Part 5 now emphasizes the importance of using sources to make the student's own ideas convincing to readers. This emphasis can be seen in coverage of:

- choosing the types of sources (primary versus secondary, scholarly versus popular versus reference, books versus articles versus media) that are most appropriate to the writing situation,
- evaluating sources for relevance and reliability, using the critical reading tools covered in Part 1,
- working with sources to take careful and useful notes that avoid plagiarism and include source information,
- working with sources to evaluate notes and synthesize information from sources to create original work, and
- structuring a supporting paragraph in a research project to make sure each body paragraph states the student's idea, uses information from sources to support that idea, explains how the source information relates to the student's main point, and uses in-text citations to clearly differentiate the student's ideas from those of the source authors.

New online tutorials in LaunchPad demonstrate how to avoid plagiarism and how to cite just about anything, and LearningCurve activities provide useful practice in working with sources. Both the online tutorials and LearningCurve activities in eleven core topics are available free when LaunchPad is packaged with the text.

New! **Updated coverage of online presentations and business writing.** Chapter 27 has been updated to include a revised discussion of best practices for making presentations using PowerPoint and Prezi. Coverage of business writing now emphasizes writing and delivering business correspondence online.

ACKNOWLEDGMENTS

A number of instructors and students from across the country have helped me to develop and revise *Successful College Writing*. I would like to express my gratitude to the following instructors, who served as members of the advisory board for the first edition. They provided detailed, valuable comments and suggestions about the manuscript as well as student essays and additional help and advice during its development: Marvin Austin, Columbia State Community College; Sarah H. Harrison, Tyler Junior College; Dan Holt, Lansing Community College; Michael Mackey, Community College of Denver; Lucille M. Schultz, University of Cincinnati; Sue Serrano, Sierra College; Linda R. Spain, Linn-Benton Community College; and Jacqueline Zimmerman, Lewis and Clark Community College. I would also like to thank the following instructors and their students, who class-tested chapters from *Successful College Writing* and provided valuable feedback about how its features and organization worked in the classroom: Mary Applegate, D'Youville College; Michael Hricik, Westmoreland County Community College; Lee Brewer Jones, DeKalb College; Edwina Jordan, Illinois Central College; Susan H. Lassiter, Mississippi College; Mildred C. Melendez, Sinclair Community College; Steve Rayshich, Westmoreland County Community College;

Barbara J. Robedeau, San Antonio College; and Deanna White, University of Texas at San Antonio.

I am indebted to the valuable research conducted by George Jensen, John DiTiberio, and Robert Sternberg on learning-style theory that informs the pedagogy of this book. For their comments on the coverage of learning styles in this text, I would like to thank John DiTiberio, Saint Louis University; Ronald A. Sudol, Oakland University; and Thomas C. Thompson, The Citadel. My thanks go to Mary Jane Feldman, Niagara County Community College, for designing the field test of the Learning Styles Inventory and conducting the statistical analysis of the results. I would also like to thank the instructors and students who participated in a field test of the Learning Styles Inventory: Laurie Warshal Cohen, Seattle Central Community College; Lee Brewer Jones, DeKalb College; Edwina Jordan, Illinois Central College; Jennifer Manning, John Jay College; Mildred Melendez, Sinclair Community College; Paul Resnick, Illinois Central College; and Deanna M. White, University of Texas at San Antonio.

I benefited from the experience of those instructors who reviewed the fifth edition and the manuscript for the sixth edition, and I am grateful for their thoughtful comments and helpful advice:

Irene Anders, Indiana University–Purdue University Fort Wayne; Angie Asmussen, Oklahoma State University Institute of Technology; Kathryn Benchoff, Hagerstown Community College; Mary Bowman, University of Wisconsin–Stevens Point; Bridget Brennan, Prince George; Mark Brock-Cancellieri, Harford Community College; Darci Cather, South Texas College; Mary Cavanaugh, Harford Community College; Sharon Cavusgil, Georgia State University; Michelle Conklin, Harford Community College; Michel de Benedictis, Miami Dade College; William Donovan, Idaho State University; William Duffy, Francis Marion University; Marsha Elyn Wright, Garden City Community College; Candice Floyd, Prince George's Community College; Laura Fox, Harford Community College; Linda Gary, Tyler Junior College; Edward Glenn, Miami Dade College; Michelle Green, Prince George; Danielle Griffin, Shelton State Community College; Courtney Harned, University of Maryland–Eastern Shore; Candice Hill, Montgomery College; Katherine Hoerth, University of Texas–Pan American; Vicki Holmes, University of Nevada–Las Vegas; Jay Johnson, Gateway Technical College; Michael Johnson, Muskegon Community College; Beth Jones, Wor-Wic Community College; Ken Kerr, Frederick Community College; Eric Leuschner, Fort Hays State University; Mitzi Litton, Concord University; Meredith Love-Steinmetz, Francis Marion University; Melinda May, Hagerstown Community College; Torria Norman, Black Hawk College; Summerlin Page, Central Carolina Community College; Karen Patterson, Ohio University; Charles Porter, Wor-Wic Community College; Ben Railton, Fitchburg State University; Alison Reynolds, University of Florida; Gina Santoro, Community College of Rhode Island; Arvis Scott, McLennan Community College; Stacy Seibert, Waukesha County Technical College; Lisa Shaw, Miami Dade College; Laurie Sherman, Community College of Rhode Island; Bonnie Startt, Tidewater Community College; Rebecca Stephens, University of Wisconsin–Stevens Point; Saralyn E. Summer, Georgia Perimeter College; Lori Truman, Kilgore College; Leslie Umschweis, Broward College; Victor Uszerowicz, Miami-Dade College; Jennifer Vanags, Gateway Technical College; Samantha Veneruso, Montgomery College; Scott West, Harford Community College; Concetta Williams, Chicago State University.

I also want to thank Elizabeth Gruchala-Gilbert for her research assistance, Charlotte Smith for her revision of the Teaching Tips that appear in the Instructor's Annotated Edition of the book and for writing the reading comprehension quizzes, and Jamey Gallagher for writing new material on teaching a co-requisite (or *ALP*) course alongside a freshman writing course. I also want to thank Kathy Tyndall for her valuable assistance in helping me revise portions of the manuscript.

Many people at Bedford/St. Martin's have contributed to the creation and development of *Successful College Writing*. Each person with whom I have worked is a true professional: Each demonstrates high standards and expertise; each is committed to producing a book focused on student needs.

My thanks to Denise Wydra, former president of Bedford/St. Martin's, for overseeing the project and making valuable contributions to the revision. I value her editorial experience and appreciate her creative energy. Joan Feinberg, formerly co-president of Macmillan Higher Education, has been another trusted advisor. I also must thank Molly Parke, executive editor for rhetorics and business/tech writing, for her forthright advice and for valuable assistance in making some of the more difficult decisions about the book. Special thanks to Melissa Skepko-Masi, new media editor, for her careful and talented work on the new e-book version.

I also appreciate the advice and guidance that Emily Rowin in the marketing department at Bedford/St. Martin's has provided at various junctures in the revision of this text. Leah Rang, associate editor, has helped improve and prepare the manuscript in innumerable ways. Kendra LeFleur, production editor, deserves special recognition for guiding this revision through the production process.

I owe the largest debt of gratitude to Jane Carter, my developmental editor, for her valuable guidance and assistance in preparing this revision. Her careful editing and attention to detail have strengthened the sixth edition significantly. She helped me to reinforce the book's strengths and to retain its focus on providing extra help to the student. Finally, I must thank the many students who inspired me to write this book. From them I have learned how to teach, and they have shown me how they think and learn. My students, then, have made the largest contribution to this book, for without them I would have little to say and no reason to write.

Kathleen T. McWhorter

Features of *Successful College Writing*, 6e, Correlated to the Writing Program Administrators (WPA) Outcomes Statement (2014)

Desired Student Outcomes	Relevant Features of *Successful College Writing*
Rhetorical Knowledge	
Learn and use key theoretical concepts through analyzing and composing a variety of texts.	• Chapter 1: Covers academic expectations (pp. 2–20). • Chapter 2: Discusses the range of settings in which college students will be expected to write, the types of writing college students are likely to encounter, and the kinds of writing employees are likely to be expected to produce (p. 25); strategies for succeeding in a range of writing situations, especially writing in college (pp. 25–30). • Chapter 3: Offers advice for reading academic and other challenging texts, including instruction on active reading (previewing, annotating, summarizing, and keeping a response journal) and critical reading (pp. 40–72). • Chapter 4: Offers advice for reading texts and visuals critically, including drawing reasonable inferences (pp. 74–75), assessing the evidence (pp. 76–77), distinguishing fact from opinion (p. 78), analyzing the author's language (pp. 78–81), and reading photos and graphics actively and critically (pp. 88–95). • Chapters in Parts 3 and 4: Includes reading selections for a variety of audiences, from popular to more scholarly, followed by scaffolded apparatus to help students read actively and critically (see, for example, "The Psychology of Stuff and Things," pp. 356–61); writing essays using a variety of rhetorical modes (see the Guided Writing Assignment and student essay in Chapter 15, pp. 343–48, for example); "Scenes from College and the Workplace" boxes (for example, on p. 264). Also includes multimedia selections (one per mode), on topics from across the disciplines (via LaunchPad*). • Part 5: Offers advice for writing using sources and citing sources in MLA and APA style. • Part 6: Offers advice about writing in specific academic contexts (Chapter 25, "Reading and Writing about Literature"; Chapter 26, "Essay Examinations and Portfolios"); and about writing in the workplace (Chapter 27, "Multimedia Presentations and Business Writing").
Gain experience reading and composing in several genres to understand how genre conventions shape and are shaped by readers' and writers' practices and purposes.	• Chapter 2: Covers reading a syllabus (pp. 26–28). • Chapter 3: Covers reading and analyzing different genres, including the writing of other students (pp. 40–72). • Chapter 4: Offers instruction in reading texts critically and reading visuals (both images and graphics) actively and critically (pp. 73–96). • Chapters 20–21: Covers reading arguments (pp. 499–525) and writing arguments (pp. 526–56). • Chapter 24: Covers writing a research project, with example research projects in MLA and APA style (pp. 598–656). • Chapter 25: Writing literary analyses, with sample essays (pp. 658–88) • Chapter 26: Covers writing essay examinations, with sample essay answers (pp. 689–98). • Chapter 27: Covers creating multimedia presentations using presentation slides (PowerPoint and Prezi) (pp. 706–13); writing résumés and job application letters; and writing in electronic media for business (pp. 713–18).

*Additional resource, available free when packaged with the text. See p. xxiii for details.

cont.

Desired Student Outcomes	Relevant Features of *Successful College Writing*
Rhetorical Knowledge	
Develop facility in responding to a variety of situations and contexts calling for purposeful shifts in voice, tone, level of formality, design, medium, and/or structure.	• Chapter 4: Covers reading critically, particularly by paying attention to the author's use of language (pp. 78–81). • Chapter 5: Offers techniques for generating ideas that are appropriate to the writing situation (pp. 98–117). • Chapter 10: Offers instruction on editing words and sentences, including editing to create an appropriate tone and level of diction (pp. 206–11). • Chapter 24: Covers appropriate formats for writing a paper using sources, in MLA and APA style (pp. 598–656). • Chapter 27: Covers appropriate business writing formats and styles for résumés, job application letters, and electronic business correspondence (pp. 713–18); appropriate design and formatting of slides in presentation software, such as PowerPoint and Prezi (pp. 706–13).
Understand and use a variety of technologies to address a range of audiences.	• Chapter 4 (via LaunchPad*): Includes tutorials in critical reading and digital writing; LearningCurve activities in critical reading, topic sentences and supporting details, topics and main ideas, and issues of correctness. • Chapter 10: Discusses computer-aided proofreading (including the pitfall of relying too heavily on spell-check and grammar-check software (p. 213). • Parts 3 and 4 (via LaunchPad*): Includes multimedia selections in each of the modes of development from across the disciplines. • Part 5 (via LaunchPad*): Offers tutorials in documenting and working with sources in both MLA and APA style. • Chapter 27 (via LaunchPad*): Offers tutorials in making multimedia presentations, job searching, and personal branding.
Match the capacities of different environments (e.g., print and electronic) to varying rhetorical situations.	• Chapter 2: Covers writing and researching online (pp. 23–24). • Chapter 24: Covers using appropriate formats (MLA or APA) for writing a paper using sources (pp. 598–656). • Chapter 26: Covers using print and digital portfolios for assessment and learning. • Chapter 27: Covers planning, drafting, and delivering a multimedia presentation using visual aids (objects and presentation slides), whether face to face or via the Web (pp. 706–13); creating effective résumés and job application letters, whether printed or uploaded electronically, and using electronic media for business writing (pp. 713–18). • *ix visualizing composition 2.0**: Interactive assignments and guided analysis, practice with multimedia texts. • *Instructor's Resource Manual for Successful College Writing,* Sixth Edition (for instructors): Covers teaching and learning online (pp. 20–22, 147–48). • LaunchPad*: Offers tutorials on digital writing, including photo and audio editing, making presentations, word processing, using online research tools, and job search/personal branding.

*Additional resource, available free when packaged with the text. See p. xxiii for details.

cont.	
Desired Student Outcomes	**Relevant Features of *Successful College Writing***

Critical Thinking, Reading, and Composing

Use composing and reading for inquiry, learning, critical thinking, and communicating in various rhetorical contexts.	• The entire book is informed by the connection between reading critically and writing effectively. • Chapter 2: Covers the importance of reading and writing for college success and the distinctive qualities and demands of academic reading and writing. • Chapter 3: Covers reading actively (pp. 43–60) by understanding and responding to reading in writing (pp. 60–65); analyzing and responding to other students' writing (pp. 69–72). • Chapter 4: Covers thinking critically about text and images by analyzing the author's ideas (pp. 74–78), use of language (pp. 78–82), assumptions, generalizations, and omissions (pp. 82–85), synthesizing ideas (pp. 87–88); and analyzing photographs and graphics by reading them actively and critically (pp. 88–95). Via LaunchPad*: Offers tutorials and activities in Learning Curve on reading critically. • Parts 3 and 4: Covers thinking critically about the features of the genre, including thinking critically about characteristic flaws in the chapter's pattern (for example, the Making Connections box on p. 277, and the Synthesizing Ideas box on p. 296).
Read a diverse range of texts, attending especially to relationships between assertion and evidence, to patterns of organization, to interplay between verbal and nonverbal elements, and to how these features function for different audiences and situations	• Chapter 3: The entire chapter focuses on strategies for reading and responding to text and visuals, including understanding expectations for reading academic texts and texts written in a variety of genres or purposes (pp. 41). • Chapter 4: Includes coverage of assessing evidence (pp. 76–77), distinguishing between fact and opinion (p. 78), the role patterns of development play (pp. 86–88), and the role illustrations (photographs and graphics) play in writing (pp. 88–95). • Chapter 5: Includes coverage of the importance of audience, purpose, point of view, genre, and medium in reading and writing (pp. 103–07). • Chapter 6: Emphasizes the importance of supporting a thesis with evidence. • Chapter 8: Focuses on the relationship between a paragraph's topic and use of supporting evidence. • Parts 3 and 4: Each of the chapters in these parts focuses on a pattern of organization, with each including a section that asks students to consider the role of the audience and situation (see Chapter 13, pp. 276–78, for example.) Readings in these chapters range from popular to accessible scholarly selections (see "The Brains of the Animal Kingdom," pp. 302–05; "The Psychology of Stuff and Things," pp. 356–61, for example.) Where appropriate, activities following the readings also ask students to think critically about the relationship between text and visuals (see Chapter 15, pp. 362–63, for example). Via LaunchPad*, each chapter includes a multimedia reading selection with scaffolded activities that challenge students to analyze the selection and its use of the medium in which it was created. • Chapter 20: Covers supporting an arguable claim (p. 504), appeals (pp. 505–06), and responses to alternative views (pp. 506–07). • Chapter 24: Addresses appropriate tone for essays addressed to academic audiences (p. 603), the role of reasons and evidence in supporting the writer's ideas (pp. 605, 608–12).

*Additional resource, available free when packaged with the text. See p. xxiii for details.

cont.

Desired Student Outcomes	Relevant Features of *Successful College Writing*
Critical Thinking, Reading, and Composing	
Locate and evaluate (for credibility, sufficiency, accuracy, timeliness, bias, and so on) primary and secondary research materials, including journal articles, essays, books, databases, and informal electronic networks and Internet sources.	• Chapter 4: Focuses on analyzing a selection critically, including assessing the quality of the evidence and the author's use of language to discover bias or faulty reasoning (pp. 74–78). • Chapter 22: Emphasizes choosing appropriate source types for the project (primary vs. secondary sources, p. 566; scholarly vs. popular sources, pp. 566–68; books vs. articles vs. media sources, pp. 568–69); evaluating sources for relevance, including timeliness and appropriateness for the audience (p. 569), and reliability, including fairness and objectivity, verifiability, and bias (pp. 570–71). • Chapter 23: Provides instruction on using library resources including using key words effectively for searching catalogs and databases (pp. 576–81), using and choosing appropriate research tools such as subject guides, government documents, Listservs, newsgroups, and so on (pp. 581–84), and conducting field research (pp. 584–86).
Use strategies—such as interpretation, synthesis, response, critique, and design/redesign—to compose texts that integrate the writer's ideas with those from appropriate sources.	• Chapter 3: Covers a variety of strategies, including synthesis, response, and critique in its Guide to Responding to Text (pp. 60–65). • Chapter 4: Covers using synthesis and other techniques to read critically (pp. 74–78). • Chapters 12-19: Each chapter contains a section on thinking critically about the rhetorical mode (see Ch. 13, p. 277, for example) and a "Synthesizing Ideas" box (see Ch. 13, p. 296, for example). The apparatus following reading selections in the second half of each chapter also includes activities for analyzing the writer's technique thinking critically about the rhetorical mode, and responding to the reading (see Ch. 12, pp. 293–94). • Chapter 23: Covers evaluating notes and synthesizing sources (pp. 592–95). • Chapter 24: Covers integrating information from sources with the students' own ideas (pp. 605–08); integrating quotations, paraphrases, and summaries (pp. 608–12) while avoiding plagiarism (pp. 602–03). Via LaunchPad*, tutorials in documenting and working with sources are available. • *i-cite: visualizing sources**: Tutorials and practice on citing all kinds of sources.
Processes	
Develop a writing project through multiple drafts.	• Part 2: Chapter 5 focuses on finding and focusing ideas; Chapter 6—developing and supporting a thesis; Chapter 7—organizing and drafting an essay; Chapter 8—writing focused, well supported paragraphs; Chapter 9—revising an essay for content and organization, including benefits and processes of peer revising; Chapter 10—reading and revising a draft critically. One student's writing process, from idea generation through revision, is depicted across the chapters in Part 2. • Parts 3-4: The Guided Writing Assignments in each chapter stress the writing process. (See, for example, Ch. 15, pp. 343–48.) • Chapter 26: Coverage of developing a portfolio emphasizes the importance of demonstrating and reflecting on the writing process (pp. 698–701). • *Portfolio Keeping,* Second Edition†: Emphasizes the importance of portfolio keeping as a reflection of the writing processes.

*Additional resource, available free when packaged with the text. See p. xxiii for details.
†Available as a select value package. See p. xxiv for more information.

cont.	
Desired Student Outcomes	**Relevant Features of *Successful College Writing***

Processes

Desired Student Outcomes	Relevant Features of *Successful College Writing*
Develop flexible strategies for reading, drafting, reviewing, collaborating, revising, rewriting, rereading, and editing.	• Chapter 2: Introduces the idea of learning styles (pp. 30–39). • Part 2: Provides an overview of the writing process, with activities and student samples punctuating the process. • Parts 3 and 4: A Guided Writing Assignment in each chapter offers pattern-specific coverage of prewriting, drafting, revision, editing, and proofreading (for example, pp. 343–48). Learning styles options (see p. 89, for example) provide opportunities to tailor the writing process to the writer's needs. • Chapter 26: Coverage of developing a portfolio emphasizes the importance of demonstrating and reflecting on the student's writing process (pp. 698–701). • *Portfolio Keeping,* Second Edition*: Emphasizes the importance of portfolio keeping as a reflection of the writing process.
Use composing processes and tools as a means to discover and reconsider ideas.	• Chapter 5: Covers finding and focusing ideas. • Chapter 9: Focuses on revising for content and organization. • Parts 3-4: The chapters in these parts offer pattern-specific coverage of prewriting, drafting, revision, editing, and proofreading (for example, pp. 343–48). Learning styles options (see p. 345, for example) provide opportunities to tailor the writing process to the writer's needs. • Chapter 26: Coverage of developing a portfolio emphasizes the importance of demonstrating and reflecting on the student's writing process (pp. 698–701). • Part 5: Chapters in this part cover writing a research project, from planning (pp. 658–73), finding and evaluating sources (pp. 574–97), and synthesizing information to support the writer's own ideas (pp. 560–61, 592–95, 605–06), drafting and revising the research project (pp. 598–656), and citing sources in a style that is appropriate to the discipline (pp. 616–56). Student samples in these chapters provide appropriate models for college-level research projects. • *Portfolio Keeping,* Second Edition*: Discusses portfolio keeping as a reflection of writing processes. • *Teaching Composition (for instructors)*: Chapter 2 covers thinking about the writing process.
Experience the collaborative and social aspects of writing processes.	• Opportunities to work collaboratively appear in exercises throughout the book, with additional ideas for collaboration available in the annotated instructor's edition. • Chapter 1: Provides advice for collaborating effectively with classmates (pp. 17–18). • Chapter 5: Provides instruction for brainstorming in groups (p. 111). • Chapter 9: Includes coverage of peer review and tips for getting the best result from collaborative editing (pp. 182–84). • *Instructor's Resource Manual for Successful College Writing, Sixth Edition (for instructors)*: Chapter 6 offers tips on managing the peer review process.

*Available as a select value package. See p. xxiv for more information.

cont.	
Desired Student Outcomes	**Relevant Features of *Successful College Writing***

Processes

Learn to give and to act on productive feedback on works in progress.	• Chapter 9: Includes coverage of peer review and tips for getting the best result from collaborative editing (pp. 182–84), using the instructor's comments (pp. 184–86). • Parts 3 and 4: The chapters in these parts provide Guided Writing Assignments, offering pattern- and genre-specific advice on peer review and revision (for example, pp. 343–48), with revision flowcharts that can be used to guide peer-review process (for example, pp. 347–48). • *Instructor's Resource Manual for Successful College Writing* (for instructors): Chapter 6 offers tips on managing the peer review process.
Adapt composing processes to a variety of technologies and modalities.	• The entire book assumes that students will be using technology for writing and research. • Chapter 1: Emphasizes the importance of avoiding the distractions that can arise from multitasking (pp. 3–7); provides tips for using digital tools (including course management software) appropriately in the classroom (pp. 14–15, 20); and provides advice for avoiding common pitfalls (p. 20). • Chapter 2: Provides advice for choosing and using the most appropriate writing tools, whether digital or analog (pp. 28–29). • Part 5: Chapter 22 provides special tips for evaluating resources in a digital landscape (p. 571); Chapter 23—searching strategies for online research including unified searching of catalogs and databases (pp. 576–81), searching the Web (pp. 581–83), using citation managers for managing the research process (p. 587), and using online communities for research (pp. 583–84); Chapter 24—instruction on organizing notes regardless of the medium in which they were taken (pp. 586–92) and avoiding plagiarism by cutting and pasting carelessly (pp. 602–03). • Chapter 27: Covers making multimedia presentations, using presentation slides (pp. 706–13), making a Web-based presentation (pp. 713–18), submitting a résumé and cover letter online, and using electronic media (such as email, Twitter, Facebook) for business (pp. 713–18). • LaunchPad*: Offers tutorials on digital writing, including photo and audio editing, making presentations, word processing, using online research tools, and job search/personal branding. • *ix visualizing composition 2.0**: Provides interactive assignments and guided analysis of multimedia texts.

Knowledge of Conventions

Develop knowledge of linguistic structures, including grammar, punctuation, and spelling, through practice in composing and revising.	• Chapter 10: Covers editing words and sentences, including writing concisely, varying sentences, editing to create an appropriate tone and level of diction, choosing appropriate words, and editing to avoid errors of grammar, punctuation, and mechanics (pp. 194–214). • Parts 3 and 4: Guided Writing Assignments offer pattern- and genre-specific advice about editing and proofreading (for example, pp. 346–48). • Handbook (full edition): Provides instruction in correcting errors of grammar, punctuation, mechanics, and spelling. • LaunchPad*: Provides access to LearningCurve for Readers and Writers, adaptive game-like quizzing that provides opportunities for learning to identify and correct common writing problems.

*Additional resource, available free when packaged with the text. See p. xxiii for details.

cont.

Desired Student Outcomes	Relevant Features of *Successful College Writing*
Knowledge of Conventions	
Understand why genre conventions for structure, paragraphing, tone, and mechanics vary.	• Coverage of audience is infused throughout the text. • Chapter 2 highlights differences in expectations for writing as students move from high school to college, including expecting to find differences among genres (pp. 22–23) and between disciplines (p. 23). • Chapter 10 covers editing to create an appropriate tone and level of diction (whether the level is formal, popular, informal, or academic) (pp. 206–09), choosing appropriate words depending on the audience and purpose (pp. 209–12).
Gain experience negotiating variations in genre conventions.	• Parts 3 and 4: Each chapter in Parts 3 and 4 includes a box highlighting how the rhetorical mode could be used in college and in the workplace (see p. 264, for example); a range of readings are provided so students gain experience reading selections written for sophisticated popular audiences as well as more academic audiences (see "The Brains of the Animal Kingdom" by animal behaviorist Franz de Waal, pp. 302–05, and "The Psychology of Stuff and Things," by Christian Jarrett, pp. 356–61, for example), and apparatus following the readings in the second half of each chapter helps students gain experience in negotiating variations in the conventions. Multimedia selections (available via LaunchPad*) also provide opportunities for students to become familiar with the benefits of creating in multiple media. • Chapter 27: Highlights style choices that are appropriate for writing in a business context (p. 713).
Learn common formats and/or design features for different kinds of texts.	• Chapter 24: Highlights variations in formatting depending on expectations in the discipline for which the text was created (pp. 614–15, 632–38, 650–56). • Chapter 27: Covers formatting expectations for PowerPoint and Prezi slides, business writing formats for résumés, job application letters, and other forms of electronic business writing. • LaunchPad*: Provides tutorials on photo and audio editing, creating presentations, and personal branding
Explore the concepts of intellectual property (such as fair use and copyright) that motivate documentation conventions.	• Chapter 24: Covers concepts underlying plagiarism including common knowledge (pp. 602, 603).
Practice applying systematic citation conventions to a range of source material in their own work.	• Chapter 24: Covers documenting sources in MLA (pp. 617–38) and APA (pp. 638–56) style. • LaunchPad*: Offers tutorials in documentation and working with sources. • *ix visualizing composition 2.0*: Offers tutorials on and practice citing a variety of sources.

*Additional resource, available free when packaged with the text. See p. xxiii for details.

GET THE MOST OUT OF YOUR COURSE WITH *SUCCESSFUL COLLEGE WRITING*, SIXTH EDITION

Bedford/St. Martin's offers resources and format choices that help you and your students get even more out of the book and your course. To learn more about or to order any of the following products, contact your Bedford/St. Martin's sales representative, e-mail sales support (sales_support@macmillanhighered.com), or visit the catalog page at **macmillanhighered.com/successfulwriting/catalog**.

LAUNCHPAD FOR *SUCCESSFUL COLLEGE WRITING*: WHERE STUDENTS LEARN

LaunchPad provides engaging content and new ways to get the most out of your course. Get an **interactive e-book** combined with **unique**, **book-specific materials** (listed on the last page of this book) in a fully customizable course space; then assign and mix our resources with yours.

- Eleven **multimedia selections** — one for each rhetorical mode and one that demonstrates a mixing of modes — include videos, animated graphics, podcasts, and more. Selections range from a video narrative about a surprising, accidental revelation to a podcast that explains why movie sound effects have become so gruesome.

  Just like the readings in the printed text, each multimedia selection is preceded by a headnote and accompanied by activities that ask students to analyze the writer's technique and think critically about the patterns of development used in the selection.
- **Pre-built units** — including readings, videos, quizzes, discussion groups, and more — are **easy to adapt and assign** by adding your own materials and mixing them with our high-quality multimedia content and ready-made assessment options, such as **LearningCurve** adaptive quizzing.
- **LaunchPad** also provides access to a **gradebook** that provides a clear window on the performance of your whole class, individual students, and even individual assignments. A **streamlined interface** helps students focus on what's due, and social commenting tools let them engage, make connections, and learn from each other. Use LaunchPad on its own or integrate it with your school's learning management system so that your class is always on the same page.

To get the most out of your course, order LaunchPad for *Successful College Writing* **packaged with the print book** *at no additional charge.* (LaunchPad for *Successful College Writing* can also be purchased on its own.) An activation code is required. To order LaunchPad for *Successful College Writing*, Sixth Edition (with handbook), use ISBN 978-1-319-09240-5; to order LaunchPad for *Successful College Writing*, Brief Sixth Edition (without handbook), use ISBN 978-1-319-09238-2.

CHOOSE FROM ALTERNATIVE FORMATS OF *SUCCESSFUL COLLEGE WRITING*

Bedford/St. Martin's offers a range of affordable formats, allowing instructors to choose the one that works for their students. For details, visit **macmillanhighered.com /successfulwriting/formats**.

- *Paperback*   To order *Successful College Writing*, Sixth Edition (with the handbook), use ISBN 978-1-319-08774-6; to order *Successful College Writing*, Brief Sixth Edition (without the handbook), use ISBN 978-1-319-08775-3.

- *LaunchPad*   An online course space that integrates interactive tools and content, including an e-book (see below for details). To order LaunchPad packaged with the print text of *Successful College Writing*, Sixth Edition (with handbook), use ISBN 978-1-319-09240-5; to order LaunchPad packaged with the print text of *Successful College Writing*, Brief Sixth Edition (without handbook), use ISBN 978-1-319-09238-2. To order LaunchPad for *Successful College Writing* without a print book, contact your Bedford/St. Martin's sales representative, e-mail sales support (**sales_support@bfwpub.com**), or visit the Web site at **macmillanhighered.com/theguide/catalog**.

- *Popular e-book formats*   For details, visit **macmillanhighered.com/ebooks**.

SELECT VALUE PACKAGES

Add value to your text by packaging one of the following resources with *Successful College Writing*. To learn more about package options for any of the following products, contact your Bedford/St. Martin's sales representative or visit **macmillanhighered.com /successfulwriting/catalog**.

- *LearningCurve for Readers and Writers,* Bedford/St. Martin's adaptive quizzing program, quickly learns what students already know and helps them practice what they don't yet understand. Game-like quizzing motivates students to engage with their course, and reporting tools help teachers discern their students' needs. *LearningCurve for Readers and Writers* can be packaged with *Successful College Writing* at a significant discount. An activation code is required. For details, visit **learningcurveworks.com**.

- *Portfolio Keeping*, **Third Edition, by Nedra Reynolds and Elizabeth Davis** provides all the information students need to use the portfolio method successfully in a writing course. *Portfolio Teaching*, a companion guide for instructors, provides the practical information instructors and writing program administrators need to use the portfolio method successfully in a writing course.

MAKE LEARNING FUN WITH *RE:WRITING 3*

bedfordstmartins.com/rewriting

New, open online resources with videos and interactive elements engage students in new ways of writing. You'll find tutorials about using common digital writing tools, an interactive peer review game, *Extreme Paragraph Makeover*, and more—all for free and for fun. Visit **bedfordstmartins.com/rewriting**.

ADDITIONAL RESOURCES

macmillanhighered.com/successfulwriting

You have a lot to do in your course. Bedford/St. Martin's wants to make it easy for you to find the support you need—and to get it quickly.

The Instructor's Resource Manual for Successful College Writing is available as a PDF that can be downloaded from the Bedford/St. Martin's online catalog at the URL above. In addition to tips for teaching with *Successful College Writing*, the *Instructor's Resource Manual* includes advice for helping underprepared students, sample assessment tests to determine student skill level, reading quizzes to check understanding, sample syllabi, advice for teaching as an adjunct, and more.

Reading Quizzes—including five multiple-choice questions and summary practice (with a model answer as feedback), and an open-ended response prompt—are available for each print and multimedia reading selection. They are available in LaunchPad and in the Instructor's Resource Manual and they can be downloaded from Bedford/St. Martin's online catalog at the URL above.

Teaching Co-Requisite (ALP) Writing Classes, a new supplement by Jamey Gallagher (co-director of the Accelerated Learning Program at the Community College of Baltimore County) helps instructors who will be teaching a co-requisite, or ALP, course alongside a first-year writing class. Gallagher offers practical advice on how to align the co-requisite class with the first-year writing course, how to use the time effectively to help developmental writers build skills, how to avoid common mistakes, and how to build a community.

Teaching Central offers the entire list of Bedford/St. Martin's print and online professional resources in one place. You'll find landmark reference works, sourcebooks on pedagogical issues, award-winning collections, and practical advice for the classroom—all free for instructors.

Bits collects creative ideas for teaching a range of composition topics in an easily searchable blog format at **bedfordbits.com**. A community of teachers—leading scholars, authors, and editors—discuss revision, research, grammar and style, technology, peer review, and much more. Take, use, adapt, and pass the ideas around. Then come back to the site to comment or share your own suggestions.

Additional Exercises for Successful College Writings, Sixth Edition, provides students with more practice for writing skills covered in the text, especially those covered in Part 7, the Handbook (available in the full edition), but also skills covered in Chapters 7, 9, and 10 of the text.

CONTENTS

PART 3   Patterns of Development   215

PART 7   Handbook: Writing Problems and How to Correct Them 719

THEMATIC CONTENTS

part one
Reading, Writing, and Learning for College Success

AP Photo/Jeff Roberts

1

Succeeding in College

The photographs to the right show two first-year college students. One is a successful student, and the other is less so. What factors could explain why one student excels academically and the other does not?

Write a paragraph based on your experiences with education up to this point that explains which factors you think contribute to academic success and which lead to frustration. Be specific: You might discuss tasks that students need to know how to perform, offer tips, identify pitfalls, or consider nonacademic factors, such as jobs and family responsibilities.

What skills did you identify as contributing to college success? Some you may have mentioned include the following:

- being motivated and organized
- using your time effectively
- being able to focus on a task

© Martin Heitner/Aurora Photos; © Sonda Dawes/The Image Works

- studying and learning efficiently
- knowing how to read critically
- performing well in class and on exams
- knowing how to write papers and essay exams

All of these skills, and many others, contribute to academic success. This chapter begins with a reading that discusses several key factors that contribute to college success. The remainder of the chapter presents numerous other strategies for success to help you develop the skills you need for a successful college career.

- discover the factors that contribute to college success,
- learn strategies for becoming a successful student, and
- develop classroom skills for college success.

FACTORS THAT CONTRIBUTE TO SUCCESS

Read "The New Marshmallow Test," the article that follows. As you read, highlight the main points the writer is making about multitasking and academic success, and write notes, questions, and comments in the margin about your own media multitasking habits and your ability to devote your undivided attention to class lectures and course materials during your study time. You'll be glad you did!

READING

The New Marshmallow Test: Students Can't Resist Multitasking

ANNIE MURPHY PAUL

Annie Murphy Paul is an author, journalist, and contributing writer for *Time* magazine and often writes about learning and its improvement. She also blogs about learning at CNN.com, Forbes.com, and HuffingtonPost.com and has written several books including *The Cult of Personality*, which explores the historical quirks of how personality tests were developed and critiques their value; *Origins: How the Nine Months before Birth Shape the Rest of Our Lives*, a book about the science of prenatal influences; and *Brilliant: The New Science of Smart*.

Living rooms, dens, kitchens, even bedrooms: Investigators followed students 1 into the spaces where homework gets done. Pens poised over their "study observation forms," the observers watched intently as the students—in middle school, high school, and college, 263 in all—opened their books and turned on their computers.

For a quarter of an hour, the investigators from the lab of Larry Rosen, a psychology 2 professor at California State University–Dominguez Hills, marked down once a minute what the students were doing as they studied. A checklist on the form included: reading a book, writing on paper, typing on the computer—and also using email, looking at Facebook, texting, talking on the phone, watching television, listening to music, surfing the Web. Sitting unobtrusively at the back of the room, the observers

Attending to multiple streams of information and entertainment while studying, doing homework, or even sitting in class has become a common behavior among college students. © Jared Leeds/Aurora Photos

counted the number of windows open on the students' screens and noted whether the students were wearing earbuds.

Although the students had been told at the outset that they should "study something important, including homework, an upcoming examination or project, or reading a book for a course," it wasn't long before their attention drifted: Students' "on-task behavior" started declining around the two-minute mark as they began responding to arriving texts or checking their Facebook feeds. By the time the 15 minutes were up, they had spent only about 65 percent of the observation period actually doing their schoolwork.

Rosen's study, published in the May issue of *Computers in Human Behavior*, is part of a growing body of research focused on a very particular use of technology: media multitasking *while learning*. Evidence from psychology, cognitive science, and neuroscience suggests that when students multitask while doing schoolwork, their learning is far spottier and shallower than if the work had their full attention. They understand and remember less, and they have greater difficulty transferring their learning to new contexts. So detrimental is this practice that some researchers are proposing that a new prerequisite for academic and even professional success — the new marshmallow test of self-discipline — is the ability to resist a blinking inbox or a buzzing phone.

The media multitasking habit extends into the classroom. While most middle and high school students don't have the opportunity to text, email, and surf the Internet during class, studies show the practice is nearly universal among students in college and professional school. One large survey found that 80 percent of college students admit to texting during class; 15 percent say they send 11 or more texts in a single class period.

During the first meeting of his courses, Rosen makes a practice of calling on a student who is busy with his phone. "I ask him, 'What was on the slide I just showed to the class?' The student always pulls a blank," Rosen reports. "Young people have a wildly inflated idea of how many things they can attend to at once, and this demonstration helps drive the point home: If you're paying attention to your phone, you're not paying attention to what's going on in class." Other professors have taken a more surreptitious approach, installing electronic spyware or planting human observers to record whether students are taking notes on their laptops or using them for other, unauthorized purposes.

In a study involving spyware, for example, two professors of business administration at the University of Vermont found that "students engage in substantial multitasking behavior with their laptops and have non-course-related software applications open and active about 42 percent of the time." Another study, carried out at St. John's University in New York, used human observers stationed at the back of the classroom to record the technological activities of law students. The spies reported that 58 percent of second- and third-year law students who had laptops in class were using them for "non-class purposes" more than half the time. Texting, emailing, and posting on Facebook and other social media sites are by far the most common digital activities students undertake while learning, according to Rosen. That's a problem, because these operations are actually quite mentally complex, and they draw on the same mental resources — using language, parsing meaning — demanded by schoolwork.

David Meyer, a psychology professor at the University of Michigan who's studied   8
the effects of divided attention on learning, takes a firm line on the brain's ability to multitask: "Under most conditions, the brain simply cannot do two complex tasks at the same time. It can happen only when the two tasks are both very simple and when they don't compete with each other for the same mental resources. An example would be folding laundry and listening to the weather report on the radio. That's fine. But listening to a lecture while texting, or doing homework and being on Facebook — each of these tasks is very demanding, and each of them uses the same area of the brain, the prefrontal cortex."

Young people think they can perform two challenging tasks at once, Meyer acknowl-   9
edges, but "they are deluded," he declares. It's difficult for anyone to properly evaluate how well his or her own mental processes are operating, he points out, because most of these processes are unconscious. And, Meyer adds, "there's nothing magical about the brains of so-called 'digital natives' that keeps them from suffering the inefficiencies of multitasking. They may like to do it, they may even be addicted to it, but there's no getting around the fact that it's far better to focus on one task from start to finish."

Researchers have documented a cascade of negative outcomes that occurs when   10
students multitask while doing schoolwork. First, the assignment takes longer to complete, because of the time spent on distracting activities and because, upon returning to the assignment, the student has to refamiliarize himself with the material.

Second, the mental fatigue caused by repeatedly dropping and picking up a mental   11
thread leads to more mistakes. Third, students' subsequent memory of what they're working on will be impaired if their attention is divided. As the unlucky student spotlighted by Rosen can attest, we can't remember something that never really entered our consciousness in the first place. And a study last month showed that students who multitask on laptops in class distract not just themselves but also their peers who see what they're doing.

Fourth, some research has suggested that when we're distracted, our brains actu-   12
ally process and store information in different, less useful ways. In a 2006 study in the *Proceedings of the National Academy of Sciences*, Russell Poldrack of the University of Texas–Austin and two colleagues asked participants to engage in a learning

activity on a computer while also carrying out a second task, counting musical tones that sounded while they worked. Brain scans taken during Poldrack's experiment revealed that different regions of the brain were active under the two conditions, indicating that the brain engages in a different form of memory when forced to pay attention to two streams of information at once. The results suggest, the scientists wrote, that "even if distraction does not decrease the overall level of learning, it can result in the acquisition of knowledge that can be applied less flexibly in new situations."

Finally, researchers are beginning to demonstrate that media multitasking while learning is negatively associated with students' grades. In Rosen's study, students who used Facebook during the 15-minute observation period had lower grade-point averages than those who didn't go on the site. Meyer, of the University of Michigan, worries that the problem goes beyond poor grades. "There's a definite possibility that we are raising a generation that is learning more shallowly than young people in the past," he says. "The depth of their processing of information is considerably less, because of all the distractions available to them as they learn." 13

Given that these distractions aren't going away, academic and even professional achievement may depend on the ability to ignore digital temptations while learning — a feat akin to the famous marshmallow test. In a series of experiments conducted more than forty years ago, psychologist Walter Mischel tempted young children with a marshmallow, telling them they could have two of the treats if they put off eating one right away. Follow-up studies performed years later found that the kids who were better able to delay gratification not only achieved higher grades and test scores but were also more likely to succeed in school and their careers. 14

Two years ago, Rosen and his colleagues conducted an information-age version of the marshmallow test. College students who participated in the study were asked to watch a 30-minute videotaped lecture, during which some were sent eight text messages while others were sent four or zero text messages. Those who were interrupted more often scored worse on a test of the lecture's content; more interestingly, those who responded to the experimenters' texts right away scored significantly worse than those participants who waited to reply until the lecture was over. 15

The ability to resist the lure of technology can be consciously cultivated, Rosen maintains. He advises students to take "tech breaks" to satisfy their cravings for electronic communication: After they've labored on their schoolwork uninterrupted for 15 minutes, they can allow themselves two minutes to text, check websites, and post to their hearts' content. Then the devices get turned off for another 15 minutes of academics. Over time, Rosen says, students are able to extend their working time to 20, 30, even 45 minutes, as long as they know that an opportunity to get online awaits. Device-checking is a compulsive behavior that must be managed, he says, if young people are to learn and perform at their best. 16

UNDERSTANDING THE READING

1. **Main idea** Explain the author's main point in your own words.
2. **Effects** According to the reading selection, what are some of the short-term effects of multitasking while studying? What may be some of the long-term effects?
3. **Comparison** What was the original Marshmallow Test, and what did it show? How would the new Marshmallow Test work?

ANALYZING THE WRITER'S TECHNIQUE

1. **Evidence** What evidence does the author supply to support the claims about multitasking while learning? How convincing do you find that evidence and why?
2. **Purpose** Why do you think the author wrote this article? What clues in the text lead you to this conclusion?
3. **Audience** Who do you think is the main audience for this article? What clues in the text lead you to this conclusion?

RESPONDING TO THE READING

Explore your media multitasking habits by trying to replicate Larry Rosen's investigation. For fifteen minutes while you are at home studying, use the following categories to mark down once per minute what you are doing as you study:

❏ reading a book
❏ writing on paper
❏ typing on the computer
❏ reading or writing email
❏ texting
❏ talking on the phone
❏ reading or writing on Facebook (or another social media site)
❏ watching television
❏ listening to music
❏ surfing the Web

At the end of the fifteen-minute period, analyze your findings.
- What percentage of your fifteen-minute study time did you devote to studying?
- How long were you able to go without a distraction?
- What was your primary distraction?

Finally, write a paragraph or two explaining how well you think you "learned" what you were studying and what lessons you will take away from this exercise. What changes will you make in your study habits (if any), and how will you make them?

STRATEGIES FOR SUCCESS

"The New Marshmallow Test" demonstrates the importance of focusing your attention while in the classroom, but there are strategies for college success that you can embrace even before you enter the classroom that will help you learn more effectively and efficiently. These strategies are presented in this section.

MANAGE YOUR TIME EFFECTIVELY

As you discovered in "The New Marshmallow Test," using your study time efficiently, without media distractions, is important. Setting aside enough time—for every hour spent in class, *plan to work two to three hours outside of class*—and planning that time carefully are also crucial. The best way to get started is to establish goals and create a workable plan for achieving those goals.

Examine the two student schedules shown in Figures 1.1 and 1.2. Which student is more likely to meet his or her deadlines? Why?

The planner in Figure 1.1 shows only test dates and assignment deadlines, whereas the planner in Figure 1.2 includes not only tests and deadlines but also details showing how and when the student will meet those deadlines. The student who uses the planner in Figure 1.2 is more likely to complete his or her work on time—and with less worry.

FIGURE 1.1 Planner with Due Dates

NOVEMBER	NOVEMBER
10 Monday	**Thursday 13**
	10 am Essay 3 due
11 Tuesday	**Friday 14**
3 pm History exam	
	1 pm Anthro quiz
12 Wednesday	**Saturday 15**
	Sunday 16

FIGURE 1.2 Planner with Detailed Schedule

NOVEMBER	NOVEMBER
10 Monday	**Thursday 13**
am—Outline English Essay 3	*10 am Essay 3 due*
6 pm History study group	*5–8 pm Work*
	9–10 pm Study Anthro chapters
11 Tuesday	**Friday 14**
am—Draft Essay 3	*am—Review Anthro notes and*
3 pm History exam	*chapter highlighting*
6–8 pm Work	
Read Anthro Ch. 20	*1 pm Anthro quiz*
12 Wednesday	**Saturday 15**
10 am Writing Center—Review	*9–4 Work*
Essay 3	**Sunday 16**
Read Anthro Chs. 21–22	*Read Bio Ch. 17*
	Review Bio lab
	Read History Ch. 15

Plan your schedule. Each time you sit down to study for a class, assess what you need to do, and determine the most effective order in which to do it. Work on the most challenging assignments first, when your concentration is at its peak. You should plan to study six to eight hours per week for each course. Study for each course during the same time period each week, if possible, to establish a routine. Alternatively, you may want to take ten minutes at the beginning of each week to specify the six to eight hours in which you'll work on each course.

Avoid procrastination. Procrastination is putting off things that need to be done; you know you should work on an assignment, but you do something else instead. To avoid procrastination, try these tips.

- Divide the task into manageable parts.
- Avoid making excuses. It is easy to say you don't have enough time to get everything done, but often that is not true.
- Avoid escaping into routine tasks such as shopping, cleaning, or washing your car rather than completing the task.

ORGANIZE A WRITING AND STUDY AREA

You don't need a lot of room to create an appropriate space for studying and writing, but you do need a space that is conducive to writing and studying. Your work area should be:

- quiet so you won't be disturbed by family or roommates or be tempted to turn on your television or play with your cat,
- well lit and spacious enough to accommodate your books, notebooks, and computer, and
- equipped with all the tools you need: a clock, a computer, a calculator, pens, pencils, paper, a pencil sharpener.

If your home does not fit the bill, consider studying in the library. Libraries offer carrel space, and many also offer study rooms for group work or secluded areas with comfortable chairs if you do not need a desk. The library also offers a convenient spot to study between classes.

> **EXERCISE 1.1**   **Organizing a Study Area**

Using the suggestions listed above, write a paragraph describing what you can do to organize an area that is conducive to writing and studying.

STUDY MORE EFFICIENTLY

Does either of these situations sound familiar?

"I just read a whole page, and I can't remember anything I read!"

"Every time I start working on this assignment, my mind wanders."

If so, you may need to improve your concentration. No matter how intelligent you are or what skills or talents you possess, if you cannot keep your mind on your work, your classes—including your writing class—will be unnecessarily difficult. In addition to shutting down distracting media, try the following strategies to help you "study smarter," not harder.

- **Work at peak periods of attention.** Identify the time of day or night that you are most efficient and focused. Avoid working when you are tired, hungry, or distracted.
- **Vary your activities.** Do not complete, say, three reading assignments consecutively. Instead, alternate assignments: for example, read, then write, then work on math problems, then read another assignment, and so on.
- **Use writing to keep you mentally and physically active.** Highlight, annotate, and take notes as you read. These processes will keep you mentally alert.
- **Approach assignments critically.** Ask yourself questions as you read. Make connections with what you have already learned and with what you already know about the subject. You will learn more about synthesis, a crucial component of learning effectively, later in this chapter (p. 17).
- **Challenge yourself with deadlines.** Before beginning an assignment, estimate how long it should take and work toward completing it within that time limit.
- **Keep a to-do list.** When you are working on an assignment, stray thoughts about other pressing things (tomorrow's car inspection, next week's birthday party for your mother) are bound to zip through your mind. When these thoughts occur to you, jot them down so that you can unclutter your mind and focus on your work.
- **Reward yourself.** As Professor Rosen (in "The New Marshmallow Test") suggests, use a fun activity, such as texting a friend or getting a snack, as a reward for reaching your goal or completing your assignment.

> **EXERCISE 1.2**   **Selecting Study Strategies**

Not all students study the same way, and most students study differently for different courses. List below the courses you are taking this semester. For each, identify a study strategy that works for that course. Compare your list with those of other students and add useful techniques you learn from them.

Course	Study Strategies to Try
1.	
2.	
3.	
4.	
5.	

LEARN TO MANAGE STRESS

Stress is a natural reaction to the challenges of daily living, but if you are expected to accomplish more or perform better than you think you can, stress can become overwhelming. As a successful student, you need to monitor your stress. Take the "How Stressed Are You?" quiz on the next page to assess your stress level.

Quiz: How Stressed Are You?	Always	Sometimes	Never
1. I worry that I do not have enough time to get everything done.	❏	❏	❏
2. I regret that I have no time to do fun things each week.	❏	❏	❏
3. I find myself losing track of details and forgetting due dates, promises, and appointments.	❏	❏	❏
4. I worry about what I am doing.	❏	❏	❏
5. I have conflicts or disagreements with friends or family.	❏	❏	❏
6. I lose patience with small annoyances.	❏	❏	❏
7. I seem to be late, no matter how hard I try to arrive on time.	❏	❏	❏
8. I have difficulty sleeping.	❏	❏	❏
9. My eating habits have changed.	❏	❏	❏
10. I find myself needing a cigarette, drink, or prescription drug.	❏	❏	❏

You can use stress to motivate yourself to start a project or assignment, or you can let it interfere with your ability to function mentally and physically. If you answered "Always" or "Sometimes" to more than two or three items in the "How Stressed Are You?" quiz, you may be reacting to stress negatively. Here are some effective ways to change your thinking and habits to reduce stress.

- **Establish your priorities.** Let's say, for example, that you decide college is more important than your part-time job. Once you have decided this, you won't worry about requesting a work schedule to accommodate your study schedule because studying is your priority.
- **Be selfish and learn to say no.** Use your priorities to guide you in accepting new responsibilities.
- **Simplify your life by making fewer choices.** For example, instead of deciding what time to set your alarm clock each morning, get up at the same time each weekday. Set fixed study times and stick to them.
- **Focus on the positive.** Instead of saying "I'll never be able to finish this assignment on time," ask yourself, "What do I have to do to finish this assignment on time?"
- **Separate work, school, and social problems.** Create mental compartments for your worries. Don't spend time in class thinking about a problem at work or a conflict with a friend. Deal with problems at the appropriate time.
- **Keep a personal journal.** Writing down details about your worries and emotions can go a long way toward relieving stress, but be sure to include notes about how you can resolve problems too.

CLASSROOM SKILLS

"The New Marshmallow Test" showed that what you do within the classroom contributes significantly to your success in college. But there are other classroom skills besides paying attention in class that are important to success. A number are discussed below.

POLISH YOUR ACADEMIC IMAGE

Your academic image is the way your instructors and other students see you as a student. How you act and respond in class creates this image. This list of do's and don'ts can help you improve your academic image.

Do . . .	Don't . . .
Prepare for class fully.	Read, send text messages, surf the Web, or check Facebook during class.
Make thoughtful contributions based on your understanding of the material and refer to assigned readings in class.	Work on homework during class.
Maintain eye contact with instructors.	Sleep or daydream in class.
Ask questions when information is unclear.	Remain silent during class discussion.
Treat classmates respectfully.	Interrupt others or criticize their contributions.

A committed student is more likely to be taken seriously and to get the assistance he or she needs. One way to demonstrate your seriousness is to participate regularly in class. If you are nervous about joining in discussion, try reflecting on assigned readings or taking notes before class so you will feel prepared. Saying something early in the discussion can also help: The longer you wait, the more difficult it is to say something that has not already been said.

Showing your commitment involves more than just speaking out. It also involves the following:

- focusing and taking notes on the discussion,
- recording what the instructor writes or projects on the board or shows on presentation slides,
- keeping handouts,
- jotting down ideas for future writing assignments,
- connecting what you're learning with your own experiences, and
- taking responsibility for getting help when you need it.

EXERCISE 1.3 **Rating Your Academic Image**

Rate your academic image by checking "Always," "Sometimes," or "Never" for each of the following statements.

	Always	Sometimes	Never
I arrive at classes promptly.	❑	❑	❑
I sit near the front of the room.	❑	❑	❑
I look and act alert and interested in the class.	❑	❑	❑
I complete reading assignments before class.	❑	❑	❑
I ask thoughtful questions.	❑	❑	❑
I participate in class discussions.	❑	❑	❑
I take careful notes and retain handouts.	❑	❑	❑
I complete all assignments on time.	❑	❑	❑
I turn in neat, complete, well-organized, and carefully edited papers.	❑	❑	❑
I seek out the instructor if I need help understanding the reading, discussion, or assignments.	❑	❑	❑

EXERCISE 1.4 **Analyzing Your Academic Image**

Write a brief statement about how you think others perceive you as a student and why. Refer to the list of tips about building a positive academic image on page 12. What tips do you normally follow? Which do you most need to work on?

DEMONSTRATE ACADEMIC INTEGRITY

Demonstrating academic integrity means conducting yourself in an honest and ethical manner. It involves avoiding the obvious forms of classroom dishonesty such as copying homework, buying a paper on the Internet, and cheating on exams or helping others do so. It also means not plagiarizing, using the ideas or language of others — deliberately or unintentionally — without giving credit. An example of intentional plagiarism is cutting and pasting information into your paper from the Internet without indicating that it is borrowed. Unintentional plagiarism occurs when you use language too similar to that of the original source, inadvertently omit a citation, or forget to place quotation marks around a quotation.

To learn how to avoid unintentional plagiarism, see Chapter 24, p. 603.

COMMUNICATE EFFECTIVELY WITH YOUR INSTRUCTORS

Meeting with your instructor outside class, especially if you have questions or concerns about the material, will demonstrate your commitment to succeeding in college and help you understand and meet the course objectives. Use the following tips to communicate effectively with your instructors.

- **Don't be afraid to approach your instructors.** Most instructors enjoy teaching and working with students and will happily work with you to understand a reading or an assignment and to provide information on research, academic decisions, and careers in their fields. But you need to take the initiative. Find out when your instructors hold office hours, and note their email addresses someplace you can find easily.
- **Prepare for meetings with your instructor.** Consider your questions in advance. If you need help with a paper, bring along all the work (drafts, outlines, research sources) you have done so far and explain specifically the trouble you are having and what you'd like the instructor to help you with.
- **Stay in touch with your instructor.** Unexcused absences generally lower your grade and suggest that you are not taking your studies seriously. If you absolutely cannot attend class for a particular reason, notify your instructor and explain why. In addition, if personal problems interfere with your schoolwork, let your instructors know. They can refer you to counseling services on campus and may grant you an extension for work you missed for a documented emergency.

USE ELECTRONIC TOOLS EFFECTIVELY

Email and texting are now widely used for academic purposes. Some college libraries offer students online help from reference librarians, and many instructors use course management systems to post syllabi and assignments, to host online discussions or post study questions, and to enable students and professors to communicate electronically. You can use Google Drive and similar systems effectively for collaborating on writing assignments. If your instructor uses electronic classroom tools, the following guidelines will help you use them effectively.

- **Text your instructor only if invited.** Even then, text only when you are certain that it's appropriate to do so. For example, it would be inappropriate to try to get your instructor to respond to texts the night before a paper is due.
- **Use appropriate language.** The abbreviations, emoticons (like smiley faces), and slang often used in texting and email among friends are not appropriate for formal writing, such as course assignments. Even emails to instructors should use formal language unless the instructor has set a less formal tone in his or her own emails to you.

See Chapter 3, p. 51, for suggestions on learning vocabulary.

- **Become familiar with the software or course management system.** Take responsibility for figuring out how to use the software by reading the instructions or viewing a model or demo, checking FAQs (frequently asked questions), or getting help from your campus computer center, classmates, or technical support personnel.
- **Show respect and consideration for others.** Make it easy for classmates and your instructor to read your postings. Think through what you want to say

before you say it; use correct spelling and grammar; and format your comments using spacing, boldface, numbered lists, and so on as appropriate. Be polite, even when you are disagreeing with an earlier comment, and always reread your comments before posting them.

EXERCISE 1.5 | **Working Together**

The following chart lists options for communicating electronically with classmates and instructors. Check the possible benefits and drawbacks of each method. When would it be effective and appropriate to use each option? In what circumstances should you *not* use an option? When is it best to have a face-to-face meeting? Compare your completed chart with those of classmates.

Options	Communicating with Classmates		Communicating with Instructors	
	Benefits	Drawbacks	Benefits	Drawbacks
Email	❑	❑	❑	❑
Phone	❑	❑	❑	❑
Text messages	❑	❑	❑	❑
Social networks (examples: Facebook, Twitter)	❑	❑	❑	❑
Discussion board in a course management system (such as Blackboard or Moodle)	❑	❑	❑	❑

LISTEN CAREFULLY AND CRITICALLY

Of the most common ways people communicate — reading, writing, speaking, and listening — listening is the skill that you perform most frequently in a classroom. Because you learn so much through listening, learning to listen carefully and critically — grasping what is said and questioning and reacting to what you hear — is a crucial college skill.

Listening carefully. Did you know that you can process information faster than speakers can speak? As a result, your mind has time to wander while listening. Try using the following suggestions to maintain your attention in the classroom.

- **Sit comfortably, but do not sprawl.** A serious posture puts your mind in gear for serious work.
- **Focus on the lecture.** Shutting off distracting media (your phone and your Web applications), sitting toward the front of the room (not among a group of friends), and maintaining eye contact with the speaker will all make you feel more involved and less likely to drift off mentally.
- **Try to anticipate the ideas the speaker will address next.** Doing so will keep your mind active.

Listening critically. In many classes, you are expected both to understand what the speaker is saying and respond to it. Here are a few suggestions for developing your critical-listening skills.

- **Focus on the message, not the speaker.** Try not to be distracted by the speaker's clothing, mannerisms, speech patterns, or annoying quirks or to be lulled into accepting a message simply because the speaker is attractive or dynamic.
- **Maintain an open mind.** It is easy to shut out ideas and opinions that do not conform to your own values and beliefs. Try to avoid evaluating a message as positive or negative until it is complete and understandable, and strive to understand the speaker's viewpoint, even if you think you disagree.
- **Take notes.** Noting questions or creating an informal outline of the speaker's main points can hold off a knee-jerk reaction and give you a starting point for participating in the discussion. (See pp. 18–20.)
- **Identify and assess the speaker's main point and key supporting evidence.** The speaker is likely to repeat his or her main point in a different form throughout the presentation. Consider how well the reasons and evidence support the speaker's main point. Is the presentation convincingly argued? When listening to difficult, unpleasant, emotional, or complex messages, think about how (or whether) they add to your understanding of the speaker's experience.

> **EXERCISE 1.6** | **Improving Your Note-Taking Skills**
>
> Review the advice given above. Then choose at least three points to apply in the next two lectures you attend for one of your other courses. Finally, write a paragraph reflecting on what you learned from the experience.

ASK AND ANSWER QUESTIONS APPROPRIATELY

You can learn more from your classes if you develop or polish your questioning skills. This means asking questions when you need information and clarification and answering questions posed by the instructor to demonstrate and evaluate your knowledge and express interest in the class. Use the following tips to strengthen your questioning and answering skills.

- **Conquer your fear of speaking in class.** Stop worrying what your friends and classmates will think: Speak out.
- **As you read assignments, jot down questions as they occur to you.** Bring your list to class, and use it when your instructor invites questions.
- **Form your questions concisely.** Don't ramble.
- **Don't worry if your questions seem unimportant or silly.** Don't apologize for asking; other students probably have the same questions but are reluctant to ask them.
- **Focus on critical questions.** Instead of asking factual questions, think how the information can be used, how ideas fit together, how things work, what might be relevant problems and solutions, or what the long-term value and significance of the information are.
- **Think before responding.** When answering questions, try to compose your response before volunteering to answer.

EXERCISE 1.7   **Working Together**

Working with a classmate, brainstorm a list of questions you could ask about the content presented in this chapter.

SYNTHESIZE YOUR IDEAS AND EXPERIENCES WITH WHAT YOU ARE LEARNING

Completing assignments, writing papers, and taking exams are all tasks in which instructors will expect you not only to repeat what you have learned in class, but also to **synthesize**, or pull together, ideas from your reading assignments, your class lectures, and your own experience. When you synthesize ideas, you analyze similar or competing ideas and use them to extend or challenge your understanding, and you connect them to your own experience to see the practical consequences of an idea. Consider again "The New Marshmallow Test" (pp. 3–6). If reading that article prompted you to consider your own media multitasking or complete the checklist in "Responding to the Reading," then you were synthesizing the reading with your own experience.

Often, you will be asked to put ideas from multiple readings in conversation, compare and integrate ideas from several sources, draw conclusions, and generate new ideas based on those sources. For example, you might be asked to read "The New Marshmallow Test" (pp. 3–6), "Internet Addiction" (pp. 131–34), and "Alone Together: Why We Expect More from Technology and Less from Each Other" (pp. 324–27) and to write an essay developing your own thesis about the value or risks of this technology in students' lives. Here are some other common assignments that require you to synthesize ideas.

- For a biology class, you might be asked to conduct a lab experiment and write a paragraph or two explaining the principles the experiment demonstrated.
- For an American history class, you might be asked to read a letter from a freed slave, a diary of a plantation owner, and a speech by an abolitionist and then write about what life as a slave was like prior to the Civil War.
- For an abnormal psychology class, you might be asked to read a case study and then diagnose the patient based on the symptoms described.

COLLABORATE WITH CLASSMATES

Many college assignments and class activities involve working with other students. For example, many exercises in this chapter ask you to share ideas and writing with other students. Many students expect to learn from their instructors but do not realize they can learn from one another as well. In your writing class, your instructor may encourage you to ask other students to read and comment on your draft. Group projects enable students to share experiences, understand classmates' thinking, and evaluate new ideas and approaches to completing a task.

Group projects vary, and therefore your approach may vary depending on the discipline, the course, the membership of the group, and the instructor, but whatever type of group project you undertake, the tips on the next page may help you get the most out of working together:

For more about peer review, see Chapter 9, p. 182; for more about collaboration, see Chapter 3, p. 68.

- **Understand the purpose.** To benefit most from group projects, be sure you understand the task, and then ask yourself, "What can I learn from this?" You will get more out of an assignment if you focus on outcomes.
- **Establish a cohesive group.** To work well together, start your project by meeting face-to-face, at least for the first meeting if possible. Have all team members say a bit about themselves so you all get to know each other, and share contact information (email address, home phone or cell number, best times to call or text).
- **Set the ground rules.** Discuss the issues that are likely to derail the project, such as members skipping meetings or consistently arriving late, one member dominating the discussion or not participating actively, members not completing assigned work on time or doing the work badly. Then decide as a group what you should do to address the potential problems you have identified. Once you agree, put your decisions in writing and have all group members sign the document.
- **Determine and assign tasks, and set a realistic schedule.** Brainstorm project ideas, making sure everybody has a voice. Make a list of all the tasks that need to be accomplished, and divide the work among group members. Be sure to consider what members are good at, what they enjoy doing, and what they can accommodate given their schedules. Finally, establish a schedule with due dates that everyone in the group can stick to, and distribute copies or post the schedule online.

TAKE GOOD NOTES IN CLASS

Good note-taking is a hallmark of a successful student. Why? Researchers have shown that most people retain far more information when they interact with it using more than one sense. For instance, a student who only listens to a lecture or discussion will probably forget most of it within a couple of weeks, well before the next exam. Students who take accurate notes and review them regularly are likely to retain the main points and supporting details needed to understand the concepts discussed in class. Reviewing notes regularly also replaces the inefficient and exhausting strategy of cramming for exams—a strategy that loads information into your memory only temporarily—with a system of learning that allows deeper, longer-term retention of information. Here are some useful note-taking tips.

- **Read assignments before the lecture.** Familiarity with the topic will make note-taking easier.
- **Record only main ideas and key details.** Avoid writing in complete sentences; instead use words and phrases, and develop a system of abbreviations, signs, and symbols. Developing your own symbols over time will help make note-taking quicker and more consistent for you.
- **Pay attention to your instructor's cues about what is important.** These cues include repetition of points, changes in voice or rate of speech, listing or numbering of points, and information written on the board or presented in slides.
- **Review notes immediately after the lecture.** While your memory is fresh, amend your notes to clarify relationships, add examples, or fill in information you missed during the lecture. (If you wait a day or more, your memory of the class will fade.) If you are taking hand-written notes, leave plenty of blank space for additions.
- **If you must miss class, borrow notes from a classmate who is a good student.**

Two of the most popular and efficient methods of taking notes are discussed on the next page.

Two-column method. This note-taking method is valuable for all learners. Draw a vertical line down a notebook page or create a two-column table in a word-processing document. Make the left-hand column about half as wide as the right-hand column.

In the wider, right-hand column, record ideas and facts as they are presented in a lecture or a discussion. In the narrower, left-hand column, note your own questions as they arise during the class. When you review your notes after class, add summaries of major concepts and sections to the left-hand column. You can get a quick overview of a lecture by reading the left-hand column, and you can study specific information and examples in the right-hand column.

THE TWO-COLUMN METHOD OF NOTE-TAKING

Writing process	Prewriting — taking notes, writing ideas, drawing a cluster diagram, researching, writing questions, noting what you already know, outlining, etc.
	Writing — drafting
(How many drafts does the average writer complete?)	Rewriting — revision = "to see again" 2 types: global = major rehaul (reconsidering, reorganizing) local = rewording, correcting grammar (editing for correctness & style)
NOT linear	Writing is not a linear process. May go back to prewriting after writing, etc.

Modified outline method. The modified branch or outline method uses bullets, dashes, and indentations to indicate main ideas and supporting information. The more detailed the information gets, the farther to the right you indent your outline entries.

THE MODIFIED OUTLINE METHOD OF NOTE-TAKING

Writing is a process.

- Prewriting
  - Taking notes
  - Writing ideas
  - Drawing a cluster diagram
  - Researching
  - Writing questions
  - Noting what you already know
  - Outlining
- Writing
  - First drafts
    - On paper
    - On computer
  - Later drafts
- Rewriting, or revision (means "to see again")
  - Global
    - Major revision
    - Reconsidering ideas
    - Reorganizing
  - Local
    - Rewording for style
    - Rewriting for correct grammar, spelling, punctuation

If you take notes electronically, use the tips in the following box to make the process work for you.

Do . . .	Don't . . .
Make sure you can plug in your laptop or that you have sufficient battery power.	Allow distracting programs such as email, Facebook, or Twitter to compete for your attention.
Set up a folder for each course. Create a separate file for each day's notes, and include the date of the lecture in naming the file.	Risk interrupting the class with annoying beeps and buzzes. Turn off the sound.
Keep a pen and paper handy to record diagrams, drawings, and other nonverbal material in case the computer malfunctions.	Type every word the speaker says.
Save your document frequently so you don't lose anything.	Condense ideas; do not transcribe them. (Taking notes in outline format can help.)

MANAGE ONLINE COURSES RESPONSIBLY

Online courses, which continue to grow in popularity, are convenient, but they require more self-direction and ability to work alone than traditional classes do. They also require a great deal of online writing, reading, and research, so they may prove to be more work than a traditional class. Here are some tips for succeeding in online courses.

- **Try to avoid taking online courses during your first term in college.** First learn what is expected in college courses by attending traditional classes. When you are familiar with college expectations, you will be better prepared to take an online course.
- **Set regular hours to devote to your online course.** Most students who fail online courses do so because they fall hopelessly behind on reading and assignments. Even if a class does not meet at a specified time, build blocks of time for the course into your schedule (two to three hours of study time for each hour of class time) to avoid procrastinating on classwork.
- **Plan on doing a lot of reading and writing.** You will read your textbooks and posts from your professor and other students. In addition to papers, your class "discussions" will also be in written form.
- **Maintain your concentration.** Turn off cell phones, music, and email while working on your online course.
- **Make sure your online postings are serious and do not waste classmates' time.** Respond directly to previous posts and any instructor writing prompts, and summarize the discussion before moving on to a new topic.

2 Writing in College

The photograph to the right shows a college student taking notes in class. When else do you use writing? Brainstorm a list of other situations. For example, do you write emails at work, blog about an interest or hobby, or text friends and relatives? What does your list reveal about the importance of writing in your life?

Most college classes require some form of writing—exams, essays, journals, reports, and so forth—because instructors see writing not just as a means of evaluating what students have learned but also as a means for their students to learn. Because strong writing skills are essential to success in college (and at work), the time and effort you spend in improving your

© Phil Boorman/Getty

writing are valuable investments. The main purpose of this chapter—and of this entire book—is to help you succeed in your writing class as well as in other classes that involve writing.

IN THIS CHAPTER YOU WILL LEARN TO

- understand what academic writing involves,
- grasp the importance of improving your writing skills,
- develop strategies to improve your writing skills, and
- assess your learning style using a Learning Style Inventory.

ACADEMIC WRITING: WHAT TO EXPECT

In college you will probably do more writing than you did in high school, and the expectations instructors will have of your writing will also be different. This section explains what you can expect about writing in college.

EXPECT YOUR WRITING TO BECOME LESS PERSONAL

Much of your writing up to now may have been about yourself and your experiences. In college you may be asked to share your ideas and opinions, which will be based on your experiences, but you will need to support these ideas and opinions with good reasons and objective evidence, such as examples, observations, facts, statistics, and expert opinion. As a result, you will find that college writing uses third person (*it, they, he, she*) much more than first person (*I, me*).

In some cases, your main reason, or purpose, for writing in college may be to *express your thoughts and feelings*, but in most cases it will be to *inform* or *persuade*.

- **Informative writing** presents information about a subject in an objective, nonpersonal way. For example in a sociology class, you might write an essay defining generation 1.5. You could offer examples of friends and relatives who are members of generation 1.5, but you would focus mostly on characterizing that generation as a whole.
- **Persuasive writing** attempts to convince readers to think or act a certain way. For example, you might write an essay for your criminal justice class arguing that the penalties for drunk driving should be increased. In writing this essay, you could draw on your personal knowledge of drunk driving, but you would need to supply mostly objective evidence to persuade your readers.

As you analyze a writing assignment, determine how much of your personal experience and personal opinion (if any) are appropriate for the assignment.

EXPECT TO WRITE IN DIFFERENT FORMS, OR *GENRES*

In college you will write much more than essays and exam answers. Depending on your program of study or major, you may also write in a variety of specialized **genres** (or types):

- essays and essay exams
- abstracts and research projects

- case studies and observational or laboratory reports
- diagnostic evaluations

Each genre has its own set of conventions and expectations. For example, a lab report:
- has a specific purpose (to report the results of a laboratory experiment),
- follows a specific format (it includes sections with headings such as *Introduction, Materials and Methods,* and *Observation*),
- has an expected style of writing (brief, factual, and concise), and
- uses technical and specialized language (names specific instruments and refers to elements as abbreviated in the periodic table, for example).

As you encounter new genres, read samples that can serve as models for your own writing.

EXPECT TO USE THE LANGUAGE OF THE DISCIPLINE

Each academic discipline has its own language—words and phrases that are used only or primarily in that discipline. The words *photosynthesis* and *homeostasis,* for example, are used primarily in biology, and the words *allegory, symbolism,* and *personification* are used in literature. When you write in a particular discipline, you are expected to use the language of that discipline. Concentrate first on expressing your ideas clearly. As you revise, check to be sure you have used the language of the discipline correctly.

See Chapter 3, pp. 51–52, for suggestions on learning vocabulary.

EXPECT TO USE STANDARD AMERICAN ENGLISH

Although nonstandard English (slang, incorrect grammar, intentional or unintentional misspellings) may be appropriate in some settings (such as text messages and emails to friends), students in an academic context are expected to write in standard, correct American English. As you proofread your writing, concentrate on correctness. Refer to a grammar handbook or consult an online writing resource for help.

For help with sentence-level problems, see Chapter 10 and, unless you are using the Brief Edition, the handbook at the back of this book.

EXPECT TO READ, WRITE, AND THINK CRITICALLY

In college, instructors will expect you to go beyond merely repeating what you hear in class or read in the textbook; they'll expect you to demonstrate understanding by being able to draw your own inferences based on what you have learned and to synthesize information from sources to support your ideas and to come up with new ideas.

For more on reading actively and critically, see Chapters 3 and 4.

EXPECT TO USE AND DOCUMENT SCHOLARLY SOURCES

Many college writing assignments require you to conduct research to acquire the information you need to support your ideas. College writing often requires the use of **scholarly sources** (books and articles written by experts and published in scholarly journals and university presses). In many cases **popular sources** (magazines like *People* or *Sports Illustrated,* newspapers like the *Los Angeles Times* or *USA Today*) may not be

For guidance in locating and using scholarly sources, see Chapters 22 and 23.

appropriate because they may not offer expert information or sufficient detail. Consult your reference librarian if you need help finding scholarly sources. Google may be familiar and easy to use, but it may not be the best place to find the scholarly sources you need. You will likely search for sources online, using your library's online catalog of books and databases listing scholarly articles. Keep in mind that the best sources for your research may (still) be available only in print.

For help with citing sources, see Chapter 24.

Whether you quote directly or express ideas from a source in your own words through a summary or paraphrase, your instructors will expect you to **credit** the sources you use by including an in-text citation and a list of works cited (or references).

EXPECT TO WRITE MULTIPLE DRAFTS

For more about the writing process, see Part 2.

College instructors will expect you to write multiple drafts, so that the essay you turn in is thoughtful, appropriate to the assignment, clearly organized, and free from errors of grammar, punctuation, and spelling. They will expect you also to write using a computer, which will help with writing multiple drafts. If you are new to using a computer for writing, your college writing or computer lab may offer resources and advice to help you get started.

WHY IMPROVE YOUR WRITING SKILLS?

Most college students ask themselves the following two questions.
1. How can I improve my grades?
2. How can I improve my chances of getting a good job after college?

The answer to both questions is the same: Improve your writing skills. The following sections explain why writing well is essential to your success in college and on the job.

WRITING HELPS YOU LEARN AND REMEMBER

In general, the more senses you use in learning, the more easily you learn and the more you will remember. Writing facilitates learning by engaging two senses at once: You take in information visually while reading, and you engage your sense of touch as you put your pen to paper or your fingers on a keyboard while writing. Taking notes, outlining, summarizing, and annotating enhance learning by engaging your attention and getting you to think about the subject matter as you connect, define, and evaluate ideas. Writing paragraphs and essays helps you think through issues in a sustained way, challenging you to devise reasons and find appropriate supporting evidence.

WRITING HELPS YOU THINK AND SOLVE PROBLEMS

Writing also helps you think and solve problems by forcing you to define issues or problems and allowing you to see new aspects of them. For example, one student had a father-in-law who seemed hostile and uncooperative. The student described her problem in an email to a friend: "He looks at me as if I'm going to take his son to the end of the earth and never bring him back." When she reread what she had written, she realized that her father-in-law might resent her because he was afraid of losing contact with his son. She looked for ways to reassure her father-in-law and strengthen their relationship. Writing about the problem helped the student define it and discover ways to solve it.

WRITING SKILLS HELP YOU SUCCEED IN COLLEGE AND CAREER

Writing well allows you to demonstrate what you've learned in the many college courses (such as psychology, biology, and political science) that require you to read articles, essays, reports, and textbooks and then write about what you've read. Writing is important on the job as well. In almost all jobs, workers need to communicate effectively with supervisors, coworkers, patients, clients, and customers. You can expect to write plenty of letters, email messages, and reports. A study conducted by the Collegiate Employment Research Institute found that employers consistently want the "total package"—both technical knowledge *and* strong oral and written communication skills—in recent college graduates.* Because your writing course offers both immediate and long-range benefits, it is one of the most important college courses you will take.

DEVELOPING STRATEGIES FOR WRITING

Chapter 1 provided some general strategies for success in college, such as managing your time effectively, establishing a study area, studying more efficiently, and learning to manage stress. The section below covers strategies that will make a big difference in your writing.

START WITH A POSITIVE ATTITUDE

You have the ability to be a successful writer. To approach your writing course with a positive attitude and get the most out of it, use the following suggestions.

1. **Think of writing as a process.** Writing is not a single act of getting words down on paper. It is a series of steps—planning, organizing, drafting, revising, and editing and proofreading—all of which can be done in whatever order makes sense and repeated as needed. (Most writers go back and forth among these steps.)

   For more about the writing process, see Part 2.

2. **Be patient.** Writing is a skill that improves with practice. On some days, writing will be easier than on other days, but as you draft and revise your essays, your writing will improve in small ways that build on one another.

3. **Expect writing to take time, often more time than you planned.** Build in extra time for completing writing assignments.

---

*Betsy Stevens, "What Communication Skills Do Employers Want? Silicon Valley Recruiters Respond," *Journal of Employment Counseling* 42 (2005): 2–9.

4. **Focus on learning.** When you are given a writing or reading assignment, ask, "What can I learn from this task?" As you learn more about your own reading and writing processes, write down your observations. (See the section on journal writing on p. 29.)

5. **Attend all classes, and use the support and guidance available to you outside class.** Writing is a skill that is best learned through practice and feedback from readers, such as your instructor and classmates, so being prepared for class, attending regularly, and participating fully are crucial to your success. You can also get help outside class by talking to your instructor during office hours, visiting the writing center at your school, and taking advantage of the guidance in this book and online. (In Parts 3 and 4 of this book, Guided Writing Assignments and Revision Flowcharts provide tips, advice, and alternative ways of approaching assignments.)

USE YOUR COURSE SYLLABUS

The most important document you will receive in your first week of class is your course **syllabus**, a document that describes how the course operates and directs you through your class. A typical syllabus includes information on required texts, attendance and plagiarism policies, grading system, course objectives, weekly assignments or readings, due dates, and dates of exams. Here are some tips for using a syllabus to maximize your learning and your course grade.

- Read the syllabus carefully at the beginning of the course, and check it regularly so that you are prepared for class.
- Mark all deadlines on your calendar.
- Ask your instructor any questions you may have about the syllabus, course structure, deadlines, and expectations about course objectives. Note the answers on the syllabus or in your course notebook.
- Pay close attention to the course objectives, which outline what you are expected to learn in the course. Papers and exams will measure how well you meet them.
- Scan or copy each course syllabus. Keep one copy in the front of your notebook for easy reference during class or while you are studying; keep the other in a file folder at home or on your computer in case you lose your notebook.

A sample syllabus is shown in Figure 2.1.

EXERCISE 2.1 | **Getting the Most from Your Syllabus**

Review the syllabus that your writing class instructor distributed. Write a paragraph describing your expectations and concerns about your writing course based on the syllabus. Be sure to answer the following questions.

1. What are you expected to learn in the course?
2. What kinds of essays will you write?
3. What are the grading and attendance policies?
4. Is class participation expected and required? Is it part of your grade?
5. Is research required? Is Internet use required or expected?

FIGURE 2.1 Excerpted Sample Syllabus for a College Writing Course

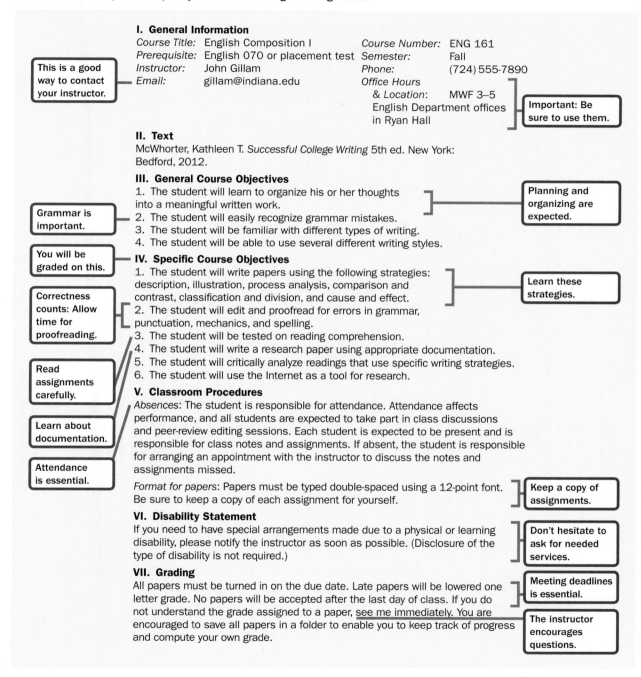

I. General Information

Course Title: English Composition I   *Course Number:* ENG 161
Prerequisite: English 070 or placement test   *Semester:* Fall
Instructor: John Gillam   *Phone:* (724) 555-7890
Email: gillam@indiana.edu   *Office Hours*
    & Location: MWF 3–5
    English Department offices
    in Ryan Hall

> This is a good way to contact your instructor.

> Important: Be sure to use them.

II. Text

McWhorter, Kathleen T. *Successful College Writing* 5th ed. New York: Bedford, 2012.

III. General Course Objectives

1. The student will learn to organize his or her thoughts into a meaningful written work.
2. The student will easily recognize grammar mistakes.
3. The student will be familiar with different types of writing.
4. The student will be able to use several different writing styles.

> Planning and organizing are expected.

> Grammar is important.

IV. Specific Course Objectives

1. The student will write papers using the following strategies: description, illustration, process analysis, comparison and contrast, classification and division, and cause and effect.
2. The student will edit and proofread for errors in grammar, punctuation, mechanics, and spelling.
3. The student will be tested on reading comprehension.
4. The student will write a research paper using appropriate documentation.
5. The student will critically analyze readings that use specific writing strategies.
6. The student will use the Internet as a tool for research.

> You will be graded on this.

> Correctness counts: Allow time for proofreading.

> Learn these strategies.

> Read assignments carefully.

> Learn about documentation.

V. Classroom Procedures

Absences: The student is responsible for attendance. Attendance affects performance, and all students are expected to take part in class discussions and peer-review editing sessions. Each student is expected to be present and is responsible for class notes and assignments. If absent, the student is responsible for arranging an appointment with the instructor to discuss the notes and assignments missed.

> Attendance is essential.

Format for papers: Papers must be typed double-spaced using a 12-point font. Be sure to keep a copy of each assignment for yourself.

> Keep a copy of assignments.

VI. Disability Statement

If you need to have special arrangements made due to a physical or learning disability, please notify the instructor as soon as possible. (Disclosure of the type of disability is not required.)

> Don't hesitate to ask for needed services.

VII. Grading

All papers must be turned in on the due date. Late papers will be lowered one letter grade. No papers will be accepted after the last day of class. If you do not understand the grade assigned to a paper, <u>see me immediately.</u> You are encouraged to save all papers in a folder to enable you to keep track of progress and compute your own grade.

> Meeting deadlines is essential.

> The instructor encourages questions.

(Figure 2.1 continued)

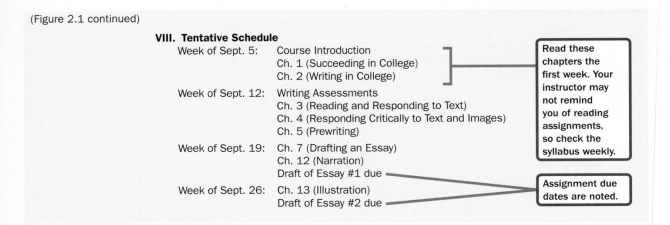

VIII. Tentative Schedule

Week of Sept. 5:	Course Introduction
	Ch. 1 (Succeeding in College)
	Ch. 2 (Writing in College)
Week of Sept. 12:	Writing Assessments
	Ch. 3 (Reading and Responding to Text)
	Ch. 4 (Responding Critically to Text and Images)
	Ch. 5 (Prewriting)
Week of Sept. 19:	Ch. 7 (Drafting an Essay)
	Ch. 12 (Narration)
	Draft of Essay #1 due
Week of Sept. 26:	Ch. 13 (Illustration)
	Draft of Essay #2 due

> Read these chapters the first week. Your instructor may not remind you of reading assignments, so check the syllabus weekly.

> Assignment due dates are noted.

USE THE RIGHT WRITING TOOLS

To be successful in college, you need the right learning tools. Your textbooks are essential, but you also need quick access to other sources of information.

If you have access to a computer, bookmark the following:

- a good online dictionary (such as *Merriam-Webster Online*),
- an online desk reference, such as www.refdesk.com, for factual information,

A sample definition from Merriam-Webster Online

By permission. From Merriam-Webster's Collegiate® Dictionary, 11th Edition. © 2013 by Merriam-Webster, Inc. (www.Merriam-Webster.com).

- the home page of your college library,
- DVDs or USB drives for backing up and transporting your work (unless you save your work in the "cloud"), and
- classmates' and instructors' email addresses.

Be sure you have each of the following tools handy in your writing and study area:
- a reliable collegiate dictionary, such as *Merriam-Webster's Collegiate Dictionary* or *Webster's New World Dictionary,* and
- a thesaurus (dictionary of synonyms), such as *Roget's Thesaurus.*

> **EXERCISE 2.2**   **Examining Online Reference Sources**
>
> Record below the online reference sources that you have found useful. Compare your list with other students' lists. Add any sources that seem useful to your list.
>
> **ONLINE REFERENCE SOURCES**
>
> 1.
> 2.
> 3.
> 4.

USE THE COLLEGE WRITING CENTER

Many colleges have a writing center that offers help with any college writing assignment, not just assignments for your writing class. Writing centers generally provide trained student tutors and professional staff, who can help you do the following:
- understand an assignment,
- organize your ideas,
- revise a draft,
- use appropriate format and documentation, and
- understand errors on a graded paper.

However, do not expect them to write your paper or correct all of its errors. Some writing centers offer their tutorial services online or face-to-face, others only face-to-face; some offer walk-in help, and others require an appointment. When you visit the writing center, be sure to bring all of the following:
- your assignment,
- all drafts of your essay,
- any articles or essays to which the assignment refers, and
- paper and pen or pencil.

KEEP A WRITING JOURNAL

Keeping a **writing journal** will help you improve your writing by giving you a judgment-free place to practice. In your journal, you can experiment with voice, topics, or approaches to a topic; reflect on a reading selection or assignment; record your impressions and observations; or explore relationships among people or ideas. Here's how to get started.

1. **Write in a spiral-bound notebook or create a computer file.** Date each entry.
2. **Set aside five to ten minutes for journal writing each day.** You don't need a long block of time; instead, you can write while waiting for a bus or for class to start.
3. **Concentrate on capturing your ideas, not on being grammatically correct.** Try to write correct sentences, but don't focus on grammar and punctuation. (If you are not sure what to write about, consult Figure 2.2.)
4. **Reread your journal entries regularly.** Rereading entries will bring back vivid snippets of the past for reflection and provide ideas and insights for upcoming assignments.

Writing Activity 1

Write a journal entry describing your reaction to one or more of your classes this term. For example, you might write about which classes you expect to be most or least difficult, most or least enjoyable, and most or least time-consuming.

GET THE MOST OUT OF WRITING CONFERENCES

Many writing instructors require writing conferences with individual students to discuss the student's work and his or her progress in the course. If the conferences are optional, be sure to schedule one.

The following tips will help you get the most out of a writing conference.

1. **Reread recently returned papers ahead of time, so that your instructor's comments are fresh in your mind.** Review your notes from any previous conferences.
2. **Arrive on time or a few minutes early, and bring copies of the essay you are currently working on, as well as previously graded papers.** Have these materials in hand, not buried in your backpack, when your conference begins.
3. **Allow your instructor to set the agenda,** but come prepared with questions.
4. **Take notes either during or immediately after the conference.** Include the comments and suggestions that your instructor offered. You might also write a journal entry that summarizes the conference.
5. **Revise the draft essay you and your instructor discussed as soon as possible,** while your instructor's suggestions are still fresh in your mind.

WHAT IS YOUR LEARNING STYLE?

Have you noticed that you do better with some types of academic assignments than with others? For example, you may prefer hands-on assignments to conducting research or vice versa. Do you find it is easier to learn from some instructors than from others?

FIGURE 2.2 Starting Points for Journal Writing

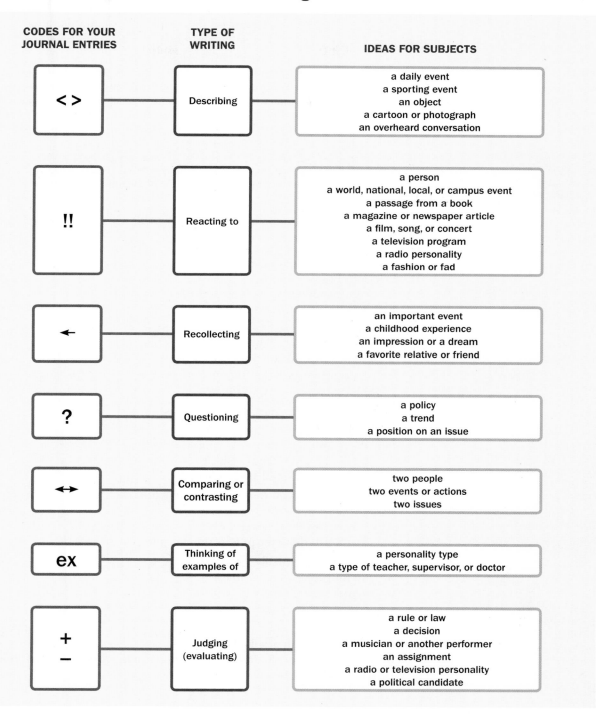

CODES FOR YOUR JOURNAL ENTRIES	TYPE OF WRITING	IDEAS FOR SUBJECTS
< >	Describing	a daily event a sporting event an object a cartoon or photograph an overheard conversation
!!	Reacting to	a person a world, national, local, or campus event a passage from a book a magazine or newspaper article a film, song, or concert a television program a radio personality a fashion or fad
←	Recollecting	an important event a childhood experience an impression or a dream a favorite relative or friend
?	Questioning	a policy a trend a position on an issue
↔	Comparing or contrasting	two people two events or actions two issues
ex	Thinking of examples of	a personality type a type of teacher, supervisor, or doctor
+ −	Judging (evaluating)	a rule or law a decision a musician or another performer an assignment a radio or television personality a political candidate

For example, you may prefer instructors who provide real-life examples or those who show relationships by drawing diagrams. Have you noticed that your friends study, solve problems, and approach assignments differently than you do? For example, you may be able to read printed information and recall it easily, but a friend may find it easier to learn from class lectures or an online video.

Each person learns and writes in a unique way, depending in part on his or her experiences, personality, and prior learning. Discovering the **learning style** that is right for you will give you an important advantage in all of your college courses. To assess your learning style, complete the Learning Style Inventory below.

LEARNING STYLE INVENTORY

Directions: Each numbered item presents two choices. Select the alternative that describes you better. There are no right or wrong answers. In cases in which neither choice suits you, select the one that is closer to your preference. Check the letter of your choice next to the question number on the answer sheet on page 35.

1. In a class, I usually
   a. make friends with just a few students.
   b. get to know many of my classmates.

2. If I were required to act in a play, I would prefer to
   a. have the director tell me how to say my lines.
   b. read my lines the way I think they should be read.

3. Which would I find more helpful in studying the processes by which the U.S. Constitution can be amended?
   a. a one-paragraph summary
   b. a diagram

4. In making decisions, I am more concerned with
   a. whether I have all the available facts.
   b. how my decision will affect others.

5. When I have a difficult time understanding how something works, it helps most if I can
   a. see how it works several times.
   b. take time to think the process through and analyze it.

6. At a social event, I usually
   a. wait for people to speak to me.
   b. initiate conversation with others.

7. I prefer courses that have
   a. a traditional structure (lectures, assigned readings, periodic exams, and assignments with deadlines).
   b. an informal structure (class discussions, flexible assignments, and student-selected projects).

8. If I were studying one of the laws of motion in a physics course, I would prefer to have my instructor begin the class by
   a. stating the law and discussing examples.
   b. giving a demonstration of how the law works.

9. Which set of terms describes me better?
   a. fair and objective
   b. sympathetic and understanding

10. When I learn something new, I am more interested in
    a. the facts about it.
    b. the principles behind it.

11. As a volunteer for a community organization that is raising funds for a hospice, I would prefer the following tasks:
    a. stuffing envelopes for a mail campaign
    b. making phone calls asking for contributions

12. I would begin an ideal day by
    a. planning what I want to do during each hour of the day.
    b. doing whatever comes to mind.

13. If I wanted to learn the proper way to prune a rosebush, I would prefer to
    a. have someone explain it to me.
    b. watch someone do it.

14. It is more important for me to be
    a. consistent in thought and action.
    b. responsive to the feelings of others.

15. If I kept a journal or diary, it would most likely contain entries about
    a. what happens to me each day.
    b. the insights and ideas that occur to me each day.

16. If I decided to learn a musical instrument, I would prefer to take
    a. one-on-one lessons.
    b. group lessons.

17. If I worked in a factory, I would prefer to be a
    a. machine operator.
    b. troubleshooter.

18. I learn best when I
    a. write down the information.
    b. form a mental picture of the information.

19. If I gave a wrong answer in class, my main concern would be
    a. finding out the correct answer.
    b. what others in class thought of me.

20. I prefer television news programs that
    a. summarize events through film footage and factual description.
    b. deal with the issues behind the events.

21. Whenever possible, I choose to
    a. study alone.
    b. study with a group.

22. In selecting a topic for a research paper, my more important concern is
    a. choosing a topic for which there is adequate information.
    b. choosing a topic I find interesting.

23. To help me reassemble a complicated toy or machine I took apart to repair, I would
    a. write a list of the steps I followed when taking the toy or machine apart.
    b. draw a diagram of the toy or machine.

24. As a member of a jury for a criminal trial, I would be primarily concerned with
    a. determining how witness testimony fits with the other evidence.
    b. judging the believability of witnesses.

25. If I were an author, I would most likely write
    a. biographies or how-to books.
    b. novels or poetry.

26. A career in which my work depends on that of others is
    a. less appealing than working alone.
    b. more appealing than working alone.

27. When I am able to solve a problem, it is usually because I
    a. worked through the solution step-by-step.
    b. brainstormed until I arrived at a solution.

28. I prefer to keep up with the news by
    a. reading a newspaper.
    b. watching television news programs.

29. If I witnessed a serious auto accident, my first impulse would be to
    a. assess the situation.
    b. comfort any injured people.

30. I pride myself on my ability to
    a. remember numbers and facts.
    b. see how ideas are related.

31. To solve a personal problem, I prefer to
    a. think about it myself.
    b. talk it through with friends.

32. If I had one last elective course to take before graduation, I would choose one that presents
    a. practical information that I can use immediately.
    b. ideas that make me think and stimulate my imagination.

33. For recreation, I would rather do a
    a. crossword puzzle.
    b. jigsaw puzzle.

34. I can best be described as
    a. reasonable and levelheaded.
    b. sensitive and caring.

35. When I read a story or watch a film, I prefer one with a plot that is
    a. clear and direct.
    b. intricate and complex.

Answer Sheet

Directions: Check either *a* or *b* in the boxes next to each question number.

	Column One			Column Two			Column Three			Column Four			Column Five	
	a	*b*		*a*	*b*		*a*	*b*		*a*	*b*		*a*	*b*
1			2			3			4			5		
6			7			8			9			10		
11			12			13			14			15		
16			17			18			19			20		
21			22			23			24			25		
26			27			28			29			30		
31			32			33			34			35		
Total														

Directions for Scoring

1. On your answer sheet, add the checkmarks in each *a* and *b* column, counting first the number of *a*s checked and then the number of *b*s.
2. Enter the number of *a*s and *b*s you checked in the boxes at the bottom of each column.
3. Transfer these numbers to the Scoring Grid on page 36. Enter the number of *a* choices in column one in the blank labeled "Independent," the number of *b* choices in column one in the blank labeled "Social," and so on.
4. Circle your higher score in each row. For example, if you scored 2 for Independent and 5 for Social, circle "5" and "Social."
5. Your higher score in each row indicates a characteristic of your learning style. Scores that are close, such as 3 and 4, probably do not indicate a strong preference for either approach to learning. Scores that are far apart, such as 1 and 6, suggest a strong preference.

Scoring Grid

Column	Number of Checkmarks	
	Choice *a*	Choice *b*
One	_____ Independent	_____ Social
Two	_____ Pragmatic	_____ Creative
Three	_____ Verbal	_____ Spatial
Four	_____ Rational	_____ Emotional
Five	_____ Concrete	_____ Abstract

INTERPRETING YOUR SCORES

Each question in the Learning Style Inventory assesses one of five aspects of your learning style. Here is how to interpret the five aspects of your learning style.

1. **Independent or Social** These scores indicate your preferred level of interaction with others. *Independent* learners prefer to work and study alone. They focus on the task at hand rather than on the people around them. Independent learners are often goal oriented and self-motivated. *Social* learners are more people oriented and prefer to learn and study with classmates. They often focus their attention on those around them and see a task as an opportunity for social interaction.

2. **Pragmatic or Creative** These scores suggest how you prefer to approach learning tasks. *Pragmatic* learners are practical and systematic. They approach tasks in an orderly, sequential manner. They like rules and learn step-by-step. *Creative* learners approach tasks imaginatively. They prefer to learn through discovery or experiment. They enjoy flexible, open-ended tasks and tend to dislike following rules.

3. **Verbal or Spatial** These scores indicate the way you prefer to take in and process information. *Verbal* learners rely on language, usually written text, to acquire information. They are skilled in the use of language and can work with other symbol systems (such as numbers) as well. *Spatial* learners prefer to take in information by studying graphics such as drawings, diagrams, films, or videos. They can visualize in their minds how things work or how they are positioned in space.

4. **Rational or Emotional** These scores suggest your preferred approach to decision making and problem solving. *Rational* learners are objective; they rely on facts and information when making decisions or solving problems. Rational learners are logical, often challenging or questioning a task. They enjoy prioritizing, analyzing, and arguing. *Emotional* learners are subjective; they focus on feelings and values. Emotional learners are socially conscious and consider what others think. They seek harmony and may base a decision in part on its effect on others. Emotional decision makers are often skilled at persuasion.

5. **Concrete or Abstract** These scores indicate how you prefer to perceive information. *Concrete* learners pay attention to what is concrete and observable. They focus on details and tend to perceive tasks in parts or steps. Concrete learners prefer specific, tangible tasks and usually take a no-nonsense approach to learning. *Abstract* learners tend to focus on the "big picture" — large ideas, meanings, and relationships.

The results of the Learning Style Inventory probably confirmed some things you already knew about yourself as a learner and provided you with some new insights as well. Keep in mind, though, that there are other ways to measure learning style.

- The inventory you completed is an informal measure of your learning style. Other, more formal measures including Kolb's Learning Style Inventory, the Canfield Instructional Styles Inventory, and the Myers-Briggs Type Indicator may be available at your college's counseling or academic skills center.
- The inventory you completed measures the five aspects of learning style that are most relevant to the writing process, but many other aspects exist.
- You are the best judge of the accuracy of the results of this inventory and how they apply to you. If you think that one or more of the aspects of your learning style indicated by the inventory do not describe you, trust your instincts.

APPLYING YOUR LEARNING STYLE TO YOUR WRITING

Writing is a process that involves planning, organizing, drafting, revising, editing, and proofreading. You'll learn more about each of these steps in Chapters 5 to 10. Each step in the writing process can be approached in more than one way. For example, one of the first steps in writing an essay is selecting a topic to write about.

- A social learner may prefer to brainstorm possible topics with a friend.
- A verbal learner may flip through a news magazine for topics.
- A spatial learner may see a photograph that generates ideas.
- A social, spatial learner may prefer to discuss photographs with a classmate.

Let's consider an example involving two hypothetical students, Yolanda and Andrea. These classmates in a first-year writing course are given the same assignment: "Write an essay describing an event that has influenced your life." Although Yolanda and Andrea approach the same assignment in different ways, they both write effective essays.

Yolanda, a *pragmatic learner,* prefers a deliberate and systematic approach:

- She writes a list of possible events and arranges them in order of importance.
- After selecting one of these events, she draws a diagram showing the circumstances that led up to the event and the effects of that event.
- Before she begins writing, she decides on the best way to organize her ideas and creates an outline.

Andrea, a *creative learner,* prefers to experiment before deciding on the best approach to her essay:

- She lets her mind roam freely while jogging. All of a sudden an event comes to mind.
- She jots down everything she can recall about the event.
- From these notes, she selects ideas and writes her first draft.
- She experiments with different organizations and revises twice before she is satisfied.

Because learning styles differ, this book presents alternative strategies for generating ideas and revising your writing. These choices are indicated by the marginal note "Learning Style Options" (see p. 60 for an example). The following advice will help you take advantage of these learning style alternatives.

1. **Your learning style profile indicates your strengths as a writer.** Try to build on your strengths, which Figure 2.3 (p. 39) can help you identify. First circle the learning style characteristics that correspond to you. Then refer to the right-hand column to see your strengths as a writer in each area.
2. **Experiment with options.** Some students find that when they try a new approach, it works better than they expected. Sometimes choose an activity that does not match your preferred learning style.
3. **Don't expect the option that is consistent with your learning style to require less attention or effort.** Even if you are a social learner, an interview must still be carefully planned and well executed.
4. **Keep logs of the skills and approaches that work for you and the ones you need to work on.** The logs may be part of your writing journal. (See p. 29.) Be specific: Record the assignment, the topic, and the skills you applied. Analyze your log, looking for patterns. Over time, you will discover more about the writing strategies and approaches that work best for you.

Writing Activity 2

Write a two-page essay describing your reactions to the results of the Learning Style Inventory. Explain how you expect to use the results in your writing course or other courses.

Writing Activity 3

Using your responses to the Writing Quick Start on page 21 and the results of the Learning Style Inventory, write a two-page profile of yourself as a student or as a writer.

FIGURE 2.3 **Your Strengths as a Writer**

LEARNING STYLE CHARACTERISTIC	STRENGTHS AS A WRITER
Independent	You are willing to spend time thinking about a topic and are able to pull ideas together easily.
Social	You usually find it easy to write from experience. Writing realistic dialogue may be one of your strengths. You tend to have a good sense of whom you are writing for (your audience) and what you hope to accomplish (your purpose).
Pragmatic	You can meet deadlines easily. You recognize the need for organization in an essay. You tend to approach writing systematically and work through the steps in the writing process.
Creative	You tend to enjoy exploring a topic and often do so thoroughly and completely. Your writing is not usually hindered or restricted by rules or requirements.
Verbal	You may have a talent for generating ideas to write about and expressing them clearly.
Spatial	You can visualize or draw a map of the organization of your paper. Descriptions of physical objects, places, and people come easily.
Rational	You tend to write logically developed, well-organized essays. You usually analyze ideas objectively.
Emotional	Expressive and descriptive writing usually go well for you. You have a strong awareness of your audience.
Concrete	You find it easy to supply details to support an idea. You are able to write accurate, detailed descriptions and observations. You can organize facts effectively and present them clearly.
Abstract	You can develop unique approaches to a topic; you can grasp the point to which supporting ideas lead.

3

Reading and Responding to Text

Your Mass Communication instructor has asked your class to study the photograph at the right and discuss its meaning. Write a paragraph explaining what the photograph suggests to you about mass communication and evaluate why the instructor might have asked you to study it. Be detailed and specific. Study the photograph's content, trying to discover what statement it makes about communication.

© Purepix/Alamy

To explain the photograph, you had to think beyond the obvious. You had to interpret the photograph to arrive at its possible meaning. To complete this analysis, you did two things. First, you understood what the photograph shows: a shepherd using a mobile telephone. Then you evaluated why your instructor asked you to reflect on the photo: He or she probably wanted you to realize how communications have changed in the twenty-first century. Now, people from all walks of life, and all over the globe, communicate using mobile telephones and other devices.

Reading involves a similar process of comprehension and evaluation. First, you must understand what the author *says;* then you must interpret and respond to what the author *means.* Both parts of the process are essential.

IN THIS CHAPTER YOU WILL LEARN TO

- understand what academic reading involves and develop an active approach to reading,
- learn how to draw a *graphic organizer* that will help you grasp both the content and the organization of an assignment,
- learn how to write a paper in response to a reading assignment, and
- learn how to respond effectively to other students' writing.

ACADEMIC READING: WHAT TO EXPECT

EXPECT TO BE RESPONSIBLE FOR YOUR OWN LEARNING

College instructors generally offer less help with reading assignments than high school teachers do. If you have questions, they will answer them, but they won't remind you to do the reading, and they often won't check to see if you are keeping up with the assignments. They will expect you to understand the reading and be able to apply it, and you may be called on in class to demonstrate your understanding through discussion or quizzes. So use the time-management suggestions in Chapter 1 (pp. 8–9) to schedule time to complete all your assignments, and leave extra time for challenging selections.

EXPECT TO READ SELECTIONS FOR ACADEMIC AUDIENCES

The reading you will be assigned in college will likely be more challenging than the reading you were assigned in high school. As you progress through college, you will read increasingly challenging selections, many of which are written for specialized or academic audiences. These take more time to read than do less challenging selections: You may need to look up unfamiliar vocabulary as you master the language of the discipline. You may also need to think about each sentence or paragraph before you understand it well enough to move on to the next. Your instructors will expect you to make an effort to understand the reading and to engage with it critically, so plan to read assignments more than once.

EXPECT TO READ SELECTIONS IN DIFFERENT GENRES AND WITH DIFFERENT PURPOSES

In college, you will encounter a wide range of reading material. In addition to reading textbooks, you may read scholarly articles, essays, critiques, field reports, and scientific studies. You will need to use different strategies for reading each type, or **genre** of material. Begin by noticing how each genre is organized. Then determine the writer's purpose: Is the reading selection mainly **informative** or mainly **persuasive**? Next, devise a strategy for identifying what is important to learn and remember about it. (The suggestions elsewhere in this chapter and in this book will help you with this task.)

EXPECT TO READ CRITICALLY

In college, understanding the literal content of reading assignments is often not enough. You must go beyond what an article or essay *says* to understand what it *means*. You also need to think about how true, useful, and important the information is. Instructors expect you to interpret, evaluate, and respond to the ideas you have read about. They expect you to read and think critically, questioning and challenging ideas as you encounter them. The advice in this chapter and the next will help you read critically.

Many reading assignments include illustrations, photographs, charts, and graphs. Writers use these visuals to clarify or emphasize ideas, condense information, explain a complicated process, or illustrate a viewpoint. Think about the purpose of each visual you encounter and the way that it relates to the text that accompanies it. Chapter 4 discusses interpreting visuals in detail.

To read actively and critically, you will need to write as you read. Try taking notes on assignments, highlighting, outlining or drawing a graphic organizer, summarizing, and annotating texts to engage with them actively. Try also to synthesize, or connect, what you're reading with what you've learned in other classes or elsewhere.

EXPECT TO USE READINGS AS MODELS

By studying what others have written, you can improve your own writing. As you read an article, essay, or textbook assignment, take note of the writer's techniques. For example, notice how paragraphs are organized, how language is used to express ideas, and how ideas are developed. Then practice these techniques, in either your writing journal or your draft essays.

AVOIDING MISCONCEPTIONS

Much misinformation exists about how to read effectively and efficiently. This section dispels some popular misconceptions about reading.

MISCONCEPTION: You must read, understand, and remember everything.

TRUTH: Most texts contain a mixture of important and not-so-important ideas and information. Your job is to sort through the material and evaluate what you need to know.

MISCONCEPTION: You should read everything the same way.

TRUTH: Your purpose for reading should guide the way you read. The type of material, your familiarity with the subject, and what you are expected to do when you have finished reading (take a test or participate In a class discussion, for example) should determine how you read.

MISCONCEPTION: Reading an assignment once is enough.

TRUTH: Reading an assignment once is often not sufficient. You will need to reread to discover the author's position, summarize the author's key ideas, and analyze the strength of the supporting evidence.

MISCONCEPTION: If it's in print or online, you can trust it.	**TRUTH:** Not everything in print or online is true. Just as you shouldn't believe everything you hear, neither should you believe everything you read. Read with a critical, questioning eye. To evaluate a text, consider the author's credibility and purpose for writing.

EXPECT TO RESPOND TO READINGS IN WRITING

Many instructors will ask you to respond in writing to assigned readings. They may ask you to take a brief quiz based on the reading, for example, or to prepare a list of questions or issues that the reading raises in preparation for class discussion. The purpose of such activities is to make sure you understand the reading and are ready to analyze and evaluate it. Instructors may also require you to write a response paper. (See the Guide to Responding to Text later in this chapter on pp. 60–65.)

A GUIDE TO ACTIVE READING

When you attend a ball game or watch a TV show, do you get actively involved? Baseball fans cheer some players and boo others, evaluate plays and calls, and shout out advice. Similarly, fans of TV shows react to sudden turns of events, sympathizing with some characters and despising others. By contrast, if you are not a fan of a baseball team or TV show, you might watch the game or show passively, letting it take its course with little or no personal involvement or reaction (and little recollection of key events a few days later).

APPROACHES TO READING: ACTIVE VERSUS PASSIVE

Passive Reading	**Active Reading**
Passive readers begin reading.	Active readers begin by reading the title, evaluating the author, and thinking about what they already know about the subject. Then they decide what they need to know before they begin reading.
Passive readers read the essay only because it is assigned.	Active readers read the essay while looking for answers to questions and key elements.
Passive readers read but do not write.	Active readers read with a pen or pencil in hand. They highlight or underline, annotate, and write notes as they read.
Passive readers close the book when finished.	Active readers review, analyze, and evaluate the essay.

Like fans of a sports team or TV show, active readers get involved with the material they read. They question, think about, and react to ideas using the process outlined in Figure 3.1. Their active involvement in what they read helps them understand and remember the selection long after they finish the page. The sections that follow explain in detail each of the steps in reading actively.

BEFORE READING

Never start reading an essay or other reading assignment without preparation. Your mind isn't ready. Instead, use previewing and guide questions to discover what the reading is about and focus your mind on the topic.

FIGURE 3.1 The Active Reading Process

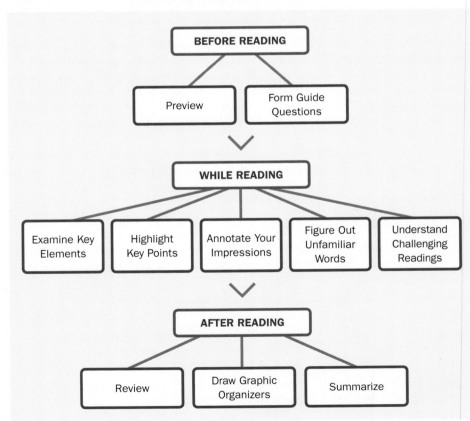

Previewing. Previewing is a quick way of familiarizing yourself with an essay's content and organization. It helps you decide what you need to learn, and it has a number of other benefits as well.

- It helps you get interested in the material.
- It helps you concentrate on the material because you have a mental outline of it before you begin reading and therefore know what to expect.
- It helps you remember more of what you read.

To preview a reading selection, use the guidelines in the following list. When previewing, remember to read *only* the parts of an essay that are listed:

1. **Read the title, subtitle, and author.** The title and subtitle may tell you what the reading is about. Check the author's name to see if it is one you recognize.
2. **Read the introduction or the first paragraph.** These sections often provide an overview of the selection.
3. **Read any headings and the first sentence following each one.** Taken together, headings often form a mini-outline of the selection. The first sentence following a heading often explains the heading further.
4. **For selections without headings, read the first sentence in a few of the paragraphs on each page.**
5. **Look at the photographs, tables, charts, and drawings.**
6. **Read the conclusion or summary.** A conclusion draws the selection to a close and may repeat the main idea (or thesis) of the essay and the key supporting ideas, providing a summary.
7. **Read any end-of-assignment questions.** These questions will help focus your attention on what is important and what you might be expected to know after you have read it.

The following essay has been highlighted to illustrate the parts you should read while previewing. Preview it now.

READING

American Jerk: Be Civil, or I'll Beat You to a Pulp

TODD SCHWARTZ

Todd Schwartz is a writer based in Portland, Oregon. A longer version of this essay originally appeared in the *Oregon Humanities Review* in 2008 under the title "The Great Civility War." The version below was published in 2009 in *The Utne Reader*.

It was the most civil of times, it was the least civil of times, it was the age of politeness, it was the age of boorishness, it was the epoch of concern, it was the epoch of who cares, it was the season of hybrid, it was the season of Hummer, it was the spring of Obama, it was the winter of hate speech . . .   1

Jesse Kuhn/RawToastDesign

With apologies to Mr. Dickens (or not: screw him), we have arrived at simultaneously the most and least civil moment in U.S. history. A moment when a roomful of even relatively evolved people will react with discomfort to an off-color joke about people of color—and when those same people have no compunction whatsoever about loudly ignoring one another as they blather into their cell phones. 2

We have never been more concerned about the feelings of minority groups, the disabled, and the disadvantaged. Yet we have never been less concerned about the feelings of anyone with whom we share the road, the Internet, or the movie theater. 3

Political correctness holds such sway that holidays go unnamed for fear of insulting or excluding someone. Schools won't let teachers use red pens to correct papers, because little Ethan's or Emily's self-esteem might be bruised. No one is "poor," but many are "socioeconomically disadvantaged." Civility and thoughtfulness in speech have never been so complete or so codified. 4

All of which is well intentioned and mostly a wonderful thing. I'm all for being polite and caring and Golden Rule-ish. Sadly, like a lovely field of wildflowers—which in reality is filled with bloodsucking ticks and noxious pollen—we live oh-so-politely in what must certainly be the rudest era in recorded history. Maybe even prehistory. 5

Neanderthals were probably nicer to each other than we are. 6

Pick your poison: reality television, slasher movies, video games, online porn, cell phones, automated answering systems, giant assault vehicles for trips to the grocery store, car stereos played at volumes easily heard on Jupiter, web-powered copyright infringement, people who will not shut their inane traps in movie theaters, and, lord help us, now even people who won't shut their inane traps during live theater. 7

We're all talking to someone all the time, but it's ever more rarely to the people we are   8
actually with. Our cell phones blare ringtones that no one else wants to hear. We love
to watch TV shows about the stunningly predictable results of hand-feeding a grizzly
bear or lighting a stick of dynamite with a cigarette. We also love shows where people
lie to others for money and programs where snarky, slightly talented folks say vicious
things to hopeful, and usually more talented, contestants.

Civility rules, friends.   9

Civility is dead, jerks.   10

Why? I have a few theories.   11

The first is that America is in the same position as Rome found itself in about 420 CE,   12
meaning that we've reached the peak of our civilization and now everything is going
to Tartarus in a chariot. We're too far from our food and energy sources, and fewer and
fewer of the Druids and Visigoths like us anymore. So we desperately cling to a patina of
civility while we grab a snack and watch large, toothy predators devour people.

The second is that sunlight contains tiny spores that lodge in the cerebellum,   13
making the infected believe they are the center of the universe.

My final and somewhat less cutting edge theory is that a large percentage of people   14
are just clueless, distracted, and self-absorbed, unable to process concepts such as spatial
awareness (for example: when you are walking in the same direction with several hundred
people in, say, an airport terminal, DON'T JUST STOP IN THE MIDDLE OF THE FLOW!).

But I digress.   15

I am not here to judge whether being civil and considerate is somehow better than   16
being a mindless dillweed. You must make that choice for yourself. We inhabit the
most civil of times and the least—and I completely honor and respect your freedom to
choose your side in the Great Civility War.

Just don't get in my way. I'm on my cell in the Escalade, and I can't be bothered.   17

EXERCISE 3.1   **Testing Recall after Previewing**

Based only on your preview of the essay "American Jerk," indicate whether each of the following
statements is true or false. If most of your answers are correct, you will know that previewing
helped you gain a sense of the essay's context and organization. (For the answers to this exercise, see p. 72.)

_____ 1. The reading is primarily about civility and the lack of it.
_____ 2. The author blames the Internet for our society's lack of civility.
_____ 3. The author suggests that political correctness does not go far enough.
_____ 4. People are often not intentionally rude but simply are distracted or unaware.
_____ 5. Society is unconcerned about minorities.

Form questions to guide your reading. Before you begin reading, devise questions about the selection based on sections you previewed (see pp. 45–47). Then, as you read, answer those questions. This process of asking and answering questions will strengthen your comprehension and recall of the material. The following examples will help you start devising your questions.

Essay Titles	*Questions*
"Part-time Employment Undermines Students' Commitment to School"	Why does part-time employment undermine commitment to school?
"Human Cloning: Don't Just Say 'No'"	What are good reasons to clone humans?

Headings	
"Types of Territoriality"	What are the types of territoriality?
"Territorial Encroachment"	What is territorial encroachment and how does it occur?

Not all essays lend themselves to these techniques. In some essays, you may need to dig deeper into the introductory and final paragraphs to form questions, or you may discover that the subtitle is more useful than the title. Look again at your preview of "American Jerk." Using the introductory paragraphs of that essay, you might decide to look for answers to this question: *Why is the author, Todd Schwartz, negative toward Americans?*

WHILE READING

While you are reading, figure out which ideas are important and which are less so by
- examining key elements,
- recording your thoughts and reactions to the reading,
- highlighting key points, and
- annotating the reading.

As you read, identify unfamiliar vocabulary to figure out or look up later, and be prepared to take action to strengthen your comprehension of challenging reading assignments.

Examine key elements. As you read assigned articles and essays, pay particular attention to the following key elements:
1. **The title and subtitle.** Often the title announces the topic and reveals the author's point of view. Sometimes, though, the meaning or significance of the title becomes clear only as you read the text.
2. **The introduction.** The opening paragraph or paragraphs often provide background information, announce the topic, and grab the reader's attention.
3. **The author's main point.** In most essays, a **thesis statement** directly expresses the one big idea that the essay explains, explores, or supports. Writers often place the thesis in the first or second paragraph to let readers know what lies ahead. But the thesis may appear at the end of an essay, and occasionally a thesis may be implied or suggested rather than stated directly.

For more about thesis statements, see Chapter 6.

4. **The support and explanation.** The body of an essay should support the author's main point with convincing evidence or examples. Each paragraph in the body usually has a **topic sentence** stating what the paragraph is about. Each topic sentence in some way explains or supports the essay's thesis statement.

5. **The conclusion.** The essay's final paragraph or paragraphs often restate the author's main point or offers ideas for further thought.

You'll learn much more about each part of an essay in Chapters 6 to 8.

Now read the "American Jerk" again, paying attention to the marginal notes that identify and explain the various parts of it.

American Jerk: Be Civil, or I'll Beat You to a Pulp

TODD SCHWARTZ

Todd Schwartz is a writer based in Portland, Oregon. A longer version of this essay originally appeared in the *Oregon Humanities Review* in 2008 under the title "The Great Civility War." The version below was published in 2009 in *The Utne Reader*.

Title and subtitle: suggest idea of conflict over behavior

1   It was the most civil of times, it was the least civil of times, it was the age of politeness, it was the age of boorishness, it was the epoch of concern, it was the epoch of who cares, it was the season of hybrid, it was the season of Hummer, it was the spring of Obama, it was the winter of hate speech . . .

Introduction: Illustration suggest contradictory attitudes.

2   With apologies to Mr. Dickens (or not: screw him), we have arrived at simultaneously the most and least civil moment in U.S. history. A moment when a roomful of even relatively evolved people will react with discomfort to an off-color joke about people of color—and when those same people have no compunction whatsoever about loudly ignoring one another as they blather into their cell phones.

Main idea: Thesis states main idea and refers to Dickens, who used "It was the best of times, it was the worst of times. . . ." in his novel *A Tale of Two Cities*.

3   We have never been more concerned about the feelings of minority groups, the disabled, and the disadvantaged. Yet we have never been less concerned about the feelings of anyone with whom we share the road, the Internet, or the movie theater.

Support: Offers examples of contradictory attitudes toward groups

4   Political correctness holds such sway that holidays go unnamed for fear of insulting or excluding someone. Schools won't let teachers use red pens to correct papers, because little Ethan's or Emily's self-esteem might be bruised. No one is "poor," but many are "socioeconomically disadvantaged." Civility and thoughtfulness in speech have never been so complete or so codified.

5   All of which is well intentioned and mostly a wonderful thing. I'm all for being polite and caring and Golden Rule-ish. Sadly, like a lovely field of wildflowers—which in reality is filled with bloodsucking ticks and noxious pollen—we live oh-so-politely in what must certainly be the rudest era in recorded history. Maybe even prehistory.

6   Neanderthals were probably nicer to each other than we are.

7   Pick your poison: reality television, slasher movies, video games, online porn, cell phones, automated answering systems, giant assault vehicles for trips to the grocery

Support: Provides examples of rudeness

store, car stereos played at volumes easily heard on Jupiter, web-powered copyright infringement, people who will not shut their inane traps in movie theaters, and, lord help us, now even people who won't shut their inane traps during live theater.

Support: More examples

We're all talking to someone all the time, but it's ever more rarely to the people   8 we are actually with. Our cell phones blare ringtones that no one else wants to hear. We love to watch TV shows about the stunningly predictable results of hand-feeding a grizzly bear or lighting a stick of dynamite with a cigarette. We also love shows where people lie to others for money and programs where snarky, slightly talented folks say vicious things to hopeful, and usually more talented, contestants.

Contradictions: Refer back to information and introduce reasons to follow

Civility rules, friends.   9

Civility is dead, jerks.   10

Why? I have a few theories.   11

Support: First reason

The first is that America is in the same position as Rome found itself in about 420   12 CE, meaning that we've reached the peak of our civilization and now everything is going to Tartarus in a chariot. We're too far from our food and energy sources, and fewer and fewer of the Druids and Visigoths like us anymore. So we desperately cling to a patina of civility while we grab a snack and watch large, toothy predators devour people.

Support: Second reason

The second is that sunlight contains tiny spores that lodge in the cerebellum,   13 making the infected believe they are the center of the universe.

Support: Third reason

My final and somewhat less cutting edge theory is that a large percentage of people   14 are just clueless, distracted, and self-absorbed, unable to process concepts such as spatial awareness (for example: when you are walking in the same direction with several hundred people in, say, an airport terminal, DON'T JUST STOP IN THE MIDDLE OF THE FLOW!).

But I digress.   15

Conclusion: Affirms thesis statement and ends on a humorous note

I am not here to judge whether being civil and considerate is somehow better than   16 being a mindless dillweed. You must make that choice for yourself. We inhabit the most civil of times and the least—and I completely honor and respect your freedom to choose your side in the Great Civility War.

Just don't get in my way. I'm on my cell in the Escalade, and I can't be bothered.   17

Highlight key points. As you read, you will encounter many new ideas, some more important than others. You will agree with some and disagree with others. Later, as you write about what you have read, you will want to return to the main points to refresh your memory. To locate and remember these points easily, read with a highlighter or pen in hand. **Highlighting** is an active reading strategy *only* when you use it to distinguish important ideas from less important ideas, so be selective. (If you highlight every idea, none will stand out.) The following guidelines will make your highlighting as useful as possible:

1. **Before you begin reading, decide what kinds of information to highlight.** What types of tasks will you do as a result of your reading? Will you write a paper, participate in a class discussion, or take an exam? Think about what you need to know, and tailor your highlighting to the needs of the task.

2. **Read first; then highlight.** First read a paragraph or section; then go back and mark what is important within it. This approach will help you control the tendency to highlight too much.

3. **Highlight key elements, words, and phrases.** Mark the thesis statement, the topic sentence in each paragraph, important terms and definitions, and key words and phrases that relate to the thesis.

Annotate to record your impressions. When you **annotate** a reading assignment, you jot down your reactions to the reading in the margins or in a reading journal. Think of your annotations as a personal response to the author's ideas. Your annotations can take many forms:

For more about keeping a journal, see Chapter 2, p. 29.

- important points (such as the thesis) to which you react emotionally,
- places where you want or need further information,
- places where the author reveals his or her reasons for writing,
- passages that raise questions or that intrigue or puzzle you, and
- ideas you disagree or agree with or that seem inconsistent.

Later, when you are ready to write about or discuss the reading, your annotations will help you focus on major issues and questions. Sample annotations for a portion of "American Jerk" are shown below.

SAMPLE ANNOTATIONS

Civility rules, friends.
Civility is dead, jerks.
Why? I have a few theories.

> What examples are there other than political correctness?

The first is that America is in the same position as Rome found itself in about 420 CE, meaning that we've reached the peak of our civilization and now everything is going to Tartarus in a chariot. We're too far from our food and energy sources, and fewer and fewer of the Druids and Visigoths like us anymore. So we desperately cling to a patina of civility while we grab a snack and watch large, toothy predators devour people.

> Need more information

The second is that sunlight contains tiny spores that lodge in the cerebellum, making the infected believe they are the center of the universe.

My final and somewhat less cutting edge theory is that a large percentage of people are just clueless, distracted, and self-absorbed, unable to process concepts such as spatial awareness (for example: when you are walking in the same direction with several hundred people in, say, an airport terminal, DON'T JUST STOP IN THE MIDDLE OF THE FLOW!).

> Does distractedness and lack of awareness excuse poor behavior?

EXERCISE 3.2 | **Practice with Annotating**

Reread "American Jerk" on pp. 49–50. Highlight and annotate the essay as you read.

Figure out the meaning of unfamiliar words. Before looking up an unfamiliar word in a dictionary, use one of these strategies to figure it out for yourself:

- **Look for clues in surrounding text.** Sometimes the author provides a brief definition or synonym.

BRIEF DEFINITION	Janice *prefaced,* or introduced, her poetry reading with a personal story. [*Prefaced* means "introduced."]

Other times a less obvious clue reveals meaning or you can figure out meaning by considering how the word is used in the passage.

> **CONTEXT**   In certain societies young children are always on the
> **CLUE**   *periphery,* never in the center, of family life. [*Periphery* means "the edges or the fringe," far away from the center.]

- **Try pronouncing the word aloud.** By pronouncing the word *magnific,* you may hear part of the word *magnify* and know that it has something to do with enlargement. *Magnific* means "large," "imposing," and "impressive."
- **Look at parts of the word.** For example, in the word *nonresponsive* you can see the verb *respond,* which means "act or react." *Non* means "not," so you can figure out that *nonresponsive* means "not acting or reacting."

Understand challenging readings. At one time or another, all students encounter challenging reading assignments. Perhaps the language is unfamiliar or you just can't connect with the author, the topic, or the writing style. Regardless of the problem, however, you know you must complete the assignment. The Troubleshooting Guide in Table 3.1 (p. 53) lists some typical problems that students experience with challenging reading material and identifies strategies for solving them.

AFTER READING

When you finish reading an assignment, it may be tempting to close the book, periodical, or browser window and move immediately to another task. However, doing so increases the likelihood that you will forget most of what you have read because your brain will not have had time to process the material. To improve your comprehension and recall, take a few minutes to review the material and draw a graphic organizer.

Review. Review immediately after you finish reading. Reviewing should not take much time; your goal is to touch on each main point one more time, not to embark on a long and thorough study. To review material after reading, use the same steps you used to preview the reading. (See p. 45). Pay particular attention to the following elements:

- the headings,
- your highlighting,
- your annotations, and
- the conclusion.

Draw a graphic organizer. Think of a graphic organizer as a means of tracking the author's flow of ideas. Your graphic organizer should include all the key elements of an

e **macmillanhighered.com/successfulwriting**
Tutorials > Critical Reading > Active Reading Strategies

TABLE 3.1 Challenging Readings: A Troubleshooting Guide

Problems	Strategies for Solving Them
The sentences are long and confusing.	1. Read aloud. 2. Divide each sentence into parts, and analyze the function of each part. 3. Express each sentence in your own words.
The ideas are complicated and hard to understand.	1. Reread the material several times. 2. Rephrase or explain each idea in your own words. 3. Make outline notes. 4. Study with a classmate; discuss difficult ideas. 5. Look up the meanings of unfamiliar words in a dictionary.
The material seems disorganized or poorly organized.	1. Study the introduction for clues to organization. 2. Pay more attention to headings. 3. Read the summary or conclusion. 4. Try to discover the organization by writing an outline or drawing a graphic organizer (see pp. 144 and 146).
The material contains many unfamiliar words.	1. Look for clues to meaning in the surrounding text. 2. Try pronouncing words aloud to see if they remind you of related words. 3. Break words into parts whose meaning you know. 4. Use a dictionary when necessary.
You cannot get interested in the material.	1. Think about something you've experienced that is related to the topic. 2. Work with a classmate, discussing each section as you go.
You cannot relate to the writer's ideas or experiences.	1. Find out some background information about the writer. 2. Imagine having the writer's experiences. How would you react differently?
The subject is unfamiliar; you lack background information on the subject.	1. Obtain a more basic text or other source that moves slower, offers more explanation, and reviews fundamental principles and concepts. 2. Look up unfamiliar terminology in a specialized dictionary. 3. Ask your instructor to recommend useful references.

essay listed on pages 48–49. Figure 3.2 (p. 54) shows the correct format for a graphic organizer. An example of a graphic organizer for "American Jerk" appears in Figure 3.3 (p. 55). Work through the organizer, rereading the essay paragraph by paragraph at the same time.

Summarize to Check Your Understanding. If you are expected to be able to discuss a reading with other students or write about it in a response paper or on an exam, writing a **summary** (a brief restatement of the major points) of what you have read is a good idea. Summarizing can help improve your retention of the material. It is also an excellent way to check whether you have understood what you have read. If you have difficulty writing a summary, you probably do not understand what is important in the reading.

FIGURE 3.2 **Graphic Organizer: Key Elements to Include**

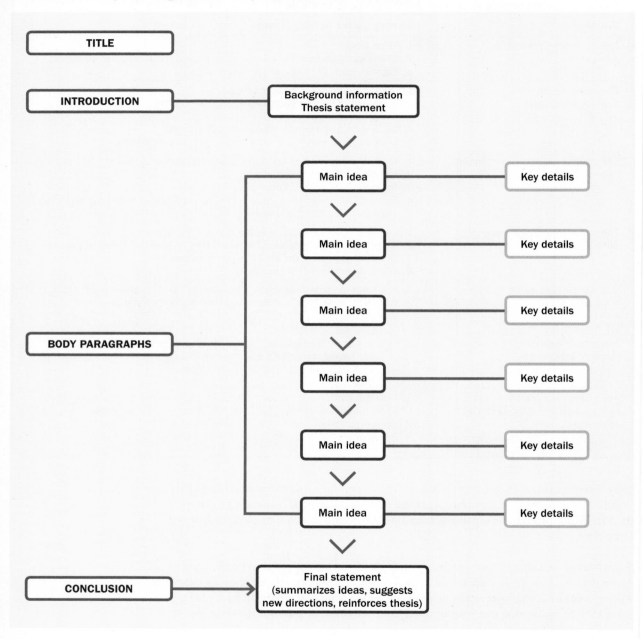

FIGURE 3.3 **Graphic Organizer for "American Jerk"**

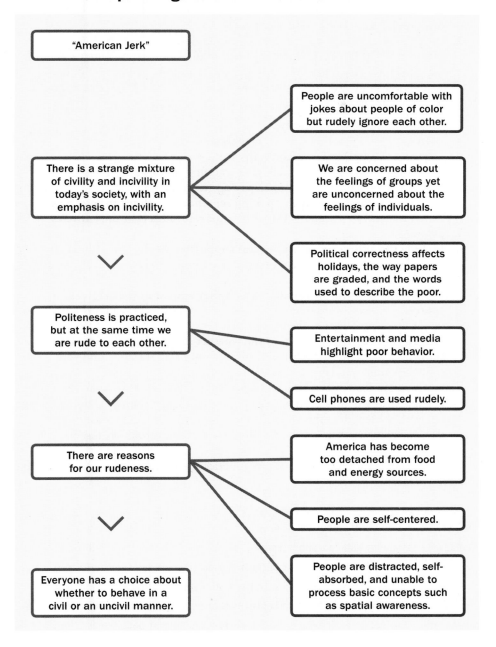

To write an effective summary, use the following guidelines:

1. **Review annotations and highlights.** Be sure to identify the topic sentence or main idea of each paragraph.
2. **Write your summary as you reread each paragraph.** Good marginal summary notes briefly restate the content of each paragraph. Below is a list of marginal summary notes for the essay "American Jerk," pages 49–50. If you write notes similar to those below, you can easily convert them into sentences for your summary.

   MARGINAL SUMMARY NOTES
   (para. 2)   politeness and rudeness together
   (para. 4)   political correctness in excess
   (para. 12) being out of touch with real survival causes rudeness
   (para. 14) people have stopped paying attention

3. **Start your summary with an opening sentence that states *in your own words* the author's thesis — the most important idea that the entire essay explains.**
4. **Include the author's most important supporting ideas.** Use either highlighted topic sentences or marginal summary notes (from Step 2, above) as a guide for what to include.
5. **Present the ideas in the order in which they appear in the original source.** Use transitions (connecting words and phrases) as you move from one major supporting idea to the next.
6. **Reread your summary to determine whether it contains sufficient information.** Ask yourself: Would someone who has not read the essay find your summary understandable and meaningful? If not, revise it to include additional information. Remember: Your summary should include only the main ideas and key supporting points. A good rule of thumb is that a summary should be about one-fifth the length of the original. If your summary is longer (or shorter) than this, consider whether you should delete (or add) ideas from the essay.

Here is a sample summary of the essay "American Jerk." It was written by a student using the preceding six steps.

The writer expresses Schwartz's thesis in her own words.

Although people believe they are acting politely, rudeness and incivility are on the rise. We overdo political correctness, yet we behave rudely to everyone around us. Media, entertainment, and cell-phone usage illustrate improper behavior and support

The order of ideas parallels the order in Schwartz's essay.

our rudeness. The author believes that because our civilization has evolved to the point that we are no longer concerned with basic survival, we can act selfishly while pretending to be civil. The author also contends that people are simply distracted and

The writer continues to use her own words — not those of Schwartz.

self-absorbed but not intentionally rude. The bottom line is that people must choose their own behavior and decide how they will act.

Many students keep a journal in which they write summaries and other responses to what they've read. These journal entries can serve as useful sources of ideas for writing papers.

EXERCISE 3.3   **Writing a Summary**

Read "American Jerk," p. 49, or another reading selection your instructor has chosen, and summarize it.

Keep a response journal. A **response journal** is a section of your writing journal in which you record summaries of readings as well as your reactions to and questions about readings. Experiment with the following two ways to organize a response journal entry to discover the one that works better for you.

For more about keeping a journal, see Chapter 2, p. 29.

The Open-Page Format

On a blank page, write, outline, draw, or create a diagram to express your reactions to an essay. Because the open-page format encourages you to let your ideas flow freely, it may work well for creative and spatial learners. Figure 3.4 shows one student's open-page response journal entry for "American Jerk." This entry suggests several possible topics to write about: identifying generational differences in defining civility, determining standards for civility, and recognizing subjectivity in evaluating behavior.

FIGURE 3.4 Sample Open-Page Journal Format

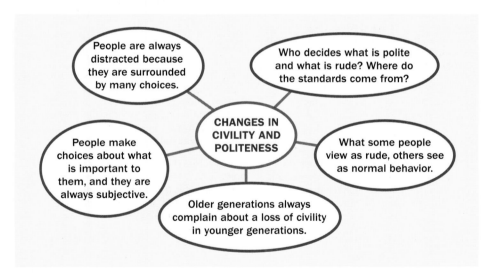

The Two-Column Format

Divide several pages of your journal into two columns. If you journal on a computer, you can insert a table with two columns. Label the left side "Quotations" and the right side "Responses." Under "Quotations," jot down five to ten quotations from the text. Choose remarks that seem important—that state an opinion, summarize a viewpoint, and so forth.

In the right column, next to each quotation, write your response to the quotation. You might explain it, disagree with or question it, relate it to other information in the reading or in another reading, or tie it to your experiences. The two-column format forces you to think actively about an essay while you question what you have read and draw connections. Because it provides more structure than the open-page format, the two-column format may be ideal for pragmatic or concrete learners.

Figure 3.5 follows the two-column format. In this journal entry, the writer has uncovered several possible topics: types or degrees of rudeness, the meaning of "socio-economically disadvantaged," and self-centered behavior.

For more on paraphrasing, see Chapter 23, p. 589.

You may find it useful to paraphrase the quotation before writing your response. Paraphrasing forces you to think about the meaning of the quotation, and ideas for writing may come to mind as a result. To use paraphrasing, add a "Paraphrases" column to your journal between the "Quotations" column and the "Responses" column.

FIGURE 3.5 Sample Two-Column Journal Format

QUOTATIONS	RESPONSES
"A moment when a roomful of even relatively evolved people will react with discomfort to an off-color joke about people of color—and when those same people have no compunction whatsoever about loudly ignoring one another as they blather into their cell phones."	This statement implies that racial jokes and talking on your cell phone are somehow on the same level of rudeness.
"No one is 'poor,' but many are 'socioeconomically disadvantaged.'"	There is a distinction between "poor" and "socioeconomically disadvantaged," and it's an important one. The first term has to do with money, but the second one also has to do with culture and opportunities.
"The second is that sunlight contains tiny spores that lodge in the cerebellum, making the infected believe they are the center of the universe."	This is a joke, but the author is saying that everyone sees themselves as important; this is a bad thing; and schools, churches, and parents teach this message to children to build self-esteem.

Essay in Progress 1

For "American Jerk" or another essay chosen by your instructor, write a response in your journal using the open-page or the two-column format.

Use a reading-response worksheet. A reading-response worksheet allows you to record all your ideas about a reading in one place. The worksheet guides your response while directing your thinking. Figure 3.6, a blank worksheet, includes space for recording your first impressions, a summary, connections to your experiences, ideas for analysis, and additional sources.

FIGURE 3.6 Reading-Response Worksheet

READING-RESPONSE WORKSHEET

TITLE: _____

AUTHOR: _____

FIRST IMPRESSIONS: _____
_____
_____

SUMMARY: _____
_____
_____
_____

CONNECTIONS TO YOUR OWN EXPERIENCES: _____
_____
_____
_____

ANALYSIS (issue, aspect, feature, problem)

1. _____
_____
_____
_____

2. _____
_____
_____
_____

ADDITIONAL SOURCES OR VISUALS (if needed)

1. _____
_____

2. _____
_____

3. _____
_____

Use your learning style. If you are a *verbal* or *social* learner, you probably find reading a comfortable and convenient way to obtain information. But even if you prefer a different learning style, most of your assignments will be in print form. So it's important that you use your learning style in a way that enhances reading and writing.

Learning Style Options

- *Spatial* learners can enhance reading and writing by creating mental pictures of people and places. For example, while reading "American Jerk," create a mental image of a person behaving rudely. Graphic organizers and diagrams can help you organize the ideas in an essay. As you annotate, use symbols to connect the ideas within and between paragraphs. (See the symbols listed for the reading-response journal on p. 31.)
- *Social* learners can preview reading assignments with a classmate and discuss your reactions to it after reading. (Use the Guide to Active Reading, p. 43, and the Guide to Responding to Text below to get started.)
- *Abstract* and *creative* learners may overlook details and instead focus on the reading's "big ideas" and overall message, so highlight important points and key supporting facts and details.
- *Concrete* and *pragmatic* learners may focus on details instead of seeing how ideas fit together and contribute to the author's overall message. Graphic organizers can help you see the larger picture. Try to make the essay as "real" as possible by visualizing events occurring or the author writing, or by visualizing yourself interviewing the author, alone or with a panel of classmates.
- *Emotional* learners may focus on feelings about people or events in the essay and overlook the way the author uses them to convey an overall message. Keep this question in mind: How does the author use these people or events to get his or her message across?
- *Rational* learners may focus on the logic or clarity of the ideas and overlook more subtle shades of meaning. Annotating the essay will draw out your personal reactions to a piece of writing.

Essay in Progress 2

Discuss "American Jerk" or another essay chosen by your instructor with a classmate. Make notes as you discuss. If you chose another essay, pair up with a classmate who also chose that essay, or choose an essay to read together.

A GUIDE TO RESPONDING TO TEXT

When an instructor assigns a reading, some form of response is always required. For example, you might be expected to participate in a class discussion, analyze the reading on an essay exam, or research the topic further and report your findings. By responding to material, you understand and learn it better. A common assignment is a **response paper**, which requires you to read an essay, analyze it, and write about some aspect of it.

ANALYZE THE ASSIGNMENT AND DECIDE ON AN APPROACH

Before beginning a response paper, make sure you understand the assignment.

- Has your instructor suggested a particular direction for the paper, or should you decide on your own approach?
- What page or word count is expected?
- Are you expected to do additional research, or is research not allowed?

If you are uncertain about your instructor's expectations, be sure to ask.

When writing your response paper, you may include a brief summary as part of your introduction. (See the section on summarizing, pp. 53–57.) But concentrate on interpreting and evaluating what you have read. Rather than attempting to discuss all of your reactions, focus on one of the following:

- a key idea,
- a question the essay raises, or
- an issue it explores.

For example, suppose your instructor asks you to read an article entitled "Advertising: A Form of Institutional Lying," which argues that advertisements deceive consumers by presenting half-truths, distortions, and misinformation. Your instructor asks you to write a two-page paper responding to the essay but gives you no other directions. In writing this paper, you might take one of the following approaches.

- Discuss how you were once deceived by an advertisement, as a means of confirming the author's thesis and main points.
- Evaluate the evidence and examples the author provides, and determine whether the evidence is relevant and sufficient to support the claim.
- Discuss the causes or effects of deception in advertising that the author overlooks. (You may need to consult other sources to take this approach).
- Evaluate the assumptions the author makes about advertising or consumers.

For an assignment like this one, or for any response paper, how should you decide what to write about? How can you come up with ideas about a reading? Figure 3.7 presents an effective, step-by-step process for discovering ideas for response. Writing an effective summary is discussed on pp. 53–57. Each of the other steps is discussed, within the context of a reading and writing assignment, in the sections that follow.

FIGURE 3.7 **Active Response to a Reading**

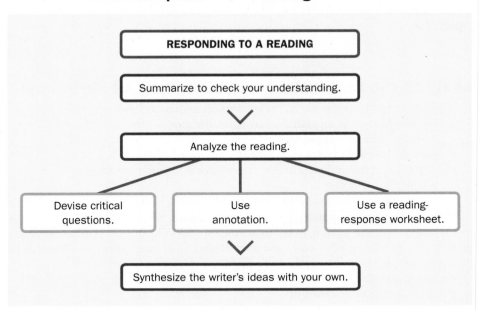

SYNTHESIZE THE WRITER'S IDEAS WITH YOUR OWN

One way to start ideas flowing for a response paper is to connect, or **synthesize**, the ideas expressed in the reading with your own ideas, knowledge, and experiences. Doing so builds a bridge between your ideas and the author's. To begin synthesizing ideas, follow these steps.

1. **Look for useful information in the essay that you could apply or relate to other real-life situations.** Think of familiar situations or examples that illustrate the subject. For example, for "American Jerk," which considers incivility in society, you might write a journal entry about incivility among college students.

2. **Think beyond the reading.** Recall other material you have read and events you have experienced that relate to the reading. In thinking about "American Jerk," for example, you might recall the behavior of students in the classroom, as described in the reading "The New Marshmallow Test" from Chapter 1 (pp. 3–6). How does student use of digital technology in the classroom relate to the topic of "American Jerk," for example?

For more on freewriting, see Chapter 5, p. 108.

3. **Use the key-word response method for generating ideas.** Choose one or more key words that describe your initial response, such as *angered, amused, surprised, confused, annoyed, curious,* or *shocked.* For example, fill in the following blank with one or more key words describing your response to "American Jerk."

"After reading the essay, I felt _____."

The key-word response you just wrote will serve as a point of departure for further thinking. Start by explaining your response; then write down ideas as they come to you, trying to approach the reading from many different perspectives. Here is the result of one student's key-word response to "American Jerk."

> After reading "American Jerk," <u>I felt annoyed and insulted</u>. I agree that the world has changed because of cell phones, but I don't think that these changes have made people ruder. Each generation creates its own rules and values, and the cell-phone generation is doing that. If media and entertainment were horrible and insulting, then people wouldn't watch them. Humans are evolving, and our expectations have to evolve with technology. Some people act like they are polite when they actually do rude things all the time. Behavior comes from people. People have to change it.
>
> Possible Topic #1: How generations create their own values
>
> Possible Topic #2: How behavior changes with changes in technology

> **Essay in Progress 3**
> Use synthesis to draw connections between the ideas expressed in "American Jerk" (or another essay assigned by your instructor) and your own ideas and experiences.

ANALYZE THE READING

After you see a movie, you ask a friend, "What did you think of it?" Your friend may praise the plot, criticize the acting, or comment on the characters' behavior. Your friend is analyzing the film, breaking the film down into its component parts and assessing how well they work together. When you analyze a reading, you may focus on any aspect of the selection, such as the author's fairness or accuracy, the method of presentation, the quality of the supporting evidence provided, or the intended audience. To discover ideas for analysis, try devising critical questions, using annotation, keeping a response journal, or using a reading-response worksheet.

Devise critical questions. Asking critical questions and then answering them is a useful method for analysis and for discovering ideas for a response paper. Here are three sample questions and the answers that one student wrote after reading "American Jerk."

> <u>Can we turn the tide and find a way to return to a polite society?</u>
> I think that adults emphasize politeness less than in the past. Parents and teachers hardly try to instill it in children. People no longer have to learn etiquette. To improve manners would require us to rethink how we raise and educate children.

Possible topic: how to teach politeness and effective methods

> <u>Is technology causing people to be less civil, or is it just an excuse?</u>
> Technology has changed the way that people communicate with one another. Technology makes it easier to have less personal contact with others, but it does not encourage rudeness. It's possible to use technology and still be civil to other people.

Possible topic: the effects of technology on human behavior

Possible topic: the effect of distractions on the ways that people interact with one another

Why are people more distracted and thoughtless now than they used to be?
People have probably always been distracted and thoughtless, but today so many things clamor for our attention that it is easier than ever to be distracted. We are focused less on the people around us and more on the electronics we use throughout the day.

> **Essay in Progress 4**
> Write a list of critical questions about "American Jerk" or another essay assigned by your instructor.

Use annotation.   In the Guide to Active Reading earlier in this chapter (pp. 43–60), you learned to annotate as you read. Use these annotation skills to analyze and respond to a reading you are preparing to write about. As you read an essay the second time, record additional reactions that occur to you. Some students prefer to use a different color of ink to record their second set of annotations. (Refer to the sample student annotation shown on p. 51.)

> **Essay in Progress 5**
> Reread "American Jerk" or another essay chosen by your instructor, this time adding annotations that record your reactions to and questions about the essay as you read.

Use a reading-response worksheet.   In the Guide to Active Reading above, you learned about keeping a response journal and using a Reading-Response Worksheet, like the one shown in Figure 3.6 (p. 59). Because it enables you to pull together so many of the elements of your response, the reading-response worksheet provides a convenient jumping off place for beginning your response essay.

> **Essay in Progress 6**
> Complete a Reading Response Worksheet to capture one or more aspects of your response to "American Jerk" or another essay you have been assigned.

For more on each aspect of the writing process, see Part 2 of this book.

> **Essay in Progress 7**
> Write a two- to four-page paper in response to "American Jerk" or another essay chosen by your instructor. Use the following steps to shape the ideas you generated in Essays in Progress 1 to 6.
>
> 1. Reread the writing you did in response to the selection. Look for related ideas. Try to find ideas that fit together to produce a viewpoint or position toward the reading. (Do not attempt to cover all your ideas. Your essay should not analyze every aspect of the essay. Instead, you should focus on one feature or aspect.)
> 2. Write a sentence that states your central point. This sentence will become your thesis statement. It should state what your essay will assert or explain.
> 3. Collect ideas and evidence from the reading to support your thesis. Your thesis should be backed up by specifics in the reading.
> 4. Organize your ideas into essay form. Your paper should have a title, introduction, body, and conclusion.

5. Revise your essay. Be sure that you have explained your ideas clearly and have provided support from the reading for each one.

6. Proofread for accuracy and correctness. Use the Suggestions for Proofreading in Chapter 10 (pp. 211–13).

WORKING WITH TEXT

While reading the selection below, apply the processes you have learned for reading and responding to an essay.

BEFORE READING

1. Preview the reading using the steps listed on pp. 50–51 and write three questions you expect to be able to answer after reading the essay.

WHILE READING

1. Highlight the key elements of the essay, as described on pp. 50–51.
2. Record your thoughts as you read using annotations.
3. Circle any unfamiliar words. Figure out their meanings using the techniques on pp. 51–52 or by using a dictionary.

READING

Superhero or Supervillain? If science gives people superpowers, will they use them for good or evil?

WILL OREMUS

This essay originally appeared in the online magazine *Slate* in May 2013. *Slate's* Web site describes the magazine as a "general-interest publication offering analysis and commentary about politics, business, technology, and culture." Will Oremus is a staff writer for this magazine, writing about science and technology.

From invisibility to superhuman strength to telekinesis, a wave of emerging technologies promises to give people powers once reserved for comic-book characters. Which raises an important question: If humans become superhuman, will we turn out to be superheroes — or supervillains? 1

You might think the answer would depend on each individual's moral compass. Batman uses human-enhancement technologies to fight crime because he loathes injustice, while the Joker uses them to wreak mayhem because he's a psychopath. In reality, though, most people possess the capacity for both good and evil. Which one wins out at any given time depends not only on our genes and our upbringing, but the circumstances in which we find ourselves. For Peter Parker, a shy and neurotic kid, the transformation into Spider-Man brings out a deep sense of social responsibility. For Otto Octavius, once a respected scientist, becoming Dr. Octopus means becoming a 2 vengeful megalomaniac. Comic books typically provide pop-psychological back stories to explain the choices each character makes in response to the pressure of being extraordinary. But what if it also turns out that some types of powers inherently lend themselves to altruism, while others make us more likely to lie, cheat, steal, or kill?

Last year, Stanford researchers recruited 60 volunteers for an experiment on how virtual superpowers could influence moral decisions. In an immersive virtual-reality simulation, 30 of the subjects were granted the power of flight, like Superman, while the other 30 rode as passengers in a helicopter. Each volunteer had the same mission — to cruise over a city following an earthquake in search of a stranded child. The experiment was rigged so that everyone would find the boy in the same amount of time and save his life. 3

(Top) Participant "flying" in virtual reality; (bottom) virtual child after being "rescued." Courtesy of Cody Karutz; Stanford Virtual Human Interaction Lab

After the simulation, an experimenter sat down to debrief each subject. As they talked, the experimenter "accidentally" knocked over a canister full of pens, then waited five seconds before beginning to pick them up. The volunteers in the helicopter group took an average of six seconds to start helping clean up the spill, and some didn't pitch in at all. But those in the Superman group jumped right in, with most coming to the experimenter's aid even before she started gathering the pens herself. 4

The findings suggest that acquiring a superpower can spark benevolent tendencies. Give someone Superman's abilities, and she'll start to behave a little more like Superman. Clinical psychologist Robin Rosenberg, who helped design the experiment, said its outcome supported her hypothesis that people might treat an extraordinary ability as a sort of gift that brings with it a responsibility to help others. That's an encouraging finding, particularly in light of Lord Acton's maxim that power corrupts. 5

But wait — what if the researchers had given their subjects a different superpower? Rosenberg's co-author, Stanford communications professor Jeremy Bailenson, explained that they chose the power of flight partly because it seemed like a classic "do-gooder" sort of ability. "We thought about giving them X-ray vision, but that would have been a little creepy," he noted. 6

It would be nice to think that morality emanates from the sheer goodness of people's souls, but research has consistently shown that people behave far better when they think they're being watched. In a 2010 study, Newcastle University researchers found that just hanging posters of a pair of staring eyes on the walls of a cafeteria was enough to cut littering in half. That's why Rosenberg, who has written a book on the psychology of superheroes, draws a distinction between visible powers and stealth powers. Soaring above the masses is a highly conspicuous activity, so it would behoove the flyer to be on his best behavior. X-ray vision is stealthier — you could use it for nefarious purposes without making a scene. 7

The ultimate stealth power, of course, is invisibility. Its promise is that of impunity — the ability to do things that would otherwise get you in trouble. In Plato's *Republic*, Glaucon recounts the story of an otherwise decent shepherd who came into possession of an invisibility ring. Unable to resist temptation, he used it to seduce the queen, kill the king, and claim the crown for himself. H.G. Wells' invisible man went on a similar spree. And in a classic episode of *This American Life*, John Hodgman went around asking people which superpower they'd prefer: flight or invisibility. Those who pondered invisibility couldn't resist premeditating a slew of illicit deeds. One fellow was so spooked by his own impulses that he ended up changing his answer to "flight" because the mere thought of invisibility "leads me down a dark path." 8

Powers that inherently violate other people's autonomy, like mind control, would also seem to lend themselves to abuse. A utilitarian might be able to dream up some applications that redound to the public welfare, but the German philosopher Immanuel Kant would argue that mind control is immoral no matter how it's used. Mind-reading would be similarly invasive. A form of telepathy that required both parties' active participation, on the other hand, might be stealthy, but it would be fundamentally social and consensual. That ups the odds that it would be used for virtuous ends. Other powers, like supreme 9 intelligence, time travel, and indestructibility, are morality-agnostic and could be employed equally for good or ill. Likewise incredible strength, which Bruce Banner's Hulk uses mostly for good but which also bedevils him by amplifying the consequences of his rage.

That example suggests another way of looking at the risks and benefits of human-   10
enhancement technologies. By definition, they enable people to transcend their natural limitations. That can obviously be a good thing, but it also carries heightened risks, because civil society and human morality have evolved against a background in which those constraints are taken for granted. That's why emerging technologies like drones and 3-D printing scare so many people — they enable behaviors that our laws and norms have not evolved to regulate. Imagine the panic that would ensue if hypothetical superpowers like mind-reading suddenly became widely available.

It's probably fortunate, then, that we're nowhere near as close to the technological   11
singularity as Ray Kurzweil would have us believe. We have jet packs, but they're grossly impractical. Headlines about real-life invisibility cloaks tend to be exaggerated. Muscle suits so far are clunky enough that they're only really useful for people with disabilities. Brain-computer interfaces let you move things with your mind, but only if you're willing to undergo brain surgery and practice for months just to feed yourself a bite of chocolate. Promises of super-longevity or immortality are premature.

That said, each of these human-enhancement technologies, and several more that   12
Slate will explore in the coming weeks, are progressing at various rates along a path that could someday lead to real-world viability. Before they do, it might be wise to take a little time to think about whether each one is likely to make people better — or just more potent.

AFTER READING

1. **Review** Reread your highlighting and annotations for "Superhero or Supervillain?"
2. **Organization** Draw a graphic organizer of the essay.
3. **Summary** Write a summary of the essay's main points.
4. **Journal** Write an entry in your response journal or complete the Reading-Response Worksheet on page 59.

RESPONDING TO THE READING

1. **Synthesis** Synthesize the writer's ideas with your own, using the suggestions on pages 62–63.
2. **Questions** Write a list of critical questions.
3. **Essay** Write a brief essay in response to this essay. Follow the steps listed in Essay in Progress 7 on page 64.

WORKING TOGETHER

Contact five people of varying ages (such as a child, a college student, a mature adult) and ask them the following question:

If you could have any superpower, what would it be and how would you use it?

Record your responses in the chart below.

Age of Respondent	Desired Superpower	Proposed Use of Superpower

In class, join a small group of your peers to combine your charts and analyze the responses. Does your group's chart reveal any trends? Be prepared to share your results and any trends you noticed with the rest of the class.

ANALYZE STUDENT ESSAYS

Helping other students improve their writing—by participating actively in peer review or by analyzing the model essays in this book—will better equip you to analyze and improve your own writing. (The student essays in this book are reasonably good models, but they are not perfect.) Use the following suggestions when reading student essays, either in this book or when working with classmates:

- **Read the essay several times.** During your first reading, concentrate on the writer's message. Then reread the essay as many times as necessary to analyze its writing features. For example, first identify the writer's thesis statement and notice how the writer supports the thesis, and then look at the language used to create a particular impression.
- **Annotate the essay as you read.** Use a pen or pencil, or use the Comment feature in your word-processing software.
- **Use graphic organizers to grasp the essay's method of organization.** Each chapter in Part 3 of this book presents the characteristics of a particular method of organization (such as narration, description, comparison-contrast, and definition) and provides one or more graphic organizers for each pattern. Identify which method of organization the writer has chosen, and compare the essay to the graphic organizer, noticing whether the essay contains each element.
- **Focus on techniques.** Each chapter in Part 3 of this book offers specific techniques and suggestions for writing a particular type of essay. Review these techniques and observe how the writer applies them.

- **Focus on what is new and different.** Ask yourself the following questions as you read: What is the writer doing that you haven't seen before? What catches your attention? What works particularly well? What writing techniques might be fun to try? What techniques would be challenging to try? For example, if a writer begins his or her essay with a striking statistic, consider whether you could use a striking statistic to begin your essay.

READING: STUDENTS WRITE

"American Jerk"? How Rude! (but True)

KAREN VACCARO

Karen Vaccaro wrote the following essay in response to "American Jerk." As you read, notice how Vaccaro analyzes Schwartz's points about civility and the lack of it in our society.

Introduction: Identifies the article Vaccaro is responding to

Vaccaro's thesis statement indicates how her ideas differ from Schwartz's.

Vaccaro agrees with Schwartz.

Vaccaro offers examples of lack of concern.

In his article "American Jerk," Todd Schwartz claims that Americans today are both the most and the least civil we have ever been. Although the painful truth in these observations is a bit hard to take, Schwartz eases the reality by providing a great deal of humorous relief. Schwartz's claim is an apt one, and most of his observations about our current culture are accurate, but some of his observations and accusations are broad generalizations that don't always hold true.

"We have never been more concerned about the feelings of minority groups, the disabled, and the disadvantaged," Schwartz writes in paragraph 3, and he is right. We have become a culture obsessed with being PC (politically correct). I often carefully choose and often second-guess the words I use to describe anyone of a different race or physical or mental ability, for fear of offending anyone. And yet many people I encounter seem hardly concerned about offending me. Schwartz is right that "we have never been less concerned about the feelings of anyone with whom we share the road, the Internet, or the movie theater" (para. 3). Cyclists seem to have taken over city streets and even shout insults at me when I am walking in a crosswalk (and they are breaking the law by ignoring a red light). Despite many methods used to discourage theater goers from using their cell phones, cell phones ring during films, concerts, and plays. In fact, last week I was at a live theater performance, and in the middle of an important scene, a cell phone rang in the audience — twice.

1

2

In another example of how (overly) civil we've become, Schwartz writes, "Schools won't let teachers use red pens to correct papers because . . . self-esteem might be bruised" (para. 4). This reminded me of the teaching internship I did while studying abroad in China one semester. I taught an English writing course to Chinese high school students. One day I was marking up the students' papers with a red pen (as I thought teachers were supposed to do). Another American teacher said, "I thought teachers weren't supposed to mark students' papers with red pens anymore." I asked if red was offensive to Chinese students. "No," she answered. "Some of my teachers back home in America said it's because red is a harsh color that really stands out from the black and white." "Well, yes, I thought that was the point," I said. "But it can make some students feel bad," she responded. "That's the silliest thing I've ever heard," I said as I went back to marking my students' papers with the red pen. Have we become so "civil" that we're afraid to teach students? Don't young men and women come to class expecting to learn something, knowing that at some point they will need to be corrected to see their mistakes so that they can truly learn?

3

Vaccaro connects Schwartz's ideas to her own experience and affirms his ideas.

Then there are the less civil aspects of our culture, as Schwartz so accurately points out. We Americans have become obsessed with reality television shows that often take advantage of the misfortune and embarrassment of others. In addition, "giant assault vehicles" (para. 7) dwarf other cars on the road, guzzle gas, often take up more than one parking space, and seem unnecessary on city streets in a time of environmental awareness and concern. Furthermore, we are so interested in our technological gadgets that we ignore real human-to-human interactions. "We're all talking to someone all the time," Schwartz writes, "but it's ever more rarely to the people we are actually with" (para. 8). I have noticed that my boyfriend often whips out his new iPhone. Even when we're walking and talking, catching up after days of not seeing one another, he's playing a new game, downloading a new app, or chatting with his friends. I myself can be guilty of this rude behavior. Sometimes I am spending time with one friend but will be texting another friend. I know it's rude, but I do it anyway (usually because the friend I'm with is doing the same thing and therefore it seems okay). We no longer realize how rude it is to divide our attention between two sources instead of giving our friend or loved one our full, undivided attention.

4

Vaccaro identifies another of Schwartz's points that she agrees with and admits that she is guilty of it as well.

Where I must disagree with Schwartz, though, is his sweeping, unfounded statement that we are now living in "what must certainly be the rudest era in

5

Vaccaro moves to points with which she disagrees.

history" (para. 5). Really? Are we ruder than people who enslaved others and denied them any and all rights, including the right to be treated like human beings and not animals? Are people who refuse to "shut their inane traps" (para. 7) ruder than people in the time of segregation? It might be easy to convince ourselves that the present must be the rudest time in our history, since it is freshest in our minds, and we know it very well. But if Schwartz took time to flesh out his observations and accusations with concrete examples, he might rethink such a generalization.

Conclusion: Vaccaro points out the value of Schwartz's article.

Even if it doesn't fix the problems it calls attention to, Schwartz's enter- 6 taining and witty article forces us to stop and think about how contemporary American culture straddles the line between civility and rudeness. Many of his examples illustrate the hypocrisy of our behaviors and ways of thinking. Ulti- mately, Schwartz is correct in his claim that "we have arrived at simultaneously the most and least civil moment in U.S. history" (para. 2). I doubt, though, that Neanderthals—with their barbaric weapons and primitive hunting instincts— "were probably nicer to each other than we are" (para. 6).

ANALYZING THE WRITER'S TECHNIQUE

1. Express Vaccaro's thesis (central point) in your own words.
2. What kinds of information does Vaccaro include to support her thesis?
3. Where would additional examples help Vaccaro support her thesis?

RESPONDING TO THE READING

1. Vaccaro admits to texting one friend while spending time with another. Are you also guilty of acts of incivility? If so, describe one.
2. What steps or actions could be taken to build Americans' awareness of their lack of civility?
3. Do you agree or disagree that our culture is obsessed with political correctness? Give examples to support your answer.
4. Write a journal entry describing an act of incivility that you have observed or expe rienced that particularly disturbed or annoyed you.

4

Thinking Critically about Text and Visuals

Suppose you are taking a sociology class and are studying popular culture. Your instructor asks you to examine publications such as those shown in the photograph to the right, read and evaluate a few articles, and be prepared to discuss in class what they reveal about Americans' values.

Write a list of questions about one or two of the articles whose titles are legible in the photograph. Include questions that would help you evaluate the articles' purpose—to express the writer's thoughts and feelings? to inform? to persuade?—and intended audience. Then write a few sentences explaining why the illustrations may have been included and what they accomplish.

As you analyzed and wrote about the titles of the articles and the photos that accompany them, you had to question, evaluate, and respond critically. In this chapter you will learn strategies for thinking and reading

© Frank Siteman Photography, 2014

critically that you can apply to reading essays, newspaper and magazine articles, textbook selections, works of literature, and visuals, including photographs and graphics.

- determine whether authors make reasonable inferences and use appropriate evidence,
- analyze the author's tone, assumptions, generalizations, and omissions, and
- interpret and think critically about photographs and graphics.

THINKING AND READING CRITICALLY

We live in a world of overload, surrounded by news, opinions, advertisements, and other kinds of information everywhere we look (or listen). Sometimes the information we encounter presents ideas fully and fairly. More often, writers and speakers present only their own views on a topic, without fully exploring the range of positions. And sometimes writers and speakers present their positions in such a way as to make their viewpoint sound like the only logical option. So it is important to assess carefully the ideas and information we encounter. And since writers may not always be aware when unfair bias creeps in, it is also important to assess carefully the way you present your own ideas, making sure that you have presented them clearly and fairly. The sections that follow provide the tools you need to evaluate texts critically—both those you create and those you consume.

ANALYZE THE AUTHOR'S IDEAS

To analyze an essay, begin by examining the author's ideas closely and critically. This involves knowing what the author *says,* and, more important, it involves making inferences about what the author *means*. It also involves examining the supporting evidence an author offers, distinguishing between fact and opinion, and identifying bias.

Make reasonable inferences. Some writers (for example, textbook authors) present information in a straightforward manner, spelling everything out clearly and directly so that you don't have to guess at their conclusions. Other writers directly state some ideas but hint at, or *imply*, other ideas. Critical readers must be sure to pick up on the clues that will allow them to determine the writer's unstated messages.

An **inference** is a reasonable guess based on the available facts and information, including content directly provided in the reading. Inferences are logical connections between what the writer states directly and what he or she implies. Consider the following situation:

You have been cutting your history class all semester because you find the instructor boring. You skip your reading assignments, and your score on the midterm exam was 46 out of 100. You wrote one paper for the class and got a D on it. One morning, you read an email from your history instructor asking you to come to her office.

In this situation, you can reasonably infer that you are likely to fail the course and that your instructor wants to discuss the situation with you. It would not be reasonable to infer that the instructor wants to offer you an internship or wants your advice about research she is conducting.

Making inferences requires active reading and critical thinking. Here are some guidelines for making reasonable inferences.

1. **Understand the author's purpose and literal meanings.** Before you can make reasonable inferences, you need a clear understanding of the author's purpose and the reading's thesis statement, main ideas, and supporting details.

2. **Pay attention to details.** Sometimes details offer a hint regarding what the writer has implied or left unsaid. When you notice a striking or unusual detail, ask yourself: Why is this detail included? For example, read the following passage.

> Maria attends college, has a full-time job, takes care of her two children, cooks dinner for her family every night, and pays taxes. She doesn't *look* like an illegal immigrant, but this is how the U.S. government classifies her.

What is the writer's reason for including the detail about Maria's immigration status? Perhaps the writer is implying that undocumented workers are just like everyone else: They go to school, work, and have families. You might also reasonably infer that the writer disagrees with or questions this classification.

3. **Consider the facts.** Consider the complete set of facts provided in the reading. What is the writer trying to suggest with these facts? What conclusions does the complete set of facts support? Suppose a writer presents the following facts.

> Dr. Tannenbaum is an old-school doctor. His staff greets you by name and offers you a cup of coffee when you arrive for your appointment. A receptionist answers the phone and returns all calls promptly. Dr. Tannenbaum talks to you as if you're a human being, not just a medical chart, and he'll make house calls if you live alone and have no transportation to his office.

From these sentences, the conclusion is clear: The writer considers Dr. Tannenbaum an excellent doctor who treats his patients with respect.

4. **Examine word choices.** A writer's choice of words often conveys his or her feelings toward the topic. Look for words that are heavy with connotations and ask yourself why the writer chose these words. For example, in the paragraph about Dr. Tannenbaum, the author uses the adjective *old-school* to imply a traditional doctor who cares about his patients.

For more on connotation, see p. 79.

5. **Support your inference with specific evidence.** Valid inferences are based on fact, context, and personal experiences. Be sure you have ample evidence to back up any inference you make. It would be incorrect to infer that Dr. Tannenbaum is highly skilled at diagnosing rare illnesses, for example, based on the information presented.

EXERCISE 4.1 **Making Reasonable Inferences**

Read the following excerpt from "American Jerk" (p. 49) and answer the questions that follow.

Pick your poison: reality television, slasher movies, video games, online porn, cell phones, automated answering systems, giant assault vehicles for trips to the grocery store, car stereos played at volumes easily heard on Jupiter, web-powered copyright infringement, people who will not shut their inane traps in movie theaters, and, lord help us, now even people who won't shut their inane traps during live theater.

We're all talking to someone all the time, but it's ever more rarely to the people we are actually with. Our cell phones blare ringtones that no one else wants to hear. We love to watch TV shows about the stunningly predictable results of hand-feeding a grizzly bear or lighting a stick of dynamite with a cigarette. We also love shows where people lie to others for money and programs where snarky, slightly talented folks say vicious things to hopeful, and usually more talented, contestants.

1. What reasonable inferences can you make about the author's opinion of the typical American? Provide three adjectives that the author would use to describe Americans.
2. Which specific words or phrases in the selection provide hints regarding the author's attitude toward "American jerks"?
3. What details are particularly revealing about Americans' behavior?

Assess the evidence. In general, the most reliable information is based on solid *evidence*. Just as police assess the evidence to discover who committed a crime, you must assess it to determine whether:

- the evidence is reliable,
- the evidence supports the writer's assertions, and
- enough evidence has been provided to make a strong case.

The following list of pros and cons will help you determine the reliability of some of the most common types of evidence.

Type	Pros	Cons
Personal experience or examples	• Can be powerful: No one understands cancer, for example, like a person who has survived the disease.	• Is subjective: Two people can experience the same event very differently. • May not offer enough examples to support a broad generalization.
Eyewitness reports	• May be powerful: Witnesses often have strong convictions that their memories are reliable.	• Are often inaccurate: Many studies have shown that memory is easily influenced. • May be subjective: If two people see a man running from a burning building, one may think, "What a lucky man! He escaped from the burning building," while the other may think, "That man started the fire."

Type	Pros	Cons
Surveys	• May be highly reliable when conducted by experienced researchers who collect responses from a wide array of subjects.	• May be misleadingly worded or administered inconsistently, or may include responses from too narrow a spectrum of respondents.
Data and statistics	• Tend to be collected by academic researchers and members of professional research organizations who try to be as objective and accurate as possible.	• Can be used in ways that hide the truth. Example: A soda company may claim that "90% of the people in a taste test preferred our cola to the competitor's." This may be true, but consider how many subjects were tested, whether the test was run in a neutral location, and so on.
Evidence from scientific experiments and studies	• Usually considered highly reliable because they are based on the scientific method, a set of procedures that researchers follow to investigate their hypotheses and test the results of other experiments and studies.	• May apply to only a narrow range of cases. • Can be influenced by uncontrollable factors. Example: Studies on drug safety are often contradictory. • May reflect the economic or political biases of scientists conducting the study; occasionally, results may be falsified or outcomes misrepresented.

For more about analyzing data in graphics, see pp. 91–95.

EXERCISE 4.2 **Evaluating Statements**

Consider each of the following statements and the context in which it is made. List what types of information are missing that would help you weigh the evidence and evaluate the claim being made. What further types of evidence would you need to accept or reject the statement?

1. On the label of a bag of cookies: "CONTAINS 45% LESS FAT and 0 grams of TRANS FAT!"
2. In a printed campaign flyer for mayoral candidate Mary Johnson: "My opponent, Joe Smith, has been accused of serious conflicts of interest in the awarding of city contracts during his term as mayor."
3. In large print on the cover of a novel you see at the supermarket checkout: "'This novel is a . . . wild and exciting . . . ride through the rough-and-tumble days of the Gold Rush . . . full of . . . adventure and excitement. . . . Memorable.'—*New York Times*"

Distinguish fact from opinion. In order to determine whether an opinion has been adequately supported by facts, first you must be able to distinguish facts from opinions. The chart below will help:

Facts . . .	Opinions . . .
. . . are objective statements of information that can be verified—that is, their truth can be established with evidence. Facts can be checked in trustworthy sources such as online dictionaries and Web reference sources like refdesk.com.	. . . are subjective—that is, they differ by individual. They make a claim based on attitudes, feelings, or beliefs. These claims cannot be established definitely as either true or false, at least at the present time. Often they put forth a particular position or agenda.
Examples	**Examples**
• Many people who smoke marijuana do not go on to use more dangerous drugs. • Texting while driving has caused many accidents.	• Marijuana use will probably be legalized in all fifty states by 2020. • People who text while driving should be fined and have their driver's licenses revoked.

When writers want to limit the extent of a claim, they often use qualifying words and phrases. For example, an expert on government debt may write, "*It seems likely* that Social Security payments will decline for future generations of Americans." Using such words and phrases limits the writer's responsibility for providing solid evidence to support the claim and allows other viewpoints to be acceptable.

EXERCISE 4.3 **Distinguishing between Facts and Opinions**

Label each of the following statements as fact (F) or opinion (O).

1. The best symphonies are shorter than twenty minutes.
2. About half the population of Uruguay lives in Montevideo.
3. More women earned doctoral degrees in engineering in 2012 than in 1995.
4. Private companies should not be allowed to operate concessions inside our national parks.
5. The mountains of northern Idaho contain the most scenic landscapes in the country.

EXERCISE 4.4 **Writing Facts and Opinions**

For two of the following topics, write one statement of fact and one statement of opinion.

1. voter turnout rates in presidential elections
2. alternative energy solutions
3. the Super Bowl

ANALYZE THE AUTHOR'S LANGUAGE

Authors often convey their message through the language they use, choosing words to create impressions, express feelings, even shape the readers' attitudes and feelings toward the topic. When analyzing language, be sure to consider denotative versus connotative meanings, figurative language, and euphemisms and doublespeak, as well as the writer's overall tone.

Consider denotation versus connotation. A **denotation** is the literal meaning of a word. For example, the denotation of the word *talking* is "expressing ideas using speech." A **connotation** is the set of additional meanings or associations that a word has taken on. Often a word's connotation has a much stronger effect on readers or listeners than its denotation does. The manner in which a politician talks to his or her audience might be described as "responding to ideas" (which carries a positive connotation), "discussing ideas" (which is an objective-sounding statement of fact), or "ranting" or "lecturing" (which gives readers a negative impression). As you read, ask yourself, "What effect is the writer's word choices likely to have on readers?"

EXERCISE 4.5 | **Analyzing Denotation and Connotation**

For each of the following words, think of one word with a similar denotation but a positive connotation and another word with a similar denotation but a negative connotation.

- **Example: Group (of people): positive connotation, *audience*; negative connotation, *mob***

  1. choosy
  2. cheap
  3. thin
  4. bold
  5. walk

Assess figurative language. **Figurative language** is language used in a nonliteral way to create a striking impression. For example, "The teenage boy tore into his sandwich like a hyena into a fallen zebra" creates a stronger image and conveys a more meaningful description than, "He quickly ate his sandwich." The four common types of figurative expressions are:

1. **Personification:** Giving an object human qualities or characteristics. For example, in the sentence, "The urn glared at me from the mantelpiece," an urn (an inanimate object) is made to seem ominous.
2. **Symbolism:** Using one thing to represent something else. For instance, the White House is often considered a symbol of the United States. For many people, a car symbolizes freedom.
3. **Simile:** Comparing two items using the word *like* or *as*. For example, in *Peter Pan*, J. M. Barrie describes Mrs. Darling's mind with the following simile: "Her romantic mind was like the tiny boxes, one within the other, that come from the puzzling East."
4. **Metaphor:** Comparing two objects without using the word *like* or *as*. For example, Shakespeare wrote in *Romeo and Juliet*, "But soft, what light through yonder window breaks? / It is the east and Juliet is the sun." Here the speaker compares Juliet to the sun.

Most writers use figurative language to add color and shades of meaning to their writing. Carefully chosen, figurative language can persuade or convey a certain impression.

For example, a political party may use powerful patriotic images, such as the White House or the bald eagle, to convey the idea that their agenda is "what's right for America." In the quote from *Peter Pan* on page 79, the author uses figurative language to convey a strong impression of Mrs. Darling: Her mind is "romantic" (which may connote "unrealistic" or "out of touch"), and it is similar to tiny boxes from the "puzzling East." Through this simile, Barrie implies that Mrs. Darling's thought processes are puzzling to the people who know her.

When you encounter figurative language, ask yourself the following questions.

- How does it affect the writer's tone?
- Does it advance the author's agenda?
- Does it reveal bias?
- Is the author using figurative language to inform and delight or to hide something?

EXERCISE 4.6 **Recognizing Similes and Metaphors**

Identify each of the following excerpts as a simile or metaphor and explain the items being compared. What is the tone of each excerpt? How does the figurative language help to convey a particular impression?

1. "She entered with ungainly struggle like some huge awkward chicken, torn, squawking, out of its coop." —Sir Arthur Conan Doyle, "The Adventure of the Three Gables"
2. "Her father had inherited that temper; and at times, like antelope fleeing before fire on the slope, his people fled from his red rages." —Zane Grey, *Riders of the Purple Sage*
3. "Shall I compare thee to a summer's day? / Thou art more lovely and more temperate." —William Shakespeare, Sonnet 18

Identify euphemisms and doublespeak. A **euphemism** is a word or phrase that is used to avoid a word that is unpleasant, embarrassing, or otherwise objectionable. For example, many people think it is more considerate to say that a loved one "passed away" rather than "died." Many people prefer the terms *disabled* and *person with disabilities* to the word *handicapped*.

Doublespeak is a type of euphemism that uses deliberately unclear or evasive language to sugar-coat an unpleasant reality. As a critical thinker you should always be alert for it, particularly when reading about business and politics. For example, a government may say that it is engaging in *enhanced interrogation* when it is torturing prisoners; a corporation may tell employees that the company will be *downsizing* or *smart-sizing* instead of saying that some of them will be laid off.

Euphemisms and doublespeak use roundabout, indirect, or neutralized language to avoid stating the facts directly. Any time you encounter such language, your critical thinking skills should kick into gear. Ask yourself questions like these.

- What is the author trying to prevent me from knowing?
- Why is the author hiding something: to spare my feelings, avoid personal embarrassment, hide something nasty about the author or the group the author represents?

EXERCISE 4.7 **Recognizing Euphemisms and Doublespeak**

Answer each of the following questions.

1. The media often report about people from other countries who come to the United States without permission from the U.S. government or who stay here after their permission to visit has expired. Two terms are used to refer to these people: *illegal aliens* and *undocumented immigrants*. Discuss which term seems to have a more negative connotation and which seems more neutral. Why does each term carry the connotations it does? Is the more neutral term a euphemism? Why or why not?

2. Working with a classmate, brainstorm a list of euphemisms and doublespeak currently in use in the media. Be prepared to share your list with the class.

Analyze the author's tone. **Tone** refers to how a writer sounds to readers, and it is influenced by how the writer feels about his or her topic and readers and the language the writer uses to convey that attitude.

Tone is constructed primarily by:
- choosing words with the appropriate connotation,
- using figurative language effectively,
- using euphemism and doublespeak, and
- using stylistic features such as sentence patterns and length to lend emphasis.

For more on sentence patterns and length, see Chapter 10, p. 197.

Using these strategies effectively, a writer can communicate surprise, disapproval, disgust, admiration, gratitude, or amusement. These are just a few of the words commonly used to describe tone; Table 4.1 lists many others. Recognizing an author's tone will help you interpret and evaluate the message and its effect on you.

TABLE 4.1 Words Commonly Used to Describe Tone

angry	detached	impassioned	objective
arrogant	earnest	indignant	sarcastic
bitter	forgiving	informative	serious
compassionate	frustrated	joyful	sympathetic
condescending	hateful	mocking	worried

EXERCISE 4.8 **Analyzing Tone**

Read each of the following statements and describe its tone. Which words in the statement provide clues to the tone? (Refer to Table 4.1 if necessary.)

1. Do you eat canned tuna? Then you are at least partially responsible for the deaths of thousands of innocent dolphins, which are mercilessly slaughtered by fishermen in their quest for tuna.

2. The penalty for creating and launching a computer virus should include a personal apology to every person who was affected by the virus, and each apology should be typed—without errors!—on a manual typewriter.

3. Piles of solid waste threaten to ruin our environment, pointing to the urgent need for better disposal methods and strategies for lowering the rate of waste generation.
4. All poets seek to convey emotion and the complete range of human feeling, but the only poet who fully accomplished this goal was William Shakespeare.

EXERCISE 4.9 **Experimenting with Tone**

Consider the following situation: A developer has received permission to bulldoze an entire city block filled with burned-out tenement buildings and abandoned factories. In their place, the developer is going to build a community of 300 upscale condominiums for people who work in the city and want to live close to their jobs.

Write three different sentences (or paragraphs) that react to this news. Make the tone of your first sentence *outraged*. Make the tone of your second sentence *joyful*. Make the tone of your third sentence *nostalgic*.

ANALYZE THE AUTHOR'S ASSUMPTIONS, GENERALIZATIONS, AND OMISSIONS

Authors make decisions or take short cuts that can influence readers' understanding. For example, they make assumptions and generalizations, and they decide which information to include or exclude. As a critical reader, you should analyze the author's assumptions and assess whether the generalizations the author makes are fair and whether he or she omits any information that is important to a full understanding of the subject.

Recognize the author's assumptions. An **assumption** is an idea or principle the writer accepts as true and makes no effort to prove. Often the writer implies assumptions rather than stating them directly.

Some assumptions are fair and reasonable; others are not. For example, it is reasonable to assume that most of the people who read *People* magazine are interested in celebrities. It is not reasonable to assume that readers of *People* magazine are Republicans.

Assumptions can be based on any combination of the following:

- anecdotal evidence,
- facts,
- opinions,
- religious beliefs,
- personal experiences, and
- background.

Writers often make assumptions at the beginning of an essay and then base the rest of the essay on that assumption. If the assumption is false or cannot be proven, then the ideas that flow from it may also be incorrect. For instance, the following excerpt begins with an assumption (highlighted) that the writer makes no attempt to prove or justify.

> Childbirth is a painful experience, intolerable even with appropriate medications. In response to this pain, modern women should accept the painkillers offered to them by their doctors. Why be a martyr? You have to suffer sleepless nights because of your child for the rest of your life; bring them into this world on your terms—pain free. Women should not be embarrassed or reluctant to request anesthesia during labor.

The author assumes that all women find childbirth intolerably painful and then argues that women should request anesthesia during labor. But if the writer's initial assumption is false, much of the argument that follows should be questioned.

As you read, identify the author's assumptions (especially those at the start of an essay) and then decide whether these assumptions are realistic and reasonable by asking questions like these.

- How do these assumptions reinforce or challenge social norms (or standards)?
- What effects do these assumptions have on the essay?
- What information, if any, would raise doubts about this assumption?

The answers to these questions will help you determine whether arguments or opinions based on these assumptions make sense. If you disagree with some of the assumptions in a source, check other sources to obtain different viewpoints.

EXERCISE 4.10 **Identifying Assumptions**

Each of the following statements contains one or more assumptions. Identify the assumption(s) made in each statement.

1. Computer users expect Web sites to entertain them with graphics, sound, and video.
2. In response to the problem of ozone depletion, the U.S. Environmental Protection Agency has designed various programs to reduce harmful emissions. It wants to stop the production of certain substances so that the ozone layer can repair itself over the next fifty years.
3. Only the routine vaccination of all children can eliminate the threat of serious disease and ensure optimum public health. These shots should be administered without hesitation. Parents must have full confidence in their doctors on this matter.
4. Since so many athletes and coaches approve of the use of performance-enhancing drugs, these substances should be allowed without regulation.
5. Because they recognize that meat consumption is environmentally damaging, environmentalists are often vegetarians.

> **EXERCISE 4.11** Identifying Assumptions in a Reading
>
> Reread "American Jerk" on pages 49–50. What assumptions does the author make in the first four paragraphs of the essay?

Assess the author's generalizations. A **generalization** is a claim based on one or more specific examples and applied more widely. Many writers generalize to argue a point, and generalizations may be reasonable or not. They are unreasonable when they are based on too little evidence or when all the variables are not taken into consideration (hasty generalization) and also when the conclusion is applied more widely than the evidence supports (sweeping generalization). Here's an obvious example of sweeping generalization: A woman who feels unfulfilled in her emotional life divorces her husband, leaves her children, and decides to travel the world. As she travels, she learns more about herself and falls in love with a new man. Based on this one woman's experience, is it safe to assume that all women in search of a richer emotional life should leave their husbands and travel the world? Of course not.

For more about problems of logical reasoning, see Chapter 20, pp. 517–18.

Most generalizations, however, are not so clearly reasonable or unreasonable. Imagine you are reading an article by a writer who argues that cars should be prohibited in congested cities. To support this claim, the writer cites studies showing the benefits of banning cars in three European cities. Is such a generalization fair? The reader must decide whether these three case studies provide *sufficient* evidence for such a generalization.

When assessing generalizations, ask yourself the following questions to determine whether such generalizations are justified.

- How many examples has the author provided?
- Are these examples representative of the situation? That is, do the examples represent most people's experiences?
- Can the generalization be proved scientifically? In other words, is there a scientific consensus about the generalization?

Generalizations can provide many ideas for your own writing. An essay might respond to a generalization, looking at the evidence that supports it and the evidence that contradicts it. A research paper might include details about what others have said about the topic.

> **EXERCISE 4.12** Identifying Generalizations
>
> Label each of the following statements fact (F) or generalization (G). Indicate what support or documentation would be necessary for you to evaluate its accuracy.
>
> 1. Many women want to become pilots.
> 2. Elephants can vocalize at frequencies below the range of human hearing.
> 3. In certain parts of the Red Sea, the temperature of the water can reach 138 degrees Fahrenheit.
> 4. Most people who live in San Diego are associated with the U.S. Navy.
> 5. People all over the world showed sympathy by donating money to survivors of Hurricane Sandy.

Look for purposeful omissions. Writers and speakers sometimes mislead by omission.

- They leave out essential information, background, or context, or include only the details that favor their position.
- They adopt the passive voice to avoid taking or assigning responsibility for an action (*a decision was made*).
- They use vague nouns and pronouns to avoid specifying exactly what or whom they are referring to (*they are bleeding our city's coffers dry*).

Consider an article written by a parent who has home-schooled her children. As an advocate of home schooling, she is likely to emphasize her children's educational progress and her own sense of personal fulfillment achieved by teaching her children. However, she may omit information—for example, that home-schooled children sometimes feel lonely or isolated from their peers. She also may refer to home schooling as "better" for children without specifying exactly what it is better than (her local public school, public schools in general, or any kind of school) or in what ways it is better.

Regardless of what you are reading, ask yourself the following questions to be sure you are getting full and complete information.

- Has any important information or contradictory evidence been omitted? What, if anything, am I not being told?
- Is it clear to whom actions or thoughts are being attributed? If not, why not?
- Is there another side to this argument or aspect to this topic that I should consider?
- Based on my own knowledge and experience, how do I evaluate this material?

To answer these questions, you may need to do some additional reading or research.

| **EXERCISE 4.13** | **Identifying Purposeful Omissions**

Read the following scenarios and determine what information is being withheld from you. What additional information do you need to determine whether you are being misled?

1. You see a TV ad for a fast-food restaurant that shows a huge hamburger topped with pickles, onions, and tomatoes. The announcer says, "For a limited time, get your favorite burger for only 99 cents!"
2. You open your mailbox and find a letter from a credit-card company. The letter invites you to open a charge card with no annual fee and offers you instant credit if you return the attached card in a postage-paid envelope.
3. You get an offer from a DVD club that appears to be a good deal. As part of your introductory package, you can buy five DVDs for only ninety-nine cents, plus shipping and handling.

USE THE PATTERNS OF DEVELOPMENT TO THINK AND READ CRITICALLY

The patterns you will learn to identify and use in Part 3 suggest useful questions for critical reading, questions that highlight aspects of the reading selection you might not otherwise have considered.

Pattern	Questions
Narration (recounting events)	• Were any events glided over or given special emphasis? If so, why? • What events in your life experience confirm or challenge the writer's ideas? • Were any of the events surprising or unconvincing? Why?
Description (painting a mental picture)	• Why did the author choose the particular sensory images used? • What was the effect of these details on the reader?
Illustration (explaining by example)	• Why were these examples, and not others, chosen? • Are the examples representative? Are they relevant?
Process analysis (explaining how something works or is done)	• Why is the process worth knowing? • Were any steps missing or over- (under-) developed?
Comparison and contrast (showing similarities and differences)	• Why did the author choose to focus on these similarities or differences? What makes them unique, important, or surprising? • How is what the author describes similar to or different from your own experience?
Classification or division (explaining by categories or parts)	• Why is it useful to classify or divide this topic? • What categories or parts does the author identify? Were any of them surprising? • Were each of the categories or parts equally convincing?
Definition (explaining what you mean)	• What terms were defined? Are the definitions clear and objective? Were any of the definitions surprising?
Cause and effect (using reasons and results to explain)	• What are the relationships among the events described in the reading? • What else could have been a cause (or effect)? • Could the causes or effects just have happened at the same time by coincidence or for some other reason the writer does not investigate?

Refer back to this list as you work through readings in the remainder of the book. Each chapter in Part 3 includes a section called "Thinking Critically about [the name of pattern]." These sections explore in more depth the concerns critical readers and thinkers should address as they analyze and evaluate readings using each pattern.

> **EXERCISE 4.14** | **Identifying Bias in a Reading Selection**

Reread the excerpt from "American Jerk" in Exercise 4.1. Using the techniques described in "Analyze the Author's Language," write a paragraph explaining whether you detect hidden bias in the selection or whether the writer makes clear that he is expressing only one viewpoint among others. If you detect bias, point to purposeful omissions or other strategies (such as his word choices) the writer uses to hide his biases. If you do not, explain why you feel the excerpt is not biased.

USE SYNTHESIS TO THINK AND READ CRITICALLY

At times you may realize that you do not have sufficient knowledge or experience to analyze and evaluate an author's ideas. In such cases, you may need to locate additional sources to fill in the gaps, provide additional viewpoints, challenge the author's assumptions or speculations, or offer more detailed evidence. When you synthesize information from sources to assess or challenge a writer's assumptions or claims, you must do two things.

1. Synthesize, or merge, information from sources with your existing, but limited, knowledge and experience.
2. Test the evidence or claims from the original reading against your own experience and what you've learned from the new sources.

Use the following questions as guidelines.

See Chapter 23, p. 592, for more about synthesis.

- On what do two or more of the sources agree? On what, if anything, do they disagree?
- What new information or perspectives did you encounter? Did they reinforce or challenge information or ideas in the other source(s)?
- In what ways do the new sources help you understand the original reading? Do they provide context, expand upon a topic, or challenge the writer's interpretation, for example?

> **EXERCISE 4.15** | **Synthesizing Your Skills**

As a cumulative activity and to synthesize all the critical thinking strategies you have learned in this chapter, refer to the reading "Superhero or Supervillain?" (Chapter 3, pp. 65–68) to answer the following questions.

1. Using the information you find in the introduction to the reading and in the reading itself, evaluate Will Oremus's qualifications to write about human enhancement technologies.
2. What types of evidence does Oremus use to support his ideas? Give several examples, and explain in a sentence or two whether the evidence is relevant.
3. List at least two inferences Oremus makes and at least one inference the researchers he discusses make. Identify at least three statements of fact and three statements of opinion.
4. Identify at least five words with positive or negative connotations.

5. Describe the author's tone. What effect does the tone have on you as a reader? How effective do you find it?
6. Identify at least one assumption the author makes.
7. What generalizations does the author make? List two.
8. What additional information would you need to evaluate Oremus's claims about the likelihood of certain kinds of superpowers being used for good or evil?
9. Based on your analysis, do you think Oremus seems fair or biased? Write a paragraph justifying your answer.

READING VISUALS CRITICALLY

Visuals appear everywhere—on television and in movies; in magazines, newspapers, textbooks, and presentation slides; on signs, flyers, and billboards; in print and online. They may appear on their own, but often they are combined with text to make a message even more effective. Visuals are used so widely because they can convey information and impressions, sell products and ideas, raise questions, and trigger emotions. Because they are so powerful, make sure you study them as carefully as you read, analyze, and evaluate written text. You should also choose them carefully when you use them in your own essays.

For more on using visuals in your writing, see Chapter 6, pp. 128–30.

Consider, for example, the public service advertisement (PSA) from LoveIsRespect.org. What did you notice first? Perhaps you noticed the headline with its shocking statistic: "Dating Abuse Affects 1 in 3 Young People." Or perhaps you noticed the photographs of hands holding speech bubbles telling viewers what love really is ("the closest thing we have to magic," "caring enough to ask," "respect," "playing fair"). Or maybe the white shape in the bottom-left corner caught your eye, with its message: "Connect NOW!"

Whatever you noticed first, second, or third, when you put the text and images together, you recognized the purpose of the ad: to help young people who may be involved in abusive relationships understand what a loving relationship should be all about and to provide them with help to

Courtesy of loveisrespect.org and the National Domestic Violence Hotline

"break the cycle." The design, the colors, the headline contrasting with the photos arranged in the shape of a heart below: Together these elements make a dramatic statement about love and self-respect. By combining words and images, this PSA makes the issue of dating abuse much more compelling and engaging than it would have been with written text alone.

TABLE 4.2 Analyzing Photographs
Guidelines for reading photographs actively and critically

1. **Preview the visual.** What is its main subject? What did you notice first, and how did it affect you?

2. **Study the visual as a whole, and then examine its parts**. What is its focal point? What details appear in the foreground and the background? (If you are a verbal learner, translating the photo into words may be helpful.) Is it a close-up or a distance shot? (Close-ups may reveal emotions; distance shots provide more context.)

3. **Read the caption and any accompanying text, consider the context, and make connections**. What information about time, place, or subject is provided? What does the author want to emphasize? How does the photo relate to the ideas presented in the surrounding text? What happened before or after the photo was taken? Is any other context provided?

4. **Determine the author's purpose and intended message.** Is the purpose to inform, amuse, shock, persuade, or some combination of these or other motives? Is the photo intended to elicit a powerful reaction from viewers or to provide information?

Learning Style Options

READING PHOTOGRAPHS ACTIVELY

Use the guidelines in Table. 4.2 when reading photographs and any words (a caption, labels, slogans, text) that accompany them. What do you learn when you apply them to the photograph in Figure 4.1?

FIGURE 4.1 Reading Happens Anytime, **Anywhere** © Hola/Superstock RF

> **EXERCISE 4.16** **Analyzing a Textbook Photo**

Analyze Figure 4.2, using the guidelines in Table 4.2 on p. 89. Then answer the following questions.

1. Describe your first impression of the photo.
2. Summarize what is happening in the photo. What details convey this impression? Is it a close-up or distance shot? What is revealed (or hidden) about the subject of the photograph as a result?
3. What does the caption or any context contribute to your understanding of the photo? (This photograph appeared in an economics textbook in a chapter titled "Factor Markets and Distribution of Income.")
4. Why did the author include this photo? Does it reveal any assumptions or biases?
5. Does the photo look staged, edited, or touched up? If so, what details convey this impression?
6. Does the photo achieve the author's purpose? What other kinds of photos or visuals might the writer have used to make the same point? (Provide reasons or use details from the photograph to support your claim.)

FIGURE 4.2 **The Value of a Degree**
If you have doubts about completing college, consider this: Factory workers with high school diplomas earn much less than college graduates. The present discounted value of the difference in lifetime earnings is as much as $1 million. © Monika Graff/The Image Works

EXERCISE 4.17 | **Writing about Photos**

Examine one of the photographs that accompanies the reading "Superhero or Supervillain?" in Chapter 3 (pp. 65–68), or another reading chosen by your instructor. Then write a paragraph explaining what the photo shows and analyzing the factors that contribute to the impression it makes.

READING GRAPHICS ACTIVELY

Graphics organize and condense information, making lengthy or complicated data and concepts easier to understand. Writers use many types of graphics; the purpose of each of the common types is summarized in Table 4.3.

TABLE 4.3 Graphics and Their Purposes

Type of Graphic	Purpose	Example
Pie (circle) chart	To show the relationships among parts of a whole; to show how given parts of a unit are divided or classified	A chart showing the proportions of different racial and ethnic groups in the U.S. population
Bar graphs	To make comparisons between quantities or amounts	A graph comparing the number of calories needed by men and women leading sedentary lives
Line graphs	To show changes in a variable over time or to compare relationships between two or more variables	A graph showing variations in quiz scores
Tables	To organize and condense data; to compare and classify information	A table showing how many calories men and women need daily for various age groups with either an active or a sedentary lifestyle
Diagrams and flowcharts	To explain processes or procedures or show how things work	A diagram showing the parts of an essay

Use the guidelines in Table 4.4 when analyzing graphics and any words (a caption, labels, slogans, text) that accompany them.

TABLE 4.4 Analyzing Graphics

Guidelines for reading tables and charts actively and critically

1. **Preview the table or chart.** Read the title and caption (if any) and look quickly at the table or chart. What is it supposed to show?

2. **Look at the headings (of tables/charts), labels (of figures), and legends (of charts/figures) to determine how the data are organized.** The headings and labels should indicate the variables. The legend (or guide to the colors, symbols, terms, or other information) should show what is being analyzed. A scale shows how measurements should be read.

3. **Read the caption (if any) and any discussion of the graphic in the text, and make connections.** Does the text explain why the graphic was included or what it is intended to show? (If not, make your own connections between the text and graphic.) To understand a complicated graphic, you may need to study the text and graphic carefully several times. Read the whole explanation in the text before looking back at the graphic.

4. **Study the data to try to identify trends or patterns.** Note unexpected changes (such as sudden increases or decreases in amounts), surprising statistics, or unexplained variations. Summarize any trends and note any patterns you find. Writing will crystallize the idea in your mind, and your notes will be useful for review.

5. **Check the source of the data.** Are the data from a reliable source? Are they up to date?

EXERCISE 4.18 **Analyzing a Table**

Use the guidelines in Table 4.4 to analyze Table 4.5.

TABLE 4.5 U.S. Household Internet Usage by Age, 2011

Age of householder	Internet use at home (%)	Dial-up at home (%)	Broadband at home (%)	Internet use anywhere (%)	No Internet use anywhere (%)
Under 25	69.53	1.18	66.68	85.09	14.91
25 to 34	77.75	1.36	75.33	87.35	12.65
35 to 44	81.86	1.53	79.45	89.55	10.45
45 to 54	77.93	2.43	74.59	84.44	15.56
55 years +	61.68	3.05	58.00	66.21	33.79

Source: U.S. Department of Commerce, National Telecommunications and Information Administration, *Exploring the Digital Nation: America's Emerging Online Experience,* June 2013. See also <http://www.ntia.doc.gov/report>. Based on the July 2011 Current Population Survey Computer and Internet Use Supplement. See text, Section 1 and Appendix III. For more information: http://www.ntia.doc.gov/report/2013/exploring-digital-nation-americas-emerging-online-experience

EXERCISE 4.19   **Working with Tables and Figures**

Study the figure below, which converts some of the data from Table 4.5 into a line graph, and answer the following questions.

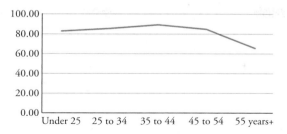

1. Compare this figure with Table 4.5. What variables does this figure use? Which data from that table were used to create this figure?
2. What title would you give this figure? The title should accurately describe the information conveyed by the figure.
3. Write a caption for this figure that accurately describes the trend(s) it shows.

THINKING CRITICALLY ABOUT PHOTOS AND GRAPHICS

Just as you should critically examine all the words you read, you should also critically examine all visuals that accompany a reading. Photographs and graphics may reflect bias or distort information, either intentionally or unintentionally. For example, an author may choose more or less powerful photographs demonstrating one side of an issue or another. (See Figure 4.3 below.)

Disabled Army veteran Jim Champion at a hearing on medical marijuana at the Illinois State Capitol, May 8, 2013. Champion hopes his story will help convince Illinois's governor, Pat Quinn, to legalize medical marijuana in his state. AP Photo/Seth Perlman

Marijuana advocates march along Monroe Center in downtown Grand Rapids, Thursday, December 6, 2012. Kent County prosecutor William Forsyth recently filed a lawsuit to block a voter-approved city amendment to decriminalize marijuana. AP Photo/The Grand Rapids Press, Ciry Morse

FIGURE 4.3 The power of pictures

FIGURE 4.4 Cropping photographs to affect viewers' reactions © John Hasselt/Corbis

Or an author may crop a photo to distort the viewer's perception. Compare the photographs in Figure 4.4. These photos show a rally to free thirty Greenpeace activists who were arrested for piracy by Russia. The photo on the left provides a clear sense of the size of the rally, whereas the photo above, taken from a different angle and cropped tight, could mislead some readers into believing the rally was more extensive than it really was. The close-up of the activists' photos is also likely to make viewers more sympathetic.

When reading graphics, consider also whether showing the data in a different type of graphic would change the reader's perception of the information. Compare Figure 4.5 (below), with the figure in Exercise 4.19 (p. 93). The downward-slanting line may suggest a greater difference in usage by age group than the bar graph suggests.

Percentage of U.S. Households Using the Internet, by Age (2011)

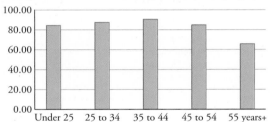

FIGURE 4.5 Shaping readers' perceptions through depiction of the data

Finally, consider whether the scale or units of measurement are misleading in any way. Reducing the scale, for example, can make differences seem huge, and expanding the scale can make them seem tiny. Compare the bar graph in Figure 4.6 with that in Figure 4.5 (on the previous page). The data used in both charts are the same, but because the chart below reduces the scale, it looks as if the difference between the groups is more dramatic than it is.

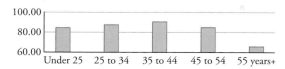

FIGURE 4.6 Misleading by adjusting the scale

Be especially careful when pictures are used in graphics instead of lines or bars (Figure 4.7). The labels in this graphic clearly indicate that more U.S. households own dogs (36.5%) than own cats (30.4%). But the relative size of the two animals suggests that the percentage difference is much greater than 6.1% (36.5–30.4%). If you looked only at the images, you might assume that dog ownership is much greater than it really is. You might also reasonably conclude that there are more pet dogs than pet cats in the United States, but the labels indicate that the pictures represent households that own *at least one* cat or dog. Some households may own two, six, or even ten cats. In fact, as of 2013 the American Pet Products Association estimates that there were over 10 million more pet cats than pet dogs in the United States. But you wouldn't know this from a glance at this graphic.

30.4% of U.S. households own at least one cat   36.5% of U.S. households own at least one dog

FIGURE 4.7 Cat and Dog Ownership in the United States

Source: American Pet Products Association, American Veterinary Medicine Association, and The Humane Society of the United States. http://www.humanesociety.org/issues/pet_overpopulation/facts/pet_ownership_statistics .html, https://www.avma.org/KB/Resources/Statistics/Pages/Market-research-statistics-US-pet-ownership.aspx © Benjamin Simeneta/Shutterstock.com; © ARTSILENCE/Shutterstock.com

© Creative RF/iStockphoto/Getty

part two
Strategies for Writing Essays

5 Prewriting
How to Find and Focus Ideas

Study the photo on this page. What is happening? What do you think the man could be reacting to? Write whatever comes to mind. You might write about times when you've felt the same emotions you think the man is expressing, or about times when you've seen others express strong emotions in public. Try to write nonstop for at least five minutes. Don't stop to evaluate your writing or worry about grammar. Just record your thoughts.

©Caro/Alamy

You have just used **freewriting**, a method of discovering ideas about a topic by writing without stopping for a set period of time. Read over what you wrote. Suppose you are now asked to write an essay about joy or exuberance. Do you see some starting points and usable ideas in your freewriting?

Generating ideas, considering your writing situation (your purpose, audience, point of view, and genre), and choosing and narrowing a topic are all part of the writing process, as illustrated in Figure 5.1 (p. 100). Although writing is often described as a step-by-step process, writers often move back and forth between the steps and return to an earlier step to cut and paste material they previously developed. This movement is designated by arrows pointing in both directions in the figure.

98

IN THIS CHAPTER YOU WILL LEARN TO

- choose and narrow a topic,
- consider audience, purpose, point of view, genre, and medium, and
- discover ideas to write about.

CHOOSING A TOPIC

In some writing situations, your instructor will assign the topic. In others, your instructor will allow you to choose your own topic, perhaps selecting from a number of possibilities. When you choose your own topic, don't just grab the first one that comes to mind. Rather, look for a topic that

- is appropriate to the assignment,
- you know something about or want to learn about, and
- will maintain your interest.

In addition to Internet browsing to search for a topic, don't overlook topics discussed in your classes or related to your entries in your writing journal, daily activities such as sports or social events, programs you've heard or seen on radio or television, or the world around you: people, objects, and social interactions.

For more on keeping a journal, see Chapter 2, pp. 29–30, and Chapter 3, pp. 57–58.

> **Essay in Progress 1**
> List at least three broad essay topics.

NARROWING A TOPIC

Once you have chosen a topic, narrow it to make it manageable within the required length of your essay. For example, if you are assigned a two- to four-page essay, a broad topic such as divorce is too large. However, you might write about one specific cause of divorce or its effects on children. *Skipping this step is one of the biggest mistakes you can make.* You can waste a great deal of time working on an essay only to discover later that the topic is too broad.

To narrow a topic, limit it to a specific part or aspect. Two techniques—branching and questioning—will help you. The idea-generating techniques covered later in the chapter (pp. 107–16) may also be used to narrow a broad topic.

e macmillanhighered.com/successfulwriting
LearningCurve > Topics and Main Ideas

FIGURE 5.1 **An Overview of the Writing Process**

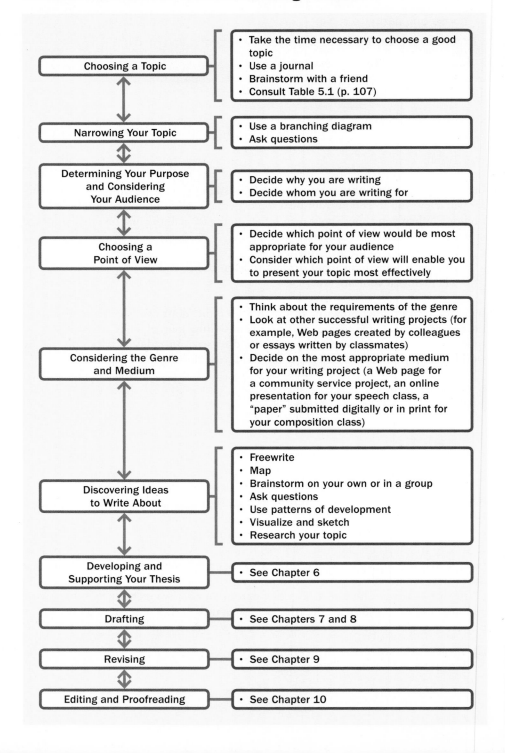

USING A BRANCHING DIAGRAM

Start by writing your broad topic at the far left side of your paper or computer screen. Then subdivide the topic into three or more subcategories or aspects. Here is an example for the broad topic of wild-game hunting.

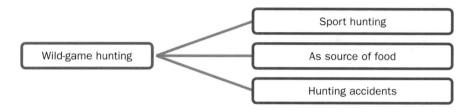

Then choose one subcategory and subdivide it further, as shown here.

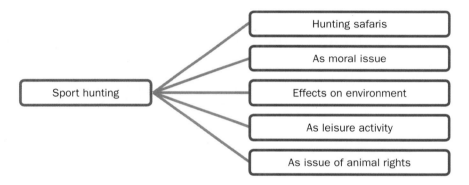

Continue narrowing the topic in this way until you feel you have found one that is interesting, appropriate to your assignment, and manageable. The following example shows narrowed topics that would be workable for a two- to four-page essay on the effects of sport hunting on the environment.

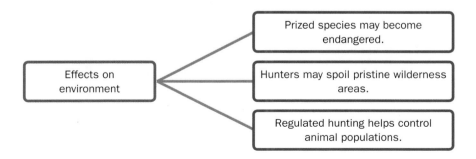

Note: Did you notice that as the narrowing progressed, the topics changed from words and phrases to statements of ideas?

Once you begin planning, researching, and drafting your essay, you may need to narrow your topic even further.

EXERCISE 5.1 **Branching**

Use branching diagrams to narrow three of the following broad topics to more manageable topics for a two- to four-page essay.

1. Manned space travel
2. School lunches
3. Air travel safety measures
4. Campaign finance rules
5. Alternative energy sources

Essay in Progress 2

Narrow one of the broad topics you chose in Essay in Progress 1 to a topic manageable for a two- to four-page essay.

ASKING QUESTIONS TO NARROW A BROAD TOPIC

Use questions that begin with *who, what, where, when, why,* and *how* to narrow your topic. Questioning will lead you to consider and focus your attention on specific aspects of the topic. Here is an example of questioning for the broad topic of divorce:

Questions	Narrowed Topics
Why does divorce occur?	• Lifestyle differences as a cause of divorce • Infidelity as a cause of divorce
How do couples divide their property?	• Division of assets after a divorce
Who can help couples work through a divorce?	• Role of friends and family • Role of mediator • Role of attorney
What are the effects of divorce on children?	• Emotional effects of divorce on children • Financial effects of divorce on children
When might it be advisable for a couple considering divorce to remain married?	• Couples who stay together for the sake of their children • Financial benefit of remaining married

Sometimes you may need to ask additional questions to limit the topic sufficiently. The topic "emotional effects of divorce on children," for example, is still too broad for an essay. Asking questions such as "What are the most common emotional effects?" and "How can divorcing parents prevent emotional problems in their children?" can lead to more specific topics.

| **EXERCISE 5.2** | **Questioning** |

Use questioning to narrow three of the following subjects to topics that would be manageable within a two- to four-page essay.

1. Senior citizens
2. Mental illness
3. Environmental protection
4. Cyberbullying
5. Television programming

THINKING ABOUT YOUR WRITING SITUATION

Once you have decided on a manageable topic, you are ready to consider your writing situation: Your purpose, audience, point of view, genre, and medium.

DETERMINING YOUR PURPOSE

A well-written essay should have a specific purpose or goal. There are three main purposes for writing.

1. **To *express* yourself:** For example, to express the writer's feelings about an incident of road rage that he or she observed.
2. **To *inform* your reader:** For example, to inform readers about the primary causes of road rage.
3. **To *persuade* your reader:** For example, to persuade readers to vote for funding to investigate the problem of road rage in the community.

To identify your purpose, ask yourself the following questions.

1. Why am I writing this essay?
2. What do I want this essay to accomplish?

Some essays can have more than one purpose. An essay on snowboarding, for example, could be both informative and persuasive: It could explain the benefits of snowboarding and urge readers to take up the sport because it is good exercise.

CONSIDERING YOUR AUDIENCE

Considering your **audience** (the people who will read your essay) is an important part of the writing process. Many aspects of your writing—how you express yourself, which words you choose, which details and examples you include, which types of sentences you use, and what attitude you take toward your topic—depend on the audience. Your **tone** (how you sound to your audience) is especially important. If you want your audience to feel comfortable with your writing, you need to write in a manner that your readers can understand and that appeals to them.

For more on tone, see Chapter 4, p. 81.

If you were describing a student orientation session to a friend, you would use a different tone and select different details than you would if you were describing the orientation in an article for the student newspaper:

Telling a Friend	Writing for the Student Newspaper
Remember I told you how nervous I am about attending college in the fall? Well, guess what? I went to my student orientation over the weekend, and it was much better than I expected! I even met one of my teachers—they call them "instructors" here—and he was so nice and down-to-earth that now I'm starting to get excited about going to college.	College student orientations are often thought to be stuffy affairs where prospective students attempt to mix with aloof professors. For this reason, I am pleased to report that the college orientation held on campus last weekend was a major success and not a pointless endeavor after all. Along with my fellow incoming first-year students, I was impressed with the friendliness of instructors and the camaraderie that developed between students and faculty.
Language: casual **Sentence Structure:** shorter sentences **Tone:** familiar, friendly	**Language:** more formal **Sentence Structure:** longer sentences **Tone:** serious, formal

How to consider your audience. As you consider your audience, keep the following points in mind.

- **Your readers are not present and cannot observe or participate in what you are writing about.** If you are writing about your apartment, for example, they cannot visualize it unless you describe it in detail.
- **Your readers do not know everything you know.** They may not have the same knowledge about and experience with the topic that you do, so you will have to define specialized terms, for example, if readers are unlikely to know what they mean.
- **Your readers may not share your opinions and values.** If you are writing about raising children and assume that strict discipline is undesirable, for example, some readers may not agree with you.
- **Your readers may not respond in the same way you do to situations or issues.** Some readers may not see any humor in a situation that you find funny. An issue that you consider only mildly disturbing may upset or anger some readers.

For a helpful list of questions you can ask to analyze your audience, consult the box on the next page.

ANALYZING YOUR AUDIENCE

When analyzing your audience, ask yourself the following questions:

- **What does my audience know (or not know) about my topic?** If you are proposing a community garden project to an audience of city residents who know little about gardening, you will need to describe the pleasures and benefits of gardening to capture their interest.

- **What is the education, background, and experience of my audience?** If you are writing your garden-project proposal for an audience of low-income residents, you might emphasize how much money they could save by growing vegetables, and if you are proposing the project to middle-income residents, you might stress is how relaxing gardening can be and how a garden can beautify a neighborhood.

- **What attitudes, beliefs, opinions, or biases are my audience likely to hold?** Suppose your audience believes that most development is harmful to the environment. If you are writing an essay urging your audience to sponsor a new community garden, consider emphasizing how the garden will benefit the environment and decrease development.

- **What tone do my readers expect?** Suppose you are writing to your local city council urging council members to approve the community garden. Although the council has been stalling on the issue, your tone should be serious and not accusatory. As community leaders, the council members expect to be treated with respect.

- **What tone will help me achieve my purpose?** If you are writing to your city counselor to urge her to support the community garden, a respectful tone is more likely to achieve your goal than a hostile one.

Considering your audience when it is composed of one person: your instructor. Instructors occasionally direct students to write for a particular audience, such as readers of a certain magazine or newspaper, but you can often assume that your main audience is your instructor. In most cases, it is best to write as if your instructor were unfamiliar with your topic. He or she wants to see if you understand the topic and can write and think clearly about it. For academic papers, provide enough information to demonstrate your knowledge of the subject (including background information, definitions of technical terms, and relevant details), make sure your essay is clear and understandable, maintain a reasonable tone, provide evidence from soures that are appropriate to your discipline, and treat alternative views fairly.

> **EXERCISE 5.3** **Considering Your Audience**
>
> 1. Write a one-paragraph description of a current television commercial for a particular product. Your audience is another college student.
> 2. Write a description of the same commercial for one of the following writing situations:
>   a. An assignment in a business marketing class: Analyze the factors that make the advertisement interesting and appealing. Your audience is a marketing instructor.
>   b. A letter to the company that produces the product: Describe your response to the advertisement. Your audience is the consumer relations director of the company.
>   c. A letter to your local television station: Comment favorably on or complain about the advertisement. Your audience is the station director.

CHOOSING A POINT OF VIEW

Point of view is the perspective from which you write an essay. There are three types: first, second, and third person. In choosing a point of view, consider your topic, your purpose, and your audience.

Think of point of view as the "person" you become as you write.

- **First person** uses first-person pronouns (*I, me, mine, we, ours*). First person is often effective and appropriate in an essay narrating an event in which you participated. For formal essays, many instructors prefer that you not write in the first person.
- **Second person** uses second-person pronouns (*you, your, yours*). Second person is appropriate when giving directions, as in an essay explaining how to build a fence: "First, *you* should measure . . ." Sometimes the word *you* may be understood but not directly stated, as in, "First, measure . . ." Many textbooks, including this one, use the second person to address student readers; however, many instructors prefer that you avoid using the second person in formal essays.
- **Third person** uses people's names and third-person pronouns (*he, she, it*). Third person is prevalent in academic writing. It is less personal and more formal than first person and second person. Think of the third person as public rather than private or personal. The writer reports what he or she sees.

> **EXERCISE 5.4** **Point of View**
>
> Working with a classmate, discuss which point of view (first, second, or third person) would be most appropriate in each of the following writing situations.
>
> 1. An essay urging students to participate in a march against hunger to support a local food drive
> 2. A description of a car accident on a form that your insurance company requires you to submit in order to collect benefits
> 3. A paper for an ecology course on the effects of air pollution caused by a local industry

CONSIDERING THE GENRE AND MEDIUM

Genre is a term used to classify types of text—for example, laboratory reports, proposals, or blog posts. Each genre has its own conventions, or ways of doing things. A laboratory report, for example, has a specific purpose: To inform readers about how an experiment was conducted so that it can be repeated and to tell readers the results. It takes the third-person point of view, uses technical language, and includes the following sections:

- introduction,
- methods,
- results, and
- discussion.

To write effectively you need to understand the conventions of the genre and follow them closely. Reviewing samples of effective writing in the genre, either by classmates or those posted on reliable Web pages, can be helpful.

Medium refers to the means through which ideas are expressed and information conveyed. In your writing class, your primary medium will be printed text, but your essays may include visuals, and if assignments are submitted or viewed electronically, you may also include audio or visual files, animations, or hyperlinks to Web sites. Be sure to choose a medium that suits your purpose and your audience. (For example, consider whether your readers will have high-speed Internet access when reading your assignment.) Also consider the conventions of the genre in which you are writing.

DISCOVERING IDEAS TO WRITE ABOUT

Discovering ideas to write about is a process of gathering all of your separate but related ideas on a topic and fitting them together. For example, you may know a lot about biking, but all your knowledge is not stored in one place in your brain: Verbal information is stored in one place; sensory impressions are stored in another. Be sure to draw on verbal information stored as words (facts, concepts), but do not overlook other sources of ideas as well. Table 5.1 shows the ideas one student developed on bicycling, tapping numerous sources of ideas. Together, all of these sources provide a wealth of ideas to write about on the topic of bicycling.

TABLE 5.1 Synthesizing Your Ideas on a Topic	
To Discover Ideas, Draw Upon Your . . .	**Example Topic: Bicycling**
Verbal Knowledge: facts, dates, numbers, concepts, definitions, reasons, and so forth	Types of bikes, costs, speeds, repairs, convenience, bike races
Personal Knowledge: events you have experienced	A bike trip to Yellowstone National Park, pedaling to school
Mental Images: pictures in your mind, recollections of images on television, videos	A mental image of the first bike you rode; a video of the Tour de France
Sensory Impressions: recollections of tastes, smells, touch, and sound	The feel of wind in your face as you ride, the roar of a truck coming up behind you
Motor Skills: memory of physical actions	Keeping your balance, steering, braking, changing gears

In the following sections, you will learn a number of specific strategies for discovering and recording ideas to write about. Depending on your learning style, you will probably find that some strategies work better than others. Experiment with each before deciding which will work for you. You may also find that the technique you choose for a given essay may depend on your topic.

FREEWRITING

When you use freewriting, you write for a specific period of time, usually five to ten minutes. Freewriting allows you to explore ideas and make associations, jumping from one idea to another. If nothing comes to mind, just write the topic, your name, or "I can't think of anything to write" until something occurs to you. The following tips will help you.

- **Write or type nonstop.** Writing often forces thought, so keep going, even after you think you have nothing more to say.
- **Don't be concerned with grammar, punctuation, or spelling.**
- **Write or type fast!** Try to keep up with your thinking. (Most people can think faster than they can write or type.)
- **Record ideas as they come to you** and in whatever form they appear—words, phrases, questions, sentences—or pictures and doodles.
- **If you are freewriting on a computer, darken the screen** so that you are not distracted by errors, formatting issues, and the words you have already written.

When you are done, reread your freewriting, and highlight or underline ideas that seem useful. Look for patterns and connections: Do several ideas together make a point; reflect a sequence; or suggest a larger, unifying idea? Here is an excerpt from one student's freewriting on the broad topic of violence in the media.

There seems to be a lot of violence in the media these days, particularly on TV. For example, last night when I watched the news, the camera man showed people getting shot in the street. What kind of people watch this stuff? I'd rather watch a movie. It really bothered me because people get so turned off by such an ugly, gruesome scene that they won't want to watch the news anymore. Then we'll have a lot of uninformed citizens. There are too many already. Some people do not even know who the vice president of the U.S. is. A negative thing—the media has a negative impact on any person or group who wants to do something about violence in the inner city. And they create negative impressions of minority and ethnic groups, too. If the media shows one Latino man committing a crime, viewers falsely assume all Latinos are criminals. It's difficult to think of something positive that can be done when you're surrounded by so much violence. It's all so overwhelming. What we need in the inner city is not more coverage of violence but <u>viable solutions</u> to the violence we have. The media coverage of violent acts only serves to make people think that this <u>violence is a normal state of affairs and nothing can be done</u> about it.

A number of subtopics surfaced from this student's freewriting:
- the media's graphic portrayal of violence,
- the negative effect of media violence on viewers, and
- the media's portrayal of minority and ethnic groups.

Any one of these topics could be narrowed to a manageable topic for an essay.

If you are a creative learner or feel restricted by organization and structure, freewriting may appeal to you because it allows you to give your imagination free rein.

Learning Style Options

EXERCISE 5.5 **Freewriting**

Set a clock or timer for five minutes and freewrite on one of the following broad topics. Then review and highlight your freewriting, identifying usable ideas with a common theme that might serve as a topic for an essay. Starting with one of the potential topics from your freewriting, freewrite for another five minutes to narrow your topic further and develop your ideas.

1. Hip-hop music
2. Facebook
3. How to be self-sufficient
4. Pressures on college students
5. Job interviews

MAPPING

Mapping, or **clustering**, is a visual way to discover ideas and relationships. Here is how to create a map.

1. Write your topic in the middle of a blank sheet of paper, and draw a box or circle around it. (You may also want to experiment with mapping on a computer, using a graphics program such as bubbl.us or smartdraw.com. You could then cut and paste items from your map into an outline or draft of your essay.)
2. Think of ideas that are related to or suggested by your topic. As you think of them, write them down in clusters around the topic, connecting them to the topic with lines (Figure 5.2). Think of your topic as a tree trunk and the related ideas as branches.
3. Draw arrows and lines or use highlighting to show relationships and connect groups of related ideas.
4. Think of still more ideas, clustering them around the ideas already on your map.

FIGURE 5.2 **Sample Map**

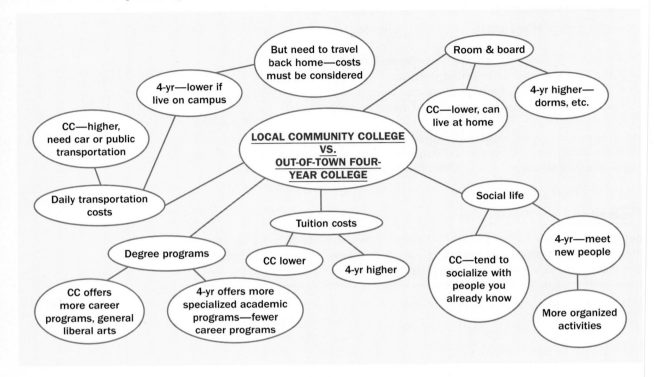

The sample map in Figure 5.2 was done by a student working on the topic of the costs of higher education. In this map, the student compared attending a local community college and attending an out-of-town four-year college. A number of different subtopics evolved, including the following:

- Transportation costs,
- Social life,
- Availability of degree programs, and
- Room and board costs.

Learning Style Options

Mapping may appeal to you if you prefer a spatial method of dealing with information and ideas. It also appeals to creative learners who like to devise their own structure or framework within which to work.

> **EXERCISE 5.6** | **Mapping**

Narrow one of the following topics. Then draw a map of related ideas as they come to mind.

1. Presidential politics
2. Daydreaming
3. Tattoos
4. Cable TV
5. Year-round schooling

BRAINSTORMING

When you **brainstorm**, you list everything that comes to mind when you think about your topic: facts, impressions, emotions, and reactions. Record words or phrases rather than sentences, and give yourself a time limit; this will force ideas to come faster. If you use a computer, you might use bullets or the indent function to brainstorm.

The following example shows a student's brainstorming on the narrowed topic of the disadvantages of home schooling.

Topic: Disadvantages of Home Schooling

- Parent may not be an expert in every subject
- Libraries not easily accessible
- Wide range of equipment, resources not available
- Child may be confused by parent playing the role of teacher
- Child does not learn to interact with other children
- Child does not learn to compete against others
- Parents may not enforce standards
- Parents may not be objective about child's strengths and weaknesses
- Child may learn only parent's viewpoint — not exposed to wide range of opinions
- Special programs (art, music) may be omitted
- Services of school nurse, counselors, reading specialists not available

Three clusters of topics are evident: unavailable services and resources (highlighted in purple), limits of parents (not highlighted), and problems of social development (highlighted in green). Once the student selected a cluster of topics, he did further brainstorming to generate ideas about his narrowed topic.

Brainstorming is more structured than freewriting because the writer focuses only on the topic at hand instead of writing whatever comes to mind. If you are a pragmatic learner, brainstorming may help you release your creative potential.

Brainstorming can also work well when it is done in groups of two or three classmates. Use a chalkboard or whiteboard in an empty classroom, share a large sheet of paper, sit together in front of a computer screen, or use networked computers. Say your ideas aloud as you write. You'll find that your classmates' ideas will trigger more of your own. Group brainstorming often appeals to students who are social learners and who find it stimulating and enjoyable to exchange ideas with other students.

Learning Style Options

EXERCISE 5.7   **Brainstorming**

Choose one of the following subjects and narrow it to a manageable topic for a two- to four-page paper. Then brainstorm, either alone or with one or two classmates, to generate ideas to write about.

1. Value of music
2. National parks
3. Credit-card fraud
4. Texting
5. Web advertising

QUESTIONING

Questioning is another way to discover ideas about a narrowed topic. Working either alone or with a classmate, write down every question you can think of about your topic. Focus on ideas, not correctness. Don't judge or evaluate ideas as you write. It may help to imagine that you are asking an expert on your topic anything that comes to mind.

Here is a partial list of questions one student generated on the narrow topic of the financial problems that single parents face.

Why do many female single parents earn less than male single parents?

How can single parents afford to pay for day care?

How do single parents find time to attend college to improve their employability and earning power?

How can women force their former husbands to keep up with child support payments?

Are employers reluctant to hire women who are single parents?

Beginning a question with "What if . . ." is a particularly good way to extend your thinking and look at a topic from a fresh perspective. Here are a few challenging "What if . . ." questions about the financial situation of single parents.

What if the government provided national day care or paid for day care?

What if single parents were not allowed to deduct more than one child on their income tax?

What if single parents were entitled to special tax rebates?

Another way to stimulate your thinking is to ask questions that approach the topic from a number of different perspectives. For the topic of the increased popularity of health foods, you could write questions about human motivation to purchase, marketing strategies, or nutritional value, for instance.

You may find questioning effective if you are an analytical, inquisitive person. Social learners will enjoy using this technique with classmates. Because questions often tend to focus on specifics and details, questioning is also an appealing strategy for concrete learners.

After devising a number of questions, you may want to write tentative answers, or hypotheses. If you need to conduct research, you can use these hypotheses as a guide.

Learning Style Options

To learn more about using research questions and hypotheses, see Chapter 22, pp. 522–23.

EXERCISE 5.8 **Questioning**

Working either alone or with a classmate, choose one of the following topics, narrow it, and write a series of questions to discover ideas about it.

1. The campus newspaper
2. Learning a foreign language
3. Financial aid regulations
4. Late-night talk radio shows
5. Government aid to developing countries

USING THE PATTERNS OF DEVELOPMENT

In Parts 3 and 4 of this book, you will learn nine ways to develop an essay or a paragraph.

- narration
- description
- illustration
- process analysis
- comparison and contrast
- classification and division
- definition
- cause and effect
- argument

These methods are often called *patterns of development.*

In addition to providing ways to develop an essay or a paragraph, the patterns of development may be used to generate ideas about a topic. Think of the patterns as doors through which you gain access to your topic. The list of questions in Table 5.2 (p. 115) will help you approach your topic through these different "doors." For any given topic, some questions work better than others. If your topic is voter registration, for example, the questions listed for definition and process analysis would be more helpful than those listed for description. (You might choose the definition or process analysis pattern if you are a pragmatic learner who enjoys structured tasks or a creative learner who likes to analyze ideas from different viewpoints.)

Learning Style Options

EXERCISE 5.9 **Patterns of Development**

Use the patterns of development to generate ideas on one of the following topics. Refer to Table 5.2 to form questions based on the patterns.

1. Buying only American-made products
2. Community gardens in urban areas
3. How high-speed trains would change travel
4. Cell-phone usage
5. Effects of a computer virus

VISUALIZING OR SKETCHING

Visualizing or **sketching** may be effective ways to discover ideas about your topic. To visualize a person, for example, close your eyes and picture that person in your mind. Imagine what he or she is wearing and what his or her facial expressions and gestures might look like.

Here is what one student "saw" when visualizing a shopping mall. Possible subtopics are annotated.

As I walked through the local mall, I crossed the walkway to get to Target and noticed a large group of excited women all dressed in jogging suits; they were part of a shopping tour, I think. I saw a tour bus parked outside. Across the walkway was a bunch of teenagers, shouting and laughing and commenting on each other's hairstyles. They all wore T-shirts and jeans; some had body adornments — pierced noses and lips. They seemed to have no interest in shopping. Their focus was on one another. Along the

Possible Subtopics:
Tour-group shopping

Teenage behavior

Body piercing

walkway came an obvious mother-daughter pair. They seemed to be on an outing, escaping from their day-to-day routine for some shopping, joking, and laughing. Then I noticed a tired-looking elderly couple sitting on one of the benches. They seemed to enjoy just sitting there and watching the people walk by, every now and then commenting on the fashions they observed people wearing.

Learning Style Options

Visualization is a technique particularly well suited to spatial and creative learners.

The technique of sketching, or storyboarding, uses a series of sketches to show the sequence of events or relationships among ideas. Visual learners may find it easier to draw sketches than to formulate ideas in words, and once the ideas are on paper in sketch form, they can be converted to text.

> **EXERCISE 5.10** **Visualizing and Sketching**
>
> Visualize one of the following situations. Make notes on or sketch what you "see." Include as many details as possible.
>
> 1. A couple obviously "in love"
> 2. A class you recently attended
> 3. The campus snack bar
> 4. A traffic jam
> 5. A sporting event

RESEARCHING YOUR TOPIC

For more about finding, using, and citing sources, see Chapters 21 and 23.

To learn more about avoiding plagiarism, see Chapter 24, pp. 601–03.

Do some preliminary research on your topic. Reading what others have written about your topic may suggest new approaches, reveal issues or controversies, and help you determine what you already know (or do not know) about the topic.

Take notes while reading sources, and be sure to record the publication data you will need to cite each source (author, title, publisher, page numbers, and so on). If you use ideas or information from sources in your essay, you must give credit to those sources of the borrowed material. Make sure to avoid simply cutting and pasting material from your sources directly into your notes to avoid plagiarizing inadvertently. Plagiarism, even by accident, carries serious penalties.

Learning Style Options

While research may be particularly appealing to concrete or rational learners, all students may need to use it at one time or another depending on their topic.

> **EXERCISE 5.11** **Researching a Topic**
>
> Do library or Internet research to generate ideas on one of the narrowed topics listed here.
>
> 1. Reducing the federal deficit
> 2. Preventing terrorism in public areas
> 3. Controlling children's access to television programs
> 4. A recent local disaster (flood, earthquake)
> 5. Buying clothing on eBay

TABLE 5.2 Using the Patterns of Development to Explore a Topic

Pattern of Development	Questions to Ask
Narration (Chapter 12)	What stories or events does this topic remind you of?
Description (Chapter 13)	What does the topic look, smell, taste, feel, or sound like?
Illustration (Chapter 14)	What examples of this topic are particularly helpful in explaining it?
Process Analysis (Chapter 15)	How does this topic work? How do you do this topic?
Comparison and Contrast (Chapter 16)	To what is the topic similar? In what ways? Is the topic more or less desirable than those things to which it is similar?
Classification and Division (Chapter 17)	Of what larger group of things is this topic a member? What are its parts? How can the topic be subdivided? Are there certain types or kinds of the topic?
Definition (Chapter 18)	How do you define the topic? How does the dictionary define it? What is the history of the term? Does everyone agree on its definition? Why or why not? If not, what points are in dispute?
Cause and Effect (Chapter 19)	What causes the topic? How often does it happen? What might prevent it from happening? What are its effects? What may happen because of it in the short term? What may happen as a result of it over time?
Argument (Chapters 20 and 21)	What issues surround this topic?

One student who was investigating the topic of extrasensory perception (ESP) decided to use the questions for definition and cause and effect. Here are the answers she wrote:

Definition (How can my topic be defined?)

- ESP, or extrasensory perception, is the ability to perceive information not through the ordinary senses but as a result of a "sixth sense" (as yet undeveloped in most people).
- Scientists disagree on whether ESP exists and how it should be tested.

Cause and Effect (What causes my topic? What may happen because of it?)

- Scientists do not know the cause of ESP and have not confirmed its existence, just the possibility of its existence.
- Some people with ESP claim to have avoided disasters such as airplane crashes.

(**EXERCISE 5.12**) **Prewriting**

Choose two prewriting techniques discussed in this chapter that appeal to you. Experiment with each method by generating ideas about one of the topics from the previous exercises in the chapter. Use a different topic for each prewriting technique you choose.

> **Essay in Progress 3**
> Keeping your audience and purpose in mind, use one of the prewriting strategies discussed in this chapter to generate details about the topic you narrowed in Essay in Progress 2.

STUDENTS WRITE

In this and the remaining five chapters of Part 2, we will follow the work of Latrisha Wilson, a student in a first-year writing course who was assigned to write about surveillance and loss of privacy.

Wilson decided to use questioning to narrow her topic and freewriting to generate ideas about her narrowed topic. Here is an example of her questioning.

LATRISHA WILSON'S QUESTIONING

<u>What are some examples of surveillance in the US?</u>

Cameras in retail stores and at bank cash machines

Cell phone surveillance and tracking

Airport security checkpoints

Online surveillance

Nanny cams

Traffic cameras and street corners

GPS devices worn by people on probation

Undercover police

Cameras in government buildings

Cameras on school buses

Wilson decided to explore further the types of surveillance commonly conducted in the United States. She did so by asking another question:

<u>Which of these types of surveillance are the least "obvious"?</u>

1. Undercover police

   They disguise their identity.

   They often become friends with the people they are investigating.

   They participate in drug deals.

   Oftentimes, their family members do not even know about their assignments.

   They become the "bad guy" in order to get the "bad guy."

2. Online surveillance

   Who is hiding behind our computer screens?

   Valuable information about us is gathered from the Web.

   Lots of information is gathered without our consent.

   Google studies gmail accounts for keywords and sells the information to companies.

   Information on Facebook is also sold to marketers.

After looking over the answers to her questions, Wilson decided to focus on types of surveillance. The following excerpt from her freewriting shows how she started to develop her topic.

LATRISHA WILSON'S FREEWRITING

I feel like I have no privacy. Just the other day I read how the mayor of my city brags of his new plan to put surveillance cameras on all the big street corners. There are already lots of traffic and security cameras. Soon there won't be anywhere I can walk without being monitored by some government employee sitting behind his desk. My life is like a movie anybody can watch. A reality tv show. If I'm not breaking the rules, what right does anyone have to track me? I'm not even safe going online. Netflix and YouTube keep suggesting movies to me. Stores where I have only shopped once keep e-mailing me about their new products. I get so much junk mail that Gmail just created a folder in my inbox just for "promotions." And right beside my inbox I see all those ads targeted specifically to me. If I write my mom "happy birthday" the next day I see ads for places to buy birthday hats. That's really creepy. I use Google for everything but that doesn't give them the right to pour through all my messages in search of information they can sell. I thought Google was a free service. To the mayor I'm just a potential criminal and to Google I'm just a potential consumer. What happened to my right to privacy?

As you work through the remaining chapters of Part 2, you will see how Wilson develops her tentative thesis statement in Chapter 6, her first draft in Chapter 7, a specific paragraph in Chapter 8, and her final draft in Chapter 9. In Chapter 10, you will see a paragraph from her final draft, edited and proofread to correct sentence-level errors.

6

Developing and Supporting a Thesis

Study the cartoon on this page, which humorously depicts a serious situation. Working alone or with one or two class-mates, write a statement that expresses the main point of the cartoon. Your statement should not only describe what is happening in the cartoon but also state the idea that the cartoonist is trying to communicate to his audience.

The statement you have just written is an assertion around which you could build an essay. Such an assertion is called a *thesis statement.* Developing a thesis is an important part of the writing process shown in Figure 6.1 (p. 120), which lists the skills presented in this chapter while placing them within the context of the writing process.

© Mike Baldwin / Cornered

"That's not what it says on the Web."

©CartoonStock.com

- write effective thesis statements, and
- support your thesis statement with evidence.

WHAT IS A THESIS STATEMENT?

A **thesis statement** is the main point of an essay. It is usually expressed in a single sentence. An effective thesis statement should accomplish three goals. It should:
1. introduce your narrowed topic,
2. reveal what your essay is about, and
3. state the point you will make about that topic.

It may also forecast how the essay will be organized.
    Here is a sample thesis statement:

Topic   Position
↓   ↓

Playing team sports, especially football and baseball, develops skills

and qualities that can make you successful in life because these sports

Forecast
↓

demand communication, teamwork, and responsibility.

When you write, think of a thesis statement as a promise to your reader. The rest of your essay delivers on your promise. The example thesis promises the audience, that by reading this essay, they will discover how football and baseball players learn communication, teamwork, and responsibility and how these skills and qualities contribute to the players' success in life.

DEVELOPING YOUR THESIS STATEMENT

Keep the following guidelines in mind as you develop your thesis statement.
- **Expect your thesis statement to evolve during prewriting.** Exploring your topic may lead you to discover a new focus or a more interesting way to approach your topic.

For more on prewriting, see Chapter 5.

- **Expect to do research to revise your thesis.** You may need to do some reading or research to learn more about your topic or tentative thesis.

For more on research, see Chapter 22.

- **Expect to revise your thesis as you draft and revise your essay.** You may write several versions of a thesis statement before you find one that works, and you may revise your thesis as you gather and organize supporting evidence, draft, and revise your essay.

For more on drafting and revision, see Chapters 7 and 9.

FIGURE 6.1 **An Overview of the Writing Process**

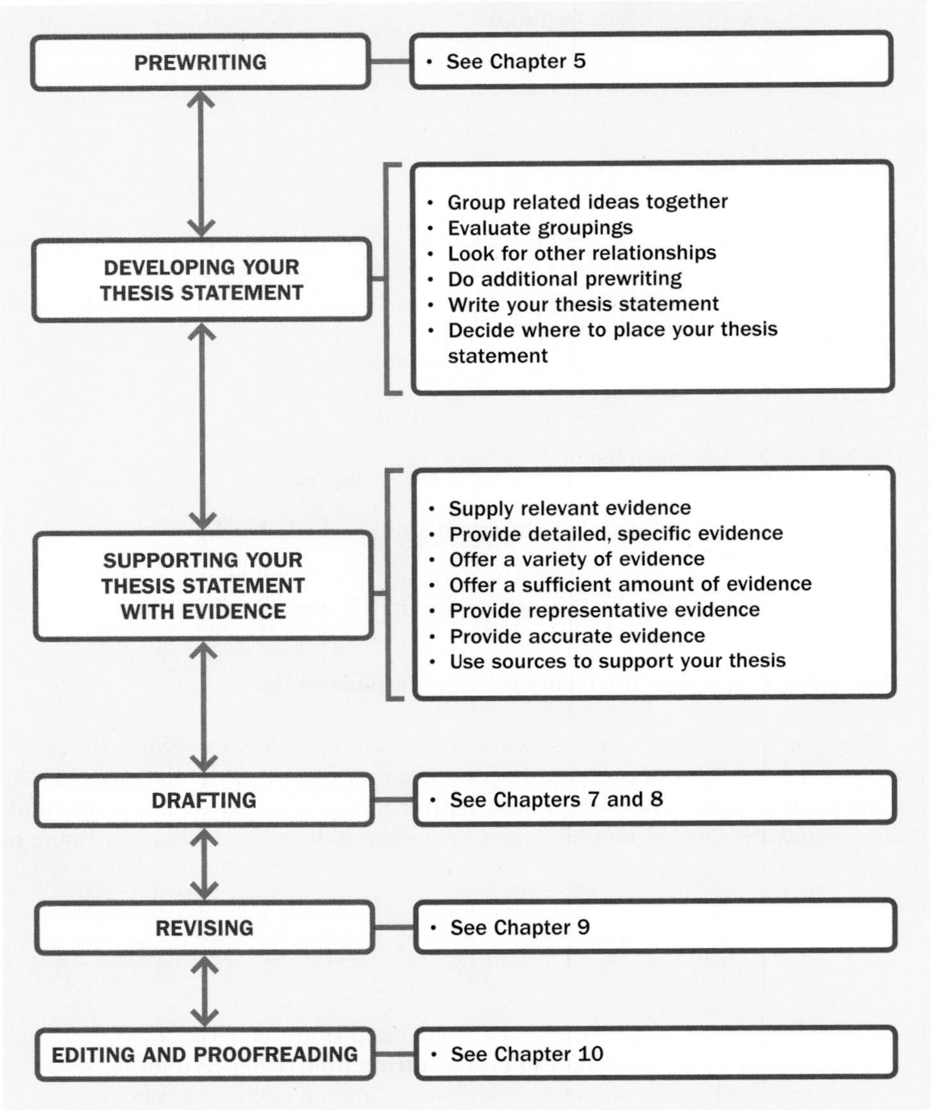

| PREWRITING | • See Chapter 5 |

| DEVELOPING YOUR THESIS STATEMENT | • Group related ideas together
• Evaluate groupings
• Look for other relationships
• Do additional prewriting
• Write your thesis statement
• Decide where to place your thesis statement |

| SUPPORTING YOUR THESIS STATEMENT WITH EVIDENCE | • Supply relevant evidence
• Provide detailed, specific evidence
• Offer a variety of evidence
• Offer a sufficient amount of evidence
• Provide representative evidence
• Provide accurate evidence
• Use sources to support your thesis |

| DRAFTING | • See Chapters 7 and 8 |

| REVISING | • See Chapter 9 |

| EDITING AND PROOFREADING | • See Chapter 10 |

Learning Style Options

Your learning style can influence how you develop a thesis statement. Pragmatic and concrete learners find it helpful to generate facts and details about a narrow topic and then write a thesis statement that reveals a large idea that is demonstrated by the details. Creative and abstract learners find it easier to begin with a broad idea, focus it in a thesis statement, and then generate details to support the thesis.

SYNTHESIZING IDEAS TO GENERATE A WORKING THESIS STATEMENT

Coming up with a working thesis statement involves reviewing your prewriting to determine how some or all of the ideas you discovered fit together. It is a process of looking for similarities among ideas and grouping them in related categories. Use the following steps, adapting the process to your learning style.

1. **Reread your prewriting, identify details that relate to the same subtopic, and cut and paste them so they appear together; then write a word or phrase that describes each of the two groups of related ideas.**
   A student working on the topic of intelligence in dogs noticed in her brainstormed list that the details could be grouped into two general categories: (1) details about learning and (2) details about instinct. Here is how she arranged her ideas.

   Learning

   follow commands

   read human emotions

   get housebroken

   serve as guide dogs for blind people

   Instinct

   females deliver and care for puppies

   avoid danger and predators

   seek shelter

   automatically raise hair on back in response to aggression

2. **Decide which group(s) of ideas best represents the focus your paper should take.** Sometimes, one group of details will be enough to develop a working thesis. Other times, you'll need to use the details in two or three groups. The student working on a thesis for the topic of intelligence in dogs evaluated her grouped details and decided that learning provided enough material to write about.

3. **Consider whether you have enough relevant details.** If your list of details is thin, you may not have enough details to come up with a good working thesis. Delete any details that do not work, and use prewriting to generate more ideas, trying a different prewriting strategy from the one you used previously. A new strategy may help you see your narrowed topic from a different perspective. If your second prewriting does not produce better results, consider refocusing or changing your topic.

Essay in Progress 1

If you used a prewriting strategy to generate details about your topic in response to Essay in Progress 3 in Chapter 5 (p. 116), review your prewriting, highlight useful ideas, and identify several sets of related details among those you have highlighted.

WRITING AN EFFECTIVE THESIS STATEMENT

Use the following guidelines to write an effective thesis statement or to evaluate and revise your working thesis.

1. **An effective thesis makes an assertion.** Rather than stating a fact, a thesis should take a position, express a viewpoint, or suggest your approach toward the topic.

LACKS AN ASSERTION	Hollywood movies, like *127 Hours* and *Jersey Boys*, are frequently based on true stories.
REVISED ASSERTIVE	Hollywood movies, like *127 Hours* and *Jersey Boys*, manipulate true stories to cater to the tastes of the audience.

2. **An effective thesis is specific.** Provide as much information as possible about your main point.

TOO GENERAL	I learned a great deal from my experiences as a teenage parent.
REVISED	From my experiences as a teenage parent, I learned to accept responsibility for my own life and for that of my son.

EXERCISE 6.1   Identifying and Revising Thesis Statements That Lack Assertions

First, determine which of the following is a statement of fact and which is an assertion. Then revise each statement of fact, making it an assertion that could be an effective thesis statement for a brief (two- to four-page) college writing assignment.

1. By budgeting time and money, students can avoid stress and enjoy the holidays.
2. The viewers were moved by pictures of the devastation in the Philippines following Typhoon Haiyan.
3. Levying a fine on college students who cheat on an assignment might help improve academic integrity.
4. Taking a class online can be convenient, but succeeding in online classes requires self-discipline and motivation.
5. As a result of taking care of her family's dog, Adrian developed a strong desire to rescue abandoned pit bulls.

EXERCISE 6.2   Identifying and Revising Overly General Thesis Statements

First, determine which of the following thesis statements are too general for a brief (two- to four-page) college-level writing assignment. Then narrow the overly general thesis statements using the strategies for narrowing topics discussed above and in Chapter 5 (pp. 99–103).

1. Unfortunately, discrimination exists in many forms in today's society.
2. The demands of my job undermined my relationship with my family.

3. The experience of living in a dorm provides students with opportunities to develop valuable people skills that will serve them well throughout their lives.
4. Violent storms can have devastating effects on communities.
5. Although it seemed unwise at the time, postponing college was one of the wisest decisions I ever made.

3. **Focus on one central point.** Limit your essay to one major idea.

FOCUSES ON SEVERAL POINTS	This college should improve its tutoring services, sponsor more activities of interest to Latino students, and speed up the registration process for students.
REVISED	To better represent the student population it serves, this college should sponsor more activities of interest to Latino students.

4. **Offer an original perspective on your topic.** If your thesis seems dull or ordinary, it probably needs revision. Search your prewriting for an interesting angle on your topic.

TOO ORDINARY	Many traffic accidents are a result of carelessness.
REVISED: MORE INTERESTING	An automobile accident can change a driver's entire approach to driving.

EXERCISE 6.3 **Identifying and Revising Thesis Statements That Focus on Several Points**

The following thesis statements focus on more than one central point. Revise them so that each focuses clearly on only one point.

1. In order to be more successful in college, students must learn time management strategies, curtail their social life during the week, and learn to balance work and school obligations so that they are able to enjoy all parts of their life.
2. The Internet has revolutionized the way friends communicate, but it has also made children more sedentary, which has had negative health effects, and it has also made people in the workforce more solitary, which has undermined teamwork.
3. Movie theaters continue to attract viewers to new releases although many of them are simply remakes of older movies and ones that appeal only to those who like graphic violence.
4. Although the tornado destroyed the entire town and seriously injured hundreds of people, the local townspeople grew closer as they tended to the injured, helped to rebuild houses, and shared their financial resources with one another.
5. Although the company has made strides in repairing its reputation in the community, it still needs to pay its employees a fair salary, restructure management, and conduct business with more reputable vendors.

5. **Avoid making an announcement.** Don't use phrases such as "This essay will discuss" or "The subject of my paper is." Instead, state your main point directly.

MAKES AN ANNOUNCEMENT	The point I am trying to make is that people should not be allowed to smoke on campus.
REVISED: MAIN POINT STATED DIRECTLY	The college should prohibit smoking on campus.

6. **Use your thesis to preview the organization of the essay.** Consider using your thesis to mention the two or three key concepts on which your essay will focus, in the order in which you will discuss them.

EXERCISE 6.4   **Evaluating Thesis Statements**

Working in a group of two or three students, discuss what is wrong with each of the following thesis statements. Then revise each thesis to make it more effective.

1. In this paper, I will discuss the causes of asthma, which include exposure to smoke, chemicals, and allergic reactions.
2. Jogging is an enjoyable aerobic sport.
3. The crime rate is increasing in U.S. cities.
4. Living in an apartment has many advantages.
5. Children's toys can be dangerous, instructional, or creative.

Essay in Progress 2
Keeping your audience in mind, select one or more of the groups of ideas you identified in Essay in Progress 1. Write a working thesis statement based on these ideas.

PLACING THE THESIS STATEMENT

Your thesis statement can appear anywhere in your essay, but it is usually best to place it in the first paragraph as part of your introduction. When your thesis appears at the beginning of the essay, your readers will know what to pay attention to and what to expect in the rest of the essay. If you place your thesis later in the essay, you need to build up to it gradually in order to prepare readers for it.

USING AN IMPLIED THESIS

In some professional writing, especially in narrative or descriptive essays, the writer may not state the thesis directly. Instead, the thesis may be strongly implied by the details the writer chose and the way he or she organized them. Although some professional writers use an implied thesis, academic writers, including professors and students, generally state their thesis. You should always include a clear statement of your thesis in your college papers.

SUPPORTING YOUR THESIS STATEMENT WITH EVIDENCE

After you have written a working thesis statement, the next step is to develop evidence that supports your thesis. **Evidence** is any type of information, such as examples and anecdotes, facts and statistics, or expert opinion, that will convince your reader that your thesis is reasonable or correct. This evidence, organized into well-developed paragraphs, makes up the body of your essay. To visualize the basic structure of an essay, look ahead to Figure 7.2 on page 140.

TAILORING THE EVIDENCE TO YOUR WRITING SITUATION

Your writing situation—that is your purpose, audience, point of view, genre, and medium—will determine which types of evidence will be most effective. For example,

- if your purpose is to persuade, using comparison and contrast to highlight advantages and disadvantages, giving examples of problems, citing statistics to support your claim, and using quotations from experts may help make your argument convincing.
- if your audience is unfamiliar with your topic, providing definitions, historical background, an explanation of a process, and factual and descriptive details may be necessary.

Table 6.1 lists various types of evidence and gives examples of how each type could be used to support a working thesis on acupuncture. **Note:** Many of the types of evidence correspond to the patterns of development discussed in Parts 3 and 4.

| EXERCISE 6.5 | **Choosing the Best Evidence for Your Writing Situation**

1. In groups of two or three students, discuss and list the types of evidence that could be used to support the following thesis statement for an informative essay.

    The need to become financially independent is a challenge for many young adults and often causes them to develop social and emotional problems.

2. For each audience, discuss and record the types of evidence that would offer the best support for the preceding thesis.
    a. Young adults
    b. Parents of young adults
    c. Counselors of young adults

TABLE 6.1 Types of Evidence Used to Support a Thesis

Working Thesis:	Acupuncture, a form of alternative medicine, is becoming more widely accepted in the United States.
Types of Evidence	**Example**
Definitions	Explain that in acupuncture, needles are inserted into specific points of the body to control pain or relieve symptoms.
Historical background	Explain that acupuncture is a medical treatment that originated in ancient China.
Explanation of a process	Explain the principles on which acupuncture is based and how scientists think it works.
Factual details	Explain who uses acupuncture, on what parts of the body it is used, and under what circumstances it is applied.
Descriptive details	Explain what acupuncture needles look and feel like.
Narrative story	Relate a personal experience that illustrates the use of acupuncture.
Causes or effects	Discuss one or two theories that explain why acupuncture works. Offer reasons for its increasing popularity.
Classification	Explain types of acupuncture treatments.
Comparison and contrast	Compare acupuncture with other forms of alternative medicine, such as massage and herbal medicines. Explain how acupuncture differs from these other treatments.
Advantages and disadvantages	Describe the pros (nonsurgical, relatively painless) and cons (fear of needles) of acupuncture.
Examples	Describe situations in which acupuncture has been used successfully—by dentists, in treating alcoholism, for pain control.
Problems	Explain that acupuncture is not always practiced by medical doctors; licensing and oversight of acupuncturists may thus be lax.
Statistics	Indicate how many acupuncturists practice in the United States.
Quotations	Quote medical experts who attest to the effectiveness of acupuncture as well as those who question its value.

COLLECTING EVIDENCE TO SUPPORT YOUR THESIS

Learning Style Options

Depending on your learning style, select one or more of the following suggestions to generate evidence that supports your thesis.

1. Complete the worksheet in Figure 6.2 on page 129. For one or more types of evidence listed in the left column, provide examples that support your thesis in the right column. Collect evidence only for the types that are appropriate for your thesis.
2. Picture yourself speaking to your audience. What would you say to convince your audience of your thesis? Jot down ideas as they come to you.

3. Develop a skeletal outline of major headings. Leave plenty of blank space under each heading, and fill in ideas about each heading as they come to you.

For more on outlining, see Chapter 7.

4. Draw a graphic organizer of your essay, filling in supporting evidence as you think of it.

For more on drawing a graphic organizer, see Chapter 7.

5. Discuss your thesis statement with a classmate; try to explain why he or she should accept your thesis as valid.

Essay in Progress 3

Using the preceding list of suggestions and Table 6.1, generate at least three different types of evidence to support the working thesis statement you wrote in Essay in Progress 2.

CHOOSING THE BEST EVIDENCE

In collecting evidence in support of a thesis, you will probably generate more than you need. Consequently, you will need to identify the evidence that (1) best supports your thesis and (2) best suits your purpose and audience. Your learning style can influence the way you select evidence and the kinds of evidence you favor. If you are a creative or an abstract learner, for example, you may tend to focus on large ideas and overlook the need for supporting detail. If you are a pragmatic or concrete learner, you may tend to include too many details or fail to organize them logically.

Learning Style Options

The following guidelines will help you select the types of evidence that will best support your thesis.

1. **Make sure the evidence is relevant.** All of your evidence must clearly and directly support your thesis. Irrelevant evidence will distract and puzzle (or annoy) your readers. If your thesis is that acupuncture is useful for controlling pain, you would not need to describe other alternative therapies.

2. **Provide specific evidence.** Avoid general statements that will not help you make a convincing case for your thesis. For instance, to support the thesis that acupuncture is becoming more widely accepted by patients in the United States, citing statistics that demonstrate an increase in the number of practicing acupuncturists in the United States over the past five years would be most convincing. (You may need to return to your prewriting or conduct research to find evidence for your thesis.)

For more on conducting, incorporating, and citing research, see Chapters 21–23.

3. **Offer a variety of evidence.** Using different kinds of evidence increases the likelihood that your evidence will convince your readers. If you provide only four examples of people who have found acupuncture helpful, for instance, your readers may conclude that four people's experiences do not mean that acupuncture is becoming more popular nationally. If you also provide statistics and quotations from experts, however, more readers will be likely to accept your thesis. Using different types of evidence also enhances your credibility, showing readers you are well informed about your topic.

4. **Provide a sufficient amount of evidence.** The amount of evidence you need varies according to your audience and your topic. To discover whether you have provided enough evidence, ask a classmate to read your essay and tell you

whether he or she is convinced. If your reader is not convinced, ask him or her what additional evidence is needed.

5. **Provide representative evidence.** Do not provide unusual, rare, or exceptional situations as evidence. Suppose your thesis is that acupuncture is widely used for various types of surgery. An example of one person who underwent painless heart surgery using only acupuncture will not support your thesis unless the use of acupuncture in heart surgery is common. Including such an example would mislead your reader and may bring your credibility into question.

6. **Provide accurate evidence from reliable sources.** Do not make vague statements, guess at statistics, or make estimates. For example, do not simply say that many medical doctors are licensed to practice acupuncture in the United States or estimate the number. Instead, find out exactly how many U.S. physicians are licensed for this practice.

For more about choosing reliable evidence, see Chapter 21.

CHOOSING EVIDENCE FOR ACADEMIC WRITING

For most kinds of academic writing, certain types of evidence are preferred over others. In general, your personal experiences and opinions are not considered as useful as more objective evidence such as facts, statistics, historical background, and expert testimony.

Suppose you are writing an academic paper on the effects of global warming. Your observations about climate changes in your city would not be considered adequate or appropriate evidence to support the idea of climatic change as an effect of global warming. To support your thesis, you would need to provide facts, statistics, and expert testimony on climatic change in a wide geographic area and demonstrate their relationship to global warming.

> **Essay in Progress 4**
>
> Evaluate the evidence you generated in Essay in Progress 3. Select the evidence that you could use to support your thesis in a two- to four-page essay.

INCORPORATING VISUALS INTO AN ESSAY

Today's readers are used to seeing more than words on a page, and since your task is to engage readers and communicate meaning effectively, using appropriate visuals can help. Of course, a visual is not a substitute for an explanation in your essay, and including a visual merely to brighten up your document is inappropriate in academic writing projects. But visuals can complement and support your ideas if they

- support the purpose of your writing and your point of view,
- appeal to your readers,
- are appropriate to the genre and medium in which you are writing,
- complement and enhance the meaning of your writing,
- are easy to understand and interpret, and
- are relevant.

e **macmillanhighered.com/successfulwriting**
Tutorials > Digital Writing > Photo Editing Basics with GIMP

FIGURE 6.2 A Worksheet for Collecting Evidence

Purpose: _____

Audience: _____

Point of View: _____

Thesis Statement: _____

_____

TYPE OF EVIDENCE	ACTUAL EVIDENCE
Definitions	
Historical background	
Explanation of a process	
Factual details	
Descriptive details	
Narrative story	
Causes or effects	
Classification	
Comparison and contrast	
Advantages and disadvantages	
Examples	
Problems	
Statistics	
Quotations	

To incorporate a visual effectively within your essay, reference the visual (*for example, see fig. 1*) and briefly explain its intended message. Place the visual as close after the reference in the text as possible to ensure readers can connect the visual with the part of the text in which it is discussed. Include the figure number and a brief explanatory caption below.

One final word of caution: Unless the visual is a photograph you took or a graphic created from data you collected, you must credit the source. For academic papers, include complete source information at the end of the caption (unless your instructor provides other instructions).

USING SOURCES TO SUPPORT YOUR THESIS

For many topics, you will need to conduct research to collect enough evidence to support your thesis. Chapter 23 provides a thorough guide to finding reliable sources by using library catalogs and databases and Internet search engines (pp. 579–84), and it also includes tips for accomplishing firsthand (or primary) research by conducting interviews, surveys, and observations (pp. 584–86). Chapter 24 provides guidelines for integrating and documenting sources (pp. 606–12). Also see "Writing from Sources: Using Sources to Make Your Own Ideas Convincing," in Chapter 22, pp. 560–61. As you use sources, be sure to record complete source information so you can credit them.

Note: Cutting and pasting information directly from sources into your notes and papers can lead to accidental plagiarism, so always be sure to put borrowed material in quotation marks or to rephrase it in your own words.

> **Essay in Progress 5**
> Locate and consult at least two sources to find evidence that supports the working thesis statement you wrote in Essay in Progress 2.

STUDENTS WRITE

In the Students Write section of Chapter 5, you saw how Latrisha Wilson narrowed her topic and generated ideas for her essay on surveillance. You also saw how she explored types of surveillance as they affect her privacy. After reviewing her responses to questions about her topic and her freewriting, Wilson drafted the following working thesis.

These new digital technologies have both benefits and drawbacks.

She realized that her thesis was overly general and too broad, so she did more freewriting and brainstorming to help her recall details about types of surveillance. Here's an excerpt from her brainstorming:

- Spies like James Bond are no longer necessary. Movies and video games fool us into believing they are, but mainly spying is done by computers.
- The National Security Agency (NSA) watches everything we do on the Internet and everything we say on our phones.

- Edward Snowden, a recent NSA whistleblower, is a current newsmaker. He exposed the NSA's secret surveillance.
- Google has access to everything about us, and they sell the information to other companies.
- If we want to communicate through a screen or a phone, we have to give up our privacy.
- We seldom are asked for our consent to share information about ourselves.
- Twitter, Flickr, YouTube, Facebook, and other new media also provide lots of information about our daily lives, and not just to our "friends."
- Because we enjoy sharing our lives and learning about the lives of others, we forget about where the information is going.
- In reality, we have very little privacy if we use digital devices.

After brainstorming, she decided that she should focus on the drawbacks of digital communications technology. She narrowed her thesis even further to focus on the subtle forms of surveillance new communications technology enable:

Often advertised as free services, new ways of communicating put us under more invasive but less obvious forms of surveillance.

Internet Addiction

GREG BEATO

The following essay by Greg Beato was first published in 2010 in *Reason*, a magazine that offers updates on current developments in politics and culture from a libertarian perspective. Beato, a contributing editor for *Reason*, supports the essay's thesis with a variety of evidence. As you read, highlight the thesis statement and notice the types of evidence used to support it.

In 1995, in an effort to parody the way the American Psychiatric Association's hugely influential *Diagnostic and Statistical Manual of Mental Disorders* medicalizes every excessive behavior, psychiatrist Ivan Goldberg introduced on his website the concept of "Internet Addiction Disorder." Last summer Ben Alexander, a 19-year-old college student obsessed with the online multiplayer game *World of Warcraft*, was profiled by CBS News, NPR, the Associated Press, and countless other media outlets because of his status as client No. 1 at reSTART, the first residential treatment center in America for individuals trying to get themselves clean from Azeroth, iPhones, and all the other digital narcotics of our age.

At reSTART's five-acre haven in the woods near Seattle, clients pay big bucks to detox from pathological computer use by building chicken coops, cooking hamburgers, and engaging in daily therapy sessions with the program's two founders, psychologist Hilarie Cash and clinical social worker and life coach Cosette Rae. With room for just six addicts at a time and a $14,500 program fee, reSTART isn't designed for the masses, and so far it seems to have attracted more reporters than paying clients. When I spoke with Rae in May, she said "10 to 15" people had participated in the 45-day program to date.

Still, the fact that reSTART exists at all shows how far we've progressed in taking Dr. Goldberg's spoof seriously. You may have been too busy monitoring Kim Kardashian's every passing thought-like thing on Twitter to notice, but Digital Detox Week took place in April, and Video Game Addiction Awareness Week followed on its heels in June. Internet addiction disorder has yet to claim a Tiger Woods of its own, but the sad, silly evidence of our worldwide cyber-bingeing mounts on a daily basis. A councilman in

3

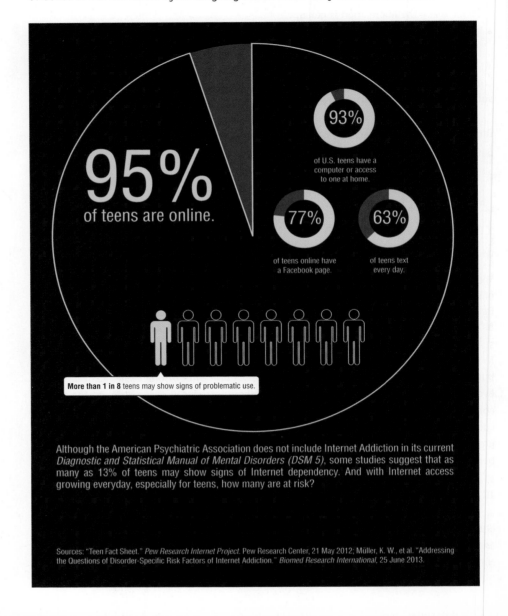

95%
of teens are online.

93%
of U.S. teens have a
computer or access
to one at home.

77%
of teens online have
a Facebook page.

63%
of teens text
every day.

More than 1 in 8 teens may show signs of problematic use.

Although the American Psychiatric Association does not include Internet Addiction in its current *Diagnostic and Statistical Manual of Mental Disorders (DSM 5)*, some studies suggest that as many as 13% of teens may show signs of Internet dependency. And with Internet access growing everyday, especially for teens, how many are at risk?

Sources: "Teen Fact Sheet." *Pew Research Internet Project.* Pew Research Center, 21 May 2012; Müller, K. W., et al. "Addressing the Questions of Disorder-Specific Risk Factors of Internet Addiction." *Biomed Research International,* 25 June 2013.

the Bulgarian city of Plovdiv is ousted from his position for playing *Farmville* during budget meetings. There are now at least three apps that use the iPhone's camera to show the world right in front of you so you can keep texting while walking down the street, confident in your ability to avoid sinkholes, telephone poles, and traffic. Earlier this year, 200 students taking a class in media literacy at the University of Maryland went on a 24-hour media fast for a group study, then described how "jittery," "anxious," "miserable," and "crazy" they felt without Twitter, Facebook, iPods, and laptops. "I clearly am addicted," one student concluded, "and the dependency is sickening."

In the early days of the Web, dirty talk was exchanged at the excruciatingly slow rate   4 of 14.4 bits per second, connectivity charges accrued by the hour instead of the month, and the only stuff for sale online was some overpriced hot sauce from a tiny store in Pasadena. It took the patience of a Buddhist monk, thousands of dollars, and really bad TV reception to overuse the Web in a self-destructive manner. Yet even then, many people felt Ivan Goldberg's notes on Internet addiction worked better as psychiatry than comedy. A year before Goldberg posted his spoof, Kimberly Young, a psychologist at the University of Pittsburgh, had already begun conducting formal research into online addiction. By 1996 the Harvard-affiliated McLean Hospital had established a computer addiction clinic, a professor at the University of Maryland had created an Internet addiction support group, and *The New York Times* was running op-eds about the divorce epidemic that Internet addiction was about to unleash.

Fifteen years down the line, you'd think we'd all be introverted philanderers by now,   5 isolating ourselves in the virtual Snuggie of *World of Warcraft* by day and stepping out at night to destroy our marriages with our latest hook-ups from AshleyMadison.com. But the introduction of flat monthly fees, online gaming, widespread pornography, MySpace, YouTube, Facebook, WiFi, iPhones, netbooks, and free return shipping on designer shoes with substantial markdowns does not seem to have made the Internet any more addictive than it was a decade ago.

In 1998 Young told the Riverside *Press-Enterprise* that "5 to 10 percent of the   6 52 million Internet users [were] addicted or 'potentially addicted.' " Doctors today use similar numbers when estimating the number of online junkies. In 2009 David Greenfield, a psychiatrist at the University of Connecticut, told the *San Francisco Chronicle* that studies have shown 3 percent to 6 percent of Internet users "have a problem." Is it possible that the ability to keep extremely close tabs on Ashton Kutcher actually has reduced the Internet's addictive power?

Granted, 3 percent is an awful lot of people. Argue all you like that a real addiction   7 should require needles, or spending time in seedy bars with people who drink vodka through their eyeballs, or at least the overwhelming and nihilistic urge to invest thousands of dollars in a broken public school system through the purchase of lottery tickets. Those working on the front lines of technology overuse have plenty of casualties to point to. In our brief conversation, Cosette Rae tells me about a Harvard student who lost a scholarship because he spent too much time playing games, a guy who spent so many sedentary hours at his computer that he developed blood clots in his leg and had to have it amputated, and an 18-year-old who chose homelessness over gamelessness when his parents told him he either had to quit playing computer games or move out.

A few minutes on Google yields even more lurid anecdotes. In 2007 an Ohio teen-   8
ager shot his parents, killing his mother and wounding his father, after they took away
his Xbox. This year a South Korean couple let their real baby starve to death because
they were spending so much time caring for their virtual baby in a role-playing game
called *Prius Online*.   9

On a pound-for-pound basis, the average *World of Warcraft* junkie undoubtedly
represents a much less destructive social force than the average meth head. But it's
not extreme anecdotes that make the specter of Internet addiction so threatening;
it's the fact that Internet overuse has the potential to scale in a way that few other
addictions do. Even if Steve Jobs designed a really cool-looking syringe and started
distributing free heroin on street corners, not everyone would try it. But who among
us doesn't already check his email more often than necessary? As the Internet weaves
itself more and more tightly into our lives, only the Amish are completely safe.

As early as 1996, Kimberly Young was promoting the idea that the American Psychi-   10
atric Association (APA) should add Internet addiction disorder to the *Diagnostic and
Statistical Manual of Mental Disorders* (*DSM*). In February, the APA announced that
its coming edition of the *DSM*, the first major revision since 1994, will for the first
time classify a behavior-related condition—pathological gambling—as an "addiction"
rather than an "impulse control disorder." Internet addiction disorder is not being
included in this new category of "behavioral addictions," but the APA said it will
consider it as a "potential addition . . . as research data accumulate."

If the APA does add excessive Internet use to the *DSM*, the consequences will be   11
wide-ranging. Health insurance companies will start offering at least partial coverage
for treatment programs such as reSTART. People who suffer from Internet addiction
disorder will receive protection under the Americans With Disabilities Act if their
impairment "substantially limits one or more major life activities." Criminal lawyers
will use their clients' online habits to fashion diminished capacity defenses.

Which means that what started as a parody in 1995 could eventually turn more   12
darkly comic than ever imagined. Picture a world where the health care system goes
bankrupt because insurers have to pay for millions of people determined to kick their
Twitter addictions once and for all. Where employees who view porn at work are legally
protected from termination. Where killing elves in cyberspace could help absolve
you for killing people in real life. Is it too late to revert to our older, healthier, more
balanced ways of living and just spend all our leisure hours watching *Love Boat* reruns?

EXAMINING THE READING

1. **Definition** Define the term *Internet addiction*.
2. **Examples** What are some examples of dangerous behavior caused by Internet
   addiction?
3. **Meaning** Why does adding Internet addiction to the *DSM* have important social
   consequences?
4. **Vocabulary** Define each of the following words as they are used in the essay: *parody*
   (para. 1), *pathological* (2), *nihilistic* (7), *lurid* (8), and *specter* (9).

ANALYZING THE WRITER'S TECHNIQUE

1. **Thesis** State the author's thesis in your own words. Then, using the guidelines on pages 122-24, evaluate the effectiveness of the thesis.
2. **Rhetorical Situation** To what audience does Beato address this essay? What purpose does the essay fulfill? How do you think the writing situation affects the author's choice of evidence?
3. **Support** Cite one paragraph from the essay in which you think the author provides detailed, specific information. Explain why you chose that paragraph. Does it support the thesis? Why or why not?

VISUALIZING THE READING

In the chart below, supply an example of each type of evidence the author has used in the reading. The first one has been done for you.

Type of Evidence	Example
Historical background	Website parody of the *DSM* in 1995 included Internet addiction and 1996 McLean Hospital program for Internet addiction
Descriptive details	
Statistics	
Examples	
Comparison and contrast	
Quotations	

THINKING CRITICALLY ABOUT THE READING

1. **Sources** Evaluate the sources that Beato uses to support his thesis. Are they trustworthy and reliable?
2. **Tone** Describe the author's tone. How does it affect your response to the reading?
3. **Opinion** Identify at least one statement of opinion in paragraph 9. Does the author offer evidence to support the opinion?

For more about connotation and tone, see Chapters 4 and 10, pp. 81, 206–08; for more about distinguishing between facts and opinions, see Chapter 4, p. 78.

4. **Connotation** What is the connotation of the word *junkies* in paragraph 6? Identify at least four other words in the selection with strong positive or negative connotations.
5. **Evaluation** How useful are the anecdotes in paragraphs 7 and 8 as evidence?

INTERPRETING A GRAPHIC

1. **Meaning** The text below the large pie chart on page 132 reports that "13% of teens show signs of Internet dependency," and the pictogram says that "1 in 8 individuals may show signs of problematic use." What is the difference between the terms *dependency* and *problematic use*?
2. **Source** How reliable do the sources for this graphic seem? What other sources might you use for a paper on Internet dependency among teens?

RESPONDING TO THE READING

1. **Audience** How do you think this essay would change if the author wrote it for *Parents* magazine?
2. **Discussion** Why do you think the number of people addicted to the Internet has actually lessened since 1998? What might it mean that the American Psychological Association is not ready to include Internet addiction in the *DSM*? What does this say about the disorder?
3. **Journal** In your journal, write about ways you use the Internet that may not be healthy. How does it negatively affect your life? Do you feel it has more positive than negative effects on your life? Explain.

WORKING TOGETHER

1. Imagine that you and a classmate are authors of an advice column for your college newspaper. Write a letter responding to a reader who asked for advice about kicking her Internet addiction. Working with your partner, draft a one-paragraph reply, suggesting steps the person can take to break free of her addiction. Be creative in your response. Be prepared to share your advice with the class.
2. Working with two or three of your classmates, spend 5 to 10 minutes brainstorming a list of positive and negative effects of Internet use among college students. Then

write a thesis statement based on the ideas you generated. Compare your list with the lists of other groups in the class.

3. In groups of two or three, examine the cartoon below. Together, come up with a one-sentence thesis statement (or punch line) that expresses the main point of the cartoon. Do not describe the cartoon: rather, convey the underlying message the cartoonist is trying to communicate—humorously, if you can. (To see the caption the cartoonist supplied, turn to the Acknowledgments page at the end of the book.)

© Cartoonbank.com

Thesis/Punch line: _____

7

Drafting an Essay

The photographs here show two examples of green initiatives at colleges around the country. Study these images of composting and bicycle sharing. Then, working alone or with classmates, write a sentence that states your opinion of these initiatives and how likely they are to succeed. Support this opinion with details (evidence) from the photographs and from your own knowledge of green initiatives. Number your best evidence 1, your second-best evidence 2, and so on. Cross out any details that do not support your opinion, or adjust the sentence if the evidence disagrees with it. Finally, write a paragraph that begins with the sentence you wrote and includes your evidence in order of importance.

The paragraph you just wrote could be part of an essay on how colleges are making

© Stefano Politi Markovina/Alamy; © Jim West/Alamy

IN THIS CHAPTER YOU WILL LEARN TO

- structure an essay effectively,
- organize supporting details, and
- write effective introductions, conclusions, and titles.

campuses environmentally sustainable. To write an essay you would need to do the following.

- Do additional prewriting and research to learn more about this topic.
- Write a thesis statement and develop supporting paragraphs.
- Write an effective introduction and conclusion.
- Choose a good title.

This chapter will guide you through the process of developing an essay as part of the writing process shown in Figure 7.1.

THE STRUCTURE OF AN ESSAY

Think of an essay as a complete piece of writing, with a title, an introduction and thesis statement, several paragraphs supporting the thesis, and a conclusion. (See Figure 7.2.)

FIGURE 7.1 An Overview of the Writing Process

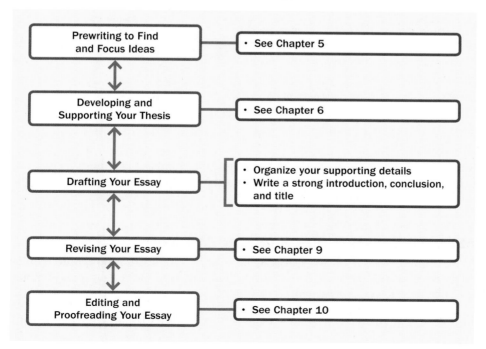

FIGURE 7.2 **The Structure of an Essay: Parts and Functions**

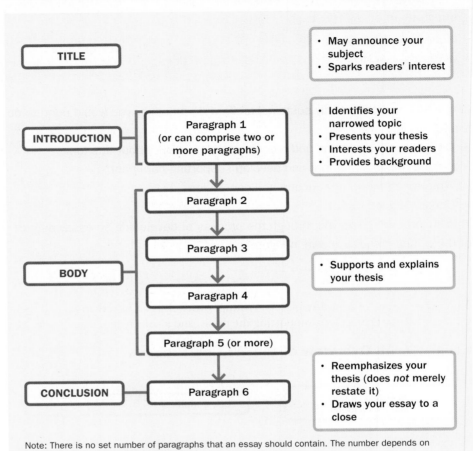

Note: There is no set number of paragraphs that an essay should contain. The number depends on your narrowed topic, purpose, and audience.

ORGANIZING YOUR SUPPORTING DETAILS

For more on developing a thesis and selecting evidence to support it, see Chapter 6.

The body of your essay contains the paragraphs that support your thesis. Before you begin writing these paragraphs, decide on the supporting evidence you will use and the order in which you will present your evidence.

SELECTING A METHOD OF ORGANIZATION

Three common ways to organize ideas are most-to-least (or least-to-most) order, chronological order, and spatial order. To decide which to use, consider your topic and how it can be most logically presented.

Most-to-least (or least-to-most) order When you choose this method of organizing an essay, you arrange your supporting details moving gradually from most to least (or

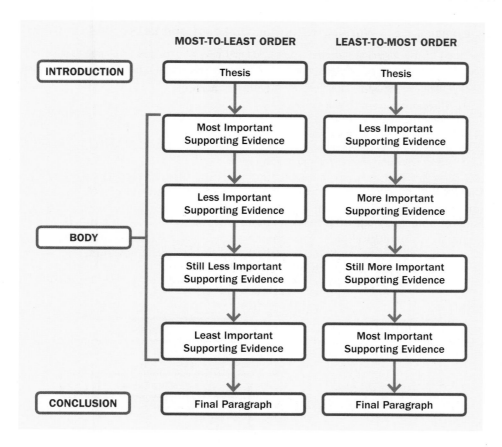

least to most) important, familiar, or interesting. If you need to entice readers or expect they will read only the beginning of your essay, you might include your strongest evidence first. If readers are interested in the topic and likely to read on, you might hold your most memorable evidence for last. You can visualize these two options as follows:

A student, Robin Ferguson, devised this thesis statement: "Working as a literacy volunteer taught me more about learning and friendship than I ever expected." She identified four primary benefits related to her thesis.

- I learned about the learning process.
- I developed a permanent friendship with my student, Marie.
- Marie built self-confidence.
- I discovered the importance of reading for Marie.

Ferguson then chose to arrange the supporting evidence from least to most important.

LEAST	Paragraph 1: Learned about the learning process
TO MOST	Paragraph 2: Discovered the importance of reading for Marie
IMPORTANT	Paragraph 3: Marie increased her self-confidence
	Paragraph 4: Developed a permanent friendship with Marie

EXERCISE 7.1 **Working with Most-to-Least and Least-to-Most Order**

For each of the following narrowed topics, identify several qualities or characteristics that you could use to organize details in most-to-least or least-to-most order. For each, would you choose most-to-least or least-to-most order? Why?

1. Three stores in which you shop
2. Three friends
3. Three members of a sports team
4. Three fast-food restaurants
5. Three television shows you watched this week

Chronological order When you arrange your supporting details in **chronological** (or time) **order**, you put them in the order in which they happened, beginning the body of your essay with the first event and progressing through the others as they occurred. Chronological order is commonly used in narrative essays (essays that tell a story or recount events) and process analyses (essays that explain how something works or is done). You can visualize chronological order as follows.

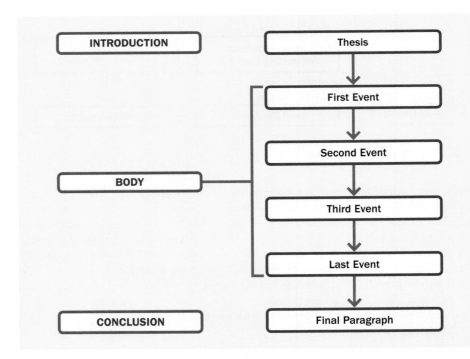

Suppose that Robin Ferguson, writing about her experiences as a literacy volunteer, decides to demonstrate her thesis by relating the events of a typical tutoring session. In this case, she might organize her essay by narrating the events in the order in which they usually occur, using each detail about the session to demonstrate what tutoring taught her about learning and friendship.

EXERCISE 7.2 **Working with Chronological Order**

Alone or with a classmate, identify at least one thesis statement from those listed below that could be supported with paragraphs organized in chronological order. Explain how you would use chronological order to support this thesis.

1. European mealtimes differ from those expected by many American visitors, much to the visitors' surprise and discomfort.
2. Despite the many pitfalls that await those who shop at auctions, people can find bargains if they prepare in advance.
3. My first day of kindergarten was the most traumatic experience of my childhood, one that permanently shaped my view of education.
4. Learning how to drive a car increases a teenager's freedom and responsibility.

Spatial order When you use **spatial order**, you organize details about your subject by location. Spatial organization is commonly used in descriptive essays (essays that portray people, places, and things) as well as in classification and division essays (essays that explain categories or parts). Consider, for example, how you might use spatial order to support the thesis that movie theaters are designed to shut out the outside world and create a separate reality within. You could begin by describing the ticket booth, then the lobby, and finally the theater. Similarly, you might describe a person from head to toe. Robin Ferguson, writing about her experiences as a literacy volunteer, could describe her classroom or meeting area from front to back or left to right.

Visualize spatial organization by picturing your subject in your mind or by sketching it. "Look" at your subject systematically—from top to bottom, inside to outside, front to back. Cut it into imaginary sections or pieces and describe each piece. Here are two possible options for visualizing an essay that uses spatial order.

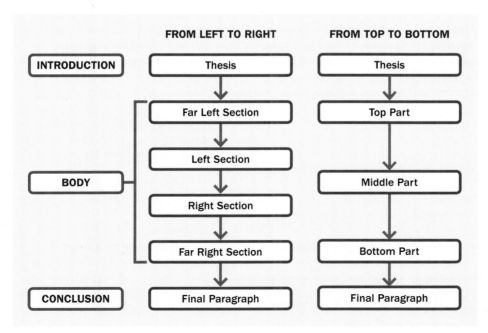

| EXERCISE 7.3 | **Working with Spatial Order** |

Alone or with a classmate, identify one thesis statement listed below that could be supported by means of spatial organization. Explain how you would use spatial order to support this thesis.

1. Our family's yearly vacation at a cabin in Maine provides us with a much-needed opportunity to renew family ties.
2. The Civic Theatre of Allentown's set for Tennessee Williams's play *A Streetcar Named Desire* was simple yet striking and effective.
3. Although a pond in winter may seem frozen and lifeless, this appearance is deceptive.
4. A clear study space can cut down on time-wasting distractions.

Essay in Progress 1

Choose one of the following activities.

1. Using the thesis statement and evidence you gathered for the Essay in Progress activities in Chapter 6, choose a method for organizing your essay.
2. Choose one of the following narrowed topics:
   a. Positive or negative experiences with computers
   b. Stricter (or more lenient) regulations for teenage drivers
   c. Factors that account for the popularity of action films
   d. Discipline in public elementary schools
   e. Advantages or disadvantages of instant messaging

Then, using the steps in Figure 7.1 (p. 139), prewrite to produce ideas, develop a thesis, and generate evidence to support the thesis. Next, choose a method for organizing your essay. Explain briefly how you will use that method of organization.

PREPARING AN OUTLINE OR A GRAPHIC ORGANIZER

After you have written a thesis statement and chosen a method of organization, take a few minutes to create an outline or graphic organizer of the essay's main points in the order you plan to discuss them. This is especially important when your essay is long or complex. Outlining or drawing a graphic organizer can help you see how ideas fit together and may reveal places where you need to add supporting information.

Outlining There are two types of outlines: informal and formal. An **informal** (or **scratch**) **outline** uses key words and phrases to list main points and subpoints. Below is an informal outline of Robin Ferguson's essay. Recall that Ferguson chose to use the least-to-most-important method of organization.

| SAMPLE INFORMAL OUTLINE |

Thesis: Working as a literacy volunteer taught me more about learning and friend-ship than I ever expected.

Paragraph 1: Learned about the learning process

– Went through staff training program
– Learned about words "in context"

Paragraph 2: Discovered the importance of reading for Marie

- Couldn't take bus, walked to grocery store
- Couldn't buy certain products
- Couldn't write out grocery lists

Paragraph 3: Marie increased her self-confidence

- Made rapid progress
- Began taking bus
- Helped son with reading

Paragraph 4: Developed a permanent friendship with Marie

- Saw each other often
- Both single parents
- Baby-sat each other's children

Conclusion: I benefited more than Marie did.

Formal outlines use Roman numerals (I, II), capital letters (A, B), Arabic numbers (1, 2), and lowercase letters (a, b) and indentation to designate levels of importance. Formal outlines fall into two categories.

- *Sentence outlines* use complete sentences.
- *Topic outlines* use only key words and phrases.

Here is a sample topic outline that a student wrote for an essay for her interpersonal communication class.

SAMPLE FORMAL (TOPIC) OUTLINE

First Topic   I. Types of listening

  First Subtopic   A. Participatory

    First Detail   1. Involves the listener responding to the speaker

    Second Detail   2. Has expressive quality

      Detail or Example   a. Maintain eye contact

      Detail or Example   b. Express feelings using facial expressions

  Second Topic   B. Nonparticipatory

    First Detail   1. Involves the listener listening without talking or responding

    Second Detail   2. Allows speaker to develop his or her thoughts without interruption

For more on parallel structure, see Chapter 10.

All items at the same level should be at the same level of importance, and each must explain or support the topic or subtopic under which it is placed. All items at the same level should also be grammatically parallel.

NOT **PARALLEL**	I. Dietary Problems
	   A. Consuming too much fat
	   B. High refined-sugar consumption

PARALLEL	I. Dietary Problems
	   A. Consuming too much fat
	   B. Consuming too much refined sugar

If your instructor allows, you can use both phrases and sentences within an outline, as long as you do so consistently. You might write all subtopics (designated by capital letters A, B, and so on) as sentences and all supporting details (designated by 1, 2, and so on) as phrases, for instance.

Learning Style Options

To learn more about creating a graphic organizer, see Chapter 3.

Preparing a graphic organizer If you have a pragmatic learning style, a verbal learning style, or both, preparing an outline will probably appeal to you. If you are a creative or spatial learner, however, you may prefer to draw a graphic organizer. Figure 7.3 shows the graphic organizer that Robin Ferguson created for her essay. Notice that it follows the least-to-most-important method of organization, as did her informal outline on page 144.

Whichever method you find more appealing, begin by putting your working thesis statement at the top of a page and listing your main points below. Leave plenty of space between main points. While you are filling in details that support one main point, you will often think of details or examples to use in support of a different one. As these details or examples occur to you, jot them down under or next to the appropriate main point on your outline or graphic organizer.

Essay in Progress 2

For the topic you chose in Essay in Progress 1, prepare an outline or draw a graphic organizer to show your essay's organizational plan.

WRITING YOUR INTRODUCTION, CONCLUSION, AND TITLE

When you write an essay, you don't have to start with the title and introduction and write straight through to the end. Some students prefer to write the body of the essay first and then return to the introduction. (Often your true thesis emerges only in the conclusion.) Others prefer to write a tentative introduction as a way of getting started. Some students think of a title before they start writing; others find it easier to add a title when the essay is finished. Regardless of when you write them, the introduction, conclusion, and title are important components of a well-written essay.

FIGURE 7.3 **Sample Graphic Organizer**

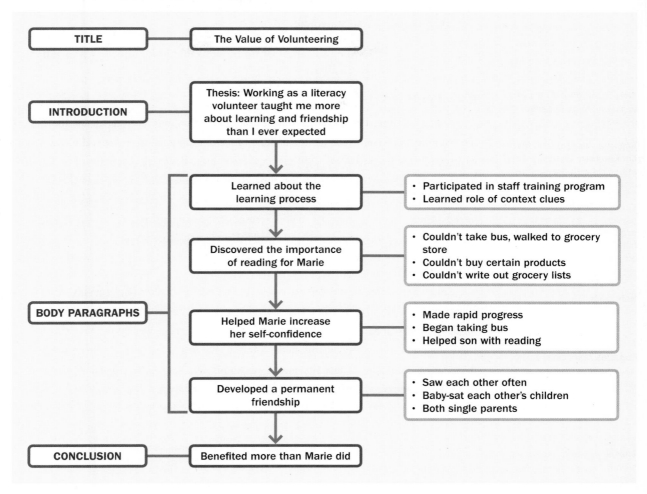

WRITING A STRONG INTRODUCTION

Introductions often start with a fairly general statement of the topic and narrow their focus until they reach the thesis statement at the end of the paragraph. However you begin, your readers should be able to form an expectation of what the essay will be about from this section. Because the introduction creates a first, and often lasting, impression, take the time to get it right.

An effective introduction should:

- establish your topic and indicate your focus, approach, and point of view,
- set the tone of your essay—how you "sound" to your readers and what relationship you have with them,

For more about tone, see Chapters 4 and 10, pp. 81 and 206–08.

- interest your readers and provide any background information they may need, and
- present your thesis statement.

Notice how each of the two sample introductions that follow, both on sexual harassment, creates an entirely different impression and set of expectations.

INTRODUCTION 1

Sets tone: Tone is reasonable yet with mild sense of disbelief

Engages readers/provides background: Grabs readers' attention with provocative example

Thesis: Thesis prepares readers for an essay that examines definitions of sexual harassment and perhaps offers one.

Sexual harassment has received a great deal of attention in recent years. From the highest offices of government and the military to factories in small towns, sexual harassment cases have been tried in court and publicized on national television for all Americans to witness. This focus on sexual harassment has been, in and of itself, a good and necessary thing. However, when a first-grade boy makes national headlines because he kissed a little girl of the same age and is accused of "sexual harassment," the American public needs to take a serious look at the definition of sexual harassment.

INTRODUCTION 2

Sets tone: Tone is outraged, angry

Engages readers/provides background: Provides specific, distressing examples

Thesis: Thesis prepares readers for an essay that suggests ways women can speak out against sexual harassment.

Sexual harassment in the workplace seems to happen with alarming frequency. As a woman who works part time in a male-dominated office, I have witnessed at least six incidents of sexual harassment aimed at me and my female colleagues on various occasions during the past three months alone. For example, in one incident, a male coworker repeatedly made kissing sounds whenever I passed his desk, even after I explained that his actions made me uncomfortable. A female coworker was invited to dinner several times by her male supervisor; each time she refused. The last time she refused, he made a veiled threat: "You obviously aren't happy working with me. Perhaps a transfer is in order". These incidents were not isolated, did not happen to only one woman, and were initiated by more than one man. My colleagues and I are not the only victims. Sexual harassment is on the rise and will continue to increase unless women speak out against it loudly and to a receptive audience.

An introduction can be difficult to write. If you have trouble, return to it later, once you have written the body of your essay. As you draft, you may think of a better way to grab your readers, set your tone, and establish your focus.

The following suggestions for writing a strong introduction will help you capture your readers' interest:

1. **Ask a provocative or disturbing question, or pose a series of related questions to direct readers' attention to your key points.**

   Should health insurance companies pay for more than one stay in a drug rehabilitation center? Should insurance continue to pay for rehab services when patients consistently put themselves back into danger by using drugs again?

2. **Begin with a dramatic or engaging anecdote or an example that is relevant to your thesis.**

> The penal system sometimes protects the rights of the criminal instead of those of the victim. For example, during a rape trial, the defense attorney can question the victim about his or her sexual history, but the prosecuting attorney is forbidden by law to mention that the defendant was charged with rape in a previous trial. In fact, if the prosecution even hints at the defendant's sexual history, the defense can request a mistrial.

3. **Offer a quotation that illustrates or emphasizes your thesis.**

> As Indira Gandhi once said, "You cannot shake hands with a clenched fist." This truism is important to remember whenever people communicate with one another but particularly when they are attempting to resolve a conflict. Both parties need to agree that there is a problem and then agree to listen to each other with an open mind. Shaking hands is a productive way to begin working toward a resolution.

4. **Cite a little-known fact or shocking statistic.**

> Recent research has shown that the color pink has a calming effect on people. In fact, a prison detention center in western New York was recently painted pink to make prisoners more controllable in the days following their arrest.

5. **State a commonly held misconception, and correct this misconception in your thesis.**

> Many people have the mistaken notion that only homosexuals and drug users are in danger of contracting AIDS. In fact, many heterosexuals also suffer from this debilitating disease. Furthermore, the number of heterosexuals who test HIV-positive has increased substantially over the past decade. It is time the American public became better informed about the prevention and treatment of AIDS.

6. **Describe a hypothetical situation.**

> Suppose you were in a serious car accident and became unconscious. Suppose further that you slipped into a coma, with little hope for recovery. Unless you had a prewritten health-care proxy that designated someone familiar with your wishes to act on your behalf, your fate would be left in the hands of doctors who knew nothing about you or your preferences for treatment.

7. **Compare your topic with one that is familiar or of special interest to your readers.**

> The process a researcher uses to locate a specific piece of information in the library is similar to the process an investigator follows in tracking a criminal; both pose a series of questions and follow clues to answer them.

WRITING AN EFFECTIVE CONCLUSION

Write a **conclusion** that brings your essay to a satisfying close. For most essays, your conclusion should reaffirm your thesis without directly restating it. For lengthy essays, you may want to summarize your main points. Shorter essays can be ended more memorably and forcefully by using one of the following suggestions.

1. **Take your readers beyond the scope and time frame of your essay.**

> For now, then, the present system for policing the Internet appears to be working. In the future, though, it may be necessary to put a more formal, structured procedure in place.

2. **Remind readers of the relevance of the issue or suggest why your thesis is important.**

> As stated earlier, research has shown that the seat-belt law has saved thousands of lives. These lives would almost certainly have been lost had this law not been enacted.

3. **Offer a recommendation or urge your readers to take action.**

> To convince the local cable company to eliminate pornographic material, concerned citizens should organize, contact their local cable station, and threaten to cancel their subscriptions.

4. **Discuss broader implications not fully addressed in the essay (but do not introduce a completely new issue).**

> When fair-minded people consider whether the FBI should be allowed to tap private phone lines, the issue inevitably leads them to the larger issue of First Amendment rights.

5. **Conclude with a fact, quotation, anecdote, or example that emphasizes your thesis.**

> The next time you are tempted to send a strongly worded email, consider this fact: Your friends and your enemies can forward those messages, with unforeseen consequences to you.

**INTRODUCTIONS AND CONCLUSIONS:
FOUR COMMON MISTAKES TO AVOID**

	In your introduction, don't . . .	In your conclusion, don't . . .
1.	**make an announcement.** Avoid opening comments such as "I am writing to explain . . ." or "This essay will discuss . . ."	**make an announcement or a restate your thesis directly.** Statements like "In my essay I have shown. . . ." are dull and mechanical.
2.	**prolong your introduction unnecessarily.** An introduction that is longer than two paragraphs will probably sound long-winded and make your readers impatient.	**introduce major points or supporting evidence.** Reasons and evidence that support your thesis belong in the body of your essay.
3.	**discourage your readers from continuing.** Statements such as "This process may seem complicated, but . . ." may make your readers apprehensive.	**apologize or weaken your stance.** Do not say, for example, "Although I am only twenty-one, . . ." or back down after criticizing someone by saying "After all, she's only human."
4.	**use a casual, overly familiar, or chatty tone, especially in academic writing.** Openings such as "You'll never in a million years believe what happened . . ." are generally not appropriate for college essays.	**use standard phrases.** Don't use phrases such as "To sum up," "In conclusion," or "It can be seen, then." They are routine and tiresome.

WRITING A GOOD TITLE

The title of your essay should indicate your topic and prepare readers for what follows. Titles such as "Baseball Fans" or "Gun Control," which just indicate the topic, provide readers with little information or incentive to continue reading. For academic essays, write straightforward titles that accurately describe your topic and approach.

<u>Why</u> State Lotteries Are an <u>Unfair</u> Tax on the Poor

Topic — Suggests a cause-effect analysis

Position — Suggests an argument

For other writing situations—depending on your purpose, audience, stance, genre, and medium—your title may be direct, informative, witty, intriguing, or a combination of these. The following suggestions will help you write effective titles.

- **Ask a question that your essay answers.**

  Who Plays the Lottery?

- **Use alliteration.** Repeating initial sounds often produces a catchy title.

  Lotteries: Dreaming about Dollars

- **Use a play on words or a catchy or humorous expression.** This technique may work well for less formal essays.

  Playing to Lose

- **Use a brief quotation.** You will likely need to mention the quotation in your essay and indicate there who said it and where.

  The Lottery: "A Surtax on Desperation"?

EXERCISE 7.4 **Writing Titles**

For each of the following essays, suggest a title. Use each of the above suggestions at least once.

1. An essay explaining tenants' legal rights
2. An essay opposing drug testing on animals
3. An essay on the causes and effects of road rage
4. An essay comparing fitness routines
5. An essay explaining how to choose a primary care physician

> Essay in Progress 3
>
> Using the outline or graphic organizer you created in Essay in Progress 2, write a first draft of your essay.

READING: STUDENTS WRITE

No Place Left for Privacy

LATRISHA WILSON

The first draft of an essay by Latrisha Wilson follows. Wilson used her freewriting (see Chapter 5) and her working thesis (see Chapter 6) as the basis for her draft, adding details that she came up with by doing additional brainstorming (see Chapter 6). Because she was writing a first draft, Wilson did not worry about correcting the errors in grammar, punctuation, and mechanics. (You will see an excerpt from her revised draft and her final draft in Chapter 9, p. 190, and an excerpt that shows Wilson's final editing and proofreading in Chapter 10, p. 213.)

First Draft

Do we need to talk? There are plenty of exciting new ways to do it. We can communicate by talking on our iPhones, but there are dangers there. Our conversations can be recorded, and the GPS function on the phone allows our whereabouts to be tracked. We can chat on Skype, Gmail, Facebook message, read each other's Twitter or Blog posts. These new digital technologies are incredibly useful; however, they also come at a hidden cost.

When the word surveillance comes up, maybe you think of some thrilling and dangerous activity, like the kind of spying on foreign terrorists that goes on in James Bond movies. In the US today, most spying is done by surveillance computers. Edward Snowden bounced around for weeks from one airport to another, and lived for a while in the Moscow airport, eating who knows what and sleeping who knows where. The NSA seems to be able to do whatever it wants without having to answer to anyone or suffer any consequences. But we can't say the same for whistleblowers. Just look what they did to Bradley Manning! And now, the US government is aggressively pursuing Snowden. The NSA is more and more aggressively protecting its own secrecy, by punishing whistleblowers, and lying to Congress and, it seems as if they are more concerned about themselves than the people they are spying on.

The NSA isn't the only organization to be spying on us. You got companies like Google and other companies doing it to. The next time you pull up your Gmail account, go to your inbox and click on a message. Do you see all those advertisements to the right of your inbox? There directly related to the message you are reading. (I wish my mom "Happy Birthday!" and now I see ads for places to buy birthday hats. This creepy connection is because Google is a major online marketing business, and it automatically scans all of our e-mails for keywords and phrases all at the same time. Companies are paying Google tons of money to record our search histories and pore over our personal messages. Spokesmen for Google reassure us that only computers, no human beings, are reading our e-mails.

Google and other corporations could do more do inform it's users about privacy concerns. How much personal information are we giving away when we make an account with G-mail, Facebook, or NetFlix? What kind of controls keep employees at this companies from accessing our viewing histories, profiles, or private communications? Its never easy to tell.

The terms are long legal documents written in a lingo your everyday person doesn't have the time or energy to decipher. We just check a box.

Well, what's the big deal? you might say. I have nothing to hide from neither the government nor companies like Google and Facebook. Neither do I, I would say in response. But I don't like the idea of having people I don't know constantly looking over my shoulder. When I'm researching my next poli sci paper on alternate forms of government, will I set off alarms in Washington by typing words like "anarchism" or "Marxism" into my browser? When I'm writing a Facebook message to my boyfriend, do I need to worry about getting blackmailed by some Facebook employee, who got bored on a break and decided to do some browsing? Less and less is there any kind of privacy, online or in real life.

ANALYZING THE FIRST DRAFT

1. **Title and Introduction** Evaluate Wilson's title and introduction.
2. **Thesis** Evaluate Wilson's thesis statement.
3. **Support** Does Wilson provide adequate details in her essay? If not, which paragraphs need more detail? What additional information might she include?
4. **Organization** How does Wilson organize her ideas?
5. **Conclusion** Evaluate the conclusion.

READING

Black Men and Public Space

BRENT STAPLES

Brent Staples is a journalist who has written numerous articles and editorials as well as a memoir, *Parallel Time: Growing Up in Black and White* (1994). He holds a Ph.D. in psychology and is a member of *The New York Times* editorial board and a regular contributor to its Commentary section. This essay, first published in *Harper's* magazine in 1986, is a good model of a well-structured essay. As you read the selection, highlight or underline the author's thesis.

My first victim was a woman—white, well dressed, probably in her early twenties. I came upon her late one evening on a deserted street in Hyde Park, a relatively affluent neighborhood in an otherwise mean, impoverished section of Chicago. As I swung onto the avenue behind her, there seemed to be a discreet, uninflammatory distance between us. Not so. She cast back a worried glance. To her, the youngish black man—a broad six feet two inches with a beard and billowing hair, both hands shoved into the pockets of a bulky military jacket—seemed menacingly close. After a few more quick glimpses, she picked up her pace and was soon running in earnest. Within seconds she disappeared into a cross street.

That was more than a decade ago. I was twenty-two years old, a graduate student   2
newly arrived at the University of Chicago. It was in the echo of that terrified woman's
footfalls that I first began to know the unwieldy inheritance I'd come into—the ability
to alter public space in ugly ways. It was clear that she thought herself the quarry of
a mugger, a rapist, or worse. Suffering a bout of insomnia, however, I was stalking
sleep, not defenseless wayfarers. As a softy who is scarcely able to take a knife to a
raw chicken—let alone hold one to a person's throat—I was surprised, embarrassed,
and dismayed all at once. Her flight made me feel like an accomplice in tyranny. It
also made it clear that I was indistinguishable from the muggers who occasionally
seeped into the area from the surrounding ghetto. That first encounter, and those that
followed, signified that a vast, unnerving gulf lay between nighttime pedestrians—
particularly women—and me. And I soon gathered that being perceived as dangerous
is a hazard in itself. I only needed to turn a corner into a dicey situation, or crowd
some frightened, armed person in a foyer somewhere, or make an errant move after
being pulled over by a policeman. Where fear and weapons meet—and they often do
in urban America—there is always the possibility of death.

In that first year, my first away from my hometown, I was to become thoroughly   3
familiar with the language of fear. At dark, shadowy intersections, I could cross in
front of a car stopped at a traffic light and elicit the *thunk, thunk, thunk, thunk* of
the driver—black, white, male, or female—hammering down the door locks. On less
traveled streets after dark, I grew accustomed to but never comfortable with people
crossing to the other side of the street rather than pass me. Then there were the standard unpleasantries with policemen, doormen, bouncers, cabdrivers, and others whose
business it is to screen out troublesome individuals *before* there is any nastiness.

I moved to New York nearly two years ago and I have remained an avid night   4
walker. In central Manhattan, the near-constant crowd cover minimizes tense one-on-
one street encounters. Elsewhere—in SoHo, for example, where sidewalks are narrow
and tightly spaced buildings shut out the sky—things can get very taut indeed.

After dark, on the warrenlike streets of Brooklyn where I live, I often see women who   5
fear the worst from me. They seem to have set their faces on neutral, and with their purse
straps strung across their chests bandolier-style, they forge ahead as though bracing
themselves against being tackled. I understand, of course, that the danger they perceive
is not a hallucination. Women are particularly vulnerable to street violence, and young
black males are drastically overrepresented among the perpetrators of that violence. Yet
these truths are no solace against the kind of alienation that comes of being ever the
suspect, a fearsome entity with whom pedestrians avoid making eye contact.

It is not altogether clear to me how I reached the ripe old age of twenty-two   6
without being conscious of the lethality nighttime pedestrians attributed to me.
Perhaps it was because in Chester, Pennsylvania, the small, angry industrial town
where I came of age in the 1960s, I was scarcely noticeable against a backdrop of
gang warfare, street knifings, and murders. I grew up one of the good boys, had
perhaps a half-dozen fistfights. In retrospect, my shyness of combat has clear sources.

As a boy, I saw countless tough guys locked away; I have since buried several, too.   7
They were babies, really—a teenage cousin, a brother of twenty-two, a childhood

friend in his mid-twenties—all gone down in episodes of bravado played out in the streets. I came to doubt the virtues of intimidation early on. I chose, perhaps unconsciously, to remain a shadow—timid, but a survivor.

The fearsomeness mistakenly attributed to me in public places often has a perilous flavor. The most frightening of these confusions occurred in the late 1970s and early 1980s, when I worked as a journalist in Chicago. One day, rushing into the office of a magazine I was writing for with a deadline story in hand, I was mistaken for a burglar. The office manager called security and, with an ad hoc posse, pursued me through the labyrinthine halls, nearly to my editor's door. I had no way of proving who I was. I could only move briskly toward the company of someone who knew me. 8

Another time I was on assignment for a local paper and killing time before an interview. I entered a jewelry store on the city's affluent Near North Side. The proprietor excused herself and returned with an enormous red Doberman pinscher straining at the end of a leash. She stood, the dog extended toward me, silent to my questions, her eyes bulging nearly out of her head. I took a cursory look around, nodded, and bade her good night. 9

Relatively speaking, however, I never fared as badly as another black male journalist. He went to nearby Waukegan, Illinois, a couple of summers ago to work on a story about a murderer who was born there. Mistaking the reporter for the killer, police officers hauled him from his car at gunpoint and but for his press credentials would probably have tried to book him. Such episodes are not uncommon. Black men trade tales like this all the time. 10

Over the years, I learned to smother the rage I felt at so often being taken for a criminal. Not to do so would surely have led to madness. I now take precautions to make myself less threatening. I move about with care, particularly late in the evening. I give a wide berth to nervous people on subway platforms during the wee hours, particularly when I have exchanged business clothes for jeans. If I happen to be entering a building behind some people who appear skittish, I may walk by, letting them clear the lobby before I return, so as not to seem to be following them. I have been calm and extremely congenial on those rare occasions when I've been pulled over by the police. 11

And on late-evening constitutionals I employ what has proved to be an excellent tension-reducing measure: I whistle melodies from Beethoven and Vivaldi and the more popular classical composers. Even steely New Yorkers hunching toward nighttime destinations seem to relax, and occasionally they even join in the tune. Virtually everybody seems to sense that a mugger wouldn't be warbling bright sunny selections from Vivaldi's *Four Seasons*. It is my equivalent of the cowbell that hikers wear when they know they are in bear country. 12

EXAMINING THE READING

1. **Paraphrase** Explain what Staples means by "the ability to alter public space" (para. 2).
2. **Details** Staples considers himself a "survivor" (para. 7). To what does he attribute his survival?
3. **Examples** What does Staples do to make himself seem less threatening to others?
4. **Vocabulary** Explain the meaning of each of the following words as it is used in the reading: *uninflammatory* (para. 1), *unwieldy* (2), *vulnerable* (5), *retrospect* (6), and *constitutionals* (12).

ANALYZING THE WRITER'S TECHNIQUE

1. **Introduction** Evaluate Staples's opening paragraph. Does it spark your interest? Why or why not?
2. **Thesis** Identify Staples's thesis statement. How does the author support his thesis? What types of information does he include?
3. **Supporting Details** Cite several examples of places in the essay where Staples uses specific supporting details effectively. Explain your choices.
4. **Conclusion** Evaluate Staples's conclusion. Does it leave you satisfied? Why or why not?
5. **Method of Organization** What is Staples's method of organization in this essay? What other method of organization could he have used?

THINKING CRITICALLY ABOUT THE READING

1. **Word Choice** Why did Staples choose the word *victim* in paragraph 1? What connotations does it have? What images does he create through its use?
2. **Fact and Opinion** Highlight the facts about what Staples sees during his night walks, and underline his opinions about what he sees. Evaluate the evidence for his interpretations and opinions and consider the following question: Is he also prejudging people?
3. **Sources** What other kinds of sources might Staples have considered in formulating his views? How would including such sources have changed his essay?
4. **Tone** Describe the tone of the essay. What effect does the tone have on you as a reader? How effective do you find it?
5. **Omissions** What information has Staples omitted that would help you further understand his thesis, if any?

VISUALIZING THE READING

Review the reading and supply the missing information in the graphic organizer on the next page.

RESPONDING TO THE READING

1. **Reaction** Why is Staples's whistling of classical music similar to hikers wearing cowbells in bear country?
2. **Discussion** In what other ways can an individual "alter public space"?
3. **Journal** Do you think Staples should alter his behavior in public to accommodate the reactions of others? Write a journal entry explaining whether you agree or disagree with Staples's actions.
4. **Essay** Staples describes himself as a "survivor" (para. 7) of the streets he grew up on. In a sense, everyone is a survivor of certain decisions or circumstances that, if played out differently, might have resulted in misfortune. Write an essay that explains how and why you or someone you know is a survivor.

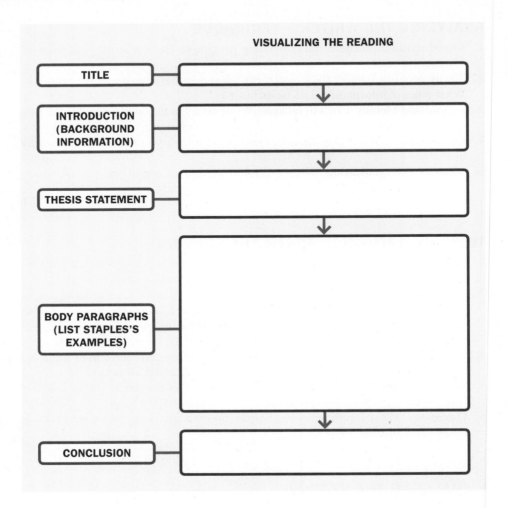

VISUALIZING THE READING

TITLE

INTRODUCTION
(BACKGROUND
INFORMATION)

THESIS STATEMENT

BODY PARAGRAPHS
(LIST STAPLES'S
EXAMPLES)

CONCLUSION

WORKING TOGETHER

Working in a group with two or three of your classmates, come up with an alternate title (one that will spark your readers' interest) for the article "Black Men and Public Space." Be prepared to share your title and explain the reason your group chose it.

8 Writing Effective Paragraphs

Study the photograph on this page. At what kind of event does it seem to have been taken? Write a sentence that states the main point of the photograph. Then write several more sentences explaining what is happening in the photograph. Describe what details in the photo helped you identify the event.

In much the same way as a photograph does, a paragraph makes an overall impression, or main point, and includes details that support this main point. Your first sentence, or **topic sentence**, states the main idea, and the other sentences you write provide the details that support it.

AL Photo/NAM Y. Huh, File

- understand the structure of a paragraph,
- write effective topic sentences,
- select supporting details that support the paragraph's main idea, and
- use transitions and repetition effectively.

THE STRUCTURE OF A PARAGRAPH

A paragraph is a group of connected sentences that develop a single idea about a topic. Each paragraph in your essay should support your thesis and contribute to the overall meaning and effectiveness of your essay. A well-developed paragraph contains:

- a well-focused topic sentence,
- specific supporting details (definitions, examples, facts and statistics, explanations, or other evidence),
- transitions and strategic repetition that show how the ideas are related, within and across paragraphs.

For a paragraph to develop a single idea, it must have **unity**: It must stay focused on one idea, without switching or wandering from topic to topic. A paragraph also should be of a reasonable length, neither too short nor too long. Short paragraphs are often underdeveloped; long paragraphs may be difficult for readers to follow. Note that what is an appropriate length may change across genres (or types) of writing — college essays usually have longer paragraphs than newspaper articles, and scholarly articles usually have longer paragraphs than college essays.

Here is a sample paragraph from a college textbook with its parts labeled.

Topic sentence: Main idea

Repetition: Key terms

Transitions: Guideposts

Audiences gather with varying degrees of willingness to hear a speaker. Some are anxious to hear the speaker, and may even have paid a substantial admission price. The "lecture circuit," for example, is a most lucrative aspect of public life. But whereas some audiences are willing to pay to hear a speaker, others don't seem to care one way or the other. Other audiences need to be persuaded to listen (or at least to sit in the audience). Still other audiences gather because they have to. For example, negotiations on a union contract may require members to attend meetings where officers give speeches.

DeVito, *The Essential Elements of Public Speaking*

Notice also how the writer repeats the words *audience(s)* and *speaker,* along with the synonyms *lecture* and *speeches,* to help tie the paragraph to the idea in the topic sentence. To visualize the structure of a well-developed paragraph, see Figure 8.1.

FIGURE 8.1 **The Structure of a Paragraph**

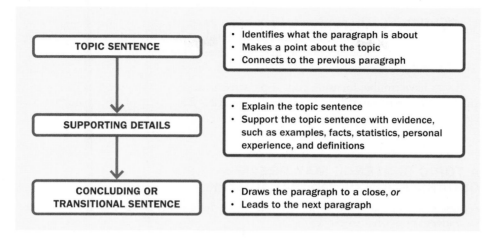

WRITING A TOPIC SENTENCE

A **topic sentence** is to a paragraph what a thesis statement is to an essay. Just as a thesis announces the main point of an essay, a topic sentence states the main point of a paragraph. In addition, each paragraph's topic sentence must support the thesis of the essay. An effective topic sentence should be focused, support the thesis, and be placed appropriately (usually at the beginning of the paragraph).

A TOPIC SENTENCE SHOULD BE FOCUSED

A topic sentence should make clear what the paragraph is about (its topic) and express a view or make a point about the topic.

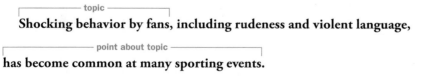

It should use specific and detailed language to tell readers what the paragraph is about. Avoid vague, general, or unfocused statements.

UNFOCUSED	Some members of minority groups do not approve of affirmative action.
FOCUSED	Some members of minority groups disapprove of affirmative action because it implies that they are not capable of obtaining employment based on their own accomplishments.

UNFOCUSED	Many students believe that hate groups shouldn't be allowed on campus.
FOCUSED	The neo-Nazis, a group that promotes hate crimes, should not be permitted to speak in our local community college because most students find its members' views objectionable.

If you have trouble focusing your topic sentences, review the guidelines for writing an effective thesis statement in Chapter 6 (pp. 122–24), many of which also apply to writing effective topic sentences.

A TOPIC SENTENCE MAY PREVIEW THE ORGANIZATION OF THE PARAGRAPH

A topic sentence may suggest the order in which details are discussed in the paragraph, so readers know what to expect.

Teaching employees how to handle conflicts through
┌──── detail 1 ────┐   ┌─ detail 2 ─┐
anger management and mediation is essential in high-stress jobs.

Readers can expect a discussion of anger management first, followed by a discussion of mediation.

EXERCISE 8.1 **Working with Topic Sentences**

Revise each of the following topic sentences to make it focused and specific. At least two of your revised topic sentences should also preview the organization of the paragraph.

1. In society today, there is always a new fad or fashion in clothing.
2. People watch television talk shows because they find them irresistible.
3. Tattoos are a popular trend.
4. Procrastinating can have a negative effect on your success in college.
5. In our state, the lottery is a big issue.

A TOPIC SENTENCE SHOULD SUPPORT YOUR THESIS

Each topic sentence must in some way explain the thesis or show why the thesis is believable or correct. For example, this sample thesis could be supported by the topic sentences that follow it.

THESIS	Adoption files should not be made available to adult children who are seeking their biological parents.

TOPIC SENTENCES
- Research has shown that not all biological parents want to meet with the sons or daughters they gave up many years before.
- If a woman gives up a child for adoption, it is probable that she does not ever intend to have a relationship with that child.
- Adult children who try to contact their biological parents often meet resistance and even hostility, which can cause them to feel hurt and rejected.
- A woman who gave up her biological child because she became pregnant as a result of rape or incest should not have to live in fear that her child will one day confront her.

All of these topic sentences support the thesis because they offer valid reasons for keeping adoption files closed.

EXERCISE 8.2 **Using Topic Sentences to Support a Thesis**

For each of the following thesis statements, identify the topic sentence in the list below it that does not support the thesis.

1. To make a marriage work, a couple must build trust, communication, and understanding.
   a. Knowing why a spouse behaves as he or she does can improve a relationship.
   b. People get married for reasons other than love.
   c. The ability to talk about feelings, problems, likes, and dislikes should grow as a marriage develops.
   d. Marital partners must rely on each other to make sensible decisions that benefit both of them.
2. Internet sales are capturing a larger market share relative to in-store sales.
   a. Internet retailers that target a specific audience tend to be most successful.
   b. The convenience of ordering any time of day or night accounts, in part, for increased Internet sales.
   c. Many customers use PayPal for online purchases.
   d. Websites that locate and compare prices for a specified item make comparison shopping easier on the Internet than in retail stores.

A TOPIC SENTENCE SHOULD BE STRATEGICALLY PLACED

The beginning of the paragraph is the most common and often the best position for a topic sentence: You state your main point, and then you explain it. The topic sentence tells readers what to expect in the rest of the paragraph, making it clear and easy for them to follow.

Advertising is first and foremost based on the principle of visibility—the customer must notice the product. Manufacturers often package products in glitzy, even garish, containers to grab the consumer's attention. For example, one candy company always packages its candy in reflective wrappers. When the hurried and hungry consumer glances at the candy counter, the reflective wrappers are easy to spot. It is only natural for the impatient customer to grab the candy and go.

Topic sentence: Appears at beginning of paragraph

Email and texting are important technological advances, but they have hidden limitations, even dangers. It is too easy to avoid talking to people face to face.

and text messaging are important

Does not provide any evidence of how or why they can be addictive

Emailing and texting can be addictive, too. Plus, they encourage ordinary people to ignore others while typing on a keyboard.

DEVELOPED PARAGRAPH

States reason that emailing and texting are disadvantageous

Provides further information about the addictive qualities of texting and email

Explains the qualities of face-to-face interaction that are absent from email and texting

Email and texting are important technological advances, but they have hidden limitations, even dangers. While email and texting allow fast and efficient communication and exchange of information, they provide a different quality of human interaction. It is too easy to avoid talking to people. It is easier to click on a phone number and text a friend to see if she wants to meet for dinner than it would be actually to talk to her. In fact, using these services can become addictive. For example, some students on campus are obsessed with checking their email and sending, reading, or checking for texts many times throughout the day, even during class lectures and small group discussions. They spend their free time texting with acquaintances across the country while ignoring interesting people right in the same room. There is something to be said for talking with a person who is sitting next to you and responding to his or her expressions, gestures, and tone of voice.

The first paragraph has skeletal ideas that support the topic sentence, but it does not explain those ideas. The second paragraph fleshes out the ideas by providing examples and explanations.

To discover if your paragraphs are well developed, ask yourself the following questions.

- Have I provided enough evidence to achieve my purpose?
- Have I given my readers enough information to make my ideas understandable and believable?
- Have I provided the amount and type of evidence that readers of a college essay will expect?
- Do I jump quickly from one idea to another without explaining each idea first? (Reading your essay aloud, or asking a friend to do so, can help you hear gaps.)

To learn more about prewriting strategies, see Chapter 4; for more on research, see Part 5; for a list of evidence that can be used to support a paragraph, see Table 6.1, p. 126.

To develop your paragraphs further, you can use a prewriting strategy or do some research to find supporting evidence for your topic sentence. The same types of evidence that can be used to support a thesis can be used to develop a paragraph.

> **EXERCISE 8.4**   Using Evidence to Develop a Paragraph

Use Table 6.1 (p. 126) to suggest the type or types of evidence that might be used to develop a paragraph based on each of the following topic sentences.

1. Many people have fallen prey to fad diets, risking their health and jeopardizing their mental well-being.
2. One can distinguish experienced soccer players from rookies by obvious signs.
3. To begin a jogging routine, take a relaxed but deliberate approach.
4. The interlibrary loan system is a fast and convenient method for obtaining print materials from libraries affiliated with the campus library.
5. Southwest Florida's rapid population growth poses a serious threat to its freshwater supply.

EXERCISE 8.5 | **Using Details to Develop a Paragraph**

Create a well-developed paragraph by adding details to the following paragraph.

Although it is convenient, online shopping is a different experience than shopping in an actual store. You don't get the same opportunity to see and feel objects. Also, you can miss out on other important information. There is much that you miss. If you enjoy shopping, turn off your computer and support your local merchants.

EFFECTIVE PARAGRAPHS PROVIDE SUPPORTING DETAILS AND ARRANGE THEM LOGICALLY

The evidence you provide to support your topic sentences should be concrete and specific. Specific details interest your readers and make your meaning clear and forceful. Compare the following two examples.

VAGUE

Many people are confused about the difference between a psychologist and a psychiatrist. Both have a license, but a psychiatrist has more education than a psychologist. Also, a psychiatrist can prescribe medication.

General statements that do not completely explain the topic sentence

CONCRETE AND SPECIFIC

Many people are confused about the difference between psychiatrists and psychologists. Both are licensed by the state to practice psychotherapy. However, a psychiatrist has earned a degree from medical school and can also practice medicine. Additionally, a psychiatrist can prescribe psychotropic medications. A psychologist, on the other hand, usually has earned a Ph.D. but has not attended medical school and therefore cannot prescribe medication of any type.

Concrete details make clear the distinction between the two terms

To make your paragraphs concrete and specific, use the following guidelines.

1. **Focus on *who, what, when, where, how,* and *why* questions.** Ask yourself these questions about your supporting details, and use the answers to expand and revise your paragraph.

   VAGUE   Some animals hibernate for part of the year. (What animals? When do they hibernate?)

   SPECIFIC   Some bears hibernate for three to four months each winter.

2. **Name names.** Include the names of people, places, brands, and objects.

   VAGUE   When my sixty-three-year-old aunt was refused a job, she became an angry victim of age discrimination.

   SPECIFIC   When my sixty-three-year-old Aunt Angela was refused a job at Vicki's Nail Salon, she became an angry victim of age discrimination.

3. **Use action verbs.** Select strong verbs that help your readers visualize the action.

VAGUE	When Silina came on stage, the audience became excited.
SPECIFIC	When Silina burst onto the stage, the audience screamed, cheered, and chanted, "Silina, Silina!"

4. **Use descriptive language that appeals to the senses (smell, touch, taste, sound, sight).** Words that appeal to the senses help your readers feel as if they are observing or participating in the experience you are describing.

VAGUE	It's relaxing to walk on the beach.
SPECIFIC	I walked in the sand next to the ocean, breathing in the smell of the salt water and listening to the rhythmic sound of the waves.

5. **Use adjectives and adverbs.** Carefully chosen adjectives and adverbs in your description of a person, place, or experience can make your writing more concrete.

VAGUE	As I weeded my garden, I let my eyes wander over the meadow sweets and hydrangeas, all the while listening to the chirping of a cardinal.
SPECIFIC	As I slowly weeded my perennial garden, I let my eyes wander over the pink meadow sweets and blue hydrangeas, all the while listening absent-mindedly to the chirping of a bright red cardinal.

For more on organization, see Chapter 7, pp. 139–44.

The details in a paragraph should also follow a logical order. You might arrange the details from most to least (or least to most) important, in chronological order, or in spatial order.

EXERCISE 8.6   **Providing Concrete, Specific Details**

Alone or in a group of two or three students, revise and expand each sentence in the following paragraph to make it specific and concrete. Feel free to add new information and new sentences, and be sure to arrange the supporting details logically.

I saw a great concert the other night in Dallas. Two groups were performing. The music was great, and there was a large crowd. In fact, the crowd was so enthusiastic that the second group performed one hour longer than scheduled.

Essay in Progress 2

For the draft you worked with in Essay in Progress 1 (p. 164), evaluate the supporting details you used in each paragraph. Revise as necessary to make each paragraph unified and logically organized. Make sure you have provided concrete, specific details.

USING TRANSITIONS AND REPETITION

All the details in a paragraph must fit together and function as a connected unit of information. When a paragraph has **coherence**, its ideas flow smoothly, allowing readers to follow its progression with ease. Two useful devices for linking details are transitions between sentences and repetition of key terms.

Transitions are words, phrases, or clauses that lead your reader from one idea to another. Think of transitions as guideposts, or signals, of what is coming next in a paragraph. Some commonly used transitions are shown in Table 8.1, which groups transitions according to the type of connections they show.

Table 8.1 Commonly Used Transitional Expressions	
Type of Connection	**Transitions**
Logical Connections	
Items in a series	then, first, second, next, another, furthermore, finally, as well as
Illustration	for instance, for example, namely, that is
Result or cause	consequently, therefore, so, hence, thus, then, as a result
Restatement	in other words, that is, in simpler terms
Summary or conclusion	finally, in conclusion, to sum up, all in all, evidently, actually
Similarity/agreement	similarly, likewise, in the same way
Difference/opposition	but, however, on the contrary, nevertheless, neither, nor, on the one/other hand, still, yet
Spatial Connections	
Direction	inside/outside, along, above/below, up/down, across, to the right/left, in front of/behind
Nearness	next to, near, nearby, facing, adjacent to
Distance	beyond, in the distance, away, over there
Time Connections	
Frequency	often, frequently, now and then, gradually, week by week, occasionally, daily, rarely
Duration	during, briefly, hour by hour
Reference to a particular time	at two o'clock, on April 27, in 2010, last Thanksgiving, three days ago
Beginning	before then, at the beginning, at first
Middle	meanwhile, simultaneously, next, then, at that time
End	finally, at last, eventually, later, at the end, subsequently, afterward

In the two examples that follow, notice that the first paragraph is disjointed and choppy because it lacks transitions. The revised version is more coherent and therefore easier to follow.

WITHOUT TRANSITIONS

Most films are structured much like a short story. The film begins with an opening scene that captures the audience's attention. The writers build up tension, preparing for the climax of the story. They complicate the situation by revealing other elements of the plot, perhaps by introducing a surprise or additional characters. They introduce a problem. It will be solved either for the betterment or to the detriment of the characters and the situation. A resolution brings the film to a close.

WITH TRANSITIONS

Repetition: Key words and pronouns

Transitions: Guideposts

Most films are structured much like a short story. The film begins with an opening scene that captures the audience's attention. Gradually the writers build up tension, preparing for the climax of the story. Soon after the first scene, they complicate the situation by revealing other elements of the plot, perhaps by introducing a surprise or additional characters. Next, they introduce a problem. Eventually the problem will be solved either for the betterment or to the detriment of the characters and the situation. Finally, a resolution brings the film to a close.

Notice that the repetition of key terms (*film(s)*, *writers*), as well as pronouns that stand in for the key terms (*they* for *writers*), also lends coherence to the paragraph.

> **Essay in Progress 3**
> For the draft you worked with in Essay in Progress 2 (p. 168), evaluate your use of transitions within each paragraph, adding them where needed to make the relationship among your ideas clearer.

STUDENTS WRITE

Chapters 5 to 7 show Latrisha Wilson's progress in planning and drafting an essay on surveillance. Below you can see her first-draft paragraph (also included in Chapter 7 as part of her first draft essay, p. 153) and her revision to strengthen the paragraph.

FIRST-DRAFT PARAGRAPH

Transition needed

Need to explain who Snowden is, what he did, and when; also add transition to make connection clear

Snowden's travels irrelevant

Need to explain what NSA is, what it did

When the word surveillance comes up, maybe you think of some thrilling and dangerous activity, like the kind of spying on foreign terrorists that goes on in James Bond movies. In the US today, most spying is done by surveillance computers. Edward Snowden bounced around for weeks from one airport to another, and lived for a while in the Moscow airport, eating who knows what and sleeping who knows where. The NSA seems to be able to do whatever it wants without having to answer to anyone or suffer any consequences. But we can't say the same for whistleblowers. Just look what they did to Bradley Manning! And now, the US government is aggressively pursuing Snowden. The NSA is more and more aggressively protecting its own secrecy, by punishing whistleblowers, and lying to Congress and, it seems as if they are more concerned about themselves than the people they are spying on.

> Relevance of Bradley Manning not made clear; explain or delete

> Detail needed to support claim about spying by surveillance computers in topic sentence

Revised Paragraph

When the word *surveillance* comes up, people think of some thrilling and dangerous activity, like the spying on foreign terrorists that goes on in James Bond movies. But in the U.S. today, most spying isn't done by handsome secret agents out to save the world; it's done by surveillance computers, and they monitor U.S. citizens, not just foreign terrorists. For example, consider what we learned from the whistleblower Edward Snowden, who sacrificed his career as a contractor for the National Security Agency (NSA) to alert the public to the deals the NSA makes with companies like Microsoft, Facebook, and Verizon to collect personal information and monitor everything their customers do on the internet or speak into a telephone.

ANALYZING THE WRITER'S TECHNIQUE

1. **Topic Sentence** Identify Wilson's topic sentence. How did she strengthen it in her revision?
2. **Details** What irrelevant details did she delete?
3. **Transitions** What transitions did she add to provide coherence?
4. **Repetition** What words are repeated, thus contributing to coherence?
5. **Further Revision** What further revisions do you recommend?

> **EXERCISE 8.7** **Evaluating Paragraphs, Unity, and Coherence**

The following student essay by Robin Ferguson on volunteering in a literacy program was written using the graphic organizer shown in Chapter 7 (p. 147). Read the essay and answer the questions that follow.

READING

The Value of Volunteering

Robin Ferguson

I began working as a literacy volunteer as part of a community service course I was taking last semester. The course required a community service project, and I chose literacy volunteers simply as a means of fulfilling a course requirement. Now I realize that working as a literacy volunteer taught me more about learning and friendship than I ever expected.   1

When I first went through the training program to become a literacy volunteer, I learned   2
about the process of learning -- that is, the way in which people learn new words most
effectively. To illustrate this concept, the person who trained me wrote a brief list of simple
words on the left side of a chalkboard and wrote phrases using the same words on the right
side of the chalkboard. She instructed us to read the words and then asked which words
we would be most likely to remember. We all said the words on the right because they
made more sense. In other words, we could remember the words in the phrases more easily
because they made more sense in context. The trainer showed us several more examples
of words in context so we could get a grasp of how people learn new information by
connecting it to what they already know.

The training I received, though excellent, was no substitute for working with a real   3
student, however. When I began to discover what other people's lives are like because they
cannot read, I realized the true importance of reading. For example, when I had my first
tutoring session with my client, Marie, a forty-four-year-old single mother of three, I found
out she walked two miles to the nearest grocery store twice a week because she didn't know
which bus to take. When I told her I would get her a bus schedule, she confided to me that it
would not help because she could not read it and therefore wouldn't know which bus to take.
She also said she had difficulty once she got to the grocery store because she couldn't always
remember what she needed. Since she did not know words, she could not write out a grocery
list. Also, she identified items by sight, so if the manufacturer changed a label, she could not
recognize it as the product she wanted.

As we worked together, learning how to read built Marie's self-confidence, which   4
gave her an incentive to continue in her studies. She began to make rapid progress
and was even able to take the bus to the grocery store. After this successful trip, she
reported how self-assured she felt. Eventually, she began helping her youngest son,
Mark, a shy first grader, with his reading. She sat with him before he went to sleep,
and together they would read bedtime stories. When his eyes became wide with excitement as she read, her pride swelled, and she began to see how her own hard work in
learning to read paid off. As she described this experience, I swelled with pride as
well. I found that helping Marie to build her self-confidence was more rewarding than
anything I had ever done before.

As time went by, Marie and I developed a friendship that became permanent.   5
Because we saw each other several times a week, we spent a lot of time getting to
know each other, and we discovered we had certain things in common. For instance,
I'm also a single parent. So we began to share our similar experiences with each other.
In fact, we have even baby-sat for each other's children. I would drop my children off

at her house while I taught an evening adult class, and in return, I watched her children while she worked on Saturday mornings.

As a literacy volunteer, I learned a great deal about learning, teaching, and helping others. I also established what I hope will be a lifelong friendship. In fact, I may have benefited more from the experience than Marie did.   6

1. Highlight each of the topic sentences in the body of the essay (between the introduction and the conclusion). Evaluate how well each supports the thesis.
2. What type(s) of evidence does Ferguson use to support each topic sentence?
3. What method(s) does Ferguson use to arrange her details logically within paragraphs?
4. Highlight transitions that Ferguson uses to connect her ideas, both within and between paragraphs.

WORKING TOGETHER

Working in a group with two or three of your classmates, return to the essay "Black Men and Public Space" by Brent Staples in Chapter 7 (pp. 154–56) and examine Staples's use and placement of topic sentences. As you read, identify each topic sentence and discuss how effectively it is supported with concrete, specific details.

9

Revising Content and Organization

©Cavan Images/Getty

Looking at the photograph on this page from top to bottom, list everything that is happening. Now, write a few sentences summarizing what you think is happening, and then add details to your original list to describe the photo more fully. After you add these details, will it be easier for a reader who has not seen the photo to picture what is happening in it?

Exchange papers with a classmate and examine how your classmate organized ideas and what details he or she included. Look for parts that you find confusing and that need more detail. Write down your comments for your classmate. Finally, using your own comments and those of the classmate who examined your list, make changes to improve your own description of the photograph.

When you changed your list, did you include more details from the photo? Leave some unimportant details out? Change or rearrange any details? If so, you *revised* the description of the photo. **Revision** is a process of making changes to improve what your essay says and how you say it. Revising an essay works in much the same way as the revision of your list did. As Figure 9.1 shows, revision is an essential part of the writing process.

174

- ask key questions to revise,
- work with your classmates to revise,
- use your instructor comments to revise, and
- consider your learning style when revising.

WHY REVISE?

A thorough, thoughtful revision can change a C paper to an A paper! Revising can make a significant difference in how well your paper
- achieves your purpose,
- expresses your ideas to your intended audience, and
- reflects your reader's expectations of your genre.

FIGURE 9.1 An Overview of the Writing Process

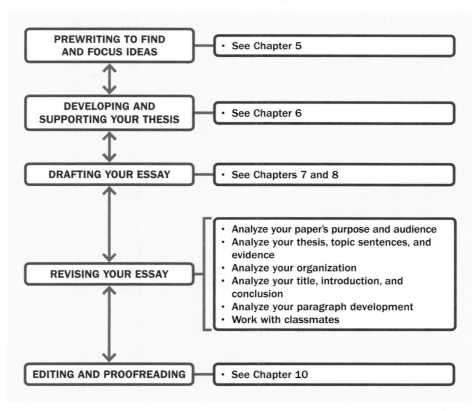

This difference is why most professional writers—and successful student writers—revise frequently and thoroughly.

Revising is not a process of correcting surface errors, such as spelling mistakes or punctuation errors. Rather, it is a process of looking at your *ideas* and finding ways to make them clearer and easier to understand. This may mean adding, eliminating, or reorganizing key elements within the essay, even revising your thesis statement and refocusing the entire essay.

Learning Style Options

The amount of revision you need to do depends in part on how you approach the task of writing. Some writers spend more time planning; others spend more time revising. For example, pragmatic learners tend to take a highly structured approach to writing. They plan in detail what they will say before they draft. In contrast, creative learners may dash off a draft as ideas come to mind. A well-planned draft usually requires less revision than one that was spontaneously written. Regardless of how carefully planned an essay may be, any first draft requires at least some revision.

USEFUL TECHNIQUES FOR REVISION

The following techniques will help you evaluate and revise your essays.

- **Allow time between drafting and revising, so you can approach your essay from a fresh perspective.** Try to leave enough time to set your draft aside overnight if possible.
- **Listen for problems as you or a friend reads your draft aloud.** Listening carefully can help you identify awkward wording, vague or overused expressions, or main points that are unclear or lack adequate support. A reader less familiar with the text than you may also slow down when reading or misread confusing passages, providing a hint for areas that need revision.
- **Ask a classmate to read and comment on your paper.** This process, called **peer review**, is discussed in detail later in this chapter (p. 182).
- **Look for consistent problem areas in your writing.** Develop a checklist of common problems—such as confusing organization or a lack of concrete supporting details—by listing issues from several essays you have written; then check for these problem areas as you revise.
- **Read a printed copy.** You will be able to analyze and evaluate your writing more impartially, and you can write marginal annotations, circle troublesome words or sentences, and draw arrows to connect details more easily.

For more about creating a graphic organizer, see Chapter 3, pp. 52–55; for more on outlining, see Chapter 7, pp. 144–46.

- **Draw a graphic organizer or outline your draft.** A graphic organizer or outline allows you to see how your thesis and topic sentences relate to one another and helps you evaluate content and organization. If you spot a problem, such as a detail or an example that does not support a topic sentence, write notes to the right of your organizer (or outline), as shown in Figure 9.2.

FIGURE 9.2 **Sample Graphic Organizer for Revision**

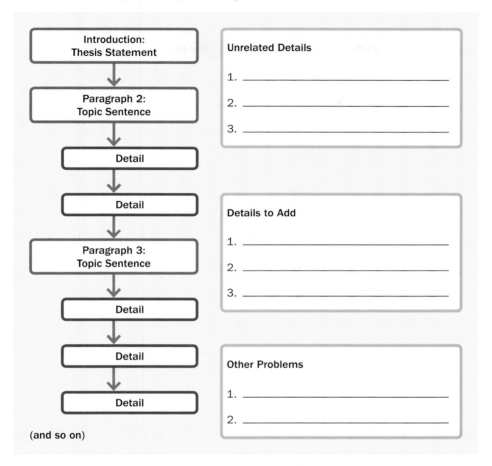

KEY QUESTIONS FOR REVISION

To identify broad areas of weakness in your essay, ask yourself these five key questions.

1. Does my essay clearly convey a purpose, address an appropriate audience, and follow the conventions of the genre?
2. Does my essay state a clear, well-focused thesis and provide enough reasons and evidence to support the thesis?
3. Does each paragraph include a clear main idea (usually stated in a topic sentence) and enough details to develop the idea fully?
4. Do the ideas in my essay fit together logically?
5. Does my essay have a strong introduction and conclusion, and an appropriate title?

After you have identified areas that need reworking, refer to the self-help flowcharts that follow.

ANALYZING YOUR PURPOSE AND AUDIENCE

For more about purpose and audience, see Chapter 5; for more about developing a thesis, see Chapter 6.

First drafts often lack focus. They may go off in several directions rather than have a clear purpose. For instance, one section of an essay on divorce may inform readers of its causes, and another section may argue that it harms children. A first draft may also contain sections that appeal to different audiences. For instance, one section of an essay on counseling teenagers about drug abuse might seem to be written for parents; other sections might be more appropriate for teenagers.

To determine if your paper has a clear focus, write a sentence stating what your essay is supposed to accomplish. If you cannot write such a sentence, your paper probably lacks a clear purpose. To find a purpose, reread your draft. Does one purpose predominate? If so, revise the sections that do not fit in. If not, do some additional thinking or brainstorming, listing as many possible purposes as you can think of and revising to address the purpose you find most appropriate.

To determine if your essay is directed to a specific audience, write a few sentences describing your intended readers. Describe their knowledge, beliefs, and experience with your topic. If you are unable to do so, focus on a particular audience and revise your essay with them in mind.

> **Essay in Progress 1**
> Evaluate the purpose and audience of the draft essay you wrote in Essay in Progress 3 in Chapter 7 (p. 152) or another essay that you have written. Make notes on your graphic organizer or annotate your outline.

ANALYZING YOUR THESIS, TOPIC SENTENCES, AND EVIDENCE

Use Figure 9.3 to examine your thesis statement, topic sentences, and evidence.

> **Essay in Progress 2**
> Using Figure 9.3, evaluate the thesis statement, topic sentences, and evidence of the essay you began assessing in Essay in Progress 1 above. Make notes on your graphic organizer or annotate your outline.

ANALYZING YOUR ORGANIZATION

Your readers will not be able to follow your ideas if your essay is not unified. To assess your essay's unity, examine its organization. Your graphic organizer or outline (see p. 144) will help you discover any flaws.

You can also ask a classmate to read your essay and explain how it is organized. If your classmate cannot describe your essay's organization, it probably needs further work. Use one of the methods in Chapter 7 (pp. 140–44) or one of the patterns of development described in Parts 3 and 4 to reorganize your ideas.

FIGURE 9.3 **Flowchart for Evaluating Your Thesis Statement, Topic Sentences, and Evidence**

QUESTIONS		REVISION STRATEGIES

1. Does your essay have a thesis that identifies your topic and position and suggests your slant? (To find out, state your thesis; then highlight the sentence in your draft that comes closest to what you just said. If you cannot find such a sentence, you probably do not have a well-focused thesis).

 NO

- Reread your essay and answer this question: What is the essay's one main point?
- Write a thesis statement that expresses that main point.
- Revise your paper to focus on that main point.
- Delete parts of the essay that do not support your thesis statement.

YES

2. Do your readers have the background they need to understand your thesis? (To find out, ask someone unfamiliar with your topic to read your essay, and get feedback.)

 NO

- Answer *who, what, when, where, why,* and *how* questions to discover more background information.

YES

3. Have you presented enough evidence to support your thesis? (Place a ✔ beside the evidence that supports your thesis. For paragraphs with few ✔s, ask yourself: Do they need more evidence to be convincing?)

 NO

- Use prewriting strategies or do additional research to discover more supporting evidence.
- Evaluate this new evidence and add the most convincing evidence to your essay.

YES

4. Does each topic sentence logically connect to and support the thesis? Read the thesis, and then read each topic sentence. Revise when the connection is not obvious.

 NO

- Rewrite the topic sentence so that it clearly supports the thesis.
- If necessary, broaden your thesis so that it encompasses all your supporting points.

YES

5. Is your evidence specific and detailed? Reread paragraphs where you placed ✔s. Does each item answer one of these questions: *Who? What? When? Where? Why? How?* For paragraphs with few or no ✔s, add more detailed evidence.

 NO

- Answer *who, what, when, where, why,* and *how* questions to discover more detailed evidence. Name names, give dates, specify places.
- Use action verbs and descriptive language, including carefully chosen adjectives and adverbs.

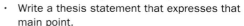

ANALYZING YOUR INTRODUCTION, CONCLUSION, AND TITLE

The following questions can help you evaluate your introduction, conclusion, and title.

1. **Will your introduction interest your reader and provide needed background information?** If your essay jumps into the topic without preparing readers for it, your introduction needs to be revised. Ask the questions *who, what, when, where, why,* and *how* to determine the background information your readers will need. Then use the suggestions in Chapter 7 (pp. 148–50) to create interest.

2. **Does your conclusion draw your essay to a satisfactory close, reinforce your thesis statement, and follow logically from the introduction?** If not, try imagining yourself explaining the significance or importance of your essay to a friend, and use this explanation to rewrite your conclusion. Then use the suggestions for writing conclusions in Chapter 7 (pp. 150–51) to add interest.

3. **Does your title accurately reflect the content of your essay?** Write a few words that "label" your essay. Mine your thesis statement for a few key words that can serve as part of your title. Finally, use the suggestions in Chapter 7 (pp. 151–52) to help you write a title.

> **Essay in Progress 3**
> Evaluate the organization of your essay in progress. Make notes on your draft copy.

ANALYZING YOUR PARAGRAPH DEVELOPMENT

See Chapter 8 for more on paragraph development.

Each paragraph in your essay must fully develop a single idea that supports your thesis. (Exception: Each paragraph of a narrative essay focuses on a separate part of the action; see Chapter 11.) In a typical first draft, paragraphs are often weak or loosely structured. They may contain irrelevant information or lack a clearly focused topic sentence.

Study each paragraph in conjunction with your thesis statement. Consider whether your topic sentence supports your thesis and whether the reasons and evidence in the paragraph support the topic sentence. You may need to delete or combine some paragraphs, rework or reorganize others, or move paragraphs to more appropriate placement in the essay. If you need to supply additional information to support your thesis, you may need to add paragraphs to the draft. Use Figure 9.4 to analyze and revise your paragraphs.

> **Essay in Progress 4**
> Using Figure 9.4, examine each paragraph of your essay in progress, and make notes on your draft.

FIGURE 9.4 Flowchart for Evaluating Your Paragraphs

QUESTIONS	REVISION STRATEGIES
1. Does each paragraph have a clear topic sentence that supports the thesis? <u>Underline the topic sentence in each paragraph.</u> Then evaluate whether the topic sentence makes a statement that supports the main idea of the essay.	• Revise a sentence within the paragraph so that it clearly states the main point. • Write a new sentence that supports the thesis and states the main point of the paragraph.

 NO

YES

2. Do all sentences in each paragraph support the topic sentence? To find out, read the topic sentence and each supporting sentence in turn.	• Revise supporting sentences to make their connection to the topic sentence clear. • Delete any sentences that do not support the topic sentence.

 NO

YES

3. Does the paragraph offer adequate explanation and supporting details? Place ✔'s beside supporting details. Then ask yourself: Will readers want or need to know anything else?	• Add more details if your paragraph seems skimpy. • Use either the *who, what, when, where, why,* and *how* questions or the prewriting strategies in Chapter 5 to generate the details you need.

 NO

YES

4. Will it be clear to your reader how each sentence and each paragraph connects to those before and after it? (To find out, read your paper aloud to see if it flows smoothly or sounds choppy.)	• Add transitions where they are needed. Refer to the list of common transitions on page 169.

 NO

WORKING WITH CLASSMATES TO REVISE YOUR ESSAY

Many instructors ask students to use **peer review**, a process in which two or more students read and comment on one another's papers. Working with classmates is an excellent way to get ideas for improving your essays and your approach to the writing process. Peer review can also hone your critical reading skills. The following suggestions will help writers and reviewers get the most from peer review.

HOW TO FIND A GOOD REVIEWER

Your instructor may pair you with another class member or let you find your own reviewer, either a classmate or someone outside class. If you can select your own reviewer, use these tips.

- Select a classmate who is attentive in class, so he or she will be familiar with the assignment and with what you have learned so far in the course. If you need to find someone outside of class, choose a person who has already taken the course, preferably someone who did well in it.
- Avoid choosing close friends; they are not necessarily the best reviewers because they may be reluctant to offer criticism or may be too critical. Instead, choose someone who is serious, skillful, objective, and willing to spend the time needed to provide useful comments.
- If your college has a writing center, ask a tutor in the center to read and comment on your draft.
- Use more than one reviewer if possible, so you can get several perspectives.

SUGGESTIONS FOR WRITERS

To get the greatest benefit from peer review, use the following suggestions.

1. **Provide readable copy.** A typed, double-spaced draft is best.
2. **Do some revision yourself first.** Think through your draft, and try to fix obvious problems. The more developed your draft is, the more helpful your reviewer's comments will be.
3. **Offer specific questions or guidelines.** Give your reviewer a copy of the "Questions for Peer Reviewers" below, and add other questions that you want answered. You might also give your reviewer one of the revision flowcharts in this (or another) chapter.
4. **Be open to criticism and new ideas.** Try not to be defensive. Look at your essay objectively, seeing it from your reader's perspective.
5. **Don't feel obligated to accept all of the advice you are given.** A reviewer might suggest a change that will not work well in your paper or wrongly identify something as an error. If you are uncertain about a suggestion, discuss it with your instructor or other reviewers.

QUESTIONS FOR PEER REVIEWERS

1. What is the purpose of the essay?
2. Who is the intended audience?
3. What expectations are associated with this genre?
4. Is the introduction fully developed?
5. What is the main point or thesis? Is it easy to identify?
6. Does each paragraph offer a clear topic sentence and relevant and convincing evidence to support the main point? Where is more evidence needed? (Identify specific paragraphs.)
7. Is each paragraph clear and well organized? Are transitions needed to connect ideas within paragraphs?
8. Is the organization easy to follow? Where might it be improved, and how? Are transitions needed to connect ideas between paragraphs?
9. Does the conclusion draw the essay to a satisfying close?
10. What do you like about the draft? What could be improved? Underline or highlight passages that are unclear or confusing.

SUGGESTIONS FOR REVIEWERS

Reviewers should be honest but tactful. Criticism is never easy to accept, so keep your reader's feelings in mind. These tips will help you provide useful comments.

1. **Read the draft through twice before making any judgments or comments.**
2. **Focus on the main points and how clearly they are expressed.** If you notice a misspelling or a grammatical error, you can circle it, but correcting errors is not your primary task.
3. **Offer praise.** It will help the writer to know what works as well as what needs improvement.
4. **Be specific.** For instance, instead of saying that more examples are needed, tell the writer which ideas in which paragraphs are unclear or unconvincing without examples. Suggest useful examples in each case.
5. **Use the Questions for Peer Reviewers above as well as any additional questions that the writer provides to guide your review.** If the essay was written in response to an assignment in one of the chapters in Part 3 or 4, consult the revision flowchart in that chapter.
6. **Write notes and comments directly on the draft.** At the end of the essay, write a note that summarizes your overall reaction, pointing out both strengths and weaknesses. Here is one reviewer's sample final note:

> Overall, I think your paper has great ideas. It definitely held my interest, and the example about the judge proved your point well. But it could be organized better. The last three paragraphs don't seem connected to the rest of the essay. Maybe better transitions would help. Also the conclusion just repeats your thesis statement. It needs to be developed more.

7. **Use the Comments feature or insert comments in brackets or in a different color following the passage.** Make it easy for the writer to find and delete your comments after reading them.

8. **Do not rewrite paragraphs or sections of the essay.** Instead, suggest how the writer might revise them.

Essay in Progress 5

Give your essay in progress to a classmate to read and review. Ask your reviewer to respond to the Questions for Peer Reviewers (p. 183). Revise your essay using your revision outline, Figures 9.3 and 9.4, and your reviewer's suggestions.

USING YOUR INSTRUCTOR'S COMMENTS

The comments your instructor provides are an important resource to use in revising your essays. You can use them not only to revise an essay but also to improve your writing throughout the course.

REVISING AN ESSAY USING YOUR INSTRUCTOR'S COMMENTS

Often your instructor's comments provide a road map for you to begin your revision. An essay by a student, Kate Atkinson, appears in Figure 9.5. Her assignment was to write an essay defining a specialized term, and Kate chose "guerrilla street art" as her subject. In the marginal comments, Kate's instructor comments on a range of elements in the essay, including the effectiveness of the introduction, paragraph unity and development, word choice, and source citations. Atkinson read the comments carefully and used them to revise her essay. Her final draft appears in Chapter 18 (pp. 449–51).

FIGURE 9.5 Using Your Instructor's Comments to Revise Your Essay

Guerrilla Street Art: Definition Essay Rough Draft

Comment [KM1]: Good opening sentence. It gives readers a reason for wanting to know more about it and challenges them to look for it.

Comment [KM2]: This term is not yet defined. I know it is defined later, but readers will wonder what it is now. Perhaps choose a different example here?

Comment [KM3]: This is your thesis, but it is not very detailed. What about combining it with the following sentence to create a stronger thesis?

Guerrilla street art is everywhere, if you look for it. There are countless examples in   1
the small college town where I grew up, where the dense population of college students
and artists breeds creativity. Just around the corner from my school there are stickers
littering sign posts, colorful graffiti tags on exposed brick walls, homemade posters
advertising local bands at the bus stop, and a cheerful Dr. Seuss character stenciled on
the sidewalk. These small works of art can go easily unnoticed, but they bring an unexpected vibrancy to the city that is unique. Guerrilla street art is any unauthorized art in
a public space . By taking art out of the traditional context, guerrilla street artists create
controversy and intrigue by making art free and accessible to a broad audience.

Graffiti is unauthorized writing or drawing on a public surface. It dates back centu-   2

ries and artists have been know to use chalk, markers, paint, and even carving tools to

inscribe their messages on public property. Common techniques used by street artists today

include graffiti, stenciling, poster art, sticker art, and wheat pasting. Graffiti is so common

that it is difficult to travel far in most urban settings without coming across a word or

image scrawled in spray paint on a public a surface. Stenciling is a form of graffitti in

which artists use pre-cut stencils to guide their work, and pre-made stickers and posters are

popular because they can be quickly appled and are easy to mass produce. "Wheat pasting"

refers to the use of a vegetable-based adhesive to adhere posters to walls. Using a less

common technique called "yarn bombing," crafty artists knit colorful sheaths of wool and

acrylic and wrap them around telephone poles and park benches. The finished pieces are

eye-catching and unusual, but not permanent or damaging to public property.

The various motives behind guerilla street art are as diverse as the artwork itself   3

and range from social and political activism to self-promotion of the artist. Artist embellish

telephone poles with colorful yarn or train carriges with ornate murals as a way to reclaim and

beautify public space. Others use public space as a billboard ~~for~~ *to advocate for a* cause.

An example of street art as propaganda is artist Shepard Fairey's iconic image of Barack

Obama. The simple design combines a striking red, white, and blue portrait of Obama with

the word "Hope." With the nod of approval from Obama's campaign team, Fairey and his team

dispersed and glue, stencilled, and tacked the image onto countless public surfaces across

the US until it became an important facet of the campaign. The picture itself is powerful, but

what made it even more effective as a campaign tool was the distribution of the image by

supporters and the youth appeal that it garnered as a result.

Street Art is also an easy way for new artists to gain notoriety withouth revealing who   4

they really are. A tag, which is an artists signature or symbol, is the most prevalent type

of graffitti. Before the Obama campaign, Shepard Fairey gained international acclaim for

a sticker depicting wrestler Andre the Giant and the word "Obey." The image soon became

his tag and can be found in almost all of his work, making it instantly recognizable. The

anonymity of street art also gives artists the freedom to express themselves without fearing

the judgement of their peers. At worst, this freedom can result in crude or offensice inscrip-

tions on public property but at best, it can produce bold statements.

Due to the illicit nature of their art, the street artist community is shrouded in   5

secrecy. In the film "Exit through the Gift Shop," a documentary by notorious British street

artist Banksy, hooded figures in ski masks are shown scaling buildings and perched precari-

ously on ledges, armed with spray cans and buckets of industrial paste and always on the

lookout for the police. Despite his celebrity, Banksy has managed to keep his identity

---

Comment [KM4]: This sentence defining graffiti is almost the same definition as your definition of guerrilla street art in para. 1.

Comment [KM5]: The paragraph is about graffiti-writing or drawing. Do wheat pasting and yarn bombing fall into this category? If so, can you expand the definition to fit them? Or are they other forms of guerrilla street art? If so, I'd put them in a separate paragraph. Right now you only mention one form of guerrilla art—graffiti—yet your title suggests the essay is about street art. Are there other forms you haven't mentioned?

Comment [KM6]: This is a strong topic sentence.

Deleted: a

Comment [KM7]: Are all causes propaganda? You might want to chose a different word here or introduce propaganda and a separate motive first.

Comment [KM8]: Add source citation

Comment [KM9]: This sentence leads me to believe that the para. will be about secrecy, but midway through the topic seems to switch to reasons for street art's appeal. Maybe make this part into a separate paragraph?

Comment [KM10]: Add source citation

anonymous and his face is never shown in the film. It is common for street artists to be arrested for trespassing and vandalism, and the risk and intentional disobience involved in street art adds to its appeal, especially amoung young people. Another appeal of guerrilla street art is that it is comtemporary and can be enjoyed without a visit to a museum. It is free and encourages the belief that art should be accessible and available to everyone. It is also a movement that anyone can take part in and that challenges traditional standards of art.

> Guerrilla street art has blossomed from and underground movement to a cultural   6
> phenomenon. At the very least, it brings up the controversial questions of what constitutes art, and whether public space is an appropriate place for it. It brings beauty and intrigue to urban spaces that would otherwise go unnoticed and it is a tool for artists to exercise freedom of speech and expression.

Comment [KM11]: I am glad you raised this question. I kept wondering about it all along as I read the essay. Can you raise it earlier? And should you try to answer this knotty question of "What is art"? Maybe just recognize that the question exists?

EXERCISE 9.1 **Comparing a First Draft and a Final Draft**

Either alone or in small groups, compare Kate Atkinson's first draft with her final draft on pp. 449–51. Make a list of the changes she made to her essay in response to her instructor's comments. Also, put a checkmark next to any problems that recur throughout the first draft of the essay.

USING YOUR INSTRUCTOR'S COMMENTS TO IMPROVE FUTURE ESSAYS

When you receive a graded essay back from an instructor, it is tempting to note the grade and then file away the essay without reading any accompanying notes or suggestions. To improve your writing, however, take time to study each comment. Use the following suggestions to improve future essays.

- **Reread your essay at least twice.** It takes more than one reading to process numerous comments on a wide range of topics. Read your essay once to note grammatical corrections. Then read it a second time to study comments about organization or content.
- **If you did not get a high grade, try to determine why.** Was the essay weak in content, organization, or development?
- **Make sure you understand (and can correct) each grammatical error.** If you cannot, check a grammar handbook or ask a classmate. If you still do not understand your error, check with your instructor.
- **Record grammar errors in an error log.** When you proofread your next essay, look carefully for each type of error.

- **Using Figures 9.3 (p. 179) and 9.4 (p. 181), highlight or mark weaknesses that your instructor identified.** When writing your next essay, refer back to these flowcharts. Pay close attention to the areas you had trouble with as you revise your next paper.
- **If any comments are unclear, first ask a classmate if he or she understands them.** If not, talk to your instructor, who will be pleased that you are taking time to study the comments.

EXERCISE 9.2 | **Using Your Instructor's Comments on a Draft**

If your instructor has returned a marked-up first draft to you, read the comments carefully. Then draw a line down the middle of a blank sheet of paper. On the left, write the instructor's comments; on the right, jot down ways you might revise the essay in response to each comment. Put a checkmark next to any problems that recur throughout your essay; these are areas to which you will want to pay particular attention in your future writing.

CONSIDERING YOUR LEARNING STYLE WHEN YOU REVISE

Depending on your learning style, you may need to address specific kinds of problems in your drafts. The following revision tips for various learning styles may help.

Learning Style Options

- *Creative* learners sometimes write drafts that lack organization, so they will benefit greatly from preparing outlines and graphic organizers.
- *Independent* learners often need time for reflection, so they should allow extra time between drafting and revising.
- *Verbal* learners may prefer to outline drafts to check the organization.
- *Rational* learners should be sure their drafts do not seem dull or impersonal, adding vivid descriptions and personal examples where appropriate.
- *Concrete* learners tend to focus on specifics, so they should check that their thesis and topic sentences are clearly stated.

- *Pragmatic* learners tend to write tightly organized drafts that may lack interest, originality, or content, so they should make sure their draft offers interesting and relevant supporting details.
- *Social* learners often find discussing revision plans with classmates helpful, so they should add time to get feedback from classmates.
- *Spatial* learners may prefer to draw a graphic organizer to check the organization.
- *Emotional* learners should check to make sure they have stated their ideas directly, without hedging or showing undue concern for those who disagree.
- *Abstract* learners tend to focus on general ideas, so they should be sure their essay has enough supporting details.

STUDENTS WRITE

After writing her first draft, which appears in Chapter 7 (pp. 153–54), Latrisha Wilson used the guidelines and revision flowcharts in this chapter to guide her revision. For example, she decided that she needed to focus more on how communications technologies allow greater surveillance. She added details and examples, including a visual to show what she was describing.

Wilson asked a classmate to review her essay. A portion of his comments is shown below.

> ### REVIEWER'S COMMENTS
>
> I like your topic. It's current and interesting, but maybe your thesis could be more specific? Maybe it should focus on how new ways of communicating put us at risk of surveillance? Or you could revise your intro to focus on whistleblowers (that's what your first body paragraph talks about), but you'd need to add a lot of information. Since I have a gmail account and a Facebook page, I'd like to know more about how those sites use our personal information to make money, and maybe you could include a screenshot of a gmail page to show where the ads are. That might be helpful for the 5 people in the world (like the teacher?) who don't have gmail accounts. The only other thing that I think may be a problem is the tone. It's kind of casual for an essay for class. Maybe you could make your tone more formal?

Using her own analysis and her classmate's suggestions, Wilson created a graphic organizer (Figure 9.6) to help her decide how to revise her draft. She used the format for an illustration essay provided in Chapter 14 (p. 306).

FIGURE 9.6 Graphic Organizer for Latrisha Wilson's Revision Plans

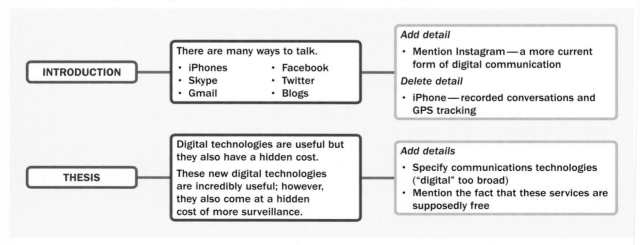

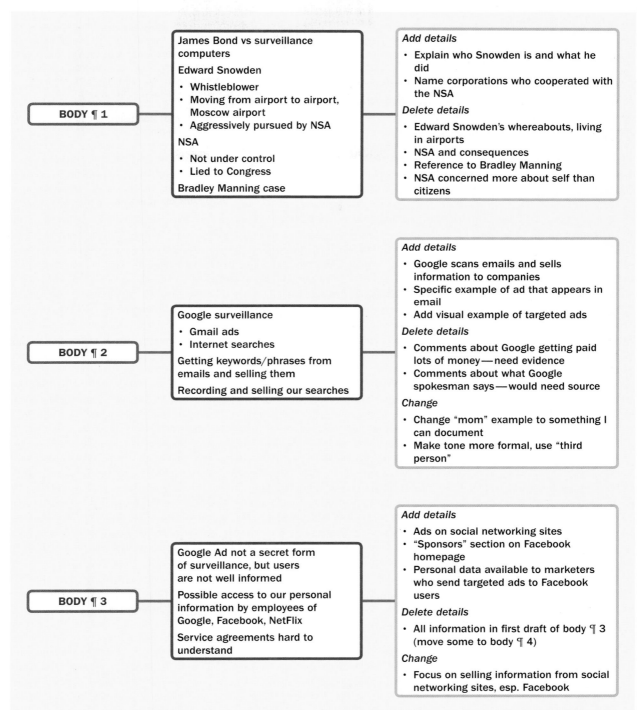

BODY ¶ 1

James Bond vs surveillance computers

Edward Snowden
- Whistleblower
- Moving from airport to airport, Moscow airport
- Aggressively pursued by NSA

NSA
- Not under control
- Lied to Congress

Bradley Manning case

Add details
- Explain who Snowden is and what he did
- Name corporations who cooperated with the NSA

Delete details
- Edward Snowden's whereabouts, living in airports
- NSA and consequences
- Reference to Bradley Manning
- NSA concerned more about self than citizens

BODY ¶ 2

Google surveillance
- Gmail ads
- Internet searches

Getting keywords/phrases from emails and selling them

Recording and selling our searches

Add details
- Google scans emails and sells information to companies
- Specific example of ad that appears in email
- Add visual example of targeted ads

Delete details
- Comments about Google getting paid lots of money—need evidence
- Comments about what Google spokesman says—would need source

Change
- Change "mom" example to something I can document
- Make tone more formal, use "third person"

BODY ¶ 3

Google Ad not a secret form of surveillance, but users are not well informed

Possible access to our personal information by employees of Google, Facebook, NetFlix

Service agreements hard to understand

Add details
- Ads on social networking sites
- "Sponsors" section on Facebook homepage
- Personal data available to marketers who send targeted ads to Facebook users

Delete details
- All information in first draft of body ¶ 3 (move some to body ¶ 4)

Change
- Focus on selling information from social networking sites, esp. Facebook

(continued on next page)

(Figure 9.6 continued)

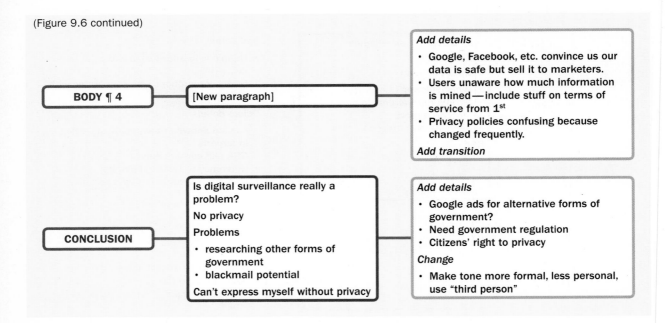

After creating the graphic organizer, Wilson revised her first draft. A portion of her revised draft, with her revisions indicated using the Track Changes function, follows.

REVISED DRAFT

Do we need to talk? There are plenty of exciting new ways to do it. We can ~~communicate by talking on~~ use our iPhones, chat on Skype, Gmail, Facebook message or read each other's Twitter, or blog posts, or share pictures on Instagram. ~~but there are dangers there. Our conversations can be recorded, and the GPS funtion on the phone allows our whereabouts to be tracked. We can chat on Skype, Gmail, Facebook message, or read each other's Twitter or blog posts.~~ These new digital technologies are incredibly useful; however, they also come at a hidden cost. Often advertised as free services, new ways of communicating put us under more invasive but less obvious forms of ~~more~~ surveillance.

Before Wilson submitted her final draft, she read her essay several more times, editing it for sentence structure and word choice. She also proofread it to catch errors in grammar and punctuation as well as typographical errors. (A portion of Wilson's revised essay, with editing and proofreading changes marked, appears in Chapter 10, p. 213.) The final version of Wilson's essay follows.

FINAL DRAFT

No Place Left for Privacy

Do we need to talk? There are plenty of exciting new ways to do it. We can use our iPhones, chat on Skype, Gmail, Facebook message, or read each other's

Twitter feed or blog posts, or share pictures on Instagram. These new digital technologies are incredibly useful; however, they also come at a hidden cost. Often advertised as free services, new ways of communicating put us under more invasive but less obvious forms of surveillance.

When the word *surveillance* comes up, people think of some thrilling and dangerous activity, like the spying on foreign terrorists that goes on in James Bond movies. But in the U.S. today, most spying isn't done by handsome secret agents out to save the world; it's done by surveillance computers, and they monitor U.S. citizens, not just foreign terrorists. For example, consider what we learned from the whistleblower Edward Snowden, who sacrificed his career as a contractor for the National Security Agency (NSA) to alert the public to the deals the NSA makes with companies like Microsoft, Facebook, and Verizon to collect personal information and monitor everything their customers do on the Internet or speak into a telephone.

2

The NSA, of course, isn't the only organization spying on us. Another kind of surveillance, which doesn't make top press, is the eavesdropping that Google and other communication service providers regularly do on their users. Google software, for example, automatically scans the content of all Gmail for keywords and phrases that then must get sold or rented to other companies because users of Gmail regularly see targeted advertisements related to what they've written about: If a user wishes her friend "Happy Birthday!" she now sees advertisements for party clowns and birthday packages. (See Fig. 1.)

3

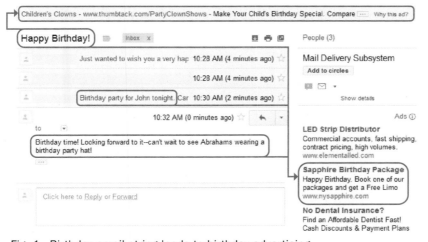

Fig. 1. Birthday email string leads to birthday advertising

Advertisers pay social networking sites to do something similar, which is why users might have noticed that section of "sponsors" to the right of your Facebook homepage. Everything public on a typical person's profile page—their age, relationship status, favorite music, education history—is available to marketers (for a price), so they can send their ads to specific people. 4

In this way, Facebook, Google, and other digital service providers sell advertisers intimate data about us, while also attempting to convince us that all our personal data is safe. Most people have little to no idea how much data they give up when they get on the Internet. How would they? Facebook and Google constantly change their privacy policies, and the terms-of-service agreements are long legal documents written in a language which your everyday person doesn't have the time or energy to decipher. So they just check a box. 5

"What's the problem?" you might say. "I have nothing to hide from either the government or companies like Google and Facebook." But think about it for a few minutes: When researching a political science paper on alternate forms of government, will typing words like "anarchism" or "Marxism" into a search box set off warning signals at the NSA or trigger Google to send advertisements for *The Anarchist's Handbook* (which might set off warning signals)? To honestly express ourselves, we need privacy. But less and less is there any kind of space for it online, where most of us read, write, and communicate. There needs to be some space online where all our activity is not recorded and sold (or taken by government agencies). But unless more rules and regulations are put in place to govern the behavior of Internet service providers and governmental data miners, privacy will become a thing of the past, and people will forget that they are not just consumers, but also citizens with rights, like the right to privacy.

ANALYZING THE REVISION

1. **Revision** Identify the major revisions that Wilson made from the earlier draft in Chapter 7. Explain why you think she made the changes she did. Are there other changes she could have made to make the final draft even better?

2. **Introduction and Conclusion** Examine Wilson's introduction and conclusion. In what ways are they more effective than the introduction and conclusion in her first draft? What additional improvements could she make?

3. **Details** Choose one paragraph, and compare the details provided in it with those in the corresponding paragraph of the first draft. Which added details are particularly effective, and why?

4. **Tone** Consider the differences in tone between Wilson's first draft and her revised draft. What changes affected her tone? (List three.) Given that she was writing this essay for a college course and that her instructor was her main audience, how effective is the tone of the revised essay?

WORKING TOGETHER

In groups of two or three classmates, use the questions below to analyze two paragraphs from the essay "The New Marshmallow Test: Students Can't Resist Multitasking" (p. 3) or another essay.

- What is the topic sentence of each paragraph?
- How are the paragraphs organized?
- What transitions does the author use in the paragraphs?
- What action verbs (if any) does the author use in the paragraphs? (Give an example from each paragraph.)
- Does the author use descriptive language (language that appeals to the senses)? If so, give an example of such language in each paragraph.

Be prepared to share your responses with the rest of the class.

ARE YOUR SENTENCES CONCISE?

Concise sentences convey their meaning in as few words as possible. Use the following suggestions to make your sentences concise.

1. Avoid wordy expressions. Omit words and phrases that contribute little or no meaning. If a sentence is clear without a particular phrase or if the phrase can be replaced by a more direct word or phrase, take it out or replace it:

- ~~In the near future,~~ another revolution in computer technology is bound to occur. *soon.*

- ~~In light of the fact that~~ computer technology changes ~~every month or so,~~ *monthly* *Since* software upgrades are ~~what everybody has to do.~~ *necessary*

2. Eliminate redundancy. Look for places where you have repeated an idea unnecessarily by using different words that have the same meaning:

- ~~My decision to choose~~ accounting as my major will lead to steady, rewarding employment. *Choosing*

- Teenagers use slang to establish ~~who they are and what~~ their identity ~~is.~~

3. Eliminate unnecessary sentence openings. Look for words you have expressed indirectly or tentatively. As you revise, edit to make them more direct:

- ~~It is my opinion that~~ fast-food restaurants should post nutritional information for each menu item. *F*

- ~~Many people would agree that~~ selecting nutritious snacks is a priority for health-conscious people. *S*

An **adverb** modifies a verb, an adjective, or another adverb.

4. Eliminate unnecessary adverbs. Using too many **adverbs** can weaken your writing. Adverbs such as *extremely*, *really*, and *very* add nothing and can weaken the words they modify. Notice that the following sentence is stronger without the adverb:

- The journalist was ~~very~~ elated when he learned that he had won a Pulitzer Prize.

Other adverbs, such as *somewhat*, *rather*, and *quite* also add little or no meaning and are often unnecessary.

- The college president was ~~quite~~ disturbed by the findings of the Presidential Panel on Sex Equity.

5. Eliminate unnecessary phrases and clauses. Wordy phrases and clauses make it difficult for readers to find and understand the main point of your sentence. This problem often occurs when you use too many **prepositional phrases** and clauses that begin with *who*, *which*, or *that*.

- The complaints ~~of students~~ ^{students} ~~in the college~~ encouraged the dean to create additional parking spaces.

- The ~~teenagers who were~~ ^{teenage} mall walkers disagreed with the editorial ~~in the newspaper that supported the~~ ^{newspaper} ^{supporting} shopping mall regulations.

6. Avoid weak verb-noun combinations. Weak verb-noun combinations such as *wrote a draft* instead of *drafted* or *made a change* instead of *changed* tend to make sentences wordy.

- The attorney ~~made an assessment of~~ ^{assessed} the company's liability in the accident.

- The professor ~~gave a lecture~~ ^{lectured} on Asian American relations.

> A **prepositional phrase** is a group of words that begins with a preposition and includes the object or objects of the preposition and all their modifiers: *above the low wooden table.*

EXERCISE 10.1

Edit the following sentences to make them concise.

1. Due to the fact that Professor Wu assigned twenty-five math problems for tomorrow, I am forced to make the decision to miss this evening's lecture to be given by the vice president of the United States.
2. In many cases, workers are forced to use old equipment that needs replacing despite the fact that equipment malfunctions cost the company more than the price of new machines.
3. Miley Cyrus is one of the best examples of an entertainment celebrity being given too much publicity.
4. The president of Warehouse Industries has the ability and power to decide who should and who should not be hired and who should and who should not be fired.
5. The soccer league's sponsor, as a matter of fact, purchased league jerseys for the purpose of advertisement and publicity.

ARE YOUR SENTENCES VARIED?

Sentences that are varied will help hold your reader's interest and make your writing flow more smoothly. Vary the type, length, and pattern of your sentences.

How to vary sentence type There are four types of sentences: *simple, compound, complex,* and *compound-complex.* Each type consists of one or more clauses. A **clause** is a group of words with both a subject and a verb. There are two types of clauses:
- An **independent clause** can stand alone as a complete sentence.
- A **dependent clause** cannot stand alone as a complete sentence. It begins with a subordinating conjunction (for example, *because* or *although*) or a relative pronoun (for example, *when, which,* or *that*).

A brief summary of each sentence type and its clauses appears in Table 10.1.

TABLE 10.1 Sentence Types

Sentence Type	Clauses	Example
Simple	One independent clause and no dependent clauses	Credit-card fraud is increasing in the United States.
Compound	Two or more independent clauses and no dependent clauses	Credit-card fraud is increasing in the United States; it is a violation of financial privacy.
Complex	One or more dependent clauses and one independent clause	Because credit-card fraud is increasing in America, consumers must become more cautious.
Compound-complex	One or more dependent clauses and two or more independent clauses	Because credit-card fraud is increasing in America, consumers must be cautious, and retailers must take steps to protect consumers.

Use the following suggestions to vary your sentence types.

1. Use simple sentences for emphasis and clarity. A **simple sentence** contains only one independent clause, but it is not necessarily short. It can have more than one subject, more than one verb, and several modifiers.

- Both retailers and consumers have and must exercise the responsibility to curtail fraud by reporting suspicious use of credit cards.

A short, simple sentence can be used to emphasize an important point or to make a dramatic statement.

- Credit-card fraud is rampant.

If you use too many simple sentences, however, your writing will sound choppy and disjointed.

DISJOINTED	It was a cold, drizzly spring morning. I was driving to school. A teenage hitchhiker stood alongside the road. He seemed distraught.
BETTER	I was driving to school on a cold, drizzly spring morning when I saw a teenage hitchhiker standing alongside the road. He seemed distraught.

2. Use compound sentences to show relationships among equally important ideas. A **compound sentence** consists of two or more independent clauses joined in one of the following ways:

- With a comma and **coordinating conjunction**:

  - Leon asked a question, *and* the whole class was surprised.

- With a semicolon:

  - Graffiti had been scrawled on the subway walls; passersby ignored it.

- With a semicolon and a **conjunctive adverb**:

  - Each year thousands of children are adopted; *consequently*, adoption service agencies have increased in number.

- With a **correlative conjunction**:

  - *Either* the jury will reach a verdict tonight, *or* it will recess until Monday morning.

Notice that in each example, both clauses are equally important and receive equal emphasis.

You can also use compound sentences to explain *how* equally important ideas are related. For example, you can use different coordinating conjunctions to show the relationship between two important related ideas. (See Table 10.2.)

Coordinating conjunctions (*and, but, or, nor, for, so, yet*) connect sentence elements that are of equal importance.

A **conjunctive adverb** is a word (such as *also, however,* or *still*) that links two independent clauses.

A **correlative conjunction** is a word pair (such as *not only . . . but also*) that works together to join elements within a sentence.

TABLE 10.2 Selecting Coordinating Conjunctions to Convey Relationships

Coordinating Conjunction	Relationship	Example
and	Additional information	The three teenage vandals were apprehended, *and* their parents were required to pay damages.
but, yet	Contrast or opposition	No one wants to pay more taxes, *yet* taxes are necessary to support vital public services.
for, so	Causes or effects	Text messages can disrupt a student's concentration, *so* turning your cell phone off in class is essential to learning.
or, nor	Choices or options	Quebec may become a separate country, *or* it may settle its differences with the Canadian government.

3. Use complex sentences to show that one or more ideas are less important than (or subordinate to) another idea. A **complex sentence** consists of one independent clause and at least one dependent clause. Either type of clause may come first. When the dependent clause comes first, it is usually followed by a comma. When the independent clause comes first, a comma is usually not used.

- Because the dam broke, the village flooded.

- The village flooded because the dam broke.

In the preceding sentences, the main point is that the village flooded. The dependent clause explains *why* the flood happened. A dependent clause often begins with a *subordinating conjunction* that indicates how the less important (dependent) idea is related to the more important (independent) idea. Table 10.3 lists some subordinating conjunctions and the relationships they suggest.

TABLE 10.3 Selecting Subordinating Conjunctions to Convey Relationships

Subordinating Conjunction	Relationship	Example
as, as far as, as soon as, as if, as though, although, even though, even if, in order to	Circumstance	*Even though* cable television has expanded, it is still unavailable in some rural areas.
because, since, so that	Causes or effects	*Because* the movie industry has changed, the way theaters are built has changed.
before, after, while, until, when	Time	*When* prices rise, demand falls.
whether, if, unless, even if	Condition	More people will purchase hybrid cars *if* these cars become less expensive.

Dependent clauses can also begin with a relative pronoun (*that, who, which*).

- Many medical doctors *who are affiliated with a teaching hospital* use interns in their practices.

To see how complex sentences can improve your writing, study the following two paragraphs:

ORIGINAL

Monotonous use of simple and compound sentences

Are you one of the many people who has tried to quit smoking? Well, don't give up trying. Help is here in the form of a nonprescription drug. A new nicotine patch has been developed. This patch will help you quit gradually. That way, you will experience less severe withdrawal symptoms. Quitting will be easier than ever before, but you need to be psychologically ready to quit smoking. Otherwise, you may not be successful.

REVISED

If you are one of the many people who has tried to quit smoking, don't give up trying. Help is now here in the form of a nonprescription nicotine patch, which has been developed to help you quit gradually. Because you experience less severe withdrawal symptoms, quitting is easier than ever before. However, for this patch to be successful, you need to be psychologically ready to quit.

Varied sentence types convey relationship among ideas

4. Use compound-complex sentences occasionally to express complicated relationships. A **compound-complex sentence** contains one or more dependent clauses and two or more independent clauses.

- If you expect to study medicine, you must take courses in biology and chemistry, and you must prepare for four more years of study after college.

Use compound-complex sentences sparingly. When overused, they make your writing hard to follow.

> **EXERCISE 10.2**

Combine each of the following sentence pairs into a single compound or complex sentence.

1. A day-care center may look respectable. Parents assume a day-care center is safe and run well.
2. In some states, the training required to become a day-care worker is minimal. On-the-job supervision and evaluation of day-care workers are infrequent.
3. Restaurants are often fined or shut down for minor hygiene violations. Day-care centers are rarely fined or closed down for hygiene violations.
4. More and more mothers have entered the workforce. The need for quality day care has increased dramatically.
5. Naturally, day-care workers provide emotional support for children. Few day-care workers are trained to provide intellectual stimulation.

How to vary sentence length If you vary sentence type, you often automatically vary sentence length as well. Simple sentences tend to be short, while compound and complex sentences tend to be longer. Compound-complex sentences tend to be the longest.

You can use sentence length to achieve a specific effect: Short sentences tend to be sharp and emphatic; they move ideas along quickly, creating a fast-paced essay. In the following example, a series of short sentences creates a dramatic pace:

- The jurors had little to debate. The incriminating evidence was clear and incontrovertible. The jury announced its verdict with astonishing speed.

Longer sentences, in contrast, move the reader more slowly through the essay. Notice that the lengthy sentence in this example suggests a leisurely, unhurried pace:

- While standing in line, impatient to ride the antique steam-powered train, the child begins to imagine how the train will crawl deliberately, endlessly, along the tracks, slowly gathering speed as it spews grayish steam and emits hissing noises.

How to vary sentence pattern   A sentence is usually made up of one or more subjects, verbs, and modifiers. **Modifiers** are words (adjectives or adverbs), phrases, or clauses that describe or limit another part of the sentence (a noun, pronoun, verb, phrase, or clause). Here are some examples of modifiers in sentences.

WORDS AS MODIFIERS	The *empty* classroom was unlocked. [adjective]
	The office runs *smoothly*. [adverb]
PHRASES AS MODIFIERS	The student *in the back* raised his hand.
	Schools should not have the right *to mandate community service*.
CLAUSES AS MODIFIERS	The baseball *that flew into the stands* was caught by a fan.
	When the exam was over, I knew I had earned an A.

As you can see, the placement of modifiers may vary, depending on the pattern of the sentence.

1. Modifier last: subject-verb-modifier.   The main message (expressed in the subject and verb) comes first, followed by information that clarifies or explains the message.

- ⌐— subject —⌐ ⌐ verb ⌐ ⌐— modifier —⌐
- The instructor walked into the room.

In some cases, a string of modifiers follows the subject and verb.

- ⌐— subject —⌐ ⌐— verb —⌐   ⌐— modifier —⌐
- The salesperson demonstrated the word-processing software, creating and deleting files, moving text, creating directories, and formatting tables.

2. Modifier first: modifier-subject-verb (periodic sentences).   Information in the modifier precedes the main message, elaborating the main message but slowing the overall pace. The emphasis is on the main message at the end of the sentence.

- ⌐—————— modifier ——————⌐ ⌐ subject ⌐verb⌐
- Tired and depressed from hours of work, the divers left the scene of the accident.

Use periodic sentences sparingly: Too many will make your writing sound stiff and unnatural.

3. Modifier in the middle: subject-modifier-verb. The modifier interrupts the main message and tends to slow the pace of the sentence. The emphasis is on the subject because it comes first in the sentence.

- ┌── subject ──┐ ┌─────── modifier ───────┐┌ verb ┐
  The paramedic, trained and experienced in water rescue, was first on the scene of the boating accident.

Avoid placing too many modifiers between the subject and verb in a sentence. Doing so may cause your reader to miss the sentence's key idea.

4. Modifiers used throughout.

- ┌──────── modifier ────────┐┌──── subject ────┐
  Because human organs are in short supply, awarding an organ transplant,
  ┌──── modifier ────┐┌── verb ──┐
  especially hearts and kidneys, to patients has become a controversial issue,
  ┌──────── modifier ────────┐
  requiring difficult medical and ethical decisions.

By varying the order of subjects, verbs, and modifiers, you can give emphasis where it is needed as well as vary sentence patterns as shown in the paragraphs that follow.

ORIGINAL

Theme parks are growing in number and popularity. Theme parks have a single purpose — to provide family entertainment centered around high-action activities. The most famous theme parks are Disney World and Disneyland. They serve as models for other, smaller parks. Theme parks always have amusement rides. Theme parks can offer other activities such as swimming. Theme parks will probably continue to be popular.

Monotonous use of same subject-verb-modifier pattern

REVISED

Theme parks are growing in number and popularity. Offering high-action activities, theme parks fulfill a single purpose — to provide family entertainment. The most famous parks, Disney World and Disneyland, serve as models for other, smaller parks. Parks always offer amusement rides, which appeal to both children and adults. Added attractions such as swimming, water slides, and boat rides provide thrills and recreation. Because of their family focus, theme parks are likely to grow in popularity.

Ideas come alive through use of varied sentence patterns

EXERCISE 10.3

Add modifiers to the following sentences to create varied sentence patterns.

1. The divers jumped into the chilly waters.
2. The beach was closed because of pollution.

3. Coffee-flavored drinks are becoming popular.
4. The dorm was crowded and noisy.
5. The exam was more challenging than we expected.

ARE YOUR SENTENCES PARALLEL IN STRUCTURE?

Parallelism means that similar ideas in a sentence are expressed in similar grammatical form. It means balancing words with words, phrases with phrases, and clauses with clauses. Parallel sentences flow smoothly and make your thoughts easy to follow. Study the following sentence pairs. Which sentence in each pair is easier to read?

- The horse was large, had a bony frame, and it was friendly.

- The horse was large, bony, and friendly.

- Maria enjoys swimming and sailboats.

- Maria enjoys swimming and sailing.

In each pair, the second sentence sounds better because it is balanced grammatically. *Large*, *bony*, and *friendly* are all adjectives. *Swimming* and *sailing* are nouns ending in *-ing*. The following sentence elements should be parallel in structure.

1. **Nouns in a series**
   - A thesis statement ~~that is clear,~~ *clear* strong supporting paragraphs, and ~~a~~ *an interesting* conclusion ~~that should be interesting~~ are all elements of a well-written essay.

2. **Adjectives in a series**
   - The concertgoers were rowdy and ~~making a great deal of noise.~~ *noisy.*

3. **Verbs in a series**
   - The sports fans jumped and ~~were applauding.~~ *applauded.*

4. **Phrases and clauses within a sentence**
   - The parents who supervised the new playground were pleased ~~about~~ *that* the preschoolers ~~playing~~ *played* congenially and that everyone enjoyed the sandbox.

5. **Items being compared**
   - It is usually better to study for an exam over a period of time than ~~cramming~~ *to cram* the night before.

EXERCISE 10.4

Edit the following sentences to eliminate problems with parallelism.

1. The biology student spent Saturday morning reviewing his weekly textbook assignments, writing a research report, and with lab reports.
2. The career counselor advised Althea to take several math courses and that she should also register for at least one computer course.
3. Three reasons for the popularity of fast-food restaurants are that they are efficient, offer reasonable prices, and most people like the food they serve.
4. Driving to Boston is as expensive as it is to take the train.
5. While at a stop sign, it is important first to look both ways and then proceeding with caution is wise.

DO YOUR SENTENCES HAVE STRONG, ACTIVE VERBS?

Strong, active verbs make your writing lively and vivid. By contrast, *to be* verbs (*is, was, were, has been,* and so on) and other **linking verbs** (*feels, became, seems, appears*) — which connect a noun or pronoun to words that describe it — can make your writing sound dull. Linking verbs often contribute little meaning to a sentence. Whenever possible, use stronger, more active verbs.

"TO BE" VERB	The puppy *was* afraid of thunder.
ACTION VERBS	The puppy *whimpered* and *quivered* during the thunderstorm.
LINKING VERB	The child *looked* frightened as she boarded the bus for her first day of kindergarten.
ACTION VERBS	The child *trembled* and *clung* to her sister as she boarded the bus for her first day of kindergarten.

To strengthen your writing, use active verbs rather than passive verbs as much as possible. A **passive verb** is a form of the verb *to be* combined with a past participle (*killed, chosen, elected*). In a sentence with a passive verb, the subject does not perform the action of the verb but instead receives the action. By contrast, in a sentence with an **active verb**, the subject performs the action.

PASSIVE	It *was claimed* by the cyclist that the motorist failed to yield the right of way.
ACTIVE	The cyclist *claimed* that the motorist failed to yield the right of way.

Notice that the first sentence emphasizes the action of claiming, not the person who made the claim. In the second sentence, the person who made the claim is the subject.

Unless you decide deliberately to deemphasize the subject, try to avoid using passive verbs. On occasion, you may need to use passive verbs, however, to emphasize the object or person receiving the action.

For more about possible problems with using passive voice, see p. 85.

- The Johnsons' house *was destroyed* by the flood.

macmillanhighered.com/successfulwriting
LearningCurve > Active and Passive Voice

Passive verbs may also be appropriate if you do not know or choose not to reveal who performed an action. Journalists often use passive verbs for this reason.

- It *was confirmed* late Tuesday that Senator Kraemer is resigning.

> **EXERCISE 10.5**

Edit the following sentences by changing passive verbs to active ones, adding a subject when necessary.

1. Songs about peace were composed by folk singers in the 1960s.
2. The exam was thought to be difficult because it covered thirteen chapters.
3. For water conservation, it is recommended that low-water-consumption dishwashers be purchased.
4. The new satellite center was opened by the university so that students could attend classes nearer their homes.
5. In aggressive telemarketing sales calls, the consumer is urged by the caller to make an immediate decision before prices change.

> **Essay in Progress 1**
> For your essay in progress (the one you worked on in Chapters 7–9) or any essay you are working on, evaluate and edit your sentences.

ANALYZING YOUR WORD CHOICE

Each word in your essay contributes to your essay's meaning. Consequently, when you are revising, be sure to analyze your word choice, or **diction**. The words you choose should suit your purpose, audience, tone, and genre. This section describes four aspects of word choice to consider as you evaluate and revise your essay.

1. Tone and level of diction
2. Word connotations
3. Concrete and specific language
4. Figures of speech

ARE YOUR TONE AND LEVEL OF DICTION APPROPRIATE?

Imagine that as a technician at a computer software company, you discover a time-saving shortcut for installing the company's best-selling software program. Your supervisor asks you to describe your discovery and how it works for two audiences—your fellow technicians at the company and customers who might purchase the program. Would you say the same thing in the same way? Definitely not. Your writing would differ not only in content but also in tone and level of diction. The writing addressed to the other technicians would be technical and concise, explaining how to use the shortcut and why it works. The writing directed to customers would praise the discovery, mention the time customers will save, and explain in nontechnical terms how to use the shortcut.

Tone refers to how you sound to your readers. Your word choice should be consistent with your tone. When writing to the technicians, you would use a direct, matter-of-fact tone. When writing to the customers, your tone would be enthusiastic. There are three common **levels of diction**: formal, popular, and informal.

For more about tone, see p. 81.

Formal diction The **formal** level of diction is serious and dignified. Think of it as the kind of language that judges use in interpreting laws, presidents employ when greeting foreign dignitaries, or speakers choose for commencement addresses. Formal diction is often written in the third person, tends to include long sentences and multisyllabic words, and contains no slang or contractions. It has a slow, rhythmic flow and an authoritative, distant, and impersonal tone. Here is an example taken from *The Federalist, No. 51*, a political tract written by James Madison in 1788 to explain constitutional theory:

> It is of great importance in a republic, not only to guard the society against the oppression of its rulers, but to guard one part of the society against the injustice of the other part. Different interests necessarily exist in different classes of citizens. If a majority be united by a common interest, the rights of the minority will be insecure.

Formal diction is also used in scholarly publications, operation manuals, and most academic fields. Notice in the following excerpt from a chemistry textbook that the language is concise, exact, and marked by specialized terms, called *jargon*, used within the particular field of study. The examples of jargon are in italics.

> A *catalyst* is classified as *homogeneous* if it is present in the same *phase* as that of the *reactants*. For reactants that are *gases*, a *homogeneous catalyst* is also a *gas*.
>
> Atkins and Perkins, *Chemistry: Molecules, Matter, and Change*

Popular diction **Popular**, or casual, diction is common in magazines and newspapers. It sounds more conversational and personal than formal diction. In popular diction, sentences tend to be shorter and less varied than in formal diction. The first person (*I, me, mine, we*) or second person (*you, your*) may be used. Consider this example taken from a popular arts magazine, *Paste Magazine*.

> "Concert for George" pays tribute to not only one of the greatest musicians in history, but one of the freakin' Beatles. The performance took place in honor of the first anniversary of George Harrison's death, with Eric Clapton and Jeff Lynne serving as musical directors.
>
> Wyndham Wyeth, "The 11 Best Concert Films"

Informal diction **Informal** diction, also known as *colloquial language*, is the language of everyday speech and conversation. It is friendly and casual. Contractions (*wasn't, I'll*), slang expressions (*selfie, YOLO, tat*), sentence fragments, and first-person and second-person pronouns are all common. Informal diction should not be used in essays and academic writing, except when it is part of a quotation or a block of dialogue. Also inappropriate for essays and academic writing is the use of language shortcuts typically used in email and texting. These include abbreviations (*u* for *you, r* for *are*) and emoticons (☺).

Here is an example of informal diction. Notice the use of the first person, slang expressions, and a loose sentence structure.

Contractions are acceptable

> This guy in my history class is a psycho. He doesn't let anybody talk but him. I mean, this guy interrupts all the time. Never raises his hand. He drives us nuts—what a loser.

Diction in academic writing When you write academic papers, essays, and exams, you should use formal diction and avoid flowery or wordy language. Here are some guidelines.

- Use the third person (*he, she, it*) rather than the first person (*I, we*), unless you are expressing a personal opinion.
- Use standard vocabulary, not slang or a regional or an ethnic dialect.
- Use correct grammar, spelling, and punctuation.
- Aim for a clear, direct, and forthright tone.

One of the most common mistakes students make in academic writing is trying too hard to sound "academic." Be sure to avoid writing stiff, overly formal sentences, using big words just for the sake of it, and expressing ideas indirectly.

INAPPROPRIATE DICTION

Language is stiff, pompous

> Who among us would be so bold as to venture to deny that inequities are rampant in our ailing health- and medical-care system? People of multiethnic composition overwhelmingly receive health care that is not only beneath the standard one would expect, but even in some cases threatening to their very lives. An abundance of research studies and clinical trials prove beyond a doubt that a person of non-European descent residing in the United States of America cannot rely on doctors, nurses, physician assistants, nurse practitioners, and other health-care workers to provide treatment free of invidious discrimination.

REVISED DICTION

Language is formal but clear

> Who can deny that inequities are common in our ailing medical care system? Racial and ethnic minorities receive health care that is substandard and in some cases life-threatening. Many research studies and clinical trials demonstrate that minorities in the United States cannot rely on doctors, nurses, physician assistants, nurse practitioners, and other health-care workers to provide unbiased treatment.

:e: **macmillanhighered.com/successfulwriting**
LearningCurve > Appropriate Language

EXERCISE 10.6

Revise the following informal statement by giving it a more formal level of diction.

> It hadn't occurred to me that I might be exercising wrong, though I suppose the signs were there. I would drag myself to the gym semi-regularly and go through the motions of walking (sometimes jogging) on the treadmill and doing light weight training. But I rarely broke a sweat. I just didn't have the energy. "Just doing it" wasn't cutting it. My body wasn't improving. In fact, certain areas were getting bigger, overly muscular. I needed someone to kick my butt—and reduce it too.
>
> <div align="right">Wendy Schmid, "Roped In," <i>Vogue</i></div>

DO YOU USE WORDS WITH APPROPRIATE CONNOTATIONS?

Many words have two levels of meaning—a denotative meaning and a connotative meaning. A word's **denotation** is its precise dictionary definition. For example, the denotative meaning of the word *mother* is "female parent." A word's **connotation** is the collection of feelings and attitudes the word evokes—its emotional colorings or shades of meaning. A word's connotation may vary from one person to another. One common connotation of *mother* is a warm, caring person. Some people, however, may think of a mother as someone with strong authoritarian control. Similarly, the phrase *horror films* may conjure up memories of scary but fun-filled evenings for some people and terrifying experiences for others.

Since the connotations of words can elicit a wide range of responses, be sure the words you choose convey only the meanings you intend. In each pair of words that follows, notice that the two words have a similar denotation but different connotations.

For more about analyzing connotative meanings, see p. 79.

artificial/fake	firm/stubborn	lasting/endless

EXERCISE 10.7

Describe the different connotations of the three words in each group of words.

1. crowd/mob/gathering
2. proverb/motto/saying
3. prudent/penny-pinching/frugal
4. token/gift/keepsake
5. display/show/expose

DO YOU USE CONCRETE LANGUAGE?

Specific words convey much more information than general words. The following examples show how you might move from general to specific word choices.

General	Less General	More Specific	Specific
store	department store	Sears	Sears at the Galleria Mall
music	popular music	country rock music	Taylor Swift's "Eyes Open"

Concrete words add life and meaning to your writing. In each of the following sentence pairs, notice how the underlined words in the first sentence provide little information, whereas those in the second sentence provide interesting details.

GENERAL	Our <u>vacation</u> was <u>great fun</u>.
CONCRETE	Our <u>rafting trip</u> was filled with <u>adventure</u>.
GENERAL	The <u>red and white flowers</u> were blooming in our yard.
CONCRETE	<u>Crimson and white petunias</u> were blooming in our yard.

Suppose you are writing about a shopping mall that has outlived its usefulness. Instead of saying "a number of stores were unoccupied, and those that were still in business were shabby," you could describe the mall in concrete, specific terms that would enable your readers to visualize it:

The vacant storefronts with "For Rent" signs plastered across the glass, the half-empty racks in the stores that were still open, and the empty corridors suggested that the mall was soon to close.

> **EXERCISE 10.8**

Revise the following sentences by adding concrete, specific details.

1. The book I took on vacation was exciting reading.
2. The students watched as the instructor entered the lecture hall.
3. The vase in the museum was an antique.
4. At the crime scene, the reporter questioned the witnesses.
5. Although the shop was closed, we expected someone to return at any moment.

DO YOU USE FRESH, APPROPRIATE FIGURES OF SPEECH?

A **figure of speech** is a word or phrase that makes sense imaginatively or creatively but not literally. For example, if you say "the movie was *a roller coaster ride,*" you do not mean the movie was an actual ride. Rather, you mean it was thrilling, just like a ride on a roller coaster. This figure of speech, like many others, compares two seemingly unlike objects or situations by finding one point of similarity.

Fresh and imaginative figures of speech can help you create vivid images for your readers. However, overused figures of speech can detract from your essay. Be sure to avoid **clichés** (trite or overused expressions) such as *blind as a bat, green with envy, bite the bullet,* or *sick as a dog.*

Three common figures of speech are simile, metaphor, and personification. A **simile** uses words such as *like* or *as* to make a direct comparison of two unlike things.

The child acts *like a tiger.*

The noise in a crowded high school cafeteria is as deafening *as a caucus of crows.*

A **metaphor** also compares unlike things but does not use *like* or *as*. Instead, the comparison is implied.

> That child is a tiger.

> If you're born in America with black skin, you're born in prison.
>
> Malcolm X, "Interview"

Personification describes an idea or object by giving it human qualities.

> A sailboat devours money.

In this example, the ability to eat is ascribed to an inanimate object, the sailboat.

When you edit an essay, look for and eliminate overused figures of speech, replacing them with creative, fresh images. If you have not used any figures of speech, look for descriptions that could be improved by using a simile, a metaphor, or personification.

For more on figures of speech, see Chapter 13, p. 268.

EXERCISE 10.9

Invent fresh figures of speech for two items in the following list.

1. Parents of a newborn baby
2. A lengthy supermarket line or a traffic jam
3. A relative's old refrigerator
4. A man and woman obviously in love
5. Your team's star quarterback or important player

EVALUATING YOUR WORD CHOICE

Use Figure 10.2 (p. 212) to help you evaluate your word choice. If you have difficulty identifying which words to revise, ask a classmate or friend to evaluate your essay by using the flowchart as a guide and marking any words that may need revision.

Essay in Progress 2

For the essay you worked on in Essay in Progress 1, use Figure 10.2 to evaluate and edit your word choice.

SUGGESTIONS FOR PROOFREADING

When you are satisfied with your edited words and sentences, you are ready for the final step of the writing process—*proofreading*. By proofreading, you make sure your essay is error free and presented in acceptable manuscript format. Your goals are to catch and correct surface errors—such as errors in grammar, punctuation, spelling, and mechanics—as well as keyboarding or typographical errors. An essay that is free of surface errors gives readers a favorable impression of the essay and of you as its writer.

FIGURE 10.2 Flowchart for Evaluating Your Word Choice

QUESTIONS

1. Have you used an appropriate tone and level of diction? (To find out, imagine that you are talking to a member of your audience. Look for and circle any words or phrases that seem too formal or too informal, especially any slang or jargon.)

 NO

REVISION STRATEGIES

· Replace circled words and phrases with language appropriate for your audience.

 YES

2. Have you chosen words with appropriate connotations? (To find out, look for and circle any words whose connotations do not fit your intended meaning and whose connotations you are unsure of.)

 NO

· Check a dictionary, if necessary, and replace circled words with more appropriate words.

 YES

3. Is your language concrete and specific? (To find out, look for and circle any general, vague words that contribute little or no meaning.)

 NO

· Replace circled words with concrete, specific words.

 YES

4. Have you used fresh, appropriate figures of speech? (To find out, look for and underline any expressions that sound trite or overused.)

NO

· Replace the underlined expressions with fresh and appropriate figures of speech.

Spotting errors is easier when working with a clean, printed copy, so start with a fresh printout. Do not attempt to work with a previously marked-up copy or on a computer screen. Be sure to double-space the copy to allow room to mark corrections between lines.

Use the following suggestions to produce an error-free essay.

1. Review your paper once for each type of error. Because it is difficult to spot all types of surface errors simultaneously, read your essay several times, each time focusing on *one* error type—errors in spelling, punctuation, grammar, mechanics, and so on. Then read once more, focusing on just the errors you make most often. (Keep a list of your most common errors in your writing journal, and update it as each assignment is returned.)

2. **Read your essay backward, from the last sentence to the first.** Reading in this way will help you spot errors without being distracted by the flow of ideas.

3. **Use the spell-check and grammar-check functions cautiously.** The spell-check function can help you spot some—but not all—spelling and keyboarding errors. For example, it cannot detect the difference in meaning between *there* and *their* or *to* and *too*. Similarly, the grammar-check function can identify only certain kinds of errors and is not a reliable substitute for a careful proofreading.

4. **Read your essay aloud.** By reading aloud slowly, you can catch certain errors that sound awkward, such as missing words, errors in verb tense, and errors in the singular or plural forms of nouns.

5. **Ask a classmate to proofread your paper.** Another reader may spot errors you have overlooked.

STUDENTS WRITE

Recall that Latrisha Wilson's essay, "No Place Left for Privacy," was developed, drafted, and revised in the Students Write sections of Chapters 6 to 9. Below is a body paragraph from Wilson's essay with her final editing and proofreading changes shown. The reasons for each change, identified by number, are noted in the margin. The final draft of Wilson's essay, with these changes incorporated into it, appears in Chapter 9 (pp. 190–92).

The NSA isn't the only organization ~~to be~~ spying on us another kind of surveillance, a ~~kind that~~ which doesn't always make top press, is the ~~kind of~~ eavesdropping that companies like Google, and other ~~companies~~ communication service providers regularly do on their users. Google software automatically scans the content of all Gmail for keywords and phrases that and they then must get sold or rented to other companies, because I regularly see targeted advertizements related to what they've written about: If I wish my friend "Happy Birthday!" I now see advertizements for party clowns, and birthday pack-ages. (See Fig. 1.)

1. Added transition
2. Edited for wordiness
3. Fixed run-on
4. Edited for repetition
5. Deleted unnecessary comma
6. Revised to make more specific
7. Revised to avoid 1st person (/)
8. Corrected misspelling

![e] **macmillanhighered.com/successfulwriting**
LearningCurve > Commas; Fragments; Run-Ons and Comma Splices; Subject-Verb Agreement

part three
Patterns of Development

© WILDLIFE GmbH/Alamy

11

An Introduction to Patterns of Development

Suppose your instructor asks you to write a paragraph about one or both of the photos on this page.

To write your paragraph, you had to decide on an approach to the topic that would be appropriate to your writing situation, your purpose, audience, genre, and medium. For example, if you wanted to write a blog post to express your thoughts and feelings to your friends, you might have chosen to tell a story about what the people in one of the photographs are doing or how they got there (*narration*). If you were writing an exam for your psychology instructor, you might have described the response to environmental cues (*process analysis*) or analyzed the differences among responses in the two settings (*comparison and contrast*).

© RIA-Novosti/The Image Works; © Carsten Peter/Getty

IN THIS CHAPTER YOU WILL LEARN TO

- recognize common patterns of development,
- identify patterns of development in essays that use more than one pattern, and
- write an essay using more than one pattern.

Many paragraphs and essays use specific **patterns of development** (also called **rhetorical modes**, or just **modes**) like narration, process analysis, and comparison or contrast, because they help the writer

To learn more about the writing situation, see Chapter 5, p. 113.

- devise a strong thesis or topic sentence,
- select appropriate evidence, and
- create a unified paragraph or essay.

The patterns also help readers understand by comparing something they know well with something unfamiliar or describing a place they've never been so that they can picture it, for example.

While some authors write essays that focus mainly on a single mode, many others create essays from paragraphs in a variety of patterns, choosing among the patterns that will best help them achieve their goals.

In Chapters 11 to 20, you will read and write essays that focus mainly on one mode. In this chapter, you will find one mixed-mode reading, and the chapters in Parts 3 and 4 also include a reading that uses a variety of patterns to supplement the main one. As you read these essays and write your own mixed-mode essay later in this chapter, think about how writers use patterns to achieve their goals.

AN OVERVIEW OF THE PATTERNS OF DEVELOPMENT

The most common patterns are:

- narration,
- description,
- illustration (or exemplification),
- process analysis,
- comparison and contrast,
- classification and division,
- definition,
- cause and effect, and
- argument.

NARRATION

Narration uses a sequence of events—a story—to make a point. The following excerpt from a narrative essay tells the story of one man's experience with the police.

EXAMPLE   Friday for me usually means a trip to the bank, errands, the gym, dinner, and then off to the theater. On this particular day, I decided to break my pattern of getting up and running right out of the house. Instead, I took my time, slowed my pace, and splurged by making strawberry pancakes. Before I knew it, it was 2:45; my bank closes at 3:30, leaving me less than 45 minutes to get to midtown Manhattan on the train. I was pressed for time but in a relaxed, blessed state of mind. When I walked through the lobby of my building, I noticed two light-skinned Hispanic men I'd never seen before. Not thinking much of it, I continued on to the vestibule, which is separated from the lobby by a locked door.

— Alton Fitzgerald White, "Right Place, Wrong Face" (para. 5, p. 234)

When to use it. Use narration when you want readers to learn something by experiencing an episode or sequence of events from your life. In the Writing Quick Start, you could use narration to tell a story of how the people in the photos got to their location. You might begin with their trip to the airport and end at the moment the photo was taken.

DESCRIPTION

Description uses words that appeal to the five senses to create a word-picture for readers. The following excerpt from a descriptive essay introduces readers to the kitchen of a busy diner, using specific details to emphasize how tightly everything is crammed in.

EXAMPLE The kitchen space I spend eight hours a day in is about the size of my one-room apartment, which is slightly larger than your <u>average prison cell</u>. Three people, and more on horribly busy days, work in that space, crammed in with four fryers, a massive grill, a griddle, an oven, a microwave, two refrigeration units with prep counters, bins of tortilla chips, a burning-hot steam table bigger than the grill, and vast tubs of bacon. If I put both arms out and rotated, I'd severely injure at least two people.

— Ted Sawchuck, "Heatstroke with a Side of Burn Cream" (para. 3, p. 283)

When to use it. Use description when you want to emphasize the sensory aspects of an object or experience. In the Writing Quick Start, you could use description to convey in detail what the winter landscape or the rain forest looked, smelled, or felt like.

ILLUSTRATION

Illustration uses examples to explain unfamiliar topics, concepts, or terms. In the following excerpt from an illustration essay, the author provides a specific example (*illustration*) to support his thesis that road rage represents a decline in civilized society.

EXAMPLE A most amazing example of driver rage occurred recently at the Manhattan end of the Lincoln Tunnel. We were four cars abreast, stopped at a traffic light. And there was no moving even when the light had changed. A bus had stopped in the cross traffic, blocking our paths: it was a normal-for-New-York-City gridlock. Perhaps impatient, perhaps late for important appointments, three of us nonetheless accepted what, after all, we could not alter. One, however, would not. He would not be helpless. He would go where he was going even if he couldn't get there. A Wall Street type in suit and tie, he got out of his car and strode toward the bus, rapping smartly on its doors. When they opened, he exchanged words with the driver. The doors folded shut. He then stepped in front of the bus, took hold of one of its large windshield wipers and broke it.

— Martin Gottfried, "Rambos of the Road" (para. 8, p. 308)

When to use it. Use illustration when you want to provide specific, sometimes extended, examples to support your thesis statement. In the Writing Quick Start, in an essay about how rain forests are threatened by development, you might provide examples of the plants and animals whose habitats are endangered.

PROCESS ANALYSIS

Process analysis explains step by step how something works, is done, or is made. In the following how-to essay, the writer describes the process of writing a second draft.

> **EXAMPLE**   The next day, I'd sit down, go through it all with a colored pen, take out everything I possibly could, find a new lead somewhere on the second page, figure out a kicky place to end it, and then write a second draft. It always turned out fine, sometimes even funny and weird and helpful. I'd go over it one more time and mail it in.
>
> — Anne Lamott, "Shitty First Drafts" (para. 8, p. 339)

When to use it. Use process analysis when you want to provide step-by-step instructions or a part-by-part analysis. In the Writing Quick Start, you might discuss rain forest exploration as a sport and provide instructions on how to prepare for a strenuous climb.

COMPARISON AND CONTRAST

Writers compare or contrast to examine closely what two things have in common or what their differences are. Many essays use both comparison and contrast. In the following excerpt from a comparison-contrast essay, the author compares the satirical newspaper *The Onion* with other newspapers.

> **EXAMPLE**   It's easy to see why readers connect with *The Onion*, and it's not just the jokes: Despite its "fake news" purview, it's an extremely honest publication. Most dailies, especially those in monopoly or near-monopoly markets, operate as if they're focused more on not offending readers (or advertisers) than on expressing a worldview

of any kind. The Onion takes the opposite approach. It delights in crapping on pieties and regularly publishes stories guaranteed to upset someone: "Christ Kills Two, Injures Seven, in Abortion-Clinic Attack." "Heroic PETA Commandos Kill 49, Save Rabbit." "Gay Pride Parade Sets Mainstream Acceptance of Gays Back 50 Years." There's no predictable ideology running through those headlines, just a desire to express some rude, blunt truth about the world.

> —Greg Beato, "Amusing Ourselves to Depth: Is *The Onion* Our Most Intelligent Newspaper?" (para. 9, p. 371)

When to use it. Use comparison and contrast to provide an in-depth analysis that explores the similarities and/or differences between two things. In the Writing Quick Start, there is opportunity to explore the differences between the two activities shown, but an essay that examines the similarities among participants might be just as revealing.

CLASSIFICATION AND DIVISION

Classification groups things into categories; division breaks a single item down into its component parts. In the following excerpt from a classification essay, a college instructor groups the types of excuses she receives into several categories (the family, the best friend, the evils of dorm life, the evils of technology, and the totally bizarre).

EXAMPLE   Taped to the door of my office is a cartoon that features a cat explaining to his feline teacher, "The dog ate my homework." It is intended as a gently humorous reminder to my students that I will not accept excuses for late work, and it, like the lengthy warning on my syllabus, has had absolutely no effect. With a show of energy and creativity that would be admirable if applied to the (missing) assignments in question, my students persist, week after week, semester after semester, year after year, in offering excuses about why their work is not ready. Those reasons fall into several broad categories: the family, the best friend, the evils of dorm life, the evils of technology, and the totally bizarre.

> —Carolyn Foster Segal, "The Dog Ate My Flash Drive, and Other Tales of Woe" (para. 1, p. 423)

When to use it. Use classification or division when you want to look closely at the subcategories or parts of a particular topic. In the Writing Quick Start, you might classify activities by seasons, pointing to the top photo as an example of a winter activity and the bottom photo as an example of a summer activity.

EXTENDED DEFINITION

An extended definition explains in detail how a term is used or differentiates among its shades of meaning. The following excerpt from an extended definition begins the process of explaining what the word *dude* means by showing how it is used and how its meaning has changed over time.

EXAMPLE   Originally meaning "old rags," a "dudesman" was a scarecrow. In the late 1800s, a "dude" was akin to a dandy, a meticulously dressed man, especially in the western United States. *Dude* became a slang term in the 1930s and 1940s among black zoot suiters and Mexican American pachucos. The term began its rise in the teenage lexicon with the 1982 movie *Fast Times at Ridgemont High*. Around the same time, it became an exclamation as well as a noun. Pronunciation purists say it should sound like "duhd"; "dood" is an alternative, but it is considered "uncool" or old.

—Mike Crissey, "Dude, Do You Know What You Just Said?" (para. 2, p. 439)

When to use it. Use an extended definition when you want to conduct a close analysis of a complicated word, phrase, or phenomenon. In the Writing Quick Start, you might use the photos as a jumping-off point to define the word *ecotourism*, which means environmentally friendly tourism that has limited impact on the land and local communities.

CAUSE AND EFFECT

Causes are the reasons that an event or phenomenon happens and effects are what happen because of the event or phenomenon. Often, causes and effects are discussed together. The following excerpt points to a single cause (a diet rich in vitamins, minerals, and fatty acids) leading to a single effect (psychological health).

EXAMPLE   The best way to curb aggression in prisons? Longer jail terms, maybe, or stricter security measures? How about more sports and exercise? Try fish oil. How can children enhance their learning abilities at school? A well-balanced diet and safe, stimulating classrooms are essential, but fish oil can provide an important extra boost. Is there a simple, natural way to improve mood and ward off depression? Yoga and meditation are great, but—you guessed it—fish oil can also help do the trick. A diet rich in vitamins, minerals, and fatty acids like omega-3 is the basis for physical well-being. Everybody knows that. But research increasingly suggests that these same ingredients are crucial to psychological health too. And that's a fact a lot of people seem to find hard to swallow.

—Juriaan Kamp, "Can Diet Help Stop Depression and Violence?" (para. 1, p. 485)

When to use it. Use cause and effect to show how one (or more) thing(s) leads to another or many other things. In the Writing Quick Start, you might use the bottom photo as inspiration for writing about what causes deforestation or what is lost as a result of it.

ARGUMENT

Writers use arguments to persuade readers to adopt (or at least to consider) their position on an issue. In the following excerpt from an argument essay, the author tries to persuade readers that the size of the tip does not correspond to the quality of service a customer receives. This is one reason that tipping, which is supposed to motivate wait staff to provide good service, should be abolished.

> **EXAMPLE** Tipping does not incentivize hard work. The factors that correlate most strongly to tip size have virtually nothing to do with the quality of service. Credit card tips are larger than cash tips. Large parties with sizable bills leave disproportionately small tips. We tip servers more if they tell us their names, touch us on the arm, or draw smiley faces on our checks. Quality of service has a laughably small impact on tip size. According to a 2000 study, a customer's assessment of the server's work only accounts for between 1 and 5 percent of the variation in tips at a restaurant.
>
> —Brian Palmer, "Tipping Is an Abomination" (para. 3, p. 511)

When to use it. Use argumentation when you are trying to convince your readers that your point of view is correct or when you want them to take action. In the Writing Quick Start, you might use the bottom photo to convince people to become more active in rain forest conservation and preservation efforts.

COMBINING THE PATTERNS

Some essays use only one major pattern, but many writers combine several patterns to engage their readers and support their ideas. For example, an essay may mainly tell a story (the primary pattern), but it may also include description and illustration (secondary patterns). The following excerpt is from an essay that mainly uses cause-and-effect but also uses several other patterns of development.

Narration: The writer tells the story of restaurant meals.

Description: The writer helps you picture the child's behavior.

Process: The writer explains how they proceeded through a meal.

Comparison-Contrast: The writer contrasts her child's behavior with that of French children.

1   We ate breakfast at the hotel, but we had to eat lunch and dinner at the little seafood restaurants around the old port. We quickly discovered that having two restaurant meals a day with a toddler deserved to be its own circle of hell.

2   Bean would take a brief interest in the food, but within minutes she was spilling salt shakers and tearing apart sugar packets. Then she demanded to be sprung from her high chair so she could dash around the restaurant and bolt dangerously toward the docks.

3   Our strategy was to finish the meal quickly. We ordered while being seated, then begged the server to rush out some bread and bring us our appetizers and main courses at the same time. While my husband took a few bites of fish, I made sure Bean didn't get kicked by a waiter or lost at sea. Then we switched. We left enormous, apologetic tips to compensate for the arc of torn napkins and calamari around the table.

4   After a few more harrowing restaurant visits, I started noticing that the French families around us didn't look like they were sharing our mealtime agony. Weirdly, they looked like they were on vacation. French toddlers were sitting contentedly

in their high chairs, waiting for their food, or eating fish and even vegetables. There was not shrieking or whining. And there was no debris around their tables.

—Pamela Druckerman, *Bringing Up Bébé*

WRITING AN ESSAY THAT COMBINES THE PATTERNS OF ORGANIZATION

Recognizing that many writers combine patterns, Chapters 12–21 offer not only detailed instructions on how to write an effective essay in each pattern but how to combine the patterns into a **mixed-mode** essay. Each of these chapters also offers readings that show multiple patterns at work in a single essay. Use the following guidelines, along with the detailed instructions on writing in each mode in the chapters that follow, to plan and write a mixed-mode essay.

A GUIDED WRITING ASSIGNMENT*
MULTIPLE PATTERNS OF ORGANIZATION

Prewriting

1 **Choose and narrow a topic, and select a main pattern of organization.**

Chapter 5 can help you narrow your topic. Many essays benefit from following **one dominant pattern** of organization. Select the major pattern of organization that best fits your **purpose**.

2 **Write a preliminary thesis, and generate details to support it.**

Chapter 6 can help with devising a thesis and generating details. You may also want to consult the chapter in Part 3 or 4 that corresponds to your main mode of development.

3 **Determine which secondary patterns will help you support your thesis.**

The idea-generating strategies from **Chapter 5**, especially using the modes of development, can help you flesh out your ideas with specific evidence. Be cautious about using too many patterns of organization, though, which can make your essay difficult to follow.

*The writing process is *recursive*; that is, you may find yourself revising as you draft or prewriting as you revise. This is especially true when writing on a computer. Your writing process may also differ from that of your classmates, depending on your preferred learning style.

4 **Prepare a graphic organizer or an outline of your essay.**

Make sure your graphic organizer or outline
- clearly indicates the essay's **organization** and each paragraph's **relationship to the thesis statement**, and
- includes only details that **support your thesis**.

The chapter in Part 3 or 4 that corresponds to your main mode of development can provide a model graphic organizer.

5 **Keep your purpose and audience in mind.**

Do not worry about grammar or spelling at this point. Instead, focus on the following:
- using **supporting details** that help you achieve your purpose with your readers,
- making sure your **introduction** and **conclusion signal your primary pattern** of organization, so readers know what to expect or experience a satisfying sense of closure,
- using **transitions** to signal that you are moving from one pattern to another, so readers can follow your train of thought.

6 **Evaluate your draft and revise as necessary.**

As you reread your essay, ask yourself questions like these.
- Have I **fully developed** my primary pattern?
- Have I **effectively used secondary patterns** to support my thesis?

Then ask a classmate or friend to read your essay and answer your questions. Refer to **Chapter 9** for help with revising, and use the **flowchart for revising essays** from **Chapters 12 to 21** that corresponds to your main pattern of development.

7 **Edit the words and sentences of your essay, and then proofread carefully.**

As you edit your essay, ask yourself questions like these.
- Are my sentences **concise**, **varied** (in type, length, and sentence pattern), and **parallel**?
- Do they use **strong active verbs**?
- Are my words at an appropriate **level of diction** for my readers?
- Do I use concrete language, with appropriate **connotations** and fresh **figures of speech**?

As you **proofread**, look for errors in **grammar**, **punctuation**, and **spelling**. Look for the kinds of errors you regularly make, and do not rely too heavily on spell- or grammar-checkers, which can lead you astray.

For additional help, refer to **Chapter 10**, "Editing Sentences and Words," and to the guided writing assignment in the chapter that corresponds to your main pattern of development.

In the following reading, note how the author effectively combines multiple patterns of organization.

Against Forgetting: Where Have All the Animals Gone?

DERRICK JENSEN

Derrick Jensen writes about environmental issues for a number of publications, including *Audubon* and *The Sun* magazine. He is the author of *Endgame* (2006), *Resistance against Empire* (2010), and *Truths among Us: Conversations on Building a New Culture* (2011). This article originally appeared in *Orion* (July/August 2013). According to the magazine's mission statement, "It is *Orion*'s fundamental conviction that humans are morally responsible for the world in which we live and that the individual comes to sense this responsibility as he or she develops a personal bond with nature." As you read, examine how the author combines patterns of development to persuade readers that declining baselines is a serious problem and convince them that something needs to be done about it.

1   Last night a host of nonhuman neighbors paid me a visit. First, two gray foxes sauntered up, including an older female who lost her tail to a leghold trap six or seven years ago. They trotted back into a thicker part of the forest, and a few minutes later a raccoon ambled forward. After he left I saw the two foxes again. Later, they went around the right side of a redwood tree as a black bear approached around the left. He sat on the porch for a while, and then walked off into the night. Then the foxes returned, hung out, and, when I looked away for a moment then looked back, they were gone. It wasn't too long before the bear returned to lie on the porch. After a brief nap, he went away. The raccoon came back and brought two friends. When they left the foxes returned, and after the foxes came the bear. The evening was like a French farce: As one character exited stage left, another entered stage right.

> **Narration:** Tells a story in chronological (time) order, to establish baseline
>
> **Description:** Uses concrete details to help readers picture animal parade

2   Although I see some of these nonhuman neighbors daily, I was entranced and delighted to see so many of them over the span of just one evening. I remained delighted until sometime the next day, when I remembered reading that, prior to conquest by the Europeans, people in this region could expect to see a grizzly bear every 15 minutes.

> **Comparison-contrast:** Contrasts number of animals today with number in the past

3   This phenomenon is something we all encounter daily, even if some of us rarely notice it. It happens often enough to have a name: declining baselines. The phrase describes the process of becoming accustomed to and accepting as

> **Definition:** Provides definition of key term to be used in his thesis/argument

Cause-effect: Explains a chain of causes and effects to explain declining baselines

normal worsening conditions. Along with normalization can come a forgetting that things were not always this way. And this can lead to further acceptance and further normalization, which leads to further amnesia, and so on. Meanwhile the world is killed, species by species, biome by biome. And we are happy when we see the ever-dwindling number of survivors.

Comparison-contrast: Contrasts number of animals today with number at various times in the past to dramatize declining

I've gone on the salmon-spawning tours that local environmentalists give, and I'm not the only person who by the end is openly weeping. If we're lucky, we see 15 fish. Prior to conquest there were so many fish the rivers were described as "black and roiling." And it's not just salmon. Only five years ago, whenever I'd pick up a piece of firewood, I'd have to take off a half-dozen sowbugs. It's taken me all winter this year to see as many. And I used to go on spider patrol before I took a shower, in order to remove them to safety before the deluge. I still go on spider patrol, but now it's mostly pro forma. The spiders are gone. My mother used to put up five hummingbird feeders, and the birds would fight over those. Now she puts up two, and as often as not the sugar ferments before anyone eats it. I used to routinely see bats in the summer. Last year I saw one.

Process analysis: Shows process of decline in songbird populations

Cause-effect: Shows causes of huge declines in songbird populations (effects)

You can transpose this story to wherever you live and whatever members of the nonhuman community live there with you. I was horrified a few years ago to read that many songbird populations on the Atlantic Seaboard have collapsed by up to 80 percent over the last 40 years. But, and this is precisely the point, I was even more horrified when I realized that *Silent Spring* came out more than 40 years ago, so this 80 percent decline followed an already huge decline caused by pesticides, which followed another undoubtedly huge decline caused by the deforestation, conversion to agriculture, and urbanization that followed conquest.

Comparison-contrast: Contrasts number of animals today with number at various times in the past to dramatize declining

My great-grandmother grew up in a sod house in Nebraska. When she was a tiny girl — in other words, only four human generations ago — there were still enough wild bison on the Plains that she was afraid lightning storms would spook them and they would trample her home. Who in Nebraska today worries about being trampled by bison? For that matter, who in Nebraska today even thinks about bison on a monthly, much less daily, basis?

Cause-effect: Effects of declining baselines

This state of affairs is problematic for many reasons, not the least of which is that it's harder to fight for what you don't love than for what you do, and it's hard to love what you don't know you're missing. *It's harder still to fight an injustice you do not perceive as an injustice* but rather as just the way things are. How can you fight an injustice you never think about because it never occurs to you that things have ever been any different?

4

5

6

7

Declining baselines apply not only to the environment but to many fields. Take surveillance. Back in the 1930s, there were people who freaked out at the notion of being assigned a Social Security number, as it was "a number that will follow you from cradle to grave." But since 9/11, according to former National Security Agency official William Binney, the U.S. government has been retaining every email sent, in case any of us ever does anything the government doesn't like. How many people complain about that? And it's not just the government. I received spam birthday greetings this year from all sorts of commercial websites. How and why does ESPN.com have my birth date? And remember the fight about GMOs? They were perceived as scary (because they are), and now they're all over the place, but most people don't know or don't care. The same goes for nanotechnology.   **8**

Yesterday I ate a strawberry. Or rather, I ate a strawberry-shaped object that didn't have much taste. When did we stop noticing that strawberries/plums/tomatoes no longer taste like what they resemble? In my 20s I rented a house where a previous resident's cat had pooped all over the dirt basement, which happened to be where the air intakes for the furnace were located. The house smelled like cat feces. After I'd been there a few months, I wrote to a friend, "At first the smell really got to me, but then, as with everything, I got used to the stench and it just doesn't bother me anymore."   **9**

This is a process we need to stop. Milan Kundera famously wrote, "The struggle of man against power is the struggle of memory against forgetting." Everything in this culture is aimed at helping to distract us from — or better, help us to forget — the injustices, the pain. And it is completely normal for us to want to be distracted from or to forget pain. *Pain hurts*. Which is why on every level from somatic reflex to socially constructed means of denial we have pathways to avoid it.   **10**

But here is what I want you to do: I want you to go outside. I want you to listen to the (disappearing) frogs, to watch the (disappearing) fireflies. Even if you're in a city — especially if you're in a city — I want you to picture the land as it was before the land was built over. I want you to research who lived there. I want you to feel how it was then, feel how it wants to be. I want you to begin keeping a calendar of who you see and when: the first day each year you see buttercups, the first day frogs start singing, the last day you see robins in the fall, the first day for grasshoppers. In short, I want you to pay attention. If you do this, your baseline will stop declining, because you'll have a record of what's being lost.   **11**

Do not go numb in the face of this data. Do not turn away. I want you to feel the pain. Keep it like a coal inside your coat, a coal that burns and burns. I want all of us to do this, because we should all want the pain of injustice to stop.   **12**

Illustration: Examples to help readers understand how baselines decline

Comparison-contrast: Contrasting responses today with responses previously

Argument: Thesis states author's position

Cause-effect

Argument: Uses repetition to persuade readers to take steps

Cause-effect

Argument: Uses comparison to persuade readers to take steps

IN THIS CHAPTER YOU WILL LEARN TO

- understand the purpose and function of narrative essays,
- use graphic organizers to visualize narrative essays,
- integrate narration into an essay,
- read and think critically about narration, and
- plan, organize, draft, revise, and edit essays using narration.

USING NARRATION IN COLLEGE AND THE WORKPLACE

- Each student in your *business law course* must attend a court trial and complete the following written assignment: "Describe what happened and how the proceedings illustrate the judicial process."

- Your *sociology instructor* announces that the class session will focus on the nature and types of authority figures in U.S. society. She begins by asking class members to describe situations in which they found themselves in conflict with an authority figure.

- Your *job in sales* involves frequent business travel, and your company requires you to submit a report for each trip. You are expected to recount the meetings you attended, your contacts with current clients, and the new sales leads you developed.

CHARACTERISTICS OF A NARRATIVE

A narrative does not merely report events; it is *not* a transcript of a conversation or a news report. Instead, it is a story that conveys a particular meaning. It presents actions and details that build toward a *climax*, the point at which the conflict of the narrative is resolved. Most narratives also use dialogue to present portions of conversations that move the story along.

NARRATIVES MAKE A POINT

A narrative makes a point by telling readers about an event or a series of events. The point may be to describe the significance of the event(s), make an observation, or present new information. The writer may state the point directly, using an explicit thesis statement, or leave it unstated, using an implied thesis. Either way, the point should always be clear to the audience by the details selected and the way they are presented.

The following excerpt comes from "The Lady in Red" (p. 253). It tells the story of a homeless man's first attempt to beg, the rejection he faces, and the kindness of one woman. Notice how he chooses vocabulary to reinforce his own sense of defeat and his miraculous rescue by the "lady in red."

I closed my eyes for a moment against the failure and fatigue, and then I felt a tap on my shoulder. "Sir," a lady was saying. As I opened my eyes and turned around, a lady in a red hat and an old red coat with a big brooch of an angel pinned to her lapel was standing there. She was digging through her purse as she talked. (para. 20)

Details that reinforce the main point

NARRATIVES CONVEY ACTION AND DETAIL

Narratives present a detailed account of an event or a series of events, using *dialogue*, *physical description*, and *action verbs* to make readers feel as if they are watching the scene or experiencing the action.

" Because you were born over two months premature, the doctors told your parents that you might be deaf or blind, or have other serious disabilities. Your parents seemed worried about what people in their community would think if they brought home a baby with special needs. . . . "

Dialogue

Alone in my room, I gripped the phone tightly, my head whirling. Years ago, when a friend asked me if I had an "idealized" view of my birthparents, I had scoffed and said no. Yet now, confronted with notes from my unearthed adoption file, I realized that my imagination had nonetheless cast my birthparents as courageous people who made a terribly difficult decision out of love, as many birthparents do. . . . It had never occurred to me that their decision might also have been motivated by the fact that I was a girl— a girl whose potential health problems could prove embarrassing to them. ("The Alternate History of Susan Chung," p. 257)

Action verbs

Physical description

NARRATIVES PRESENT A CONFLICT AND CREATE TENSION

An effective narrative presents a **conflict**—such as a struggle, question, or problem— and works toward its resolution. The conflict can be between participants or between a participant and some external force, such as a law, value, tradition, or an act of nature. (In the example paragraph, the conflict is between the adopted woman's beliefs about her birth parents and what she learns from the adoption file.) **Tension** is the suspense created as the story unfolds and the reader wonders how the conflict will be resolved. The height of the action—the point just before the resolution of the conflict—is the **climax**.

> **EXERCISE 12.1**   **Building Conflict**
>
> Working alone or with a classmate, complete each of the following statements by setting up a conflict. Then, for one of the completed statements, write three to four sentences that build tension through action, physical description, or dialogue (or some combination of the three).
>
> 1. You are ready to leave the house when . . .
> 2. You have just turned in your math exam when you realize that . . .
> 3. Your spouse suddenly becomes seriously ill . . .
> 4. Your child just told you that . . .
> 5. Your best friend phones you in the middle of the night to tell you . . .

NARRATIVES SEQUENCE EVENTS

A narrative often presents events in **chronological order**—the order in which they happened. Some narratives use flashback and foreshadowing to add tension and drama. A **flashback** returns readers to events that took place in the past; **foreshadowing** hints at events that will occur in the future. Both techniques are used frequently in fiction and film. For example, an episode of a soap opera might open with a woman lying in a hospital bed, flash back to a scene showing the accident that put her there, and then return to the scene in the hospital. When used sparingly, flashback and foreshadowing can build interest and add variety to a narrative, especially a lengthy chronological account.

NARRATIVES USE DIALOGUE

Just as people reveal much about themselves by what they say and how they say it, dialogue can reveal much about the characters in a narrative. The use of dialogue can also dramatize the action, emphasize the conflict, and reveal the personalities or motives of the key participants in a narrative. Dialogue can be strategically inserted to heighten the drama and help characterize the people depicted.

NARRATIVES ARE TOLD FROM A PARTICULAR POINT OF VIEW

Most narratives use either the first-person or third-person point of view.

- The **first-person** point of view ("I first realized the problem when . . .") allows you to assume a personal tone and speak directly to your audience, permitting you to express your attitudes and feelings and offer your interpretation and commentary. A drawback to using the first person is that you cannot easily convey the inner thoughts of other participants (unless they have shared their thoughts with you). When you narrate an event that occurred in your life, the first person is probably your best choice.

- The **third-person** point of view ("The problem began when Saul Overtone . . .") gives the narrator more distance from the action and often provides a broader, more objective perspective. When you narrate an event that occurred in someone else's life, the third person is likely to be the natural choice.

EXERCISE 12.2   **Choosing a Point of View**

Discuss the advantages and disadvantages of using the first- and third-person points of view for each of the following situations, and then decide which point of view would work better.

1. The day you and several friends played a practical joke on another friend
2. An incident of sexual or racial discrimination that happened to you or someone you know
3. An incident at work that a coworker told you about

The following readings demonstrate the techniques discussed above for writing effective narratives. The first reading is annotated to point out how Alton Fitzgerald White uses these techniques to help readers understand how his encounter with the police changed his life. As you read the second essay, try to identify how the writer uses the techniques of narrative writing to help readers understand what his father's gloves meant to him.

READING

Right Place, Wrong Face

ALTON FITZGERALD WHITE

Alton Fitzgerald White is an actor, singer, and dancer and has appeared in several Broadway shows. He is also the author of *Uncovering the Heart Light*, a collection of poems and short stories.

As the youngest of five girls and two boys growing up in Cincinnati, I was raised to believe that if I worked hard, was a good person, and always told the truth, the world would be my oyster. I was raised to be a gentleman and learned that these qualities would bring me respect.

While one has to earn respect, consideration is something owed to every human being. On Friday, June 16, 1999, when I was wrongfully arrested at my Harlem apartment building, my perception of everything I had learned as a young man was forever changed — not only because I wasn't given even a second to use the manners my parents taught me, but mostly because the police, whom I'd always naively thought were supposed to serve and protect me, were actually hunting me.

1

Point of view: Uses first person for this personal essay

Provides background information readers need to understand main point

2

Thesis: Main point

I had planned a pleasant day. The night before was a payday, plus I had received a standing ovation after portraying the starring role of Coalhouse Walker Jr. in the Broadway musical *Ragtime*. It is a role that requires not only talent but also an honest emotional investment of the morals and lessons I learned as a child.

Details: Includes background of character he plays in *Ragtime* to reinforce main point, foreshadow his own experiences, and build tension

Coalhouse Walker Jr. is a victim (an often misused word, but in this case true) of overt racism. His story is every black man's nightmare. He is hardworking, successful, talented, charismatic, friendly, and polite. Perfect prey for someone with authority and not even a fraction of those qualities. On that Friday afternoon, I became a real-life Coalhouse Walker. Nothing could have prepared me for it. Not even stories told to me by other black men who had suffered similar injustices.

Organization: Narrates events in chronological order; uses transitions of time, contrast

Friday for me usually means a trip to the bank, errands, the gym, dinner, and then off to the theater. On this particular day, I decided to break my pattern of getting up and running right out of the house. Instead, I took my time, slowed my pace, and splurged by making strawberry pancakes. Before I knew it, it was 2:45; my bank closes at 3:30, leaving me less than 45 minutes to get to midtown Manhattan on the train. I was pressed for time but in a relaxed, blessed state of mind. When I walked through the lobby of my building, I noticed two light-skinned Hispanic men I'd never seen before. Not thinking much of it, I continued on to the vestibule, which is separated from the lobby by a locked door.

Action and detail: Uses detailed descriptions and action verbs to involve readers, heighten drama

As I approached the exit, I saw people in uniforms rushing toward the door. I sped up to open it for them. I thought they might be paramedics, since many of the building's occupants are elderly. It wasn't until I had opened the door and greeted them that I recognized that they were police officers. Within seconds, I was told to " hold it "; they had received a call about young Hispanics with guns. I was told to get against the wall. I was searched, stripped of my backpack, put on my knees, handcuffed, and told to be quiet when I tried to ask questions.

With me were three other innocent black men who had been on their way to their U-Haul. They were moving into the apartment beneath mine, and I had just bragged to them about how safe the building was. One of these gentlemen got off his knees, still handcuffed, and unlocked the door for the officers to get into the lobby where the two strangers were standing. Instead of thanking or even acknowledging us, they led us out the door past our neighbors, who were all but begging the police in our defense.

Action and detail: Uses details, examples to reinforce main point and build tension

The four of us were put into cars with the two strangers and taken to the precinct station at 165th and Amsterdam. The police automatically linked us, with no questions and no regard for our character or our lives. No consideration was given to where we were going or why. Suppose an ailing relative was waiting upstairs, while I ran out for her medication? Or young children, who'd been told that Daddy was running to the corner store for milk and would be right back? My new neighbors weren't even allowed to lock their apartment or check on the U-Haul.

After we were lined up in the station, the younger of the two Hispanic men was   9
identified as an experienced criminal, and drug residue was found in a pocket of the other. I now realize how naive I was to think that the police would then uncuff me, apologize for their mistake, and let me go. Instead, they continued to search my backpack, questioned me, and put me in jail with the criminals.

The rest of the nearly five-hour ordeal was like a horrible dream. I was handcuffed,   10
strip-searched, taken in and out for questioning. The officers told me that they knew exactly who I was, knew I was in *Ragtime,* and that in fact they already had the men they wanted.

How then could they keep me there, or have brought me there in the first place? I   11
was told it was standard procedure. As if the average law-abiding citizen knows what that is and can dispute it. From what I now know, "standard procedure" is something that every citizen, black and white, needs to learn, and fast.

I felt completely powerless. Why, do you think? Here I was, young, pleasant, and   12
successful, in good physical shape, dressed in clean athletic attire. I was carrying a backpack containing a substantial paycheck and a deposit slip, on my way to the bank. Yet after hours and hours I was sitting at a desk with two officers who not only couldn't tell me why I was there but seemed determined to find something on me, to the point of making me miss my performance.

It was because I am a black man!   13   **Climax**

I sat in that cell crying silent tears of disappointment and injustice with the real-   14
ization of how many innocent black men are convicted for no reason. When I was handcuffed, my first instinct had been to pull away out of pure insult and violation as a human being. Thank God I was calm enough to do what they said. When I was thrown in jail with the criminals and strip-searched, I somehow knew to put my pride aside, be quiet, and do exactly what I was told, hating it but coming to terms with the fact that in this situation I was a victim. They had guns!

Before I was finally let go, exhausted, humiliated, embarrassed, and still in shock,   15   **Resolution:** Tension relieved
I was led to a room and given a pseudo-apology. I was told that I was at the wrong   when author released from jail
place at the wrong time. My reply? "I was where I live."

Everything I learned growing up in Cincinnati has been shattered. Life will never be   16
the same.

VISUALIZING A NARRATIVE: A GRAPHIC ORGANIZER

For more on creating a graphic organizer, see pp. 52–53.

Seeing the content and structure of an essay in simplified, visual form can help you analyze a reading, recall key events as you generate ideas for an essay, and structure your own writing. The graphic organizer in Figure 12.1 diagrams the basic structure of a narrative. You can use this graphic organizer as a basic model of a narrative, but keep in mind that narrative essays vary widely in organization and therefore may lack one or more of the elements included in the model.

FIGURE 12.1 Graphic Organizer for a Narrative Essay

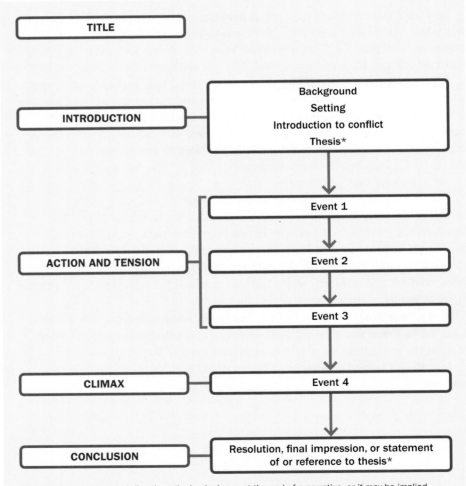

*The thesis may be stated directly at the beginning or at the end of a narrative, or it may be implied.

READING

Writing about What Haunts Us

PETER ORNER

Peter Orner is an award-winning author and essayist whose works have appeared in numerous publications, including *The Southern Review*, *The Atlantic Monthly*, and *The New York Times*. He is the author of two novels: *Love and Shame and Love* (2011) and *The Second Coming of Mavala Shikongo* (2006). Born in Chicago, Orner now lives in California, where he is a professor of creative writing at San Francisco State University. This memoir appeared in *The New York Times* online in January 2013. Figure 12.2, a graphic organizer for "Writing about What Haunts Us," appears on p. 240. Read the narrative first, and then study the graphic organizer.

1   I've been trying to lie about this story for years. As a fiction writer, I feel an almost righteous obligation to the untruth. Fabrication is my livelihood, and so telling something straight, for me, is the mark of failure. Yet in many attempts over the years I've not been able to make out of this tiny — but weirdly soul-defining — episode in my life anything more than a plain recounting of the facts, as best as I can remember them. Dressing them up into fiction, in this case, wrecked what is essentially a long overdue confession.

2   Here's the nonfiction version.

3   I watched my father in the front hall putting on his new, lambskin leather gloves. It was a sort of private ceremony. This was in early November, 1982, in Highland Park, Ill., a town north of Chicago along Lake Michigan. My father had just returned from a business trip to Paris. He'd bought the gloves at a place called Hermès, a mythical wonderland of a store. He pulled one on slowly, then the other, and held them up in the mirror to see how his hands looked in such gloves.

4   A week later, I stole them.

5   I remember the day. I was home from school. Nobody else was around. I opened the left-hand drawer of the front hall table and there they were. I learned for the first time how easy it is to just grab something. I stuffed the gloves in my pants and sprinted upstairs to my room. I hid them in the back of my closet under the wicker basket that held my license plate collection. Then I braced myself, for days. It was a warm November.

6   When we finally left that house — my mother, my brother and me — I took the gloves with me to our new place. I took them with me to college. To Boston, to Cincinnati, to North Carolina, to California. I even took them with me to Namibia for two years. I have them now, on my desk, 30 years later.

7   I've never worn them, not once, although my father and I have the same small hands. I didn't want the gloves. I never wanted the gloves. I only wanted my father not to have them.

8   Now that he is older and far milder, it is hard to believe how scared I used to be of my father. Back then he was so full of anger. Was he unhappy in his marriage? No doubt. He and my mother never had much in common. But his anger — sometimes it was rage — went beyond this not so unusual disappointment. My own totally

unscientific, armchair diagnosis is that like other chronically unsatisfied people, the daily business of living caused my father despair. At no time did this manifest itself more powerfully than when he came home from work. A rug askew, a jacket not hung up, a window left open — all could set off a fury. My brother once spilled a pot of ink on the snowy white carpet of my parents' bedroom: Armageddon.

His unpredictability is what made his explosions so potent. Sometimes the bomb   9
wouldn't go off, and he'd act like my idea of a normal dad. When he finally noticed those precious gloves were missing, he seemed only confused.

"Maybe they're in the glove compartment," my mother said.   10

"Impossible. I never put gloves in the glove compartment. The glove compartment   11
is for maps."

"Oh, well," my mother said.   12

He kept searching the front hall table, as if he had somehow overlooked them amid   13
all the cheap imitation leather gloves, mismatched mittens and tasseled Bears hats. I am certain the notion that one of us had taken the gloves never crossed his mind.

Haunted by my guilt, a frequent motivation for my fiction in general, I've tried to   14
contort my theft into a story, a made-up story.

In my failed attempts, the thief is always trying to give the gloves back. In one   15
abandoned version, the son character (sometimes he's a daughter) mails the gloves back to the father, along with a forged letter, purportedly written by a long-dead friend of the father, a man the father had once betrayed. I liked the idea of a package arriving, out of the blue, from an aggrieved ghost. I'm returning your gloves, Phil. Now at least one of us may be absolved.

The problem was that it palmed off responsibility on a third party. And it muddied   16
the story by pulling the thief out of the center of what little action there was.

In a simpler but equally bad version, the son character, home for Thanksgiving,   17
slips the gloves back in the top left-hand drawer of the front hall table of the house he grew up in, the house where the father still lives. This attempt was marred not only by cooked-up dialogue but also by a dead end.

"Dad! How about we take a walk by the lake?"   18

"It's been years, Son, since we've taken a walk."   19

"Pretty brisk out. Maybe you need your gloves?"   20

The moment arrives: the father slides open the drawer. Voilà! (Note the French.)   21
Cut to the father's face. Describe his bewilderment. I must have checked this drawer a hundred thousand times. Decades drop from the father's eyes, and both father and son face each other as they never faced each other when both were years younger. The son stammers out a confession I could somehow never get right. He tries to explain himself, but can't. Why did he take the gloves? My character could never express it in words and the story kept collapsing.

This is where the truth of this always derails the fiction. I can't give the gloves   22
back, in fiction or in this thing we call reality. If I did, I'd have to confront something I've known all along but have never wanted to express, even to myself alone. My father would have given me his gloves. All I had to do was ask. He would have been so

pleased that for once we shared a common interest. This happened so few times in our lives. All the years I've been trying to write this, maybe I've always known that this essential fact would stick me in the heart.

Our imaginations sometimes fail us for a reason. Not because it is cathartic to tell the truth (I finally told my father last year) but because coming clean may also be a better, if smaller, story. A scared (and angry) kid rips off his father's gloves, carries them around for decades. Sometimes he takes them out and feels them but never puts them on. When I see my father these days, we graze each other's cheeks, a form of kissing in my family. I love my father. I suppose I did even then, in the worst moments of fear.   23

Well-made things eventually deteriorate. The Hermès gloves are no longer baby-soft. All the handless years have dried them up.   24

In 1982, my father wasn't much older than I am at this moment. I think of him now, standing in the front hall. He's holding his hands up in the mirror, pulling on his beautiful gloves, a rare stillness on his face, a kind of hopeful calm. Was this what I wanted to steal?   25

> **EXERCISE 12.3** **Drawing a Graphic Organizer**

Using the graphic organizer in Figure 12.1 or 12.2 as a basis, draw a graphic organizer for "Right Place, Wrong Face" (pp. 233–35).

INTEGRATING NARRATION INTO AN ESSAY

In many of your essays, you will want to use both narration and one or more other patterns of development to support your thesis. For example, although "Right Place, Wrong Face" is primarily a narrative, it also uses cause and effect to explain why the author was detained despite evidence that he was a respectable, law-abiding citizen. Similarly, "Writing about What Haunts Us" is a narrative that also uses cause and effect to explain why the author stole from his dad and how this act affected him.

Although most of your college essays will not be primarily narrative, you can use stories — to illustrate a point, clarify an idea, support an argument, or capture readers' interest — in essays that rely mainly on another pattern of development or use several patterns. Here are a few suggestions for combining narration effectively with other patterns of development:

1. **Use a story.** It should illustrate your main point (or thesis) accurately and well (not just because it's funny or interesting).
2. **Keep the narrative short.** Include only the details readers need to understand the events you are describing.
3. **Introduce the story with a transitional sentence or clause.** It should indicate that you are about to shift to a narrative and make clear the connection between the story and the point it illustrates.
4. **Use descriptive language, dialogue, and action.** These will make your narrative vivid, lively, and interesting.

The essay "The Alternate History of Susan Chung: One Woman's Quest to Find Her Birth Parents" later in this chapter (pp. 257–59) uses multiple patterns of development to convey her ideas.

FIGURE 12.2 **Graphic Organizer for "Writing about What Haunts Us"**

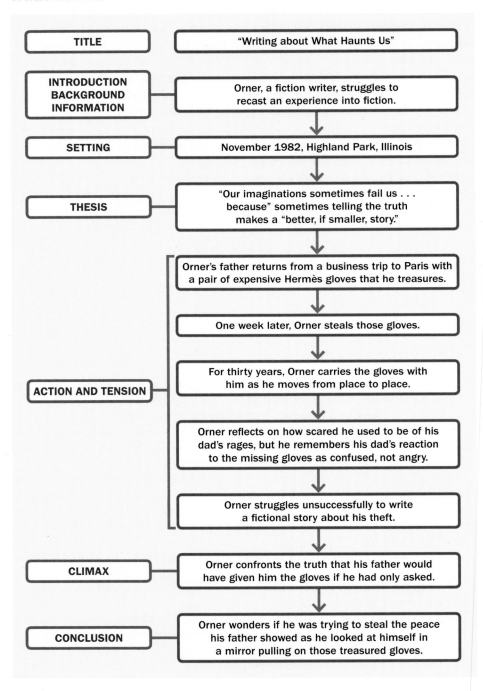

| TITLE | "Writing about What Haunts Us" |

| INTRODUCTION BACKGROUND INFORMATION | Orner, a fiction writer, struggles to recast an experience into fiction. |

| SETTING | November 1982, Highland Park, Illinois |

| THESIS | "Our imaginations sometimes fail us . . . because" sometimes telling the truth makes a "better, if smaller, story." |

ACTION AND TENSION

- Orner's father returns from a business trip to Paris with a pair of expensive Hermès gloves that he treasures.
- One week later, Orner steals those gloves.
- For thirty years, Orner carries the gloves with him as he moves from place to place.
- Orner reflects on how scared he used to be of his dad's rages, but he remembers his dad's reaction to the missing gloves as confused, not angry.
- Orner struggles unsuccessfully to write a fictional story about his theft.

| CLIMAX | Orner confronts the truth that his father would have given him the gloves if he had only asked. |

| CONCLUSION | Orner wonders if he was trying to steal the peace his father showed as he looked at himself in a mirror pulling on those treasured gloves. |

READING ACTIVELY AND THINKING CRITICALLY

Reading and thinking critically about a narrative requires you to read the selection and reflect on its meaning, consider it in terms of your own experience, and, finally, examine and challenge the author's attitude as it is shown in the selection.

For more on reading actively, see Chapter 3. For more on thinking critically, see Chapter 4.

WHAT TO LOOK FOR, HIGHLIGHT, AND ANNOTATE

Use these guidelines to read narratives actively.

1. **Preview.** Preview the essay to get an overview of its content and organization.

For more on previewing, see Chapter 3, pp. 45–48.

2. **Understand the sequence of events.** Read the narrative thoroughly to familiarize yourself with the events and action, noting who did what, when, where, and how. Focus on the sequence of events. Hint: Especially for lengthy or complex narratives and for those that flash back and forward among events, try drawing a graphic organizer or numbering the sequence of events in the margins.

3. **Think about the meaning.** Reread the narrative, this time concentrating on its meaning, by answering the following questions:
   - What is the writer's thesis? Is it stated directly or implied?
   - What is the author's purpose in writing this narrative? For what audience is it intended? What techniques does the writer use to achieve his or her purpose with this audience?
   - What is each participant's role in the story? What does the dialogue reveal about the participants or contribute to the main point?
   - What is the conflict, and how is it resolved? How does the writer create tension? When does the climax occur? Pay attention to the issue, struggle, or dilemma.
   - What broader issue is the essay concerned with? For example, in a story about children who dislike eating vegetables, the larger issue might be food preferences, nutrition, or parental control.

   You may want to highlight sentences or sections that reveal or suggest the answers.

4. **Consider your reactions.** As you read, write down your reactions to and feelings about the events, participants, and outcome of the narrative, both positive and negative. Do not hesitate to question or challenge participants, their actions, and their motives. Once you've identified the larger issue, try relating it to your own experiences. Finally, ask yourself what the lasting value or merit of this essay is. What does it tell you about life, people, jobs, or friendships, for example?

ANALYZING NARRATIVES

A nonfiction narrative is often one writer's highly personal, subjective account of an event or a series of events. Unless you have reason to believe otherwise, assume that the writer is honest—that he or she does not lie about the experiences or incidents presented in the essay. You should also assume, however, that the writer chooses details selectively, with the goal of advancing his or her narrative point. Use the following questions to think critically about the narratives you read.

How objective is the writer? Because a narrative is often highly personal, readers must recognize that the information it contains is likely influenced by the author's values, beliefs, and attitudes. Two writers may present two very different versions of a single incident. In "Right Place, Wrong Face," for example, the author presents the police officers as uncaring and insensitive, but imagine how the officers would describe the same incident.

What is the writer's tone? *Tone* refers to how the author sounds to his or her readers or how he or she feels about the topic: angry, joyous, fearful, or some combination. Writers establish tone through word choice, sentence structure, and formality or informality. The author's tone often affects the reader's attitude toward the topic. In "Writing about What Haunts Us," for example, Orner gains his readers' sympathy by creating a tone of regret and sadness.

What does the writer leave unspoken or unreported? A writer usually cannot report all conversations and events related to the narrative; however, the author should report everything that is *relevant*. Pay attention to what is said and reported but also to what might be left unsaid and unreported. For example, In "Writing about What Haunts Us," Orner does not tell his reader what happened when he told his dad about the stolen gloves. He only tells us that he told his dad, and he leaves the details of that confession to our imagination.

A GUIDED WRITING ASSIGNMENT*
NARRATION

YOUR ESSAY ASSIGNMENT

Write a narrative essay about an experience that had a significant effect on you or that changed your views in some important way. Choose an experience that . . .

- taught you something about yourself,
- revealed the true character of someone you know,
- helped you discover a principle to live by,
- helped you appreciate your ethnic identity,
- has become a family legend (one that reveals the character of a family member or illustrates a clash of generations or cultures), and
- explains the personal significance of a particular object.

*The writing process is *recursive*; that is, you may find yourself revising as you draft or prewriting as you revise. This is especially true when writing on a computer. Your writing process may also differ from that of your classmates, depending on your preferred learning style.

Prewriting

1 Select a topic from the list on p. 242, or create your own.

Use one or more of the following suggestions to choose an experience to write about.

1. Alone or with another student, **list one or more broad topics**—for example, *Learn about Self*, *A Principle to Live By*, *Family Legend*—and then **brainstorm** to come up with **specific experiences** in your life for each category. (Rational and pragmatic learners may prefer this kind of listing.)
2. Flip through a **family photo album**, or page through a **scrapbook**, **diary**, or **yearbook** to remind you of events from the past. Other prewriting strategies, like freewriting or questioning, may also help trigger memories of experiences. (Spatial and emotional learners may prefer reviewing memorabilia.)
3. **Work backward**: Think of a principle you live by, an object you value, or a family legend. How did it become so? (Abstract and independent learners may prefer working backward.)

After you have chosen your topic, make sure that it is **memorable and vivid** and that you can develop your main idea into a **working thesis**.

2 Consider your purpose and audience, and choose a point of view.

Ask yourself these questions.

- Will my essay's **purpose** be to **express myself**, **inform**, or **persuade**?
- Who is my **audience**? Will readers need any **background information** to understand my essay? Am I **comfortable writing about my experience** for this audience?
- What **point of view** best suits my purpose and audience? (In most cases, you will use **first person** to relate a personal experience.)

3 Gather details about the experience or incident.

Use idea-generating strategies to recollect as many details about the experience or incident as possible.

1. Replay the experience or incident in your mind's eye. Jot down what you see, hear, smell, and feel—colors, dialogue, sounds, odors, and sensations—and how these details make you feel. (A broad range of learners—spatial, concrete, creative, and emotional—may prefer to generate ideas using mental imaging.)
2. Write down the following headings: *Scene, Key Actions, Key Participants, Key Lines of Dialogue, Feelings*. Then brainstorm ideas for each and list them. (Pragmatic and rational learners may prefer to use brainstorming.)
3. Describe the incident or experience to a friend. Have your friend ask you questions as you tell the story. Jot down the details that the telling and questioning helped you recall. (Social and verbal learners may prefer to use storytelling.)

Prewriting

As you gather details for your narrative, be sure to include those that are essential to an effective narrative.

- *Describe the scene:* Include relevant **sensory details** to allow your readers to feel as if they are there. Choose details that point to or hint at the narrative's main point, and avoid those that distract readers from the main point.
- *Include key actions:* Choose actions that **create tension**, **build it to a climax**, and **resolve it**. Answer questions like these:

  Why did the experience or incident occur?

  What events led up to it, what was the turning point, and how was it resolved?

  What were its short- and long-term outcomes? What is its significance?
- *Describe key participants:* Concentrate on the **appearance** and **actions** of only those people who were directly involved, and include details that help highlight relevant character traits.
- *Quote key lines of dialogue:* Include dialogue that is **interesting**, **revealing**, and **related to the main point** of the narrative. To make sure the dialogue sounds natural, read the lines aloud or ask a friend to do so.
- *Capture feelings:* How did you feel during the incident, how did you reveal your feelings, and how did others react to you? How do you feel about the incident now? What have you learned from it?

Use at least two idea-generating strategies, and then work with a classmate to evaluate your ideas.

4 Evaluate your ideas to make sure they describe your experience or incident vividly and meaningfully.

Try these suggestions to help you evaluate your ideas.

- **Reread** everything you have written. (Sometimes reading your notes aloud is helpful.)
- **Highlight** the most relevant material, and **cross out** any material that does not directly support your main point. Then **copy** and **paste** the usable ideas to a new document to consult while drafting.
- **Collaborate** in small groups, take turns **narrating your experience** and **stating its main point** and having classmates tell you . . .
  1. how they react to the story.
  2. what more they need to know about it.
  3. how effectively the events and details support your main point.

Organizing & Drafting

5 Focus and place your thesis effectively.

Make the main point of your narrative clear and effective by focusing your thesis. For example, a student who decided to write about a robbery at her family's home devised the following focused thesis statement for her narrative.

─ *focuses on 1 object* ─ ┌─── *explains value* ───

Example: The silver serving platter, originally owned by my great-grandmother,

┌──── *introduces experience & expresses main point* ────

became our most prized family heirloom after a robbery terrorized our family.

Team up with classmates to test your thesis. Is it clear? Is it interesting? Provide feedback to help your partner focus the thesis more effectively.

Organizing & Drafting

Consider the best placement for your thesis. A thesis statement may be placed at the beginning (as in "Right Place, Wrong Face," page 233) or at the end of a narrative, or it may be implied. (Even if you don't state your thesis explicitly in your essay, having a focused thesis written down can help you craft your narrative.)

(**Note:** Once you have a focused thesis, you may need to do some additional prewriting, or you may need to revise your thesis as you draft. Return to the steps above as needed.)

 Choose a narrative sequence.

Organize your narrative. You may use **chronological order** from beginning to end or present some events using **flashbacks** or **foreshadowing** for dramatic effect. To help you determine the best sequence for your narrative, try the following.

1. Write a brief description of each event on an index card. Highlight the card that contains the climax. Experiment with various ways of arranging your details by rearranging the cards. (Pragmatic learners may benefit from using index cards this way.)
2. Draw a graphic organizer of the experience or incident using Figure 12.1 on page 236 as a model. (Spatial learners may benefit from drawing a graphic organizer.)
3. Create a list of the events, and then cut and paste them to experiment with different sequences. (Verbal learners may benefit from creating a list.)

 Write a first draft of your narrative essay.

Use the following guidelines to keep your narrative on track.

- The **introduction** should set up the sequence of events. It may also contain your **thesis**.
- The **body paragraphs** should **build tension** and follow a clear order of progression. Use **transitional words and phrases**, such as *during*, *after*, and *finally*, to guide readers. Most narratives use the past tense ("Yolanda discovered the platter . . ."), but fast-paced, short narratives may use the present ("Yolanda discovers the platter . . ."). Avoid switching between the two unless the context clearly requires it.
- The conclusion is unlikely to require a summary. Instead, try . . .
  - **making a final observation about the experience or incident**, (Example: "Overall, I learned a lot more about getting along with people than I did about how to prepare fast food.")
  - **asking a probing question**, (Example: "Although the visit to Nepal was enlightening for me, do the native people really want or need us there?")
  - **suggesting a new but related direction of thought**, (Example: An essay on racial profiling might conclude by suggesting that police sensitivity training might have changed the outcome of the situation.)
  - **referring to the beginning of the essay**, (Example: "Right Place, Wrong Face" (para. 16, p. 233) or **restating the thesis in different words** (Example: "Being Double" (para. 22, pp. 251–52).

Revising

8 **Evaluate your draft and revise as necessary.**

Use **Figure 12.3, "Flowchart for Revising a Narrative Essay,"** to evaluate and revise your draft.

Editing & Proofreading

9 **Edit and proofread your essay.**

Refer to Chapter 10 for help with . . .
- **editing sentences** to avoid wordiness, make your verb choices strong and active, and make your sentences clear, varied, and parallel, and
- **editing words** for tone and diction, connotation, and concrete and specific language.

Pay particular attention to **dialogue:**
- Each quotation by a new speaker should start a **new paragraph**.
- Use **commas** to separate each quotation from the phrase that introduces it unless the quotation is integrated into your sentence. If your sentence ends with a quotation, the **period** should be inside the quotation marks.

Example: The wildlife refuge guide noted, "American crocodiles are an endangered species and must be protected."

Example: The wildlife refuge guide noted that "American crocodiles are an endangered species and must be protected".

FIGURE 12.3 **Flowchart for Revising a Narrative Essay**

QUESTIONS		REVISION STRATEGIES

1. Highlight the sentence(s) that express the main point of your narrative. Is the main point clear?

NO

· Rework your thesis to make it more explicit.

YES

2. *Write* a brief sentence that summarizes the conflict of your narrative. Is the conflict clear? Is it directly related to the main point?

NO

· Add events and dialogue specific to the conflict.
· Rework your thesis to make it better relate to the conflict.

YES

3. Place an ✗ by each important scene, person, or action. Is it clear how each relates to both the main point and the *conflict*?

NO

· Delete scenes, persons, or actions that don't help you make your main point or establish conflict.

YES

4. Place a checkmark ✔ by each descriptive word or phrase. Is each important scene, person, or action vividly described?

NO

· Brainstorm to discover more vivid details.
· Consider adding dialogue to bring people and events to life.

YES

5. *Number* the major events in the narrative in chronological order. Is the sequence of events clear? If you use foreshadowing or flashbacks, is it clear where you do so?

NO

· Look for gaps in the sequence, and add any missing events.
· Consider rearranging the events.
· Use transitions to clarify the sequence of events.

YES

6. Underline the topic sentence of each paragraph. Is each paragraph focused on a separate part of the action?

NO

· Be sure each paragraph has a topic sentence and supporting details. (See Chapter 7.)
· Consider combining closely related paragraphs.
· Split paragraphs that cover more than one event.

YES

(continued on next page)

(Figure 12.3 continued)

QUESTIONS		REVISION STRATEGIES

7. <u>Wavy-underline</u> the dialogue. Does it sound realistic? Does it directly relate to the *conflict*?

 NO

- Revise by telling someone what you want your dialogue to express. Record what you say.
- Eliminate dialogue that does not help you make your main point or add drama.

YES

8. each personal pronoun and each verb. Do you use a consistent point of view and verb tense?

 NO

- Check for places where your point of view shifts for no reason, and revise to make it consistent.
- Check for places where the tense changes for no reason, and revise to make it consistent.

YES

9. Look at your introduction and conclusion. Do they address each other and the main point? Does the conclusion resolve the *conflict*?

 NO

- Revise your introduction and conclusion. (See pp. 146–51.)

READINGS: NARRATIVE IN ACTION

Being Double

SANTIAGO QUINTANA

Santiago Quintana, a junior literature major, wrote this essay for an assignment given by his first-year writing instructor. He had to describe a situation that challenged him and taught him a valuable lesson. As you read the essay, notice how Quintana's narrative creates conflict and tension and builds to a climax and resolution. Highlight the sections(s) where you think the tension is particularly intense.

Details: Exact details help readers imagine the scene.

Dialogue: Quotations sound natural and capture the relationship between mother and son.

A summer sun shone on the Wisconsin Indian mounds and the grass poked its little blades through my sandaled toes. "College, finally," said mom and her hand fell slowly on my hair. I couldn't stop the shaking. It was inside me though; outside I was as still as a statue, with a smile frozen on my lips. 1

"Hey, should we leave some stuff in the car and come get it later or should we all help you carry it to the building?" asked my brother as he held two crates, one with my sheets in it and the other with books. The idea of having my family parade around campus yelling in Spanish, being "those loud Mexicans" I'd seen in American movies, and carrying all my stuff with me sounded terrifying. At the same time, I thought, why not? I didn't know anyone on campus, so there was no reason for me to be concerned about what others thought of me or my family. In Mexico City, I would have been mortified to be seen walking around high school with my whole family. Then again, that was high school, that was teenage Santiago, and that was Mexico City. I was in college now, in America; it was the time to read more, stop smoking, make friends, and do all those things that I had postponed beyond the imaginary line of "when I go to college."

With Wisconsin as our final destination, my family and I had been traveling around the Midwest for a week. I spoke the best English, so for the whole trip, I had been translating directions and ordering food for all. In my bilingual high school, I had the top grades in English, and hours watching You Tube videos and standing in front of a mirror had made my accent one of the least recognizable among my friends. Now, in America, all that obsession with language was paying off. My lighter skin and over rehearsed accent baffled many a waiter and cab driver when they discovered I was Mexican. My English was the reason I had chosen and been able to get into an American college. Now, here I was, my accent and lexicon ready to be put to the test.

The room was larger than I thought it would be, and my roommate quieter. My parents and I set the room up and left for coffee.

"Your roommate seems nice," said my mom.

"Yeah, a little quiet," I said, "and way younger than me."

"Everyone will be younger than you here," said my dad, "and you didn't really talk much either. You're usually so talkative."

"He's nervous dad," said my brother.

"I'm not. It's just, I don't know, weird. I don't know what to say to them," I said.

"Them? As in?" asked my dad.

"As in Americans. I don't know what to say to them, what they think is funny, and what is too much. You know my humor; I can go way overboard sometimes, and I don't want to mess up," I said.

Conflict: Description of Quintana's feelings introduces conflict and foreshadows the process he will undergo during his first year in college.

2 **Background:** Provides background about his English skills

Details: Exact details help readers imagine the writer's appearance and language.

3 **Tension:** Quintana anticipates the challenge of putting his English skills to work and builds tension.

4 **Tension:** Dialogue helps build tension

5

6

7

8

9

10

"I see. Well, I'm sure it'll come with time. You'll get used to it," said my mom.   11

After my parents left I sat on my dorm bed for two or three hours and had three cups of tea. I then decided to go out for a walk and try to talk to people. I closed the door behind me and was greeted by a long empty hallway in muted colors with doors on both sides. I walked quietly down the hallway to the stairs without meeting anyone. I went down the stairs and out the back door of the building. The air was more humid that I had ever felt, and the sun burnt my skin. I eventually found my way to the Office of International Education, where I saw a crowd of similarly terrified students standing at the door. I approached them, not sure how I would introduce myself, or what excuse I'd have for talking to them. In the end, I didn't need an excuse. One of the students recognized me from orientation and called out to me. "Hey! You're from Mexico aren't you?"   12

"Yeah," I answered.   13

"Come, I'm from Salvador. We were just talking about how different it is to learn English in class and have to speak it all the time with other Americans and also in class. I mean, you haven't had class yet, but you'll see. It's different," he said.   14

"I've already gotten lost like three times because I couldn't understand directions," said Amy, from Japan.   15

"It's the intonation. It's all wrong," said Matej from the Czech Republic.   16

"Also, they go too fast." All of the international students had stories of struggling with English, and they all had theories for the difference.   17

Finally, the time came for my first class—Mythology. I nervously entered the classroom, took a seat, and with pen and notebook ready, prepared to take notes. As I looked around, I noticed that there were only about ten students in the class. This only added to my nervousness; I would not be able to hide. I knew college in America would be difficult, but I could not have ever imagined how difficult it would actually be. Before class, I had made myself the promise that I would ask at least one question, or participate at least once. By the end of class, I had, at the most, one sentence scribbled on the page, and I had participated much more than once. I had asked the professor to explain terms and phrases, and sometimes even to repeat himself. I knew this was annoying for the rest of the students, and I apologized profusely through my blush. The professor assured me that it was fine, that he'd rather have us know the first half of the material really well, than go through the whole of it with only a vague inkling of what we were talking about. After   18

Transitions: Transitions of time help sequence events.

Details: Exact details help readers visualize situation.

Tension: Dialogue reinforces Santiago's struggle and builds tension.

Transitions: Transitions of time help sequence events.

Details: Detailed description helps build tension.

he let us out of class, I stopped another student, a junior, and ask him to
repeat what the homework assignment was, because I hadn't understood
the professor. He smiled and said I didn't need to apologize, that it was only
natural I would struggle with the language for the first week or so.

At the end of class, I was physically, mentally, and emotionally exhausted.   19
Wanting to be alone, I went back to my room, lay down for a bit, and then made
some tea. It was early afternoon now, and I had another class after lunch. I tried
to relax. My head thumped from the adrenaline, and my heart hurt from the
loneliness. My roommate came in and asked if I was doing fine and if I wanted
to have lunch with him and his friends. "Friends, friends, how can he have friends
already?" I thought, "We've been here for less than a week and you call them
friends." I said yes anyway. I knew I had to get out and walk it off, so to speak.
Lunch was equally stressful, but being a less formal situation, I couldn't raise my
hand and ask my roommate's friends to define terms and explain phrases and
repeat themselves. So I just smiled and let most of the conversation go without
participating. One of my roommate's friends must have seen confusion written on
my face for she took her food and sat across from me and started talking to me.
I asked her to go slowly, and told her that I was just getting used to English and
that I was sorry for being a nuisance. She laughed. "The first thing you need to do
is stop apologizing. We are not cold heartless people. Well, most of us aren't. We
understand. I can enunciate more clearly and speak more slowly, and it won't be a
problem. Tell me, you went to high school in Mexico City?"

I was hesitant at first and thought about every word and whether it was   20
appropriate. My new friend was incredibly patient with me, and she made me
feel fine about my English. I don't know when or how, but eventually I was
laughing at her jokes and the others joined in on our conversation, and I stopped
thinking about every word I said. The words seemed to fall effortlessly out of
my mouth already strung into phrases. I told them about Mexico City and how
crazy everything is, and no it's not nearly as dangerous as reporters make it seem
in the news. I learned about their home towns, their interests, and what they did
for fun. I was thinking about the conversation rather than the words. I forgot
myself and only then did the English that I knew finally make an appearance.

It wasn't permanent though. It still took me a while to switch from   21
translating to talking. I still struggled in class for the rest of the month, but
the moments when I forgot myself and flowed with the conversation began
happening more often. They happened when I didn't apologize for my "bad

Details: Exact details help
readers understand Quintana's
experience.

Climax

Conclusion: Transitions highlight what Quintana has learned—that he must relearn confidence each year.

English," when I didn't talk myself down, when I knew myself capable, and when I trusted the years and years of English lessons behind me, rather than searching for words like papers in a file cabinet.

Now, I am about to start my third year of college. I have increased my vocabulary and improved my style immensely. Nevertheless, there is always a week or two at the beginning of school when I have to tell myself to find that confidence again, to not apologize, and to trust my knowledge. Sometimes I still apologize and struggle when choosing words, but it has become easier and easier to find those moments when I forget it's me talking, and I just let the talking happen.

22

ANALYZING THE WRITER'S TECHNIQUE

1. **Thesis** Evaluate the strength of Quintana's thesis. How clear and specific is it?
2. **Details** How effectively does Quintana use details to reinforce his main point and to help readers visualize key people and places? Did you feel more details were needed? If so, where? Which details, if any, would you suggest he add or delete?
3. **Conflict and Tension** How does Quintana establish conflict and create tension?
4. **Foreshadowing** Where does Quintana use foreshadowing? How effective is it?
5. **Title, Introduction, and Conclusion** Evaluate the title, introduction, and conclusion of the essay.

THINKING CRITICALLY ABOUT NARRATION

1. **Tone** Describe Quintana's tone. What words convey his attitude or perspective? Does the tone change over the course of the essay? If so, how? Does it seem appropriate for the topic?
2. **Connotation** What connotation does the phrase "those loud Mexicans" (para. 1) have in the context of the paragraph?
3. **Fact and Opinion** In paragraph 2, Quintana writes, "My English was the reason I had chosen and been able to get into an American college." Is this statement a fact or an opinion? How do you know?

RESPONDING TO THE READING

1. **Reaction** Quintana mentions one experience with other international students, but he ends up bonding with a group of Americans. Why do you think this happened?
2. **Discussion** International students have a sizable presence on most college campuses in America. What can American colleges do to better meet the needs of these students?
3. **Journal** Write a journal entry about someone you befriended when others may have brushed him or her aside. How did you reach out to the individual, and what were the results?

4. **Essay** Quintana felt lonely and anxious as he began college in a new country with a new language. Write a narrative essay about a time when you felt like an outsider, lonely and anxious about making friends and fitting in.

READING

The Lady in Red

RICHARD LEMIEUX

Richard LeMieux was a successful businessman who operated his own publishing company and lived a life of comfort and even luxury. After his business failed, however, he was evicted from his home and became homeless, living out of his car with his dog, Willow. LeMieux details his experiences in a book titled *Breakfast at Sally's: One Homeless Man's Inspirational Journey* (2009), from which this excerpt is taken.

It went back to last Thanksgiving Day, 2002. That was the day I learned to beg.   1

I was up in Poulsbo. I had used the last of my change to buy Willow a hamburger   2
at the McDonald's drive-thru. My gas tank was almost empty, and my stomach was growling. Desperate for money just to keep moving and get something to eat, I began to consider the only option I seemed to have left: begging.

My whole life I had been a people person. As a sportswriter for the *Springfield Sun*,   3
I had seen Woody Hayes motivate players at Ohio State and Sparky Anderson put the spark into Pete Rose. As a sales rep, I had sold hundreds of thousands of dollars of advertising, convincing people they needed to invest in the product I was publishing. I wore the right suits and ties and kept my cordovans shined and did the corporate dance for twenty years. But this, this *begging*, was far more difficult.

I had given to others on the street. They had all types of stories: "I need to buy   4
a bus ticket to Spokane so I can go visit my dying mother." "I lost my wallet this morning, and I need five dollars for gas." I had always given, knowing all along that their tales were suspect. So I decided to just straight-up ask for money. No made-up stories. No sick grandmas waiting for my arrival. No lost wallets.

I started at the store I had shopped at for many years — Central Market. It was a   5
glitzy, upscale place with its own Starbucks, $120 bottles of wine, fresh crab, line-caught salmon, and oysters Rockefeller to go. It was a little bit of Palm Springs dropped into Poulsbo. The parking lot was full of high-priced cars: two Cadillac Escalades, three Lincoln Navigators, and a bright yellow Hummer. I had spent at least $200 a week there ($800 a month, $9,600 a year, $192,000 in twenty years), so I rationalized that I could beg there for *one* day — Thanksgiving Day at that.

I was wrong.   6

After watching forty people walk by, I finally asked a lady for help. "Ma'am, I'm   7
down on my luck. Could you help me with a couple of dollars?" I blurted out.

"Sorry," she said. "All I have is a credit card," and she moved on.   8

A man in a red Porsche pulled in. I watched him get out of his car, lock the doors   9
from his key-chain remote, and head for the store. "Sir, I hate to bother you. This is

the first time I have ever done this, and I'm not very good at it. But I am down on my luck and need help. Could you —"

"Get a Goddamned job, you bum!" he interrupted and kept walking. 10

Stung, I wanted to run to the van and leave, but I knew I couldn't go far; I barely had enough gas to leave the parking lot. 11

I spent the next twenty minutes trying to recover from the verbal blast I had received and could not approach anyone else. But the exclamation point had not yet been slapped in place on my failure at begging. The young manager of the store, maybe twenty-five years old, came out to do the honors. "Sir, sir," he called out to me as he approached. "We have a . . ." He halted mid-sentence. "Don't I know you?" he asked instead. 12

"Probably," I replied. "I've been shopping here for twenty years." 13

"I thought I'd seen you in the store," he said. "Well," he sighed heavily, "a man complained about you begging in front of the store. You're going to have to move on." 14

I could tell he didn't want to hear about the $192,000 I had spent in his store. He just wanted to hear what I was going to spend today. So I said, "Okay." He didn't offer me a sandwich, a loaf of bread, a soy latte, or even a plain old cup of coffee. 15

I had no choice. I had to keep trying. I decided to go across the street to Albertsons. As I walked back to the van, tears filled my eyes. I remembered Thanksgivings of the past. By now, I would be pouring wine for our family and friends, rushing to the door to welcome guests, and taking their coats to be hung in the hall closet. My home would be filled with the smells of turkey and sage dressing. At least twenty people would be there. Children would be jumping on the sofa and racing up and down the hallways and stairs. The football game between the Cowboys and the Packers would be blaring in the background. There would be a buzz. A younger, friskier Willow would stay close to the kitchen, hoping for the first bites of the bird from the oven. 16

But that was yesterday. Today, I drove across the highway to the "down-market" store, nestled in the strip mall between the drugstore and the card shop. I stepped out of the van to try my luck again. It was getting late, and the shoppers were rushing to get home to their festivities. I had little time to succeed. 17

I saw an old friend of mine pull into the parking lot and get out of her car. She headed for the grocery store. I turned my back to her and hid behind a pillar. I waited for her to enter the store, and then I approached a man as he walked toward the entrance. "Sir, I'm down on my luck. Could you help me with a little money for food?" I asked. 18

He walked away muttering, "Jesus Christ, now we've got worthless beggars on the streets of *Poulsbo*." 19

I closed my eyes for a moment against the failure and fatigue, and then I felt a tap on my shoulder. "Sir," a lady was saying. As I opened my eyes and turned around, a lady in a red hat and an old red coat with a big brooch of an angel pinned to her lapel was standing there. She was digging through her purse as she talked. 20

"I overheard your conversation with that man. I hope you don't mind. I — well, 21
I can help you a little bit," she said, holding out some rolled-up bills. Her presence
and the offered gift surprised me. I stood there a moment, looking into her eyes.
"Here," she said, reaching her hand out again. "Take it."

I reached out my hand and took the money from her. "Thank you so much," I 22
said softly. "This is very kind of you."

"Thank you. I know what . . ." she began, and then her sentence was inter- 23
rupted by a cough. She clutched her purse to her chest with one hand and did
her best to cover her mouth with the other. She stiffened and then bent her head
toward the pavement as the cough from deep in her chest consumed her. She
moved her hand from her mouth to her bosom and just held it there. When the
cough subsided, she took a deep breath. She looked up at me with watery eyes.
"I've had this darned hacking cough for a month or more now," she said after she
recovered. "I can't seem to shake this cold. It's going to be the death of me," she
added with a smile. "I'm going back to the doctor after the holiday."

"I hope you get better soon," I said. 24

The lady then moved her purse from her chest and opened it again. "Wait," she 25
said, looking inside her bag and then reaching in. "I might have some change in
here too." She dug to the bottom of her purse. She took out a handful of change
and handed it to me. I put my hands together and held them out, and she poured
the coins into them. "I hope this helps you," she said, gently placing her hand on
mine. "Remember me. I'll see you in heaven. Happy Thanksgiving!" She turned and
walked away.

I watched her disappear into her car before I counted the money she had given 26
me. It was sixty-four dollars and fifty cents. I was stunned! I walked back to the
van, counted the money again, and then counted my blessings.

I sat there in the drizzle, contemplating what had just happened. A sporadic 27
churchgoer my entire life, I had spent recent months asking God to send his angels
to me. But no angels came. Maybe *I* had to go looking for *them*.

With the glimmer of faith I still had left on that Thanksgiving Day, I said a 28
prayer, thanking God for the visit from the Lady in Red.

And now, in the church parking lot, it was time to sleep. I closed the doors of 29
my mind, one by one, and snuggled with Willow.

EXAMINING THE READING

1. **Background** What circumstances led LeMieux to resort to begging?
2. **Reasons** Why does the author begin begging at Central Market?
3. **Details** How does the author's emotional state change as the essay progresses?
4. **Details** What details of the essay identify the author as a different kind of beggar
   from what you would expect to find on the street?
5. **Vocabulary** Explain the meaning of each of the following words as it is used in the
   reading: *rationalized* (para. 5), *halted* (12), *nestled* (17), *brooch* (20), *sporadic* (27).
   Refer to your dictionary as nee ded.

ANALYZING THE WRITER'S TECHNIQUE

1. **Thesis** In your own words, restate LeMieux's thesis.
2. **Details** Why does the author include the detail that he bedded down for the night in his car, parked in the church parking lot?
3. **Patterns of Development** What other patterns of development does the author use? Provide examples of two, and explain how they contribute to the narrative.

VISUALIZING THE READING

Record below two or three particularly effective examples of each characteristic of narrative that LeMieux uses in "The Lady in Red."

Narrative Characteristic	Examples (Paragraph Number)
Dialogue	
Sensory details	
Action	
Sequence of events	
Tension	

THINKING CRITICALLY ABOUT NARRATION

1. **Tone** Describe the tone of LeMieux's essay. Highlight key phrases that reveal his attitude toward begging.
2. **Connotation** What connotation does the phrase "down on my luck" (para. 9) have?
3. **Inference** What can be inferred about the health of the lady in red? What details allow you to draw this inference?
4. **Fact or Opinion** In paragraph 3, is the author's statement about begging fact or opinion?
5. **Discussion** Discuss why LeMieux includes the detail that the lady in red wore a "big brooch of an angel pinned to her lapel."
6. **Climax** What is the climax of the story? How is the tension resolved?

RESPONDING TO THE READING

1. **Reaction** How do you think LeMieux was changed by his experience?
2. **Journal** Using information from the essay, write a journal entry in which you analyze the lady in red. Who is she? What kind of illness might she have? What kind of life might she have led before and after her encounter with LeMieux? What evidence from the essay helps create this impression?
3. **Discussion** Imagine you have no option but to become a beggar. Discuss the strategies you would use to convince people to give you money.
4. **Essay** Write a narrative essay about a time you encountered a beggar. Describe the circumstances in which you encountered the beggar. Choose vocabulary with the correct connotation to convey your feelings toward the beggar. Use dialogue to

capture the beggar's request and your response. Indicate what you learned from the experience.

WORKING TOGETHER

1. **Response** Suppose you witnessed the scene between the grocery store manager and LeMieux. Working with a partner, write a letter to the grocery store manager that conveys your reaction and your recommendations for how he should treat beggars in the future. Be prepared to share your letter with the class.
2. **Discussion** In groups of two or three, brainstorm ideas for helping beggars. List several options and then discuss them to determine which response you think will be most effective and why. Be prepared to share with the class your preferred option and the reason(s) you chose it.

READING: NARRATION COMBINED WITH OTHER PATTERNS

The Alternate History of Susan Chung: One Woman's Quest to Find Her Birthparents

NICOLE SOOJUNG CALLAHAN

Nicole Soojung Callahan is a writer, editor, and graduate student in the Writing Program at Johns Hopkins University. Her essays have appeared in several publications, including *The Atlantic*, *Salon*, and *The New York Times*. Callahan lives outside Washington, D.C., with her husband and two children.

© AtnoYdur/iStockphoto

My search for my birthparents began when I got pregnant. 1

I was born to Korean immigrants in Seattle, and my confidential or "closed" adoption at the age of 2 months severed all ties between my birth family and me — until I set out to restore those ties a few years ago. Though I was always curious about my first parents and their reasons for giving me up, I had been focused on other things — going to school, graduating from college, finding a job, getting married. But after years of wondering, I finally had a compelling, undeniable reason to look for my birthparents, a reason I thought about night and day (and every time I caught a glimpse of my expanding waistline in the mirror): I was expecting my first child. 2

I fully expected my life to change when I became pregnant. But the strong desire to find out more about my original family was not something I had anticipated. After a lifetime of trying to convince myself that blood connections were unnecessary, at least to me personally, I was just months away from meeting my first biological family member. I couldn't deny how closely our lives and our histories were already entwined; as an adoptee, I had almost no way to comprehend it. I could no longer believe that my biological connections weren't of great importance, responsible in many ways for the person I became. My daughter and I had yet to meet, but I knew that we *were* connected; that I was a part of her. The deep love her father and I felt for her — had my birthparents felt that way about me? Even if they hadn't, shouldn't I know why, and what happened to our family that made my adoption seem necessary? 3

So, in between work and childbirth classes and endless discussions with my husband about the merits of various baby names, I began the search for a suitable intermediary. Finally I found Donna, who seemed to possess good intentions and a willingness to proceed slowly and respectfully with my birthparents. I sent her requested $500 fee and a notarized form authorizing her to petition the court for my file. 4

She called two months later, when I was in my third trimester, to announce that she had found my birth family and could forward a letter to them as soon as I wrote it. "Did you know that you have *five* sisters?" she exclaimed. "The social worker wasn't sure, but she got the impression that your parents might have wanted a boy, not another girl." 5

I felt irritated with her for sharing such hurtful speculation at the very start, but it also made me snort — after five daughters, I thought, my birthparents should have recognized a clear pattern when they saw one. "What else does it say in the file?" I asked. 6

"Because you were born over two months premature, the doctors told your parents that you might be deaf or blind, or have other serious disabilities. Your parents seemed worried about what people in their community would think if they brought home a baby with special needs. They thought it would be easier if they told everyone that you died at birth — that appears to be what they told your sisters." 7

Alone in my room, I gripped the phone tightly, my head whirling. Years ago, when a friend asked me if I had an "idealized" view of my birthparents, I had scoffed and said no. Yet now, confronted with notes from my unearthed adoption file, I realized that my imagination had nonetheless cast my birthparents as courageous people who made a terribly difficult decision out of love, as many birthparents do. Over the years, as my adoptive parents shared snippets of information culled from the attorney who handled 8 my adoption — *your birthparents were recent immigrants; they worked 14 hours a day and had no health insurance; the doctors told them you would struggle all your life* — I had used these facts to bolster my view of them. I pictured defiantly strong people who made the decision to place me for adoption so that another family could provide the care I needed should the doctors' predictions prove correct. It had never occurred to me that their decision might also have been motivated by the fact that I was a girl — a girl whose potential health problems could prove embarrassing to them.

Hearing the intermediary read my adoption file over the phone left me doubting my birthparents, doubting their intentions, for the first time. Did they give me up because I wasn't the son they'd hoped for? Would they have been embarrassed to have a child who was deaf or disabled? I thought about my own daughter, not yet born or named but very much wanted, and felt disappointment well inside of me.   9

Eventually I realized that Donna was still waiting for me to say something. "Is there anything else I should know before I write my letter?" I asked. I was no longer certain I wanted to write it — perhaps no answers were better than ones I might hate.   10

"Just one more thing," she said. I heard paper rustling through the phone. "There's a name here. Your parents chose it for you before you were adopted."   11

"A name." My heart thumped once, hard. "What is it?"   12

"Susan."   13

Susan. I didn't know many Susans. I was sure that I didn't look like one. But it was the name my birthparents had chosen for me — the name they gave me in the hospital.   14

With tears in my eyes, I tried, as I had many times before, to imagine myself in their place. I tried to imagine being parted from my own daughter, a thought too painful to consider. If I were giving up the right to raise my child, if I knew I might not see her again after her birth, would I bother giving her a name — one she wasn't going to keep? Would it help, somehow, to remember her by name?   15

Maybe my parents would have preferred a son instead of a daughter. Maybe they felt ashamed for having a child they couldn't keep. But as I thought about them, and my own baby whose birth I looked forward to with so much excitement and hope, I felt sure that my parents would not have named a child they didn't love. I said good-bye to Donna and hung up the phone, fingers already roving over my laptop keys. A quick search told me that the name Susan meant "lily." I wondered what it had meant to my birthparents.   16

I'll have to ask them in my letter.   17

I opened a new file and began to write.   18

EXAMINING THE READING

1. **Reason** Why does the author decide to search for her birthparents? Why did her birthparents give her up for adoption?
2. **Detail** What did the doctors tell the author's birthparents about their daughter? Was their prediction correct?
3. **Detail** How does Callahan react when she hears her birth name?
4. **Vocabulary** Explain the meaning of each of the following words as it is used in the reading: *intermediary* (para. 4), *speculation* (6), *scoffed* (8), *culled* (8).

ANALYZING THE WRITER'S TECHNIQUE

1. **Thesis** What is Callahan's thesis? Is it stated or implied?
2. **Audience** Who is Callahan's intended audience? How do you know?
3. **Description** How does Callahan use description and other strategies to make her experience vivid and engaging? Cite several examples.
4. **Patterns of Organization** Identify at least two other patterns of organization Callahan uses, and explain the benefit of including these other patterns.
5. **Reaction** Explain the author's feelings about being put up for adoption. Does she understand what motivated her birthparents? Is she sympathetic toward them? How do you know? Cite details from the reading.

THINKING CRITICALLY ABOUT TEXT AND VISUALS

1. **Fact or Opinion** The author writes, "Maybe my parents would have preferred a son instead of a daughter" (para. 16). Is this a statement of fact or opinion?
2. **Visual** A photo appears on p. 257. Why do you think it was included? How does the inclusion of this photograph affect your response to the reading?
3. **Inference** What can you infer from the last sentence of Callahan's essay?
4. **Conflict and Tension** How does the author build tension? What is the climax of the story, and how does she resolve the tension?
5. **Writing** Write the letter that you think Callahan would have written to her birthparents, given what she learned from her adoption file. Be prepared to share your letter with the class, and discuss the reasons you wrote the letter you did.

RESPONDING TO THE READING

1. **Discussion** Based on the reading selection, consider why Callahan's Korean parents named her Susan or gave her a name at all. What do you think Callahan will tell her own children about why her birthparents gave her up for adoption?
2. **Journal** Write a journal entry in which you speculate about why Callahan's birthparents told their other daughters that "Susan" had died? How do you think they would react when they learned that in fact "Susan" was not dead but had been given up for adoption?
3. **Essay** The author had to make a very difficult decision about whether to contact her birthparents. Write a narrative essay in which you discuss a difficult decision you or someone you know had to make. Be sure to explain in detail both the process of making the decision and the decision itself.

WORKING TOGETHER

Role-play In a small group, role-play the first meeting between Callahan and her birthparents.

:e **macmillanhighered.com/successfulwriting**
E-readings > *Discussing Family Trees in School Can Be Dangerous* (video), Paul Nurse

DESCRIPTION USES SENSORY DETAILS

Sensory details appeal to one or more of the five senses—sight, sound, smell, taste, and touch—and help your readers experience the object, sensation, event, or person you are describing.

Sight. When you describe what something looks like, you help your reader create a mental picture of the subject. In the following excerpt, notice how Loren Eiseley uses visual detail—shape, color, action—and specific nouns and noun phrases to describe what he comes across in a field.

> One day as I cut across the field which at that time extended on one side
>
> of our suburban shopping center, I found a giant slug feeding from a
>
> funnel of pink ice cream in an abandoned Dixie cup. I could see his
>
> eyes telescope and protrude in a kind of dim, uncertain ecstasy as his dark
>
> body bunched and elongated in the curve of the cup.
>
> Loren Eiseley, "The Brown Wasps"

Noun and noun phrases

Descriptive adjectives of shape and color

Active verbs depicting motion

This description allows the reader to imagine the slug eating the ice cream in a way that a bare statement of the facts—"On my way to the mall, I saw a slug in a paper cup"—would not.

Sound. Sound can also be a powerful descriptive tool. Can you "hear" the engines in the following description?

> They were one-cylinder and two-cylinder engines, and some were make-and-
>
> break and some were jump-spark, but they all made a sleepy sound across the
>
> lake. The one-lungers throbbed and fluttered, and the twin-cylinder ones *purred*
>
> and *purred*, and that was a quiet sound too.
>
> E. B. White, "Once More to the Lake"

Descriptive adjectives

Action verbs used to evoke specific sounds; some are onomatopoetic—they sound like what they describe

Smell. Smells are sometimes difficult to describe, partly because the English language does not have as many adjectives for smells as it does for sights and sounds. Smell can be an effective descriptive device, however, as shown here.

> Driving through farm country at summer sunset provides a cavalcade
>
> of smells: manure, cut grass, honeysuckle, spearmint, wheat
>
> chaff, scallions, chicory, tar from the macadam road.
>
> Diane Ackerman, *A Natural History of the Senses*

Nouns used to evoke distinct odors

Notice how Diane Ackerman lists nouns that evoke distinct odors and leaves it to the reader to imagine how they smell.

Taste. Words that evoke the sense of taste can make descriptions lively. Consider this restaurant critic's description of Vietnamese cuisine.

Descriptive adjectives of taste

In addition to balancing the primary flavors — the sweet, sour, bitter, salty

and peppery tastes whose sensations are, in the ancient Chinese system,

directly related to physical and spiritual health — medicinal herbs were used

in most dishes. . . . For instance, the orange-red annatto seed is used for its

"cooling" effect as well as for the mildly tangy flavor it lends and the orange

color it imparts.

Molly O'Neill, "Vietnam's Cuisine: Echoes of Empires"

Touch. Annie Dillard's descriptions of texture, temperature, and weight allow a reader not only to visualize but also to experience what it feels like to hold a Polyphemus moth cocoon:

Descriptive adjectives of weight and texture

Active verbs conveying temperature and motion

Nouns and noun phrases

We passed the cocoon around; it was heavy. As we held it in our hands, the

creature within warmed and squirmed. We were delighted, and wrapped it

tighter in our fists. The pupa began to jerk violently, in heart-stopping knocks.

Who's there? I can still feel those thumps, urgent through a muffling of spun

silk and leaf, urgent through the swaddling of many years, against the curve of

my palm.

Annie Dillard, *Pilgrim at Tinker Creek*

DESCRIPTION USES ACTIVE VERBS AND VARIED SENTENCES

For more on using active verbs, see Chapter 10.

Sensory details are often best presented through active, vivid verbs. In fact, active verbs are often more effective than adverbs in creating striking and lasting impressions, as the following example demonstrates.

	adverb
ORIGINAL	The team captain *proudly* accepted the award.

	verb		verb
REVISED	The team captain marched to the podium, grasped the trophy,

verb

and saluted his teammates.

Using varied sentences also contributes to the effective expression of sensory details. Be sure to use different types and patterns of sentences and to vary their lengths.

> **EXERCISE 13.1** **Using Sensory Details, Active Verbs, and Varied Sentences**

Using sensory details, active verbs, and varied sentences, describe one of the common objects in the following list or one of your own choosing. Do not name the object in your description. Exchange papers with a classmate. Your reader should be able to guess the item you are describing from the details you provide.

1. A piece of clothing
2. A food item
3. An appliance
4. A plant
5. An animal

DESCRIPTION CREATES A DOMINANT IMPRESSION

An effective description leaves the reader with a **dominant impression** — an overall attitude, mood, or feeling about the subject. The impression may be awe, inspiration, anger, or distaste, for example.

For more on thesis statements, see Chapter 6.

Let's suppose that you are writing about an old storage box you found in your parents' attic. The aspect of the box you want to emphasize (your *slant, angle,* or *perspective*) is memories of childhood. Given this slant, you might describe the box in several ways, each of which would convey a different dominant impression.

- "A box filled with treasures from my childhood brought back memories of long, sunny afternoons playing in our backyard."
- "Opening the box was like lifting the lid of a time machine, revealing toys and games from another era."
- "When I opened the box, I was eight years old again, fighting over my favorite doll with my twin sister, Erica."

Notice that each example provides a different impression of the box's contents and would require a different type of support. That is, only selected objects from within the box would be relevant to each impression. Note, too, that in all of these examples, the dominant impression is stated directly in a thesis statement rather than implied.

To write an effective description, select details carefully, including only those that contribute to the dominant impression you are trying to create. Notice that Dillard, in the paragraph above, does not clutter her description by describing the physical appearance of the cocoon. Instead, she focuses on its movement and how it feels in her hand.

> **EXERCISE 13.2** **Focusing the Dominant Impression**

As you read the following paragraph, cross out details that do not contribute to the dominant impression.

All morning I had had a vague sense that bad news was on its way. As I stepped outside, the heat of the summer sun, unusually oppressive for ten o'clock, seemed to sear right through me. In fact, now that I think about it, everything seemed slightly out of kilter that morning. The car, which had been newly painted the week before, had stalled several times. The flowers in the garden, planted for me by my husband, purchased from a nursery down the road, were drooping. It was as though they were wilting before they even had a chance to grow. Even my two cats, who look like furry puffballs, moved listlessly across the room, ignoring my invitation to play. It was then that I received the phone call from the emergency room telling me about my son's accident.

DESCRIPTION USES CONNOTATIVE LANGUAGE EFFECTIVELY

As noted in Chapter 4, most words have two levels of meaning: denotative and connotative. The *denotation* of a word is its precise dictionary meaning. Often, however, feelings and attitudes — emotional colorings or shades of meaning — are also associated with a word. These are the word's *connotations*.

WORD	DENOTATION	CONNOTATIONS
Flag	A piece of cloth used as a national emblem	patriotism, love, and respect for one's country

For more on connotation versus denotation, see Chapter 4.

As you write, be careful to select words with connotations that strengthen the dominant impression you are creating.

DESCRIPTION USES COMPARISONS

For more on simile, metaphor, personification, and analogy, see Chapter 4.

Comparing the person or object you are describing to something your readers are familiar with can help them visualize your subject. Several types of comparisons are used in descriptive writing: similes, metaphors, personification, and analogies.

FIGURE OF SPEECH	DEFINITION	EXAMPLE
Simile	a direct comparison introduced by words such as *like* or *as*	*His lips were as soft as a rosebud's petals.*
Metaphor	an indirect comparison describing one thing as if it were another	*. . . his rosebud lips . . .*
Personification	a comparison that gives human qualities or characteristics to an inanimate object	*The television screen stared back at me.*

> **EXERCISE 13.3**   **Appealing to the Senses**

Write a paragraph describing an animal or pet. Focus on one sense or appeal to several. If possible, include a simile or a metaphor.

DESCRIPTION FOLLOWS A METHOD OF ORGANIZATION

For more on methods of organization, see Chapter 7.

Effective descriptions must follow a clear method of organization. Three common methods of organization used in descriptive writing are spatial order, chronological order, and most-to-least or least-to-most order.

- When you use **spatial order**, you describe a subject from top to bottom, from left to right, from near to far away, or from a central point outward. For example, if you are describing a college campus, you might start by describing a building at the center of the campus—the library, perhaps—and then move to surrounding buildings.

In writing a description using spatial order, you can use either a fixed or a moving **vantage point**. With a fixed vantage point, you describe what you see from a particular position. With a moving vantage point, you describe your subject from different positions. A fixed vantage point is like a stationary camera trained on a subject from one direction. A moving vantage point is like a hand-held camera that captures the subject from many directions.

- **Chronological order** works well when you need to describe events or changes that occur over a period of time. You might use chronological order to describe the changes in a puppy's behavior as it grows or to relate changing patterns of light and shadow as the sun sets.
- You might use **most-to-least** or **least-to-most order** to describe the smells in a flower garden or the sounds of an orchestra tuning up for a concert.
- Clustering details by the **five senses**—how your subject looks, sounds, smells, tastes, and feels—might make sense for a topic such as a hot fudge sundae or a delicious meal at a restaurant.

The following readings demonstrate the techniques discussed above for writing effective descriptive essays. The first reading is annotated to point out how Rachel Maizes uses these techniques to make the depiction of her dog, Chance, come alive. As you read the second essay, try to identify for yourself how the writer uses the techniques of descriptive writing to help readers imagine her prized bicycle.

READING

Bad Dog

RACHEL MAIZES

Rachel Maizes is an attorney, a writer, and a dog lover who currently lives in Boulder, Colorado. Her essay "Bad Dog" was published in the "My Story" section of *The New York Times* online in September 2013.

© Jill Bielawski

My dog, Chance, is old. White fur circles his eyes, coats his muzzle, sprouts between his toes. Although still alive, he looks like a ghost. He used to stand like a champion, his chest and muzzle forward, his hind legs back. Now he can hardly support himself when he sits, balancing precariously like a pile of kindling propped against itself.

1

Sensory details: Appeals to the reader's sense of sight

Comparisons: Uses similes to compare Chance with a ghost, a champion

He takes an anti-inflammatory medication for arthritis and pumpkin for constipa-
tion and fish oil and glucosamine for his

2

joints and mind, though it may be too late for the latter. He walks an endless circuit between the guest room and bedroom and master bath searching for what I don't know. When he tires, he lies next to me as I work. Sometimes he groans.

Comparison: Uses comparison to highlight author's identification with Chance

I think about what it means to have cared for Chance for most of his life. It confirms that I, too, am growing older. I turned 50 a few months ago. Overnight, wiry gray hair has sprouted at my temples. Always a theater buff, now I attend matinees. My back stiffens after weeding. In the mirror, I see a face rearranged by gravity's heavy hand. I remember Chance as a gangly puppy with floppy ears. I keep a picture of myself as a young woman, a 20-something with spiky hair, my arm around my mother, now dead 10 years. A dog's life is shorter than ours, but ours is, as the Talmud says, "k'heref aiyen," like the blink of an eye.   3

Sensory details: Appeals to reader's sense of sight, touch

Chance's fur is long and mats easily. I brush it, collecting thick, webby piles. My second husband, Steve, saved the fur of a dog he once owned and a friend wove it into cloth. It's one of the things I love about Steve, the over-the-top affection he bestows on animals. I toss Chance's hair into the trash or scatter it outside for birds to install in their nests.   4

Dominant impression: Uses anecdote to reinforce main idea

Fourteen years ago my ex-husband and I adopted Chance from a shelter. He was a 4-month-old puppy, an Australian Shepherd mix, with brindle fur. We had another dog, Tilly, a 2-year-old black Lab, who trained him. When we told Chance to sit, he glanced at Tilly and followed her lead. We crated Chance, as the shelter recommended, keeping him in an enclosure for brief periods of time to housebreak him and give him a sense of security. Once I left him in the crate for several hours. I returned to find him trembling, squeezed into a corner of the crate to avoid the puddles and piles he had made. No emergency had kept me. I had been chatting with a friend and time got away. It wasn't the only time I failed Chance. It was easy to fail him, a mere dog, who couldn't insist that I return, who couldn't even embarrass me by telling the story.   5

Organization: Uses transition to suggest chronological organization

Sensory details: Appeals to reader's sense of sound, sight, touch

When Chance turned 2 he became aggressive. He growled at other dogs and bared his teeth. He flattened puppies under his heavy paws. He chased children and cyclists, clamped down on their ankles and knocked them over. He even bit Tilly in a scuffle over my bed.   6

When I tired of apologizing for him, I hired a trainer. She told me his aggression was set off by fear. She said to keep him away from unfamiliar dogs and people, for their sake and his.   7

Active verbs: Uses striking verbs to present details

I fled when other dogs approached. If I was distracted and we crossed paths with another dog, I ordered Chance to sit and rewarded him with meaty treats if he stayed calm. Most days he preferred the fight. He hurled himself at the other dog, barely restrained by the leash. He barked furiously, drowning out my attempt to explain to the other dog's owner, "Chance doesn't like to socialize."   8

I didn't know when I adopted Chance that puppies need to interact with other dogs to learn social cues. A well-socialized dog employs a soft growl to tell another dog "you're in my space." A puppy who interacts with a variety of other dogs learns to   9 roughhouse in a playful, rather than a threatening, way. Chance had Tilly for company and I mistakenly thought that was enough. I was depressed and in a bad marriage. Nothing got me off the couch. By the time I started taking better care of myself and walking the dogs every day, it was too late.

I divorced my first husband and the dogs took care of me. Chance made me feel   10
safe in a large, empty house. Tilly shared my bed, resting her head on my ex-husband's pillow. But I hated being the owner of a bad dog. I felt ashamed turning away someone whose dog wanted to play and telling a schoolchild she couldn't pet Chance. I lived in constant fear of him attacking someone.

> **Dominant impression:** Uses anecdote to reinforce main idea

Yet in some ways, I am the perfect owner for Chance. An introvert, I identify with   11
his desire to be left alone. I empathize with his feelings of jealousy. When Steve and I married and Tilly transferred her loyalty to him, lying at his feet instead of mine, I could hardly suppress my rage.

It's easy to love a well-behaved dog. It's harder to love Chance, with his bristly   12
personality and tendency toward violence. Yet in the end, I measure the success of my relationship with Chance by its challenges, because if I can't love him at his most imperfect what use is love?

A few years ago, an old yellow Lab got loose. The dog lunged at Chance, sinking   13
his teeth into the soft flesh of his throat. He bit his head and tore at his face. The Lab foamed, reveling in the attack. I kept hold of Chance's leash and screamed at the owner, but she was frozen. I didn't see how Chance could survive multiple, vicious bites.

> **Connotation:** Chooses words with powerful connotations

Finally, the owner pulled the Lab off by his hind legs. Chance whimpered. He hadn't   14
fought back. What saved him were the other dog's teeth, so worn by age they were mostly ineffective. Chance's teeth were sharp and he was young and strong. Why had he held back? Perhaps he wasn't such a bad dog after all.

In his old age Chance has mellowed. When we walk, he attends to what is directly   15
in front of him, a flagpole or a mailbox, barely sensing other dogs. It takes us 40 minutes to go around the block, but when I look at him he grins. It's his favorite time of day and mine.

I try to be gentle with Chance, hoping when the time comes others will be gentle   16
with me. When I catch myself tugging his leash, I remind myself these are his last days and to enjoy them. The night before Tilly died she tried to get my attention, resting her muzzle on my keyboard. I moved her aside. I was busy writing and I thought there would be time to play, not knowing her cancer would take a dramatic turn in the morning and we would have to euthanize her.

> **Comparison:** Uses comparison to show that the author identifies with Chance
>
> **Dominant impression:** Uses anecdote to reinforce main idea

I often think back to that night, wishing I had cuddled and cradled my girl. I   17
hope not to make the same mistake with Chance. Steve scratches his belly every night before we go to bed. Chance deserves at least as much from me.

He is, after all, my good dog.   18

VISUALIZING A DESCRIPTION: A GRAPHIC ORGANIZER

For more on creating a graphic organizer, see pp. 52–53.

Seeing the content and structure of an essay in simplified, visual form can help you analyze a reading, recall key images as you generate ideas for an essay, and structure your own writing. The graphic organizer in Figure 13.1 diagrams the basic structure of a descriptive essay. When you write an essay in which your primary purpose is to describe something, you will need to follow the standard essay format—title, introduction, body, and conclusion—with slight adaptations and adjustments.

- The **introduction** should provide a context for the description and present the thesis statement, which states or suggests the dominant impression.
- The **body** of the essay should present sensory details that support the dominant impression.
- The **conclusion** draws the description to a close and makes a final reference to the dominant impression. It may offer a final detail or make a closing statement.

When you incorporate a description into an essay in which you also use other patterns of development, you will probably need to condense or eliminate one or more of the elements of your descriptive essay.

FIGURE 13.1 **Graphic Organizer for a Descriptive Essay**

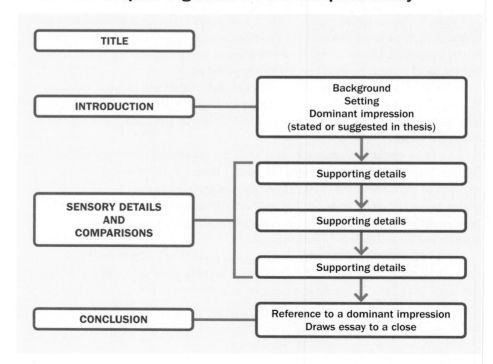

READING

You Are Your Bike

MARY ROACH

Mary Roach is a *New York Times* best-selling author of several books of popular science, including *Stiff* (2003), *Spook* (2005), *Bonk* (2008), *Packing for Mars: The Curious Science of Life in the Void* (2010), and *Gulp: Adventures on the Alimentary Canal* (2013). This essay appeared in the October 2005 issue of *Bicycling* magazine. As you read, highlight the details that help you visualize her beloved Schwinn Sting-Ray I. Then, after reading the essay, study the graphic organizer for it that appears on p. 275.

1   A stingray is a flat, gray marine creature with little about it to capture one's fancy. Bottomfeeder. Sits on its mouth. You could name a rubber bathtub mat after the stingray, and I wouldn't question your logic. But not a bike. Not a bike with a four-foot chrome sissy bar and a chopper handlebar and a glitter-gold banana seat. There is no fish as cool as the Schwinn Sting-Ray I got in sixth grade.

2   In my neighborhood, circa 1972, there was serious bike culture going down. Every day after school, around 4, the phone would ring. It would be one of the Balch kids, my neighbors: "Wanna come out and ride around?" That's what we did in those days. We watched tv and we rode around. There were six of us. We had a route: over the dirt path between our houses, down the Balch's rock-studded, rain-gullied driveway, through the pinewoods across the street (Did we invent mountain biking?), up onto the road, and back over to my driveway. The summer my parents repaved the blacktop, we'd linger at the top of the driveway where it widened out and turn laps for a while, savoring the velvet glide and leaning into the turns like the racers we'd seen on ABC's Wide World of Sports. No one spoke during these moments. There was a religious quality to our concentration, an absurd intensity that even now I can't bring to bear on my athletic pursuits.

3   As all Sting-Ray owners must, I mastered the wheelie. I was coming off a four-year horse fixation, and the wheelie held a secret thrill for me: The bike became my horse, rearing up onto its back legs, mane streaming, nostrils flared. I kept this to myself.

4   Becky Balch had a Sting-Ray too, but hers was girlie. The sissy-bar was only four inches high, and her basket had plastic flowers sewn into the fake white wicker. She earned my tomboy scorn. As tough and as cool as my Sting-Ray was, it wasn't what the Balch boys were riding. Bernie and Jeff Balch blew out so many tires on the trails that they started riding on their rims. They called their tireless, gearless junk jobs "Peelers" and took to launching them off the banks of a cattail-fringed pond at the end of our road. They'd build up speed, leap off at the last possible second, and watch the bike sink into the muck. The littlest Balch, Johnny, would wade in waist-deep and drag their Peelers out — the price he paid to hang with the big boys.

5   One day Jeff Balch convinced me to cast the Sting-Ray into the muck. I loved my Sting-Ray, but I loved Jeff Balch more. It was an unrequited love, not all that different

from the love I'd felt for horses. I can recall to this day the site of the glitter-gold seat sinking from view and the sick feeling inside me. Jeff Balch continued to ignore me and soon started going out with a glossy-haired cheerleader three houses down from us. Though she surely owned a bicycle, she did not ride around.

Shortly after the pond debacle, I wiped out in a sand patch going no-hands down   6
a hill about a half-mile down the road. This was a hill so steep and treacherous that it was known by name: Connie Elder's Hill. It was Connie Elder, a kind, quiet spinster, who pressed a wad of gauze to my chin and drove me home, leaving behind the Sting-Ray and a persistent rumor that "a piece of Mary Roach's chin" had been spotted on the pavement. I wound up with six stitches and a scar that to this day brings to mind the little gold Sting-Ray and my reckless need to impress. This had been another ill-guided effort to capture Jeff's heart. It was around then that it began to dawn on me that boys weren't interested in girls that acted like boys. They wanted girls that giggled and brushed their hair a lot and kept their bicycles out of the mud. The Sting-Ray never felt quite right after the accident, and only partly because the fork was crooked.

My tomboy years were coasting to a stop, and the Sting-Ray would eventually be   7
replaced by a 10-speed. More than most objects, the bikes we own in certain periods of our lives define who we are and what we're about. They are more like lovers or pets than things we simply own. I've long held the fantasy that I'll come across a gold, glitter-seat Sting-Ray at a local flea market. I won't go so far as to buy it, but I'll give the guy who's selling it five bucks to let me go off to the empty fringes of the parking lot and ride around.

> **EXERCISE 13.4**   **Drawing a Graphic Organizer**
>
> Using the graphic organizer in Figure 13.1 or 13.2 as a basis, draw a graphic organizer for "Bad Dog" (pp. 269–71).

INTEGRATING DESCRIPTION INTO AN ESSAY

The essay "Speaking Quiché in the Heart of Dixie" later in this chapter (pp. 289–93) uses multiple patterns of development to convey the author's ideas.

Sometimes description alone fulfills the purpose of an essay. In most cases, however, you will use description in essays that mainly rely on a different mode. For instance, in a narrative essay, description helps readers experience events, reconstruct scenes, and visualize action. Although most of your college essays will not be primarily descriptive, you can use description in essays that explain the causes or effects of a phenomenon, compare or contrast animal species, or illustrate defensive behavior in children, for example.

Here are a few suggestions for combining description effectively with other patterns of development.

1. **Include only relevant details.** Whether you describe an event, a person, or a scene, the sensory details you choose should enhance the reader's understanding of your subject.

FIGURE 13.2 **Graphic Organizer for "You Are Your Bike" by Mary Roach**

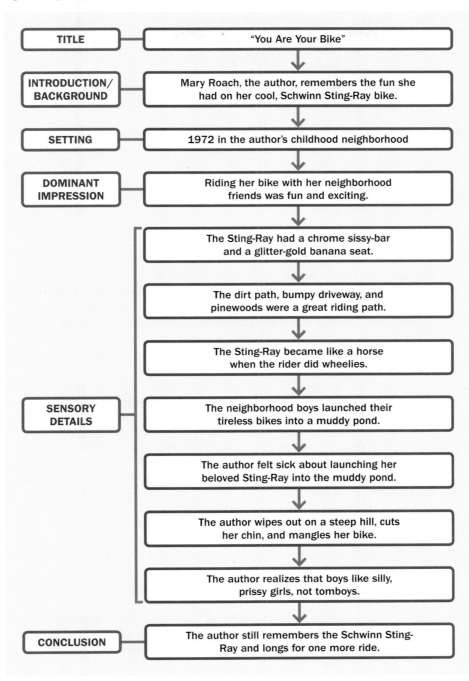

TITLE	"You Are Your Bike"
INTRODUCTION/ BACKGROUND	Mary Roach, the author, remembers the fun she had on her cool, Schwinn Sting-Ray bike.
SETTING	1972 in the author's childhood neighborhood
DOMINANT IMPRESSION	Riding her bike with her neighborhood friends was fun and exciting.
SENSORY DETAILS	The Sting-Ray had a chrome sissy-bar and a glitter-gold banana seat.
	The dirt path, bumpy driveway, and pinewoods were a great riding path.
	The Sting-Ray became like a horse when the rider did wheelies.
	The neighborhood boys launched their tireless bikes into a muddy pond.
	The author felt sick about launching her beloved Sting-Ray into the muddy pond.
	The author wipes out on a steep hill, cuts her chin, and mangles her bike.
	The author realizes that boys like silly, prissy girls, not tomboys.
CONCLUSION	The author still remembers the Schwinn Sting-Ray and longs for one more ride.

2. **Keep the description focused.** Select enough details to make your essential points and dominant impression clear. Readers may become impatient if you include too many descriptive details.
3. **Make sure the description fits the essay's tone and point of view.** A personal description, for example, is not appropriate in an essay explaining a technical process.

READING ACTIVELY AND THINKING CRITICALLY

For more on reading actively, see Chapter 3; for more on thinking critically, see Chapter 4.

When you read descriptive essays, you are often more concerned with impressions and images than you are with the logical progression of ideas. To get the full benefit of descriptive writing, you need to read actively to connect what you are reading to your own senses of sight, sound, smell, touch, and taste. But you must also examine and challenge the author's attitude as it is shown in the selection. Below are some guidelines for reading and thinking critically about descriptive essays.

WHAT TO LOOK FOR, HIGHLIGHT, AND ANNOTATE

For more on previewing, see p. 45.

1. **Preview the essay to get an overview of its content and organization.**
2. **Identify the dominant impression.** As you read, identify the subject of the description and try to determine the dominant impression the writer creates. If it is not directly stated in a thesis statement, try the following:
   - Pay attention to sensory details and highlight particularly striking ones. How do the sensory details contribute to the dominant impression?
   - Observe how the writer uses language to achieve an effect. Make an ✘ or ✔ in the margin next to effective comparisons. Underline or circle powerful word choices. How do they contribute to the dominant impression?
   - Consider the introduction, conclusion, and title. How does the introduction hint at the dominant impression or indicate the subject of the description? How does the conclusion relate to the dominant impression? How does the title suggest the essay's dominant impression?
3. **Think about the meaning.** Concentrate on the essay's meaning by answering the following questions:
   - What is the thesis? If it is not stated directly, write a sentence stating what you think the main point of the essay is.
   - What is the author's purpose in writing this description? For what audience is it intended? What techniques does the writer use to achieve her or his purpose with this audience?
4. **Consider your reactions.** Think about how the description relates to your own experience:
   - Have any situations you've experienced evoked similar images or feelings for you?
   - What thoughts and feelings does the essay evoke in you? What did you feel as you read? What feelings were you left with after reading the essay?

ANALYZING DESCRIPTIONS

A description will be colored by the writer's personal, subjective experience. Unless you have reason to believe otherwise, assume that the writer is honest—that he or she is presenting the subject accurately. But also keep in mind that the writer chooses details selectively, with the goal of advancing his or her agenda.

What is the writer's attitude toward the subject? The words a writer chooses to describe a subject can largely determine how readers view and respond to that subject and often reveal the writer's feelings and attitudes toward the subject. A description of a car as "fast and sleek" suggests approval, while the phrase "slick and glitzy" suggests a less favorable attitude. You can make the subject seem attractive and appealing or ugly and repellent, depending on the details you choose and the words you select.

APPEALING	The stranger had an impish, childlike grin, a smooth complexion with high cheekbones, and strong yet gentle hands.
REPELLENT	The stranger had limp blond hair, cold vacant eyes, and teeth stained by tobacco.

As you read, pay attention to connotations; writers often use them intentionally to create a particular emotional response. Highlight words with strong connotations or annotate them in the margin. Ask yourself whether the writer is presenting a neutral, objective description or a subjective, possibly biased, one. For example, when reading "Bad Dog" (para. 6), you might wonder how Maizes's ex-husband or pet owners whose puppies Chance "flattened" (6) might have described Chance.

What details does the writer omit? As you read an essay, ask yourself questions like these:

- What hasn't the writer told me?
- What else would I like to know about the subject?

Writers often omit details because they are not relevant, but they may also omit details that would contradict the dominant impression they intend to convey. You have probably noticed that news outlets on television or online offer slightly different slants on a news event, each providing different details or film footage. By combining or synthesizing the various reports, you can form your own impression. Often you must do the same thing when reading descriptions. Pull together information from several sources to form your own impression.

YOUR ESSAY ASSIGNMENT

Write a descriptive essay about something you can picture clearly or that you can readily observe. Choose one of the following to describe in detail:

- an unusual, striking, or surprising object,
- a place that has significance to you, your family, or your cultural group, and
- a person who influenced you (for good or ill).

Examples: A robot you built from a kit; a playground you hung around in as a child; a teacher who changed your expectations about school or learning.

Prewriting

1 Select a topic from the list above, or create your own.

Use one or more of the following suggestions to choose a subject to describe.

1. **List one or more broad topics**, such as *An Unusual Object, A Place with Personal Significance,* or *An Influential Person.* Then alone or with another student, **brainstorm a list of objects, activities,** or **people** that fit the assignment. Other prewriting strategies, like freewriting or questioning, may also help you generate topic ideas. (Rational, pragmatic, and concrete learners may prefer listing. Creative, emotional, and abstract learners may prefer freewriting or questioning.)
2. **Picture the objects in your room** or on your desk and ask yourself questions, such as, "Who gave me that object?" or "Why did I buy [or make] it?" (Spatial, creative, or emotional learners may prefer picturing.)
3. **Work backward**: Think about the most influential people or most important values in your life, and then think about a place or object that represents them in your mind. (Abstract and independent learners may prefer working backward.)

2 Consider your purpose and audience, and choose a perspective and point of view.

Ask yourself these questions.

- Will my essay's **purpose** be to **express myself**, **inform**, or **persuade**?
- Who is my **audience**? Will readers need any **background information** to understand my essay? Have I chosen a person, place, or thing that I can write about honestly for this audience?
- What **point of view** best suits my purpose and audience? The first person (*I, we*) will work best if describing an object with personal significance or if your purpose is expressive; third person (*it, they, he/she*) will be most appropriate if describing something objectively, of if your purpose is informative.

*The writing process is *recursive*; that is, you may find yourself revising as you draft or prewriting as you revise. This is especially true when writing on a computer. Your writing process may also differ from that of your classmates, depending on your preferred learning style.

Prewriting

3 **Choose an aspect of your subject to emphasize, and collect sensory details.**

Choose one trait or aspect of your subject to focus on.

If it's a . . .	try focusing on . . .
person	a character trait
thing	its usefulness, value, or beauty

Then record details that support the slant you have chosen.

1. **Describe your subject to a friend**, concentrating on the slant you have chosen, and make notes on your comments and your friend's response.
2. **Draw a quick sketch** of your subject and label the parts.
3. **Make a table** and label each section with one of the senses. Then list the sensory details associated with your subject.

Generate comparisons. Think of appropriate comparisons—**similes**, **metaphors**, **personifications**—for as many details in your list as possible. Then select the one or two strongest comparisons and try to use them in your essay. Use at least 2 prewriting strategies to generate details. (More prewriting strategies appear in Chapter 5, pp. 107–16.)

4 **Evaluate your details.**

Reread your notes, highlighting the **vivid**, **concrete details** that will create pictures in your reader's mind. Cross out the following:

- vague details,
- irrelevant details, and
- details that do not support your slant.

Then copy and paste the remaining details to a new document for easy access when drafting.

In small groups, share your ideas and details.

1. Have each writer **explain her or his slant** on the subject and **provide a list of details**.
2. As a group, **evaluate each writer's details** in terms of her or his slant and suggest improvements.

(continued on next page)

Organizing & Drafting

5 Create a dominant impression.

Your **dominant impression** should
- appeal to **your audience**,
- offer an **unusual perspective**, and
- provide **new insights** on your subject.

Description often includes an element of surprise; a description with an unexpected slant and new insights is more likely to engage the readers' imagination.

Think of the dominant impression as . . .
1. **a thesis** that conveys your main point and pulls your details together.
2. **a mood or feeling about the subject**, which all the details in your essay explain or support.

Team up with a classmate to evaluate each other's dominant impression. Underline or highlight any problematic wording and give feedback.

6 Choose a method of organization.

Select the **method of organization** that will best support your dominant impression. For example:
- If you are focusing on a person's slovenly appearance, then a **spatial** (top to bottom, left to right) organization may be effective. If using spatial organization, also consider what **vantage point(s)** will provide the most useful information or from which vantage point(s) you can provide the most revealing or striking details.
- If you are describing a visit to a wildlife preserve, **chronological** order might be a useful method of organization.
- A **most-to-least** or **least-to-most** arrangement might work best for a description of the symptoms of pneumonia.
- If you are describing a chocolate chip cookie, you may want to organize by the **five senses**, clustering details about how it looks, smells, tastes, and feels in your mouth.

7 Write a first draft of your descriptive essay.

Use the following guidelines to keep your narrative on track.
- The **introduction** should set up your **dominant impression**, which you may choose to state in a thesis.
- The **body paragraphs** should include **striking sensory details** that support your **dominant impression**. Be sure to include **enough details** that readers can picture your subject but not so many that readers will get bored. Try to work your one or two strongest comparisons into your draft. Organize each body paragraph so that it focuses on a **single topic**, and use **transitions** (*first, next, above, below, before, after*) to make relationships among details clear.
- The **conclusion** should **revisit your dominant impression**. You may also want to refer to the beginning of your essay or make a final observation about the significance of your subject.

Revising

8 Evaluate your draft and revise as necessary.

Use **Figure 13.3, "Flowchart for Revising a Descriptive Essay,"** to help you discover the strengths and weaknesses of your descriptive essay.

Editing & Proofreading

9 Edit and proofread your essay.

Refer to Chapter 10 for help with . . .
- **editing sentences** to avoid wordiness, making your verb choices strong and active, and making your sentences clear, varied, and parallel, and
- **editing words** for tone and diction, connotation, and concrete and specific language.

Pay particular attention to the **punctuation of adjectives**

1. Use a comma between **coordinate adjectives** that are not joined by *and*.
   - **Singh was a *confident, skilled* pianist.**
   Coordinate adjectives are a series of adjectives whose order can be changed (*skilled, confident* pianist or *confident, skilled* pianist).
2. Do not use commas between **cumulative adjectives** whose order cannot be changed.
   - ***Two frightened brown* eyes peered at us from under the sofa.**
   You would not write *frightened two* brown eyes.
3. Use a hyphen to connect two words that work together as an adjective before a noun *unless* the first word is an adverb ending in -*ly*.
   - ***well-used* book**
   - ***foil-wrapped* pizza**
   - ***perfectly thrown* pass**

FIGURE 13.3 **Flowchart for Revising a Descriptive Essay**

QUESTIONS

1. Without looking at your essay, *state* the dominant impression in a sentence. Then highlight the sentences in the essay that express the *dominant impression*. Do these sentences successfully convey the impression?

NO

YES

REVISION STRATEGIES

- Reread your essay. Make a list of the different impressions it conveys.
- Choose one impression that you have the most to say about, and brainstorm to develop additional details that support it.

(continued on next page)

(Figure 13.3 continued)

QUESTIONS		REVISION STRATEGIES

2. Place a ✔ by each sensory detail. Does each detail support your *dominant impression*?

 NO

- Eliminate irrelevant sensory details.

 YES

3. Review the sensory details you have ✔'d. Is your language vivid enough to help readers visualize the topic? Are the connotations of your language appropriate?

 NO

- Brainstorm additional sensory details.
- Replace passive verbs with active ones.
- Vary your sentences.
- Replace words with inappropriate connotations with words that better support your dominant impression.

 YES

4. [Bracket] each comparison—simile, metaphor, and analogy. Is each fresh and effective?

 NO

- Eliminate clichés.
- Brainstorm fresh comparisons.
- Instead of writing, try speaking to a friend.

 YES

5. *Write* a brief outline showing how you have organized your details. Is it clear from your essay how the details are organized?

 NO

- Rearrange your details in a different order. Experiment to see which works best.
- Add transitions where necessary to connect your ideas.

 YES

6. Underline the topic sentence of each paragraph. Compare the sensory details (✔) to the topic sentence. Does the topic sentence make clear what the paragraph is describing?

 NO

- Revise so that each paragraph has a clear topic sentence and supporting details clearly relate to the topic sentence.

 YES

7. Reread your introduction and conclusion. Is each effective?

 NO

- Revise your introduction and conclusion so that they meet the guidelines in Chapter 7.

READINGS: DESCRIPTION IN ACTION

Heatstroke with a Side of Burn Cream

TED SAWCHUCK

Ted Sawchuck, a journalism student at the University of Maryland at College Park, wrote this essay in response to an assignment in one of his classes. He was asked to describe a workplace situation that he had experienced. As you read, study the annotations and pay particular attention to Sawchuck's use of sensory language that helps you see and feel what he has experienced.

I sprinkle the last layer of cheese on top of my nachos--no time to watch the cheddar melt--and turn sideways, nearly falling face-first on grimy, spongy rubber mats. Catching my fall and the plate, I whip a towel from my belt with my free hand, open the scalding-hot oven door, and slide in the chips to toast before slapping a palm on top of the now-light-brown quesadilla on the rack below and pulling it out onto a clean part of the towel for a 180 degree turn to the counter behind. A pizza cutter makes three smooth cuts; the quesadilla is plated with three small cups (guac, salsa, sour cream) and handed to the window. I slap the bell, bellow "Jamie! Nachos!", and spin back to my station too fast to see a gorgeous grad student scoop up the plate and scoot it out to her table.

Welcome to a restaurant kitchen during lunch or dinner rush, the time when the restaurant is packed with hungry people and the kitchen is maniacally cranking away at their orders. I'm thrashing appetizers, trying to keep up with college students' demands for fried goodies, nachos, and quesadillas. My friend A is working the grill, cooking fifteen burgers and a couple chicken breasts for sandwiches, and M, a mutual friend, is buzzing around prepping plates, flirting with waitresses, and handling salads and desserts, both of which require time away from the main preparation line.

The kitchen space I spend eight hours a day in is about the size of my one-room apartment, which is slightly larger than your average prison cell. Three people, and more on horribly busy days, work in that space, crammed in with four fryers, a massive grill, a griddle, an oven, a microwave, two refrigeration units with prep counters, bins of tortilla chips, a burning-hot steam table bigger than the grill, and vast tubs of bacon. If I put both arms out and rotated, I'd severely injure at least two people.

1   **Introduction:** Sawchuck builds toward his dominant impression by describing a hectic evening in a restaurant kitchen.

2   **Dominant impression:** Thesis identifies the topic of the description, and vivid, active verbs help create the dominant impression.

3   **Sensory details:** Topic sentences in paragraphs 3 and 4 introduce sensory details that help readers imagine the kitchen. A comparison adds humor and realism to visual details.

The most common problem for nonchefs is dealing with the heat. On one side of my work station are four fryers full of 350-degree oil. On the other, there is the steam table, so named because it boils water to keep things warm--especially deadly for forearms. Burns aren't the worst of it. You'll lose some skin, but you won't die. Overheating or dehydration can kill. When it's over 110 degrees in your workplace, fluid consumption is essential. I start gushing sweat the second I clock in and don't stop until about half an hour after clocking out. Even though we have huge buzzing exhaust fans to suck the greasy smoke away from our lungs and a warehouse-sized room fan to keep it at a low triple digits, I drink enough water to fill the steam table twice during busy times. My bandana frequently restrains ice cubes as well as rapidly tangling hair.

The fans add to the noise, as do the chattering servers, the head chef yelling out orders, other cooks yelling out updates, and the music. Some kitchens run on music, others don't. I like to blare NPR when it is just me and A working, but on nights with a full staff, the rap music that gives rap music a bad name is trotted out--you know the kind I mean--the mainstream, with pre-choreographed dances, predictable couplets about the joys of 'caine and loose women, and frequently more bleeped words than heard. The volume at which such music is played means I have to scream everything and never hear orders. It's like playing tennis with a ball that randomly disappears.

There are uncountable ways to damage yourself in a restaurant kitchen. If you didn't touch anything--just stood there--you'd still be at risk for smoke inhalation, steam burns, knife cuts from other people, spills, splatters, and being bowled over--because no one stands still in a professional kitchen. Even walking in a kitchen is dangerous. The only time the kitchen floor at the to-remain-nameless restaurant at which I cook is clean is immediately after washing, a process that results in innumerable gallons of grody gray water and the inadvertent freeing of at least one mouse from his glue trap. Moving in that kitchen is a constant struggle. Because the floor is slippery red tile, we put down thick rubber mats, which make standing for eight hours much easier on the knees. Unfortunately, these mats are coated, nay permeated, with every-thing we've ever spilled on them. Moving is like trying to skate across a frying pan with butter strapped to your feet. Sometimes you'll need to use a skating-like sliding motion to get through without falling face-first in the awfulness. Falling is worse, because if you grab to catch something your options are a fryer (bad), the grill (worse), or your head chef (worst of all).

Sensory details: Topic sentences focuses attention on sounds in the kitchen

Sensory details: Topic sentences focuses attention on physical dangers of the job. Notice how the sentences in this paragraph vary in length and structure.

4

5

6

Working in a restaurant during rush makes journalism on deadline look like elementary basket-weaving. While reporters are expected to get everything right in every story, they're only writing at most three stories a day. At one point during the worst dinner rush I can remember, I was cooking five nachos, eight quesadillas, four sampler plates, and three orders of wings at the same time. I had to get every component of those dishes right, from the plate they were served on to the garnish, serving size, cooking temperature, and appearance--and I needed to have done it fifteen minutes ago because the customers have been waiting. They don't care that we're so stacked up there's no more room in the oven for the nachos and quesadillas that are stacking up. Did I mention sampler plates have four items each, all with different cooking times and prep methods?

Working in a restaurant kitchen is like speaking a foreign language. Once you stop thinking about it and just do it, you can keep up, sometimes. Other times, the pressure builds up. Maybe half the restaurant fills up in five minutes, or it's game night in a college town. Maybe the servers screwed up and gave you all their tables' orders at once instead of as they came in. Either way, you've got to shift into the next gear. Sometimes it means throwing on ten orders of wings in fryers only meant to hold eight, then garnishing a stack of plates for the main course guys so they can focus on getting twenty burgers of different doneness levels cooked properly. For the appetizer guy, it usually means never being allowed to make a mistake, because any delay in appetizer futzes the flow of the meal. The main course is being cooked at the same time, so if my stuff comes in late, then the properly cooked main course will either be overdone or arrive cold because no one wants the main course five minutes after receiving an appetizer.

When you're late in the restaurant world, it's called being in the weeds. The origin of the name is unclear, but friends of mine note that you hide bodies where weeds grow because it's a sign of low foot traffic. Being in the weeds is not as bad as rendition to Egypt, but everyone, servers and management included, can see you're behind. In addition to getting chewed out by the head chef (who would rather yell at you than help you), you lose any chance you had with that subtle, kittenish server. Not holding your own on the line means much less fun after work. When you're in the weeds (or "weeded"), you can ask for help or suck it up. Asking for help is frowned upon; your only route is taking a breath and pulling yourself out. I spend a lot of time in the weeds, unsurprising for a kid whose only chef-like

7   **Comparison:** The topic sentences in paragraphs 7 and 8 use comparisons to convey the essence of restaurant kitchen work.

8   **Organization:** After several paragraphs presenting the concrete details of the job, Sawchuck shifts to the more abstract issues of the mental complexity and time pressure.

Dominant impression: Notice how the connotations of *futzes* support the dominant impression better than a more formal word, such as *disrupts*, would.

9

Conclusion: Sawchuck offers a final comment on restaurant kitchen work and makes a direct appeal to readers.

experience was making breakfast on Sundays at home and the occasional grilled cheese sandwich.

Like print journalism and the armed forces, professional cooking requires 10 a very specific skill set. If you've got it, get a good knife and get to practicing. If not, be a little nicer next time the entree doesn't come exactly when you expect it.

ANALYZING THE WRITER'S TECHNIQUE

1. **Dominant Impression** Describe Sawchuck's dominant impression about working in a restaurant kitchen. Is it stated explicitly or implied?
2. **Sensory Language** Which examples of sensory language did you find particularly strong and engaging? What makes them effective? Which, if any, are weak, and how can they be improved?
3. **Comparisons** The annotations point out some of the numerous comparisons Sawchuck uses to explain his topic. Identify several others. Which ones are particularly effective? Do any seem ineffective? If so, why?
4. **Patterns** In addition to description, what other patterns of development does the writer use? How do these patterns make the description more effective?

THINKING CRITICALLY ABOUT DESCRIPTION

1. **Omissions** Sawchuck leaves out the name of the restaurant. What other information is omitted that might have given you a fuller understanding of Sawchuck or his job?
2. **Tone** What is Sawchuck's tone? How does it affect your attitude toward the information that is contained in the essay?
3. **Connotation** One of the annotations (para. 8) points out the connotations of a particular word Sawchuck uses. In paragraph 4, how are the connotations of "gushing sweat" different from those of other language he could have chosen, such as "sweating profusely" or "gushing perspiration"? Do you think he made the best choice, given the dominant impression he is trying to create? Why or why not?
4. **Metaphor** The phrase "in the weeds" (9) offers a visual metaphor. What connotations does this phrase have for you?

RESPONDING TO THE ESSAY

1. **Reaction** Sawchuck notes that falling behind on the job results in less fun after work. Have you found that job performance can affect off-the-job relationships with coworkers? If so, how?
2. **Discussion** Do you think Sawchuck is satisfied with his job despite the adverse working conditions? Discuss to what degree working conditions affect job performance and satisfaction.

3. **Journal** Is it possible to be "in the weeds" academically? Write a journal entry exploring either reasons for being in the weeds or ways to get yourself out of the weeds.
4. **Essay** Sawchuck describes the time pressures he experiences. Write an essay describing the time pressures you experience in either an academic or a workplace setting.

READING

Eating Chili Peppers

JEREMY MACCLANCY

Jeremy MacClancy is an anthropologist and tutor at Oxford Brookes University in England who has written several scholarly works in the field of anthropology. This essay is taken from his book *Consuming Culture: Why You Eat What You Eat* (1993). As you read the selection, underline or highlight the descriptive words and phrases that convey what it's like to eat chili peppers.

How come over half of the world's population have made a powerful chemical irritant the center of their gastronomic lives? How can so many millions stomach chilies? 1

Biting into a tabasco pepper is like aiming a flame-thrower at your parted lips. 2
There might be little reaction at first, but then the burn starts to grow. A few seconds later the chili mush in your mouth reaches critical mass and your palate prepares for liftoff. The message spreads. The sweat glands open, your eyes stream, your nose runs, your stomach warms up, your heart accelerates, and your lungs breathe faster. All this is normal. But bite off more than your body can take, and you will be left coughing, sneezing, and spitting. Tears stripe your cheeks, and your mouth belches fire like a dragon celebrating its return to life. Eater beware!

As a general stimulant, chili is similar to amphetamines — only quicker, cheaper, 3
non-addictive, and beneficial to boot. Employees at the tabasco plant in Louisiana rarely complain of coughs, hay fever, or sinusitis. (Recent evidence, however, suggests that too many chilies can bring on stomach cancer.) Over the centuries, people have used hot peppers as a folk medicine to treat sore throats or inflamed gums, to relieve respiratory distress, and to ease gastritis induced by alcoholism. For aching muscles and tendons, a chili plaster is more effective than one of mustard, with the added advantage that it does not blister the skin. But people do not eat tabasco, jalapeno, or cayenne peppers because of their pharmacological side-effects. They eat them for the taste — different varieties have different flavors — and for the fire they give off. In other words, they go for the burn.

Eating chilies makes for exciting times: the thrill of anticipation, the extremity 4
of the flames, and then the slow descent back to normality. This is a benign form of masochism, like going to a horror movie, riding a roller coaster, or stepping into a cold bath after a sauna. The body flashes danger signals, but the brain knows the threat is not too great. Aficionados, self-absorbed in their burning passion, know exactly how to pace their whole chili eating so that the flames are maintained at a steady maximum. Wrenched out of normal routines by the continuing assault on their mouths,

they concentrate on the sensation and ignore almost everything else. They play with fire and just ride the burn, like experienced surfers cresting along a wave. For them, without hot peppers, food would lose its zest and their days would seem too dull. A cheap, legal thrill, chili is the spice of their life.

In the rural areas of Mexico, men can turn their chili habit into a contest of strength by seeing who can stomach the most hot peppers in a set time. This gastro-nomic test, however, is not used as a way to prove one's machismo, for women can play the game as well. In this context, chilies are a non-sexist form of acquired love for those with strong hearts and fiery passions — a steady source of hot sauce for their lives.   5

The enjoyable sensations of a running nose, crying eyes, and dragon-like mouth belching flames are clearly not for the timorous.   6

More tabasco, anyone?   7

EXAMINING THE READING

1. **Reasons** According to the author, why do men in rural areas of Mexico eat chili peppers?
2. **Details** What are the beneficial health effects of eating chili peppers?
3. **Attitude** What is the author's attitude toward those who eat chili peppers?
4. **Explanation** How is eating chili peppers a benign form of masochism?
5. **Thesis** What is the author's thesis? Is it stated or implied?
6. **Vocabulary** Explain the meaning of each of the following words as it is used in the reading: *gastronomic* (para. 1), *palate* (2), *benign* (4), *masochism* (4), and *afi-cionados* (4).

ANALYZING THE WRITER'S TECHNIQUE

1. **Dominant Impression** Express the essay's dominant impression in your own words.
2. **Comparison** Explain the comparison between biting into a tabasco pepper and aiming a flame-thrower at your lips.
3. **Conclusion** Evaluate the essay's conclusion. If the essay had ended with paragraph 6 instead of paragraph 7, would the conclusion have been more effective or less so? Why?
4. **Audience** What audience is the author addressing? What details help you determine the audience?
5. **Title** The title of MacClancy's essay is very direct. Why do you think the author chose this title? If you had to create a title for this essay, what would it be?

THINKING CRITICALLY ABOUT DESCRIPTION

1. **Omitted Details** What details are omitted from this essay that might have been included?
2. **Connotation** What is the connotation of the phrase "chili mush" (para. 3)?

3. **Details** How does the way in which the author describes eating a chili pepper affect the way that you view eating one?
4. **Sensory Detail** Which examples of sensory language did you find particularly powerful and engaging? What makes them effective?

RESPONDING TO THE READING

1. **Reaction** How would you react if a waiter accidentally served you the wrong dish—one loaded with chili peppers—and you unsuspectingly took a big bite?
2. **Journal** Do you have a favorite food or a food that you cannot tolerate? Choose one of the two and write a journal entry that describes the food in vivid detail.
3. **Discussion** In small groups, discuss the spiciest foods that you have ever eaten and your reaction.
4. **Essay** MacClancy compares eating a chili pepper to going to a horror movie, riding a roller coaster, or stepping into a cold bath after a sauna. He says the experience of eating a chili is a cheap, legal thrill. Write an essay in which you describe a different kind of legal thrill. Be sure to use words that appeal to the senses.

WORKING TOGETHER

Collaboration Suppose you were to open a restaurant that specialized in spicy, chili-laden dishes. Working with a partner, create a name for the restaurant and a thirty-second radio advertisement for its grand opening.

READING: DESCRIPTION COMBINED WITH OTHER PATTERNS

Speaking Quiché in the Heart of Dixie

GABRIEL THOMPSON

This selection is from a book by Gabriel Thompson, *Working in the Shadows: A Year of Doing the Jobs (Most) Americans Won't Do* (2010). The book (and this excerpt from it) describes Thompson's experiences working undercover at jobs staffed mostly by undocumented immigrants. Thompson has also published two other books—*There's No José Here* (2006) and *Calling All Radicals* (2007)—as well as numerous articles in publications including *New York* magazine, *The Nation,* and *The New York Times.* As you read this excerpt, identify the dominant impression Thompson creates and the strategies he uses to reinforce it.

Superhero comics aren't complete without an evil genius. Often he seeks to construct the ultimate weapon to hold the world hostage; if he's really deranged he simply wants to use it to end human civilization. Since the construction of the weapon must be clandestine, work goes on belowground or behind hidden doors. Walk through the door and an immense world of nameless and undoubtedly evil scientists are at work, tinkering with mysterious equipment while wearing smocks and continuously checking devices. 1

That's the image that immediately comes to mind when I push through the double doors that separate the break room from the plant floor. This isn't a workplace: This is an underground lair. In the first room, workers scurry around in plastic blue smocks akin 2

that moves a continuous stream of meat, their feet planted as they arrange the pieces in a line. We weave our way around large metal machinery and step through a frothy puddle of foam that spews from a thick hose on the cement floor. The smell is a mixture of strong industrial cleaner and fresh meat. To my left is a chest-high cylinder filled to the brim with chicken bits; while it captures my attention, I step on what feels like a sponge and lift my foot to find a piece of pink meat, now flattened. Up ahead, I can see from the puffs of condensation coming from his mouth that Lonnie is saying something to our group — the temperature is frigid, probably in the low forties — but I can't hear anything. I remove my earplugs and am greeted by the roar of machinery. It's not a piercing noise, more of a loud, all-encompassing rumble: Think of the sound you hear when putting your ear to a seashell and multiply by a hundred. I put my earplugs back in.

We walk beneath a doorway and the full scale of the processing floor is revealed. I   3
see no walls in front of me, just open space filled with workers standing in various areas without moving their feet. Hundreds of dead and featherless chickens are hanging upside down from stainless steel hooks, moving rapidly across my field of vision. I hear a beeping sound and step aside from a man driving a scooter-like contraption, which is carrying a container of steaming chicken meat (the contraption turns out to be a pallet truck, and the steam is actually from dry ice). As we cross the plant floor we pass beneath a line of chickens, whirling along more steel hooks; liquid falls from their carcasses and lands with chilly plops on my scalp. Hopefully water. In front of us dozens of workers are slicing up chickens — the debone department — but we proceed further, until we're standing aside a blond-haired woman in her forties who, like Lonnie, is wearing a hard hat.

"This is your supervisor, Barbara," Lonnie tells us, "but she won't be needing you   4
tonight." He tells Ben and Diane to follow him and motions me to stay put. When he returns he leads me through another doorway. "You're going to work in a different department today, but check in with DSI tomorrow," he says. Lonnie deposits me at the end of a line where boxes are being stacked.

The nearest person is a skinny white man with the hood of his Alabama football   5
sweatshirt pulled tight over his head. I stay quiet, feeling slightly intimidated by my new coworker, who has deep lines cutting across his gaunt face and is missing a few front teeth. But when he turns to me he flashes a friendly smile. "How long you been here?" he asks.

"About five minutes."   6

He lets loose a squeaking chuckle, his shoulders bouncing up and down. "I've only   7
been here two weeks." Kyle, it turns out, is my neighbor. He lives in a trailer with his wife and two kids about half a mile from where I'm staying. "Been right at that trailer for eighteen years, on land that was my granddaddy's. I worked in the plant four years, then quit. Now I'm back . . . don't know exactly why."*

---

* A note here on accents. Kyle, like many native Alabamans at the plant, speaks in a very heavy and melodic drawl. It was beautiful to hear, but that beauty soon becomes distracting when I attempt to render it accurately on the page. For example, when he told me he had been at the trailer for eighteen years, it sounded to my ears like: "Been rahht at tha-yat trawla' for eightee-yin years." For the sake of readability, I will not try to capture every nuance of the local dialect. One final point to illustrate the strength of the country accent: It took me a week of hanging out with Kyle before I finally realized that his name wasn't, in fact, Kyle. It was Gil. Later, when I listened repeatedly to a message he left on my cell phone, I realized that it wasn't Gil, but another name entirely. Here, he will remain Kyle. [Thompson's note.]

Kyle normally works in DSI, but he says that today they're short people in the   8
IQF department, another mysterious trio of initials. In IQF, bags of chicken wings
are stuffed into boxes, taped, and shoved down on rollers to us. Our task is to
stack the forty-pound boxes onto pallets. Once a pallet is stacked with forty-nine
boxes — seven boxes to a row, seven rows high — a pallet driver whisks it away and
we start loading up another. This is almost identical to the stacking of lettuce boxes
completed by loaders on the machine, except that the pace here is much slower.
I help Kyle do this for twenty minutes, until the machine at the front of the line
breaks. A black woman with short blond hair, who has been taping the boxes shut,
lets out a good-natured curse. It takes several minutes for a group of men to fix the
machine; several minutes later it breaks down again. Over the coming month, I'll
occasionally be asked to help out in IQF, and during almost every shift the machine
breaks down — hourly. For this reason alone, it's considered a good place to work
(as one of the "good" jobs, it also doesn't have a single immigrant working in the
department).

With nothing to do, Kyle and I take a seat on the rollers. "You ever work in   9
debone?" I ask him.

"Way back when I started, they tried to get me on there. Stayed a month. They told 10
me I couldn't work fast enough so they shifted me out. I made sure I wasn't working
fast enough too. Run you like slaves over there. I already knew how they did, though,
'cause my old lady was on the debone line for years." Now, he tells me, she's working
at Wal-Mart.

The machine is finally fixed and we return to stacking boxes. After thirty minutes   11
the black woman who was cursing the contraption asks me to come up and tape boxes.
I'm happy for the change in scenery, but this task soon becomes tedious. My job is to
shake the box so that the bags lie flat, then pull the two top flaps together and shove
it through a machine that tapes it shut. Cutting lettuce confirmed in my mind that
much of what we call "low-skilled labor" is in fact quite difficult. But at the chicken
plant, I'm already learning, many of the jobs are designed so that a person off the
street, with minimal instruction, can do them correctly the very first time. I'm sure
this is considered a "breakthrough" by the managerial class, but all it does is leave me
bored within fifteen minutes.

Sometime after 2:00 a.m., I'm told to take a break. I hang up my gloves and white   12
smock on a hook and walk away from IQF. A minute later I've pushed through one
swinging door and walked beneath two other doorways, and I'm watching an endless
line of carved-up carcasses fall into a large container. I have no idea where I am. To
my left, dozens of immigrant men and women are cutting up chickens with knives and
scissors. I approach one woman who can't be much taller than four feet, and ask her in
Spanish if she can tell me how to get to the break room. She looks at me and shakes
her head.

"She doesn't speak Spanish," another woman says, in Spanish. "You go straight   13
down that row and make a left." I hear the two speak in what sounds like an Indian
dialect, thank them both, and follow her directions.

The break room is mostly empty, but I notice Ben sitting alone in a corner booth. 14
We're both struck by how disorganized everything seems to be. Like me, Ben has been
hired for one department (debone), transferred to another (DSI), and then relocated
once more, with unclear instructions along they way. He doesn't even know the name
of the department that he's in. "Whatever it is, they have me standing and watching
chickens go by."

"That's it?" I ask. "Are you supposed to *do* anything?" 15

"Uh, I think like maybe they said to look for mold." 16

"Mold? The chickens have mold?" 17

"Not yet anyway. I haven't seen any. I'm looking for green stuff." 18

"And if they have mold, what do you do?" 19

"I dunno." Ben pushes his sliding glasses up, beginning to look concerned. "I hope 20
that's what I heard. I'm pretty sure somebody said something about mold." He looks at
his watch and stands up. "I gotto go."

By now there are perhaps fifty people sitting in nearby booths, with about an equal 21
number of whites, blacks, and Latinos, who are mostly gathered in self-segregated
groups. One wall is plastered with what are meant to be inspiring corporate messages
in Spanish and English, illustrated with geometric shapes and arrows. The "Corner-
stones of Continuous Improvement" are written at each point of a large triangle:
"Quality, Process Improvement, Teamwork." Next to this diagram is a more detailed
"14 Points of Continuous Improvement," which include quizzical tips like "Drive Out
Fear." Workers pass these grand pronouncements without pause, but they take note of
a yellow flyer taped to the wall that reads "Taco Soup Wednesday Night."

I'm joined a few minutes later by a white man in a flannel coat who tells me that 22
he's been on the debone line for five months. He snorts when I tell him that I'm
impressed he's lasting so long.

"It's work release," he says. "The only reason I'm here is 'cause they locked my ass 23
up." I don't ask what landed him in prison, but he does reveal that after the death of
his father, he went on a number of epic alcohol binges. "Can't do that anymore 'cause
I'm locked up and got myself a bleeding ulcer. But I'll tell you one thing," he says
before I depart, "once I'm free you ain't never gonna see me step foot inside a chicken
plant again."

I use the bathroom and manage to find my way back to Kyle and the boxes. He is 24
seated on the rollers, hood pulled even lower on his head to ward off the cold, while a
mechanic tries to get the machine back up and working.

For reasons that aren't explained, IQF is released earlier than other departments. 25
As I walk toward the break room at 7:40 a.m., I meet a stream of men and women
heading in the other direction, getting ready to begin the day shift. I swipe my ID
card to sign out, am hit by the bright sunshine of another scorching day, hop on my
bike, and pedal home. Kyle has agreed to pick me up tonight, so I don't have to worry
about getting run over by a chicken truck. Back in my trailer I eat a quick breakfast of
cereal and a peanut butter and jelly sandwich, type up my notes, and lay down. The

sun is streaming through the window, my trailer shakes each time a truck loaded with live chickens passes, and my neighbor's roosters are engaged with a dog in some sort of noise competition. I can't be bothered; I fall asleep instantly.

EXAMINING THE READING

1. **Reasons** Why does Thompson mention and describe the two posters in paragraph 22? What is the significance of the poster describing the food?
2. **Details** In paragraph 8, Thompson mentions stacking lettuce boxes. How would he know about this job?
3. **Reasons** Why is the IQF a good place to work?
4. **Details** What erroneous assumption does the author make about the woman of whom he asks directions to the break room (para. 12)? Why did he assume this about her?
5. **Vocabulary** Explain the meaning of each of the following words or phrases as it is used in the reading: *deranged* (para. 1), *clandestine* (1), *lair* (2), *gaunt face* (5), and *pronouncement* (24). Refer to a dictionary as needed.

ANALYZING THE WRITER'S TECHNIQUE

1. **Dominant Impression** What dominant impression does Thompson convey in this essay? Is it stated or implied? Explain your answers.
2. **Title** What is the significance of the essay's title?
3. **Descriptive Language** How does Thompson's descriptive language allow you to understand and picture the processing floor (para. 3)? What words and phrases are most descriptive in this section?
4. **Patterns** What patterns other than description does Thompson use in this essay? What purposes do they serve?

VISUALIZING THE READING

Thompson conveys information about his job and surroundings by using many of the characteristics of descriptive essays. Analyze his use of these characteristics by completing the following chart. Give several examples for each type of characteristic used, including the paragraph numbers for reference. The first one has been done for you.

Descriptive Characteristic	Examples
Active verbs	1. "workers scurry around" (para. 2) 2. "I've pushed through a swinging door" (14)
Sensory details (sound, smell, touch, sight, taste)	3.
Varied sentences	4.
Comparisons	5.
Connotative language	6.

THINKING CRITICALLY ABOUT DESCRIPTION

1. **Connotation** What connotation does the word *lair* suggest (para. 2)?
2. **Detail** Why does the author make a point to say that Kyle's wife left the plant and went to work for Walmart?
3. **Connotation** Why does the author put the word *breakthrough* (para. 13) in quotations?
4. **Objective/Subjective** Is the essay objective, subjective, or a mixture of both? Explain your answer.
5. **Tone** Describe Thompson's tone in this essay. What information does his tone convey that is not directly stated?

RESPONDING TO THE READING

1. **Reaction** The author attempts to blend in with the other workers at the plant. Do you think that he is successful in doing so? Why or why not? Give examples from his behavior or his words that support your answer.
2. **Discussion** What do you think Thompson learned as a result of his undercover experience in the chicken processing plant?
3. **Journal** Thompson writes that much of what we call "low-skilled labor" is actually very difficult. Discuss some low-skilled jobs that you know about and explain what makes them so difficult.
4. **Essay** Write an essay in which you describe the worst job you or someone you know has ever had. In addition to describing the job, explain why the job was so bad.

WORKING TOGETHER

1. The poster in the break room of the chicken plant was entitled "Fourteen Points of Continuous Improvement." Working with a small group of your peers, list fourteen changes that could be implemented in that plant in order to create a better work environment.
2. Many businesses have a catchy advertising slogan that draws the public's attention to their company. Working with a small group of your peers, brainstorm slogans that you hear on TV or radio. Then assume that you are Gabriel Thompson, and you want to create a slogan for the chicken plant that will "tell it like it is." Make sure your slogan is simple, catchy, and honest. Be prepared to share your slogan with the class and explain its significance.

> **e** **macmillanhighered.com/successfulwriting**
> E-readings > *Hidden Gems of Pebble Creek* (video), National Park Service

APPLYING YOUR SKILLS: ADDITIONAL ESSAY ASSIGNMENTS

Using what you learned about description in this chapter, write a descriptive essay on one of the topics listed below. Depending on the topic you choose, you may need to conduct research.

For more on locating and documenting sources, see Part 5.

TO EXPRESS YOUR IDEAS

1. Suppose a famous person, living or dead, visited your house for dinner. Write an essay describing the person and the evening and expressing your feelings about the occasion.
2. In "You Are Your Bike," the author describes her Schwinn Sting-Ray and what it meant to her. Write an essay for your classmates describing a childhood toy that you had that still evokes fond memories.

TO INFORM YOUR READER

3. Write an essay describing destruction or devastation you have observed as a result of a natural disaster (hurricane, flood), an accident, or a form of violence.
4. Write a report for your local newspaper on a local sporting event you recently observed or participated in.

TO PERSUADE YOUR READER

5. Write a letter to persuade your parents to lend you money. The loan may be to purchase a used car or to rent a more expensive apartment, for example. Include a description of your current car or apartment.
6. "Heatstroke with a Side of Burn Cream" contains a description of the preparation of food. Do you think that Americans are overly concerned with food, or is food an important social and cultural experience? Write a persuasive essay taking a position on the role of food in American culture.

CASES USING DESCRIPTION

7. Imagine that you are a product buyer for a cosmetics distributor, a food company, or a furniture dealership. Write a descriptive review of a product recommending to the board of directors whether to distribute it. Use something that you are familiar with or come up with your own product (such as a new cosmetic, an advice book on nutrition, or an electronic gadget for the home). Describe the product in a way that will help convince the company to accept your recommendation.

- understand the purpose and function of illustration essays,
- use graphic organizers to visualize illustration essays,
- integrate illustration into an essay,
- read and think critically about illustration, and
- plan, organize, draft, revise, and edit essays using illustration.

The sentences you just wrote could be part of an illustration essay. An **illustration** essay uses examples to reveal a topic's essential characteristics and reinforce the thesis statement. By providing specific examples that make abstract ideas concrete, you help readers connect these abstract ideas to their own experience.

USING ILLUSTRATION IN COLLEGE AND THE WORKPLACE

- Your *literature instructor* assigns an analysis of metaphor and simile in the poems of Emily Dickinson. To explain your point about Dickinson's use of animal metaphors, you provide specific examples from several of her poems.
- You are studying sexual dimorphism (differences in appearance between the sexes) in a *biology course*. The following question appears on an exam: "Define sexual dimorphism and illustrate its occurrence in several different species." In your answer, you give examples of peacocks, geese, and chickens, explaining how the males and females in each species differ in physical appearance.
- As an *elementary school reading teacher,* you are writing a letter to the school board justifying the cost of the new computer software you have requested. In your letter, you provide several examples of the software's benefits to students.

CHARACTERISTICS OF ILLUSTRATION ESSAYS

Effective illustration essays support a generalization, explain, and clarify by providing examples that maintain readers' interest and achieve the author's purpose. Because a good illustration essay is more than a list of examples, a well-thought-out organization is essential.

ILLUSTRATION SUPPORTS GENERALIZATIONS

Examples are an effective way to support a **generalization**—a broad statement about a topic. Thesis statements often contain a generalization, and the body of an illustration essay contains examples that support it.

The following statements are generalizations because they make assertions about an entire group or category.

- Most college students are energetic, ambitious, and eager to get ahead in life.
- Gestures play an important role in nonverbal communication.
- Boys are more willing to participate in class discussions than girls are.

To explain and support any of these generalizations, you could provide specific examples, along with other types of evidence (facts, statistics, expert opinions), to show how or why the statement is accurate. For instance, in addition to providing relevant facts and statistics, you could also support the first generalization by providing examples of several college students who demonstrate energy and ambition.

EXERCISE 14.1 **Developing Examples to Support Generalizations**

Using one or more prewriting strategies for generating ideas, provide at least two examples that support each of the following general statements.

For more about idea-generating strategies, see Chapter 5.

  1. Television offers some programs with educational or social value.
  2. Today's parents are not strict enough with their children.
  3. The favorite pastime of most men is watching sports on television.

ILLUSTRATION EXPLAINS OR CLARIFIES

Examples are useful when you need to explain an unfamiliar topic, a difficult concept, or an abstract term.

Unfamiliar topics. Use examples to help readers understand a topic about which they know little or nothing. An instructor of abnormal psychology, for example, might provide case studies of patients with schizophrenia and other disorders to help make the characteristics of each disorder easier to understand and remember.

Difficult concepts. Many concepts are difficult to grasp by definition alone. For instance, a reader might guess that the term *urbanization*, a key concept in sociology, has something to do with cities. Defining the concept as "the process by which an area becomes part of a city" gives readers a place to begin. Providing examples of formerly suburban areas that have become urban makes the concept even more understandable.

Abstract terms. Abstract terms refer to ideas rather than to concrete things you can see and touch. Terms such as *truth* and *justice* are abstract. Because abstractions are difficult to understand, examples help clarify them. In many cases, however, abstract terms mean different things to different people. By providing examples, you can clarify what *you* mean by an abstract term. Suppose you use the term *unfair* to describe your employer's treatment of workers. Readers might have different ideas of fairness. Providing examples of the employer's unfair treatment would make your meaning clear.

> **EXERCISE 14.2** **Providing Examples to Explain and Clarify**

The following list contains a mix of unfamiliar topics, difficult concepts, and abstract terms. Choose three items from the list, and provide at least two examples of each that illustrate their meanings.

1. Phobia
2. Conformity
3. Gender role

4. Self-fulfilling prophecy
5. Sexual harassment

ILLUSTRATION CONSIDERS PURPOSE AND AUDIENCE

The number of examples a writer should include depends on his or her purpose and audience. For example, in an essay arguing that one car is a better buy than another, a series of examples explaining the various models, years, and options available to potential car buyers might be most persuasive. But if you are writing an essay for an audience of high school students about the consequences of dropping out of school, a single poignant example might be more compelling.

A careful analysis of your audience should play a key role in deciding what types of examples to include in your essay. For an expert audience, technical examples might be more appropriate; for novice readers, personal or everyday examples might be more effective. For instance, suppose you want to persuade readers that the Food and Drug Administration should approve a new cancer drug. If your audience is composed of doctors, your examples would likely include the results of scientific studies regarding the drug's effectiveness. But if your audience is the general public, your examples might focus on personal anecdotes about lives being saved.

It can be useful to provide examples that represent different aspects of or viewpoints on your topic. In writing about the new drug, for instance, you might include expert opinion from researchers as well as the opinions of doctors, patients, and a representative of the company that manufactures the drug.

> **EXERCISE 14.3** **Developing Examples for a Specific Audience**

For one of the following topics, suggest examples that would suit the different audiences listed.

1. Your college's policy on student on-campus employment:
   a. First-year students attending a college orientation session
   b. Students already working on campus
   c. Parents or spouses of students who work on campus
2. A proposal recommending that drivers over age sixty-five undergo periodic assessment of their ability to operate a motor vehicle safely
   a. senior citizens
   b. state senators
   c. adult children of elderly drivers

ILLUSTRATION USES CAREFULLY SELECTED EXAMPLES

Examples must be relevant, representative, accurate, and striking.

- *Relevant* examples have a direct and clear relationship to your thesis. If your essay advocates publicly funded preschool programs, support your case with examples of successful publicly funded programs, not privately operated programs.
- *Representative* examples show a typical or real-life situation, not a rare or unusual one. In an essay arguing that preschool programs advance children's reading skills, one example of an all-day, year-round preschool would not be representative of all or most other programs.
- *Accurate* and *specific* examples provide readers with enough information to evaluate their reliability. Notice how the second example below provides better (more specific) detail for the reader.

OVERLY GENERAL	Most students in preschool programs have better language skills than children who don't attend such programs.
SPECIFIC, DETAILED	According to an independent evaluator, 73 percent of children who attended the Head Start program in Clearwater had better language skills after one year of attendance than students who did not attend the program.

Striking and dramatic examples make a strong, lasting impression on readers. For example, in an essay about identity theft, a writer might relate shocking incidents of how victims' lives are drastically changed with the swipe of a credit card.

Sometimes it is necessary to conduct research to find examples outside your knowledge and experience. For the essay on preschool programs, you would need to do research to obtain statistical information. You might also interview a preschool administrator or teacher to gather firsthand anecdotes and opinions or visit a preschool classroom to observe the program in action.

ILLUSTRATION USES SUBEXAMPLES TO ADD DETAIL

When providing examples that are broad general categories, you will often find it helpful to include **subexamples** — specific examples that help explain the general examples. Suppose you are writing an essay about the problems that new immigrants to America face and you use three examples: problems with the language, with the culture, and with technology. For the broad culture example, you might give subexamples of how some immigrants do not understand certain American holidays, ways of socializing, and methods of doing business.

ILLUSTRATION ORGANIZES DETAILS EFFECTIVELY

When supporting a thesis with examples, organize the examples and the details that accompany them so readers can follow them easily. Often one of the methods of organization discussed in Chapter 7 will be useful:

- spatial order,
- chronological order, and
- most-to-least or least-to-most order.

For example, in an essay explaining why people wear unconventional dress, you might arrange the examples spatially, starting with outlandish footwear and continuing upward to headgear. For other writing assignments, you may want to organize your examples according to another pattern of development, such as comparison and contrast or cause and effect. For example, to support the thesis that a local department store needs to improve its customer service, you might begin by contrasting the department store with several other retailers that provide better service, offering examples of the services that each provides.

The following readings demonstrate the techniques for writing effective illustration essays. The first is annotated to point out how Frans de Waal uses these techniques to help readers understand animal intelligence. As you read the second essay, try to identify how the writer uses the techniques of illustration to help readers understand road rage.

READING

The Brains of the Animal Kingdom

FRANS DE WAAL

Frans de Waal is the C. H. Candler Professor of Primate Behavior at Emory University in Atlanta, Georgia. He is also the director of the Living Links Center at the Yerkes National Primate Research Center. He has written numerous books that chronicle his research on primate social behavior.

Introduction: Uses a surprising question to spark readers' interest

Who is smarter: a person or an ape? Well, it depends on the task. Consider Ayumu, a young male chimpanzee at Kyoto University who, in a 2007 study, put human memory to shame. Trained on a touch screen, Ayumu could recall a random series of nine numbers, from 1 to 9, and tap them in the right order, even though the numbers had been displayed for just a fraction of a second and then replaced with white squares.

I tried the task myself and could not keep track of more than five numbers — and I was given much more time than the brainy ape. In the study, Ayumu outperformed a group of university students by a wide margin.

How do you give a chimp — or an elephant or an octopus or a horse — an IQ test? It may sound like the setup to a joke, but it is actually one of the thorniest questions facing science today. Over the past decade, researchers on animal cognition have come up with some ingenious solutions to the testing problem. Their findings have started to upend a view of humankind's unique place in the universe that dates back at least to ancient Greece.

Transition: Transitional sentence prepares readers for shift from current issue to historical background.

1

2

3

A herd of elephants drink water at a dam inside the Addo Elephant National Park near Port Elizabeth, South Africa. AP Photo/Schalk van Zuydam

Aristotle's idea of the *scala naturae*, the ladder of nature, put all life-forms in rank order, from low to high, with humans closest to the angels. During the Enlightenment, the French philosopher René Descartes, a founder of modern science, declared that animals were soulless automatons. In the 20th century, the American psychologist B. F. Skinner and his followers took up the same theme, painting animals as little more than stimulus-response machines. Animals might be capable of learning, they argued, but surely not of thinking and feeling. The term "animal cognition" remained an oxymoron.

A growing body of evidence shows, however, that we have grossly underestimated both the scope and the scale of animal intelligence. Can an octopus use tools? Do chimpanzees have a sense of fairness? Can birds guess what others know? Do rats feel empathy for their friends? Just a few decades ago we would have answered "no" to all such questions. Now we're not so sure.

Experiments with animals have long been handicapped by our anthropocentric attitude: We often test them in ways that work fine with humans but not so well with other species. Scientists are now finally meeting animals on their own terms instead of treating them like furry (or feathery) humans, and this shift is fundamentally reshaping our understanding.

Elephants are a perfect example. For years, scientists believed them incapable of using tools. At most, an elephant might pick up a stick to scratch its itchy behind. In earlier studies, the pachyderms were offered a long stick while food was placed outside their reach to see if they would use the stick to retrieve it. This setup worked well with primates, but elephants left the stick alone. From this, researchers concluded that

4 **Background:** From ancient Greece to twentieth century suggests reader is well educated but not a specialist

5 **Mainpoint:** Stated in the thesis

6

Organization: States generalizations that examples in the following paragraphs support

7 **Cue:** Transitions signal supporting examples; *for years* emphasizes contrast with recent experiments

the elephants didn't understand the problem. It occurred to no one that perhaps we, the investigators, didn't understand the elephants.

Details: Specific details help to explain the example.

Think about the test from the animal's perspective. Unlike the primate hand, the   8
elephant's grasping organ is also its nose. Elephants use their trunks not only to reach food but also to sniff and touch it. With their unparalleled sense of smell, the animals know exactly what they are going for. Vision is secondary.

But as soon as an elephant picks up a stick, its nasal passages are blocked. Even   9
when the stick is close to the food, it impedes feeling and smelling. It is like sending a blindfolded child on an Easter egg hunt.

What sort of experiment, then, would do justice to the animal's special anatomy   10
and abilities?

Cue: Transition emphasizes shift to present, signals new example

Sources: Research from experts in the field enhances credibility

On a recent visit to the National Zoo in Washington, I met with Preston Foerder   11
and Diana Reiss of Hunter College, who showed me what Kandula, a young elephant bull, can do if the problem is presented differently. The scientists hung fruit high up above the enclosure, just out of Kandula's reach. The elephant was given several sticks and a sturdy square box.

Kandula ignored the sticks but, after a while, began kicking the box with his foot.   12
He kicked it many times in a straight line until it was right underneath the branch. He then stood on the box with his front legs, which enabled him to reach the food with his trunk. An elephant, it turns out, can use tools — if they are the right ones.

While Kandula munched his reward, the investigators explained how they had   13
varied the setup, making life more difficult for the elephant. They had put the box in a different section of the yard, out of view, so that when Kandula looked up at the tempting food he would need to recall the solution and walk away from his goal to fetch the tool. Apart from a few large-brained species, such as humans, apes and dolphins, not many animals will do this, but Kandula did it without hesitation, fetching the box from great distances.

Examples: Variety of species helps support thesis, reveals different aspects of the topic

We also may need to rethink the physiology of intelligence. Take the octopus.   14
In captivity, these animals recognize their caretakers and learn to open pill bottles protected by childproof caps — a task with which many humans struggle. Their brains are indeed the largest among invertebrates, but the explanation for their extraordinary skills may lie elsewhere. It seems that these animals think, literally, outside the box of the brain.

Octopuses have hundreds of suckers, each one equipped with its own ganglion with   15
thousands of neurons. These "mini-brains" are interconnected, making for a widely distributed nervous system. That is why a severed octopus arm may crawl on its own and even pick up food.

Similarly, when an octopus changes skin color in self-defense, such as by mimicking   16
a poisonous sea snake, the decision may come not from central command but from the skin itself. Could it be: an organism with a seeing skin and eight thinking arms?

Topic sentence: Identifies a significant failing of earlier animal experiments

Underlying many of our mistaken beliefs about animal intelligence is the problem   17
of negative evidence. If I walk through a forest in Georgia, where I live, and fail

to see or hear the pileated woodpecker, am I permitted to conclude that the bird is absent? Of course not. We know how easily these splendid woodpeckers hop around tree trunks to stay out of sight. All I can say is that I lack evidence.

It is quite puzzling, therefore, why the field of animal cognition has such a long 18 history of claims about the absence of capacities based on just a few strolls through the forest. Such conclusions contradict the famous dictum of experimental psychology according to which "absence of evidence is not evidence of absence."

Take the question of whether we are the only species to care about the well-being 19 of others. It is well known that apes in the wild offer spontaneous assistance to each other, defending against leopards, say, or consoling distressed companions with tender embraces. But for decades, these observations were ignored, and more attention was paid to experiments according to which the apes were entirely selfish. They had been tested with an apparatus to see if one chimpanzee was willing to push food toward another. But perhaps the apes failed to understand the apparatus. When we instead used a simple choice between tokens they could exchange for food — one kind of token rewarded only the chooser, the other kind rewarded both apes — lo and behold, they preferred outcomes that rewarded both of them.

Topic sentence: Introduces new example

Such generosity, moreover, may not be restricted to apes. In a recent study, rats freed 20 a trapped companion even when a container with chocolate had been put right next to it. Many rats first liberated the other, after which both rodents happily shared the treat.

The one historical constant in my field is that each time a claim of human unique- 21 ness bites the dust, other claims quickly take its place. Meanwhile, science keeps chipping away at the wall that separates us from the other animals. We have moved from viewing animals as instinct-driven stimulus-response machines to seeing them as sophisticated decision makers.

Aristotle's ladder of nature is not just being flattened; it is being transformed into 22 a bush with many branches. This is no insult to human superiority. It is long-overdue recognition that intelligent life is not something for us to seek in the outer reaches of space but is abundant right here on earth, under our noses.

Conclusion: Refers to idea from para. 4 to pull ideas together and restates thesis in different words

VISUALIZING AN ILLUSTRATION ESSAY: A GRAPHIC ORGANIZER

The graphic organizer shown in Figure 14.1 will help you visualize the components of an illustration essay. The structure is straightforward.

For more on creating a graphic organizer, see pp. 52–53.

- The introduction contains background information and usually includes the thesis.
- The body paragraphs provide one or more related examples. For an essay using one extended example, such as a highly descriptive account of an auto accident intended to persuade readers to wear seat belts, the body of the essay will focus on the details of that one example.
- The conclusion presents a final statement.

FIGURE 14.1 **Graphic Organizer for an Illustration Essay**

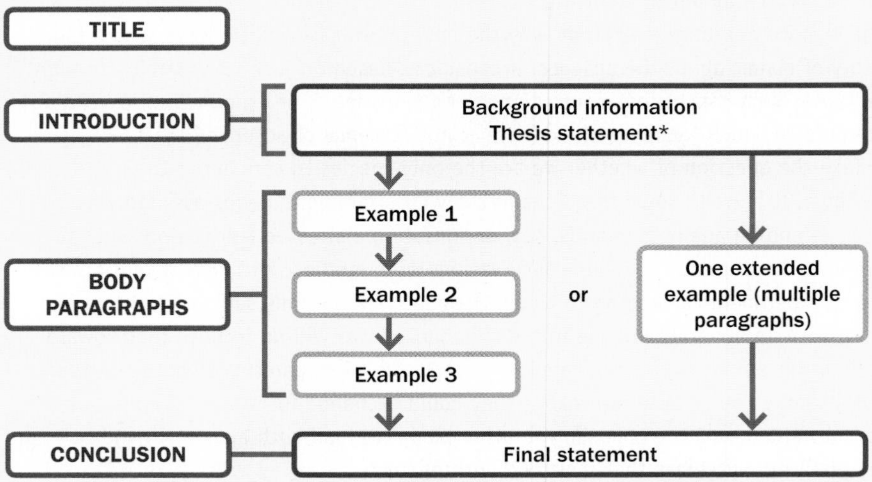

```
┌──────────────┐
│    TITLE     │
└──────────────┘

┌──────────────┐     ┌─────────────────────────────────────┐
│ INTRODUCTION │─────│      Background information          │
└──────────────┘     │      Thesis statement*              │
                     └─────────────────────────────────────┘
                              │                    │
                     ┌─────────────────┐           │
                     │    Example 1    │           │
                     └─────────────────┘           ▼
┌──────────────┐     ┌─────────────────┐   ┌──────────────────┐
│     BODY     │     │    Example 2    │ or│  One extended    │
│  PARAGRAPHS  │─────│                 │   │  example (multiple│
└──────────────┘     └─────────────────┘   │   paragraphs)    │
                     ┌─────────────────┐   └──────────────────┘
                     │    Example 3    │           │
                     └─────────────────┘           │
                              │                    │
┌──────────────┐     ┌─────────────────────────────────────┐
│  CONCLUSION  │─────│           Final statement           │
└──────────────┘     └─────────────────────────────────────┘
```

*In some essays, the thesis statement may be implied or may appear in a different position.

READING

Rambos of the Road

MARTIN GOTTFRIED

Martin Gottfried has been a drama critic for such publications as *The New York Post* and *New York* magazine. He has also written several books, including biographies of Stephen Sondheim, Arthur Miller, and Angela Lansbury. This essay was first published in *Newsweek*, the weekly news magazine, in 1986. As you read the selection, notice where Gottfried employs compelling examples to support his thesis and highlight those you find particularly striking. Figure 14.2, a graphic organizer for "Rambos of the Road," appears on p. 309. Read the illustration essay first, and then study the graphic organizer. What parts of the reading are included in the graphic organizer and why?

The car pulled up and its driver glared at us with such sullen intensity, such hatred, that I was truly afraid for our lives. Except for the Mohawk haircut he didn't have, he looked like Robert De Niro in *Taxi Driver*, the sort of young man who, delirious for notoriety, might kill a president. 1

He was glaring because we had passed him and for that affront he pursued us to the next stoplight so as to express his indignation and affirm his masculinity. I was with two women and, believe it, was afraid for all three of us. It was nearly midnight and we were in a small, sleeping town with no other cars on the road. 2

When the light turned green, I raced ahead, knowing it was foolish and that I was not in a movie. He didn't merely follow, he chased, and with his headlights turned off. 3

No matter what sudden turn I took, he followed. My passengers were silent. I knew they were alarmed, and I prayed that I wouldn't be called upon to protect them. In that cheerful frame of mind, I turned off my own lights so I couldn't be followed. It was lunacy. I was responding to a crazy *as* a crazy.

"I'll just drive to the police station," I finally said, and as if those were the magic   4
words, he disappeared.

It seems to me that there has recently been an epidemic of auto macho—a   5
competition perceived and expressed in driving. People fight it out over parking spaces. They bully into line at the gas pump. A toll booth becomes a signal for elbowing fenders. And beetle-eyed drivers hunch over their steering wheels, squeezing the rims, glowering, preparing the excuse of not having seen you as they muscle you off the road. Approaching a highway on an entrance ramp recently, I was strong-armed by a trailer truck, so immense that its driver all but blew me away by blasting his horn. The behemoth was just inches from my hopelessly mismatched coupe when I fled for the safety of the shoulder.

And this is happening on city streets, too. A New York taxi driver told me that   6
"intimidation is the name of the game. Drive as if you're deaf and blind. You don't hear the other guy's horn and you sure as hell don't see him."

The odd thing is that long before I was even able to drive, it seemed to me that   7
people were at their finest and most civilized when in their cars. They seemed so orderly and considerate, so reasonable, staying in the right-hand lane unless passing, signaling all intentions. In those days you really eased into highway traffic, and the long, neat rows of cars seemed mobile testimony to the sanity of most people. Perhaps memory fails, perhaps there were always testy drivers, perhaps—but everyone didn't give you the finger.

A most amazing example of driver rage occurred recently at the Manhattan   8
end of the Lincoln Tunnel. We were four cars abreast, stopped at a traffic light. And there was no moving even when the light had changed. A bus had stopped in the cross traffic, blocking our paths: it was a normal-for-New-York-City gridlock. Perhaps impatient, perhaps late for important appointments, three of us nonethe- less accepted what, after all, we could not alter. One, however, would not. He would not be helpless. He would go where he was going even if he couldn't get there. A Wall Street type in suit and tie, he got out of his car and strode toward the bus, rapping smartly on its doors. When they opened, he exchanged words with the driver. The doors folded shut. He then stepped in front of the bus, took hold of one of its large windshield wipers and broke it.

The bus doors reopened and the driver appeared, apparently giving the fellow a   9
good piece of his mind. If so, the lecture was wasted, for the man started his car and proceeded to drive directly *into the bus*. He rammed it. Even though the point at which he struck the bus, the folding doors, was its most vulnerable point, ramming the side of a bus with your car has to rank very high on a futility index. My first thought was that it had to be a rental car.

To tell the truth, I could not believe my eyes. The bus driver opened his doors as   10
much as they could be opened and he stepped directly onto the hood of the attacking

car, jumping up and down with both his feet. He then retreated into the bus, closing the doors behind him. Obviously a man of action, the car driver backed up and rammed the bus again. How this exercise in absurdity would have been resolved none of us will ever know for at that point the traffic unclogged and the bus moved on. And the rest of us, we passives of the world, proceeded, our cars crossing a field of battle as if nothing untoward had happened.

It is tempting to blame such belligerent, uncivil and even neurotic behavior on the nuts of the world, but in our cars we all become a little crazy. How many of us speed up when a driver signals his intention of pulling in front of us? Are we resentful and anxious to pass him? How many of us try to squeeze in, or race along the shoulder of a lane merger? We may not jump on hoods, but driving the gantlet, we seethe, cursing not so silently in the safety of our steel bodies on wheels — fortresses for cowards.

What is it within us that gives birth to such antisocial behavior and why, all of a sudden, have so many drivers gone around the bend? My friend Joel Katz, a Manhattan psychiatrist, calls it "a Rambo pattern. People are running around thinking the American way is to take the law into your own hands when anyone does anything wrong. And what constitutes 'wrong'? Anything that cramps your style."

It seems to me that it is a new America we see on the road now. It has the mentality of a hoodlum and the backbone of a coward. The car is its weapon and hiding place, and it is still a symbol even in this. Road Rambos no longer bespeak a self-reliant, civil people tooling around in family cruisers. In fact, there aren't families in these machines that charge headlong with their brights on in broad daylight, demanding we get out of their way. Bullies are loners, and they have perverted our liberty of the open road into drivers' license. They represent an America that derides the values of decency and good manners, then roam the highways riding shotgun and shrieking freedom. By allowing this to happen, the rest of us approve.

> **EXERCISE 14.4** **Drawing a Graphic Organizer**
>
> Using the graphic organizer in Figure 14.1 or 14.2 as a basis, draw a graphic organizer for "The Brains of the Animal Kingdom" (pp. 302–05).

INTEGRATING ILLUSTRATION INTO AN ESSAY

For a reading that uses illustration as well as other patterns of development, see "Alone Together: Why We Expect More from Technology and Less from Each Other" (pp. 324–27).

Examples are an effective way to support a thesis that relies on one or more other patterns of development. For instance, you might use examples in the following ways:

- to *define* a particular advertising ploy,
- to *compare* two types of small businesses,
- to *classify* types of movies,
- to *show the effects* of aerobic exercise, and
- to *argue* that junk food is unhealthy because of its high fat and salt content.

FIGURE 14.2 Graphic Organizer for "Rambos of the Road"

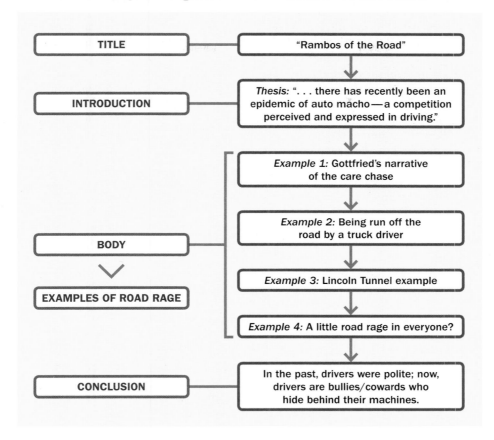

When using examples in an essay where illustration is not the main pattern of development, keep the following tips in mind:

1. **Choose effective examples.** They should be relevant, representative, accurate, specific, and striking.
2. **Use transitions such as "for instance" or "for example."** They make it obvious that an example follows.
3. **Provide enough details to help your readers understand how an example supports your point.** Do not overwhelm your readers with too many details.

READING ACTIVELY AND THINKING CRITICALLY

Reading and thinking critically about an illustration essay requires you to read the selection carefully, considering how the examples support the main point and connecting the ideas and examples to your own experience. But you must also examine and challenge the author's attitude as it is shown in the selection.

For more on reading actively, see Chapter 3; for more on thinking critically, see Chapter 4.

WHAT TO LOOK FOR, HIGHLIGHT, AND ANNOTATE

For more on previewing, see Chapter 3.

Use these guidelines to read illustration essays actively.

1. **Preview.** Preview the essay to get an overview of its content and organization.
2. **Understand the main point.** Read the essay through, highlighting the thesis or main point. If the thesis is not directly stated, ask yourself what one major point all of the examples illustrate.
3. **Identify the main supporting points and think about how the examples illustrate them.** Study and highlight the main supporting ideas in each of the body paragraphs as you reread the essay. In the margin or in your journal, note how the examples provided clarify, explain, or illustrate those ideas, and consider how each supporting paragraph supports the thesis or main idea of the essay.

    Also think about how the examples are organized: Are they arranged in order of importance, in chronological order, in spatial order, or by some other method? Hint: For especially lengthy or complex readings, creating an outline or drawing a graphic organizer can help you identify the organizational pattern. Notice, too, whether the examples fit with any other patterns of development used in the essay.
4. **Think about the meaning.** Reread the essay once again, this time concentrating on its meaning by answering the following questions:
    * What is the writer's purpose in writing this essay? For what audience is it intended? What techniques does the writer use to achieve his or her purpose with this audience?
    * How well do the examples explain or clarify the thesis? Are you convinced of the writer's thesis after reading the essay? Would more or different examples have been more effective?
5. **Consider your reactions.** Consider how the essay relates to your own experience. For example, while reading "Rambos of the Road," you might think about rude or reckless driving you have observed: drivers who are oblivious to those around them, who text or check their smartphones while driving, or who drive too slowly. Each of these examples could lead you to a thesis for an illustration essay.

ANALYZING ILLUSTRATION

When you read an essay that uses illustration to support generalizations, read with a critical eye. Examples are often dramatic, real, and concrete, and it may be tempting to focus on them exclusively. Be sure to consider the examples in terms of how well they illustrate key points of the essay. Use the following questions to think critically about the examples you read.

For more on emotional appeals, see Chapter 20, pp. 505–06.

What is the emotional impact of the examples? Writers often choose examples to manipulate their readers' feelings, especially in persuasive writing. For example, a description of a tiger pacing in a small zoo enclosure, rubbing its body against a fence, and scratching an open sore would provide a vivid example of the behaviors exhibited by some wild animals in captivity. Such an example can evoke feelings of pity, sympathy, or even outrage.

When you encounter an example that evokes an emotional response, try to set your emotions aside and look at the example objectively. In the case of the tiger, for instance, you might ask, "Why are animals held in captivity?" or "What are the benefits of zoos?"

How well do the examples support the generalization? Especially when you read persuasive writing, examine how well the examples support the author's generalizations by asking yourself questions like these:

- Are the examples *fair* and *representative*? (You may need to consult other sources to decide.) A writer who chooses dramatic but extreme examples may be attempting to make his or her case stronger than it really is. In "Rambos of the Road," Martin Gottfried presents an extreme example of road rage when describing the bus incident, but he admits it is not typical by calling it "the most amazing example."
- Would *other types of evidence*, such as statistics or expert opinion, have strengthened the essay? For instance, in "Rambos of the Road," statistics on the number of road rage incidents reported to the police (not just those observed by the writer) would be relevant.
- Are the examples *relevant* to the generalization they are illustrating? For example, in Nick Ruggia's student essay, "Conforming to Stand Out: A Look at American Beauty" (p. 318), the author uses body art as an example of Americans' obsession with making themselves physically attractive. Although this may be some people's motivation for getting tattoos and piercings, other people may be motivated by a desire to express themselves or to annoy their parents.

A GUIDED WRITING ASSIGNMENT*
ILLUSTRATION

YOUR ESSAY ASSIGNMENT

Write an illustration essay explaining a topic your readers might find unfamiliar or challenging and that you can illustrate effectively with examples. Imagine you are writing for your campus newspaper, and choose a topic that you think might interest your readers. Below are some options:

- the popularity of a certain type of sport, television show, or hobby,
- the connection between clothing and personality,
- the problems of balancing school, work, and family,
- effective (or ineffective) parenting, or
- a concept from one of your courses, such as stress management or ergonomic design.

*The writing process is *recursive*; that is, you may find yourself revising as you draft or prewriting as you revise. This is especially true when writing on a computer. Your writing process may also differ from that of your classmates, depending on your preferred learning style.

(continued on next page)

1 Select a topic from the list on page 311, or create your own.

Use one or more of the following suggestions to generate topic ideas.

1. **Peruse your textbooks**, looking for boldfaced terms that you find interesting or want to learn about. List several and then, alone or with another student, brainstorm examples that would help to illustrate or explain the concept. You may need to read your textbook for models. (If you are an abstract thinker, starting from a generalization and then coming up with examples may work better for you.)

2. **Work backward:** Make a list of the things you do for fun or find challenging and then consider what they have in common. Use that common thread as your topic.

After you have chosen your topic, make sure that you can **develop your main idea into a well-focused working thesis**.

2 Consider your purpose, audience, and point of view.

Ask yourself these questions.

- Will my essay's **purpose** be to **express myself**, **inform**, or **persuade**? Several examples may be needed to persuade. One extended example may be sufficient to inform readers about a very narrow topic (for example, how to select an educational toy for a child).

- Who is my **audience**? Will readers need any **background information** to understand my essay? **What types of examples** will be most effective with these readers? Straightforward examples, based on everyday experience, may be appropriate for an audience unfamiliar with your topic; more technical examples may be appropriate for an expert audience.

- What **other evidence** (such as facts and statistics, expert opinion) will I need to make my case with my audience? Do I have enough information to write about this topic, or must I consult additional sources? How might I use **additional patterns of development** within my illustration essay? (For example, you might use narration to present an extended example from your own life.)

- What **point of view** best suits my purpose and audience? (Unless the examples you use are all drawn from your personal experience, you will probably use the **third person** when using examples to explain.)

Prewriting

3 Narrow your topic and generate examples.

Narrow your topic. Use prewriting to make your topic manageable. Be sure you can support your topic with one or more examples.

Use idea-generating strategies to come up with a wide variety of examples.
1. Write down the generalizations your essay will make, and then **brainstorm** examples that support them.
2. **Freewrite** to bring to mind relevant personal experiences or stories told by friends and relatives.
3. **Conduct research** to find examples used by experts and relevant news reports and to locate other supporting information, like facts and statistics.
4. **Review textbooks** for examples used there.

Creative and abstract learners may have trouble focusing on details. If you have trouble, try teaming up with a classmate who has a pragmatic or concrete learning style for help.

Hint: Keep track of where you found each example so that you can cite your sources accurately.

4 Evaluate your examples.

Try these suggestions to help you evaluate your examples.
- **Reread everything you have written.** (Sometimes reading your notes aloud is helpful.)
- **Highlight examples** that are **representative** (or typical) yet **striking**. Make sure they are **relevant** (they clearly illustrate your point). Unless you are using just one extended example, make sure your examples are **varied**. Then **copy and paste** the usable ideas to a new document to consult while drafting.
- **Collaborate.** In small groups, take turns **giving examples** and having classmates tell you . . .
    1. what they think your **main idea** is. (If they don't get it, rethink your examples.)
    2. what **additional information** they need to find your main idea convincing.

Classmates can also help narrow your topic or think of more effective examples.

(continued on next page)

5 Draft your thesis statement.

Try one or more of the following strategies to **develop a generalization** that your examples support. (Your generalization will become your working thesis.)

1. Systematically **review your examples** asking yourself what they have in common.
2. **Discuss your thesis with a classmate.** Do the examples support the thesis? If not, try to improve on each other's examples or revise the thesis.
3. In a **two-column list**, write words in the left column describing how you feel about your narrowed topic. (For example, the topic *cheating on college exams* might generate such feelings as anger, surprise, and confusion.) In the right column, add details about specific situations in which these feelings arose. (For example, your thesis might focus on your surprise on discovering that a good friend cheated on an exam.)
4. **Research** your topic in the library or on the Internet to uncover examples outside your own experience. Then ask yourself what the examples from your experience and your research have in common.

Note: As you draft, you may think of situations or examples that illustrate a different or more interesting thesis. Don't hesitate to revise your thesis as you discover more about your topic.

Collaborate with classmates to make sure your examples support your thesis statement.

6 Select a method of organization.

- If you are using a **single, extended example**, you are most likely to use **chronological order** to relate events in the sequence in which they happened.
- If you are using **several examples**, you are most likely to organize the examples from most to least or least to most important.
- If you are using **many examples**, you may want to **group them into categories**. For instance, in an essay about the use of slang, you might classify examples according to regions or age groups in which they are used.

Hint: An outline or graphic organizer will allow you to experiment to find the best order for supporting paragraphs. (Spatial learners may prefer to draw a graphic organizer, while verbal learners may prefer to write an outline.)

Organizing & Drafting

7 **Write a first draft of your illustration essay.**

Use the following guidelines to keep your illustration essay on track.
- The **introduction** should spark readers' interest and include background information (if needed by readers). Most illustration essays include a **thesis** near the beginning to help readers understand the point of upcoming examples.
- The **body paragraphs** should include **topic sentences** to focus each paragraph (or paragraph cluster) on one key idea. Craft **one or more examples** for each paragraph (or cluster) to illustrate that key idea. Use **vivid descriptive language** to make readers feel as if they are experiencing or observing the situation. Include **transitions**, such as *for example* or *in particular*, to guide readers from one example to another. (Consult Chapter 8 for help with crafting effective descriptions.)
- The **conclusion** should **include a final statement** that pulls together your ideas and reminds readers of your thesis.

Revising

8 **Evaluate your draft, and revise as necessary.**

Use **Figure 14.3, "Flowchart for Revising an Illustration Essay,"** to evaluate and revise your draft.

Editing & Proofreading

9 **Edit and proofread your essay.**

Refer to Chapter 10 for help with . . .
- **editing sentences** to avoid wordiness, making your verb choices strong and active, and making your sentences clear, varied, and parallel, and
- **editing words** for tone and diction, connotation, and concrete and specific language.

Pay particular attention to the following:
1. Keep **verb tenses** consistent in your extended examples. When using an event from the past as an example, however, always use the past tense to describe it.

   Example: Special events *are* an important part of children's lives. Parent visitation day at school *was* an event my daughter *talked* about for an entire week. Children *are* also excited by . . .

(continued on next page)

Editing & Proofreading

2. Use **first person** (*I, me, we, us*), **second person** (*you*), or **third person** (*he, she, it, him, her, they, them*) consistently.

   Example: I visited my daughter's first-grade classroom during parents' week last month. Each
   parent was invited to read a story to the class, and ~~you~~ ^we^ were encouraged to ask the children questions afterward.

3. Avoid **sentence fragments** when introducing examples. Each sentence must have both a subject and a verb.

   Example: Technology has become part of teenagers' daily lives. ~~For example, high~~ ^High^ school
   students who carry iPhones^are one example.^

FIGURE 14.3 **Flowchart for Revising an Illustration Essay**

QUESTIONS

1. Highlight your thesis statement. Place a ✔ by each example. Do your examples clearly support the generalization your thesis makes?

 NO

REVISION STRATEGIES

- Revise your thesis, changing your generalization so that it fits your examples.

YES

2. *Write* a sentence describing your readers. ~~Cross out~~ any examples that won't appeal to them. Do you have enough examples left?

 NO

- Brainstorm more appealing examples.
- Add examples that represent different aspects of or viewpoints on your topic.

YES

(Figure 14.3 continued)

QUESTIONS	REVISION STRATEGIES

3. *Write* a sentence stating the purpose of your essay. ~~Cross out~~ any examples that don't fulfill your purpose. Do you have enough examples left?

 NO

- Brainstorm examples that are more appropriate to your purpose.
- Add some of these examples or consider cutting back and using one extended example.

 YES

4. Reread each example you ✔'d. Is each one accurate, relevant, striking, representative, and specific? Are the examples varied?

 NO

- Eliminate dull, irrelevant, or misleading examples.
- Brainstorm or conduct research to discover more effective examples.
- Add details to vague or misleading examples.
- Add facts, expert opinion, or statistics.

 YES

5. Underline the topic sentence of each paragraph. Does each paragraph have a topic sentence? Does each topic sentence clearly make a point that the example(s) ✔'d in that paragraph illustrate?

 NO

- Add a topic sentence or revise the existing one to clearly indicate the point each example or group of examples illustrates.
- Reorganize your essay, grouping examples according to the idea they illustrate.

 YES

6. Outline your essay. [Bracket] each transition. Is your organization clear and effective?

 NO

- Add transitions or use a different organizing strategy. (See Chapter 7.)

 YES

7. Reread your introduction and conclusion. Is each effective?

 NO

- Revise your introduction to prepare and engage readers and to provide background. Revise your conclusion so that it pulls together your ideas, reminds readers of your thesis, and creates a satisfying ending.

READINGS: ILLUSTRATION IN ACTION

STUDENTS WRITE

Title: Ruggia identifies his topic and suggests his thesis.

Conforming to Stand Out: A Look at American Beauty

NICK RUGGIA

Nick Ruggia, a student at the University of Maryland at College Park, wrote this essay in response to an assignment in which he was asked to examine an American obsession. He chose to write about Americans' obsession with physical appearance. As you read his illustration essay, notice how he supports his thesis with a variety of examples.

Introduction: Ruggia offers a biological reason for focusing on women. In his thesis statement, he makes a generalization about American women, and previews his organization by presenting his three examples in the order in which he will discuss them.

Organization: A topic sentence introduces example 1, the thin craze. In this paragraph and the next two, Ruggia uses specific celebrities and detailed statistics to support his claims.

Supporting evidence: The statistics suggest that the celebrities are representative of Americans in general. Ruggia cites the sources for his subexamples using MLA style.

In nature, two factors largely determine survival of the species: access to resources and physical attraction (necessary for the ability to mate). Humans function under the same basic rules. In modern America, where almost everyone can acquire the basic resources to live, humans are striving harder than ever to be physically attractive. Although men are increasingly caught up in its grip, the pressure to be beautiful falls most intensely on women. The thin craze, the plastic surgery craze, and the body art craze represent some of the increasingly drastic lengths American women are being driven to in their quest for physical perfection.

Since Kate Moss's wafer-thin frame took the modeling industry by storm, skinny has driven America's aesthetics. Hollywood is a mirror for our desires, and our starlets are shrinking. Nicole Ritchie and Angelina Jolie, among others, have publicly struggled with eating disorders. Jennifer Anniston and Reese Witherspoon are rumored to be following a diet of baby food to keep weight off (Crawford A1). And the stars aren't alone. According to the United States National Institutes of Mental Health, between 0.5 and 3.7 percent of American women will suffer from anorexia in their lifetimes, while another 1.1 to 4.2 percent will be bulimic and 2 to 5 percent will binge. These numbers exclude the disordered eaters who do not meet all the criteria necessary for diagnosis or do not accurately self-report. In a population of 300 million, these statistics represent millions of women struggling with eating disorders. Men are not immune either, accounting for 5 to 15 percent of bulimia and anorexia diagnoses and 35 percent of binge-eating cases. The skinny obsession is spiraling out of control as more people risk death to be thin through diet pills and gastric bypass surgery.

But for every Kate Moss idolizer, there's a would-be Pamela Anderson. This ideal, fed by porn and Hollywood, is plastic perfection: instead of anorexically denying their curves, many women choose to enhance their features through surgery. The American Society of Plastic Surgeons (ASPS) reports that in 2009, there were nearly 12.5 million cosmetic surgeries in the United States and an additional 5.2 million reconstructive plastic surgeries ("2009 Quick Facts"). While it must be remembered that the rule is not one surgery per person, so that the number of *patients* is lower than these figures, the scope of this practice is staggering nonetheless. Further evidence is provided by the surgically enhanced lips, stomachs, buttocks, and breasts that cover the pages of men's magazines all over the country. Strippers, porn stars like Jenna Jameson, and *Playboy* models like Anderson and the late Anna Nicole Smith flaunt enormous fake breasts. Clearly there is a disconnect between the sexless anorexic standard that so many women strive for and the bottle blonde bombshell that so many men favor. What everyone seems to agree on, though, is that plastic surgery is a response to the fear of aging. And in this way as well, men too are increasingly vulnerable to the superficial, with the ASPS reporting that they accounted for 9 percent of plastic surgeries in 2009.

Body art, in the form of piercing and tattoos, also illustrates (literally) Americans' obsession with physical appearance. The pierced and tattooed once jarred on public sensibilities, but now these body modifications have gone mainstream. Even "alternative" piercings are now accepted: Amy Winehouse, a heavily tattooed popular musician, has added to the popularity of the "Monroe" piercing, located above the lip where Marilyn Monroe had a mole. Nearly half the members of "Generation Next" have had a tattoo, piercing or "untraditional color" of hair ("How" 21). Once largely limited to sailors, criminals, and punk rockers--and to men--body art has become big business, drawing in more women as it spreads.

Maybe Americans have gone too far in basing their self-worth on physical appearance. Every visible part of the human body has been marketed as a fixable flaw or an opportunity for more adornment. Of course, Americans have always cared about their looks and made great efforts to improve them, but once most people kept the issue in perspective. Today, appearance rules. And men increasingly are joining women in obedience to its commands. Both sexes, though, will find that basing self-esteem on physical appearance, a fleeting commodity at best, is a recipe for misery.

3 **Organization:** A transitional sentence leads into the topic sentence for example 2, the plastic surgery craze, supported by detailed statistics.

Supporting evidence: Ruggia cites striking subexamples and detailed statistics.

4 **Organization:** A topic sentence introduces example 3, the body art craze.

Conclusion: Ruggia acknowledges that attention to appearance is nothing new, but suggests that Americans today place too much emphasis on it.

5

Sources: Ruggia lists his sources in MLA style, with the entries in alphabetical order. Notice the style for listing documents from Web sites sponsored by organizations and government agencies.

Works Cited

Crawford, Trish. "Celebrity 'Baby Food Diet' Recipe for Eating Disorder." *Toronto Star*, 18 May 2010, p. A1.

How Young People View Their Lives, Futures, and Politics: A Portrait of "Generation Next." Pew Research Center for the People and the Press, 9 Jan. 2007, www.people-press.org/files/legacy-pdf/300.pdf.

"2009 Quick Facts." American Society of Plastic Surgeons, 2010, www.plasticsurgery.org/Documents/news-resources/statistics/2009-statistics/2009quickfacts-cosmetic-surgery-minimally-invasive-statistics.pdf.

United States, National Institutes of Health, National Institutes of Mental Health. *The Numbers Count: Mental Disorders in America*. Government Printing Office, 2007.

ANALYZING THE WRITER'S TECHNIQUE

1. **Examples** Evaluate the three main examples Ruggia provides. How well do they illustrate his thesis? What other examples could he have used?
2. **Sources** Ruggia used four sources in writing the essay. What kinds of sources are they? How does his use of these sources strengthen his essay?
3. **Evidence** Ruggia uses celebrities and statistics as evidence to support each of the topic sentences about his three main examples. What other types of evidence could he have used?

THINKING CRITICALLY ABOUT ILLUSTRATION

1. **Emotional Response** Do any of Ruggia's examples or pieces of evidence create an emotional impact? If so, choose several and explain their effects.
2. **Connotation** What are the connotations of "bottle blond bombshell" (para. 3)?
3. **Alternative Viewpoints** What other types of sources could Ruggia have consulted to research and discuss alternative viewpoints?
4. **Generalization** Is the generalization in the essay's last sentence well-supported and well-explained in the essay?

RESPONDING TO THE ESSAY

1. **Discussion** Discuss the meaning and effectiveness of Ruggia's title.
2. **Journal** In your journal, respond to the following question: To what extent do you agree that piercings and tattoos are widely accepted?
3. **Thinking Critically** What do you think is the reason for the "disconnect" that Ruggia mentions in paragraph 3? Is the problem that women don't understand what men want? That men don't understand what women want? Both? Something else?
4. **Essay** Are Americans obsessed with appearances in other ways? Write an essay explaining another American obsession. Use examples to support your thesis.

Snoopers at Work

BILL BRYSON

Bill Bryson (b. 1951) grew up in the United States but lived from 1977 to 1995 in England and returned there in 2003. Originally a newspaper writer, Bryson is well known for his travel books, which include *I'm a Stranger Here Myself* (1999) and *Bill Bryson's African Diary* (2002). Some of his more recent books include *At Home: A Short History of Private Life* (2010) and *One Summer: America 1927* (2013).

The essays in *I'm a Stranger Here Myself* began as Sunday columns in a British newspaper, *The Mail*. In the following piece from that collection, Bryson discusses employers' invasion of workers' privacy. As you read, pay attention to the kinds of examples the author chooses to illustrate this disturbing trend, and notice how he uses humor to comment on the material. Consider, too, how Bryson uses the elements of illustration discussed in this chapter.

1   Now here is something to bear in mind should you ever find yourself using a changing room in a department store or other retail establishment. It is perfectly legal — indeed, it is evidently routine — for the store to spy on you while you are trying on their clothes.

2   I know this because I have just been reading a book by Ellen Alderman and Caroline Kennedy called *The Right to Privacy*, which is full of alarming tales of ways that businesses and employers can — and enthusiastically do — intrude into what would normally be considered private affairs.

3   The business of changing-cubicle spying came to light in 1983 when a customer trying on clothes in a department store in Michigan discovered that a store employee had climbed a stepladder and was watching him through a metal vent. (Is this tacky or what?) The customer was sufficiently outraged that he sued the store for invasion of privacy. He lost. A state court held that it was reasonable for retailers to defend against shoplifting by engaging in such surveillance.

4   He shouldn't have been surprised. Nearly everyone is being spied on in some way in America these days. A combination of technological advances, employer paranoia, and commercial avarice means that many millions of Americans are having their lives delved into in ways that would have been impossible, not to say unthinkable, a dozen years ago. . . .

5   Many companies are taking advantage of technological possibilities to make their businesses more ruthlessly productive. In Maryland, according to *Time* magazine, a bank searched through the medical records of its borrowers — apparently quite legally — to find out which of them had life-threatening illnesses and used this information to cancel their loans. Other companies have focused not on customers but on their own employees — for instance, to check what prescription drugs the employees are taking. One large, well-known company teamed up with a pharmaceutical firm to comb through the health records of employees to see who might benefit from a dose of antidepressants. The idea was that the company would get more serene workers; the drug company would get more customers.

According to the American Management Association two-thirds of companies in the United States spy on their employees in some way. Thirty-five percent track phone calls, and 10 percent actually tape phone conversations to review at leisure later. About a quarter of companies surveyed admitted to going through their employees' computer files and reading their e-mail.

Still other companies are secretly watching their employees at work. A secretary at a college in Massachusetts discovered that a hidden video camera was filming her office twenty-four hours a day. Goodness knows what the school authorities were hoping to find. What they got were images of a woman changing out of her work clothes and into a track suit each night in order to jog home from work. She is suing and will probably get a pot of money. But elsewhere courts have upheld companies' rights to spy on their workers.

There is a particular paranoia about drugs. I have a friend who got a job with a large manufacturing company in Iowa a year or so ago. Across the street from the company was a tavern that was the company after-hours hangout. One night my friend was having a beer after work with his colleagues when he was approached by a fellow employee who asked if he knew where she could get some marijuana. He said he didn't use the stuff himself, but to get rid of her — for she was very persistent — he gave her the phone number of an acquaintance who sometimes sold it.

The next day he was fired. The woman, it turned out, was a company spy employed solely to weed out drug use in the company. He hadn't supplied her with marijuana, you understand, hadn't encouraged her to use marijuana, and had stressed that he didn't use marijuana himself. Nonetheless he was fired for encouraging and abetting the use of an illegal substance.

Already, 91 percent of large companies — I find this almost unbelievable — now test some of their workers for drugs. Scores of companies have introduced what are called TAD rules — TAD being short for "tobacco, alcohol, and drugs" — which prohibit employees from using any of these substances at any time, including at home. There are companies, if you can believe it, that forbid their employees to drink or smoke at any time — even one beer, even on a Saturday night — and enforce the rules by making their workers give urine samples.

But it gets even more sinister than that. Two leading electronics companies working together have invented something called an "active badge," which tracks the movements of any worker compelled to wear one. The badge sends out an infrared signal every fifteen seconds. This signal is received by a central computer, which is thus able to keep a record of where every employee is and has been, whom they have associated with, how many times they have been to the toilet or water cooler — in short, to log every single action of their working day. If that isn't ominous, I don't know what is.

However, there is one development, I am pleased to report, that makes all of this worthwhile. A company in New Jersey has patented a device for determining whether restaurant employees have washed their hands after using the lavatory. Now *that* I can go for.

EXAMINING THE READING

1. **Summarizing** How did it become generally known that stores watch customers in changing rooms? According to Bryson, what are the reasons for today's high levels of spying?
2. **Details** What proportion of companies spy on their employees?
3. **Examples** Explain what an "active badge" (para. 11) is and how it works.
4. **Vocabulary** Explain the meaning of each of the following words as it is used in the reading: *surveillance* (para. 3), *avarice* (4), *delved* (4), *paranoia* (8), and *abetting* (9).

ANALYZING THE WRITER'S TECHNIQUE

1. **Introduction** The essay opens with an activity that Bryson asks readers to picture themselves doing. Why is this an effective introduction?
2. **Abstraction** "Private affairs" (para. 2) is an abstract term. How does Bryson make this term real and understandable? What is included in it, according to Bryson?
3. **Conclusion** Bryson's humorous conclusion seems somewhat at odds with the serious tone of the rest of the essay. How effective do you find it?

THINKING CRITICALLY ABOUT ILLUSTRATION

1. **Generalization** What generalization does Bryson make? How effectively is the generalization stated and supported in this essay? Are the examples relevant and representative? Does Bryson include enough examples? Explain your responses.
2. **Response** What is the emotional effect of Bryson's examples? What fears and insecurities do they play on? How might various readers (customers, employees, business owners) react to these examples?
3. **Connotation** What is the connotation of the word *tacky* (para. 3)?
4. **Alternative Examples** How would the essay be different if Bryson had included examples of surveillance that caught shoplifters, employees who were stealing, or employees who were using drugs at work? What effect would such examples have had?

RESPONDING TO THE READING

1. **Discussion** Imagine that the last time you tried on clothes in a store's dressing room you were watched by security workers. How does this make you feel? How might you behave differently the next time you are in a store?
2. **Journal** What other methods are used to spy on people? Write a journal entry describing some locations and activities that have video monitoring and your feelings about whether they are justified.
3. **Essay** What reasons might employers and store owners offer to defend the actions that Bryson describes? Write an essay from their point of view that defends it.

WORKING TOGETHER

Invention Bryson ends his essay by describing a new surveillance device that can determine whether restaurant employees washed their hands after using the restroom. In small groups, imagine a new surveillance device of your own, give it a name, and provide examples showing how it would work.

READING: ILLUSTRATION COMBINED WITH OTHER PATTERNS

Alone Together: Why We Expect More from Technology and Less from Each Other

SHERRY TURKLE

Sherry Turkle is the Abby Rockefeller Mauzé Professor of Social Studies of Science and Technology at MIT. She is also a licensed clinical psychologist and an author of numerous books, including *Life on the Screen: Identity in the Age of the Internet* (1997), *Evocative Objects: Things We Think With* (2011), and *Alone Together: Why We Expect More from Technology and Less from Each Other* (2012). The following selection is an excerpt from *Alone Together*. As you read, identify the examples Turkle uses to support her thesis and consider how effectively they support her generalization.

Online connections were first conceived as a substitute for face-to-face contact,   1
when the latter was for some reason impractical: Don't have time to make a phone call? Shoot off a text message. But very quickly, the text message became the connection of choice. We discovered the network — the world of connectivity — to be uniquely suited to the overworked and overscheduled life it makes possible. And now we look to the network to defend us against loneliness even as we use it to control the intensity of our connections. Technology makes it easy to communicate when we wish and to disengage at will.

A few years ago at a dinner party in Paris, I met Ellen, an ambitious, elegant young   2
woman in her early thirties, thrilled to be working at her dream job in advertising. Once a week, she would call her grandmother in Philadelphia using Skype, an Internet service that functions as a telephone with a Web camera. Before Skype, Ellen's calls to her grandmother were costly and brief. With Skype, the calls are free and give the compelling sense that the other person is present — Skype is an almost real-time video link. Ellen could now call more frequently: "Twice a week and I stay on the call for an hour," she told me. It should have been rewarding; instead, when I met her, Ellen was unhappy. She knew that her grandmother was unaware that Skype allows surreptitious multitasking. Her grandmother could see Ellen's face on the screen but not her hands. Ellen admitted to me, "I do my email during the calls. I'm not really paying attention to our conversation."

Ellen's multitasking removed her to another place. She felt her grandmother was   3
talking to someone who was not really there. During their Skype conversations, Ellen and her grandmother were more connected than they had ever been before, but at the same time, each was alone. Ellen felt guilty and confused: she knew that her grandmother was happy, even if their intimacy was now, for Ellen, another task among multitasks.

I have often observed this distinctive confusion: these days, whether you are online   4
or not, it is easy for people to end up unsure if they are closer together or further apart. I remember my own sense of disorientation the first time I realized that I was

"alone together." I had traveled an exhausting thirty-six hours to attend a conference on advanced robotic technology held in central Japan. The packed grand ballroom was Wi-Fi enabled: the speaker was using the Web for his presentation, laptops were open throughout the audience, fingers were flying, and there was a sense of great concentration and intensity. But not many in the audience were attending to the speaker. Most people seemed to be doing their email, downloading files, and surfing the Net. The man next to me was searching for a *New Yorker* cartoon to illustrate his upcoming presentation. Every once in a while, audience members gave the speaker some attention, lowering their laptop screens in a kind of curtsy, a gesture of courtesy.

Outside, in the hallways, the people milling around me were looking past me to   5
virtual others. They were on their laptops and their phones, connecting to colleagues at the conference going on around them and to others around the globe. There but not there. Of course, clusters of people chatted with each other, making dinner plans, "networking" in that old sense of the word, the one that implies having a coffee or sharing a meal. But at this conference, it was clear that what people mostly want from public space is to be alone with their personal networks. It is good to come together physically, but it is more important to stay tethered to our devices. I thought of how Sigmund Freud considered the power of communities both to shape and to subvert us, and a psychoanalytic pun came to mind: "connectivity and its discontents."

In corporations, among friends, and within academic departments, people readily   6
admit that they would rather leave a voicemail or send an email than talk face-to-face. Some who say "I live my life on my BlackBerry" are forthright about avoiding the "real-time" commitment of a phone call. The new technologies allow us to "dial down" human contact, to titrate its nature and extent. A thirteen-year-old tells me she "hates the phone and never listens to voicemail." Texting offers just the right amount of access, just the right amount of control. She is a modern Goldilocks: for her, texting puts people not too close, not too far, but at just the right distance. The world is now full of modern Goldilockses, people who take comfort in being in touch with a lot of people whom they also keep at bay.

Randy, twenty-seven, has a younger sister — a Goldilocks who got her distances   7
wrong. Randy is an American lawyer now working in California. His family lives in New York, and he flies to the East Coast to see them three or four times a year. When I meet Randy, his sister Nora, twenty-four, had just announced her engagement and wedding date via email to a list of friends and family. "That," Randy says to me bitterly, "is how I got the news." He doesn't know if he is more angry or hurt. "It doesn't feel right that she didn't call," he says. "I was getting ready for a trip home. Couldn't she have told me then? She's my sister, but I didn't have a private moment when she told me in person. Or at least a call, just the two of us. When I told her I was upset, she sort of understood, but laughed and said that she and her fiancé just wanted to do things simply, as simply as possible. I feel very far away from her."

Nora did not mean to offend her brother. She saw email as efficient and did not   8
see beyond. We have long turned to technology to make us more efficient in work;

now Nora illustrates how we want it to make us more efficient in our private lives. But when technology engineers intimacy, relationships can be reduced to mere connections. And then, easy connection becomes redefined as intimacy. Put otherwise, cyber-intimacies slide into cyber-solitudes.

Only a decade ago, I would have been mystified that fifteen-year-olds in my urban neighborhood, a neighborhood of parks and shopping malls, of front stoops and coffee shops, would feel the need to send and receive close to six thousand messages a month via portable digital devices or that best friends would assume that when they visited, it would usually be on the virtual real estate of Facebook. It might have seemed intrusive, if not illegal, that my mobile phone would tell me the location of all my acquaintances within a ten-mile radius. But these days we are accustomed to all this. Life in a media bubble has come to seem natural. So has the end of a certain public etiquette: on the street, we speak into the invisible microphones on our mobile phones and appear to be talking to ourselves. We share intimacies with the air as though unconcerned about who can hear us or the details of our physical surroundings.

I once described the computer as a second self, a mirror of mind. Now the metaphor no longer goes far enough. Our new devices provide space for the emergence of a new state of the self, itself, split between the screen and the physical real, wired into existence through technology.

Teenagers tell me they sleep with their cell phone, and even when it isn't on their person, when it has been banished to the school locker, for instance, they know when their phone is vibrating. The technology has become like a phantom limb, it is so much a part of them. These young people are among the first to grow up with an expectation of continuous connection: always on, and always on them. And they are among the first to grow up not necessarily thinking of simulation as second best. All of this makes them fluent with technology but brings a set of new insecurities. They nurture friendships on social-networking sites and then wonder if they are among friends. They are connected all day but are not sure if they have communicated. They become confused about companionship. Can they find it in their lives on the screen? Could they find it with a robot? Their digitized friendships — played out with emoticon emotions, so often predicated on rapid response rather than reflection — may prepare them, at times through nothing more than their superficiality, for relationships that could bring superficiality to a higher power, that is, for relationships with the inanimate. They come to accept lower expectations for connection and, finally, the idea that robot friendships could be sufficient unto the day.

Overwhelmed by the volume and velocity of our lives, we turn to technology to help us find time. But technology makes us busier than ever and ever more in search of retreat. Gradually, we come to see our online life as life itself. We come to see what robots offer as relationship. The simplification of relationship is no longer a source of complaint. It becomes what we want. These seem the gathering clouds of a perfect storm.

Technology reshapes the landscape of our emotional lives, but is it offering us the   13
lives we want to lead? Many roboticists are enthusiastic about having robots tend to
our children and our aging parents, for instance. Are these psychologically, socially,
and ethically acceptable propositions? What are our responsibilities here? And are we
comfortable with virtual environments that propose themselves not as places for recreation but as new worlds to live in? What do we have, now that we have what we say
we want — now that we have what technology makes easy? This is the time to begin
these conversations, together. It is too late to leave the future to the futurists.

EXAMINING THE READING

1. **Reasons** Explain why text messaging has become the "connection of choice" and
   how people can be "alone together."
2. **Disadvantages** What are some of the disadvantages of constant connection?
3. **Explanation** How have today's teenagers become "confused about companionship"?
4. **Vocabulary** Explain the meaning of each of the following words as it is used in the
   reading: *surreptitious* (para. 2), *titrate* (6), *intrusive* (9), *predicated* (11), and *propositions* (13).

ANALYZING THE WRITER'S TECHNIQUE

1. **Thesis** Express Turkle's thesis in your own words. Is it stated directly in the essay or
   only implied?
2. **Emotional Impact** Turkle uses a powerful example in paragraph 2. How does this
   example help convey Turkle's main point?
3. **Audience** What audience do you think Turkle is addressing in this selection? How
   do her examples address this audience?

VISUALIZING THE READING

Turkle uses cause and effect in addition to illustration in her essay. Use the chart below
to identify the causes and effects discussed in each paragraph listed. The first one has
been done for you.

Paragraph Number	Cause or Effect Discussed
Paragraph 2	Multitasking may cause a person to disengage from the person with whom he or she is communicating.
Paragraph 4	
Paragraph 5	
Paragraph 7	

THINKING CRITICALLY ABOUT ILLUSTRATION

1. **Connotation** What is the connotation of *dial down* (para. 6)? Is Turkle using it to mean something positive or negative?
2. **Sources** Turkle's examples are drawn primarily from personal interviews and her own experience. How trustworthy do you consider these sources of information? What other source types could Turkle have used to give alternative viewpoints?
3. **Examples** Does Turkle provide enough examples to support her thesis? Are the examples fair and representative of the types of people who communicate electronically?
4. **Fact or Opinion** In paragraph 4, Turkle writes: "Whether you are online or not, it is easy for people to end up unsure if they are closer together or further apart." Is this a statement of fact or opinion?

RESPONDING TO THE READING

1. **Reaction** Turkle contends that roboticists are "enthusiastic about having robots tend to our children and our aging parents." Are you comfortable with this? Is this already happening in some form? Do you believe that robotic "caregivers" are a possibility?
2. **Journal** What would your life be like without e-mail, texting, or other means of electronic communication? Write a journal entry describing a day in your life without communications technology.
3. **Essay** Sherry Turkle presents a one-sided view of the effects of technology on relationships. Write an essay illustrating the advantages of electronic communication.

WORKING TOGETHER

Imagine that a local newspaper has received a letter from a subscriber explaining that she has lost her cell phone and does not have the money to replace it. She states that she feels like she has lost her mind. Working with a partner, create both the subscriber's letter and the advice columnist's reply. Be prepared to share your work with the class.

APPLYING YOUR SKILLS: ADDITIONAL ESSAY ASSIGNMENTS

For more on locating and documenting sources, see Part 5.

Using what you learned about illustration in this chapter, write an illustration essay on one of the topics below. Depending on the topic you choose, you may need to conduct library or Internet research.

TO EXPRESS YOUR IDEAS

1. In an article for the campus newspaper, explain what you consider to be the three most important qualities of a college instructor. Support your opinion with vivid examples from your experience.

e **macmillanhighered.com/successfulwriting**
E-readings > *A Look at Vertical Patrols in Public Housing* (podcast), WNYC/Radio Rookies, Temitayo Fagbenle

2. Explain to a general audience the role played by grandparents within a family, citing examples from your own family or other families you know well.

TO INFORM YOUR READER

3. In "Rambos of the Road," Martin Gottfried explains the concept of "auto macho," also known as "road rage," using examples from his own experience. Explain the concept of *peer pressure,* using examples from your experience.
4. Describe to an audience of college students the qualities or achievements you think should be emphasized during job interviews. Give examples that show why the qualities or achievements you choose are important to potential employers.

TO PERSUADE YOUR READER

5. Argue for or against an increased emphasis on physical education in public schools. Your audience is your local school committee.
6. In a letter to the editor of a local newspaper, argue for or against the establishment of a neighborhood watch group.

CASES USING ILLUSTRATION

7. Prepare the oral presentation you will give to your local town board to convince board members to lower the speed limit on your street. Use examples as well as other types of evidence.
8. Write a letter to the parents of three-year-old children who will begin attending your day care center this year, explaining how they can prepare their children for the day care experience. Support your advice with brief but relevant examples.

SYNTHESIZING IDEAS

Civility

Both "American Jerk: Be Civil, or I'll Beat You to a Pulp" (pp. 45–47) and "Rambos of the Road" (pp. 306–09) deal with bad behavior and incivility.

Analyze the Readings

1. What types of behaviors does each reading address? Compare the authors' attitudes toward these behaviors.
2. Write a journal entry comparing the techniques that each author uses to support his thesis, especially considering the tone of each. Which is more effective? Explain your choice.

Essay Idea

Choose a public setting or forum in which selfish behavior and a lack of civility are evident to you. Write an essay illustrating the behavior.

explain how a popular radio talk show screens its callers. Your primary purpose in writing a how-it-works essay is to present the steps in the process clearly enough so that your readers can fully understand it.

Some essays contain elements of both types of process analysis. In writing about how a car alarm system works, for example, you might find it necessary to explain how to activate and deactivate the system as well as how it works.

A process analysis essay should include everything your reader needs to know to understand or perform the process. This usually means providing

- an explicit thesis statement,
- a clear, step-by-step description of the process in chronological order,
- definitions of key terms, descriptions of needed equipment, and any other important background information,
- enough detail for readers to follow the process, and
- help with avoiding potential problems.

PROCESS ANALYSES USUALLY INCLUDE AN EXPLICIT THESIS STATEMENT

A process analysis usually contains a clear thesis that identifies the process to be discussed and suggests why the process is important or useful to the reader.

HOW TO By carefully preparing for a vacation in a foreign country, *[process]*
you can save time and prevent hassles. *[why it's useful]*

HOW IT WORKS Although understanding the grieving process *[process]* will not lessen the grief

that you experience after the death of a loved one, knowing that your
experiences are normal does provide some comfort. *[why it's useful]*

PROCESS ANALYSIS IS ORGANIZED CHRONOLOGICALLY

The steps or events in a process analysis are usually organized in chronological order—that is, the order in which the steps are normally completed. For essays that explain lengthy processes, the steps may be grouped into categories or divided into substeps, with headings such as *Preparing for the Interview, During the Interview,* and *After the Interview.* Transitions, such as *Before you are called for an interview* or *Once the interview is over,* are often used to make the order of steps and substeps clear.

Sometimes the steps of a process do not have to occur in any particular order. For example, in an essay on how to resolve a dispute between two coworkers, the order of the recommended actions may depend on the nature of the dispute. In this situation, some logical progression of recommended actions should be used, such as starting with informal or simple steps and progressing to more formal or complex ones.

EXERCISE 15.1 **Writing a Thesis Statement for Process Analysis**

Choose one of the following processes. The process should be one you are familiar with and can explain to others. Draft a working thesis statement and a chronological list of the steps or stages of the process.

1. How to use a specific computer program
2. How to study for an exam
3. How to end a relationship with a friend or partner
4. How to get an A in your writing class
5. How to complete an application (for college, a job, a credit card)

PROCESS ANALYSIS PROVIDES BACKGROUND INFORMATION HELPFUL TO READERS

In some process analysis essays, readers may need additional information to understand the process. For example, in an essay explaining how scuba diving works to readers who are unfamiliar with the topic, you might need to define unfamiliar terms, such as *oxygen toxicity* or *decompression sickness*; you might need to provide background information about risks of injury or a history of the sport; and you would need to describe equipment such as dive masks, buoyancy compensators, and dive gauges. In a how-to essay, you might also need to explain where to obtain the equipment or training.

For more on defining terms, see Chapter 18.

EXERCISE 15.2 **Providing Background Information in a Process Essay**

For one of the following processes, list (a) the technical terms that you need to define in order to explain the process, (b) useful background information you might include in the essay, and (c) the types of equipment needed to perform the task.

1. How to perform a task at home or at work (such as changing the oil in a car or taking notes during a court hearing)
2. How a piece of equipment or a machine works (such as a treadmill or a lawn mower)
3. How to repair an object (such as a leaky faucet or a ripped piece of clothing)

PROCESS ANALYSIS PROVIDES AN APPROPRIATE LEVEL OF DETAIL

In deciding what to include in a process analysis essay, be careful not to overwhelm your readers with too many details. An explanation of how to perform CPR written by and for physicians could be highly technical, but the same description should be much simpler when written for volunteers in the local ambulance corps.

For a process involving many complex steps or highly specialized equipment, consider including a drawing or diagram to help your readers visualize the steps they need to follow or understand. For example, in an essay explaining how to detect a wiring problem in an electric stove, you might include a diagram of the stove's circuitry.

To keep your writing lively and interesting when explaining technical or scientific processes, use sensory details and figures of speech. Rather than giving dry technical details, try using descriptive language.

PROCESS ANALYSIS ANTICIPATES TROUBLE SPOTS AND OFFERS SOLUTIONS

A how-to essay should anticipate potential trouble spots or areas of confusion and offer advice on how to avoid or resolve problems. It should also warn readers of any difficult, complicated, or critical steps, encouraging them to pay special attention or take extra care. For instance, in a how-to essay on hanging wallpaper, you would warn readers about the difficulties of handling sheets of wallpaper and suggest folding the sheets to make them easier to work with.

> **EXERCISE 15.3** **Identifying Potential Trouble Spots in a Process**
>
> For one of the processes listed in Exercise 15.1 or Exercise 15.2, identify potential trouble spots in the process and describe how to avoid or resolve them.

The following readings demonstrate the techniques for writing effective process analyses as discussed above. The first reading is annotated to point out how Susan Silk and Barry Goldman use these techniques to help readers avoid saying the wrong thing to a suffering friend or relative. As you read the second essay, try to identify for yourself how the writer uses the techniques of process analysis to help readers understand how to transform a "shitty first draft" into a compelling piece of writing.

READING: HOW-TO ESSAY

How Not to Say the Wrong Thing

SUSAN SILK AND BARRY GOLDMAN

Susan Silk is the founder and CEO of MSI Strategic Communication, a company that provides communication consulting services. Barry Goldman is an arbitrator, mediator, and author. Using their experience, they have written an essay to help readers avoid saying the wrong thing when trying to provide comfort to someone who needs it.

Introduction: Presents an anecdote to help readers identify with the situation

When Susan had breast cancer, we heard a lot of lame remarks, but our favorite came from one of Susan's colleagues. She wanted, she needed, to visit Susan after the surgery, but Susan didn't feel like having visitors, and she said so. Her colleague's response? "This isn't just about you." 1

"It's not?" Susan wondered. "My breast cancer is not about me? It's about you?" 2

Background: Provides another anecdote to show problem is widespread

The same theme came up again when our friend Katie had a brain aneurysm. She was in intensive care for a long time and finally got out and into a step-down unit. She was no longer covered with tubes and lines and monitors, but she was still in rough shape. A friend came and saw her and then stepped into the hall with Katie's husband, Pat. "I wasn't prepared for this," she told him. "I don't know if I can handle it." 3

This woman loves Katie, and she said what she did because the sight of Katie in this condition moved her so deeply. But it was the wrong thing to say. And it was wrong in the same way Susan's colleague's remark was wrong. 4

Susan has since developed a simple technique to help people avoid this mistake. It works for all kinds of crises: medical, legal, financial, romantic, even existential. She calls it the Ring Theory.

5 **Thesis:** Thesis identifies process and indicates why it is important to learn.

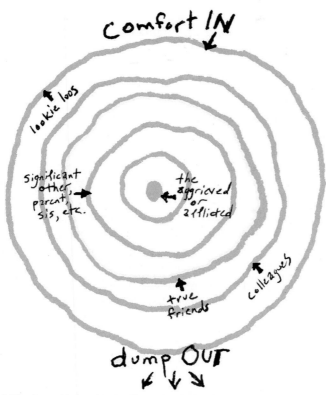

comfort IN

lookie loos

significant other, parent, sis, etc.

the aggrieved or afflicted

true friends

colleagues

dump OUT

© Wes Bausmith, Los Angeles Times, April 7, 2013

Draw a circle. This is the center ring. In it, put the name of the person at the center of the current trauma. For Katie's aneurysm, that's Katie. Now draw a larger circle around the first one. In that ring put the name of the person next closest to the trauma. In the case of Katie's aneurysm, that was Katie's husband, Pat. Repeat the process as many times as you need to. In each larger ring put the next closest people. Parents and children before more distant relatives. Intimate friends in smaller rings, less intimate friends in larger ones. When you are done you have a Kvetching Order. One of Susan's patients found it useful to tape it to her refrigerator.

6 **Organization:** Transitional words and phrases signal chronological stages of process.

Here are the rules. The person in the center ring can say anything she wants to anyone, anywhere. She can kvetch and complain and whine and moan and curse the heavens and say, "Life is unfair" and "Why me?" That's the one payoff for being in the center ring.

7

Everyone else can say those things too, but only to people in larger rings.

8

Anticipation of trouble spots: The author explains what people should avoid doing and saying.

When you are talking to a person in a ring smaller than yours, someone closer to the center of the crisis, the goal is to help. Listening is often more helpful than talking. But if you're going to open your mouth, ask yourself if what you are about to say is likely to provide comfort and support. If it isn't, don't say it. Don't, for example, give advice. People who are suffering from trauma don't need advice. They need comfort and support. So say, "I'm sorry" or "This must really be hard for you" or "Can I bring you a pot roast?" Don't say, "You should hear what happened to me" or "Here's what I would do if I were you." And don't say, "This is really bringing me down."   9

Point of view: Second person (*you*) is commonly used in how-to essays, though it may be frowned on in academic writing.

If you want to scream or cry or complain, if you want to tell someone how shocked you are or how icky you feel, or whine about how it reminds you of all the terrible things that have happened to you lately, that's fine. It's a perfectly normal response. Just do it to someone in a bigger ring.   10

Comfort IN, dump OUT.   11

There was nothing wrong with Katie's friend saying she was not prepared for how horrible Katie looked, or even that she didn't think she could handle it. The mistake was that she said those things to Pat. She dumped IN.   12

Complaining to someone in a smaller ring than yours doesn't do either of you any good. On the other hand, being supportive to her principal caregiver may be the best thing you can do for the patient.   13

Most of us know this. Almost nobody would complain to the patient about how rotten she looks. Almost no one would say that looking at her makes them think of the fragility of life and their own closeness to death. In other words, we know enough not to dump into the center ring. Ring Theory merely expands that intuition and makes it more concrete: Don't just avoid dumping into the center ring, avoid dumping into any ring smaller than your own.   14

Conclusion: Final paragraph cleverly connects to the introduction and speaks directly to the reader.

Remember, you can say whatever you want if you just wait until you're talking to someone in a larger ring than yours.   15

And don't worry. You'll get your turn in the center ring. You can count on that.   16

VISUALIZING A PROCESS ANALYSIS ESSAY: A GRAPHIC ORGANIZER

For more on creating a graphic organizer, see pp. 52–53.

Seeing the content and structure of an essay in simplified, visual form can help you analyze a reading, recall key steps as you generate ideas for an essay, and structure your own writing. The graphic organizer in Figure 15.1 shows the basic organization of a process analysis essay. When your main purpose is to explain a process, follow this standard format. When you incorporate process analysis into an essay using one or more other patterns of development, briefly introduce the process and then move directly to the steps involved. If the process is complex, you may want to add a brief summary of it before the transition back to the main topic of the essay.

FIGURE 15.1 **Graphic Organizer for a Process Analysis Essay**

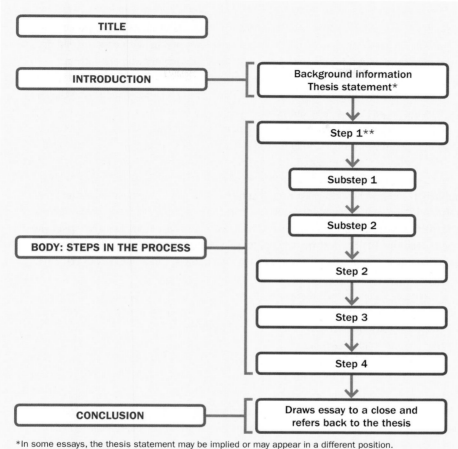

*In some essays, the thesis statement may be implied or may appear in a different position.
**In some essays, substeps may be included.

READING: HOW-IT-WORKS ESSAY

Shitty First Drafts

ANNE LAMOTT

Anne Lamott has published several nonfiction works, including *Bird by Bird: Instructions on Writing and Life* (1995), from which this essay is taken; *Traveling Mercies: Some Thoughts on Faith* (2000); *Grace (Eventually)* (2008); *Help, Thanks, Wow: The Three Essential Prayers* (2012); and *Stitches: A Handbook on Meaning, Hope, and Repair* (2013). She is also the author of several novels, including *Blue Shoe* (2002) and *Imperfect Birds* (2010). As you read this essay, notice how Lamott leads you through the steps in the writing process while at the same time revealing her attitude toward the task of writing. Figure 15.2, a graphic organizer for "Shitty First Drafts," appears on p. 340. Read the essay first, and then compare it to the graphic organizer. What was omitted and why?

Now, practically even better news than that of short assignments is the idea of shitty first drafts. All good writers write them. This is how they end up with good second drafts and terrific third drafts. People tend to look at successful writers who are getting their books published and maybe even doing well financially and think that they sit down at their desks every morning feeling like a million dollars, feeling great about who they are and how much talent they have and what a great story they have to tell; that they take in a few deep breaths, push back their sleeves, roll their necks a few times to get all the cricks out, and dive in, typing fully formed passages as fast as a court reporter. But this is just the fantasy of the uninitiated. I know some very great writers, writers you love who write beautifully and have made a great deal of money, and not one of them sits down routinely feeling wildly enthusiastic and confident. Not one of them writes elegant first drafts. All right, one of them does, but we do not like her very much. We do not think that she has a rich inner life or that God likes her or can even stand her. (Although when I mentioned this to my priest friend Tom, he said you can safely assume you've created God in your own image when it turns out that God hates all the same people you do.)

Very few writers really know what they are doing until they've done it. Nor do they go about their business feeling dewy and thrilled. They do not type a few stiff warm-up sentences and then find themselves bounding along like huskies across the snow. One writer I know tells me that he sits down every morning and says to himself nicely, "It's not like you don't have a choice, because you do — you can either type, or kill yourself." We all often feel like we are pulling teeth, even those writers whose prose ends up being the most natural and fluid. The right words and sentences just do not come pouring out like ticker tape most of the time. Now, Muriel Spark is said to have felt that she was taking dictation from God every morning — sitting there, one supposes, plugged into a Dictaphone, typing away, humming. But this is a very hostile and aggressive position. One might hope for bad things to rain down on a person like this.

For me and most of the other writers I know, writing is not rapturous. In fact, the only way I can get anything written at all is to write really, really shitty first drafts.

The first draft is the child's draft, where you let it all pour out and then let it romp all over the place, knowing that no one is going to see it and that you can shape it later. You just let this childlike part of you channel whatever voices and visions come through and onto the page. If one of the characters wants to say, "Well, so what, Mr. Poopy Pants?" you let her. No one is going to see it. If the kid wants to get into really sentimental, weepy, emotional territory, you let him. Just get it all down on paper because there may be something great in those six crazy pages that you would never have gotten to by more rational, grown-up means. There may be something in the very last line of the very last paragraph on page six that you just love, that is so beautiful or wild that you now know what you're supposed to be writing about, more or less, or in what direction you might go — but there was no way to get to this without first getting through the first five and a half pages.

I used to write food reviews for *California* magazine before it folded. (My writing food reviews had nothing to do with the magazine folding, although every single review did cause a couple of canceled subscriptions. Some readers took umbrage at my comparing mounds of vegetable puree with various ex-presidents' brains.) These reviews always took two days to write. First I'd go to a restaurant several times with a few opinionated, articulate friends in tow. I'd sit there writing down everything anyone said that was at all interesting or funny. Then on the following Monday I'd sit down at my desk with my notes and try to write the review. Even after I'd been doing this for years, panic would set in. I'd try to write a lead, but instead I'd write a couple of dreadful sentences, XX them out, try again, XX everything out, and then feel despair and worry settle on my chest like an x-ray apron. It's over, I'd think calmly. I'm not going to be able to get the magic to work this time. I'm ruined. I'm through. I'm toast. Maybe, I'd think, I can get my old job back as a clerk-typist. But probably not. I'd get up and study my teeth in the mirror for a while. Then I'd stop, remember to breathe, make a few phone calls, hit the kitchen and chow down. Eventually I'd go back and sit down at my desk, and sigh for the next ten minutes. Finally I would pick up my one-inch picture frame, stare into it as if for the answer, and every time the answer would come: all I had to do was to write a really shitty first draft of, say, the opening paragraph. And no one was going to see it.

So I'd start writing without reining myself in. It was almost just typing, just making my fingers move. And the writing would be terrible. I'd write a lead paragraph that was a whole page, even though the entire review could only be three pages long, and then I'd start writing up descriptions of the food, one dish at a time, bird by bird, and the critics would be sitting on my shoulders, commenting like cartoon characters. They'd be pretending to snore, or rolling their eyes at my overwrought descriptions, no matter how hard I tried to tone those descriptions down, no matter how conscious I was of what a friend said to me gently in my early days of restaurant reviewing. "Annie," she said, "it is just a piece of *chicken*. It is just a bit of *cake*."

But because by then I had been writing for so long, I would eventually let myself trust the process — sort of, more or less. I'd write a first draft that was maybe twice as long as it should be, with a self-indulgent and boring beginning, stupefying descriptions of the meal, lots of quotes from my black-humored friends that made them sound more like the Manson girls than food lovers, and no ending to speak of. The whole thing would be so long and incoherent and hideous that for the rest of the day I'd obsess about getting creamed by a car before I could write a decent second draft. I'd worry that people would read what I'd written and believe that the accident had really been a suicide, that I had panicked because my talent was waning and my mind was shot.

The next day, I'd sit down, go through it all with a colored pen, take out everything I possibly could, find a new lead somewhere on the second page, figure out a kicky place to end it, and then write a second draft. It always turned out fine, sometimes even funny and weird and helpful. I'd go over it one more time and mail it in.

Then, a month later, when it was time for another review, the whole process would start again, complete with the fears that people would find my first draft before I could rewrite it.

Almost all good writing begins with terrible first efforts. You need to start some-   10
where. Start by getting something — anything — down on paper. A friend of mine says
that the first draft is the down draft — you just get it down. The second draft is the
up draft — you fix it up. You try to say what you have to say more accurately. And
the third draft is the dental draft, where you check every tooth, to see if it's loose or
cramped or decayed, or even, God help us, healthy.

FIGURE 15.2 **Graphic Organizer for "Shitty First Drafts"**

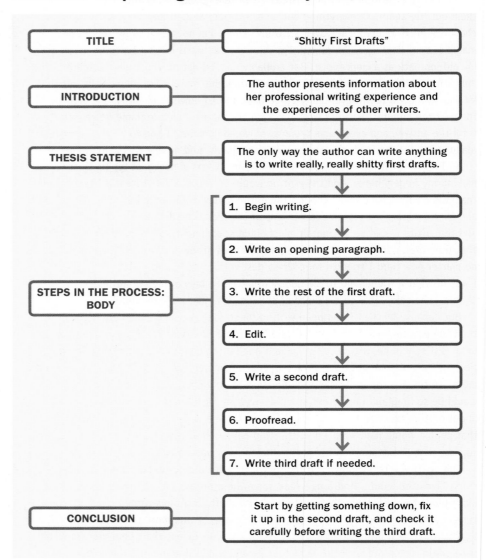

EXERCISE 15.4 **Drawing a Graphic Organizer**

Using the graphic organizer in Figure 15.1 or 15.2 as a basis, draw a graphic organizer for "How Not to Say the Wrong Thing" (pp. 334–36).

INTEGRATING PROCESS ANALYSIS INTO AN ESSAY

You may find it helpful to incorporate a process analysis into a discussion that relies on a different pattern of development. For instance, in a descriptive essay about an alcohol abuse program for high school students, you might decide to include a brief process analysis of how alcohol impairs mental functioning. Lamott incorporates illustration and description to make her process analysis engaging. Here are a few suggestions for incorporating process analysis effectively into essays based on other patterns of development.

The essay "The Psychology of Stuff and Things" later in this chapter (pp. 356–61) uses multiple patterns of development to explain how our stuff defines us across the life span.

1. **Explain only the major steps in the process rather than every step in detail to avoid diverting your readers from the primary focus of your essay.**
2. **Introduce the process analysis with a transitional sentence that alerts readers that a process analysis will follow.** For example, here is how you might introduce a brief summary of the process by which AIDS spreads through HIV (human immunodeficiency virus).

> Before you explain to teenagers *how* to avoid contracting HIV, you need to let them know *what* they are avoiding. Teenagers need to know that HIV is transmitted by . . .

3. **It is sometimes helpful to use the word *process* or *procedure* to let readers know that a process analysis is to follow.** In the preceding example, the final sentence might be revised to read as follows:

> Teenagers need to know that HIV is transmitted by the following process.

4. **Once you have completed the process analysis, alert readers that you are about to return to the main topic.** You might conclude the process with a summary statement.

> Above all, teenagers need to know that HIV is transmitted through an exchange of bodily fluids.

READING ACTIVELY AND THINKING CRITICALLY

Reading and thinking critically about process analysis requires you to read the selection and reflect on its meaning, consider it in terms of your own experience, and, finally, examine and challenge the author's attitude as it is shown in the selection.

For more on reading actively, see Chapter 3; for more on thinking critically, see Chapter 4.

For more on previewing, see pp. 45–47.

WHAT TO LOOK FOR, HIGHLIGHT, AND ANNOTATE

Use these guidelines to read process analyses effectively.

1. **Preview.** Preview the essay to get an overview of its content and organization.
2. **Identify the process.** Read the essay through. Highlight the thesis statement, and try to discover why the writer believes the process is important or useful.
3. **Understand the steps in the process.** Reread the essay, highlighting or underlining each step or set of steps. Using a different colored highlighter or an asterisk (*), mark steps that the author identifies as possibly difficult or troublesome. Circle new terms as you encounter them. Look for difficulties you might experience in the process or questions you may need to ask about it. For a complex or especially important process, try the following:
   • Explain each step in your own words, without referring to the text.
   • Imagine yourself carrying out the process as you read.
   • Annotate any sections that summarize complex steps.
   Hint: Outlining the process or drawing a graphic organizer can help you understand complex processes.
4. **Think about the meaning.** Reread the essay once again, this time concentrating on its meaning by answer the following questions:
   • What is the writer's purpose in writing this essay? For what audience is it intended? What techniques does the writer use to achieve his or her purpose with this audience?
   • How clearly is the process described? Have any steps been left out or glossed over? Could you repeat the process or explain it to someone after having read this essay several times?
5. **Consider your reactions.** Consider how the essay relates to your own experience. In what situations can you use or apply the information? Are there other processes similar to the one described in the essay? How are these processes the same as and different from the one in the essay?

ANALYZING PROCESS ANALYSIS

Although most process analyses are straightforward and informative, you should always consider the author's motives for writing and evaluate the author's level of expertise before accepting his or her advice. Use the following questions to think critically about process analysis.

What are the writer's motives? As you read, ask why the writer wants readers to understand or carry out this process and what his or her motive is. Sometimes a writer has a hidden motive for explaining a process. For example, a writer opposed to the death penalty may use graphic details about the process of executing a prisoner to shock readers and persuade them to oppose the death penalty. Even a how-to article on a noncontroversial topic can have a hidden agenda, such as one titled "How to Lose Ten Pounds" that was written by the owner of a weight-loss clinic.

Is the writer knowledgeable and experienced? Following the advice of someone who is not qualified to give it can be a waste of time or even dangerous. When you read a process analysis, consider whether the writer has sufficient knowledge about or experience with the process. Check the author's credentials, and consider whether he or she supports assertions with evidence and quotes from reliable sources and authorities.

Have any steps or important details been omitted? Authors have to make assumptions about their readers' knowledge and experience. For example, in "Shitty First Drafts" (pp. 337–40), Lamott assumes that readers have an interest in writing; she does not explain the writing terminology she uses and seems to assume that readers know something about writing and the writing process. If writers assume that their readers have more knowledge than they actually have, the audience may not understand the essay or may be unable to carry out the process.

A GUIDED WRITING ASSIGNMENT*
PROCESS ANALYSIS

YOUR ESSAY ASSIGNMENT

Write a process analysis essay explaining how something works or is done. Choose a topic you are familiar with or that you can learn about through observation or research. Try to select a topic that your readers—your instructor and your fellow students—will find interesting or useful. Below are some options to help you get started.

How-To Essay Topics

- How to improve your _____ (study habits, wardrobe, batting average)
- How to be a successful _____ (diver, parent, gardener)
- How to make or buy _____ (an object for personal use or enjoyment)

How-It-Works Essay Topics

- How a decision is made to _____ (accept a student at a college, add or eliminate a state agency)
- How _____ (a quilt, a news broadcast, a Web site, a football team) is put together
- How your college _____ (spends tuition revenues, hires professors, raises money)

*The writing process is *recursive*; that is, you may find yourself revising as you draft or prewriting as you revise. This is especially true when writing on a computer. Your writing process may also differ from that of your classmates, depending on your preferred learning style.

(continued on next page)

Prewriting

1 Select a topic from the list on p. 343, or create one of your own.

Use the following tips to select a process to write about.
- For a **how-to essay**, choose a process that you can **visualize or perform** as you write. Keep the equipment nearby for easy reference. For example, if you are writing an essay about how to scuba dive, it may be helpful to have your scuba equipment in front of you.
- For a **how-it-works essay**, choose a topic about which you **have background knowledge** or for which you can **find reliable information readily**.
- Choose a topic that is **useful** and **interesting** to your readers. Unless you can find a way to make an essay about how to do laundry interesting, do not write about it.

2 Consider your purpose, audience, and point of view.

Ask yourself these questions.
- Will my **purpose** be to **express myself**, **inform**, or **persuade**? (Process analyses tend to be informative.)
- Who is my **audience**? Will readers need any **background information** to understand my essay? Will they need me to **define terms** or **describe (or diagram) equipment**? How much **detail** do I need to go into for them to follow the steps or understand the process? Where will they need **special help** or **warnings**? (Check whether your readers will need background or definitions by asking a classmate to tell you how he or she would explain key terms to a novice.)
- What **point of view** best suits my purpose and audience? **How-to** essays commonly use the **second person**, addressing the reader directly as *you*. (Hint: Second person is often considered inappropriate in college writing.) **How-it-works** essays commonly use the **third person** (*he, she, it*).

3 Explore your subject and generate details.

Use idea-generating strategies to come up with the details your process analysis essay will use.
1. **List the steps** or **diagram the process**, keeping these questions in mind.
   - What separate actions are involved?
   - What steps are obvious to me but may not be obvious to someone unfamiliar with the process?
   - What steps, if omitted, will lead to problems or failure?
   (Listing is especially useful for pragmatic and concrete learners.)
2. Ask a friend or classmate to **act out your process**. What problems did this person encounter? What additional details did you need to tell him or her? (Acting out the process is especially useful for verbal, social, and emotional learners.)
3. Do some research to see **how others have described the process**. What details do other writers include? Do they generally add steps you've omitted or omit steps you've included? Be sure to keep track of any information you borrow from sources. (Research is useful for all learners.)

4. Alone or in pairs, list the words *looks like, sounds like, smells like,* and *feels like* across the top of a page and then **list as many words or comparisons** below as you can think of in 10 or 15 minutes. (Description is especially useful for verbal and concrete learners.)

Try taking an approach that challenges your learning style. For example, **pragmatic** and **abstract learners**—visualize steps in how-to essays; **creative learners**—slow down and set out detailed steps; **concrete learners**—convey the big picture of a social process in a how-it-works essay.

4 **Draft your thesis statement.**

Tell readers why the process is **important**, **beneficial**, or **relevant** to them.

_____ **is important/beneficial/relevant because** _____.
Name process   *state reasons audience can relate to*

Be sure to consider what *your* audience will find compelling.

5 **Organize your essay.**

Organize your ideas logically.
· For a process with **fewer than ten steps**, you can usually arrange the steps **chronologically**, devoting **one paragraph per step**.
· For a **more complicated process**, **group the steps** into three or four categories; use **one paragraph per group**, including **a topic sentence** to introduce the group and the **rest of the paragraph** to explain the individual steps involved. For an essay on how to run a garage sale, the steps might be grouped as follows:
    Group 1: Locating and collecting merchandise
    Group 2: Advertising
    Group 3: Pricing and setting up
    Group 4: Conducting the sale

Hint: An outline or graphic organizer will allow you to experiment to find the best order for supporting paragraphs.

To determine how usable your instructions are, ask a classmate to try them out.

6 **Write a first draft of your process analysis essay.**

Use the following guidelines to keep your process analysis on track.
· The **introduction** should present your **thesis statement**, include necessary **background information**, and convince readers the process is **relevant** to them.
For lengthy or complex processes, consider including an **overview** of the steps.

(continued on next page)

Organizing & Drafting

- The **body paragraphs** should **identify each step** and make clear why it is important to the process. If the process is complex, including **a drawing or diagram** to outline steps can be helpful. (If including a graphic, introduce it in your essay and refer to it by its title.)
  - Use **headings** that name your main topics and signal changes in topic. Whether your essay is brief or lengthy.
  - Use **transitions,** such as *before*, *next*, and *finally*, to signal steps in the process.
  - Make sure your **tone** is appropriate to your audience and purpose. In some situations, a matter-of-fact tone is appropriate; in others, an emotional or humorous tone may be suitable.
- The **conclusion** might emphasize the **value or importance** of the process, describe **particular situations** in which it is useful, or offer **a final amusing or emphatic comment or anecdote**. An essay that ends with the final step in the process may sound incomplete.

Revising

7 **Evaluate your draft, and revise as necessary.**

Use Figure 15.3, "Flowchart for Revising a Process Analysis Essay," to evaluate and revise your draft.

Editing & Proofreading

8 **Edit and proofread your essay.**

Refer to Chapter 10 for help with . . .
- **editing sentences** to avoid wordiness, making your verb choices strong and active, and making your sentences clear, varied, and parallel, and
- **editing words** for tone and diction, connotation, and concrete and specific language.

Look out especially for **comma splices**.

A **comma splice** occurs when two independent clauses are joined only by a comma. To correct a comma splice, . . .
- add a coordinating conjunction (*and*, *but*, *for*, *nor*, *or*, *so*, or *yet*)

Example: The first step in creating a flower arrangement is to choose an attractive container, the

but

^

container should not be the focal point of the arrangement.

Editing & Proofreading

- change the comma to a semicolon

  Example: Following signs is one way to navigate a busy airport; looking for a map is another.

- divide the sentence into two sentences

  Example: To lower fat consumption in your diet, first learn to read food product labels. *Next* ~~next~~ eliminate those products that contain trans fats or unsaturated fats.

- subordinate one clause to the other

  Example: *After you have placed* ~~Place~~ the pill on the cat's tongue, hold its mouth closed, rubbing its chin until it swallows the pill.

FIGURE 15.3 Flowchart for Revising a Process Analysis

QUESTIONS

1. Highlight your thesis statement. Does it make clear the importance of your process?

 NO

- Ask yourself: Why would readers want or need to know this process? Incorporate the answers into your thesis statement.

 YES

REVISION STRATEGIES

2. *Number* the steps of your process in the margin of your paper. Are they in chronological order (or some other logical progression)? Is the order clear?

 NO

- Study your graphic organizer or outline to determine if any steps are out of order.
- Visualize or carry out the process to discover the most sensible order.
- Rearrange the steps and add transitions if necessary.

 YES

(continued on next page)

(Figure 15.3 continued)

QUESTIONS		REVISION STRATEGIES

3. [Bracket] any background information in your introduction. Is it sufficient? Have you provided an overview of the process, if needed?

 NO

- Give an example of a situation in which the process might be used.
- Explain that related processes and ideas depend on the process you are describing.

 YES

4. Place an ✗ beside any technical terms you have used. Is each unfamiliar term defined? Are your definitions clear?

 NO

- Ask a classmate to read your draft and identify any other terms needing definitions as well as any unclear definitions.
- Add or revise definitions as needed.

 YES

5. (Circle) any equipment you have mentioned. Have you included all necessary equipment? Will all of it be familiar to readers?

 NO

- Add equipment you have overlooked.
- Describe equipment that might be unfamiliar to readers.

 YES

6. Place ✔'s beside key details of the process. Have you included an appropriate level of detail for your readers?

 NO

- Add or delete background information.
- Add or delete definitions of technical terms.
- Add or delete other detail.

 YES

7. For a how-to essay, <u>underline</u> sections where you have anticipated potential difficulties for your readers. Have you anticipated all likely trouble spots? Are these sections clear and reassuring?

 NO

- Add more detail about critical steps.
- Add warnings about confusing or difficult steps.
- Offer advice on what to do if things go wrong.

 YES

8. Reread your introduction and conclusion. Is each effective?

 NO

- Revise your introduction and conclusion so that they meet the guidelines in Chapter 7.

READINGS: PROCESS ANALYSIS IN ACTION

Going Vegan: How to Have Your Eggless Cake, and Eat It, Too!

JUSTINE APPEL

Justine Appel wrote the following essay in response to an assignment that asked her to explain a process that she had mastered. As you read the essay, consider whether the steps described in the essay clearly explain the process of adopting a vegan lifestyle.

When I finally found the courage to tell my mom I had decided to go vegan, it was in a grocery store. We were shopping for Thanksgiving dinner, and I wordlessly grabbed a carton of soy milk and stuck it in the shopping cart. My mom shot me a weary look. "Are you vegan now?" I nodded. "Well, you'll have to be in charge of your own food," she said, continuing down the aisle. "I just can't keep track of all that."

Vegans, or people who adhere to a lifestyle free of animal products, face remarks like this all the time. Although the vegetarian diet, which excludes meat, fish, and poultry, is widely accepted in many parts of the world, the idea of avoiding all foods, fabrics, and substances derived from animals often seems absurd or highly difficult in the United States. Nonetheless, for those who feel passionately about animal welfare and environmental health, adopting a vegan lifestyle doesn't have to be difficult. With some research, preparation, and the right attitude, veganism can become second nature.

As with all major lifestyle changes, the very first step is to think about the reasons for making a change. While there is a standard concept of veganism, all vegans have their own reasons for abstaining from animal products, which govern their individual choices. Some people are vegan for health reasons, and thus probably wouldn't turn down a pair of wool socks. Some are only opposed to industrial farming, and would feel comfortable eating eggs from a small, local farm. Still others don't believe in using animals for human consumption at all, and stay away from honey, glue, silk, and refined sugar (which is sometimes processed with animal bone char) on top of the usual list of animal-based food.

Once you have considered the grounds for your veganism, it is important to maintain a critical mindset towards these issues. Being vegan is a deliberate

---

1 **Introduction:** Appel grabs readers' attention with an anecdote that provides background on her decision.

2 **Background:** Defines *veganism*

Thesis: Her thesis reveals the relevance of her topic for readers who might be considering "going vegan."

3 **Organization:** Uses a transition to keep readers on track and a topic sentence to identify the step: thinking about the reasons for making a change.

4 **Organization:** Transition provides segue to step 2; topic sentence identifies main idea.

ethical choice, but that doesn't mean your ethics as a vegan cannot evolve. Staying conscious about the effects of your lifestyle is a process, so consider this first step "repeat as needed." Several months after I stopped eating animal products for environmental reasons, I realized that chowing down on bananas shipped from Ecuador is not a very environmentally conscious choice, either. Now when choosing fruit to go in my vegan breakfast smoothies, I try to use what is more locally grown. While matching up your philosophy with your day-to-day eating habits can be hard, looking at veganism as a process rather than a finish line will help you to know your limits and engage in behaviors that you feel are right.

The next step is a little easier, though it requires some investigation. Start to become familiar with the many forms of animal products and learn how to distinguish them on ingredient labels. While some animal ingredients are obvious (butter, milk, eggs), others are disguised by unfamiliar vocabulary. Gelatin, a substance used in marshmallows, jello, and gummy candy, usually comes from animal bones and cartilage. Lecithin is a common food additive that can come from animal tissue. Don't be afraid of these sneaky ingredients! A quick online search will procure several lists of hidden animal products. Fortunately, milk and eggs are common allergens, and will usually be listed in bold in the allergy warning below the ingredients list, which is much faster to find.

Once you know what to avoid, it's just as important to learn what to seek out. Since animal-based foods are good sources of several important nutrients, take the time to research some adequate substitutes to keep yourself well-fed and healthy. It is especially important to find good sources of protein and iron, since these nutrients are most easily available in animal products. Foods made from nuts, beans, or soy have high levels of protein and are usually quite filling. Meanwhile, nuts, beans, and whole grains are good sources of iron. Many fruits and vegetables are rich in other important dietary nutrients. All bodies have different needs, so if you are unsure, consult a doctor or nutritionist about how to get a healthy amount of vitamins, minerals, and other nutrients. In the meantime, eating a diverse array of foods is always a good measure.

Now that you've figured out what to eat, it's time to go food shopping. If you have a kitchen, proceed to stock it with food you like to eat. Vegan food can be found all over an average grocery store, and you will gradually learn the aisles with good vegan staples. While one of the many exciting aspects of going vegan is discovering new ingredients and dishes, forcing yourself to eat food you don't like is not a sustainable practice. For example, tempeh is a

5

6

7

Support: Offers an example to make the concept of the "critical mindset" concrete

Organization: Transition introduces step 3; topic sentence identifies it.

Background: Defines terms that may be unfamiliar to the reader

Organization: Transition introduces step 4; topic sentence, again, identifies it.

Support: Offers specific details to help readers maintain healthy protein and iron levels

Organization: Another transitional sentence introduces step 5: Go food shopping.

Support: An anecdote from her own experience supports discussion of the importance of figuring out what to buy

healthy soy product filled with protein, fiber, and vitamins that many vegans rely on for filling sandwiches and stir-fries, but I can't stand the texture of tempeh, so I stick to my favorite forms of protein, like lentils and peanut butter. There are countless vegan meals and snacks out there, so don't waste time and energy buying or preparing food you won't feel like eating.

Next, polish your cooking skills. Knowing how to cook is an empowering tool for vegans, since it allows them to make dishes they will love and can share with friends and family. The internet has tons of great cooking tutorials and blogs, which are often more personal and helpful than standard recipes. Use the internet as a resource for tips on vegan cooking, and if you wish, supplement with a few vegan cookbooks. Finding one night a week to practice cooking not only will help you improve over time, but also can result in many dinners' worth of leftovers.

As useful as it is to know how to cook, going vegan should not mean the end of going out to eat. Familiarize yourself with the good restaurants in town that have vegan options, so you can recommend them when a group of friends is going out for lunch or dinner. Once there, don't be afraid to ask the waiter about the ingredients. It's easy for them to find out, and soon you'll gain a shrewd sense of what is vegan and what isn't. For example, naan, a type of Indian bread, usually comes with butter, whereas roti, another type, does not. When in an unfamiliar city, look for Thai, Chinese, Indian, or Middle Eastern restaurants, as they are usually the most accommodating to vegan diets.

Unfortunately, you will not always find enough vegan food to satisfy your hunger, particularly if you live in or are visiting a suburban or rural region where most locals are omnivorous. While American cities and coastal regions usually contain a wider diversity of ethnic food, I have found it especially difficult to find vegan fare in southeastern, central, and Midwestern states. Make sure to carry high-protein snacks when traveling to avoid feeling starved. Being prepared with trail mix and other travel-hardy food can save the day if the grandparents you're visiting take you to a steakhouse for dinner.

Once you've successfully established a vegan lifestyle that suits you, it is time to develop your vegan etiquette. By now, you will have noticed that your veganism sometimes interferes in social situations. Perhaps someone who has graciously invited you to dinner is serving lamb, or your grandmother gives you a pair of leather shoes for your birthday. It can be upsetting to refuse kind gestures such as these, but luckily there are ways to preempt them. When

---

8   **Organization:** Transitional word introduces step 6: polishing cooking skills.

9   **Organization:** Transitional clause prepares readers for the next step (step 7): going out to eat. Offers several alternatives from which the reader may choose

10   **Organization:** Transition introduces step 8—satisfying your hunger

11   **Organization:** Step 9—How to handle potentially difficult situations
Support: Specific examples of awkward situations

Troublespots: Practical advice for avoiding pitfalls

invited to eat in a social setting, inform the host of your dietary restrictions ahead of time, and ask if they would like you to bring a dish that you will be able to eat. When your birthday or a gift-giving holiday rolls around, make sure to specify what you do or don't eat, wear, and use, so relatives and friends will not give you non-vegan gifts. They may forget or make mistakes, which is okay. If anything, take it as an opportunity to discuss why you make the choices you do. Although preaching about the moral superiority of your diet will most certainly be unwelcome, a polite explanation about the motives behind your veganism might make for interesting, friendly debate.

Final step: Be prepared to answer questions about the vegan lifestyle.

To that end, be prepared to answer many questions. Some of them may seem silly ("Is goat cheese vegan?"), but it is necessary to remember that everyone comes from a different background and therefore will have a unique set of values and beliefs. Recognize that food and clothing are political, but they also can be deeply personal or important in different cultural atmospheres. If you remain open to new thoughts and ideas and refrain from passing moral judgment on other peoples' lifestyle choices, you will find veganism much easier in social settings.   12

Conclusion: Appel offers living a vegan lifestyle as one way to live responsibly in the world.

Emphasizes the value of the process

As the twenty-first century progresses, the political, social, and environmental effects of our day-to-day decisions are becoming more evident. There is no single issue that takes precedence over another, and being vegan is just one way to live consciously in an imperfect world. However, overcoming the doubts and suspicions surrounding veganism is an important first step in challenging norms and recognizing the connections between people, animals, and the earth. Finding veganism achievable makes other positive change seem achievable, too. And, for the record, my mom has become a master at identifying vegan ingredients, and surprised me by cooking a delicious dairy-less lasagna the last time I was home.   13

Ends the essay with a final, amusing anecdote

ANALYZING THE WRITER'S TECHNIQUE

1. **Introduction** How successful are the first two paragraphs at providing a reason for learning the process?
2. **Style** Appel uses dialogue in her opening paragraph. What effect does this create?
3. **Organization** Explain how Appel has organized the steps in the process.
4. **Conclusion** Does Appel's conclusion bring the essay to a satisfying close? Why or why not?
5. **Opinion** Appel says that going vegan is an ethical choice. How does she convey her opinion? What reasons does she give?

THINKING CRITICALLY ABOUT ILLUSTRATION

1. **Response** How does Appel's use of phrases such as "gelatin . . . usually comes from animal bones" (par. 5) and "lecithin . . . can come from animal tissue" (5) affect you as a reader? Do they increase or decrease the essay's effectiveness?
2. **Tone** How would you describe Appel's tone? What words or ideas help establish the tone?
3. **Audience** Who is the intended audience for this essay? How do you know? Is the essay appropriate for this audience? Why or why not?
4. **Omissions** What has Appel omitted from her process analysis, if anything? What additional information or advice might someone who is totally ignorant about the vegan lifestyle need? Would you need any additional information?

RESPONDING TO THE ESSAY

1. **Reaction** Appel made a major lifestyle change when she chose to adhere to a vegan lifestyle. Do you think you could make the same lifestyle change? Why or why not? What would be the most difficult food for you to give up? How do you think your family and friends would respond to your lifestyle change? What would be your primary reason for making the change?
2. **Discussion** How important is it to follow the steps in the order Appel presents them? What are some other processes in which following the steps in order is especially important? List two or three.
3. **Essay** Appel sees her choice of a vegan lifestyle to be a positive change for herself. Write an essay explaining a change you have made or would like to make in your life that would change some facet of your life (your health, your sense of accomplishment) for the better. Describe the process that you would have to follow in order to make the change.

READING

Dater's Remorse

CINDY CHUPACK

Cindy Chupack (b. 1965) was born in Oklahoma. She trained as a journalist at Northwestern University because she wanted to make a living as a writer, but she found that journalism did not suit her. After working in advertising, Chupack contributed a personal essay to *New York Woman* magazine that attracted the attention of a television writer who encouraged her to create sitcom scripts. Ultimately, she became a writer and executive producer for the hit HBO show *Sex and the City*.

   This selection below appears in a collection of Chupack's writings titled *The Between Boyfriends Book* (2003). As you read, notice the way Chupack builds her humorous analogy between shopping and dating, from her opening description of her telephone-company "suitors" to her conclusion: *Caveat emptor*—"Let the buyer beware."

I never imagined this would happen, but three men are fighting over me. They call   1
me repeatedly. They ply me with gifts. They beg me for a commitment. Yes, they're just

AT&T, MCI, and Sprint salesmen interested in being my long-distance carrier, but what I'm relishing — aside from the attention — is the sense that I am in complete control.

In fact, just the other day my ex (phone carrier, that is) called to find out what went wrong. Had I been unhappy? What would it take to win me back? Turns out all it took was two thousand frequent flier miles. I switched, just like that. I didn't worry about how my current carrier would feel, or how it might affect my Friends and Family. Now if only I could use that kind of healthy judgment when it comes to my love life.

The unfortunate truth is that while most of us are savvy shoppers, we're not sufficiently selective when looking for relationships, and that's why we often suffer from dater's remorse. Perhaps we should try to apply conventional consumer wisdom to men as well as merchandise. How satisfying love might be if we always remembered to:

Go with a classic, not a trend. We all know it's unwise to spend a week's salary on vinyl hip-huggers. But when it comes to men, even the most conservative among us occasionally invests in the human equivalent of a fashion fad. The furthest I ever strayed from a classic was during college. I wrote a paper about the Guardian Angels, those street toughs who unofficially patrol innercity neighborhoods, and being a very thorough student, I ended up dating one. He wore a red beret and entertained me by demonstrating martial arts moves in my dorm room. I remember telling my concerned roommate how he was *sooo* much more interesting than those boring MBA[1] types everybody else was dating. Of course, what initially seemed like a fun, impulse buy turned out to require more of an emotional investment than I was willing to make. It took me two months to break up with him — two months of getting persistent late-night calls, angry letters, and unannounced visits to my dorm room door, which I envisioned him kicking down someday. The good thing about MBAs: They're familiar with the expression "Cut your losses."

Beware of the phrase "Some assembly required." Anyone who has tried to follow translated-from-Swedish directions for putting together a swivel chair understands that when you've got to assemble something yourself, the money you save isn't worth the time you spend. The same goes for men. Many women think that even though a guy is not exactly "together," we can easily straighten him out. The fact is that fixer-uppers are more likely to stay forever flawed, no matter what we do. My friend Jenny fell for a forty-one-year-old bachelor, despite the fact that he spent their first few dates detailing his dysfunctional family and boasting that he went to the same shrink as the Menendez brothers.[2] "Six weeks later, when he announced he couldn't handle a relationship, it shouldn't have surprised me," says Jenny, who now looks for men requiring a little less duct tape.

Make sure your purchase goes with the other things you own. I once fell in love with a very expensive purple velvet couch, and I seriously considered buying it, even though it would mean getting my cat declawed, and I had signed an agreement when I adopted her that I would never do that. But the couch . . . the couch . . . I visited it a few more times, but I didn't buy, and not just out of sympathy for my cat. I realized that if I owned that couch, I'd have to replace all my comfy, old stuff with new

---

[1] MBA: Master of Business Administration, an advanced business degree
[2] Menendez brothers: two brothers who were convicted in 1996 of killing their parents

furniture equal in quality and style to the purple couch. Men can be like that, too. You're drawn to them because they're attractively different, but being with them may mean changing your entire life. For example, while dating a long-distance bicyclist, my friend Janet found herself suddenly following his training regimen: bowing out of social events just as the fun began, rising at an hour at which she normally went to bed, and replacing fine dining with intensive carbo-loading. And the only bike she ever rode was the stationary one at the gym.

Check with previous owners. Once beyond age twenty-five, most men would have   7
to be classified as secondhand, and we all know how risky it is to buy used merchandise. Therefore, it's up to you to do some basic consumer research. Find out how many previous owners your selection has had. If he's such a steal, why is he still on the lot? Is it because his exterior is a bit unsightly, or because he's fundamentally a lemon? (Before becoming too critical, bear in mind that *you* are still on the lot.)

Caveat emptor.[3] Following these guidelines won't guarantee a great relationship,   8
but it will help you cut down on the number of times you feel dater's remorse. Obviously looking for a husband is a bit more complicated than choosing a major appliance, but since there are no lifetime guarantees or lemon laws for men, it pays to be a savvy shopper.

EXAMINING THE READING

1. **Summarizing** According to Chupack, what can happen when you date someone who is "the human equivalent of a fashion fad" (para. 4)?
2. **Analogy** Explain the connection between dating and buying furniture. Why should women to stay away from furniture with "some assembly required" (5)?
3. **Details** Explain Chupack's advice to "make sure your purchase goes with the other things you own" (6).
4. **Vocabulary** Explain the meaning of each of the following words as it is used in the reading: *relishing* (1), *classic* (4), *envisioned* (4), *dysfunctional* (5), and *regimen* (6).

ANALYZING THE WRITER'S TECHNIQUE

1. **Thesis** Chupack's thesis involves dating as well as shopping. Identify her thesis, and evaluate the effectiveness of her comparison.
2. **Organization** How does Chupack order the steps in her process analysis essay? If the essay is not organized chronologically, does the author use any sort of logical progression such as starting with simple steps and progressing to more complex ones? Is her type of organization effective? Why or why not?
3. **Level of Detail** Is there enough detail for the selection to be of practical use?
4. **Conclusion** Is Chupack's reference to lemon laws a satisfying conclusion? Why or why not?

---

[3] *Caveat emptor:* Latin phrase meaning "Let the buyer beware"

Extended Self" Russell Belk quotes from novelist Alison Lurie's book *The Language of Clothes*, in which she observes: ". . . when adolescent girls exchange clothing they share not only friendship, but also identities — they become soulmates." Similarly, in interviews with teens, Ruthie Segev at Jerusalem College of Technology found evidence that selecting and buying gifts for their friends helps adolescents achieve a sense of identity independent from their parents, and that the mutual exchange of the same or similar gifts between friends helps them to create a feeling of overlapping identities.

In the transition from adolescence to adulthood, it's the first car that often becomes the ultimate symbol of a person's emerging identity. Interviews with car owners conducted by Graham Fraine and colleagues in 2007 found that young drivers, aged 18 to 25, were particularly likely to make the effort to personalize their cars with stickers, unusual number plates and seat covers, as if marking out their territory.

ADULTHOOD

As our lives unfold, our things embody our sense of self-hood and identity still further, becoming external receptacles for our memories, relationships and travels. "My house is not 'just a thing,'" wrote Karen Lollar in 2010. "The house is not merely a possession or a structure of unfeeling walls. It is an extension of my physical body and my sense of self that reflects who I was, am, and want to be."

As our belongings accumulate, becoming more infused with our identities, so their preciousness increases. People whose things are destroyed in a disaster are traumatized, almost as if grieving the loss of their identities. Photographs from the aftermath of Hurricane Sandy, which struck the US East coast in 2012, show people standing bereft, staring in shock and bewilderment at all they've lost. Reflecting on the fire that took her home, Lollar says it was like "a form of death." Alexandra Kovach, who also lost her home in a fire, wrote in *The Washington Post* in 2007: "It isn't just a house. It's not the contents, or the walls, but the true feeling of that home — and all that it represents."

LATER LIFE AND BEYOND

Older people don't just form bonds with their specific belongings, they seem to have an affection for brands from their youth too. Usually this manifests in a taste for music, books, films and other entertainment from yesteryear, but the same has been shown for fashions and hairstyles, it has been hinted at for perfumes, and in a study published in 2003 by Robert Schindler and Morris Holbrook, it was found that it also extends to the car.

Dozens of participants aged 16 to 92 rated their preference for the appearance of 80 cars, ranging from the 1915 Dodge Model 30-35 to the 1994 Chrysler Concorde. Among men, but not women, there was a clear preference for cars that dated from the participants' youth (peaking around age 26). This was particularly the case for men who were more nostalgic and who believed that things were better in the old days. What other examples might there be? "Children of both sexes tend to have strong feelings about foods they like as they grow up," says Schindler. "Although we haven't studied food, I would expect both men and women to have a lifetime fondness for foods they enjoyed during their youth."

As with human relationships, the attachments to our things deepen with the   12
passage of time. Elderly people are often surrounded by possessions that have followed
them through good times and bad, across continents and back. In 2000, Linda Price at
the University of Arizona and her colleagues interviewed 80 older people about their

Older people don't just form bonds with their specific belongings, they seem to have an affection
for brands from their youth too. © Jeff Morgan 11/Alamy

decisions regarding these "special possessions." A common theme was the way cherished objects come to represent particular memories. "I can look at anything [in this house] and remember special occasions," recalled Diane, aged 70. "It's almost like a history of our life."

After a person dies, many of their most meaningful possessions become family heir- 13
looms, seen by those left behind as forever containing the lost person's essence. This idea is also seen in the behaviors that follow the death of a celebrity. In a process that Belk calls "sacralization," possessions owned by a deceased star can acquire astonishing value overnight, both sentimental and monetary. This is often true even for exceedingly mundane items such as President Kennedy's tape measure, auctioned for $48,875 in 1996. A study by George Newman and colleagues in 2011 provided a clue about the beliefs underlying these effects. They showed that people place more value on celebrity-owned items, the more physical contact the celebrity had with the object, as if their essence somehow contaminated the item through use.

THE FUTURE

Our relationship with our stuff is in the midst of great change. Dusty music and 14
literary collections are being rehoused in the digital cloud. Where once we expressed our identity through fashion preferences and props, today we can cultivate an online identity with a carefully constructed homepage. We no longer have to purchase an item to associate ourselves with it, we can simply tell the world via Twitter or Facebook about our preferences. The self has become extended, almost literally, into technology, with Google acting like a memory prosthetic. In short, our relationship with our things, possessions and brands remains as important as ever, it's just the nature of the relationship is changing. Researchers and people in general are gradually adjusting. The psychology of our stuff is becoming more interdisciplinary, with new generations building on the established research conducted by consumer psychologists.

Twenty-five years after he published his seminal work on objects and the "extended 15
self," Russell Belk has composed an update: "The extended self in a digital world," currently under review. "The possibilities for self extensions have never been so extensive," he says.

References

Belk, R. W. (1988). Possessions and the extended self. *Journal of Consumer Research, 15,* 139–168.

Belk, R. W. (2013). The extended self in a digital world. *Journal of Consumer Research, 40*(3), 477–500.

Carver, C. S. & Baird, E. (1998). The American dream revisited: Is it what you want or why you want it that matters? *Psychological Science, 9*(4), 289–292.

Chaplin, L. N. & John, D. R. (2007). Growing up in a material world: Age differences in materialism in children and adolescents. *Journal of Consumer Research, 34*(4), 480–493.

Cockrill, A. (2012). Does an iPod make you happy? An exploration of the effects of iPod ownership on life satisfaction. *Journal of Consumer Behaviour, 11*, 406–414.

Cova, B., Kozinets, R. & Shankar, A. (2007). *Consumer tribes*. Oxford: Butterworth-Heinemann.

Cushing, A. L. (2012). *Possessions and self extension in digital environments: Implications for maintaining personal information*. PhD thesis, University of North Carolina at Chapel Hill.

Fraine, G., Smith, S. G., Zinkiewicz, L., Chapman, R. & Sheehan, M. (2007). At home on the road? Can drivers' relationships with their cars be associated with territoriality? *Journal of Environmental Psychology, 27*(3), 204–214.

Friedman, O. & Neary, K. R. (2008). Determining who owns what: Do children infer ownership from first possession? *Cognition, 107*(3), 829–849.

Hood, B. M. & Bloom, P. (2008). Children prefer certain individuals over perfect duplicates. *Cognition, 106*(1), 455–462.

Kasser, T. (2003). *The high price of materialism*. Cambridge, MA: MIT Press.

Kovach, A. (2007, 27 October). What fire couldn't destroy. *Washington Post*. Retrieved 4 June 2013 from: www.washingtonpost.com/wpdyn/content/article/2007/10/26/AR200 7102601774.html

Lollar, K. (2010). The liminal experience: Loss of extended self after the fire. *Qualitative Inquiry, 16*(4), 262–270.

Newman, G. E., Diesendruck, G. & Bloom, P. (2011). Celebrity contagion and the value of objects. *Journal of Consumer Research, 38*(2), 215–228.

Nordsletten, A. E., Fernández de la Cruz, L., Billotti, D. & Mataix-Cols, D. (2012). Finders keepers: The features differentiating hoarding disorder from normative collecting. *Comprehensive Psychiatry*. doi:10.1016/j.comppsych.2012.07.063.

Piaget, J. (1965). *The moral judgment of the child*. New York: The Free Press. (Original work published 1932)

Price, L. L., Arnould, E. J. & Curasi, C. F. (2000). Older consumers' disposition of special possessions. *Journal of Consumer Research, 27*(2), 179–201.

Radford, S. K. & Bloch, P. H. (2012). Grief, commiseration, and consumption following the death of a celebrity. *Journal of Consumer Culture, 12*(2), 137–155.

Schindler, R. M. & Holbrook, M. B. (2003). Nostalgia for early experience as a determinant of consumer preferences. *Psychology and Marketing, 20*(4), 275–302.

Segev, R., Shoham, A. & Ruvio, A. (2012). What does this gift say about me, you, and us? The role of adolescents' gift giving in managing their impressions among their peers. *Psychology & Marketing, 29*(10), 752–764.

Shrum, L. J., Wong, N., Arif, F. et al. (2012). Reconceptualizing materialism as identity goal pursuits: Functions, processes, and consequences. *Journal of Business Research*. doi:10.1016/j.jbusres.2012.08.010

Srivastava, A., Locke, E. A. & Bartol, K. M. (2001). Money and subjective wellbeing. *Journal of Personality and Social Psychology, 80*(6), 959–971.

Steketee, G., Frost, R. O. & Kyrios, M. (2003). Cognitive aspects of compulsive hoarding. *Cognitive Therapy and Research, 27*(4), 463–479.

Van Boven, L., Campbell, M. C. & Gilovich, T. (2010). Stigmatizing materialism: On stereotypes and impressions of materialistic and experiential pursuits. *Personality and Social Psychology Bulletin, 36*(4), 551–563.

Van Boven, L. & Gilovich, T. (2003). To do or to have? That is the question. *Journal of Personality and Social Psychology, 85*(6), 1193–1202.

EXAMINING THE READING

1. **Summarizing** What are the steps in the process that Jarrett describes?
2. **Meaning** What does the author mean when he says that "our essence lives on in what once we made or owned"? (para. 1).
3. **Details** Explain the importance to sports fans of collecting paraphernalia and wearing team colors. To what part of the process does this relate?
4. **Vocabulary** Explain the meaning of each of the following words as it is used in the reading: *essence* (para. 1), *memorabilia* (4), *materialism* (5), *seminal* (6), *receptacles* (8), and *prosthetic* (16).

ANALYZING THE WRITER'S TECHNIQUE

1. **Thesis** Identify Jarrett's thesis statement. What background information does he provide to support it?
2. **Conclusion** Does Jarrett's conclusion bring the essay to a satisfying close? Why or why not?
3. **Purpose** Explain how Jarrett's citation of research supports his purpose in writing the essay.
4. **Audience** Who is Jarrett's audience? Does his advice apply to others outside this group?
5. **Patterns** What methods of development, in addition to process, does Jarrett use in this essay? What does each add to your understanding of Jarrett's explanation of how our possessions become an extension of our selves?

VISUALIZING THE READING

Jarrett uses examples and details to explain how we come to identify with our possessions. List the steps in the process and provide an example or detail for each. The first one has been done for you.

Step	Example or Detail
Childhood	Children understand ownership early; between ages two and four, children assume that the person who possesses the object owns it even if he or she gives it away later.
Adolescence	
Adulthood	
Late adulthood	

THINKING CRITICALLY ABOUT TEXT AND IMAGES

1. **Tone** How would you describe Jarrett's tone? The essay appears to have been written for students of psychology and other psychologists. How could Jarrett have made the essay easier to read for a more general audience?

2. **Conclusion** What is Jarrett suggesting about how we will identify with our posses-sions in the digital age?
3. **Visuals** What does the visual near the end of the essay contribute to the reader's understanding of how older adults relate to their belongings?
4. **Additional Evidence** What additional evidence could Jarrett have included to make his claim about our relationship with our possessions more convincing?

RESPONDING TO THE READING

1. **Discussion** Do you believe that your essence lives on in what you once made or owned? Why or why not? What do you believe your possessions say about you?
2. **Journal** How does this essay make you feel about the possessions you have accu-mulated? Will it make any difference in what you do with your accumulated posses-sions in the future?
3. **Essay** Jarrett says that "most children have an unusually intense relationship with a specific 'attachment object,' usually a favorite blanket or soft toy." Reflect on your childhood and try to remember what your favorite toy or "attachment object" was. Write an essay in which you describe this object, explain how your attachment to it developed, and include a story or two about it.

WORKING TOGETHER

If Christian Jarrett were to design a bumper sticker based on the information in this essay, what would it say? In small groups, devise a brief motto that captures the essence of this essay.

APPLYING YOUR SKILLS: ADDITIONAL ESSAY ASSIGNMENTS

Write a process analysis essay on one of the following topics. Depending on the topic you choose, you may need to conduct research.

For more on locating and docu-menting sources, see Part 5.

TO EXPRESS YOUR IDEAS

1. How children manage their parents
2. How to relax and do nothing
3. How to find enough time for your children or girlfriend/boyfriend/spouse

TO INFORM YOUR READER

4. How to avoid or speed up red-tape procedures
5. How a particular type of sports equipment protects an athlete
6. How to remain calm while giving a speech

e macmillanhighered.com/successfulwriting
E-readings > *How to Flirt and Get a Date!* (video), WrongPlanet/Alex Plank

TO PERSUADE YOUR READER

7. How important it is to vote in a presidential election
8. How important it is to select the right courses in order to graduate on time
9. How important it is to exercise every day

CASES USING PROCESS ANALYSIS

10. In your communication course, you are studying how friendships develop and the strategies that people use to meet others. Write an essay describing the strategies people use to make new friends.
11. You are employed by a toy manufacturer and have been asked to write a brochure that encourages children to use toys safely. Prepare a brochure that describes at least three steps children can follow to avoid injury.

SYNTHESIZING IDEAS

Interpersonal Relationships

Both "How Not to Say the Wrong Thing" (pp. 334–36) and "Dater's Remorse" (pp. 353–55) discuss, in part, how to deal with others. "Dater's Remorse" discusses how to select the right men to date and "How Not to Say the Wrong Thing" focuses on how to interact with people experiencing a life crisis.

Analyzing the Readings

1. Evaluate the level of detail in each essay. Which essay is more helpful?
2. Write a journal entry in which you discuss ways in which you could use the information from each of the essays in your life or how someone close to you could use the information.

Essay Idea

Think of other situations in which you need to be concerned with how to interact with others. Write a process essay explaining the steps in creating a positive interaction. For example, you might write about how to interact with an instructor, the parents of your boyfriend or girlfriend, or an elderly neighbor or relative.

16

Comparison and Contrast
Showing Similarities and Differences

Study the photograph showing a group of friends playing Rockband. Then make two lists, one of ways that playing Rockband and playing in a real band are similar and another of ways that they are different. In your lists, include details about the types of skills required, the setting, and so on. Then write a paragraph comparing playing Rockband with being in a band.

©Michael Loccisano/Getty Images

- understand the purpose and function of comparison or contrast essays,
- use graphic organizers to visualize comparison and contrast essays,
- integrate comparison and contrast into an essay,
- read and think critically about comparison and contrast, and
- plan, organize, draft, revise, and edit essays using comparison and contrast.

Using **comparison and contrast** involves looking at similarities (**comparison**), differences (**contrast**), or both. You analyze similarities and differences when you make everyday decisions (when you shop for a pair of jeans or select a sandwich in the cafeteria) as well as when you make important decisions (deciding which college to attend or which person to date). Your paragraph about playing Rockband and playing in a rock band is an example of comparison-and-contrast writing.

USING COMPARISON AND CONTRAST IN COLLEGE AND THE WORKPLACE

- For a course in *criminal justice*, your instructor asks you to participate in a panel discussion comparing organized crime in Italy, Japan, and Russia.
- For a *journalism course*, you are asked to interview two local television news reporters and write a paper contrasting their views on journalistic responsibility.
- As a *computer technician* for a pharmaceutical firm, you are asked to compare and contrast several models of tablet computers and recommend the one the company should purchase for its salespeople.

CHARACTERISTICS OF COMPARISON AND CONTRAST ESSAYS

Whether used as the primary pattern of development or alongside other patterns, successful comparison and contrast writing generally meets several criteria.

COMPARISON AND CONTRAST HAS A CLEAR PURPOSE AND IS WRITTEN FOR A SPECIFIC AUDIENCE

A comparison and contrast essay usually has one of three purposes:

- **To express ideas:** The purpose of an essay about playing Rockband could be to express the writer's love of the game, rock music, or both. The audience for

this essay might be the readers of an online forum for the discussion of video games.
- **To inform:** The purpose of an essay about playing Rockband could be to inform readers new to the game how playing Rockband differs from playing in a real band. The audience for this essay might be dedicated amateur musicians looking for an electronic alternative to joining a band.
- **To persuade:** The purpose of an essay about playing Rockband could be to persuade readers that Rockband is much more challenging in some ways than playing in an actual band. The audience for this essay might be musicians who think the game seems easy.

COMPARISON AND CONTRAST CONSIDERS SHARED CHARACTERISTICS

You cannot compare or contrast two things unless they have something in common. When making a comparison, a writer needs to choose a **basis of comparison**—a fairly broad common characteristic on which to base the essay. The paragraph you wrote comparing the Rockband game to an actual rock band may have focused on the similarities and differences in equipment required, physical exertion involved, and so forth. For another essay comparing baseball and football, for example, a basis of comparison might be the athletic skills required or the rules and logistics of each sport.

To develop a comparison-contrast essay, the writer examines two subjects using **points of comparison**—characteristics relating to the basis of comparison. In an essay using athletic skills as a basis of comparison, for example, points of comparison might be height and weight requirements, running skills, and hand-eye coordination. In an essay based on rules and logistics, points of comparison might include scoring, equipment, and playing fields.

EXERCISE 16.1 Identifying Bases of Comparison

For three items in the following list, identify two possible bases of comparison.

1. Two means of travel or transportation
2. Two means of communication (e-mails, telephone calls, letters, texts)
3. Two pieces of equipment
4. Two magazines or books
5. Two types of television programming

COMPARISON AND CONTRAST IS ORGANIZED POINT BY POINT OR SUBJECT BY SUBJECT

You probably organized your paragraph comparing playing Rockband and playing in an actual band in one of two ways.

1. Writing about playing the game and then writing about playing in an actual band (or vice versa)
2. Discussing each point of similarity or difference with examples from Rockband and playing in an actual band

Most comparison and contrast essays use one of these two primary methods of organization:

> • **Point-by-point organization**
> The writer moves back and forth between two or more subjects, comparing them on the basis of several key points or characteristics.
>
> • **Subject-by-subject organization**
> The author describes the key points or characteristics of one subject before moving on to those aspects of a second subject.

COMPARISON AND CONTRAST FAIRLY EXAMINES SIMILARITIES, DIFFERENCES, OR BOTH

Depending on their purpose and audience, writers using comparison and contrast may focus on similarities, differences, or both. In an essay intended to *persuade* readers that performers Beyoncé Knowles and Jennifer Lopez have much in common in terms of talent and cultural influence, the writer would focus on similarities: hit records, millions of fans, and parts in movies. An essay intended to *inform* readers about the singers would probably cover both similarities and differences, discussing the singers' different childhoods or singing styles.

An essay focusing on similarities often mentions a few differences, usually in the introduction, to let readers know the writer is aware of the differences. Conversely, an essay that focuses on differences might mention a few similarities.

Whether you cover similarities, differences, or both in an essay, you should strive to treat your subjects fairly. Relevant information should not be purposely omitted to show one subject in a more favorable light. In an essay about Knowles and Lopez, for instance, you should not leave out information about Lopez's charity work while mentioning Knowles's charitable causes in an effort to make Knowles appear to be the more charitable person.

COMPARISON AND CONTRAST MAKES A POINT

A successful comparison and contrast essay has a main point that sparks readers' interest in the subjects rather than boring them with a mechanical listing of similarities or differences. This main point can serve as the **thesis** for the essay, or the thesis can be implied in the writer's choice of details.

An explicit thesis has three functions:

1. **To identify the *subjects* being compared or contrasted**
2. **To suggest whether the focus is on *similarities, differences,* or *both***
3. **To state the *main point* of the comparison or contrast**

The following two sample theses meet all three criteria. Note, too, that each thesis suggests why the comparison or contrast is meaningful and worth reading about.

┌─────── similarities ───────┐ ┌─────── subjects ───────┐
Similar appeals in commercials for three popular breakfast cereals
┌─────── main point ───────┐
reveal America's obsession with fitness and health.

┌─────────────── subjects ───────────────┐
The two cities Niagara Falls, Ontario, and Niagara Falls, New York,
┌─────── differences ───────┐ ┌─────── main points ───────┐
demonstrate two different approaches to appreciating nature and

preserving the environment.

EXERCISE 16.2 | **Writing an Effective Thesis Statement**

For one of the topic pairs you chose in Exercise 16.1, select the basis of comparison that seems most promising. Then write a thesis statement that identifies the subjects, the focus (similarities, differences, or both), and the main point.

COMPARISON AND CONTRAST CONSIDERS SIGNIFICANT AND RELEVANT SHARED CHARACTERISTICS

A comparison and contrast essay considers characteristics that readers will find significant as well as relevant to the essay's purpose and thesis. In general, college writers should discuss at least three or four significant characteristics to support the thesis, describing or explaining each characteristic in detail so that readers can grasp the main point of the comparison or contrast. Writers often use sensory details, dialogue, examples, expert testimony, and other kinds of evidence to convince readers that the items being compared (or contrasted) are, in fact, similar (or dissimilar).

The following readings demonstrate the techniques discussed above for writing effective comparison and contrast essays. The first reading is annotated to show how Greg Beato uses these techniques to contrast *The Onion* with more conventional newspapers. As you read the second essay, try to identify for yourself how Ian Frazier uses the techniques of comparison and contrast to demonstrate the benefits of pay phones over cell phones.

Amusing Ourselves to Depth: Is *The Onion* Our Most Intelligent Newspaper?

GREG BEATO

Greg Beato is a San Francisco–based writer who has written for such publications as *Spin*, *Wired*, *Business 2.0*, and *The San Francisco Chronicle*. He created the webzine *Traffic* in 1995 and was a frequent contributor to the webzine *Suck.com* from 1996 to 2000. He also maintains a blog about media and culture, *Soundbitten*, which he started in 1997. This essay was published in *Reason*, a libertarian magazine for which he continues to be a contributor, in 2007. As you read, notice how Beato uses comparison and contrast to make his case for the validity of "fake news."

Purpose: To persuade readers that the troubled newspaper industry should change its approach

Basis of comparison: *The Onion*'s success versus failure of other newspapers

Thesis: Indicates subjects and key qualities that set *The Onion* apart

Organization: Alternately contrasts *The Onion*'s approach with that of other news outlets

In August 1988, college junior Tim Keck borrowed $7,000 from his mom, rented a Mac Plus, and published a twelve-page newspaper. His ambition was hardly the stuff of future journalism symposiums: He wanted to create a compelling way to deliver advertising to his fellow students. Part of the first issue's front page was devoted to a story about a monster running amok at a local lake; the rest was reserved for beer and pizza coupons. 1

Almost twenty years later, *The Onion* stands as one of the newspaper industry's few great success stories in the post-newspaper era. Currently, it prints 710,000 copies of each weekly edition, roughly 6,000 more than the *Denver Post*, the nation's ninth-largest daily. Its syndicated radio dispatches reach a weekly audience of one million, and it recently started producing video clips too. Roughly three thousand local advertisers keep *The Onion* afloat, and the paper plans to add 170 employees to its staff of 130 this year. 2

Online it attracts more than two million readers a week. Type *onion* into Google, and *The Onion* pops up first. Type *the* into Google, and *The Onion* pops up first. But type "best practices for newspapers" into Google, and *The Onion* is nowhere to be found. Maybe it should be. At a time when traditional newspapers are frantic to divest themselves of their newsy, papery legacies, *The Onion* takes a surprisingly conservative approach to innovation. As much as it has used and benefited from the Web, it owes much of its success to low-tech attributes readily available to any paper but nonetheless in short supply: candor, irreverence, and a willingness to offend. 3

While other newspapers desperately add gardening sections, ask readers to share their favorite bratwurst recipes, or throw their staffers to ravenous packs of bloggers for online question-and-answer sessions, The Onion has focused on reporting the news. The fake news, sure, but still the news. It doesn't ask readers to post their comments at the end of stories, allow them to rate stories on a scale of one to five, or encourage citizen-satire. It makes no effort to convince readers that it really does understand their needs and exists only to serve them. *The Onion*'s journalists concentrate on writing stories and then getting them out there in a variety of formats, and this relatively old-fashioned approach to newspapering has been tremendously successful. 4

Are there any other newspapers that can boast a 60 percent increase in their print circulation during the last three years ? Yet as traditional newspapers fail to draw readers, only industry mavericks like the *New York Times*' Jayson Blair and *USA Today*'s Jack Kelley have looked to *The Onion* for inspiration.

One reason *The Onion* isn't taken more seriously is that it's actually fun to read. In 1985 the cultural critic Neil Postman published the influential *Amusing Ourselves to Death*, which warned of the fate that would befall us if public discourse were allowed to become substantially more entertaining than, say, a Neil Postman book. Today newspapers are eager to entertain — in their Travel, Food, and Style sections, that is. But even as scope creep has made the average big-city tree killer less portable than a ten-year-old laptop, hard news invariably comes in a single flavor: Double Objectivity Sludge.

Too many high priests of journalism still see humor as the enemy of seriousness: If the news goes down too easily, it can't be very good for you. But do *The Onion* and its more fact-based acolytes, *The Daily Show* and *The Colbert Report*, monitor current events and the way the news media report on them any less rigorously than, say, the *Columbia Journalism Review* or *USA Today*?

During the last few years, multiple surveys by the Pew Research Center and the Annenberg Public Policy Center have found that viewers of *The Daily Show* and *The Colbert Report* are among America's most informed citizens. Now, it may be that Jon Stewart isn't making anyone smarter; perhaps America's most informed citizens simply prefer comedy over the stentorian drivel the network anchormannequins dispense. But at the very least, such surveys suggest that news sharpened with satire doesn't cause the intellectual coronaries Postman predicted. Instead, it seems to correlate with engagement.

It's easy to see why readers connect with *The Onion*, and it's not just the jokes: Despite its "fake news" purview, it's an extremely honest publication. Most dailies, especially those in monopoly or near-monopoly markets, operate as if they're focused more on not offending readers (or advertisers) than on expressing a worldview of any kind. *The Onion* takes the opposite approach. It delights in crapping on pieties and regularly publishes stories guaranteed to upset someone: "Christ Kills Two, Injures Seven, in Abortion-Clinic Attack." "Heroic PETA Commandos Kill 49, Save Rabbit." "Gay Pride Parade Sets Mainstream Acceptance of Gays Back 50 Years." There's no predictable ideology running through those headlines, just a desire to express some rude, blunt truth about the world.

One common complaint about newspapers is that they're too negative, too focused on bad news, too obsessed with the most unpleasant aspects of life. *The Onion* shows how wrong this characterization is, how gingerly most newspapers dance around the unrelenting awfulness of life and refuse to acknowledge the limits of our tolerance and compassion. The perfunctory coverage that traditional newspapers give disasters in countries cursed with relatability issues is reduced to its bare, dismal essence: "15,000 Brown People Dead Somewhere." Beggars aren't grist for Pulitzers, just punch lines: "Man Can't Decide Whether to Give Sandwich to Homeless or Ducks." Triumphs of the

---

5 **Evidence:** Provides detailed statistics to support claim of *The Onion*'s success

6 **Contrast:** Implies that humor, which includes candor, irreverence, and willingness to offend, is what sets *The Onion* apart

7

8

9 **Point of comparison 1:** candor

Point of comparison 2: irreverence

Evidence: Supports claim of *The Onion*'s irreverence with sample headlines

10 **Point of comparison 3:** willingness to offend

human spirit are as rare as vegans at an NRA barbecue: "Loved Ones Recall Local Man's Cowardly Battle with Cancer."

Fair comparison: Points out the negative effects of *The Onion*'s approach

Such headlines come with a cost, of course. Outraged readers have convinced   11
advertisers to pull ads. Ginger Rogers and Denzel Washington, among other celebrities, have objected to stories featuring their names, and former *Onion* editor Robert Siegel once told a lecture audience that the paper was "very nearly sued out of existence" after it ran a story with the headline "Dying Boy Gets Wish: To Pork Janet Jackson." But if this irreverence is sometimes economically inconvenient, it's also a major reason for the publication's popularity. It's a refreshing antidote to the he-said/she-said balancing acts that leave so many dailies sounding mealy-mouthed. And while *The Onion* may not adhere to the facts too strictly, it would no doubt place high if the Pew Research Center ever included it in a survey ranking America's most trusted news sources.

Conclusion: Restates thesis in other words

During the last few years, big-city dailies have begun to introduce "commuter"   12
papers that function as lite versions of their original fare. These publications share some of *The Onion*'s attributes: They're free, they're tabloids, and most of their stories are bite-sized. But while they may be less filling, they still taste bland. You have to wonder: Why stop at price and paper size? Why not adopt the brutal frankness, the willingness to pierce orthodoxies of all political and cultural stripes, and apply these attributes to a genuinely reported daily newspaper? Until today's front pages can amuse our staunchest defenders of journalistic integrity to severe dyspepsia, if not death, they're not trying hard enough.

VISUALIZING A COMPARISON AND CONTRAST ESSAY: TWO GRAPHIC ORGANIZERS

For more on creating a graphic organizer, see pp. 52–55.

As noted earlier, you can organize a comparison and contrast essay in one of two ways: point by point or subject by subject. ("Amusing Ourselves to Depth: Is *The Onion* Our Most Intelligent Newspaper?" is organized point by point; "Dearly Disconnected," which follows, is organized subject by subject.) Suppose you want to compare two houses (house A and house B) built by the same architect for the purpose of evaluating how the architect's style has changed over time. After brainstorming ideas, you decide to base your essay on these points of comparison:

- layout,
- size,
- building materials, and
- landscaping.

POINT-BY-POINT ORGANIZATION

Figure 16.1 shows a graphic organizer for *point-by-point organization,* in which you go back and forth between the two houses, noting similarities and differences between them on each of the four points of comparison.

FIGURE 16.1 **Graphic Organizer for a Point-by-Point Comparison and Contrast Essay***

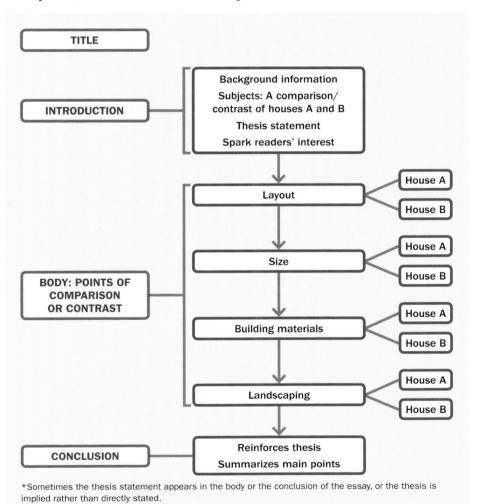

*Sometimes the thesis statement appears in the body or the conclusion of the essay, or the thesis is implied rather than directly stated.

SUBJECT-BY-SUBJECT ORGANIZATION

Figure 16.2 shows a graphic organizer for *subject-by-subject organization,* in which you first discuss the layout, size, building materials, and landscaping of house A and then do the same for house B.

FIGURE 16.2 Graphic Organizer for a Subject-by-Subject Comparison and Contrast Essay[*]

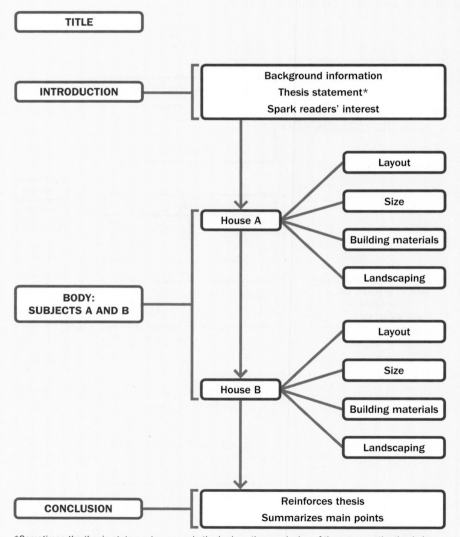

*Sometimes the thesis statement appears in the body or the conclusion of the essay, or the thesis is implied rather than directly stated.

Dearly Disconnected

IAN FRAZIER

Ian Frazier is an American writer and humorist whose books include *Great Plains* (1989), *Travels in Siberia* (2010), *The Cursing Mommy's Book of Days* (2012), and several collections of columns he wrote for *The New Yorker* magazine both as a staff writer and independently. The following essay was adapted from a column that appeared in *Mother Jones* magazine in 2000. Figure 16.3, a graphic organizer for "Dearly Disconnected," appears on p. 378. As you read, highlight the key points Frazier makes about pay phones and cell phones and his attitude toward each. Then compare your notes with the graphic organizer.

Before I got married I was living by myself in an A-frame cabin in northwestern 1
Montana. The cabin's interior was a single high-ceilinged room, and at the center
of the room, mounted on the rough-hewn log that held up the ceiling beam, was a
telephone. The woman I would marry was living in Sarasota, Florida, and the distance
between us suggests how well we were getting along at the time. We had not been in
touch for several months; she had no phone. One day she decided to call me from a
pay phone. We talked for a while, and after her coins ran out I jotted the number on
the wood beside my phone and called her back. A day or two later, thinking about the
call, I wanted to talk to her again. The only number I had for her was the pay phone
number I'd written down.

The pay phone was on the street some blocks from the apartment where she stayed. 2
As it happened, though, she had just stepped out to do some errands a few minutes
before I called, and she was passing by on the sidewalk when the phone rang. She
had no reason to think that a public phone ringing on a busy street would be for her.
She stopped, listened to it ring again, and picked up the receiver. Love is pure luck;
somehow I had known she would answer, and she had known it would be me.

Long afterwards, on a trip to Disney World in Orlando with our two kids, then 3
aged six and two, we made a special detour to Sarasota to show them the pay phone.
It didn't impress them much. It's just a nondescript Bell Atlantic pay phone on the
cement wall of a building, by the vestibule. But its ordinariness and even boringness
only make me like it more; ordinary places where extraordinary events have occurred
are my favorite kind. On my mental map of Florida that pay phone is a landmark
looming above the city it occupies, and a notable, if private, historic site.

I'm interested in pay phones in general these days, especially when I get the 4
feeling that they are about to go away. Technology, in the form of sleek little phones
in our pockets, has swept on by them and made them begin to seem antique. My
lifelong entanglement with pay phones dates me; when I was young they were just
there, a given, often as stubborn and uncongenial as the curbstone underfoot. They
were instruments of torture sometimes. You had to feed them fistfuls of change in
those pre-phone-card days, and the operator was a real person who stood maddeningly
between you and whomever you were trying to call. And when the call went wrong, as

communication often does, the pay phone gave you a focus for your rage. Pay phones were always getting smashed up, the receivers shattered to bits against the booth, the coin slots jammed with chewing gum, the cords yanked out and unraveled to the floor.

There was always a touch of seediness and sadness to pay phones, and a sense of transience. Drug dealers made calls from them, and shady types who did not want their whereabouts known, and otherwise respectable people planning assignations, and people too poor to have phones of their own. In the movies, any character who used a pay phone was either in trouble or contemplating a crime. Mostly, pay phones evoked the mundane: "Honey, I'm just leaving. I'll be there soon." But you could tell that a lot of undifferentiated humanity had flowed through these places, and that in the muteness of each pay phone's little space, wild emotion had howled. 5

The phone on the wall of the concession stand at Redwood Pool, where I used to stand dripping and call my mom to come and pick me up; the sweaty phones used almost only by men in the hallway outside the maternity ward at Lenox Hill Hospital in New York; the phone in the old wood-paneled phone booth with leaded glass windows in the drugstore in my Ohio hometown — each one is as specific as a birthmark, a point on earth unlike any other. Recently I went back to New York City after a long absence and tried to find a working pay phone. I picked up one receiver after the next without success. Meanwhile, as I scanned down the long block, I counted half a dozen or more pedestrians talking on their cell phones. 6

It's the cell phone, of course, that's putting the pay phone out of business. The pay phone is to the cell phone as the troubled and difficult older sibling is to the cherished newborn. You sometimes hear people yelling on their cell phones, but almost never yelling at them. Cell phones are toylike, nearly magic, and we get a huge kick out of them, as often happens with technological advances until the new wears off. When I see a cell-phone user gently push the little antenna and fit the phone back into its brushed-vinyl carrying case and tuck the case inside his jacket beside his heart, I feel sorry for the beat-up pay phone standing in the rain. 7

People almost always talk on cell phones while in motion — driving, walking down the street, riding on a commuter train. The cell phone took the transience the pay phone implied and turned it into VIP-style mobility and speed. Even sitting in a restaurant, the person on a cell phone seems importantly busy and on the move. Cell-phone conversations seem to be unlimited by ordinary constraints of place and time, as if they represent an almost-perfect form of communication, whose perfect state would be telepathy. 8

And yet no matter how we factor the world away, it remains. I think this is what drives me so nuts when a person sitting next to me on a bus makes a call from her cell phone. Yes, this busy and important caller is at no fixed point in space, but nevertheless I happen to be beside her. The job of providing physical context falls on me; I become her call's surroundings, as if I'm the phone booth wall. For me to lean over and comment on her cell-phone conversation would be as unseemly and unexpected as if I were in fact a wall; and yet I have no choice, as a sentient person, but to hear what my chatty fellow traveler has to say. 9

I don't think that pay phones will completely disappear. Probably they will survive   10
for a long while as clumsy old technology still of some use to those lagging behind,
and as a backup if ever the superior systems should temporarily fail. Before pay phones
became endangered I never thought of them as public spaces, which of course they are.
They suggested a human average; they belonged to anybody who had a couple of coins.
Now I see that, like public schools and public transportation, pay phones belong to a
former commonality our culture is no longer quite so sure it needs.

I have a weakness for places—for old battlefields, car-crash sites, houses where   11
famous authors lived. Bygone passions should always have an address, it seems to
me. Ideally, the world would be covered with plaques and markers listing the notable
events that occurred at each particular spot. A sign on every pay phone would describe
how a woman broke up with her fiancé here, how a young ballplayer learned that he
had made the team. Unfortunately, the world itself is fluid, and changes out from
under us. Eventually pay phones will become relics of an almost-vanished landscape,
and of a time when there were fewer of us and our stories were on an earlier page.
Romantics like me will have to reimagine our passions as they are—unmoored to
earth, like an infinitude of cell-phone messages flying through the atmosphere.

EXERCISE 16.3   Drawing a Graphic Organizer

Using the graphic organizer in Figure 16.1 as a basis, draw a graphic organizer for "Amusing
Ourselves to Depth" (pp. 370–72).

INTEGRATING COMPARISON AND CONTRAST INTO AN ESSAY

Although you will write some essays using comparison and contrast as the primary pattern of development, in most cases you will integrate comparisons or contrasts into essays that rely on other patterns, such as description, process analysis, or argument. Comparisons or contrasts can be particularly effective in persuasive essays, as "Amusing Ourselves to Depth" shows.

For a reading that uses comparison and contrast as well as other patterns of development, see "Defining a Doctor, with a Tear, a Shrug, and a Schedule" (pp. 394–96).

Use the following tips to incorporate comparison or contrast into essays based on other patterns of development.

1. **Determine the purpose of the comparison or contrast.** What will it contribute to your essay?
2. **Introduce the comparison or contrast clearly.** Use transitional words and expressions to guide readers into the comparison or contrast and then back to the essay's primary pattern of development, and tell readers how the comparison or contrast supports your main point. Do not leave it to your audience to figure out why you have included the comparison.
3. **Keep the comparison or contrast short and to the point.** Avoid distracting readers from your main message.
4. **Organize the points of the comparison or contrast appropriately.** Use point-by-point or subject-by-subject organization, even though the comparison or contrast is part of a larger essay.

FIGURE 16.3 **Graphic Organizer for "Dearly Disconnected"**

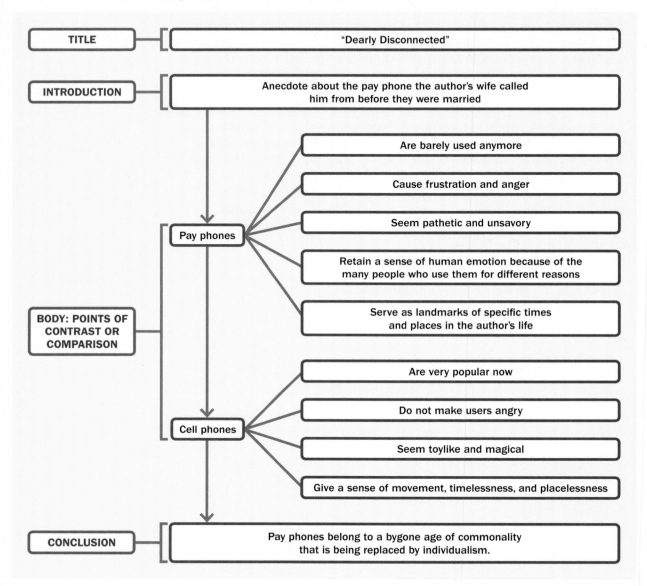

TITLE — "Dearly Disconnected"

INTRODUCTION — Anecdote about the pay phone the author's wife called him from before they were married

BODY: POINTS OF CONTRAST OR COMPARISON —

Pay phones:
- Are barely used anymore
- Cause frustration and anger
- Seem pathetic and unsavory
- Retain a sense of human emotion because of the many people who use them for different reasons
- Serve as landmarks of specific times and places in the author's life

Cell phones:
- Are very popular now
- Do not make users angry
- Seem toylike and magical
- Give a sense of movement, timelessness, and placelessness

CONCLUSION — Pay phones belong to a bygone age of commonality that is being replaced by individualism.

READING ACTIVELY AND THINKING CRITICALLY

For more on reading actively, see Chapter 3; for more on thinking critically, see Chapter 4.

Reading a comparison and contrast essay is somewhat different from reading other types of essays. First, the essay contains two or more subjects instead of just one. Second, the subjects are being compared, contrasted, or both, so you must follow the author's points of comparison between or among them.

WHAT TO LOOK FOR, HIGHLIGHT, AND ANNOTATE

Use these guidelines to read comparison-and-contrast essays actively.

1. **Preview.** As you preview the essay, determine whether it uses a point-by-point or subject-by-subject organization. Knowing the method of organization will help you move through the essay more easily.

For more on previewing, see pp. 45–48.

2. **Understand the main point.** Read the essay once to get an overall sense of how it develops. As you read, identify and highlight the thesis statement if it is stated explicitly. What does it tell you about the essay's purpose and main point? If the thesis statement is implied, write it in your own words.

3. **Identify the basis of comparison and main points of comparison.** Indicate the basis of comparison in the margin or in your journal. Highlight the main points of comparison, and underline the details that support the comparison. Review the essay by drawing a graphic organizer (see Figures 16.1 and 16.2). Doing so will help you learn and recall the key points of the essay.

4. **Think about the meaning.** Reread the essay once again, this time concentrating on its meaning by answering the following questions:
   - What is the writer's purpose in writing this essay? For what audience is it intended? What techniques does the writer use to achieve his or her purpose with this audience?
   - How well do the details support the main points of comparison or contrast? Does the comparison or contrast change your perspective on the subjects of the comparison or contrast? Would more or different supporting details have made the comparison or contrast more convincing?

5. **Consider your reactions.** Consider how the essay relates to your own experience. For example, while reading "Amusing Ourselves to Depth," you might think about your own response to the news—why you prefer *The Daily Show* or *The Colbert Report* to your hometown newspaper.

ANALYZING COMPARISON AND CONTRAST

Comparison and contrast essays can be quite straightforward when the writer's purpose is only to inform. However, when the writer's purpose is also to persuade, you need to ask critical questions.

Does the author treat each subject fairly and equally? If the author seems to favor or give special consideration to one of the subjects (or if one subject seems not to be treated fairly, fully, or adequately), the author might be *biased*—that is, introducing his or her own values or attitudes into the comparison. The lack of balance may not be intentional, and a biased piece of writing is not necessarily unreliable, but you should be aware that the author may not have presented other points of view. In "Dearly Disconnected" (pp. 375–77), for example, Ian Frazier devotes more coverage to pay phones than to cell phones. He appears to be nostalgic about pay phones but somewhat annoyed by cell phones.

For more on bias, see Chapter 4, pp. 82–87.

How does the organization affect meaning? In thinking about the question of fairness, notice whether and how the author uses a point-by-point or subject-by-subject organization. These two forms of organization provide different emphases.

- **Point by point** tends to maintain a steady balance, keeping the reader focused on both subjects simultaneously. But starting with one topic may suggest the writer's preference.
- **Subject by subject** tends to allow in-depth consideration of each subject separately. But a writer may present one subject more favorably than the other by presenting that subject and all its characteristics first, thereby shaping the reader's attitude toward it in a positive way before the reader encounters the second subject. Alternatively, a writer may present all the faults of the less favored subject first, leaving the reader with a final impression of the more favored subject.

As you consider the method of organization, ask yourself how the essay would be different if the writer had used the other method or reversed the order of the two subjects. For example, if Ian Frazier had used a point-by-point rather than subject-by-subject organization in "Dearly Disconnected," he would have found it more difficult to include his personal reflections on the meaning of the pay phone in his life.

Are important points of comparison omitted? As you evaluate a comparison or contrast essay, consider the other comparisons or contrasts that the author could have made. Ask yourself how these omissions shape the reader's impressions of the essay. In "Amusing Ourselves to Depth," for example, Greg Beato could have discussed the type of audience that would be drawn to each type of publication, but he did not.

A GUIDED WRITING ASSIGNMENT*
COMPARISON AND CONTRAST

YOUR ESSAY ASSIGNMENT

Write an essay comparing or contrasting a pair of subjects. Choose subjects to compare or contrast that your readers might find surprising or enlightening. Below are some options to help you get started:

- two forms of entertainment (movies, concerts, radio, music videos),
- two styles of communication, dress, or teaching,
- two public figures,
- the right and wrong ways of doing something, and
- two different cultures' views on the roles that should be played by men and women.

*The writing process is *recursive*; that is, you may find yourself revising as you draft or prewriting as you revise. This is especially true when writing on a computer. Your writing process may also differ from that of your classmates, depending on your preferred learning style.

Prewriting

1 Select an essay topic from the list on page 380, or create one of your own.

Consider your learning style when choosing subjects.

- Some topics are **concrete** (comparing public figures), while others are more **abstract** (comparing communication styles or cultural views). Consider your learning style and choose the option better suited to you.
- If you are a **social learner**, choose subjects with which your classmates are familiar so that you can discuss your subjects with them. Try group brainstorming about various subjects.
- **Social** and **creative learners** might prefer comparing artists' personalities or styles. **Verbal** and **rational learners** might prefer comparing opposing arguments.

Consider your interests and experiences: Choose subjects that you **already know about**, **want to learn more about**, or **have experience with**.

Brainstorm, alone or in groups, a list of subjects you would like to write about. Since comparison and contrast can work with any two comparable subjects, you should be able to find a subject you and your reader will find engaging.

2 Consider your purpose and audience, and choose a basis for comparison.

Ask yourself these questions.

- Will my essay's **purpose** be to **express myself**, **inform**, or **persuade**? What **basis of comparison** will work best, given my purpose? To **inform** readers about two football positions, you could compare the height, weight, skills, and training of players at each position. To **persuade** readers that one quarterback was better than another, you could compare the number of interceptions, completions, and passing yards of each.
- Who is my **audience**? How much do my readers **already know** about the topic? What kind of **supporting details** will they find **convincing** and **engaging**? Readers who are football fans will need different information from those who do not watch the sport.

3 Explore your subjects and develop points of comparison.

Keeping your learning style in mind, **explore how your two subjects are similar**, **how they are different**, or **both**.

- Create a **two-column list** of similarities and differences. Jot down ideas in the appropriate column. (Rational, pragmatic, and verbal learners may prefer listing.)
- Ask a classmate to help you **brainstorm** by mentioning only similarities. For each similarity, generate a difference. (Creative and social learners may prefer brainstorming.)
- **Use visualization**. Draw a sketch of your subjects. (Concrete, spatial, and creative learners may prefer visualization.)
- **Create a scenario** in which your subjects interact. For example, if your topic is the cars of today and the cars of 1950, imagine asking your grandfather to drive a 2014 luxury car. How would he react? What would he say? (Emotional learners may prefer scenarios.)

4 **Draft your thesis statement.**

Your thesis statement **should . . .**
- identify the subjects,
- suggest whether you will focus on similarities, differences, or both, and
- state your main point.

An effective thesis will also **engage your readers**, telling them why your comparison or contrast is important, surprising, or useful.

———————— subjects ————————

Example: The mystery novels of both Robert B. Parker and Sue Grafton are popular because

emphasis on similarities

main point ————————————————————————————

readers are fascinated by the intrigues of witty, independent private detectives.

Team up with a classmate to review each other's thesis statement. Try to identify the subjects for comparison, the focus, and the main point. If these are unclear or ineffective, offer suggestions for improvement.

5 **Choose a method of organization.**

Decide whether you will use **point-by-point (Figure 16.1)** or **subject-by-subject (Figure 16.2)** organization.
- **Point-by-point** often works better for lengthy essays (because it keeps both subjects current in the reader's mind) and for complicated or technical subjects.
- **Subject-by-subject** organization tends to emphasize the larger picture.

If you are not sure which will be most effective, **create an outline or graphic organizer** for both patterns to see which works better.

6 **Write a first draft of your comparison or contrast essay.**

- The **introduction** should **spark your readers' interest**, **introduce your subjects**, provide any necessary **background information**, and include your **thesis**.
- The **body paragraphs** should include **topic sentences** that focus on **a point of comparison**.
  - For **point-by-point** organization, **discuss the subjects in the same order for each point**, and **arrange your points of comparison logically**, from simplest to the most complex, for example.
  - For **subject-by-subject** organization, **cover the same points** for both subjects **in the same order** in both halves of your essay, and use **transitions** such as *similarly, in contrast, on the one hand, on the other hand*, and *not only . . . but also* to alert readers as you **switch from one subject to the other**.
- The **conclusion** should remind readers of your **thesis** and offer a **final comment** on your comparison or contrast. If your essay is lengthy or complex, consider **summarizing** your main points in the conclusion.

7 Evaluate your draft, and revise as necessary.

Use **Figure 16.4 (pp. 384–85), "Flowchart for Revising a Comparison or Contrast Essay,"** to evaluate and revise your draft.

8 Edit and proofread your essay.

Refer to Chapter 10 for help with. . .
- **editing sentences** to avoid wordiness, making your verb choices strong and active, and making your sentences clear, varied, and parallel, and
- **editing words** for tone and diction, connotation, and concrete and specific language.

When proofreading, make sure . . .
- you use the **correct form of adjectives** and **adverbs** when **comparing two items** (comparative) or **three or more items** (superlative).

	Positive	Comparative	Superlative
Adjectives	sharp	sharper	sharpest
Adverbs	early	earlier	earliest

Example: Both *No Country for Old Men* and *True Grit* were suspenseful,

but I liked *True Grit* ~~best~~.
                          ^better

Example: George, Casey, and Bob are all bad at basketball, but Bob's game

is ~~worse~~.
   ^worst

- items linked by **correlative conjunctions** (*either . . . or, neither . . . nor, not only . . . but also*) are in the **same grammatical form:**

Example: The Grand Canyon is not only a spectacular tourist attraction but also

~~scientists consider it~~ a useful geological record.
                                                     ^for scientists.

FIGURE 16.4 **Flowchart for Revising a Comparison or Contrast Essay**

QUESTIONS

REVISION STRATEGIES

1. Highlight your thesis statement. Does it identify the subjects being compared; (indicate whether you will compare, contrast, or both, and state your main point)? Does it indicate your purpose (to express ideas, inform, or persuade)?

 NO

- Revise your thesis using the suggestions on p. 382.
- Brainstorm reasons for making the comparison. Make the most promising reason your purpose.

 YES

2. *Write* the basis of comparison at the top of the page. Is your basis of comparison clear? Does it clearly relate to your thesis?

 NO

- Ask a friend or classmate to help you think of a clear or new basis for comparison.

 YES

3. *List* your points of comparison. Place a ✔ next to the sentences that focus on similarities. Mark an ✘ next to sentences that focus on differences. Have you included all significant points of comparison? Do you fairly examine similarities and differences? Is each similarity or difference significant, and does each support your thesis?

 NO

- Delete any discussion of similarities or differences that are not significant or do not support your thesis.
- Review your prewriting to see if you overlooked any significant points of comparison. If so, revise to add them.
- If you have trouble thinking of points of comparison, conduct research or ask a classmate to suggest ideas.

 YES

4. Underline the topic sentence of each paragraph. Does each paragraph have a clear topic sentence? If you are using point-by-point comparison, is each paragraph focused on a separate point or shared characteristic?

 NO

- Follow the guidelines for writing clear topic sentences (pp. 161–64).
- Consider splitting paragraphs that focus on more than one point or characteristic and combining paragraphs that focus on the same one.

 YES

(Figure 16.4 continued)

QUESTIONS		REVISION STRATEGIES

5. Draw a <u>wavy underline</u> under the concrete details in each paragraph. Do you include enough details to make your comparisons vivid and interesting? Have you provided roughly the same amount of detail for both subjects?

 NO

- Add or delete details as necessary.
- Review your prewriting to see if you overlooked any significant details.
- Research your subjects to come up with additional details. (See Chapters 22 and 23.)

 YES

6. *Draw* a graphic organizer of your essay, or review the one you did earlier. Did you use either point-by-point or subject-by-subject organization consistently throughout the essay? Will your organization be clear to your reader?

 NO

- Study your graphic organizer to find inconsistencies or gaps.
- Reorganize your essay using one method of organization consistently.
- Add transitions if necessary.

 YES

7. Reread your introduction and conclusion. Does the introduction provide a context for your comparison? Is the conclusion satisfying and relevant to the comparison?

 NO

- Revise your introduction and conclusion to meet the guidelines in Chapter 7, pp. 147–50 and 150–51.
- Consider proposing an action or way of thinking that is appropriate in light of the comparison.

READINGS: COMPARISON AND CONTRAST IN ACTION

STUDENTS WRITE

Border Bites

HEATHER GIANAKOS

Heather Gianakos was a first-year student when she wrote the following comparison-and-contrast essay for her composition course. Although she has always enjoyed both styles of cooking that she discusses, she needed to do some research to learn more about their history. As you read the essay, consider the writer's thesis and points of comparison.

Introduction: Indicates Gianakos will examine both similarities and differences but will focus on differences. Her thesis statement gives a basis of comparison of her two subjects, Mexican and southwestern cooking: the traditions and geographic locations of the people who developed them. It also makes a point: that these differences have led to the differences in the food.

Subject A: southwestern

Subject B: Mexican

Point of comparison 1: the physical conditions in which the two styles developed. Notice that Gianakos uses point-by-point comparison, discussing both subjects in each paragraph and often using transitions between them. She also cites sources for her information.

Point of comparison 2: the use of corn and wheat

Chili peppers, tortillas, tacos: All these foods belong to the styles of cooking known as Mexican, Tex-Mex, and southwestern. These internationally popular styles often overlap; sometimes it can be hard to tell which style a particular dish belongs to. Two particular traditions of cooking, however, play an especially important role in the kitchens of Mexico and the American Southwest-- native-derived Mexican cooking ("Mexican"), and Anglo-influenced southwestern cooking, particularly from Texas ("southwestern"). The different traditions and geographic locations of the inhabitants of Mexico and of the Anglo American settlers in the Southwest have resulted in subtle, flavorful differences between the foods featured in Mexican and southwestern cuisine.

Many of the traditions of southwestern cooking grew out of difficult situations--cowboys and ranchers cooking over open fires, for example. Chili, which can contain beans, beef, tomatoes, corn, and many other ingredients, was a good dish to cook over a campfire because everything could be combined in one pot. Dry foods, such as beef jerky, were a convenient way to solve food storage problems and could be easily tucked into saddlebags. In Mexico, by contrast, fresh fruits and vegetables such as avocados and tomatoes were widely available and did not need to be dried or stored. They could be made into spicy salsa and guacamole. Mexicans living in coastal areas could also enjoy fish and lobster dishes (Jamison and Jamison 5).

Corn has been a staple in the American Southwest and Mexico since the time of the Aztecs, who made tortillas (flat, unleavened bread, originally made from stone-ground corn and water) similar to the ones served in Mexico today (Jamison and Jamison 5). Southwesterners, often of European descent, adopted the tortilla but often prepared it with wheat flour, which was easily available to them. Wheat-flour tortillas can now be found in both Mexican and southwestern cooking, but corn is usually the primary grain in dishes with precolonial origins. Tamales (whose name derives from a word in Nahuatl, the Aztec group of languages) are a delicious example: A hunk of cornmeal dough, sometimes combined with ground meat, is wrapped in corn husks and steamed. In southwestern cooking, corn is often used for leavened corn bread, which is made with corn flour rather than cornmeal and can be flavored with jalapeños or back bacon.

1

2

3

Meat of various kinds is often the centerpiece of both Mexican and southwestern tables. However, although chicken, beef, and pork are staples in both traditions, they are often prepared quite differently. Fried chicken rolled in flour and dunked into sizzling oil or fat is a popular dish throughout the American southwest. In traditional Mexican cooking, however, chicken is often cooked more slowly, in stews or baked dishes, with a variety of seasonings, including ancho chiles, garlic, and onions.

Ever since cattle farming began in Texas with the early Spanish missions, beef has been eaten both north and south of the border. In southwestern cooking, steak--flank, rib eye, or sirloin--grilled quickly and served rare is often a chef's crowning glory. In Mexican cooking, beef may be combined with vegetables and spices and rolled into a fajita or served ground in a taco. For a Mexican food purist, in fact, the only true fajita is made from skirt steak, although Mexican food as it is served in the United States often features chicken fajitas.

In Texas and the Southwest United States, barbecued pork ribs are often prepared in barbecue cook-offs, similar to chili-cooking competitions. Such competitions have strict rules for the preparation and presentation of the food and for sanitation ("CTBA Rules"). However, while the BBQ is seen as a southwestern specialty, barbecue ribs as they are served in southwestern-themed restaurants today actually come from a Hispanic and Southwest Mexican tradition dating from the days before refrigeration: Since pork fat, unlike beef fat, has a tendency to become rancid, pork ribs were often marinated in vinegar and spices and then hung to dry. Later the ribs were basted with the same sauce and grilled (Campa 278). The resulting dish has become a favorite both north and south of the border, although in Mexican cooking, where beef is somewhat less important than in southwestern cooking, pork is equally popular in many other forms, such as chorizo sausage.

Cooks in San Antonio or Albuquerque would probably tell you that the food they cook is as much Mexican as it is southwestern. Regional cuisines in such areas of the Southwest as New Mexico, Southern California, and Arizona feature elements of both traditions; chimichangas--deep-fried burritos--actually originated in Arizona (Jamison and Jamison 11). Food lovers who sample regional specialties, however, will note--and savor--the contrast between the spicy, fried or grilled, beef-heavy style of southwestern food and the richly seasoned, corn- and tomato-heavy style of Mexican food.

---

4   **Point of comparison 3:** the use of chicken

Subject A: southwestern

5   **Point of comparison 4:** the use of beef

Subject A: southwestern

Subject B: Mexican

6   **Point of comparison 5:** the use of pork

Subject A: southwestern

Subject B: Mexican

7   **Conclusion:** Gianakos returns to the idea of overlap mentioned in the introduction and makes clear her purpose—to inform readers about the differences between the two cuisines.

Gianakos lists her sources at the end of her paper, following MLA style.

Works Cited

Campa, Arthur L. *Hispanic Culture in the Southwest*. U of Oklahoma P, 1979.

"CTBA Rules." *Central Texas Barbecue Association*, 16 Aug. 2004, www.ctbabbq .com/Home/Rules.

Jamison, Cheryl Alters, and Bill Jamison. *The Border Cookbook*. Harvard Common Press, 1995.

ANALYZING THE WRITER'S TECHNIQUE

1. **Background** Evaluate Gianakos's title and introduction. Do they provide the reader with enough background on her topic?
2. **Organization** Using a point-by-point organization, Gianakos presents her two subjects in the same order — first southwestern cuisine, then Mexican cuisine — for each point of comparison except in paragraph 3. Why do you think she discusses the two cuisines together in this paragraph?
3. **Sources** How does Gianakos's use of sources contribute to her essay?

THINKING CRITICALLY ABOUT COMPARISON AND CONTRAST

1. **Response** Reread the first sentence of the essay. What type of cooking is mentioned here and never discussed again in the essay? How does this decision by Gianakos affect your response to the first paragraph and to the essay as a whole?
2. **Tone** Describe Gianakos's tone. Is it effective in this essay?
3. **Language** What do phrases such as "subtle, flavorful differences" (para. 1), "Food lovers" (7), and "richly seasoned" (7) contribute to the essay? If Gianakos had included more phrases like these, how would the essay be changed?
4. **Omissions** What comparisons did Gianakos not make that she could have made?

RESPONDING TO THE ESSAY

1. **Discussion** In groups of two or three, discuss other regional cuisines that might make effective topics for a comparison and contrast essay. What traits do they share? What distinguishes them?
2. **Journal** Gianakos compares the cuisines of the American Southwest and Mexico using the traditions and geographic locations of the people who lived there as the basis of comparison. In your journal, explore several other possible bases of comparison that could be used to compare these cuisines.
3. **Essay** Write an essay comparing foods of two other regional cuisines.

His Marriage and Hers: Childhood Roots

DANIEL GOLEMAN

Daniel Goleman holds a PhD in behavioral and brain sciences and has published a number of books on psychology, including *The Brain and Emotional Intelligence: New Insights* (2011) and *Leadership: The Power of Emotional Intelligence* (2011). Goleman reported on the brain and behavioral sciences for *The New York Times* for many years and was elected a fellow of the American Association for the Advancement of Science for his efforts to bring psychology to the public. In his book *Emotional Intelligence* (1995), from which the following selection was taken, Goleman describes the emotional skills required for daily living and explains how to develop those skills. As you read the selection, notice how he uses comparison and contrast to explore his subject—differences between the sexes—and highlight his key points of comparison. Because he was writing for a general audience, he cited his sources in end notes that readers who were not interested in his citations could skip. An article in a scholarly journal would have included in-text citations and a list of works cited.

1   As I was entering a restaurant on a recent evening, a young man stalked out the door, his face set in an expression both stony and sullen. Close on his heels a young woman came running, her fists desperately pummeling his back while she yelled, "Goddamn you! Come back here and be nice to me!" That poignant, impossibly self-contradictory plea aimed at a retreating back epitomizes the pattern most commonly seen in couples whose relationship is distressed: She seeks to engage, he withdraws. Marital therapists have long noted that by the time a couple finds their way to the therapy office, they are in this pattern of engage-withdraw, with his complaint about her "unreasonable" demands and outbursts, and her lamenting his indifference to what she is saying.

2   This marital endgame reflects the fact that there are, in effect, two emotional realities in a couple, his and hers. The roots of these emotional differences, while they may be partly biological, also can be traced back to childhood and to the separate emotional worlds boys and girls inhabit while growing up. There is a vast amount of research on these separate worlds, their barriers reinforced not just by the different games boys and girls prefer but by young children's fear of being teased for having a "girlfriend" or "boyfriend."[1] One study of children's friendships found that three-year-olds say about half their friends are of the opposite sex; for five-year-olds it's about 20 percent, and by age seven almost no boys or girls say they have a best friend of the opposite sex.[2] These separate social universes intersect little until teenagers start dating.

3   Meanwhile, boys and girls are taught very different lessons about handling emotions. Parents, in general, discuss emotions—with the exception of anger—more with their daughters than their sons.[3] Girls are exposed to more information about emotions than are boys: when parents make up stories to tell their preschool children, they use more emotion words when talking to daughters than to sons; when mothers play with their infants, they display a wider range of emotions to daughters than to sons; when mothers talk to daughters about feelings, they discuss in more detail the emotional state itself

than they do with their sons — though with the sons they go into more detail about the causes and consequences of emotions like anger (probably as a cautionary tale).

Leslie Brody and Judith Hall, who have summarized the research on differences   4
in emotions between the sexes, propose that because girls develop facility with language more quickly than do boys, this leads them to be more experienced at articulating their feelings and more skilled than boys at using words to explore and substitute for emotional reactions such as physical fights; in contrast, they note, "boys, for whom the verbalization of affects is de-emphasized, may become largely unconscious of their emotional states, both in themselves and others."[4]

At age ten, roughly the same percent of girls as boys are overtly aggressive, given   5
to open confrontation when angered. But by age thirteen, a telling difference between the sexes emerges: Girls become more adept than boys at artful aggressive tactics like ostracism, vicious gossip, and indirect vendettas. Boys, by and large, simply continue being confrontational when angered, oblivious to these more covert strategies.[5] This is just one of many ways that boys — and later, men — are less sophisticated than the opposite sex in the byways of emotional life.

When girls play together, they do so in small, intimate groups, with an emphasis on   6
minimizing hostility and maximizing cooperation, while boys' games are in larger groups, with an emphasis on competition. One key difference can be seen in what happens when games boys or girls are playing get disrupted by someone getting hurt. If a boy who has gotten hurt gets upset, he is expected to get out of the way and stop crying so the game can go on. If the same happens among a group of girls who are playing, the game stops while everyone gathers around to help the girl who is crying. This difference between

© Sally and Richard Greenhill/Alamy

© Hera foto/Alamy

boys and girls at play epitomizes what Harvard's Carol Gilligan points to as a key disparity between the sexes: boys take pride in a lone, tough-minded independence and autonomy, while girls see themselves as part of a web of connectedness. Thus boys are threatened by anything that might challenge their independence, while girls are more threatened by a rupture in their relationships. And, as Deborah Tannen has pointed out in her book *You Just Don't Understand,* these differing perspectives mean that men and women want and expect very different things out of a conversation, with men content to talk about "things," while women seek emotional connection.

In short, these contrasts in schooling in the emotions foster very different skills,   7 with girls becoming "adept at reading both verbal and nonverbal emotional signals, at expressing and communicating their feelings," and boys becoming adept at "minimizing emotions having to do with vulnerability, guilt, fear, and hurt."[6] Evidence for these different stances is very strong in the scientific literature. Hundreds of studies have found, for example, that on average women are more empathic than men, at least as measured by the ability to read someone else's unstated feelings from facial expression, tone of voice, and other nonverbal cues. Likewise, it is generally easier to read feelings from a woman's face than a man's; while there is no difference in facial expressiveness among very young boys and girls, as they go through the elementary-school grades boys become less expressive, girls more so. This may partly reflect another key difference: women, on average, experience the entire range of emotions with greater intensity and more volatility than men — in this sense, women are more "emotional" than men.[7]

All of this means that, in general, women come into a marriage groomed for the role   8 of emotional manager, while men arrive with much less appreciation of the importance of this task for helping a relationship survive. Indeed, the most important element for women — but not for men — in satisfaction with their relationship reported in a study of 264 couples was the sense that the couple has "good communication."[8] Ted Huston, a psychologist at the University of Texas who has studied couples in depth, observes, "For the wives, intimacy means talking things over, especially talking about the relationship itself. The men, by and large, don't understand what the wives want from them. They say, 'I want to do things with her, and all she wants to do is talk.' " During courtship, Huston found, men were much more willing to spend time talking in ways that suited the wish for intimacy of their wives-to-be. But once married, as time went on the men — especially in more traditional couples — spent less and less time talking in this way with their wives, finding a sense of closeness simply in doing things like gardening together rather than talking things over.

This growing silence on the part of husbands may be partly due to the fact that, if anything, men are a bit Pollyannaish about the state of their marriage, while their wives are attuned to the trouble spots: in one study of marriages, men had a rosier view than their wives of just about everything in their relationship — lovemaking, finances, ties with in-laws, how well they listened to each other, how much their flaws mattered.[9] Wives, in general, are more vocal about their complaints than are their husbands, particularly among unhappy couples. Combine men's rosy view of marriage with their aversion to emotional confrontations, and it is clear why wives so often complain that their husbands try to wiggle out of discussing the troubling things about their relationship. (Of course this gender difference is a generalization and is not true in every case; a psychiatrist friend complained that in his marriage his wife is reluctant to discuss emotional matters between them and he is the one who is left to bring them up.) 9

The slowness of men to bring up problems in a relationship is no doubt compounded by their relative lack of skill when it comes to reading facial expressions of emotions. Women, for example, are more sensitive to a sad expression on a man's face than are men in detecting sadness from a woman's expression.[10] Thus a woman has to be all the sadder for a man to notice her feelings in the first place, let alone for him to raise the question of what is making her so sad. 10

Consider the implications of this emotional gender gap for how couples handle the grievances and disagreements that any intimate relationship inevitably spawns. In fact, specific issues such as how often a couple has sex, how to discipline the children, or how much debt and savings a couple feels comfortable with are not what make or break a marriage. Rather, it is how a couple discusses such sore points that matters more for the fate of their marriage. Simply having reached an agreement about how to disagree is key to marital survival; men and women have to overcome the innate gender differences in approaching rocky emotions. Failing this, couples are vulnerable to emotional rifts that eventually can tear their relationship apart. . . . [T]hese rifts are far more likely to develop if one or both partners have certain deficits in emotional intelligence. 11

Notes

1. For a useful overview of the research into the separate worlds of boys and girls, see Maccoby, Eleanor, and C. N. Jacklin. "Gender Segregation in Childhood." *Advances in Child Development and Behavior,* edited by H. Reese, Academic Press, 1987.

2. This data comes from Gottman, John. "Same and Cross Sex Friendship in Young Children." *Conversation of Friends,* edited by John M. Gottman and Jeffrey G. Parker, Cambridge UP, 1986.

3. This and the following summary of sex differences in socialization of emotions are based on the excellent review in Brody, Leslie R., and Judith A. Hall. "Gender and Emotion." *Handbook of Emotions,* edited by Michael Lewis and Jeannette Haviland, Guilford Press, 1993.

4. Brody and Hall, "Gender and Emotion," 456.

5. Girls and the arts of aggression: Cairns, Robert B., and Beverley D. Cairns. *Lifelines and Risks.* Cambridge UP, 1994.

6. Brody and Hall, "Gender and Emotion," 454.

7. The findings about gender differences in emotion are reviewed in Brody and Hall, "Gender and Emotion."

8. The importance of good communication for women was reported in Davis, Mark H., and H. Alan Oathout. "Maintenance of Satisfaction in Romantic Relationships: Empathy and Relational Competence." *Journal of Personality and Social Psychology,* vol. 53, no. 2, 1987, pp. 397-410.

9. The study of husbands' and wives' complaints: Sternberg, Robert H. "Triangulating Love." *The Psychology of Love,* edited by Robert Sternberg and Michael Barnes, Yale UP, 1988.

10. Reading sad faces: The research is by Dr. Ruben C. Gur at the University of Pennsylvania School of Medicine.

EXAMINING THE READING

1. **Summarizing** In one or two sentences, explain the differences that Goleman claims exist between men's and women's ways of expressing emotion.
2. **Causes** According to Goleman, what are the root causes of the differences between how men and women express emotion?
3. **Details** How can the emotional differences between spouses cause marital difficulties, according to the writer?
4. **Differences** Explain how boys and girls play differently, according to Goleman.
5. **Vocabulary** Explain the meaning of each of the following words as it is used in the reading: *epitomizes* (para. 1), *articulating* (4), *ostracism* (5), *vendettas* (5), *disparity* (6), and *empathic* (7).

ANALYZING THE WRITER'S TECHNIQUE

1. **Thesis** What is Goleman's thesis?
2. **Audience and Purpose** Identify the purpose of and intended audience for the essay.
3. **Points of Comparison** List the points of comparison, and for each, evaluate the evidence Goleman offers to substantiate his findings. Do you find the evidence sufficient and convincing? Why or why not? What other information might the writer have included?
4. **Objectivity** Do you think Goleman maintains an objective stance on the issue, despite his gender? Explain your answer.

THINKING CRITICALLY ABOUT TEXT AND VISUALS

1. **Organization** Discuss the type of organization the author used (point by point, subject by subject, or mixed). Does the organization seem to affect the author's fairness? Do you detect any bias? If so, explain.

2. **Language** How does the use of quotation marks around the word *unreasonable* (para. 1) affect its connotation?

3. **Tone** How does the real-life example in paragraph 1 affect the essay, especially its tone?

4. **Fact/Opinion** Do you consider the essay to be primarily fact, opinion, or informed opinion? Justify your answer.

5. **Visual** What key ideas from the essay do the photographs on pp. 390–91 illustrate?

RESPONDING TO THE READING

1. **Discussion** In groups of two or three, discuss Goleman's generalizations about men and women. Do any seem inaccurate and, if so, which one(s)? Discuss the evidence, if any, that would prove Goleman wrong.

2. **Journal** In your journal, describe a situation from your experience that either confirms or contradicts one of Goleman's generalizations.

3. **Essay** Make a list of the emotional differences and resulting behavioral conflicts between men and women that you have observed. Decide which differences Goleman explains. Write an essay reporting your findings.

WORKING TOGETHER

In small groups of three or four students, brainstorm a list of emotional differences between the sexes. Using that list as a springboard, work independently to compose a one-paragraph letter to an advice columnist describing a conflict that has arisen between a man and a woman. Trade letters with a member of your group. Then, taking on the role of the columnist, respond to your group member's letter, explaining the root of the problem — emotional differences — and offering a solution. Be creative with the name of the letter writer and the advice columnist. If your class has a blog or a discussion board, you may post these letters so that all members of the class can read them.

READING: COMPARISON AND CONTRAST COMBINED WITH OTHER PATTERNS

Defining a Doctor, with a Tear, a Shrug, and a Schedule

ABIGAIL ZUGER

Abigail Zuger is associate professor of clinical medicine at Columbia University College of Physicians and Surgeons and senior attending physician at St. Luke's–Roosevelt Hospital Center, both in New York City. She has been caring for HIV-infected patients in the New York area since 1981, and her experiences working in the early years of the AIDS epidemic led her to write *Strong Shadows: Scenes from an Inner City AIDS Clinic* (1995). Zuger is an associate editor of *Journal Watch*, an online medical digest, and blogs on wellness issues for *The New York Times*. This essay was published in *The New York Times* in 2004.

I had two interns to supervise that month, and the minute they sat down for our first meeting, I sensed how the month would unfold. 1

The man's white coat was immaculate, its pockets empty save for a sleek Palm Pilot that contained his list of patients. The woman used a large loose-leaf notebook instead, every dog-eared page full of lists of things to do and check, consultants to call, questions to ask. Her pockets were stuffed, and whenever she sat down, little handbooks of drug doses, wadded phone messages, pens, highlighters, and tourniquets spilled onto the floor. 2

The man worked the hours legally mandated by the state, not a minute more, and sometimes considerably less. He was seldom in the hospital before 8 in the morning and left by 5 unless he was on call. He ate a leisurely lunch every day and was never late for rounds. The woman got to the hospital around dawn and was on the move for the rest of the day. Sometimes she went home when she was supposed to, but sometimes, if one of her patients was particularly sick, she would sign out to the covering intern and keep working, often talking to patients' relatives long into the night. "I am now breaking the law," she would announce cheerfully to no one in particular, then trot off to do just a few final chores. 3

The man had a strict definition of what it meant to be a doctor. He did not, for instance, "do nurses' work" (his phrase). When one of his patients needed a specimen sent to the lab and the nurse didn't get around to it, neither did he. No matter how important the job was, no matter how hard I pressed him, he never gave in. If I spoke sternly to him, he would turn around and speak just as sternly to the nurse. The woman did everyone's work. She would weigh her patients if necessary (nurses' work), feed them (aides' work), find salt-free pickles for them (dietitians' work), and wheel them to X-ray (transporters' work). 4

The man was cheerful, serene, and well rested. The woman was overtired, hyperemotional, and constantly late. The man was interested in his patients, but they never kept him up at night. The woman occasionally called the hospital from home to check on hers. The man played tennis on his days off. The woman read medical articles. At least, she read the beginnings; she tended to fall asleep halfway through. 5

I felt as if I was in a medieval morality play[1] that month, living with two costumed symbols of opposing philosophies in medical education. The woman was working the way interns used to: total immersion seasoned with exhaustion and adrenaline. As far as she was concerned, her patients were her exclusive responsibility. The man was an intern of the new millennium. His hours and duties were delimited; he saw himself as part of a health-care team, and his patients' welfare as a shared responsibility. 6

This new model of medical internship got some important validation in the *New England Journal of Medicine* last week, when Harvard researchers reported the effects 7

---

[1]*morality play:* a type of play performed in the Middle Ages in which characters represent abstractions (love, death, peace, and so on); its purpose is to teach a lesson about right and wrong.

of reducing interns' work hours to 60 per week from 80 (now the mandated national maximum). The shorter workweek required a larger staff of interns to spell one another at more frequent intervals. With shorter hours, the interns got more sleep at home, dozed off less at work, and made considerably fewer bad mistakes in patient care.

Why should such an obvious finding need an elaborate controlled study to estab-   8
lish? Why should it generate not only two long articles in the world's most prestigious medical journal but also three long, passionate editorials? Because the issue here is bigger than just scheduling and manpower.

The progressive shortening of residents' work hours spells nothing less than   9
a change in the ethos of medicine itself. It means the end of Dr. Kildare, Super-star — that lone, heroic healer, omniscient, omnipotent, and ever-present. It means a revolution in the complex medical hierarchy that sustained him. Willy-nilly, medicine is becoming democratized, a team sport.

We can only hope the revolution will be bloodless. Everything will have to change.   10
Doctors will have to learn to work well with others. They will have to learn to write and speak with enough clarity and precision so that the patient's story remains accurate as care passes from hand to hand. They will have to stop saying "my patient" and begin to say "our patient" instead.

It may be, when the dust settles, that the system will be more functional, less   11
error-prone. It may be that we will simply have substituted one set of problems for another. We may even find that nothing much has changed. Even in the Harvard data, there was an impressive range in the hours that the interns under study worked. Some logged in over 90 hours in their 80-hour workweek. Some put in 75 instead. Medicine has always attracted a wide spectrum of individuals, from the lazy and disaffected to the deeply committed. Even draconian scheduling policies may not change basic personality traits or the kind of doctors that interns grow up to be.

My month with the intern of the past and the intern of the future certainly argues   12
for the power of the individual work ethic. Try as I might, it was not within my power to modify the way either of them functioned. The woman cared too much. The man cared too little. She worked too hard, and he could not be prodded into working hard enough. They both made careless mistakes. When patients died, the man shrugged and the woman cried. If for no other reason than that one, let us hope that the medicine of the future still has room for people like her.

EXAMINING THE READING

1. **Differences** How do the two interns differ in their approach to medicine? What different philosophies of medicine do the two interns represent?
2. **Details** Describe the working conditions of interns.
3. **Meaning** What do we learn about the author and her philosophy of medical practice?
4. **Vocabulary** Explain the meaning of each of the following words as it is used in the reading: *delimited* (para. 6), *ethos* (9), *omniscient* (9), *omnipotent* (9), and *draconian* (11).

ANALYZING THE WRITER'S TECHNIQUE

1. **Thesis** Highlight Zuger's thesis, and evaluate its placement.
2. **Points of Comparison** Identify the points of comparison on which the essay is based.
3. **Patterns** What other patterns of development does the author use? Give one example, and explain how it contributes to the essay.
4. **Organization** Evaluate the effectiveness of the point-by-point organization. How would the essay differ if it had been written using a subject-by-subject organization?
5. **Conclusion** Evaluate the essay's conclusion. How does it reflect the thesis and organization of the essay?

VISUALIZING THE READING

Analyze Zuger's use of point-by-point organization by listing in the box below the points of comparison she uses. The first one has been done for you. Add additional rows to the box as needed.

Points of Comparison	The Man	The Woman
Organizational styles	Efficient (Palm Pilot)	Disorganized (overstuffed pockets and notebook)

THINKING CRITICALLY ABOUT TEXT

1. **Bias** In her final sentence, Zuger reveals a bias toward one of the models of medical internship she is comparing. Is this bias apparent anywhere else? Explain.
2. **Language** What is the connotation of "nurses' work" (para. 4)?
3. **Sources** What other types of sources and information could the author have included to make this essay more comprehensive?

RESPONDING TO THE READING

1. **Discussion** In small groups, discuss the training and education you will need for the career you are interested in pursuing. What knowledge and skills will you need to succeed in the field, and how will the training provide them?
2. **Journal** Write a journal entry exploring whether medical care has become depersonalized. Give examples from your experience.
3. **Essay** Write an essay comparing or contrasting men and women in another profession (teaching, policing, nursing).

WORKING TOGETHER

In small groups of two or three, brainstorm a list of characteristics to describe the male intern and the female intern. Use this list to help your group create a vanity plate (customized license plate) for either the male or the female intern. Design your vanity plate with a word or words *and* a graphic that describe your intern. Be prepared to share your creation and explain its meaning to the class.

APPLYING YOUR SKILLS: ADDITIONAL ESSAY ASSIGNMENTS

For more on locating and documenting sources, see Part 5.

Using what you have learned in this chapter, write a comparison or contrast essay on one of the topics below. Depending on the topic you choose, you may need to conduct research.

TO EXPRESS YOUR IDEAS

1. Compare two families that you know or are part of. Include points of comparison that reveal what is valuable and important in family life.
2. Compare your values and priorities today with those you held when you were in high school.
3. Compare your lifestyle today with the lifestyle you intend to follow after you graduate from college.

TO INFORM YOUR READER

4. Compare resources available through your college library with those available on the open Web.
5. Compare two sources of information or communication as Beato does in "Amusing Ourselves to Depth" (pp. 370–72).

TO PERSUADE YOUR READER

6. Choose a technological change that has occurred in recent years, as Frazier does in "Dearly Disconnected" (pp. 375–77), and argue either that it is beneficial or that its drawbacks outweigh its usefulness compared with the old technology.

EXERCISE 17.2 | **Classifying and Dividing by Category**

Choose a principle of classification or division for two of the topics listed in Exercise 17.1. Then make a list of categories in which each item could be included or parts into which each item could be divided.

CLASSIFICATION OR DIVISION FULLY EXPLAINS EACH CATEGORY OR PART

A classification or division essay should contain enough detail for readers to understand each category or part easily. Use facts, descriptions, quotations, comparisons, or examples to help readers to "see" your categories or parts.

CLASSIFICATION OR DIVISION INCLUDES A THESIS

The thesis statement of a classification or division essay should identify the topic. It may also reveal the principle used to classify or divide the topic. In most cases it also should suggest why the classification or division is relevant or important.

Here are two examples of effective thesis statements.

Most people consider videos a form of entertainment; however, videos can also serve educational, commercial, and political functions.

Importance (implied)

Topic

Categories

The Grand Canyon is divided into two distinct geographical areas — the North Rim and the South Rim — each offering different views, activities, and climatic conditions.

Priniciple

The following readings demonstrate the techniques for writing effective classification or division essays discussed above. The first reading is annotated to point out how Jerry Newman classifies fast-food managers. As you read the second essay, try to identify for yourself how Michael Moss uses the techniques of division to show what makes potato chips nearly irresistible.

READING: CLASSIFICATION

My Secret Life on the McJob: Fast Food Managers

JERRY NEWMAN

Jerry Newman is a professor of management at the State University of New York–Buffalo and coauthor of the textbook *Compensation,* tenth edition (2010). He has also worked as a business consultant at AT&T, Hewlett-Packard, RJR Nabisco, and McDonald's. This selection is from *My Secret Life on the McJob: Lessons in Leadership Guaranteed to Supersize Any Management Style* (2007), which Newman wrote after working at various fast-food restaurants to learn about their operation and management.

Relevance: Relevance hinted at by writer's surprise at how varied stores were despite "edicts from headquarters"; for audience reading about management styles, this topic would be important

I thought all my fast food stores would be pretty similar. They weren't. Some stores made employees wear name tags, going as far as sending people home if they repeatedly didn't wear their name tags, while other stores didn't seem to care. In some stores crews socialized after work, but in others they barely talked to each other, even during work. Even though every chain had strict rules about every facet of food production and customer interaction, how employees were treated was part of an individual store culture, and this varied from store to store. These differences could often be traced to the managers' values and practices and how consistently they were applied both by the managers and by their *sensei*,[1] much more so than any edicts from headquarters. The best-run store I worked at was [a] Burger King; the worst-run store was also a Burger King. If corporate rules had a controlling impact, shouldn't stores have been much more similar? At one McDonald's the employees were extremely friendly; at another the tension between groups was palpable. The differences, I think, can be traced to the managers. The following is a sampler of the types of managers I encountered. Only the last group, performance managers, was good at finding a *sensei* and developing consistent people practices.

Thesis: Identifies topic and principle of classification

THE TOXIC MANAGER

Organization: Categories indicated by section headings

Most new employees learn through feedback. When you're first learning a job, there's relatively little ego involvement in feedback; good managers seem to know this and in early days of employment are quick to point out better ways of doing a task. [Toxic] managers, though, use sarcasm or disrespectful comments to indicate when they are unhappy with your work. One of the worst offenders I ran into was the store manager at Arby's, who admitted that the main reason he was hiring me was to change the store culture. He said he was tired of employees who were vulgar and disrespectful, but it didn't take long for me to realize that the role model for their behavior was actually the manager himself — Don. His attitude and style set the tone for everyone else in his store. Almost as bad, the key individual with the necessary attributes to be a *sensei* shared Don's disregard for the feelings of others. Don, in particular, didn't confine his wrath to "bad" employees. Bill, a diligent long-timer, messed up a coupon order. A customer had an entertainment book coupon for one Value Meal free with the purchase of another. There was a labyrinth of steps to complete some of the discounts correctly. When Bill made the error, it was right before the end of Don's shift, and Don tore into him, saying loudly enough for everyone to hear, "Well, I'm leaving before Bill can make my life any more miserable." It didn't take long to infect others with this lack of respect for employees.

Full Explanation: Uses contrast, examples, and an anecdote to explain first category fully

1

2

---

[1]*Sensei*: A Japanese word for *teacher* or *master*. Newman uses it to mean an employee who is not a manager but is both highly skilled at his or her job and socially influential among fellow employees.

THE MECHANICAL MANAGER

The most common type of manager I encountered was the Mechanical Manager, who was for the most part either an assistant manager or a shift manager, not a full store manager. You could spot the Mechanical Managers from across the room — they did their jobs, day after day, as if fast food was slow death. They didn't want to be there, and they were just going through the motions. They typically had gotten their jobs because they were reliable crew members and had put in enough time that some reward was needed to keep them working. A promotion has a certain finality, though — it makes you confront reality: Is this what I want out of life? Most say "No," and that's probably why I didn't see very many store managers who were mechanical. Before most store managers had reached that level (one store manager told me it was a ten-year journey), those who weren't interested in fast food as a lifetime career had moved on to other career pursuits. While looking for other opportunities, though, they did what was necessary to get by. Luis at McDonald's was the perfect example.

In my first McDonald's experience I made myself a grid showing all of the sandwiches and their ingredients. After a day of having instructions blasted at me, I needed a visual training aid to finally put things together. I shared this grid with Luis on my third day, expecting he might already have training materials like this (as was the case at Wendy's) or that he could use it to train other visual learners. As I handed Luis the Excel spreadsheet, I watched his face and saw no reaction. None. He told me he'd leave it for Kris, the store manager. Clearly he saw the value in it — he didn't toss it, after all — but a reinforcing response for my initiative required a level of involvement he didn't or couldn't muster.

THE RELATIONSHIP MANAGER

The Relationship Manager was a relatively rare breed in my experience. James was the prototype. He led by building relationships and demonstrating that he cared about our destinies — hard to do when it seemed like every week someone was leaving and another person was coming on board. From the first day, James was very different from what I was used to. When I first met him for my job interview, he was fifteen minutes late because he was out picking up an employee whose car had broken down. I never saw any other manager pick up or take home a crew member who had transportation problems. In fact, at one store I watched Mary, an older worker teetering on the edge of poverty, sit in a booth out front for two hours waiting for her husband to pick her up after his shift at a Sam's Club. As I came to learn, this kindness wasn't unusual for James. And in being kind, James created a culture that was much more friendly and supportive than that in many of the other fast food places I had experienced. Even the way James responded to my quitting was refreshing. With my back problems becoming increasingly worse, I called James to tell him that I was quitting and dreaded leaving him in the lurch. But he was amazingly kind, telling me to take care of myself and forcefully telling me to pick up my check.

3　**Full Explanation:** Uses definition, cause-effect, extended example (Luis), anecdote to explain second category fully

4

5　**Full Explanation:** Uses extended example (James), anecdote, contrast to explain third category fully

THE PERFORMANCE MANAGER

Purpose and Audience:
Section returns to thesis—
purpose is to explain traits
of best ("performance")
manager; audience is other
business managers or readers
interested in management

Organization: Moves from
worst (toxic managers) to best
(performance managers)

Full Explanation: Uses definition, examples, extended
example (Kris) to explain
fourth category fully

It's easy to spot the Performance Manager. Here relationships are still impor-   6
tant, but now they serve as a means to ensure performance. Through word or deed
she very quickly lets you know what is expected. I like this. No ambiguity, no doubt
about what it takes to make the grade. The best at this was Kris, who, it seemed
to me, watched for slackers much more closely than did the managers at other fast
food places. She told me during the interview that I would be watching DVDs my
first day. She also mentioned that one of the new people had taken three to four
bathroom breaks while watching the videos, which was an excessive number, she
thought. She also commented that she might be losing some people because she
thought they were slower than they should be. I got the message: She would be
watching my work and looking to see if I was going to goof off. My experience in
other places was that you got fired for only two things: not showing up and insub-
ordinate behavior. Clearly she was adding a third reason — poor performance. Good
for her!

Kris's watchful eye extended beyond bathroom breaks. I found out the hard way   7
that taking breaks, even unpaid ones, wasn't allowed unless legally required. Apparently in New York State, you're not entitled to a break until after five hours of work.
So when I asked Kris for a break before the appointed time, she answered with
an emphatic "No." Kris's message was clearly that we do our jobs by the book, no
exceptions.

Over time at this Burger King I began to notice that Kris wasn't a taskmaster all   8
the time. Sure, during busy times she was prone to exhort the staff to work faster. And
she didn't tolerate leaning (remember, "If you've got time to lean, you've got time to
clean"). But this attitude relaxed a bit during slower times, and it especially relaxed
for the better workers like Daniel, Eric, and Craig, three of the fastest guns on the
sandwich assembly board.

VISUALIZING A CLASSIFICATION OR DIVISION ESSAY: A GRAPHIC ORGANIZER

For more on creating a graphic
organizer, see pp. 52–53.

The graphic organizer shown in Figure 17.1 outlines the basic organization of a classification or division essay.

- The **introduction** announces the topic, gives background information, and
  states the thesis.
- The **body paragraphs** explain the categories or parts and their characteristics.
- The **conclusion** brings the essay to a satisfying close by reinforcing the thesis
  and offering a new insight on the topic.

FIGURE 17.1 **Graphic Organizer for a Classification or Division Essay**

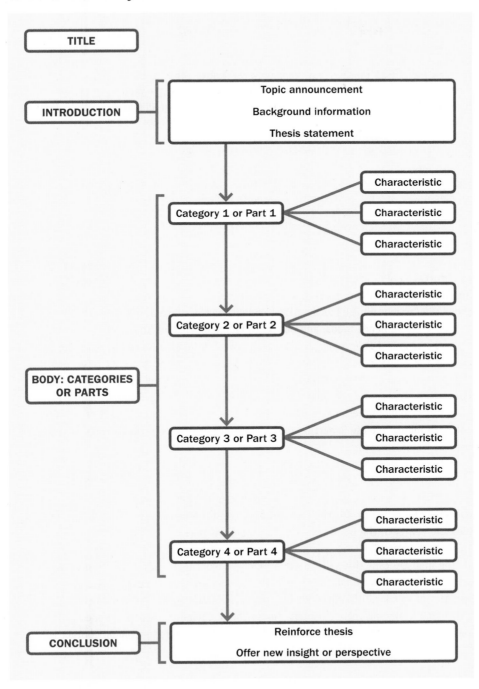

The Language of Junk Food Addiction: How to "Read" a Potato Chip

MICHAEL MOSS

Michael Moss is a Pulitzer Prize–winning investigative reporter for *The New York Times*, where he has worked since 2000. Before coming to *The Times,* he reported for publications including *The Daily Sentinel* (in Grand Junction, Colorado), *The Atlanta Journal-Constitution, New York Newsday,* and *The Wall Street Journal*. He has also published two books, *Palace Coup: The Inside Story of Harry and Leona Helmsley* (1989) and *Salt Sugar Fat: How the Food Giants Hooked Us* (2013). The interview from which this selection was taken was based on Moss's work for *Salt Sugar Fat*. Figure 17.2, a graphic organizer for "The Language of Junk Food Addiction," appears on page 410. Before studying that graphic organizer, read this division essay and try to determine what parts the author divides the topic into and what his principle of division is.

Betcha can't eat just one. 1

These five words captured the essence of the potato chip far better than anyone 2
at Frito-Lay could have imagined. In the '60s, the sentiment might have seemed cute and innocent — it's hard not to pig out on potato chips, they're tasty, they're fun. But today the familiar phrase has a sinister connotation because of our growing vulnerability to convenience foods, and our growing dependence on them.

As I researched *Salt, Sugar, Fat,* I was surprised to learn about the meticulously 3
crafted allure of potato chips (which I happen to love). When you start to deconstruct the layers of the chip's appeal, you start to see why this simple little snack has the power to make a profound claim on our attention and appetite. "Betcha can't eat just one" starts sounding less like a lighthearted dare — and more like a kind of promise. The food industry really is betting on its ability to override the natural checks that keep us from overeating.

Here's how it works. 4

It starts with salt, which sits right on the outside of the chip. Salt is the first 5
thing that hits your saliva, and it's the first factor that drives you to eat and perhaps overeat. Your saliva carries the salty taste through the neurological channel to the pleasure center of the brain, where it sends signals back: "Hey, this is really great stuff. Keep eating."

The industry calls this salty allure a food's "flavor burst," and I was surprised to 6
learn just how many variations on this effect there are. The industry creates different varieties of salt for different kinds of processed foods: everything from fine powders that blend easily into canned soups, to big chunky pyramid-shaped granules with flat sides that stick better to food (hollowed out on the inside for maximum contact with the saliva).

Then, of course, there's fat. Potato chips are soaked in fat. And fat is fasci-   7
nating because it's not one of the five basic tastes that Aristotle identified way back
when — it's a *feeling*. Fat is the warm, gooey sensation you get when you bite into
a toasty cheese sandwich — or you get just *thinking* about such a sandwich (if you
love cheese as much as I do). There's a nerve ending that comes down from the brain
almost to the roof of the mouth that picks up the feel of fat, and the industry thus
calls the allure of fat "mouthfeel."

The presence of fat, too, gets picked up by nerve endings and races along the   8
neurological channel to the pleasure center of the brain. Which lights up, as strongly
as it lights up for sugar. There are different kinds of fats — some good — but it's the
saturated fats, which are common in processed foods, that are of most concern to
doctors. They're linked to heart disease if over-consumed. And since fats have twice as
many calories as sugar, they can be problematic from an obesity standpoint.

But potato chips actually have the entire holy trinity: They're also loaded with   9
sugar. Not added sugar — although some varieties do — but the sugar in most chips is
in the potato starch itself, which gets converted to sugar in the moment the chip hits
the tongue. Unlike fat, which studies show can exist in unlimited quantities in food
without repulsing us, we do back off when a food is too sweet. The challenge is to
achieve just the right depth of sweetness without crossing over into the extreme. The
industry term for this optimal amount of sugar is called the "bliss point."

So you've got all three of the big elements in this one product. But salt, sugar, and   10
fat are just the beginning of the potato chip's allure. British researchers, for instance,
have found that the more noise a chip makes when you eat it, the better you'll like it
and the more apt you are to eat more. So chip companies spend a lot of effort creating
a perfectly noisy, crunchy chip.

The chip has an amazing textural allure, too, a kind of meltiness on the tongue. The   11
ultraprocessed food product most admired by food company scientists in this regard
is the Cheeto, which rapidly dissolves in your mouth. When that happens, it creates a
phenomenon that food scientists call "vanishing caloric density." Which refers to the
phenomenon that as the Cheeto melts, your brain interprets that melting to mean that
the calories in the Cheeto have disappeared as well. So they tend to uncouple your
brain from the breaks that keep your body from overeating. And the message coming
back from the brain is: "Hey, you might as well be eating celery for all I care about all
the calories in those disappearing Cheetos. Go for it."

Then there's the whole act of handling the chip — the fact that we move it with   12
our hand directly to the mouth. When you move a food directly to your mouth with
your hand there are fewer barriers to overeating. You don't need to wait until you have
a fork, or a spoon, or a plate to eat. You can eat with one hand while doing something else. These handheld products lead to what nutrition scientists call "mindless
eating" — where we're not really paying attention to what we're putting in our mouths.
This has been shown to be hugely conducive to over-eating. One recent example is

the Go-Gurt yogurt that comes in a collapsible tube. Once you open it, you can just squeeze out the yogurt with one hand while you're playing a computer game with the other.

The bottom line, which everyone in the food industry will tell you, is taste. They're   13 convinced that a good number of us will talk a good game on nutrition and health, but when we walk through the grocery store, we'll look for and buy the products that taste the best. And that's the cynical view: They will do nothing to improve the health profile of their products that will jeopardize taste. They're as hooked on profits as they are on salt, sugar, fat.

FIGURE 17.2 Graphic Organizer for "The Language of Junk Food Addiction"

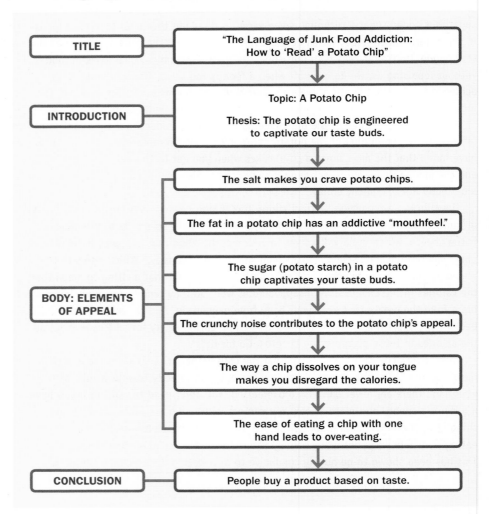

EXERCISE 17.3   **Drawing a Graphic Organizer**

Using Figure 17.1 as a basis, draw a graphic organizer for "My Secret Life on the McJob: Fast Food Managers" (pp. 403–06). Note that because "My Secret Life on the McJob" is an excerpt from a book, it does not include a conclusion.

INTEGRATING CLASSIFICATION OR DIVISION INTO AN ESSAY

Classification and division are often used along with one or more other patterns of development.

- An essay that argues for stricter gun control may categorize guns in terms of their firepower, purpose, or availability.
- A narrative about a writer's frustrating experiences in a crowded international airport terminal may describe the different parts or areas of the airport.

When incorporating classification or division into an essay based on another pattern of development, keep the following tips in mind.

1. **Avoid focusing on why the classification or division is meaningful.** When used as a secondary pattern, the significance of the classification or division should be clear from the context in which it is presented.
2. **State the principle of classification briefly and clearly.**
3. **Name the categories or parts.** In the sentence that introduces the classification or division, name the categories or parts to focus your readers' attention on the explanation that follows.

For a reading that uses classification as well as other patterns of development, see "The Dog Ate My Flash Drive, and Other Tales of Woe" (pp. 423–26).

READING ACTIVELY AND THINKING CRITICALLY

Reading and thinking critically about a classification or division essay requires you to read the selection carefully, considering how the categories or parts support the main point and connecting the ideas to your own experience. But you must also examine and challenge the author's attitude as it is shown in the selection.

For more on reading actively, see Chapter 3; for more on thinking critically, see Chapter 4.

WHAT TO LOOK FOR, HIGHLIGHT, AND ANNOTATE

Classification and division essays are usually tightly organized and relatively easy to follow. Use the following suggestions to read actively classification or division essays or any writing that uses classification or division.

For more on previewing, see pp. 45–48.

1. **Preview.** Preview the essay to get an overview of its content and organization.
2. **Understand the principle of classification or division and the category or parts used.** Read the essay through, highlighting the thesis and the name or title of each category or part. In the margin or in your journal, note the principle of classification.

3. **Identify how the writer explains each part or category.** Highlight or underline the key details of each category. Circle or asterisk any important definitions or vivid examples. In the margins or in your journal, note how the supporting evidence helps explain the categories or parts and consider how they support the essay's thesis.

4. **Think about the meaning.** Reread the essay once again, this time concentrating on its meaning by answering the following questions.
   • What is the writer's purpose in writing this essay? For what audience it is intended? How did the writer's purpose and audience influence the principle of classification or division he or she chose?
   • How well does the writer explain the categories or parts? Identify any sections where you find a category or part confusing or where you think more supporting detail is needed.

5. **Consider your reactions.** Consider how the essay relates to your own experience. For example, do the types of bosses Newman identifies in "My Secret Life on the McJob" resonate with your own experience in the workplace? To gain a different perspective on the reading, think of other ways of classifying or dividing the topic. For example, consider an essay that classifies types of exercise programs at health clubs according to the benefits they offer. Such exercise programs could also be classified according to their cost, degree of strenuousness, type of exercise, and so forth.

ANALYZING CLASSIFICATION AND DIVISION

When reading classification or division, particularly if its purpose is to persuade, focus on the essay's comprehensiveness and level of detail by asking the following questions.

Does the classification or division cover all significant categories or parts? To be fair, honest, and complete, an essay should discuss all the significant categories or parts into which the subject can be classified or divided. It would be misleading, for example, to classify unemployed workers into only two groups:
   1. Those who have been laid off or downsized
   2. Those who lack skills for employment

Many people are unemployed for other reasons.
   • Some are unable to work due to illness.
   • Some may have been fired for incompetence or laziness.
   • Some may choose not to work while they raise children or pursue an education.

When reading "My Secret Life on the McJob: Fast Food Managers," you might ask whether there are other types of managers whom Newman did not observe, recognize, or write about.

Does the writer provide sufficient detail about each category? An objective and fair classification or division requires each category to be treated with the same level of detail. Writers who provide many details for some categories and just a few details for other categories may be biased. For example, suppose a writer classifies how high school students spend their time. She goes into great detail about leisure activities but offers little detail about part-time jobs or volunteer work. The writer may be trying to create the impression that most students care only about having fun and make few meaningful contributions to society—an idea that many people would disagree with.

Is the principle of classification or division appropriate given the writer's purpose? In "My Secret Life on the McJob: Fast Food Managers," Jerry Newman classifies managers according to management style, but another principle of classification, such as productivity or experience, might also be possible. Given Newman's purpose—to recommend that readers become performance managers—his decision to use management style was appropriate. However, if his purpose had been to examine why some McDonald's franchises are more profitable than others, then classification of managers by their financial results might have been a more appropriate choice.

A GUIDED WRITING ASSIGNMENT*
CLASSIFICATION AND DIVISION

YOUR ESSAY ASSIGNMENT

Write a classification or division essay on a topic that you believe would interest other students at your college or readers who share an interest or experience of yours. Below are some options for general topics.

Classification
- types of pets
- types of sports fans
- types of movies

Division
- your family
- a sports team or extracurricular club
- a public place (building, stadium, park)

Prewriting

1 Select a topic, devise a principle of classification or division, and list the categories of which it is made up or the parts into which it breaks down.

Choose a topic idea, and then try one of the following suggestions to generate ideas for categories or parts.
- **Start from the categories or parts:** Brainstorm, freewrite, or use another idea-generating strategy to generate details describing your topic. Then categorize the details into logical groups. Look for three or four groups or parts that share a common thread.

*The writing process is *recursive*; that is, you may find yourself revising as you draft or prewriting as you revise. This is especially true when writing on a computer. Your writing process may also differ from that of your classmates, depending on your preferred learning style.

(continued on next page)

· **Start from a principle of classification or division:** Think about a trait or principle (like degrees of enthusiasm for sports fans or types of horror films) and then freewrite, brainstorm with a friend or classmate, or use another strategy to come up with the specific types or parts.

In small groups, **test your categories (classification)** or **parts (division)** to make sure that
1. **all members** of a category **fit** or **no essential parts** have been **omitted**.
2. **all categories are exclusive** (each group member fits in one category only) or **no parts overlap**.
3. categories or parts will **engage your readers**.
4. **names** of categories or parts describe them **accurately**, emphasizing their **distinguishing features**.

2 Consider your purpose, audience, and point of view.

Ask yourself these questions
· What is my **purpose**, and who is my **audience**? How do they affect my **topic**, my **principle of classification** or **division**, and my **categories** or **parts**?

Example: To *inform* novice Skype users about the software, your parts and details must be straightforward and nontechnical.

· How might **additional patterns of development** help readers understand and appreciate my topic?

Example: A classification essay might also compare and contrast types of sports fans.

· What **point of view** best suits my purpose and audience? **First person** (*I, we*) or **second person** (*you*) may be appropriate in **informal writing** if your audience has **personal knowledge** of or **experience** with the topic. **Third person** (*he, she, it, they*) is appropriate in more **formal writing** or for topics **less familiar** to your audience.

3 Generate supporting details.

Try one of the following suggestions for generating supporting details that will engage your readers and reinforce your purpose.
1. Alone or in pairs, visit a place where you can **observe your topic or the people associated with it**. For example, to generate details about pets, visit a pet store or an animal shelter. Make notes on what you see and hear. Record conversations, physical characteristics, behaviors, and so forth. (Concrete and creative learners may prefer observing; social learners may prefer observing in pairs.)
2. **Conduct research** to discover facts, examples, and other details about your topic. (All learners, but especially pragmatic and independent learners, may prefer conducting research.)
3. **Use the patterns of development** to generate details. Ask yourself how the categories or parts are **similar or different (comparison-contrast)**, what **examples** you can use to illustrate the categories or parts **(illustration)**, what **stories or anecdotes** would help you distinguish categories or parts **(narration)**, or how you would **describe parts or group members** using **language that appeals to the senses (description)**. (All learners may benefit from using the patterns of development.)

Draft your thesis statement.

Your thesis statement should **identify your topic** and **reveal your principle of division or classification**. It should also suggest why your classification or division is **useful or important**. Notice how the following weak theses are strengthened by showing both what the categories are and why they are important.

Weak
There are four types of insurance that most people can purchase.

Revised
Understanding the four common types of insurance will help you protect yourself, your family, and your property against disaster.

Working Together. In groups of two or three students, take turns reading your thesis aloud. As group members listen, have them

1. list your categories/parts
2. write down why they matter

Finally, as a group, discuss how writers could make their categories or parts more distinctive and how they could show readers why these categories or parts are useful or important.

 Choose a method of organization.

· **Least-to-most** and **most-to-least** work well in classification essays. You might arrange categories in increasing order of importance or from most to least common, difficult, or frequent.

   Example: In writing about the parts of a hospital, you might describe the most important areas first (operating rooms, emergency department) and then move to less important areas (waiting rooms, cafeterias).

· **Chronological order** works well when one category occurs or is observable before another.
· **Spatial order** works well in division essays when describing a place.

   Example: In describing the parts of a baseball stadium, you might move from stands to playing field.

Reviewing Chapter 7 may help you understand the methods of organization.

6 **Draft your classification or division essay.**

Use the following guidelines to keep your essay on track.
· The **introduction** should provide any **background** readers will need, include your **thesis statement**, and suggest why the classification or division is **useful** or **important**; it might also state your **principle of classification or division**.
· The **body paragraphs** should **name** and **elaborate on** your categories or parts, **explain the traits** they share, and **provide the details** readers need to understand and accept them. Be sure you devote roughly the **same amount of detail** to each category or part. **Headings** can help identify

(continued on next page)

Organizing & Drafting

categories or parts discussed in multiple paragraphs; a **list** can help identify a large number of categories or parts; a **diagram** or **flowchart** may help make your system of classification or division clearer to readers. Include **transitions** such as *first, next, in contrast,* and *on the one/other hand* to keep readers on track as your essay moves from one category or part to another.

- The **conclusion** should bring your essay to a satisfying close, returning to your **thesis** and elaborating on why the classification or division is **useful** and **important** or **offering a new insight** or **perspective** on the topic.

7 **Evaluate your draft and revise as necessary.**

Use **Figure 17.3, "Flowchart for Revising a Classification and Division Essay,"** to evaluate and revise your draft.

8 **Edit and proofread your essay.**

Refer to Chapter 10 for help with . . .
- **editing sentences** to avoid wordiness, make your verb choices strong and active, and make your sentences clear, varied, and parallel, and
- **editing words** for tone and diction, connotation, and concrete and specific language.

Pay particular attention to the following:

1. Avoid **short, choppy sentences,** which can make a classification or division essay sound dull and mechanical. Try combining a series of short sentences and varying sentence patterns and lengths.

Example: Working dogs ‸ are another one of the American Kennel Club's breed categories. ~~These include German shepherds and sheepherding dogs.~~
, such as German shepherds and sheepherding dogs,

Example: ‸~~One~~ standard type of writing instrument ‸ ~~is the fountain pen. It~~ is sometimes messy and inconvenient to use.
The fountain pen, one

Editing & Proofreading

2. Add a comma after **opening phrases or clauses longer than four words**.

Example: When describing types of college students, be sure to consider variations in age.

Example: Although there are many types of cameras, most are easy to operate.

FIGURE 17.3 **Flowchart for Revising a Classification and Division Essay**

QUESTIONS		REVISION STRATEGIES

1. Highlight your thesis statement. Do it and the rest of your introduction reveal your principle of classification or division and suggest why it is important?

 NO

- Revise your thesis to make your justification stronger or more apparent.
- Add explanatory information to your introduction.

 YES

2. *Write* the principle of classification you used at the top of your paper. Do you use this principle consistently throughout the essay? Does it fit your audience and purpose? Does it clearly relate to your thesis?

 NO

- Brainstorm other possible principles of classification or division, and decide if one better fits your audience and purpose.
- Revise your categories and parts to fit either your existing principle or a new one.
- Rewrite your thesis to reflect your principle of classification/division.

 YES

(continued on next page)

(Figure 17.3 continued)

QUESTIONS	REVISION STRATEGIES

3. <u>Underline</u> the names of categories or parts. Do they cover all members of the group or all major parts of the topic? Are your categories or parts exclusive (not overlapping)?

 NO

- Brainstorm or conduct research to add categories or parts.
- Revise your categories or parts so that each item fits into one group only.

 YES

4. Place a ✔ beside the details that explain each category or part. Does your essay fully explain each one? (If it reads like a list, answer "No.")

 NO

- Brainstorm or do research to generate more details.
- Add examples, definitions, facts, and expert testimony to improve your explanations.

 YES

5. *Write* the method of organization you used at the top of your essay. Is the organization clear? Does this method suit your audience and purpose? Have you followed it consistently?

 NO

- Refer to Chapter 7 to discover a more appropriate organizing plan.
- Revise the order of your categories or parts.
- Add transitions to make your organization clear.

 YES

6. <u>Underline</u> the topic sentence of each paragraph. Is each paragraph focused on a single category or part?

 NO

- Consider splitting paragraphs that cover more than one category or part.
- Consider using headings to group paragraphs on a single category or part.

 YES

7. Reread your conclusion. Does it offer a new insight or perspective on the topic or explain why your classification or division is useful or important?

 NO

- Ask yourself: "So what? What is the point I'm trying to make?" Build your answers into the conclusion.

READINGS: CLASSIFICATION AND DIVISION IN ACTION

The Use and Abuse of Facebook

ALLISON CAVA

Allison Cava wrote the following essay in response to an assignment for her writing course, in which she was asked to write an essay about a type of social media, explaining its uses or users. As you read the essay, consider how effectively Cava explains her groupings. Does her principle of classification make sense? Does she provide enough detail to convince you that the groupings exist and that her topic is useful or important?

Since its introduction in February 2004 by then Harvard University sophomore Mark Zuckerberg (along with Dustin Moskovitz, Chris Hughes, and Eduardo Saverin), Facebook has become one of the most popular social-networking websites on the Internet. At first only available to college students, the website opened to high school students in 2005, and then to everyone—including organizations, such as colleges, businesses, news outlets, political campaigns, and nonprofit organizations—shortly thereafter, and by 2012 Facebook was up to about a billion users (*The Evolution of Facebook*). Now teens are using the site to post photos of themselves (when they're not using Instagram), parents are "friending" their children, grandparents are reconnecting with lost loves, and businesses and organizations ask patrons to "like" them on Facebook.

The site's initial purpose—and the reason it grew from just a handful of users on one campus to a huge number of users across the world—was to provide an easy way for users ("friends") to keep in touch by sharing status updates, interesting links, and photos with distant friends. These constructive uses have expanded to include companies posting their mission statements and advertising their products and services; news outlets posting breaking news; colleges posting emergency alerts, closings, and course offerings; and politicians connecting with voters. In 2007, Barack Obama seemed innovative when he posted the announcement of his presidential aspirations on Facebook; now candidates are expected to have a Facebook page, and Facebook even offers tips for making the most of a post ("Less Than 100 Days"). Sadly, these constructive uses have

Title: Identifies Cava's subject

1 **Introduction:** First 2 pars. present history, original purpose, and current expanded purpose of Facebook for readers who may only know current version of software.

Support: Cava cites sources (throughout) to support her claims.

2

Thesis: Thesis identifies principle of classification and demonstrates usefulness/importance of recognizing categories of annoying and abusive practices.

been tainted by annoying and even abusive practices. An awareness of these practices is the key to the responsible and enjoyable use of Facebook.

Organization: Topic sentence: Introduces first (least offensive) category of annoying practices: over-enthusiastic posting

Among annoying Facebook practices is over-enthusiastic posting. Some users post frequent status updates about the most mundane events in their lives, continually post "cute" photos of their pets, or disproportionately message others, leading to timelines clogged with posts that just aren't that interesting. No wonder that 10 percent of adults who take a "Facebook vacation" say that they "just [weren't] interested"; 9 percent say that they stopped looking at Facebook because they were tired of the "drama" from their "friends"; and 7 percent say that they got "bored with [Facebook]" (Rainie et al.).

Support: Cava offers examples to support claim that overenthusiastic posting is boring and evidence to show boring posts drive users away

Another annoying use of Facebook is the gathering of huge quantities of "friends" in an effort to make users appear (and feel) more popular than they really are. The threshold limit of 5,000 Facebook "friends" one can acquire is far in excess of the number of friends one could possibly have in real life, but this huge number is considered normal in cyberworld (Ball), even though having a vast group of Facebook "friends" may not even be healthy: Psychotherapist Kim Schneiderman cites a study conducted at Edinburgh Napier University in which researchers saw a correlation between stress and the number of Facebook friends a person had (18). More annoying than simply *having* a vast number of "friends" is the process of *acquiring* a vast number of friends. To achieve this number, the Facebook friender must message others continually in hopes of being friended, reaching out to increasingly distant connections, like the friends of "friends" and the friends of friends of "friends."

Organization: Topic sentence: Provides transition to alert readers to second category

Support: Cava summarizes research and offers reason to support claim that over-"friending" is harmful and annoying

Organization: Topic sentence: Introduces next topic; transition indicates the method of organization (from least to most annoying)

More serious are the users who post obnoxious comments or tag "friends" in embarrassing photos. Although a "friend" may untag her- or himself or report an offensive photo or message to try and have it removed from the Internet, the effort is almost always futile (Cheng) : If someone has a direct link to the photograph, he or she can simply repost it to the detriment of others. Facebook "friends" may also cause trouble by responding nastily to another's posts. Schneiderman has noticed in her practice that Facebook has "wreaked mischief" in some of her clients' lives. For example, one client had to block her conservative brother from commenting on her statuses, as he started an argument with her politically liberal friends (Schneiderman 18).

Support: Transition introduces an example to support Cava's claim about seriousness of abuse

3

4

5

More serious still are those who use Facebook to discredit or harm others. In one court case in Arkansas, Denise New was found guilty of harassing her own son on Facebook by posting messages to his profile using his name (Lesnick). Italian teen Carolina Picchio was also a victim, receiving "a steady barrage of abusive, offensive messages" from an ex-boyfriend and his pals that ended only when the girl jumped to her death from her bedroom window (Wedeman). Her sister and friends say they asked Facebook to remove the harassing posts, but according to them, nothing happened. Similarly, business rivals can post negative comments to undermine or even ruin a competitor. In fact, Facebook may provide a forum for the spread of abuse that otherwise would not have seen the light of day, information that we may be better off never being privy to (Schneiderman 18). For instance, people's comments about their bad experiences with college professors, doctors, or companies can help to widely publicize a skewed, discriminatory, or otherwise unfair view that could very well live on the Internet forever.

For all its faults, Facebook is still the most popular social networking site online. While it could do more to enforce its policies and suppress harassing behavior by trolls, many users keep coming back because they enjoy the benefits it affords them: the easy exchange of ideas, information and photographs instantly with anyone in the world, and the opportunity to keep friendships alive across vast distances and many years. In fact, its very popularity is part of its appeal: If all their friends and relatives weren't on Facebook, users would not have as many reasons to use it.

6 **Organization:** Topic sentence: introduces last category; transition indicates that this is most abusive

Support: Cava uses examples to support claim that this category of abuse is most serious

7 **Conclusion:** Explains popularity of site despite abuses

Works Cited

Ball, Aimee Lee. "Are 5,001 Facebook Friends One Too Many?" *The New York Times*, 28 May 2010, www.nytimes.com/2010/05/30/fashion/30FACEBOOK.html?_r=0.

Cheng, Jacquie. "Over 3 Years Later, 'Deleted' Facebook Photos Are Still Online." *Ars Technica*, 5 Feb. 2012, arstechnica.com/business/2012/02/nearly-3-years-later-deleted-facebook-photos-are-still-online/.

"The Evolution of Facebook." *The New York Times*, 24 July 2013, www.nytimes.com/interactive/technology/facebook-timeline.html?ref=technology.

Lesnick, Gavin. "Mom Found Guilty in Facebook Harassment Case." *Arkansas Online*, 27 May 2010, www.arkansasonline.com/news/2010/may/27/mom-found-guilty-facebook-harassment-case/.

"Less Than 100 Days Until Election, Facebook Offers Tips for Campaigns." *Facebook*, 1 Aug. 2012, www.facebook.com/notes/government-and-politics-on-facebook/less-than-100-days-until-election-facebook-offers-tips-for-campaigns/10150937198965882/.

Rainie, Lee, et al. "Coming and Going on Facebook." Pew Research Center, 5 Feb. 2013, www.pewinternet.org/2013/02/05/coming-and-going-on-facebook/.

Schneiderman, Kim. "When Online Battles Become Offline Stresses." *Metro*, 18 July 2013, Boston ed., p. 18.

Wedeman, Benn. "Facebook May Face Prosecution over Bullied Teenager's Suicide in Italy." *CNN*, 31 July 2013, www.cnn.com/2013/07/31/world/europe/italy-facebook-suicide/.

ANALYZING THE WRITER'S TECHNIQUE

1. **Purpose** According to Cava, why is it important to understand the types of annoying and abusive practices on Facebook?
2. **Support** How does Cava explain her categories of abuse and convince readers of the relative seriousness of the abuses she cites? What types of evidence does she use?
3. **Introduction and Conclusion** Evaluate Cava's introduction and conclusion. How successful are they at engaging readers' interest? Does she convey to readers a sense of her topic's importance or a new insight or perspective? Why or why not?

THINKING CRITICALLY ABOUT CLASSIFICATION AND DIVISION

1. **Connotation** What is the connotation of the word *troll* (para. 7)?
2. **Fact or Opinion** Reread the second sentence of para. 1. Is this fact or opinion? How can you tell?
3. **Sources** Evaluate Cava's use of sources. Are her sources convincing? What additional types of sources might have made her claims more convincing? Why?
4. **Tone** Consider Cava's tone. What kind of audience does she seem to be addressing?

RESPONDING TO THE ESSAY

1. **Reaction** Cava clearly describes Internet abuses, but offers few solutions to overcome them. What are possible solutions? Would the inclusion of these have improved her essay?
2. **Discussion** Discuss other principles of classification that might be used to classify types of posts or users of Facebook.

3. **Journal** Write a journal entry describing the ideal Facebook user.
4. **Essay** Cava's essay describes abusive uses of Facebook. Write an essay classifying positive uses of Facebook or another social media site.

READING: CLASSIFICATION COMBINED WITH OTHER PATTERNS

The Dog Ate My Flash Drive, and Other Tales of Woe

CAROLYN FOSTER SEGAL

Carolyn Foster Segal is professor of English at Cedar Crest College in Allentown, Pennsylvania, where she specializes in American literature, poetry, creative writing, and women's film. She has published poems in *Buffalo Spree* magazine, *Phoebe: A Journal of Feminist Scholarship, Theory, and Aesthetics*, and *The Bucks County Writer*, as well as many essays in *The Chronicle of Higher Education*, a weekly newspaper for college faculty and administrators. The following essay appeared in *The Chronicle* in 2000. With the author's permission, it has been revised slightly to update some technological references. As you read, notice how Segal's classification essay also uses description and illustration to fully explain each category she identifies.

Taped to the door of my office is a cartoon that features a cat explaining to his feline teacher, "The dog ate my homework." It is intended as a gently humorous reminder to my students that I will not accept excuses for late work, and it, like the lengthy warning on my syllabus, has had absolutely no effect. With a show of energy and creativity that would be admirable if applied to the (missing) assignments in question, my students persist, week after week, semester after semester, year after year, in offering excuses about why their work is not ready. Those reasons fall into several broad categories: the family, the best friend, the evils of dorm life, the evils of technology, and the totally bizarre.

The Family

The death of the grandfather/grandmother is, of course, the grandmother of all excuses. What heartless teacher would dare to question a student's grief or veracity? What heartless student would lie, wishing death on a revered family member, just to avoid a deadline? Creative students may win extra extensions (and days off) with a little careful planning and fuller plot development, as in the sequence of "My grandfather/grandmother is sick"; "Now my grandfather/grandmother is in the hospital"; and finally, "We could all see it coming—my grandfather/grandmother is dead."

Another favorite excuse is "the family emergency," which (always) goes like this: "There was an emergency at home, and I had to help my family." It's a lovely sentiment, one that conjures up images of Louisa May Alcott's little women rushing off with baskets of food and copies of *Pilgrim's Progress*, but I do not understand why anyone would turn to my most irresponsible students in times of trouble.

©CartoonStock.com

The Best Friend

This heartwarming concern for others extends beyond the family to friends, as
in, "My best friend was up all night and I had to (a) stay up with her in the dorm,
(b) drive her to the hospital, or (c) drive to her college because (1) her boyfriend
broke up with her, (2) she was throwing up blood [no one catches a cold anymore;
everyone throws up blood], or (3) her grandfather/grandmother died."

At one private university where I worked as an adjunct,[1] I heard an interesting spin
that incorporated the motifs of both best friend and dead relative: "My best friend's
mother killed herself." One has to admire the cleverness here: A mysterious woman in
the prime of her life has allegedly committed suicide, and no professor can prove otherwise! And I admit I was moved, until finally I had to point out to my students that it
was amazing how the simple act of my assigning a topic for a paper seemed to drive
large numbers of otherwise happy and healthy middle-aged women to their deaths. I was
careful to make that point during an off week, during which no deaths were reported.

The Evils of Dorm Life

These stories are usually fairly predictable; almost always feature the evil roommate
or hallmate, with my student in the role of the innocent victim; and can be summed
up as follows: My roommate, who is a horrible person, likes to party, and I, who am a
good person, cannot concentrate on my work when he or she is partying. Variations
include stories about the two people next door who were running around and crying

4

5

6

---

[1]*adjunct:* A part-time instructor.

loudly last night because (a) one of them had boyfriend/girlfriend problems; (b) one of them was throwing up blood; or (c) someone, somewhere, died. A friend of mine in graduate school had a student who claimed that his roommate attacked him with a hammer. That, in fact, was a true story; it came out in court when the bad roommate was tried for killing his grandfather.

The Evils of Technology

The computer age has revolutionized the student story, inspiring almost as many   7
new excuses as it has Internet businesses. Here are just a few electronically enhanced explanations:

- The computer wouldn't let me save my work.
- The printer wouldn't print.
- The printer wouldn't print this file.
- The printer wouldn't give me time to proofread.
- The printer made a black line run through all my words, and I know you can't read this, but do you still want it, or wait, here, take my flash drive. File name? I don't know what you mean.
- I swear I attached it.
- It's my roommate's computer, and she usually helps me, but she had to go to the hospital because she was throwing up blood.
- I did write to the Listserv, but all my messages came back to me.
- I just found out that all my other Listserv messages came up under a diferent name. I just want you to know that its really me who wrote all those messages, you can tel which ones our mine because I didnt use the spelcheck! But it was yours truely :) Anyway, just in case you missed those messages or don't belief its my writting, I'll repeat what I sad: I thought the last movie we watched in clas was borring.

The Totally Bizarre

I call the first story "The Pennsylvania Chain Saw Episode." A commuter student called   8
to explain why she had missed my morning class. She had gotten up early so that she would be wide awake for class. Having a bit of extra time, she walked outside to see her neighbor, who was cutting some wood. She called out to him, and he waved back to her with the saw. Wouldn't you know it, the safety catch wasn't on or was broken, and the blade flew right out of the saw and across his lawn and over her fence and across her yard and severed a tendon in her right hand. So she was calling me from the hospital, where she was waiting for surgery. Luckily, she reassured me, she had remembered to bring her paper and a stamped envelope (in a plastic bag, to avoid bloodstains) along with her in the ambulance, and a nurse was mailing everything to me even as we spoke.

That wasn't her first absence. In fact, this student had missed most of the class meet-   9
ings, and I had already recommended that she withdraw from the course. Now I suggested again that it might be best if she dropped the class. I didn't harp on the absences (what if even some of this story were true?). I did mention that she would need time to recuperate and that making up so much missed work might be difficult. "Oh, no," she said, "I can't drop this course. I had been planning to go on to medical school and become a surgeon,

but since I won't be able to operate because of my accident, I'll have to major in English, and this course is more important than ever to me." She did come to the next class, wearing—as evidence of her recent trauma—a bedraggled Ace bandage on her left hand.

You may be thinking that nothing could top that excuse, but in fact I have one more   10
story, provided by the same student, who sent me a letter to explain why her final assignment would be late. While recuperating from her surgery, she had begun corresponding on the Internet with a man who lived in Germany. After a one-week, whirlwind Web romance, they had agreed to meet in Rome, to *rendezvous* (her phrase) at the papal Easter Mass. Regrettably, the time of her flight made it impossible for her to attend class, but she trusted that I—just this once—would accept late work if the pope wrote a note.

EXAMINING THE READING

1. **Categories** Identify the categories of student excuses that Segal identifies.
2. **Examples** Do some student excuses turn out to be legitimate? Give an example from the reading.
3. **Details** What obvious mistake was made by the student who offered the chain-saw excuse?
4. **Vocabulary** Explain the meaning of each of the following words as it is used in the reading: *bizarre* (para. 1), *veracity* (2), *conjures* (3), *motifs* (5), and *harp* (9). Refer to your dictionary as needed.

VISUALIZING THE READING

What types of supporting information does Segal supply to make her categories seem real and believable? Review the reading and complete the chart by filling in at least one type of support for each category. The first one has been done for you.

Category	Types of Support
1. The Family	Examples (death of grandmother/grandfather) Quotations
2. The Best Friend	
3. The Evils of Dorm Life	
4. The Evils of Technology	
5. The Totally Bizarre	

ie macmillanhighered.com/successfulwriting
E-readings > *What's Inside: Coffee* (animation), *Wired.*

ANALYZING THE WRITER'S TECHNIQUE

1. **Strategy** Is it helpful or unnecessary for Segal to list her five categories in her thesis?
2. **Title** What is the function of the essay's title?
3. **Audience** Who is Segal's audience? How can you tell?
4. **Patterns** What other patterns of development does Segal use in the essay?

THINKING CRITICALLY ABOUT TEXT AND VISUALS

1. **Connotation** What is the connotation of "an interesting spin" (para. 5)?
2. **Sources** Other than students, what sources does Segal use? Explain why the essay would or would not benefit from more sources.
3. **Categories** Does Segal provide sufficient detail in each category? What other kinds of details might she have included? What other categories could be included in this essay?
4. **Tone** Describe the tone of the essay. What does it reveal about Segal's attitude toward students?
5. **Visual** What does the cartoon add to the essay? Why is the boy selling "Homework Done" frowning and the boy selling "Homework Eaten" smiling? What is the implied message? What other differences do you notice between the boys?

RESPONDING TO THE READING

1. **Discussion** As a student, how do you react to the essay? Have you observed these excuses being made (or perhaps even made them yourself)? Do you agree that they are overused? Or did you find the essay inaccurate, unfair, or even upsetting?
2. **Journal** Write a journal entry exploring how you think instructors should respond to students who make false excuses.
3. **Essay** Write an essay classifying the excuses you have seen coworkers or bosses make at work to cover up or justify poor performance, tardiness, or irresponsibility.

APPLYING YOUR SKILLS: ADDITIONAL ESSAY ASSIGNMENTS

Write a classification or division essay on one of the following topics, using what you learned about classification and division in this chapter. Depending on the topic you choose, you may need to conduct research.

TO EXPRESS YOUR IDEAS

For more on locating and documenting sources, see Part 5.

1. Explain whether you are proud of or frustrated with your ability to budget money. For example, you might classify budget categories that are easy to master versus those that cause problems.
2. Explain why you chose your career or major. Categorize the job opportunities or benefits of your chosen field, and explain why they are important to you.
3. Divide a store—such as a computer store, clothing store, or grocery store—into departments. Describe where you are most and least tempted to overspend.

TO INFORM YOUR READER

4. Write an essay for the readers of your college newspaper classifying college instructors' teaching styles.
5. Explain the parts of a ceremony or an event you have attended or participated in.
6. Divide a familiar substance (like toothpaste) or object (like a Web page or a basketball team) into its component parts.

TO PERSUADE YOUR READER

7. Categorize types of television violence to develop the argument that violence on television is either harmful to children or not harmful to children.
8. In an essay that categorizes types of parenting skills and demonstrates how they are learned, develop the argument that effective parenting skills can be acquired through practice, training, or observation.

CASES USING CLASSIFICATION OR DIVISION

9. Write an essay for an introductory education class identifying a problem you have experienced or observed in the public education system. Divide public education into parts to better explain your problem.
10. You oversee the development of the annual catalog for a large community college, including the section describing the services offered to students. Decide how that section of the catalog should be organized, and then list the categories it should include. Finally, write a description of the services in one category.

SYNTHESIZING IDEAS

The Workplace

Both "Speaking Quiché in the Heart of Dixie" (pp. 289–93) and "My Secret Life on the McJob: Fast Food Managers" (pp. 403–06) deal with employment in low-level service jobs. As you answer the following questions, keep in mind that both authors are professionals who were working under the guise of learning the habits, characteristics, and problems that everyday workers face in such jobs.

Analyzing the Readings

1. What workplace problems did both Thompson and Newman observe?
2. Write a journal entry exploring the differences and/or similarities that exist between working at a chicken processing plant and working at fast-food restaurants.

Essay Idea

Write an essay in which you explore attitudes toward and expectations about work. You might consider its value, besides a weekly paycheck, or you might examine what type of work is rewarding.

18 Definition

Explaining What You Mean

©Ashley Cooper pics/Alamy

Suppose your psychology instructor showed this photograph to the class and asked, "What type of human behavior is being exhibited here?" What would be your response? You might say the people in the photograph are demonstrating cooperation, self-reliance, or compassion, for example.

Write a paragraph defining the motivations and behavior of the men pushing the car. First choose a term that describes their motivation or behavior. Then write a brief definition of the term you chose and explain the qualities or characteristics of the motivation or behavior.

- understand the purpose and function of definition essays,
- use graphic organizers to visualize definition essays,
- integrate definition into an essay,
- read and think critically about definition, and
- plan, organize, draft, revise, and edit essays using definition.

A **definition** explains the meaning of a term (or which meaning is intended when a word has several different meanings). Often a definition is intended for those who are unfamiliar with the thing or idea being defined. For example, you might define *slicing* to someone unfamiliar with golf or explain the term *koi* to a person unfamiliar with tropical fish.

You use definitions every day in a variety of situations. If you call a friend a *nonconformist,* for example, she might ask you what you mean. If you and a friend disagree over whether you are feminists, you might need to define the term in order to resolve your dispute. In the Writing Quick Start, you named and defined a motivation or behavior.

USING DEFINITION IN COLLEGE AND THE WORKPLACE

- On an exam for a *health and fitness* course, the following short-answer question appears: "Define the term *wellness.*"

- Your *psychology instructor* asks you to write a paper exploring classical conditioning. As part of the essay, you need to define the concept and provide examples from everyday life.

- As a *chemical engineer* responsible for your department's compliance with the company's standards for *safety* and *work efficiency*, you write a brief memo to your staff defining each term.

CHARACTERISTICS OF EXTENDED DEFINITIONS

If you wanted to define the term *happiness,* you would probably have trouble coming up with a brief definition because the emotion is experienced in a wide variety of situations, and the term may mean different things to different people. However, you could explore the term in an essay and explain what it means to you. Such a lengthy, detailed definition is called an **extended definition**.

Extended definitions are particularly useful in exploring a topic's various meanings and applications. Some extended definitions begin with a brief standard definition that anchors the essay's thesis statement. Other extended definitions begin by introducing a new way of thinking about the term. Whatever approach is used, the remainder of the extended definition then clarifies the term by using one or more other patterns of development.

AN EXTENDED DEFINITION IS FOCUSED AND DETAILED

An extended definition focuses on a specific term and discusses it in detail. In the first reading (pp. 434–37), for example, the author defines *freeganism*. To explain the concept, she explores the origin of the word *freegan*, describes the freegan philosophy, explains how and where freegans forage for food, and discusses safety measures.

AN EXTENDED DEFINITION OFTEN INCLUDES A STANDARD DEFINITION OF THE TERM

A **standard definition**, such as the kind found in a dictionary, consists of three parts:
- the *term* itself,
- the *class* to which the term belongs, and
- the *characteristics or details* that distinguish the term from all others in its class.

Here are two examples.

┌─── term ───┐ ┌ class ┐┌─────── distinguishing characteristics ───────┐
A wedding band is a ring, often made of gold, that brides and grooms exchange

during a marriage ceremony.

┌── term ──┐ ┌── class ──┐ ┌──── distinguishing characteristics ────┐
Dalmatian is a breed of dog that originated in Dalmatia; it has a short,

smooth coat with black or dark brown spots.

To write an effective standard definition, use the following guidelines.

1. **Describe the class as specifically as possible.** This will make it easier for your reader to understand the term you define. Notice, for example, that for *Dalmatian*, the class is not *animal* or *mammal* but rather a *breed of dog*.

2. **Do not use the term (or forms of the term) as part of your definition.** Do not write, "*Mastery* means that one has *mastered* a skill." In place of *mastered,* you could use *learned,* for example.

3. **Include enough distinguishing characteristics so that your readers will not mistake the term for something similar within the class.** If you define *a food processor* as "an appliance that purees food," your definition would be incomplete because a blender also purees food. A more complete definition would be "an appliance with interchangeable blades that shreds, dices, chops, or purees food."

4. **Do not limit the definition so much that it becomes inaccurate.** Defining *bacon* as "a smoked, salted meat from the side of a pig that is served at breakfast" would be too limited because bacon is also served at other meals. To make the definition accurate, you could either delete "that is served at breakfast" or add a qualifying expression like "usually" or "most often" before "served."

Look at the following definition of the term *bully,* taken from a magazine article on the topic. As you read it, study the highlighting and marginal notes.

Term

Three characteristics

Example of power difference

Distinguishes *bullying* from similar terms

The term *bully* does not have a standard definition, but Dan Olweus, professor of psychology at the University of Bergen, has honed the definition to three core elements—bullying involves a pattern of *repeated aggressive behavior* with *negative intent* directed from one child to another where there is a *power difference.* Either a larger child or several children pick on one child, or one child is clearly more dominant than the others. Bullying is not the same as garden-variety aggression; although aggression may involve similar acts, it happens between two people of equal status. By definition, the bully's target has difficulty defending him- or herself, and the bully's aggressive behavior is intended to cause distress.

—Hara Estroff Marano, "Big. Bad. Bully."

EXERCISE 18.1 **Writing Standard Definitions and Listing Distinguishing Characteristics**

Write a standard definition for two of the following terms, listing the distinguishing characteristics that you might use in building an extended definition.

1. Hero
2. Giraffe
3. Science fiction
4. Social media
5. Friendship

AN EXTENDED DEFINITION MAKES A POINT

The thesis of an extended definition essay conveys why the term is worth reading about. The following thesis statements include a brief definition and make a point about the term:

Informative thesis: Makes a point about hormones that most would find relevant

⌐ term ⌐   ⌐ point
Produced by the body, hormones are chemicals that are important to physical as

well as emotional development.

Persuasive thesis: Makes a judgment about an important issue about which readers are likely to care

⌐ term ⌐
Euthanasia, the act of ending the life of someone suffering from a terminal illness, is
── point ──

an issue that should not be legislated; rather, it should be a matter of personal choice.

AN EXTENDED DEFINITION USES OTHER PATTERNS OF DEVELOPMENT

To explain the meaning of a term in an extended definition, you generally must integrate one or more other patterns of development into your essay. Suppose you want to define the term *lurking* as it is used in the context of the Internet, where it usually means reading postings or comments on an online forum without directly participating in the discussion. You could use:

- **narration** (Chapter 12) to relate a story about learning something by lurking,
- **description** (Chapter 13) to describe the experience of lurking,

- **illustration** (Chapter 14) to give examples of typical situations involving lurking,
- **process analysis** (Chapter 15) to explain how to lurk in an Internet chat room,
- **comparison and contrast** (Chapter 16) to compare and contrast lurking to other forms of observation,
- **classification and division** (Chapter 17) to classify the reasons people lurk — for information, entertainment, and so on,
- **cause and effect** (Chapter 19) to explain the benefits or outcomes of lurking, and
- **argument** (Chapters 20 and 21) to argue that lurking is an ethical or unethical practice.

| EXERCISE 18.2 | **Using Additional Patterns of Development**

For one of the terms listed in Exercise 18.1 (p. 432), describe how you might use two or three patterns of development in an extended definition of the term.

AN EXTENDED DEFINITION MAY USE NEGATION AND ADDRESS MISCONCEPTIONS

Your extended definition essay may use **negation** — explaining what a term is *not* — to show how the term is different from the other terms in the same class. For example, in an essay defining rollerblading (in-line skating), you might clarify how it is unlike roller skating, which uses a different type of wheeled boot that allows different kinds of motions.

You can also use negation to clarify personal meanings. In defining what you mean by *relaxing vacation*, you might include examples of what is *not* relaxing for you: the pressure to see something new every day, long lines, crowded scenic areas, and many hours in a car each day.

In addition, your extended definition may address popular misconceptions about the term being defined. In an essay defining *plagiarism,* for instance, you might correct the mistaken idea that plagiarism only means passing off an entire paper written by someone else as your own, explaining that plagiarism also includes using excerpts from other writers' work without giving them credit.

| EXERCISE 18.3 | **Using Negation and Addressing Misconceptions**

For two of the following broad topics, select a narrowed term and develop a standard definition of it. Then, for each term, consider how you could address misconceptions and use negation in an extended definition of the term.

1. A type of dance
2. A play, call, or player position in a sport
3. A piece of clothing (hat, jacket, jeans)
4. A term related to a course you are taking
5. A type of business

The following readings demonstrate the techniques for writing effective extended definition essays discussed above. The first reading is annotated to point out how Jan Goodwin defines *freegan*. As you read the second essay, try to identify for yourself how Mike Crissey uses the techniques of extended definition to explain what *dude* means.

Freegans: They Live Off What We Throw Away

JAN GOODWIN

Jan Goodwin is a senior fellow at Brandeis University's Schuster Center for Investigative Journalism and a Soros Foundation Media Fellow. The winner of three Amnesty International UK Media Awards and a World Hunger Award, Goodwin has long been an activist for human rights and social justice. She wrote about the threat of extremism in the Muslim world in her books *Point of Honor* (1994) and *Caught in the Crossfire* (1987) and was a reporter for Lifetime Television's documentary *Defending Our Daughters* (1998). This reading was published in 2009 in the magazine *Marie-Claire*, for which Goodwin was senior international editor.

Focus: Activities and motivations of freegans

One man's trash is another man's treasure. A "freegan" climbs into a dumpster behind a West Palm Beach supermarket in search of edible food. © ZUMA Press, Inc./Alamy

It's nearly closing time on a crisp Monday night at a Midtown Manhattan supermarket, when a burly crew begins tossing bulging black bags filled with the day's   1 trash — crusty breads, salad-bar fixings, last week's fruits and vegetables — to the curb. Just then, a cadre of 15 jeans-and-sneakers-clad men and women turn the corner and quietly descend upon the heaps, gingerly opening and dissecting their contents. As they forage through the small mountains of discarded food, a 30-something woman sporting a green rain slicker calls out, "Over here, expensive Greek yogurt." Seconds later, a ponytailed guy wearing a backpack hollers, "Here's bacon and chicken for anyone who eats meat — and a perfect eggplant." Someone shouts a reminder not to tear the bags or leave litter on the ground, lest the store get fined. After less than 30 minutes, they excitedly depart the scene, each shouldering at least one tote bag filled with booty.

These urban foragers are neither homeless nor destitute. They are committed freegans, radical environmentalists (typically vegan) who reject our wasteful consumer culture by living almost entirely on what others throw away. Freegans rarely go hungry thanks to the colossal amount of food Americans dump every day — 38 million tons annually, according to the Environmental Protection Agency. Here's another way to look at it: The United Nations says our leftovers could satisfy every single empty stomach in Africa. Those castoffs are composed, in part, of the less-than-perfect products consumers instinctively reject: bruised apples, wilted lettuce, dented cans. Who hasn't passed on an entire carton of eggs after discovering a single slight fracture among the dozen? Supermarkets can't unload the quarts of milk tagged with yesterday's use-by date — which many of us interpret as a product's expiration but in fact refers to its period of peak flavor. Meaning, there's still plenty of life left in those quarts.

Freegans, like 24-year-old Leia MonDragon, a buxom Latina with a taste for heavy eye makeup, feast on those castoffs. "It's amazing what you can find and the good condition it's in," she exclaims, holding aloft a week's worth of produce, including watermelon, summer squash, kale, tomatoes, onions, and bananas. Though technically past their prime, they look pristine. MonDragon also scored half gallons of soy milk and lemonade, both unopened and still chilled, and bagels that only an hour earlier were for sale. "I once found 200 one-pound bags of organic fair-trade coffee beans just dumped outside a store with the trash," she brags, like a woman combing the racks at a Gucci clearance sale.

Aside from the $1600 a month in rent MonDragon pays for her two-bedroom Brooklyn apartment, which she shares with her boyfriend, Tate, their 1-year-old daughter, Uma, and her retired grandfather, just about everything she owns has been salvaged or handmade. She found her ivory faux-leather couch, dishes, and flatware on the street; many of Uma's clothes and toys were recovered from boxes abandoned on sidewalks and stoops, a common sight in New York, where apartment detritus — from halogen lamps to bed frames — is blithely left on the streets. MonDragon used to get around on a bicycle she and Tate cobbled together from discarded parts, but not long ago it was stolen. "So now I'm building another one," she says.

Narration: Anecdote demonstrates freegan foraging

2 **Negation:** Uses negation to address misconceptions

Definition: Thesis identifies class, distinguishing characteristics

3 **Illustration:** Examples explain motivation of freegans

Narration, description: Tells story of one freegan; describes MonDragon so readers can visualize her

4

Though official figures are hard to come by, freegan ranks are believed to be in   5
the thousands, with an estimated 500 practitioners living in New York City alone.
Born of the extreme environmentalist and anti-globalization movements of the
'90s, freeganism is a wholly modern crusade whose followers live off the grid while
simultaneously exploiting it. Freegans gravitate toward cities — and their relent-
less mounds of garbage; Web sites keep devotees in close contact with each other
so they can plan group foraging outings, recruit new members, and spread word
of upcoming events, like move-out day at a college dorm, a veritable freegan
Christmas. Using a discarded computer they restored, MonDragon and her boyfriend
routinely scour Craigslist for freebies. (The Web connection comes from a cable
package her grandfather pays for.) "The only thing I don't have yet is a skillet. But
I'll find one," MonDragon declares confidently, as she ladles dinner — tofu-and-
veggie stir-fry with lime zest — from a large stockpot.

Background: Explains history of freeganism

MonDragon first embraced freeganism five years ago as a student at a Minnesota   6
community college, where she met Tate. "We were broke, trying to find the money
for even a simple meal like rice and beans," she explains. "We saw a freegan flyer
and hooked up with some people who showed us how to do it. And just like that,
we had a source of free food. It was amazing." The more time the pair spent with
entrenched freegans, the more exposure they got to the movement's renegade
rhetoric. Since relocating to New York two years ago, they have become ardent
practitioners, positioning their lifestyle as a boycott of "corporate greed" and an
alternative to capitalism. "It's so wrong when people are losing their jobs, struggling to survive, that stores are throwing out such vast quantities of good food,"
MonDragon sighs, as Papo, her wiry gray mutt, nips the hem of her long black skirt.
She tosses him a roasted chicken leg, retrieved from her last supermarket trash run.

Narration: Continues MonDragon's story

MonDragon admits she was initially skeeved out by the prospect of eating   7
garbage — Dumpsters are a frequent freegan haunt — but says she was reassured by
the movement's common-sense safety measures. Some freegans show up for Dumpster dives armed with rubber gloves and antibacterial lotion. Produce is washed
thoroughly, withered leaves discarded; baked goods bearing even a hint of mold are
tossed. Everything undergoes a basic smell test. (Tate says he once scarfed down
day-old sushi, despite its funky aroma, and ended up with food poisoning.) And
since stores generally separate discarded food from, say, bathroom trash bins, the
ickiest finds are usually just putrid meats and dairy. MonDragon decontaminates all
salvaged housewares with a mixture of vinegar, baking soda, and hydrogen peroxide
and launders all of Uma's secondhand stuffed animals and clothes. Though she
draws the line at pre-owned underwear, instead buying new pairs from discount
stores, MonDragon makes her own reusable sanitary napkins from cloth in much
the same way women did a century ago. (Think that's hard-core? Some freegans
squat in abandoned buildings and jerry-rig toilets that compost their own waste
matter.) "People in this country are a lot more freaked out about dirt than they

need to be. We need a little dirt in our lives for our immune systems to be strong," MonDragon says.

"Freegans have been living this way for years and are very healthy," says Dr. Ruth Kava, director of nutrition at the American Council on Science and Health. "In fact, a freegan's biggest risk may be falling headfirst into a Dumpster." That, or being slapped with a fine — or worse — for trespassing on private property to scavenge. It's not uncommon for store owners, mistaking freegans for homeless people or burglars, to call the police. Two years ago, a pair of freegans in Steamboat Springs, CO, were sentenced to six months in jail after jumping a fence and taking a couple of handfuls of fruit and vegetables from a grocery store's trash. For that reason, MonDragon confines her searches to whatever she finds on the street. She and Tate get by on less than $20,000 a year — he drives a taxi, and she clerks at a nonprofit during the summer. Their meager income is earmarked for inescapable expenses, like their tuition at a community college and rent. The couple qualifies for food stamps, which pay only for Uma's formula (MonDragon stopped breastfeeding once she started working).

Though she lives hand to mouth, MonDragon insists she wants for nothing. Her family eats three hearty meals a day; their closets are crammed with wool coats, shoes, shirts with tags still dangling from their sleeves. She's got an active social life, towing Uma to playdates with other freegan moms and fielding invitations to watch DVDs with freegan friends. A week earlier, she and Tate uncovered a hoard of unopened Chinese food inside a streetside trash can, still warm in its gleaming white containers. They took it to a friend's house for an impromptu dinner party. "We usually never take more than we need," she explains, unzipping her black Patagonia shell and tossing it onto her bed — everything from the taupe sheets to the queen-size mattress were recovered from the streets of Manhattan. "We don't need to. There will be more trash out there tomorrow."

8

Background: Explains risks of freeganism

Cause-effect: Explains why MonDragon restricts her searches to the street

9

Conclusion: Ends with quotation that demonstrates lack of want (negation from para. 2)

VISUALIZING AN EXTENDED DEFINITION ESSAY: A GRAPHIC ORGANIZER

The graphic organizer in Figure 18.1 (p. 438) shows the basic organization of an extended definition essay.

For more on creating a graphic organizer, see pp. 52–53.

- The **introduction** announces the term, provides background information, and usually includes the thesis statement (which briefly defines the term and indicates its significance to readers).
- The **body paragraphs**, which use one or more patterns of development, present the term's distinguishing characteristics along with supporting details.
- The **conclusion** refers back to the thesis and brings the essay to a satisfying close.

FIGURE 18.1 **Graphic Organizer for an Extended Definition Essay**

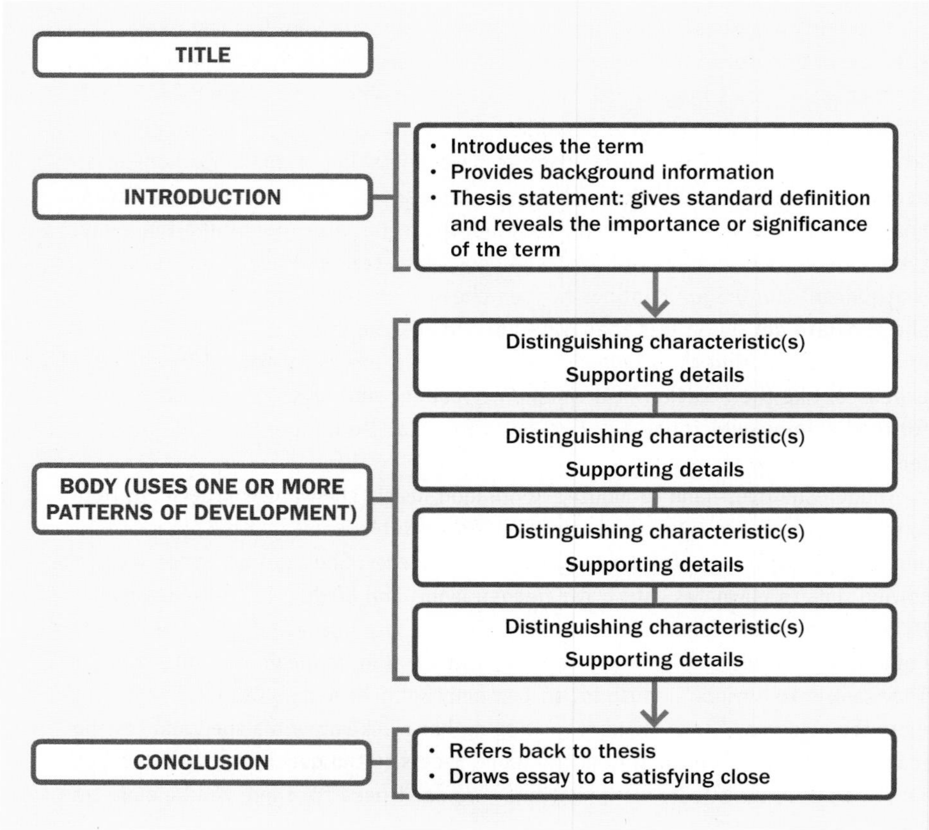

```
┌──────────────────────┐
│        TITLE         │
└──────────────────────┘

                          ┌────────────────────────────────────┐
                          │ • Introduces the term              │
                          │ • Provides background information  │
┌──────────────────────┐  │ • Thesis statement: gives standard │
│     INTRODUCTION      ├──┤   definition and reveals the       │
└──────────────────────┘  │   importance or significance       │
                          │   of the term                      │
                          └────────────────────────────────────┘
                                           │
                                           ▼
                          ┌────────────────────────────────────┐
                          │   Distinguishing characteristic(s) │
                          │         Supporting details         │
                          ├────────────────────────────────────┤
                          │   Distinguishing characteristic(s) │
┌──────────────────────┐  │         Supporting details         │
│ BODY (USES ONE OR MORE├──┤────────────────────────────────────│
│ PATTERNS OF DEVELOPMENT)│ │   Distinguishing characteristic(s) │
└──────────────────────┘  │         Supporting details         │
                          ├────────────────────────────────────┤
                          │   Distinguishing characteristic(s) │
                          │         Supporting details         │
                          └────────────────────────────────────┘
                                           │
                                           ▼
┌──────────────────────┐  ┌────────────────────────────────────┐
│     CONCLUSION        ├──┤ • Refers back to thesis            │
└──────────────────────┘  │ • Draws essay to a satisfying close│
                          └────────────────────────────────────┘
```

READING

Dude, Do You Know What You Just Said?

MIKE CRISSEY

Mike Crissey is a staff writer for the Associated Press. The following article, which appeared in *The Pittsburgh Post-Gazette* on December 8, 2004, is based on research done by Scott Kiesling, a professor of linguistics at the University of Pittsburgh. Kiesling's work focuses on the relationship between language and identity, particularly in the contexts of gender, ethnicity, and class. As you read, notice how the writer uses a combination of expert testimony, anecdotal evidence, and personal observations to support his main point.

Dude, you've got to read this. A University of Pittsburgh linguist has published   1
a scholarly paper deconstructing and deciphering *dude,* the bane of parents and
teachers, which has become as universal as *like* and another vulgar four-letter favorite.

In his paper in the fall edition of the journal *American Speech,* Scott Kiesling says *dude* is much more than a greeting or catchall for lazy, inarticulate, and inexpressive (and mostly male) surfers, skaters, slackers, druggies, or teenagers. "Without context there is no single meaning that *dude* encodes and it can be used, it seems, in almost any kind of situation. But we should not confuse flexibility with meaninglessness," Kiesling said.

Originally meaning "old rags," a "dudesman" was a scarecrow. In the late 1800s, a "dude" was akin to a dandy, a meticulously dressed man, especially in the western United States. *Dude* became a slang term in the 1930s and 1940s among black zoot suiters and Mexican American pachucos. The term began its rise in the teenage lexicon with the 1982 movie *Fast Times at Ridgemont High*. Around the same time, it became an exclamation as well as a noun. Pronunciation purists say it should sound like "duhd"; "dood" is an alternative, but it is considered "uncool" or old.

To decode *dude,* Kiesling listened to conversations with fraternity members he taped in 1993 and had undergraduate students in sociolinguistics classes in 2001 and 2002 write down the first twenty times they heard *dude* and who said it during a three-day period. He's also a lapsed *dude*-user who during his college years tried to talk like Jeff Spicoli, the slacker surfer "dude" from *Fast Times at Ridgemont High*.

According to Kiesling, *dude* has many uses: an exclamation ("Dude!" and "Whoa, Dude!"); to one-up someone ("That's so lame, dude"); to disarm confrontation ("Dude, this is so boring"), or simply to agree ("Dude"). It's inclusive or exclusive, ironic or sincere.

Kiesling says *dude* derives its power from something he calls cool solidarity: an effortless or seemingly lazy kinship that's not too intimate; close, dude, but not that close. *Dude* "carries . . . both solidarity (camaraderie) and distance (non-intimacy) and can be deployed to create both of these kinds of stance, separately or together," Kiesling wrote. Kiesling, whose research focuses on language and masculinity, said that cool solidarity is especially important to young men — anecdotally the predominant *dude*-users — who are under social pressure to be close with other young men but not enough to be suspected as gay. "It's like *man* or *buddy*. There is often this male-male addressed term that says, 'I'm your friend but not much more than your friend,'" Kiesling said. Aside from its duality, *dude* also taps into nonconformity, despite everyone using it, and a new American image of leisurely success, he said.

The nonchalant attitude of *dude* also means that women sometimes call each other *dudes*. And less frequently, men will call women *dudes* and vice versa, Kiesling said. But that comes with some rules, according to self-reporting from students in a 2002 language and gender class at the University of Pittsburgh included in his paper. "Men report that they use *dude* with women with whom they are close friends, but not with women with whom they are intimate," according to his study.

His students also reported that they were least likely to use the word with parents, bosses, and professors. "It is not who they are but what your relationship is with them. With your parents, you likely have a close relationship, but unless you're Bart Simpson, you're not going to call your parent *dude,*" Kiesling said. "There are a couple of young professors here in their thirties and every once in a while we use *dude*. Professors are dudes, but most of the time they are not."

And *dude* shows no signs of disappearing. "More and more our culture is becoming youth centered. In southern California, youth is valued to the point that even active seniors are dressing young and talking youth," said Mary Bucholtz, an associate professor of linguistics at the University of California, Santa Barbara. "I have seen middle-aged men using *dude* with each other."   8

So what's the point, dude? Kiesling and linguists argue that language and how we use it is important. "These things that seem frivolous are serious because we are always doing it. We need to understand language because it is what makes us human. That's my defense of studying *dude*," Kiesling said.   9

> **EXERCISE 18.4** **Drawing a Graphic Organizer**
>
> Using Figure 18.1 or 18.2 as a basis, draw a graphic organizer for "Freegans: They Live Off What We Throw Away" (pp. 434–37).

FIGURE 18.2 **Graphic Organizer for "Dude, Do You Know What You Just Said?"**

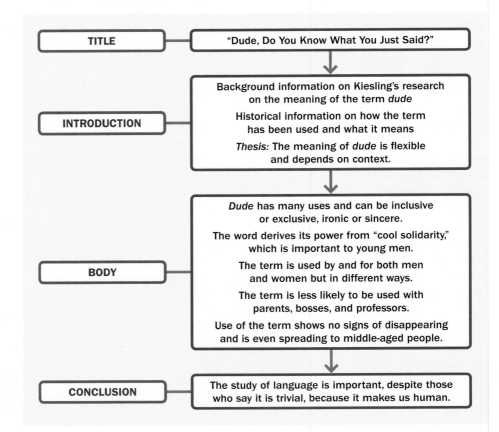

TITLE — "Dude, Do You Know What You Just Said?"

INTRODUCTION
- Background information on Kiesling's research on the meaning of the term *dude*
- Historical information on how the term has been used and what it means
- *Thesis:* The meaning of *dude* is flexible and depends on context.

BODY
- *Dude* has many uses and can be inclusive or exclusive, ironic or sincere.
- The word derives its power from "cool solidarity," which is important to young men.
- The term is used by and for both men and women but in different ways.
- The term is less likely to be used with parents, bosses, and professors.
- Use of the term shows no signs of disappearing and is even spreading to middle-aged people.

CONCLUSION — The study of language is important, despite those who say it is trivial, because it makes us human.

INTEGRATING DEFINITION INTO AN ESSAY

Including standard or extended definitions in writing that is based on other patterns of development is common. For example, you may need to include a definition in a response to an essay exam question. Definitions should also be included when terms are likely to be unfamiliar to the reader or when terms may be understood differently than intended. The following kinds of terms usually require definition.

For a reading that uses definition as well as other patterns of development, see "Dating on the Autism Spectrum" (pp. 452–56).

- **Judgmental or controversial terms.** Define terms that imply a judgment or that may be controversial. If you describe a policy as "fiscally unsound," for example, make clear whether you mean "spending more money than we earn," "paying an interest rate that is too high," or something else.
- **Technical terms.** When writing for a general audience, define specialized terms that readers may find unfamiliar. In law, for example, you may need to define terms like *writ, deposition, hearing,* and *plea* for a general audience.
- **Abstract terms.** Terms that refer to ideas or concepts, such as *loyalty, heroism,* and *conformity,* may need to be defined because they can seem vague or mean different things to different people.

In general, if you are not sure whether a term needs a definition, include one.

You may choose to provide your definition in a separate sentence or section, or you can incorporate a brief definition or synonym into a sentence, using commas, dashes, or parentheses to set off the definition, as in the following examples.

term — definition

Implicit memory, or the nonconscious retention of information about prior experiences, is important in eyewitness accounts of crimes.

term — definition

Empathy—a shared feeling of joy for people who are happy or distress for people who are in pain—explains the success of many popular films.

READING ACTIVELY AND THINKING CRITICALLY

Throughout college, you will encounter many new vocabulary words. Textbook authors and instructors usually define important terms, but articles in academic journals, which are written for an expert audience, may leave you to figure out or look up important terms for yourself.

For more on reading actively, see Chapter 3; for more on thinking critically, see Chapter 4.

If you need to learn a large number of specialized terms, try the index card system:

1. Write the words you need to learn on the front of three-by-five-inch index cards.
2. On the back, write the word's definition, pronunciation, and any details or examples that will help you remember it. Write the definition in your own words; don't copy the author's definition.
3. Test yourself by reading the front of the cards and trying to recall the definition on the back of the cards. Then reverse the process. Shuffle the pack of cards to avoid learning terms in a particular order.

WHAT TO LOOK FOR, HIGHLIGHT, AND ANNOTATE

For more on previewing, see pp. 45–47.

Use the following suggestions to read extended definition essays actively:

1. **Preview.** Preview the essay to get an overview of its content and organization and identify the term that is being defined.

2. **Understand the definition.** As you read the essay, circle the class to which the term being defined belongs, and highlight or underline its distinguishing characteristics. (See pp. 431–32) Mark any characteristics that are unclear or for which you need further information. If the reading does not sufficiently explain how two or more terms differ, check a standard or specialized dictionary. (Every academic field of study has specialized dictionaries, such as *Music Index* and *A Dictionary of Economics,* that list terms specific to the discipline.)

3. **Identify the strategies the writer uses to explain the term.** Note in the margin or in a writing journal strategies (such as negation) and patterns of development (such as narration, description, illustration, or comparison-contrast) the writer uses to distinguish the term from similar terms.

4. **Think about the meaning.** Reread the essay once again, this time concentrating on its meaning by answering the following questions:
   - What is the writer's main point? For what audience is the essay intended?
   - How might the purpose and audience have influenced the writer's choice of explanatory strategies?
   - How well do the examples and other explanatory strategies work to help you understand the term? Jot down any additional characteristics or examples that you think would help explain it to your friends, relatives, or classmates.

5. **Consider your reactions.** Try to relate the definitions to your own experience. Where or when have you observed the characteristics described? You might use your personal experiences to write an essay in which you support or challenge the writer's definitions, or you might explain how the writer's definition could be expanded to include these additional examples.

ANALYZING EXTENDED DEFINITIONS

When reading extended definitions, especially of judgmental or controversial terms, be alert to bias, euphemism, and strategic omissions by asking the following questions.

Are the definitions expressed in objective language? Especially in persuasive essays, definitions are sometimes expressed in subjective, emotional language that is intended to influence readers. For example, a writer who defines a *liberal* as "someone who wants to allow criminals to run free on the streets while sacrificing the rights of innocent victims" reveals a negative bias toward liberals and may want to make readers dislike those who describe themselves as "liberal." When reading a definition of a controversial term, ask yourself questions like these

   - Do I agree with the writer's definition of this term?
   - Do I think these characteristics apply to all members of this group?
   - Is the writer's language meant to inflame my emotions?

Are the definitions evasive? Be alert to the use of **euphemisms**, words or phrases that are used in place of an unpleasant or objectionable word. (For example, TV com-

READINGS: EXTENDED DEFINITION IN ACTION

STUDENTS WRITE

Guerrilla Street Art: A New Use of Public Space

KATE ATKINSON

Kate Atkinson wrote the following essay for an assignment to write an extended definition of a specialized term related to one of her interests. Atkinson decided to write about guerrilla street art. As you read, note how Atkinson uses other patterns of development — such as description and illustration — to define guerrilla street art as a nontraditional art form growing in popularity.

Guerrilla street art is everywhere, if you look for it. There are countless examples in the small college town where I grew up, where the dense population of college students and artists breeds creativity. Just around the corner from my school, stickers litter sign posts, colorful graffiti is scrawled on exposed brick walls, homemade posters advertise local bands at the bus stop, and a cheerful Dr. Seuss character is stenciled on the sidewalk. These small works of art can easily go unnoticed, but they bring an unexpected vibrancy to the city and raise the controversial question of what constitutes art. By taking art out of its traditional context, guerrilla street artists use public space to create controversy and intrigue while at the same time making art free and accessible to a broad audience.

Common forms used by street artists today include graffiti, stenciling, poster art, sticker art, and yarn bombing. Graffiti, the most prevalent form of guerrilla street art, is unauthorized writing or drawing on a public surface. It dates back centuries, and artists have been known to use chalk, markers, paint, and even carving tools to inscribe their messages on public property. Graffiti is so common that it is difficult to travel far in most urban settings without coming across a word or image scrawled in spray paint on a public surface. Stenciling is simply a form of graffiti in which artists use precut stencils to guide their work. Posters and stickers are popular because they can be easily mass-produced and quickly applied. Posters are usually applied with a technique called "wheat pasting" -- using a vegetable-based adhesive to attach posters to walls. Artists apply the clear paste with a roller in a thin layer to both sides of the poster, making it weather-proof and

Title: Atkinson identifies her subject and creates interest.

1 Introduction: Atkinson provides background information on guerrilla street art and explains by example what it is.

Distinguishing characteristics: Her thesis statement offers a brief definition and suggests the value and importance of guerrilla street art.

2 Distinguishing characteristics: Atkinson presents the first distinguishing characteristic and lists five examples. Notice that the first sentence in this paragraph is the topic sentence, which is supported by the rest of the paragraph — a pattern followed in each of the next three paragraphs.

durable. A less common street-art technique is "yarn bombing," in which craft artists knit colorful sheaths of wool and acrylic and wrap them around telephone poles and park benches. The finished pieces are eye-catching and unusual but not permanent or damaging to public property.

The various motives behind guerrilla street art are as diverse as the artwork itself and range from social and political activism to self-promotion of the artist. Artists embellish telephone poles with colorful yarn and train carriages with ornate murals as a way to reclaim and beautify public space. Others use public space as a billboard to advocate for a cause. An example of street art as political activism is artist Shepard Fairey's iconic image of Barack Obama (Wortham). The simple design combines a striking red, white, and blue portrait of Obama with the word "Hope." With the approval of Obama's 2008 campaign team, Fairey and his team dispersed and pasted, stenciled, or tacked the image onto countless public surfaces across the United States until it became an important facet of the campaign. The picture itself is powerful, but what made it even more effective as a campaign tool was the distribution of the image by supporters and the youth appeal that it garnered as a result.

Street art has many appeals. It is an easy way for new artists to gain notoriety, and anyone with a spray can and a flair for creativity can partake. A tag, which is an artist's signature or symbol, is the most common type of graffiti. Before the Obama campaign, Shepard Fairey gained international acclaim for a sticker depicting wrestler Andre the Giant and the word "Obey." The image soon became his tag and can be found in almost all of his work, making it instantly recognizable. The anonymity of street art also gives artists the freedom to express themselves without fearing the judgment of their peers. At worst, this freedom can result in crude or offensive inscriptions on public property; but at best, it can produce bold, striking statements. Guerrilla street art is contemporary and can be enjoyed without a visit to a museum. It is free and encourages the belief that art should be accessible and available to everyone. It is also a movement that anyone can take part in and that challenges traditional standards of art.

Due to the illicit nature of their art, the street artist community is shrouded in secrecy. In the film *Exit through the Gift Shop*, a documentary by notorious British street artist Banksy, hooded figures in ski masks

3

4

5

Distinguishing characteristic: Atkinson discusses the motives of the artists and offers examples of the various motives.

Support: Atkinson uses sources to document an example of political activism, one of the motives.

Distinguishing characteristic: Atkinson discusses the appeal of street art and gives examples.

Distinguishing characteristic: Atkinson discusses the secrecy of the artists and uses Banksy as an example.

are shown scaling buildings and perched precariously on ledges, armed with spray cans and buckets of industrial paste and always on the lookout for the police. Despite his celebrity, Banksy has managed to keep his identity anonymous, and his face is never shown in the film. It is common for street artists to be arrested for trespassing and vandalism, and the risk and intentional disobedience involved in street art adds to its appeal, especially among young people.

Guerrilla street art has blossomed from an underground movement to a cultural phenomenon. At the very least, it brings up the question of what constitutes art and whether public space is an appropriate place for it. Although it does not adhere to all traditional standards of art, guerrilla street art provokes thought, brings beauty and intrigue to urban spaces that would otherwise go unnoticed, and is a tool for artists to exercise freedom of speech and expression.

6

Conclusion: Atkinson comments on the street art movement as a cultural experience, explains its value.

Works Cited

Exit through the Gift Shop. Directed by Banksy, perfomances by Banksy and
    Thierry Guetta, Paranoid Pictures, 2010.
Wortham, Jenna. "'Obey' Street Artist Churns Out 'Hope' for Obama." *Wired*,
    21 Sept. 2010, www.wired.com/2008/09/poster-boy-shep/.

ANALYZING THE WRITER'S TECHNIQUE

1. **Definition** How does Atkinson define *guerrilla art*?
2. **Effectiveness** Evaluate the effectiveness of the title, introduction, and conclusion.
3. **Terms** Locate one of each of these in the essay—a judgment term, a technical term, an abstract term, and a controversial term.

THINKING CRITICALLY ABOUT DEFINITION

1. **Bias** Atkinson is not neutral on the subject of this essay. Explain her bias. How does this affect the essay?
2. **Sources** What other types of sources could Atkinson have included to make her essay more comprehensive? What do her two sources reveal about her attitude about the topic?

3. **Connotation** Atkinson uses words such as *vibrancy* (para. 1) and *blossomed* (6) to describe guerrilla street art. What kind of connotation do these words have, and how do the connotations play into the overall tone of the essay?
4. **Euphemism** Is "guerrilla street art" a euphemism? Why or why not? If so, how would the same idea be expressed in more direct language?
5. **Evaluation** Atkinson limits her definition of guerrilla street art to items that have no commercial or financial purpose. She does not mention posters promoting businesses or paid entertainment, signs and banners used for fund-raising by organizations, and advertising flyers, even though these items also are often displayed in the same places as those she does discuss and with the same lack of legal permission. How are these items similar to and different from the kinds of items she includes in her definition?

RESPONDING TO THE READING

1. **Reaction** Have you ever created any graffiti? Discuss how doing it made you feel. If you have ever created any, discuss how doing so might make you feel.
2. **Discussion** Discuss the value of work like Shepard Fairey's, which takes political messages and conveys them in street art. Why is this strategy effective? How does it reach a broader audience than other methods of communication?
3. **Journal** Write a journal entry discussing whether guerrilla art adds value to public space or devalues the space. How should the answer to this question be determined?

READING: DEFINITION COMBINED WITH OTHER PATTERNS

Dating on the Autism Spectrum

EMILY SHIRE

Emily Shire is a writer for *The Week* and has also published articles in a number of other publications, including *Slate* and *The Forward*. This essay appeared in *The Atlantic* in 2013. As you read, notice how Shire uses examples and quotations from personal interviews to make her extended definition vivid and convincing.

The way to Paulette Penzvalto's heart is through her Outlook calendar. "Honestly, if you want to be romantic with me, send an email through Outlook and give me all the possible dates, locations, and times, so that I can prepare," she said. 1

The former Miss America contestant and Juilliard-trained opera singer knew she had a different conception of romance than her previous boyfriends had and, for that matter, everyone else. "People tend to think of romance as spur of the moment and exciting," she told me. "I think of romance as things that make sense and are logical." However, she didn't know why until this year when, at the age of 31, she was diagnosed with autism. 2

The aspects of autism that can make everyday life challenging — reading social cues, understanding another's perspectives, making small talk and exchanging niceties — can be seriously magnified when it comes to dating. The American Psychiatric Association defines autism as a spectrum disorder: Some people do not speak at all and have disabilities that make traditional relationships (let alone romantic ones) largely unfeasible, but there are also many who are on the "high-functioning" end and do have a clear desire for dating and romance. 3

Autism diagnosis rates have increased dramatically over the last two decades (the   4
latest CDC reports show one in 50 children are diagnosed), and while much attention
has been paid to early-intervention programs for toddlers and younger children, teens
and adults with autism have largely been overlooked — especially when it comes to
building romantic relationships.

Certain characteristics associated with the autism spectrum inherently go against   5
typical dating norms. For example, while a "neuro-typical" person might think a bar
is a great place for a first date, it could be one of the worst spots for someone on the
spectrum. Dorsey Massey, a social worker who helps run dating and social programs for
adults with various intellectual disabilities, explained, "If it's a loud, crowded place,
an individual on the spectrum may be uncomfortable or distracted." Sensory issues
may also make certain lights and noises especially unpleasant.

Seemingly basic, non-sexual touching may be an issue, as well. "It may give them   6
discomfort for someone to kiss them lightly or hold their hand," Massey said. "They
need pressure, and that's not typically what you think of with tender, romantic love."

Perhaps because so much of their behavior runs counter to mainstream concep-   7
tions of how to express affection and love, people with autism are rarely considered
in romantic contexts. A constant complaint among the individuals interviewed for
this piece is the misconception that people with autism can't express love or care for
others. "I think a lot of times someone will go out on a date with someone on the
spectrum and think they're a robot," said Alex Plank, founder of WrongPlanet.net, a
popular online autism community. "It's hard to read us if we don't explicitly say what
we're feeling, but all the feelings are there."

In fact, people with autism may have greater emotional capacities. "Studies have   8
shown that people with autism can have feelings that are stronger and deeper than
those without autism," said John Elder Robison, bestselling author of *Look Me in the
Eyes* and autism advocate. "Yet those feelings may be invisible to outsiders because
we don't show them. Because we don't show them or the expected response, people
make the wrong assumption about our depth of feeling about other people."

It's not that individuals on the spectrum do not have the same desire for love; they   9
just may not know how to find it. Dr. Elizabeth Laugeson, an Assistant Clinical Professor
at UCLA said, "If you asked a person with autism if they wanted a romantic relationship,
they would probably say yes, but they would probably also say they don't know how to."

Partially from the emphasis on early intervention treatments, there's a dearth of   10
dating skills programs, or, rather, effective ones for people on the spectrum. "Early
intervention can significantly improve the outcome, but kids grow up, and we don't
have the proper services," said Laugeson, who serves as director of UCLA PEERS, a
program that teaches social, including romantic, interaction skills to teens and young
adults on the spectrum.

Central to PEERS is the promotion of "ecologically valid" social skills, traits humans   11
have been shown to exhibit in reality, rather than what we think we're "supposed"
to do. "We know people with autism think very concretely," said Laugeson. "Social
skills can be abstract behavior that's difficult to describe, but we try to break it into
concrete steps."

For example, PEERS will take the seemingly mundane, but actually complex act   12
of flirting and translate it into a step-by-step lesson. "First, a couple notices each
other across the room. They make eye contact and look away, and they look again and
they look away," said Laugeson. "The look away makes it known you're safe, but the
common error someone with autism can make is to stare, which can seem predatory
and scare a person." People with autism are also specifically instructed how to smile
and for how long, since "another common mistake is to smile really big rather than
giving a slight smile," said Laugeson. "A big smile can also be frightening."

Neuro-typical people often take flirting for granted as a fairly organic, coy, and even   13
fun back-and-forth, but for someone with autism, it is really a complex, nonsensical
interaction. "Flirting still doesn't make sense to me. It seems like a waste of time,"
said Plank, who worked on a video with Laugeson to teach his WrongPlanet community members how to flirt. "If you think about it logically, you say things you wouldn't
normally say, so it's harder. There are a whole other set of things you have to deal with."

While he didn't have PEERS to guide him, in college, Plank studied guys who were   14
always successful at picking up girls and started mimicking their behaviors. He quickly
realized acting confident was the key to dating success, especially if you're a man.

However, maintaining that confidence may be the hardest part of dating for   15
someone on the spectrum, because of their difficulty processing social cues from
others. "We will constantly not be able to read whether someone is interested, so you
can have an insecurity about whether the person you're dating likes you," said Plank.

In heterosexual courtships where men are still often expected to pursue women,   16
males with autism are at a distinct disadvantage to their female counterpart. "For guys
on the spectrum it's a one-way thing," said Robison. "We can be interested, but have
no way to tell if they're interested in us."

Some women with autism may ultimately have an edge in the dating world. A   17
common trait of people on the spectrum is being extremely logical and straightforward.
A blunt man may repulse women or get a slap in the face; think of how a woman would
react if a date told her yes, she did look fat in that dress, or consider the famous 1989
study where a female researcher received positive responses to her request for sex from
men on the street 69 to 75 percent of the time compared to her male counterpart who
received not a single yes. Women who are forward are prized for it. "Especially if they're
really attractive, neuro-typical guys appreciate when women are blunt," said Plank.

While Penzvalto doesn't necessarily think women with autism have it easier than   18
men, she has noticed that her neuro-typical dates have particularly valued many of
her autistic traits. "I've found that people who are neuro-typical really appreciate
the qualities that people on the spectrum possess: complete honesty and almost an
inability to lie," she said.

However, both sexes on the spectrum struggle equally with the fear of rejection.   19
Since so much of dating for adults with autism is trial by error, the risk of mistakes,
and often embarrassing ones, is high. Jeremy Hamburgh, a dating specialist for people
with special needs, including those on the autism spectrum, has noticed how hard
his clients take initial failure with dating. "The risk and rewards are very different for
people who are neuro-typical," he said. "The average neuro-typical person can go out

and meet ten people, and do well with one, and feel success, but for those with special needs, who have been rejected all their lives that can really hurt their self-esteem."

Plank has witnessed friends on the spectrum too quickly walk away from dating   20
for fear of rejection. "It's a numbers game in many ways and because people on the spectrum use black-and-white thinking, they think they're doing something wrong," he said. "I wish more people on the spectrum knew you need to practice, you need to go out on more dates."

Worse, is that people on the spectrum may turn the blame on themselves for not   21
exhibiting neuro-typical norms for dating and romance. While interviewing subjects on the spectrum for his documentary *Autism in Love*, filmmaker Matt Fuller noticed how, "When something is perceived as inappropriate, and it gets addressed, they will get embarrassed leading to a rabbit hole of self-deprecating thoughts." And Penzvalto, too, remembers feeling self-conscious and abnormal for her views of dating and romance. "I have struggled in the past with people telling me 'this is how it should be' and having sort of a crisis of maybe I just don't get it, maybe I'm wrong," she said.

In fact, it was during one of those types of fights in a relationship earlier this year   22
that Penzvalto decided to be evaluated for autism. She realized past boyfriends' frustrations over her "rigid thinking" and "boundary issue" could be explained by autism, and a subsequent psychological evaluation confirmed it. However, rather than alarmed, she felt relief.

Perhaps because she had spent so much of her life trying to "act" normal and conform   23
to others' expectations for romance, knowing she had autism has helped her become more comfortable with dating. It's a feeling not necessarily shared by all members on the spectrum, but realizing why she saw love and romance the way she does freed her from the pressure of neuro-typical standards. Now, she is following her own heart. "The number one freedom I found in the diagnosis is I don't need to really give into a partner's idea of what a relationship should or needs to look like," she said. "It's really liberating to know I've been living my life a certain way, and it turns out that that's okay."

EXAMINING THE READING

1. **Explanation** How do the needs of people on the autism spectrum differ from those of "neuro-typical" people (those not on the autism spectrum)?
2. **Cause** Why do uninformed people believe that an autistic person is incapable of having a romantic relationship?
3. **Characteristics** What characteristic(s) do autistic women possess that may give them an advantage in dating? How might this (these) characteristic(s) be advantageous.
4. **Vocabulary** Explain the meaning of each of the following words as it is used in the reading: *inherently* (para. 6), *dearth* (12), *mundane* (14), and *predatory* (14).

ANALYZING THE WRITER'S TECHNIQUE

1. **Source** How does the author's decision to include a quotation from a former Miss America contestant affect the reader's response to the article?

2. **Thesis** Restate Shire's thesis in your own words. How effective is it as the thesis of an extended definition essay? If you were revising her thesis, how might you change it?
3. **Introduction** Does the introduction provide all the background information you need to understand the essay? If not, what else should the author have included?
4. **Conclusion** Is the essay's conclusion satisfying? Why or why not?

VISUALIZING THE READING

Identify other patterns of development Shire uses in the essay. Complete the following chart by listing the pattern and providing an example of how each pattern is used.

Pattern of Development	Examples
Comparison-contrast	Dating for neuro-typical people vs. people on the autism spectrum (first date in a bar, para. 5; perceptions of flirting, 14; fear of rejection, 9, 21), men on the autism spectrum versus women on the autism spectrum (15–17)
Illustration	
Definition	
Process analysis	
Illustration	

FIGURE 18.4 Percentage of Children (Aged 6–17), Whose Parent(s) Report a Diagnosis of Autism Spectrum Disorder. *Source:* CDC/NCHS, *National Survey of Children's Health,* 2007 and 2001–2012.

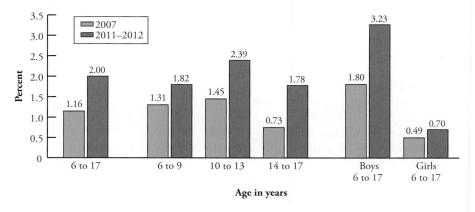

e **macmillanhighered.com/successfulwriting**
E-readings > *Chalk Talk: Tragedy of the Commons* (animation), The National Science Foundation

THINKING CRITICALLY ABOUT TEXT AND IMAGES

1. **Connotation** What connotation does the word *act* (para. 23) have? How does the use of quotation marks around the word affect your understanding of its meaning?
2. **Tone** Describe the tone of the essay. What does it reveal about Shire's attitude toward people on the autism spectrum?
3. **Sources** What types of sources does Shire use to support her thesis? What other types of sources might she have used to make her essay more convincing?
4. **Objectivity** How objective a view of people on the autism spectrum does Shire present? Identify any words, phrases, or examples that seem intended to influence the reader's emotional response to the article. Does her definition seem euphemistic or incomplete? Support your answers with evidence from the text.
5. **Visual** Examine Figure 18.4. Do you see any trends? How significant is the increase? What reasons, besides an actual increase in the number of children with autism spectrum disorder, may account for it?

RESPONDING TO THE READING

1. **Discussion** Discuss the challenges flirting, asking someone out, or even joining a conversation present. What "'ecologically valid' social skills" (para. 11) have you observed or practiced in these contexts? How would you instruct a younger friend or family member in the fine art of asking someone out on a date or joining a conversation among people you don't know well?
2. **Journal** Write a journal entry describing a time you (or someone you know) were totally misjudged or your motives were misunderstood.
3. **Essay** Write an essay defining a perfect date for your classmates.

WORKING TOGETHER

With a small group of fellow students, write a thirty-second public service announcement (PSA) promoting a class in responsible dating to share with the class. Start by naming the class, then brainstorm ideas, and write the PSA.

APPLYING YOUR SKILLS: ADDITIONAL ESSAY ASSIGNMENTS

Write an extended definition essay on one of the following topics, using what you learned in this chapter. Depending on your topic, you may need to conduct research.

For more on locating and documenting sources, see Part 5.

TO EXPRESS YOUR IDEAS

Choose a specific audience and write an essay defining and expressing your views on one of the following terms.

1. Parenting   2. Assertiveness   3. Sexual harassment

TO INFORM YOUR READER

4. Write an essay defining a term from a sport, hobby, or form of entertainment for a classmate who is unfamiliar with the term.
5. Write an essay for your instructor defining the characteristics of the "perfect job" you hope to hold after graduation.
6. Write an essay defining an important concept in a field of study, perhaps from one of your other courses. Your audience consists of students not enrolled in the course.

TO PERSUADE YOUR READER

"Freegans: They Live Off What We Throw Away" (pp. 434-37) addresses the issue of consumer waste and excess. Write an essay for readers of your local newspaper in which you define one of the terms listed below and demonstrate that the problem is either increasing or decreasing in your community.

7. Racism or ethnic stereotyping   8. Sexual discrimination   9. Age discrimination

CASES USING DEFINITION

10. You are a fifth-grade teacher working on a lesson plan entitled "What Is American Democracy?" How will you limit the term *American democracy* to define it for your audience? What characteristics and details will you include?
11. Write a press release for a new menu item as part of your job as public relations manager for a restaurant chain. First, choose the new menu item, and then define the item and describe its characteristics using sensory details.

SYNTHESIZING IDEAS

Culture

Both "Freegans: They Live Off What We Throw Away" (pp. 436–37) and "Guerrilla Street Art" (pp. 449–51) discuss the activities of a subculture: dumpster divers and graffiti artists.

Analyzing the Readings

1. In what ways does each self subgroup set itself apart from the larger society?
2. Write a journal entry exploring how some subgroups set themselves apart—for example, through dress, behavior, or language.

Essay Idea

Write an essay in which you explore a subgroup of college students, such as student democrats or vegans. Give examples of ways in which certain groups on campus set themselves apart through their language, their activities, or in some other way.

19

Cause and Effect
Using Reasons and Results to Explain

459

- understand the purpose and function of cause-and-effect essays,
- use graphic organizers to visualize cause-and-effect essays,
- integrate cause and effect into an essay,
- read and think critically about cause and effect, and
- plan, organize, draft, revise, and edit essays using cause and effect.

The paragraph you wrote in the Writing Quick Start is an example of **cause-and-effect** (or causal) **analysis** because it considered *causes* (why the disaster occurred), *effects* (what happened because of the disaster), or both. You probably use causal analysis every day. If you decide to get a good night's sleep rather than pull an all-nighter because you know you do better on exams when you're well rested, that's cause-effect analysis. Causal analysis is frequently required in college classes too, where you might be asked to analyze and write about the causes of the Civil War or the effects of oxygen deprivation on the central nervous system.

USING CAUSE AND EFFECT IN COLLEGE AND THE WORKPLACE

- For an essay exam in your *twentieth-century history course,* you are required to discuss the causes of U.S. involvement in the Korean War.

- For a *health and nutrition course*, you decide to write a paper on the relationship between diet and heart disease.

- For your job as an *investment analyst*, you need to explain why a certain company is likely to be profitable in the next year.

CHARACTERISTICS OF CAUSE-AND-EFFECT ESSAYS

A successful causal analysis essay fully explains the causes or effects that are the focus of the essay's thesis and presents those causes or effects in a logical order.

CAUSAL ANALYSIS MAY FOCUS ON CAUSES, EFFECTS, OR BOTH

Remember that *causes* are the reasons that something happened and *effects* are the results of the thing that happened. Some causes and effects are relatively easy to separate out.

CAUSE	EFFECT
You get a flat tire. ⟶	You are late for work.
You forget to mail a loan payment. ⟶	You receive a past-due notice.

EXERCISE 19.1 Identifying Causes

Alone or with a classmate, list one or more possible causes for each of the following events or phenomena.

1. You observe a peacock strutting down a city street.
2. The airline notifies you that the flight you had planned to take tonight has been canceled.
3. Your phone frequently rings once and then stops ringing.
4. Your town decides to fund a new public park.
5. A good friend keeps saying to you, "I'm too busy to get together with you."

EXERCISE 19.2 Identifying Effects

Alone or with a classmate, list one or more possible effects for each of the following events.

1. You leave your backpack containing your wallet on the bus.
2. You decide to change your major.
3. Your spouse is offered a job in a city five hundred miles away from where you live now.
4. You volunteer as a Big Brother or Big Sister.
5. A close relative becomes very ill.

But causal analysis can be complex when it deals with an event or phenomenon that has multiple causes, multiple effects, or both. For example, you probably chose the college you attend (*one effect*) for a number of reasons (*multiple causes*).

MULTIPLE CAUSES   **ONE EFFECT**

Courses available
Cost
Reputation   College attended
Distance

One cause may also have several effects. For instance, the decision to quit your part-time job (*one cause*) will have several results (*multiple effects*).

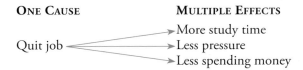

ONE CAUSE   **MULTIPLE EFFECTS**

                          More study time
Quit job   Less pressure
                          Less spending money

Related events or phenomena may have multiple causes and multiple effects. For instance, in urban areas, an increase in the number of police patrolling the street along with the formation of citizen watch groups (*multiple causes*) will result in less street crime and more small businesses moving into the neighborhood (*multiple effects*).

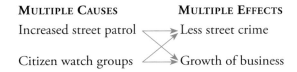

MULTIPLE CAUSES   **MULTIPLE EFFECTS**

Increased street patrol   Less street crime

Citizen watch groups   Growth of business

In some cases, a series of events forms a **chain of consequences**.

CAUSE	**EFFECT**	**EFFECT**	**EFFECT**
You cannot find your car keys.	You are late for class.	You miss a surprise quiz.	Your A quiz average is lowered to a B average.
	CAUSE	**CAUSE**	

Once you clearly identify causes and effects, you can decide whether to focus on causes, effects, or both.

CAUSAL ANALYSIS INCLUDES A CLEAR THESIS STATEMENT

An effective thesis statement for a cause-and-effect essay does the following.
- It identifies the topic.
- It makes an assertion about that topic.
- It suggests whether the essay focuses on causes, effects, or both.

CAUSES	The root *causes* of unsportsmanlike behavior lie in how society elevates athletes to positions of fame and heroism, making them unaccountable for their behavior.
EFFECTS	Unsportsmanlike behavior produces negative *effects* on fans, other players, and the institutions they represent.
CAUSES AND EFFECTS	Unsportsmanlike behavior has deep *roots* in society's inflated regard for athletes, producing negative *effects* on fans, other players, and the institutions they represent.

CAUSAL ANALYSIS IS LOGICALLY ORGANIZED

A good cause-and-effect essay is organized logically and systematically. You may present causes or effects in any logical order, but these are the most commonly used.
- *Chronological order*, the order in which causes or effects happened

   Example: An essay about causes of rising college tuition costs might begin with reasons for tuition increases in the late 1990s and move chronologically to current increases.

- *Most-to-least* or *least-to-most* order

   Example: An essay about increased immigration to the United States might begin with the most important causes and progress to less important causes.

CAUSAL ANALYSIS EXPLAINS EACH CAUSE OR EFFECT FULLY

A causal analysis essay should present each cause or effect in a detailed and understandable way. For most cause-and-effect essays, you will need to research your topic to find evidence that supports your thesis. For instance, in an essay about the effects on children of viewing violence on television, you might conduct research to locate facts or statistics that document changes in children's behavior after watching violent programs or expert opinion supporting this claim.

You might use another pattern of development (such as illustrations, descriptions, or comparisons) to explain causes or effects. For example, an essay about why dishonesty and lying are common in social media may include reasons, but also give examples or narrate incidents of dishonesty, categorize the characteristics of the social media environment that make lying easy, or contrast face-to-face communication with online communication.

CAUSAL ANALYSIS MAY CHALLENGE READERS' ASSUMPTIONS OR OFFER SURPRISING REASONS

Cause-and-effect essays that merely repeat commonplace causes or effects will discourage the audience from reading on. Engaging causal analyses, in contrast, surprise readers by challenging popular assumptions, offering surprising reasons, or including interesting evidence. For example, an essay on the effects of capital punishment might attempt to dispel the notion that it deters crime or it might surprise readers by contending that criminals are in fact deterred, but not for the reasons readers would be likely to assume.

Dealing with the causes or effects that readers assume to be primary is an effective strategy because it creates the impression that you have recognized other viewpoints and not overlooked important information. So essays that challenge readers' assumptions may first explain why the most popular explanation is false or inadequate before moving on to the writer's preferred cause or effect.

The following readings demonstrate the techniques for writing effective cause-and-effect essays. The first reading is annotated to point out how Maria Konnikova explains the connection between weather and mood. As you read the second essay, try to identify for yourself how Adam Alter uses the techniques of causal analysis to support his claim that labels shape identity.

Why Summer Makes Us Lazy

MARIA KONNIKOVA

Maria Konnikova is the author of *The New York Times* best seller *Mastermind: How to Think Like Sherlock Holmes* (2013). She has published numerous articles for publications such as *Scientific American, The Atlantic, Slate,* and *The Wall Street Journal.* In addition, she blogs for *Big Think* and *The New Yorker* magazine. The essay that appears here was originally published in *The New Yorker*'s Elements blog in 2013.

1   In his meticulous diaries, written from 1846 to 1882, the Harvard librarian John Langdon Sibley complains often about the withering summer heat: "The heat wilts & enervates me & makes me sick," he wrote in 1852. Sibley lived before the age of air-conditioning, but recent research suggests that his observation is still accurate: summer really does tend to be a time of reduced productivity. Our brains do, figuratively, wilt.

2   One of the key issues is motivation: when the weather is unpleasant, no one wants to go outside, but when the sun is shining, the air is warm, and the sky is blue, leisure calls. A 2008 study using data from the American Time Use Survey found that, on rainy days, men spent, on average, thirty more minutes at work than they did on comparatively sunny days. In 2012, a group of researchers from Harvard University and the University of North Carolina at Chapel Hill conducted a field study of Japanese bank workers and found a similar pattern: bad weather made workers more productive, as measured by the time it took them to complete assigned tasks in a loan-application process.

3   When the weather improved, in contrast, productivity fell. To determine why this was the case, the researchers assigned Harvard students data entry on either sunny or rainy days. The students were randomly assigned to one of two conditions: before starting to work, they were either shown six photographs of outdoor activities in nice weather, such as sailing or eating outdoors, or were asked to describe their daily routines. The researchers found that participants were less productive when they'd viewed pleasant outdoor photographs. Instead of focusing on their work, they focused on what they'd rather be doing—whether or not it was actually sunny or rainy outside (though the effect was stronger on sunny days). The mere thought of pleasant alternatives made people concentrate less.

4   But each season has its share of attractive days—and a skier's mind would likely have many opportunities to wander in the dead of winter. There's evidence, however, that in summer, our thinking itself may simply become lazier. In 1994, Gerald Clore, a pioneer in researching how ambient mood-altering phenomena affect cognition and judgment, found that pleasant weather can often lead to a disconcerting lapse in thoughtfulness. Clore's team approached a hundred and twenty-two undergraduates on days with either good or bad weather and asked them to participate in a survey on higher education. The better the weather, the easier it was to get the students to buy into a less-than-solid argument: on days that were sunny, clear, and warm, people were equally persuaded by both strong and weak arguments in favor of end-of-year comprehensive exams. When the weather was rainy, cloudy, and cold, their critical faculties improved: in that condition, only the strong argument was persuasive. Clore and his colleagues concluded that pleasant weather led people to embrace more heuristic-based thinking—that is, they relied heavily on mental shortcuts at the expense of actual analysis.

Thesis: Thesis suggests purpose of essay is to explain an established effect: that summer undermines productivity

Transition: "One" indicates first cause-effect relationship

Cause → Effect

Evidence: Cause-effect relationship supported by research studies (illustrations); interesting supporting evidence makes explanation of expected effect engaging. Sources cited informally; links to studies provided in original blog

Patterns of Development: Contrast, signaled by transition, indicates second cause-effect relationship

Evidence: Expert cited informally, credentials given

Summer weather—especially the muggy kind —may also reduce both our attention and our energy levels. In one study, high humidity lowered concentration and increased sleepiness among participants. The weather also hurt their ability to think critically: the hotter it got, the less likely they were to question what they were told.

The shift toward mindlessness may be rooted in our emotions. One common finding is a link between relative sunshine and happiness: although people who live in sunnier places, like Southern California, are no happier than those who live in the harsher conditions of the Midwest, day-to-day variations in sunshine make a difference. People get happier as days get longer and warmer in the approach to the summer solstice, and less happy as days get colder and shorter. They also report higher life satisfaction on relatively pleasant days. The happiest season, then, is summer.

A good mood, generally speaking, has in turn been linked to the same type of heuristic, relatively mindless thinking that Clore observed in his pleasant-weather participants. On the flip side, a bad mood tends to stimulate more rigorous analytical thought. Weather-related mood effects can thus play out in our real-life decisions—even weighty ones. In one recent project, the psychologist Uri Simonsohn found that students were more likely to enroll in a university that was famous for its academic rigor if they visited on days that were cloudy. When the weather turned sour, he concluded, the value they placed on academics increased.

There's a limit, however, to heat's ability to boost our mood: when temperatures reach the kind of summer highs that mark heat waves all over the world, the effect rapidly deteriorates. In a 2013 study of perceived well-being, the economist Marie Connolly found that on days when the temperature rose above ninety degrees, the negative impact on happiness levels was greater than the consequences of being widowed or divorced.

Conversely, the effects of heat on our brains aren't entirely negative. Many of the behaviors that psychologists study follow a so-called inverted-U pattern: as one factor steadily increases, a related behavior improves, plateaus, and then starts to deteriorate. A famous example of this is the Yerkes-Dodson curve, which charts the effect of stress on how well someone performs a given task. If we experience too little stress, or too much, our performance suffers. Like Goldilocks, we want to get it just right. Similarly, our cognitive abilities seem to improve up to a certain temperature, and then, as the temperature continues to rise, quickly diminish. An early study suggested that the optimal temperature hovered around seventy-two degrees Fahrenheit. A more recent review of the literature shows a target of twenty-seven degrees Celsius, or roughly eighty-one degrees Fahrenheit. (An important caveat, however, is that neither of these studies take humidity or sunshine into account, two major factors when it comes to assessing the influence of summer weather on behavior.)

Maybe best of all, blistering heat does give us a perfectly good reason to eat ice cream: studies have shown again and again that blood glucose levels are tied to cognitive performance and willpower. A bite of something frozen and sweet, boosting depleted glucose stores, might be just what a brain needs as the temperature spikes.

---

5 **Cause —→ Multiple Effects**

6 **Cause —→ Effect**

7 **Evidence:** Expert cited informally, credentials given

8 **Patterns of Development:** Contrast, illustration signaled by transitions

Evidence: Expert cited informally, credentials given

9 **Evidence:** Definition and illustration

Evidence: Comparison

Organization: Moves from more general cause (weather) to more specific cause (heat above/below a specific threshold) and alternates between positive and negative effects

10 **Conclusion:** Draws essay to a satisfying close providing a good reason to eat ice cream

VISUALIZING CAUSE-AND-EFFECT ESSAYS: THREE GRAPHIC ORGANIZERS

For more on creating a graphic organizer, see pp. 52–53.

The graphic organizers in Figures 19.1 through 19.3 show the basic organization of three types of causal-analysis essays.

- Figure 19.1 shows the organization of an essay that examines either causes *or* effects.
- Figure 19.2 shows the organization of an essay that examines a chain of causes and effects.
- Figure 19.3 shows two possible arrangements for an essay that focuses on multiple causes and effects.

All three types of causal analyses include an introduction (which identifies the event, provides background information, and states a thesis) as well as a conclusion. Notice in Figures 19.2 and 19.3 that causes are presented before effects. Although this is the typical arrangement, writers sometimes use the reverse organization, discussing effects first and then causes to create a sense of drama or surprise.

FIGURE 19.1 Graphic Organizer for an Essay on Causes or Effects

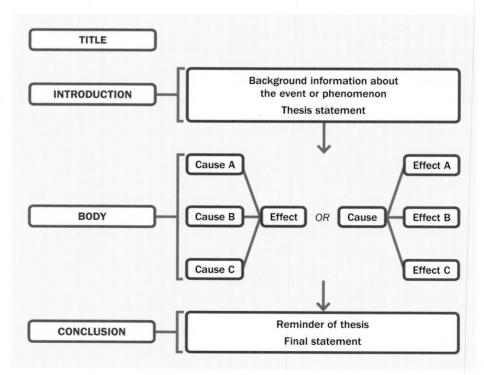

FIGURE 19.2 **Graphic Organizer for an Essay on a Chain of Causes and Effects**

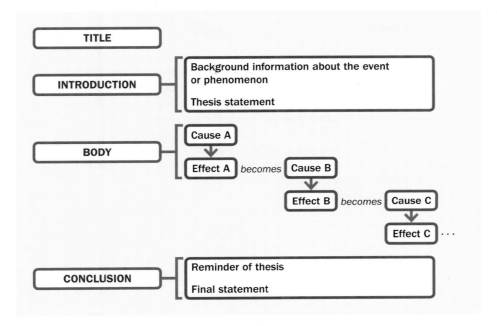

FIGURE 19.3 **Graphic Organizer for an Essay on Multiple Causes and Effects**

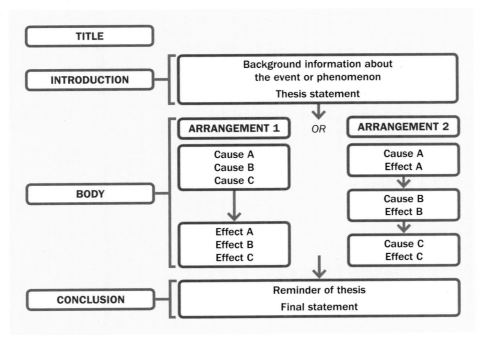

How Labels Like *Black* and *Working Class* Shape Your Identity

ADAM ALTER

Adam Alter is an assistant professor of marketing and psychology at New York University. His research focuses on decision making, and he has published numerous articles in academic journals in psychology. He has also published a number of articles for general readers in publications such as *The New York Times, The Wall Street Journal,* and *Psychology Today.* This reading is from Alter's 2013 book *Drunk Tank Pink and Other Unexpected Forces That Shape How We Think, Feel, and Behave.* Figure 19.4, a graphic organizer for "How Labels Like *Black* and *Working Class* Shape Your Identity," appears on page 471. Before studying that graphic organizer, read this causal analysis essay and highlight the effects that Alter names as resulting from racial and/or social labeling.

Long ago, humans began labeling and cataloguing each other. Eventually, lighter-skinned humans became "whites," darker-skinned humans became "blacks," and people with intermediate skin tones became "yellow-," "red-," and "brown-skinned." These labels don't reflect reality faithfully, and if you lined up 1,000 randomly selected people from across the earth, none of them would share exactly the same skin tone. Of course, the continuity of skin tone hasn't stopped humans from assigning each other to discrete categories like "black" and "white" — categories that have no basis in biology but nonetheless go on to determine the social, political, and economic well-being of their members. 1

Social labels aren't born dangerous. There's nothing inherently problematic about labeling a person "right-handed" or "black" or "working class," but those labels are harmful to the extent that they become associated with meaningful character traits. At one end of the spectrum, the label "right-handed" is relatively free of meaning. We don't have strong stereotypes about right-handed people, and calling someone right-handed isn't tantamount to calling them unfriendly or unintelligent. 2

In contrast, the terms "black" and "working class" are laden with the baggage of associations, perhaps some of them positive, but many of them negative. During the height of the civil-rights struggle, one teacher showed just how willingly children adopt new labels. On April 4, 1968, Martin Luther King Jr. was murdered, and the next day thousands of American children went to school with a combination of misinformation and confusion. In Riceville, Iowa, Stephen Armstrong asked his teacher, Jane Elliott, why "they shot that king." Elliott explained that the "king" was a man named King who was fighting against the discrimination of "Negroes." The class of white students was confused, so Elliott offered to show them what it might be like to experience discrimination themselves. 3

Elliott began by claiming that the blue-eyed children were better than the brown-eyed children. The children resisted at first. The brown-eyed majority was forced to 4 confront the possibility that they were inferior, and the blue-eyed minority faced a crisis when they realized that some of their closest friendships were now forbidden. Elliott explained that the brown-eyed children had too much melanin, a substance that darkens the eyes and makes people less intelligent. Melanin caused the "brownies," as Elliott labeled them, to be clumsy and lazy. Elliott asked the brownies to wear paper armbands — a deliberate reference to the yellow armbands that Jews were forced to wear during the Holocaust. Elliott reinforced the distinction by telling the brown-eyed children not to drink directly from the water fountain, as they might contaminate the blue-eyed children. Instead, the brownies were forced to drink from paper cups. Elliott also praised the blue-eyed children and offered them privileges, like a longer lunch break, while she criticized the brown-eyed children and forced them to end lunch early. By the end of the day, the blue-eyed children had become rude and unpleasant toward their classmates, while even the gregarious brown-eyed children were notice-ably timid and subservient.

News of Elliott's demonstration traveled quickly, and she was interviewed by Johnny   5
Carson. The interview lasted a few brief minutes, but its effects persist today. Elliott was pilloried by angry white viewers across the country. One angry white viewer scolded Elliott for exposing white children to the discrimination that black children face every day. Black children were accustomed to the experience, the viewer argued, but white children were fragile and might be scarred long after the demonstration ended. Elliott responded sharply by asking why we're so concerned about white chil-dren who experience this sort of treatment for a single day, while ignoring the pain of black children who experience the same treatment across their entire lives. Years later, Elliott's technique has been used in hundreds of classrooms and in workplace-discrimination training courses, where adults experience similar epiphanies. Elliott's approach shows how profoundly labels shape our treatment of other people and how even arbitrary damaging labels have the power to turn the brightest people into meek shadows of their potential selves.

Four years before Jane Elliott's classroom demonstration, two psychologists began   6
a remarkable experiment at a school in San Francisco. Robert Rosenthal and Lenore Jacobson set out to show that the recipe for academic achievement contains more than raw intellect and a dozen years of schooling. Rosenthal and Jacobson kept the details of the experiment hidden from the teachers, students, and parents; instead, they told the teachers that their test was designed to identify which students would improve academically over the coming year — students they labeled "academic bloomers." In truth, the test was an IQ measure with separate versions for each school grade, and it had nothing to do with academic blooming. As with any IQ test, some of the students scored quite well, some scored poorly, and many performed at the level expected from students of their age group.

The next phase of the experiment was both brilliant and controversial. Rosenthal   7
and Jacobson recorded the students' scores on the test, and then labeled a randomly chosen sample of the students as "academic bloomers." The bloomers performed

no differently from the other students — both groups had the same average IQ score — but their teachers were told to expect the bloomers to experience a rapid period of intellectual development during the following year.

When the new school year arrived, each teacher watched as a new crop of children filled the classroom. The teachers knew very little about each student, except whether they had been described as bloomers three months earlier. As they were chosen arbitrarily, the bloomers should have fared no differently from the remaining students. The students completed another year of school and, just before the year ended, Rosenthal and Jacobson administered the IQ test again. The results were remarkable. 8

The first and second graders who were labeled bloomers outperformed their peers by 10–15 IQ points. Four of every five bloomers experienced at least a 10-point improvement, but only half the non-bloomers improved their score by 10 points or more. Rosenthal and Jacobson had intervened to elevate a randomly chosen group of students above their relatively unlucky peers. Their intervention was limited to labeling the chosen students "bloomers," and remaining silent on the academic prospects of the overlooked majority. 9

Observers were stunned by these results, wondering how a simple label could elevate a child's IQ score a year later. When the teachers interacted with the "bloomers," they were primed to see academic progress. Each time a bloomer answered a question correctly, her answer seemed to be an early sign of academic achievement. Each time she answered a question incorrectly, her error was seen as an anomaly, swamped by the general sense that she was in the process of blooming. 10

During the year, then, the teachers praised these students for their successes, overlooked their failures, and devoted plenty of time and energy to the task of ensuring that they would grow to justify their promising academic labels. The label "bloomer" did not just resolve ambiguity, in other words — it changed the outcome for those students. 11

EXERCISE 19.3 | **Drawing a Graphic Organizer**

Using the graphic organizer in Figure 19.3 (Arrangement 2), draw a graphic organizer for "Why Summer Makes Us Lazy" (pp. 463–65).

INTEGRATING CAUSE AND EFFECT INTO AN ESSAY

For a reading that uses causal analysis as well as other patterns of development, see "Can Diet Help Stop Depression and Violence?" (pp. 484–87).

Although some of your essays will focus solely on causal analysis, other essays will combine cause and effect with other patterns. For example, in an essay comparing two popular magazines that have different journalistic styles, you might explain the effects of each style on the reading experience. Use the following tips to integrate causal analyses into essays that rely on other patterns of development.

1. **Introduce the causal analysis.** Use transitional words and expressions to prepare readers for a causal explanation. For example, in writing about your

FIGURE 19.4 Graphic Organizer for "How Labels Like *Black* and *Working Class* Shape Your Identity"

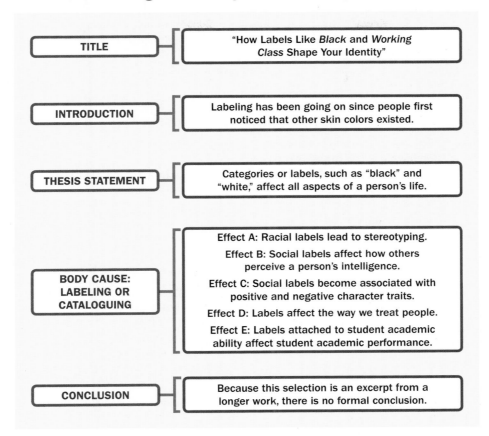

TITLE	"How Labels Like *Black* and *Working Class* Shape Your Identity"
INTRODUCTION	Labeling has been going on since people first noticed that other skin colors existed.
THESIS STATEMENT	Categories or labels, such as "black" and "white," affect all aspects of a person's life.
BODY CAUSE: LABELING OR CATALOGUING	Effect A: Racial labels lead to stereotyping. Effect B: Social labels affect how others perceive a person's intelligence. Effect C: Social labels become associated with positive and negative character traits. Effect D: Labels affect the way we treat people. Effect E: Labels attached to student academic ability affect student academic performance.
CONCLUSION	Because this selection is an excerpt from a longer work, there is no formal conclusion.

college president's decision to expand the Career Planning Center, you might introduce your discussion of causes by writing, "Three primary factors were responsible for her decision."

2. **Keep the causal explanation direct and simple.** Since your overall purpose is not to explore causal relationships, an in-depth analysis of causes and effects will distract readers from your main point. So focus on only the most important causes and effects.

3. **Use causal analysis to emphasize why particular points or ideas are important.** For example, if you are writing an explanation of how to hold a successful yard sale, your readers are more likely to follow your advice to keep the house locked and valuables concealed if you include anecdotes and statistics that demonstrate the effects of not doing so (such as thefts and break-ins during such sales).

READING ACTIVELY AND THINKING CRITICALLY

For more on reading actively, see Chapter 3; for more on thinking critically, see Chapter 4.

Reading and thinking critically about cause-effect essays requires careful analysis and close attention to detail. The overall questions to keep in mind are these.

- What is the relationship between the events or phenomena the writer is describing and the proposed causes or effects?
- Has the writer depicted this relationship accurately and completely?

WHAT TO LOOK FOR, HIGHLIGHT, AND ANNOTATE

Use the following suggestions when reading text that deals with causes and effects:

For more about previewing, see pp. 45–48.

1. **Preview.** Preview the essay to get an overview of its content and organization.
2. **Identify the causal relationship.** Read the essay through, highlighting the thesis and trying to determine whether the author is focusing on causes, effects, or both. Be alert for key words that signal a causal relationship. A writer may not always use obvious transitional words and phrases. Notice how each of the following examples suggest a cause or effect connection.

CAUSES	EFFECTS
One *source* of confusion on the issue of gun control is . . .	One *effect* of the Supreme Court decision was . . .
A court's decision *is motivated by* . . .	One *result* of a change in favored-nation status may be . . .

Draw a graphic organizer to map a complex causal relationship, sorting causes from effects (see Figures 19.1, 19.2, and 19.3).

3. **Establish the sequence of events.** Some essays may discuss effects before presenting causes; others may not mention the key events in a complex series of events in the order they occurred. Use your computer to draw a time line or write a list of the events in chronological order.
4. **Think about the meaning.** Reread the essay once again, this time concentrating on its meaning by answering the following questions:
   - What is the writer's purpose in writing this essay? For what audience is it intended? How did the writer's purpose and audience influence the causal relationship he or she analyzed?
   - How well does the writer explain the causal relationship(s)? Identify any causes or effects that you find confusing or that you do not find convincing.
5. **Consider your reactions.** Consider how the essay relates to your own experience. For example, how might your development have been influenced by labels, such as *A-student* or *difficult child*? Think of other possible causes or effects the writer does not mention. In a chain-of-events essay, think about what might have happened if the chain had been broken at some point.

ANALYZING CAUSE AND EFFECT

Reading and evaluating causal relationships involves close analysis and may require that you do research to verify a writer's assertions. Use the following questions to think critically about the causal analyses you read.

What is the writer's purpose? Consider how the writer describes certain causes or effects and how this description advances his or her purpose. For example, it may persuade readers to adopt a particular position on an issue: A detailed description of the physical effects of an experimental drug on laboratory animals may strengthen an argument against the use of animals in medical research.

Does the writer cover all major causes or effects fairly? Consider whether the writer presents a fair description of all major causes or effects. For example, a writer arguing in favor of using animals for medical research might fail to mention the painful effects of testing on laboratory animals. Conversely, a writer who opposes using animals for medical research might fail to mention that several human diseases are now controllable as a result of tests performed on animals. In either case, the writer does not offer a complete, objective, or fair account of the controversy.

Does the writer provide sufficient evidence for the causal relationship? Determine whether the writer provides *sufficient* supporting evidence to prove the existence of a causal relationship between events or phenomena. For example, suppose a writer makes this assertion: "Medical doctors waste the resources of health insurance companies by ordering unnecessary medical tests." For support, the writer relies on one example involving a grandparent who was required to undergo twenty-two tests and procedures before being approved for minor outpatient surgery. This anecdote is relevant to the writer's assertion, but one person's experience is not enough to prove a causal relationship. Consider whether the writer might have provided additional support (such as statistics and expert opinion) or whether adequate support could not be found for the assertion.

Does the writer avoid common reasoning errors? Stay alert to common errors in reasoning, such as **confusing chronology with causation** (the *post hoc, ergo propter hoc* ("after this, therefore because of this) fallacy, in which the writer assumes that event A caused event B simply because B followed A. Superstitious thought is often based on this fallacy. (Carrying a rabbit's foot, for example, does *not* cause a streak of good luck.) Similarly, a writer may **mistake correlation with causation** and assume that just because two events occur at about the same time that they are causally related. For example, an increase in sales of both snow shovels and mittens does not mean that snow shoveling causes people to buy more mittens. More likely, a period of cold, snowy weather caused the increased sales of both items. A third type of logical problem occurs when a writer **misidentifies causal relationships.** For example, consider the relationship between failure in school and personal problems. Does failure in school cause personal problems, or do personal problems cause failure in school? In some cases a third factor, such as an inappropriate classroom environment, may be the cause of both the failure and the problems. Be sure the writer provides evidence that a causal relationship not only exists but also works in the direction the writer thinks it does.

YOUR ESSAY ASSIGNMENT

Write a causal analysis essay on a topic that you believe would interest readers of your college newspaper. You may consider causes, effects, or both. Below are some options:

- the popularity (or lack of popularity) of a public figure,
- cheating on college exams,
- a current trend or fad,
- a major change or decision in your life, and
- a problem or event on campus or in the community.

Prewriting

1 **Select a topic from the list above, or create one of your own.**

Consider the **length** of your essay as you choose your **topic** and decide whether to write about **causes**, **effects**, or **both**.

Example: You couldn't explore fully both causes and effects of child abuse in a five-page paper.

2 **Consider your purpose and audience, and choose a point of view.**

Ask yourself these questions.

- What is my **purpose**? A cause-and-effect essay for a college course may be both **informative** and **persuasive**.

  Example: An essay on academic cheating could examine the causes (informative) and propose policies to help alleviate the problem (persuasive).

- Who is my **audience**? How much do my readers **already know** about the topic? If your readers are **unfamiliar** with the topic you are writing about (or if the topic is complex), limit your focus to **the most important, obvious**, and **easily understood** causes or effects. If your audience is **generally familiar** with your topic, then you can deal with **less obvious** or **more complex causes or effects**. Take into consideration what your readers will think are the most likely causes or effects.
- What **point of view** is most appropriate given my purpose and audience? Although academic writing usually uses the **third person** (*he, she, they*), you might use the **first person** (*I*) to relate relevant personal experiences.

*The writing process is *recursive*; that is, you may find yourself revising as you draft or prewriting as you revise. This is especially true when writing on a computer. Your writing process may also differ from that of your classmates, depending on your preferred learning style.

simultaneously presenting the music industry with unique opportunities to popularize new artists in ways that weren't possible before.

The most noticeable effect of the digitized music has been piracy, or the illegal downloading of music files and the subsequent decline in CD sales. At its peak in 2001, music industry revenue was $38 billion, but between 1999 and 2012, it lost almost half of that as CD sales plummeted (Pfanner 2013). Once pirating songs and albums from the Internet became an easy alternative for music consumers all over the world, CDs and other physical forms of recorded music started to become obsolete. A trade organization called the International Federation of the Phonographic Industry has claimed that digital piracy can account for the worldwide decline in music sales over the past decade (Pfanner 2010). While it's difficult to measure the financial effect on artists, the *New York Times* estimates that the music industry has lost hundreds of billions of dollars (Internet Piracy 2011). The digitization of music has enabled millions of Internet users to access music at no cost without leaving their homes, reducing sales for record companies worldwide.

The rise of legal methods of listening to digital music, a product of a rapidly evolving music industry, has also become a financial burden on musicians and their labels. As the digital piracy problem has grown, Internet companies have begun seeking ways to offer music for free, while earning money from advertising. Music streaming services such as Pandora and Spotify are available for free in certain countries to those with Internet access. However, the money they receive for playing advertisements to listeners doesn't add up to what musicians and record companies used to earn from CD sales. Music labels earn somewhere between 0.4 and 0.7 cents per stream on Spotify, which adds up to $4,000 to $7,000 per million streams. The executive of BMG Rights Management noted that with that level of payment, almost no artists could make it professionally (Sisario 2013). The shift from a CD economy to a digital music economy has decreased the profitability of music recording and distribution.

Furthermore, as the digitalization of music presents record labels with serious revenue loss, the effect is twofold. The problem of declining sales is compounded by the fact that record labels often use surplus funds to invest in new talent (Pfanner 2010). If labels are suffering shortages, there is less

---

2 **Effect 1 (negative):** Identified in topic sentence. Suggests that effects will be presented in most-to-least order

Transition: Transition emphasizes cause-effect relationship

Support: Uses evidence from sources as support

3 **Effect 2 (negative):** Announced in topic sentence

4 **Effect 3 (negative):** Announced in topic sentence

of a chance that young or up-and-coming musicians will find the means to gain new listeners. In this way, the rise of digital music exchange is actually helping to stifle new work.

Effect 4 (positive): Announced in topic sentence

Support: Uses example as evidence

Another consequence of computers and internet access becoming more widely available is that new or aspiring artists find it easier to record and circulate their own music. Tyler Ward, a 24-year-old amateur singer and songwriter featured on NPR's *The Record*, tried out recording and posting cover songs on YouTube and ended up performing on the Ellen DeGeneres Show and touring the U.S., Canada, and Europe (Nelson 2013). Whereas before the digital era, artists had to fight hard to publicize their albums, now anyone with an Internet signal and recording capability has a shot at being discovered. Big names like Justin Bieber and Soulja Boy were all made famous by the video-sharing website YouTube (Greene n.d.). While musicians used to pay to put their songs on vinyl, budding artists can now upload their music to the Internet for free and even sell their tracks from online platforms. With Bandcamp.com, musicians can upload their music and charge whatever download fee they choose. The Internet has equipped musicians with tools to help them get started.

Effect 5 (positive): Announced in topic sentence; transition highlights contrast with pre-digital era

Though the music industry has lost money because of digital piracy and declining CD sales, this very shift to a digitized economy has also produced the concept of online crowdfunding, a new way for musicians to raise money. Fundraising, too, has gone digital, and musicians can take advantage of a digitally engaged fan base and raise money electronically. Amanda Palmer, a singer and composer, raised over one million dollars through crowdfunding in the summer of 2012 and used the money to produce an album (Kelley 2012). Not only can artists reach out more directly to their fans to ask for money, but also more of those earnings go straight to the artist, rather than to record labels. Although Bandcamp takes a 15% share of its users' profits, the rest of the money goes directly to artists (Shotwell 2010). What profits the Internet has cut from the music industry by enabling piracy and low-paying streaming services, it has begun to return in the form of independent funding opportunities for new and amateur musicians.

Effect 6 (positive): Announced in topic sentence; transitions highlight shift to new effect uses contrast and examples as support

Yet another consequence of the Digital Age that boosts promising new musicians is the far-reaching effects of social media and social networks. While the charts used to be topped by big-name labels and radio hits, recent hits, such as Carly Rae Jepsen's "Call Me Maybe," have made it

5

6

7

to the mainstream with help from YouTube and Twitter (Sisario 2012). Since these marketing channels are free, artists have an easier time than ever before disseminating their songs or albums to a large audience.

Since the beginning of the Digital Age, the evolution of music production has been momentous and complex, with both serious financial repercussions and more positive effects for new musicians looking to share their art. Rather than trying to halt these changes, artists would do well to embrace the creative challenges posed by the digital music industry. While the negative effects of music's digitalization on industry profit may cloud our vision, our increasing capability to tap into a whole world's worth of musicians, and not just those signed to big labels, is exhilarating.

8   **Conclusion:** Revisits thesis and lends closure by emphasizing opportunities

Works Cited

Harmon, Amy. "Napster Users Mourn End of Free Music." *The New York Times*, 1 Nov. 2000, www.nytimes.com/2000/11/01/business/technology -napster-users-mourn-end-of-free-music.html.

Greene, Amanda. "Ten YouTube Success Stories." *Woman's Day*, 8 july 2010, www.womansday.com/life/entertainment/a1731/10-youtube-success -stories-108958/.

"Internet Piracy and How to Stop It." *The New York Times*, 8 June 2011, www.nytimes.com/2011/06/09/opinion/09thu1.html?_r=0. Editorial.

Kelley, Frannie. "Crowd Funding for Musicians Isn't the Future; It's the Present." *The Record: Music News from NPR*, 25 Sept. 2012, www.npr .org/blogs/therecord/2012/09/25/161702900/crowd-funding-for-musicians -isnt-the-future-its-the-present.

Nelson, Noah. "Covering Pop Hits on YouTube Is Starting to Pay." *The Record: Music News from NPR*, 13 May 2013, www.npr.org/sections/ therecord/2013/05/13/182880665/covering-pop-hits-on-youtube-is -starting-to-pay.

Pfanner, Eric. "Music Industry Sales Rise, and Digital Revenue Gets Credit." *The New York Times*, 26 Feb. 2013, www.nytimes.com/2013/02/27/ technology/music-industry-records-first-revenue-increase-since-1999.html.

---. "Music Industry Counts the Cost of Piracy." *The New York Times*, 21 Jan. 2010, www.nytimes.com/2010/01/22/business/global/22music.html.

Shotwell, James. "Bandcamp.com Changes Business Model." *Alternative Press,* 20 July 2010, www.altpress.com/news/entry/bandcamp.com _changes_business_model.

Sisario, Ben. "The New Rise of a Summer Hit: Tweet It Maybe." *The New York Times*, 21 Aug. 2012, www.nytimes.com/2012/08/22/business/media/ how-call-me-maybe-and-social-media-are-upending-music.html.

---. "As Music Streaming Grows, Royalties Slow to a Trickle." *The New York Times,* 28 Jan. 2013, www.nytimes.com/2013/01/29/business/media/ streaming-shakes-up-music-industrys-model-for-royalties.html.

ANALYZING THE WRITER'S TECHNIQUE

1. **Purpose** Describe Adamczak's purpose.
2. **Patterns** What other patterns of development does Adamczak use to support his thesis and maintain readers' interest?
3. **Introduction and Conclusion** Evaluate Adamczak's introduction and conclusion. How effectively do they stimulate the reader's interest and lend closure to the essay?

THINKING CRITICALLY ABOUT CAUSE AND EFFECT

1. **Tone** Describe the tone of Adamczak's essay. What words and phrases suggest his attitude toward the changes in the music industry? Given his tone, who do you think was his audience?
2. **Additional Viewpoints** In paragraph 3, Adamczak paraphrases a comment from a BMG Rights Management executive. How might Adamczak's essay have changed if he had included the viewpoints of veteran and aspiring musicians?
3. **Objectivity** How objective does Adamczak seem in his evaluation of the changes in the music industry? Use evidence from the essay to support your claim.

RESPONDING TO THE ESSAY

1. **Discussion** Do you regularly download music from the Internet? Do you use a streaming service? If so, consider how your Internet practices have contributed to the decreased profitability of the music business. Should you support musicians by buying their music from a service like Bandcamp or by contributing to crowdsourcing efforts? Why or why not?
2. **Reaction** Adamczak mentions several effects of the digitization of the music business. What other effects may he have overlooked? For example, he did not explicitly focus on the effects digitization have had on those who enjoy listening to music.
3. **Journal** Adamczak focused on both the negative and the positive effects of the Internet on the music industry. Write a journal entry describing both the negative and positive effects that some other aspect of the Internet (such as social networking or online shopping) has had on your life.

Can Diet Help Stop Depression and Violence?

JURRIAAN KAMP

Jurriaan Kamp is the author of *Because People Matter: Building an Economy That Works for Everyone* and *Small Change: How Fifty Dollars Can Change the World*. He has worked on the staff of the European Parliament; as a freelance newspaper correspondent in India; and as chief economics editor of the *NRC Handelsblad*, a leading Dutch newspaper. In 1994, Kamp and Hélène de Puy, his wife, started the progressive monthly magazine *Ode* (now, *The Intelligent Optimist*), which focuses on solutions to environmental issues and problems facing the human race. Currently, Kamp is president and editor-in-chief of *The Intelligent Optimist*. As you read the essay that follows, highlight the results of each scientific study that Kamp uses to support the cause-and-effect relationship he proposes.

1   The best way to curb aggression in prisons? Longer jail terms, maybe, or stricter security measures? How about more sports and exercise? Try fish oil. How can children enhance their learning abilities at school? A well-balanced diet and safe, stimulating classrooms are essential, but fish oil can provide an important extra boost. Is there a simple, natural way to improve mood and ward off depression? Yoga and meditation are great, but—you guessed it—fish oil can also help do the trick. A diet rich in vitamins, minerals, and fatty acids like omega-3 is the basis for physical well-being. Everybody knows that. But research increasingly suggests that these same ingredients are crucial to psychological health too. And that's a fact a lot of people seem to find hard to swallow.

2   The relationship between nutrition and aggression is a case in point. In 2002, Bernard Gesch, a physiologist at Oxford University, investigated the effects of nutritional supplements on inmates in British prisons. Working with 231 detainees for four months, Gesch gave half the group of men, ages eighteen to twenty-one, multivitamin, mineral, and fatty-acid supplements with meals. The other half received placebos. During the study, Gesch observed that minor infractions of prison rules fell by 26 percent among men given the supplements, while rule-breaking behavior in the placebo group barely budged. The research showed more dramatic results for aggressive behavior. Incidents of violence among the group taking supplements dropped 37 percent, while the behavior of the other prisoners did not change.

3   Gesch's findings were recently replicated in the Netherlands, where researchers at Radboud University in Nijmegen conducted a similar study for the Dutch National Agency of Correctional Institutions. Of the 221 inmates, ages eighteen to twenty-five, who participated in the Dutch study, 116 were given daily supplements containing vitamins, minerals, and omega-3 for one to three months. The other 105 received placebos. Reports of violence and aggression declined by 34 percent among the group given supplements; at the same time, such reports among the placebo group rose 13 percent.

4   Gesch is quick to emphasize that nutritional supplements are not magic bullets against aggression, and that these studies are just "promising evidence" of the link between nutrition and behavior. "It is not suggested that nutrition is the only explanation of antisocial behavior," he says, "only that it might form a significant part."

But Gesch is just as quick to emphasize that there is no down side to better nutrition, and in prisons in particular, the cost of an improved diet would be a fraction of the cost of other ways of addressing the problem of violence among inmates. Still, the menu in British prisons hasn't changed in the five years since Gesch published his results, even though the former chief inspector of prisons in the United Kingdom, Lord Ramsbotham, told the British newspaper the *Guardian* last year that he is now "absolutely convinced that there is a direct link between diet and antisocial behavior, both that bad diet causes bad behavior and that good diet prevents it."

Yet the effect of nutrition on psychological health and behavior is still controversial, at least in part because it is so hard to study. Our moods, emotions, and actions are influenced by so many factors: everything from our genes to our communities to our personal relationships. How can the role of diet be isolated among all these competing influences? That's exactly why Gesch conducted his study in prisons. In a prison, there are far fewer variables, since all detainees have the same routine. Do the results of the inmate trials reach beyond the prison walls? Gesch thinks so: "If it works in prisons, it should work in the community and the society at large. If it works in the United Kingdom and in the Netherlands, it should work in the rest of the world." 5

Another place improved nutrition seems to be working is in the city of Durham in northeastern England. There, Alex Richardson, a physiologist at Oxford University, conducted a study at twelve local primary schools. The research examined 117 children ages five to twelve, all of whom were of average ability but were underachieving. Instructors suspected dyspraxia, a condition that interferes with coordination and motor skills and is thought to affect at least 5 percent of British children. Possible signs of dyspraxia *may* include having trouble tying shoelaces or maintaining balance. The condition frequently overlaps with dyslexia and attention deficit hyperactive disorder (ADHD), and is part of a range of conditions that include autistic-spectrum disorders. 6

Half the group of children in Richardson's study was given an omega-3 supplement for three months; the other half received an olive oil placebo. The results: Children given the omega-3 supplements did substantially better at school than those in the control group. When it came to spelling, for example, the omega-3 group performed twice as well as expected, whereas the control group continued to fall behind. 7

Richardson came to the study of nutrition through neurology. Her interest was sparked by the rapid rise of conditions like ADHD, autism, dyslexia, and dyspraxia. The incidence of these disorders has increased fourfold in the past fifteen to twenty years. "These disorders overlap considerably," she says, "but a real solution is rarely offered. A dyslexic child is assigned a special teacher. A kid with dyspraxia is sent to a physical therapist. One with ADHD is prescribed Ritalin. And you've got to learn to live with autism." But as Richardson writes in *They Are What You Feed Them*: "There is always something that can be done. Don't ever believe it if anyone tells you otherwise." One of the things that can be done, according to Richardson, is to boost your child's intake of omega-3. 8

Of course, omega-3 is not the only answer to ADHD, autism, dyslexia, dyspraxia, or other psychological or behavioral disorders, which also include Alzheimer's disease. Studies like Richardson's suggest, however, that it may play an important role in stimulating the brain, keeping it healthy, and helping it ward off debilitating conditions. 9

And it looks like we need all the help we can get. Behavioral dysfunctions like ADHD 10 are currently the fastest-growing type of disorder worldwide. Twenty years ago, no one had even heard of ADHD. Today, everyone knows a kid who is taking Ritalin. The World Health Organization (WHO) estimates that the number of people with psychological disorders will double by 2020—and that around that time, depression will surpass heart and vascular disease as the No. 1 most preventable cause of death. The WHO adds that psychological disorders account for four of the ten most common causes of disability and that a quarter of the general population will be affected by them at some point in their lives.

So what's a consumer to do? Eat fish. Working with the U.S. National Institutes of 11 Health (NIH), American physician and psychiatrist Joseph Hibbeln compared data on fish consumption with figures on depression and murder in a large number of countries around the world. Fish are a rich and ready source of omega-3. In countries in which fish consumption is low, Hibbeln found that the likelihood of suffering from depression was up to fifty times greater than in countries where it is high.

Some 6.5 percent of New Zealanders suffer from severe depression; these citizens 12 also eat very little fish. In Japan, where fish consumption is high, 0.1 percent of the population suffers from depression. Manic depression (bipolar disorder) is rare in Iceland, which has the highest per capita fish consumption in the world, but is quite common in Brazil and Germany, where people don't eat as much fish. Hibbeln also found that, on average, the risk of being murdered is thirty times greater in countries where fish consumption is low compared to countries where it is high.

Cultural and other factors certainly influence these statistics, but the comparisons 13 are nevertheless illustrative. Overall, in subsequent trials, Hibbeln found that depressive and aggressive feelings diminished by about 50 percent after taking fish-oil capsules for two to four weeks. Based on this and other research, the WHO concluded in a report last year: "Certain dietary choices, including fish consumption, balanced intake of micronutrients, and a good nutritional status overall, also have been associated with reduced rates of violent behavior."

It almost sounds too good to be true, but research is beginning to confirm that vita- 14 mins, minerals, and fatty acids can reduce aggression and improve psychological well-being. That could be a simple recipe for a more peaceful world.

EXAMINING THE READING

1. **Summarizing** List the changes in behavior Kamp contends are affected by a diet rich in fish oil or omega-3s.
2. **Details** On what segment of the population did Bernard Gesch conduct his research? Why did he choose to use this group of people as his research subjects?
3. **Recommendations** According to Kamp, what kind of diet could help transform the world into a more peaceful place?

ANALYZING THE WRITER'S TECHNIQUE

1. **Thesis** Identify Kamp's thesis statement.
2. **Evidence** The author includes evidence from a research study conducted by Oxford University and says that the "findings were recently replicated in the

Netherlands." Why is it important for the results from scientific studies to be replicable (or repeatable)?

3. **Vocabulary** Explain the meaning of each of the following words as it is used in the reading: *placebos* (para. 2), *dyslexia* (6), *neurology* (8), *debilitating* (9), and *illustrative* (13).

THINKING CRITICALLY ABOUT CAUSE AND EFFECT

1. **Evaluation** Kamp sites research conducted in Britain and the Netherlands, but none conducted in the United States. He also includes studies that were conducted on very specific segments of the population. How might broadening his research strengthen the essay?
2. **Connotation** What is the connotation of the term *magic bullet* (para. 4)?
3. **Fact or Opinion** In paragraph 5, researcher Bernard Gesch is quoted as stating that if a change in diet "works in prisons, it should work in the community and the society at large." Is Gesch's statement fact or opinion? How do you know?
4. **Purpose** What does Kamp hope to accomplish by writing this essay?

RESPONDING TO THE READING

1. **Discussion** Kamp believes that many people are skeptical about the importance of nutrition to psychological health. Do you agree that this skepticism is widespread? Are you skeptical about the benefits of nutrition to mental health? Why or why not?
2. **Journal** Do you take vitamins or nutritional supplements? Write a journal entry in which you explain why you do or do not take them.
3. **Essay** Write an essay in which you identify one or more surprising ways in which a person could improve his or her mental health.

WORKING TOGETHER

Using the information in Kamp's essay, work with a partner to write an advertisement for fish oil. Your ad must include both words and images. Try to capture the attention of your readers and leave them with a message they will remember. Be prepared to share your advertisement with the class.

READING: CAUSE AND EFFECT COMBINED WITH OTHER PATTERNS

Dining in the Dark

CHARLES SPENCE AND **BETINA PIQUERAS-FISZMAN**

Charles Spence and Betina Piqueras-Fiszman are experimental psychologists at the Crossmodal Research Laboratory at Oxford University. Spence, the director of the laboratory, has published more than three hundred articles on multisensory research. Piqueras-Fiszman, a postdoctoral researcher for Oxford University and the New Zealand Institute for Plant and Food Research, has published numerous articles on food-related issues. This essay originally appeared in the British Psychological Society's magazine *The Psychologist* in December

2012. As you read "Dining in the Dark," highlight the reasons that people find dining in the dark to be such an appealing experience.

Many of us like to dine by romantic candlelight, but how about tucking in when it's impossible even to see your hand in front of your face? Since the opening of the Blindekuh (Blind Cow) restaurant in Zurich in 1999 and the Unsicht (which means invisible) Bar in Cologne, Germany, in 2001, the trend toward dining in the dark has become popular in the UK too, primarily in London, where several restaurants have been established since 2006. The trend has flourished too across Europe, North America and parts of Asia.

Pioneered by the likes of Axel Rudolph, psychologist, and owner of the Unsicht-Bar, the concept was developed with the idea of "shedding some light" on the sensory world of the blind. This empathic approach is meant—or better said, was originally meant—to place the blind at something of an advantage relative to their normally sighted counterparts. Nowadays, however, the dining experience at this kind of restaurant is actually very different from that of a blind person eating and drinking at a conventionally lighted establishment. The central question that we would like to address in this piece is what, exactly, makes a visit to one of these restaurants so appealing.

First off, it is worth noting that the food in such restaurants is normally served in bite-sized pieces and without bones. Thus, you are far more likely to find yourself with cubes of meat than with a T-bone steak, and with a side-serving of mashed potatoes, say, than with a helping of garden peas. It is, however, not only the presentational aspects of the food that differ when compared to a normal restaurant. Complex combinations of flavors are also notable by their absence. It turns out that diners can find it difficult to distinguish between flavors in the absence of visual cues. Nor is one offered a full menu: normally, the only decision to be made is between meat, fish, or the vegetarian option (though sometimes there may be a "surprise" option).

Furthermore, the names of the dishes often don't describe the food, or the way in which it will be (or has been) prepared. In fact, in many cases, the food descriptions are, quite simply, mystifying. Take, for example, the main course from the beef menu at Unsicht-Bar: "Upper nobility embraces the French underworld in a deep dark red river of sensuality." Here, it could be argued that the intention is to deliver a novel and surprising multisensory experience, especially since most of us are unlikely to have eaten in the dark before.

THE "EXPERIENCE ECONOMY"

One key driver behind the growth of dining-in-the-dark restaurants may be the influential idea of "The experience economy": The powerful notion here, one that has been around at least since Philip Kotler's classic paper on store atmospherics was published back in 1974, but which was re-popularized by Pine and Gilmore (1998, 1999), is that consumers are increasingly paying for "experiences" and not simply for products and services. Indeed, many of the most successful companies in recent years have managed to differentiate themselves in the marketplace by selling engaging multisensory experiences, while at the very same time offering products that aren't necessarily "la crème de la crème." Think only of Starbucks coffee (Luttinger & Dicum, 2006, p.159).

6 The dark dining concept fits right in here: what many of these contemporary restaurants are selling is very much "the experience," and one that is impossible to escape: "The mist at the Rainforest Café appeals serially to all five senses. It is first apparent as a sound: Sss-sss-zzz. Then you see the mist rising from the rocks and feel it soft and cool against your skin. Finally, you smell its tropical essence, and you taste (or imagine that you do) its freshness. What you can't be is unaffected by the mist." (Pine & Gilmore, 1998, p.104)

7 With dining in the dark, rather than delivering a more stimulating multisensory atmosphere or experience than the competition, the counterintuitive idea here is that less (intervening sensory input) can sometimes deliver more in terms of the overall customer experience. It could perhaps be argued that the dark dining concept also plays to the growing concern among some diners that delivering the "experience" has actually become more important than the food itself in certain eating establishments (e.g. Gill, 2007; Goldstein, 2005).

8 Taken together, then, there is certainly a sound business case for offering the dine-in-the-dark experience. But what is in it for the customer? Below, we critically evaluate the various arguments that have been put forward over the years in support of the concept.

WHAT HAPPENS TO OUR SENSES?

9 If, as gourmands often claim: "Eye appeal is half the meal," what happens if you cannot see the food you are eating? According to folk intuition, the result is a heightening of the other senses: "You smell better, you are more receptive to differences in texture, consistency and temperature. . . . it's a holistic experience" (Rudolph, cited in Read et al., 2011, p.16). But is it really true? The key question here concerns how the absence of one sense (in particular, vision, what many consider to be our most important sense) affects the perception of food via the other senses, and how our overall eating experiences are impacted as a consequence.

10 There are at least two competing influences on people's perception of food and drink when the lights go out. On the one hand, visual cues influence our sensory expectations regarding the taste and flavor of foods (e.g. Deliza & MacFie, 1996; Simmons et al., 2005; Spence, 2010a, 2010b). This is referred to by some as "visual flavor" (Spence et al., 2010). Our hedonic expectations (Hurling & Shepherd, 2003), our taste evaluations (Spence, 2011; Wilson & Gregson, 1967), and even our total food intake are determined, at least in part, by whatever it is that we happen to see (Linné et al., 2002; Wansink et al., 2005). In addition, a food's color often provides a reliable indicator as to its quality, to the ripeness of fruit, say, and the likely off-taint in

meat and fish. Hence, removing all such visual cues, which are normally available to us both prior to and during consumption is, we would argue, likely to diminish the overall dining experience (Spence, 2010b). No matter whether we realize it or not, sensory expectation and anticipation constitute a good part of the pleasure of a meal.

On the other hand, though, removing vision allows us to concentrate more on the taste and aroma of food and drink (Marx et al., 2003; Wiesmann et al., 2006). We humans have only limited attentional capacity, and vision tends to capitalize on the available neural resources. As a result, we often don't pay as much attention to the other senses as perhaps we should. Indeed, more often than not, what we see ultimately determines what we perceive, even when the other senses may be sending our brains a different message. Coloring certain white wines red can, for example, fool both experts and novices alike into thinking that they are actually drinking a red wine (Spence, 2010a, 2010b). [11]

The key question here then is whether the tastes, aromas and flavors associated with the consumption of food and drink really do become more intense in the absence of vision. Thus far, the limited scientific evidence argues against this intuitive claim. For example, the participants in a study by Scheibehenne et al. (2010) gave similar liking ratings to food no matter whether they ate in darkness or not. This despite the fact that the participants claimed to have paid more attention to the taste of the food in the former case. Unfortunately, though, no assessment was made in this study of whether participants' ratings of flavor intensity were affected when the lights were turned off. [12]

That said, the participants reported that it was significantly more difficult to eat, and that they paid significantly less attention to how much they ate, under cover of darkness. This could be the reason why, when served a supersized portion, those who found themselves in darkness ate almost 20 per cent more than those who could see the supersized portion in front of them. What is more, in the dark, participants tended to underestimate the amount of food that they had eaten, while the reverse was true for those who ate under normal illumination conditions. The latter results might, then, tie-in with the surprise that many of us have experienced at the cinema when, after purchasing a tub of (usually oversized) popcorn, we suddenly realize, once the final credits start to roll, that we have only a few kernels left! [13]

Another factor that makes the experience of dining in the dark unique and, for some, rather unpleasant is the uncertainty associated with not recognizing what it is that we happen to be taking into our mouths and, ultimately, swallowing. This uncertainty may lead to decreased food acceptability ratings, and a decrease in people's willingness to try the food again subsequently (Yeomans et al., 2008). In the absence of visual cues, "ambiguous foods" (such as beef enchilada) are judged as less acceptable, and what is more, are less likely to be consumed again than when consumed under normal lighting conditions (Wansink et al., 2012). However, for those foods where the initial uncertainty is low, such as, for example, crackers, no such reduction in food acceptance, or intent to consume, was observed. Could that be part of the reason, then, why popcorn has become such a staple for those wishing to snack at the cinema? [14]

Returning to our earlier discussion, this might also be one of the main reasons 15
why chefs working at dining-in-the-dark restaurants tend to deliver flavors and dishes
that are easy for diners to recognize. One can only wonder what diners choosing the
"surprise menu" have to say on this topic, given that they don't even know whether
they will be getting fish or meat.

A lack of sensory expectations can even lead to confusion and to the illusory iden- 16
tification of flavors that are actually not present (Piqueras-Fiszman & Spence, 2011).
Here, one might also want to know what happens if we discover that what we have
eaten wasn't what we originally thought it was. Whenever we consume a food that
we can't recognize, we nevertheless still tend to create post-consumption beliefs
about what the food actually was. If those beliefs don't match the reality of the situation, should we eventually find out what the food really was, what are the likely
consequences?

CONCLUSIONS

Soup, roasted potatoes and meat. Veal? Chicken? Bread, and butter, which we spread
messily. Some pudding for dessert. Vanilla? I can't remember. It tasted like vanilla but
it might have been chocolate. Maybe it wasn't pudding but it seemed that way. None of
the food tasted very good. Bland, bad texture. Indiscernible tastes and textures. (Lane,
2010, in a review of the Blindekuh)

Although it's undoubtedly true that dining in the dark can make for a memo- 17
rable multisensory experience, the available evidence suggests that you shouldn't
go to such a restaurant if you are hoping that the absence of vision will necessarily
make the food and drink taste any better. For humans, as for many other species,
visual cues play a crucial role in our perception of flavor and in the control of our
appetitive behaviors. It turns out that our sensory expectations regarding food
or drink play a surprisingly large part in how we actually experience them. Hence,
the removal of this important source of sensory information is likely to cause a
detrimental effect in terms of the correct identification, and hence enjoyment, of
whatever it is that we happen to be consuming. It may also make the diner a little
apprehensive.

So, returning to the question with which we started this piece, what exactly 18
makes it appealing to visit one of these restaurants? Rather than making the food
and drink taste better, a claim that has yet to be substantiated empirically, or even
giving one the sense of how the blind experience food, we would like to suggest
that it's the feeling of constant unexpectedness that makes the experience so interesting for diners. In this regard, and this regard alone, dining-in-the-dark shares
something with the experience of diners at a typical molecular gastronomy restaurant (see Piqueras-Fiszman & Spence, 2012). Finally, it is perhaps worth noting that
although statistics regarding repeat customers at such restaurants are hard to come
by, a straw poll of our friends and colleagues suggests that while many enjoyed the
unusual sensory experience offered by dining in the dark, few expressed any desire
to repeat it.

References

Deliza, R. & MacFie, H.J.H. (1996). The generation of sensory expectation by external cues and its effect on sensory perception and hedonic ratings: A review. *Journal of Sensory Studies, 11,* 103–128.

Gill, A.A. (2007). *Table talk: Sweet and sour, salt and bitter.* London: Weidenfeld & Nicolson.

Goldstein, D. (2005). The play's the thing: Dining out in the new Russia. In C. Korsmeyer (Ed.) *The taste culture reader: Experiencing food and drink* (pp.359–371). Oxford: Berg.

Hurling, R. & Shepherd, R. (2003). Eating with your eyes: Effect of appearance on expectations of liking. *Appetite, 41,* 167–174.

Kotler, P. (1974). Atmospherics as a marketing tool. *Journal of Retailing, 49* (Winter), 48–64.

Lane, L. (2010). Eating blind. Retrieved 20 September 2012 from www.huffingtonpost.com/lea-lane/eating-blind_b_701736.html

Linné, Y., Barkeling, B., Rossner, S. & Rooth, P. (2002). Vision and eating behavior. *Obesity Research, 10,* 92–95.

Luttinger, N. & Dicum, G. (2006). *The coffee book: Anatomy of an industry from crop to the last drop.* New York: The New Press.

Marx, E., Stephan, T., Nolte, A. et al. (2003). Eye closure in darkness animates sensory systems. *NeuroImage, 19,* 924–934.

Pine, B.J., II & Gilmore, J.H. (1998). Welcome to the experience economy. *Harvard Business Review, 76*(4), 97–105.

Pine, B.J., II & Gilmore, J.H. (1999). *The experience economy: Work is theatre and every business is a stage.* Boston, MA: Harvard Business Review Press.

Piqueras-Fiszman, B. & Spence, C. (2011). Crossmodal correspondences in product packaging: Assessing color–flavor correspondences for potato chips (crisps). *Appetite, 57,* 753–757.

Piqueras-Fiszman, B. & Spence, C. (2012). Sensory incongruity in the food and beverage sector: Art, science, and commercialization. *Petit Propos Culinaires, 95,* 74–118.

Read, S., Sarasvathy, S., Dew, N. et al. (2011). *Effectual entrepreneurship.* New York: Routledge.

Rosenblum, L.D. (2010). *See what I am saying: The extraordinary powers of our five senses.* New York: Norton.

Rosenbluth, R., Grossman, E.S. & Kaitz, M. (2000). Performance of early-blind and sighted children on olfactory tasks. *Perception, 29,* 101–110.

Scheibehenne, B., Todd, P.M. & Wansink, B. (2010). Dining in the dark: The importance of visual cues for food consumption and satiety. *Appetite, 55,* 710–713.

Simmons, W.K., Martin, A. & Barsalou, L.W. (2005). Pictures of appetizing foods activate gustatory cortices for taste and reward. *Cerebral Cortex, 15,* 1602–1608.

Spence, C. (2010a). The color of wine — Part 1. *The World of Fine Wine, 28,* 122–129.

Spence, C. (2010b). The multisensory perception of flavour. *The Psychologist, 23,* 720–723.

Spence, C. (2011). Mouth-watering: The influence of environmental and cognitive factors on salivation and gustatory/flavour perception. *Journal of Texture Studies, 42,* 157–171.

Spence, C., Levitan, C., Shankar, M.U. & Zampini, M. (2010). Does food color influence taste and flavor perception in humans? *Chemosensory Perception, 3,* 68–84.

Wansink, B., Painter, J. & North, J. (2005). Bottomless bowls: Why visual cues of portion size may influence intake. *Obesity Research, 13,* 93–100.

Wansink, B., Shimizu, M., Cardello, A.V. & Wright, A.O. (2012). Dining in the dark: How uncertainty influences food acceptance in the absence of light. *Food Quality and Preference, 24,* 209–212.

Wiesmann, M., Kopietz, R., Albrecht, J. et al. (2006). Eye closure in darkness animates olfactory and gustatory cortical areas. *NeuroImage, 32,* 293–300.

Wilson, G.D. & Gregson, R.A.M. (1967). Effects of illumination on perceived intensity of acid tastes. *Australian Journal of Psychology, 19,* 69–73.

Yeomans, M., Chambers, L., Blumenthal, H. & Blake, A. (2008). The role of expectancy in sensory and hedonic evaluation. *Food Quality and Preference, 19,* 565–573.

EXAMINING THE READING

1. **Reason** Why did Axel Rudolph, one of the pioneers of dining in the dark, develop the concept?
2. **Contrast** How does a dining-in-the-dark menu differ from a conventional menu?
3. **Conclusion** What do the authors conclude about the overall appeal of dining in the dark?

ANALYZING THE WRITER'S TECHNIQUE

1. **Thesis** Identify Spence and Piqueras-Fiszman's thesis statement.
2. **Sources** The authors include a number of references to scientific studies. How do these references affect your reaction to their analysis? How do they affect the overall tone of the selection?
3. **Vocabulary** Explain the meaning of each of the following words as it is used in the reading: *empathic* (para. 3), *counterintuitive* (6), *hedonic* (9), *olfactory* (16), and *gustatory* (16). Refer to your dictionary as needed.

VISUALIZING THE READING

Spence and Piqueras-Fiszman identify numerous effects that dining in the dark has on diners' perception of the food they eat. Use the chart below to summarize these reasons. The first one is done for you.

Causes	Effects
Cause 1	We underestimate how much we have eaten.
Cause 2	
Cause 3	
Cause 4	
Cause 5	
Cause 6	

THINKING CRITICALLY ABOUT CAUSE AND EFFECT

To learn more about evaluating sources, see Chapter 22.

1. **Objectivity** Do the authors present an objective and fair assessment of the dining-in-the-dark experience? Justify your answer with evidence from the reading.
2. **Evidence** Spence and Piqueras-Fiszman cite a number of sources that they regard as authorities on the topic. Based on the information in the references list, explain

how you could determine whether the authors of those sources were in fact authorities on the topic. Going beyond the reference list, what other information could you use to determine whether a source was authoritative?

3. **Purpose and Audience** Why do you think the authors wrote this essay? Who do you think they expected to be reading this selection, and how might their intended audience have influenced the decisions they made as writers?

4. **Tone** How would you describe the tone of the essay? Use examples from the text to support your answer.

RESPONDING TO THE READING

1. **Discussion** Do you think a dining-in-the-dark restaurant would be successful in your city or town? Why or why not?

2. **Journal** Would you choose to eat in a dining-in-the-dark restaurant? Write a journal entry in which you explain your enthusiasm or your hesitancy. What do you think you would enjoy most about the experience? What would be the greatest obstacles for you to overcome?

3. **Essay** Think of your favorite dining experience, and write an essay explaining the reasons the experience is so appealing.

WORKING TOGETHER

In paragraph 4 of "Dining in the Dark," the authors present a mystifying description of a beef dish. The only hint of the identity of the dish is the "deep dark red river," which suggests the meat may have been cooked in red wine. Working with a small group of your peers and using the menu's description as an example, choose a simple meat, vegetable, salad, or dessert dish, and then write a mystifying description of it for a dine-in-the-dark restaurant. Be sure to include a subtle hint, so your classmates will be able to guess what your mystery dish is.

APPLYING YOUR SKILLS: ADDITIONAL ESSAY ASSIGNMENTS

Write a cause-and-effect essay on one of the following topics, using what you learned about causal analysis in this chapter. Depending on your topic, you may need to conduct research.

For more on locating and documenting sources, see Chapters 23 and 24.

e macmillanhighered.com/successfulwriting
E-readings > *The Reel Sounds of Violence* (podcast), On the Media/WNYC

TO EXPRESS YOUR IDEAS

1. Write an essay explaining the causes of a "bad day" you recently experienced.
2. Suppose you or a friend or relative won a large cash prize in a national contest. Write an essay about the effects of winning the prize.

TO INFORM YOUR READER

3. Young children frequently ask "*Why?*" Choose a *why* question you have been asked by a child or think of a *why* question you have always wondered about (Examples: Why is the sky blue? Why are sunsets red? Why do parrots learn to talk?). Write an essay answering your question. Your audience is young children.
4. Write an essay explaining how you coped with a stressful situation.
5. Write a memo to your supervisor at work explaining the effects of requiring employees to work overtime.

TO PERSUADE YOUR READER

6. Write a letter to the dean of academic affairs about a problem at your school. Discuss causes, effects, or both and propose a solution to the problem.
7. Write a letter to the editor of your local newspaper explaining the possible effects of a proposed change in your community and urging citizens to take action for or against it.
8. Write a letter to the sports editor of your city's newspaper. You are a fan of a professional sports team, and you just learned that the team has been sold to new owners who may move the team to a different city. In your letter, explain the effects on the city and the fans if the team moves away.

CASES USING CAUSE AND EFFECT

9. Your psychology professor invites you to participate in a panel discussion on the psychology of humor. You are required to research this question: What makes a joke funny? Conduct research on the topic and write a paper summarizing your findings for the panel discussion.
10. A controversy has arisen concerning the use of campus computer networks. Students use the college computer system to send personal email as well as to complete course-related tasks, and some students have complained that the campus network is being used to post messages on social networking sites that defame the character of other students. In a letter to the student newspaper, either defend the students' right to use the campus computer network to post such messages or call for a policy that limits such use. Give reasons in support of your position.

FIGURE 20.1 **Graphic Organizer for an Argument Essay**

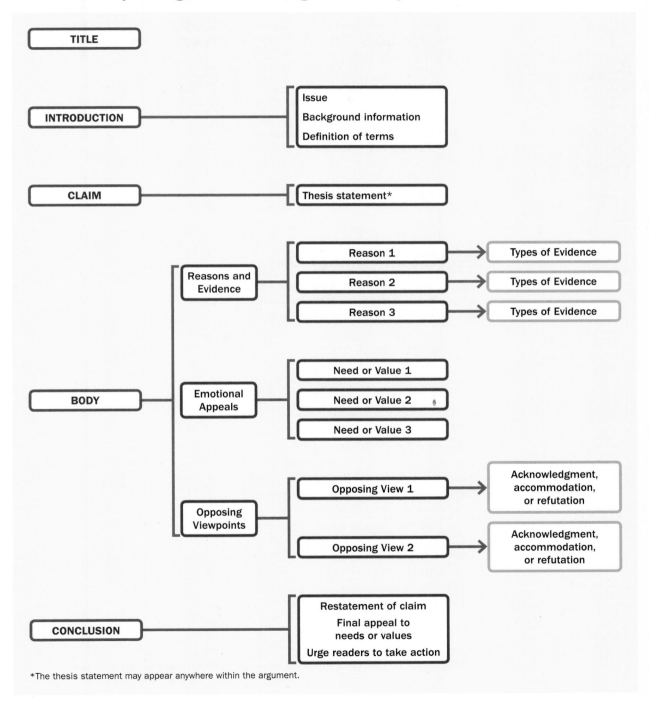

*The thesis statement may appear anywhere within the argument.

2. **Claims of value** are statements that express an opinion or judgment about whether one thing or idea is better or more desirable than other things or ideas. Issues involving questions of right or wrong, acceptable or unacceptable, often lead to claims of value. Since claims of value are subjective, they cannot be proved definitively.

> **EXAMPLE**   Doctor-assisted suicide is a violation of the Hippocratic oath and therefore should not be legalized.

3. **Claims of policy** are statements offering one or more solutions to a problem. Often the verbs *should, must,* or *ought* appear in the claim. Like claims of value, claims of policy cannot be proved definitively.

> **EXAMPLE**   The motion picture industry must accept greater responsibility for the consequences of violent films.

EXERCISE 20.1   **Writing Claims**

On your own or with one or two classmates, choose two of the following issues and write two different types of claims for each. For example, if one statement is a claim of value, the other should be a claim of policy or a claim of fact.

1. Legalization / decriminalization of marijuana
2. Stem cell research
3. Music piracy and the Internet
4. Protection for endangered species
5. Global warming and climate change

THE SUPPORT

The support in an argument consists of the ideas and information intended to convince readers that the claim is sound or believable. In Damon and Maria's conversation, Damon provides two key pieces of support.

1. People are forced to serve.
2. Potential jurors are treated like criminals.

Three common types of support are *reasons, evidence,* and *emotional appeals.*

Reasons. A **reason** is a general statement that backs up a claim. It explains why the writer's view on an issue is reasonable or correct. However, reasons alone are not sufficient support for an argument. Each reason must be supported by evidence and is sometimes accompanied by emotional appeals.

Evidence. The **evidence** provided in an argument usually consists of facts, statistics, examples, expert opinion, and observations from personal experience.

CLAIM	Reading aloud to preschool and kindergarten children improves their chances of success in school.
FACTS	First-grade children who were read to as preschoolers learned to read earlier than children who were not read to.
STATISTICS	A 1998 study by Robbins and Ehri demonstrated that reading aloud to children produced a 16 percent improvement in the children's ability to recognize words used in a story.
EXPERT OPINION	Pam Allyn, author of over sixty educational publications and well-known childhood literacy advocate urges parents to read aloud to their preschool children frequently.
EXAMPLES	Stories about unfamiliar places or activities increase a child's vocabulary. For example, reading a story about a farm to a child who lives in a city apartment will acquaint the child with such new terms as *barn, silo,* and *tractor.*
PERSONAL EXPERIENCE	When I read to my three-year-old son, I notice that he points to and tries to repeat words.

Emotional appeals. Emotional appeals evoke the **needs** or **values** that readers are likely to share.

- **Appealing to needs:** People have both physiological **needs** (food and drink, health, shelter, safety, sex) and psychological needs (a sense of belonging or accomplishment, self-esteem, recognition by others, self-fulfillment). Your friends and family, people who write letters to the editor, personnel directors who write job listings, and advertisers all appeal to needs, directly or indirectly.
- **Appealing to values:** A **value** is a principle or quality that is considered important, worthwhile, or desirable, such as freedom, justice, loyalty, friendship, patriotism, duty, and equality. Arguments often appeal to values that the writer assumes most readers will share.

The public service announcement on the following page appeals to both viewers' needs and values. The picture of the cute dog appeals to viewers' needs by evoking the emotional attachment to companion animals (either our own or other people's pets) that many of us share. The text, "a person is the best thing to happen to a shelter pet," also appeals to viewers' need to be needed. The ad appeals to values as well by evoking the principle that caring for others, including animals, is important.

> **EXERCISE 20.2** **Providing Reasons and Evidence**

Imagine you are the director of a day care center justifying expenditures to the board of directors. Choose two of the following items, and write a paragraph providing reasons for the purchases and offering evidence to show how each item would benefit the children.

1. Tropical fish tank
2. Microwave
3. Read-along books with audio recordings
4. Set of Dr. Seuss books
5. One or more tablet computers

I'VE NEVER UNDERSTOOD WHY MY HUMAN WON'T LEAVE THE HOUSE WITHOUT HER LEASH. I THINK SHE'S AFRAID OF GETTING LOST. BUT IT'S OK, I KIND OF LIKE SHOWING HER AROUND.

—HARPER
adopted 08-18-09

A PERSON IS THE BEST THING TO HAPPEN TO A SHELTER PET

adopt

theshelterpetproject.org

REFUTATION

A **refutation**, also called a *rebuttal,* recognizes and argues against opposing viewpoints. Refutation involves finding a weakness in the opponent's argument by casting doubt on the opponent's reasons or by questioning the accuracy, relevance, and sufficiency of the opponent's evidence.

Suppose you want to argue that you deserve a raise at work (your claim). To support your claim, you will remind your supervisor of the contributions and improvements you have made, your length of employment, your conscientiousness, and your promptness. But you suspect that your supervisor may still turn you down, not because you don't deserve the raise but because other employees might demand a similar raise. By anticipating this potential objection, you can build into your argument the reasons that the objection is not valid. You may have more time invested with the company and have taken on more responsibilities than the other employees, for example.

If an opponent's argument is too strong to refute, most writers will acknowledge or accommodate the opposing viewpoint in some way. They **acknowledge** an opposing view simply by stating it. They **accommodate** an opposing view by noting that it has merit and modifying their position or finding a way of addressing it. In an argument opposing hunting, for example, a writer might simply *acknowledge* the view that hunting bans would cause a population explosion among deer. The writer might *accommodate* this opposing view by stating that if a population explosion were to occur, the problem could be solved by reintroducing natural predators into the area.

The following readings illustrate the components of effective argument essays. The first reading is annotated to point out those components. As you read the second essay, try to identify for yourself the claim and the supporting reasons, evidence, and emotional appeals Brian Palmer includes. Look, too, for places where Palmer refutes, accommodates, or acknowledges opposing views on tipping.

READING

Organ Donation: A Life-Saving Gift

QUINNE SEMBER

Quinne Sember was a first-year student at the State University of New York at Buffalo when she wrote the following essay for her writing class.

The idea of helping someone less fortunate is not a novel idea in our society. However, when people think about helping someone by giving a part of their body away, they become uncomfortable. According to Donate Life America, a Web site that promotes donation, organ donation is "the process of giving an organ or a part of an organ for the purpose of transplantation into another person" ("Understanding Donation"). In addition to organs (like the heart, liver, and eye), tissue, blood, and corneas can be donated when a person dies. It is also possible to donate parts of organs or entire organs (like a kidney) while living.

Organ, eye, and tissue donation has the potential to enhance or save the lives of many people. Surprisingly, however, most people in this country will never donate. If everyone chose to donate whatever they could during their lifetimes and after their death, a lot of grief for families could be prevented.

The most compelling argument for organ donation comes from statistics. Over 100,000 people need organ transplants right now, and someone is added to the waiting list every ten minutes ("Understanding Donation").

1   **Introduction:** Sember thoroughly defines organ donation, using a quotation from a source.

2   **Claim:** In her thesis statement, Sember makes a claim of fact.

3   **Reason #1:** The topic sentence states the first reason. Statistics from two sources provide evidence.

Title: Sember clearly identifies the issue.

In 2009, a total of 7,048 patients died while waiting for an organ. This number is up from 2000, when it was only 5,000 (Delmonico). If more people were willing to donate their organs after death or even contribute while they were living, these numbers could decrease substantially.

Background: Sember offers additional background information on determining brain death, again using a quotation from a source.

The most common organ donor is someone who has experienced brain death. Brain death is "the death of the brain stem, and the diagnosis of brain death is made by examining the function of nerves that originate in the brain stem" (Kerridge 89). For someone to be considered as a donor after death, he or she must first be declared to be brain dead. Someone who is brain dead appears to be alive. The person continues to breathe with the help of a ventilator, and the body remains warm. Therefore, families often have a difficult time recognizing that the person is dead. The prospect of organ donation can be therapeutic to a family going through a difficult time. It is the one good thing that can come out of an unfortunate situation. The family may feel that by donating organs, their beloved did not die in vain.

4

Reason: The topic sentence states the second reason. An example from a source provides evidence.

Even if the person is not eligible to donate organs to someone else, he or she can donate them to research that may further medical knowledge. In 2007, researchers discovered a link between the Epstein-Barr virus and multiple sclerosis by examining the postmortem brain tissue of a donor who had MS ("Brain Tissue"). This advance occurred only because someone's family members decided that they wanted to try to help others with MS, even though their own family member could no longer be helped.

5

Evidence: Sember reports an example of how a life was saved through donation.

I have volunteered for four years with Upstate New York Transplant Services, which works to promote organ donation awareness. I have become close to a woman who chose to work with UNYTS because of a personal experience. Her four-year-old daughter was diagnosed with a failing heart and needed a transplant as soon as possible. Every day, the girl's breathing became more labored. Finally, a heart was located. After she had the transplant, however, she began to lose blood and required a large amount of blood. Because of the generosity of a family and countless individual blood donors, this young girl now lives a healthy life. Her family is forever thankful for the gift that she received. They often hold blood drives in her name.

6

Refutation: Sember's topic sentence acknowledges opposing views but says these are usually based on misconceptions. She introduces the source she will use to refute them.

Some people reject organ donation, either for themselves or for their loved ones, because they have misconceptions about it. The Mayo Clinic Web site addresses some of these mistaken ideas in "Organ Donation: Don't Let These Myths Confuse You."

7

Many people believe that if they are a registered organ donor, the hospital staff won't work as hard to save their life. This is not true. The doctor who tries to help you is not the same doctor who would be concerned with the transplantation. Your doctor's job is to save your life. In that moment, he cares about nothing else.

Others worry that they won't actually be dead when the death certificate is signed. This is highly unlikely. According to the Mayo Clinic, "people who have agreed to organ donation are given more tests (at no charge to their families) to determine that they're truly dead than are those who haven't agreed to organ donation." These tests would be reassuring to the family, as well.

Another major concern is disfiguration of the body. People believe that they won't be able to have an open-casket funeral if they donate their organs. This is untrue. The body is clothed so that no signs of organ donation can be seen. For bone donation, a rod may be inserted in place of the bone. For skin donation, a small sample of skin can be taken from the back of the donor and placed where the donated skin was taken.

Finally, many people worry whether their religion accepts organ donation. Courtney S. Campbell addresses this issue in her article "Religion and the Body in Medical Research." She recognizes two key characteristics of organ donation — "altruistic intent" and "therapeutic expectation" (281) — that explain why most religions accept it. Altruistic intent means that the donor is giving an important gift to the recipient without expecting anything in return. Therapeutic expectation means that this gift is expected to "offer a pronounced therapeutic prospect for the recipient" (281). Basically, these concepts simply mean that because the donor is trying to help someone else save his or her life, donation is acceptable in almost any situation.

Campbell also identifies the specific beliefs that some major religions hold about organ donation. In Judaism, a great deal of importance is placed on the preservation of the body after death. Campbell says, however, that "this presumption can be overridden . . . by the requirement of *pikkuah nefesh*, the saving of human life" (281). Roman Catholicism holds much the same belief. Islam believes organ donation to be acceptable as well, as long as the remaining parts of the body are buried. Most Protestant denominations have no objection to organ and tissue donation.

Most people decide not to donate their organs for reasons that are untrue. If everyone donated their organs when they died, we would make

---

8   **Refutation:** Sember refutes the opposing view that doctors don't try hard to save lives of organ donors.

9   **Refutation:** Sember refutes the opposing view that donors may not be dead when death certificates are signed. Note the transitions from one opposing view to another.

10   **Refutation:** Sember refutes the opposing view that donation causes body disfigurement.

11   **Refutation:** Sember introduces a new source to refute the opposing view that religions do not accept organ donation.

12

13   **Conclusion:** Sember explains ways to become an organ donor and urges readers to do so.

enormous advances in science as well as save countless lives. The best way to become an organ donor is to talk to your family. If they know what you want to happen when you pass away, they are much more likely to carry out your wishes. In most states, you can also sign the back of your driver's license to indicate that you would like to be an organ donor. Organ donor cards are available online, and many states have a donor registry that you can become a part of. Become an organ donor; save a life!

Works Cited

"Brain Tissue Donation Furthers MS Research." *Momentum*, vol. 2, no. 3, June 2009, p. 36. *EBSCOhost,* connection.ebscohost.com.

Campbell, Courtney S. "Religion and the Body in Medical Research." *Kennedy Institute of Ethics Journal,* vol. 8, no. 3, Sept. 1998, pp. 275-305. *Project Muse*, muse.jhu.edu/.

Delmonico, Francis L., et al. "Ethical Incentives—Not Payment—for Organ Donation." *The New England Journal of Medicine,* vol. 346, no. 25, 20 June 2002, pp. 2002-05, eml.berkeley.edu/~webfac/held/delmonico.pdf.

Kerridge, I. H., et al. "Death, Dying and Donation: Organ Transplantation and the Diagnosis of Death." *Journal of Medical Ethics,* vol. 28, no. 2, Apr. 2002, pp. 89-94. *JSTOR,* www.jstor.org/stable/27718853.

"Organ Donation: Don't Let These Myths Confuse You." *Mayo Clinic*, 3 Apr. 2010, www.mayoclinic.org/healthy-lifestyle/consumer-health/in-depth/organ-donation/art-20047529.

"Why Be a Donor?" *Donate Life America*, donatelife.net/understanding-donation/.

READING

Tipping Is an Abomination

BRIAN PALMER

Brian Palmer is a journalist and regular columnist for the online magazine *Slate,* where he writes a column, "Explainer: Answers to Your Questions about the News," and for *The Washington Post*, where he writes a "How and Why" column. The following essay appeared in *Slate* in 2013.

When wealthy Americans brought home the practice of tipping from their European 1
vacations in the late 19th century, their countrymen considered it bribery. State legislatures quickly banned the practice. But restaurateurs, giddy at the prospect of passing
labor costs directly to customers, eventually convinced Americans to accept tipping.

We had it right the first time. Tipping is a repugnant custom. It's bad for consumers 2
and terrible for workers. It perpetuates racism. Tipping isn't even good for restaurants,
because the legal morass surrounding gratuities results in scores of expensive lawsuits.

Tipping does not incentivize hard work. The factors that correlate most strongly to 3
tip size have virtually nothing to do with the quality of service. Credit card tips are
larger than cash tips. Large parties with sizable bills leave disproportionately small
tips. We tip servers more if they tell us their names, touch us on the arm, or draw
smiley faces on our checks. Quality of service has a laughably small impact on tip size.
According to a 2000 study, a customer's assessment of the server's work only accounts
for between 1 and 5 percent of the variation in tips at a restaurant.

Tipping also creates a racially charged feedback loop, based around the widely held 4
assumption — explored in an episode of *Louie*, in the Oscar-winning film *Crash*, and
elsewhere — that African-Americans tend to be subpar tippers. There seems to be some
truth to this stereotype: African-Americans, on average, tip 3 percentage points less
than white customers. The tipping gap between Hispanics and whites is smaller, but
still discernible in studies. This creates an excuse for restaurant servers to prioritize
the needs of certain ethnic groups over others.

Irrelevant or insidious factors will dominate the tipping equation until quality of work 5
becomes the main driver of tip size, but that's unlikely to happen. And tip size isn't the
real problem anyway. The real problem is that restaurants don't pay their employees a
living wage. The federal "tip credit" allows restaurants to pay their tipped employees as
little as $2.13 per hour, as long as tips make up the shortfall — which turns a customer
into a co-employer. Although federal and state law requires restaurants to ensure that
tips bring employees up to minimum wage, few diners know that. (Hosts/hostesses,
bussers, and food runners, who receive a small fraction of the servers' tips, often fall
short of minimum wage on some nights.) The tip credit has turned the gratuity into a
moral obligation, and we ought to cut it from our statute books with a steak knife.

The only real beneficiary of the preposterously complicated tip credit is lawyers. 6
Imagine what it's like for a company running restaurants in multiple states. There's no
tip credit in some states, like California and Washington, where tipped employees must
be paid the full minimum wage. Hawaii allows the tip credit only if the combined tip
and cash wage surpass the statewide minimum hourly wage by 50 cents. New York and
Connecticut have different minimum wages for servers, hotel employees, and bartenders.

Then you have to consider time that employees spend on activities not likely to 7
yield tips. Applebee's, for example, has suffered a series of legal setbacks in lawsuits
brought by tipped employees seeking back pay for time spent cleaning toilets and
washing glassware.

The laws regarding tip sharing and tip pooling, which occur in virtually every restau- 8
rant, are even more complicated. Federal law allows mandatory tip sharing, but only
among employees who customarily receive either direct or indirect tips. That means

servers, bussers, food runners, and hosts and hostesses can be required to pool their tips with each other, but not with managers. Unfortunately, the line between service and management is fuzzy in many restaurants, and differences between state laws further complicate matters. A California judge ordered Starbucks to pay $105 million in 2008 for forcing 100,000 baristas to share tips with supervisors. Last week, the New York Court of Appeals reached the opposite conclusion, ruling that New York law allows the arrangement. Chili's has also lost a multimillion dollar judgment over tip sharing.

The entire mess is begging for some certainty and predictability. Restaurants need   9 a clear set of rules to follow. Servers should have a steadier income stream. Hosts and bussers, who have relatively little interaction with customers, ought not to be involved in tipping at all. Customers need more clarity as well, instead of worrying at the end of a meal if the waiter, or your guests, approve of your 17 percent tip.

I'd like to propose a solution. First, ask your state and federal representatives to   10 abolish the tip credit, which would turn tips back into actual gratuities: something given free of obligation. Second, announce your tipping practice to your server as soon as you sit down. Virtually every other employee in America knows how much they'll be paid up front, and somehow the man who sells me shoes and the woman who does my dry cleaning still manage to provide adequate service. I have no doubt waiters and waitresses are the same. Finally, tip a flat, but reasonably generous, dollar amount per person in your party. Around 20 percent of Americans, mostly older people, tip a flat amount already, so it's not exactly revolutionary. A server's pay shouldn't be linked to whether or not you have room for dessert.

READING ACTIVELY AND THINKING CRITICALLY

For more on reading strategies, see Chapter 3.

To understand the relationships among the ideas presented in an argument essay, plan to read the argument at least twice — once to get an overview of the issue and the claim and a second time to annotate the argument and jot down your own reactions.

BEFORE YOU READ

1. Think about the title. The title may indicate the issue and claim.

claim (against)   issue

The Case against Medical Marijuana

issue   claim (for)

Voting : Why Not Make It Mandatory?

> **EXERCISE 20.3** **Predicting Issues and Claims**

For each of the following titles, predict the issue and the claim the essay would make.

1. "The Drugs I Take Are None of Your Business"
2. "Watch That Leer and Stifle That Joke at the Water Cooler"
3. "Crazy in the Streets: A Call for Treatment of Street People"
4. "Penalize the Unwed Dad? Fat Chance"
5. "A Former Smoker Applauds New Laws"

2. **Check the author's name and credentials.** If you recognize the author's name, you may have some sense of what to expect in the essay. For example, an essay written by syndicated columnist Dave Barry, who is known for his humorous articles, would likely make a point through humor or sarcasm. In contrast, an essay by former vice president Al Gore would likely take an earnest, serious approach. Also determine whether the author is qualified to write on the topic.

    Essays in newspapers, magazines, and academic journals often include a brief review of the author's credentials and experience. Books may include a biographical note about the author. When an article is published without an author's name, which often happens in newspapers, base your evaluation on the reliability of the publication in which the article appears.

    For more on evaluating sources, see Chapter 22.

3. **Look for the original source of publication, and identify its slant and intended audience.** If the essay was originally published elsewhere, use the headnote, footnotes, or list of acknowledgments (often at the end of the book) to determine the original source. Some publications have a particular viewpoint. For example, *Ms.* magazine has a feminist slant, and its intended audience is educated, professional women. *Wired* generally favors advances in technology.

4. **Check the publication date.** The more recent an article is, the more likely it is to reflect current research or debate. For instance, an essay speculating on the existence of life on other planets written in the 1980s would lack recent scientific findings that might confirm or discredit the supporting evidence. **Hint:** When obtaining information from the Internet, be especially careful to check the date the article was posted or last updated.

5. **Preview the essay.** Read the opening paragraph, headings, the first sentence of one or two paragraphs per page, and the last paragraph. Previewing may help you determine the author's claim.

6. **Think about the issue before you read.** When you think about the subject of the argument before reading, you may be less influenced by the writer's appeals and more likely to maintain an objective, critical viewpoint. Write the issue at the top of page, and then list in two or more columns as many reasons as you can come up with for supporting the main positions on the issue.

WHILE YOU READ

1. **Read first for an initial impression.** Identify the issue and the author's claim. Try to get a general feel for the essay, the author, and the author's approach to the topic. Hold off on judging or criticizing the author's take on the issue until you have analyzed it closely.

2. **Read a second time with a pen in hand.** Mark or highlight the claim, reasons, and key supporting evidence. Note appeals to needs and values, and summarize reasons and key supporting evidence as you encounter them. Understand how the writer defines key terms and concepts. If the author does not define terms precisely, look up their meanings in a dictionary, and jot down the definitions in the margins. Also jot down ideas, questions, or challenges to the writer's argument.

3. **Check your comprehension by summarizing or drawing a graphic organizer.** Use the following guidelines.
   - **Review your annotations, noting the function of each section.** Be sure you have identified the issue, the claim, sections offering reasons and evidence, opposing viewpoints, and the conclusion. (If you had trouble identifying the parts, reread the essay.) In the left-hand margin, identify the function of each section. You might write "offers examples" or "provides statistical backup," for instance.
   - **Write brief notes stating the main point of each paragraph or each related group of paragraphs.** Summarize the essay's main ideas in the right-hand margin. Be sure to use your own words, not the author's.
   - **Develop a summary from your notes or complete a graphic organizer.** Verbal and abstract learners may prefer to create a summary; concrete and spatial learners may prefer to create a graphic organizer. Social learners may prefer to work with a classmate. The following sample summary of "Tipping Is an Abomination" shows an acceptable level of detail; a graphic organizer for this selection appears in Figure 20.2.

Learning Style Options

SAMPLE SUMMARY

When the practice of tipping was introduced in the United States in the late nineteenth century, it was rejected by both state legislatures and American citizens, who considered it a form of bribery. Despite opposition, the custom made its way into American society with the help of restaurateurs, who wanted to shift labor costs to their customers. In "Tipping Is an Abomination," Brian Palmer argues that the custom is objectionable and of little benefit to anyone except lawyers for three main reasons: because it does not motivate workers to work harder or more efficiently, because the perceived tipping gap between ethnic groups creates stereotypical thinking that results in unequal levels of service, and because differences in state laws regarding the tipping credit and tip sharing leads to costly lawsuits for restaurants. To solve the problem, Palmer concludes by suggesting that states abolish the tipping credit for restaurants, which would make the rules clear for restaurants and give employees a steady income. He also suggests that customers make their tipping practice known before receiving service and that they tip a flat rate per person, despite the size of the group.

EXERCISE 20.4 **Writing a Summary**

Write a summary of "Organ Donation: A Life-Saving Gift" (pp. 507–10).

EXERCISE 20.5 **Drawing a Graphic Organizer**

Using the graphic organizer in Figure 20.1 (p. 503) or Figure 20.2 as a basis, draw a graphic organizer for "Organ Donation: A Life-Saving Gift" (pp. 507–10).

FIGURE 20.2 Graphic Organizer for "Tipping Is an Abomination"

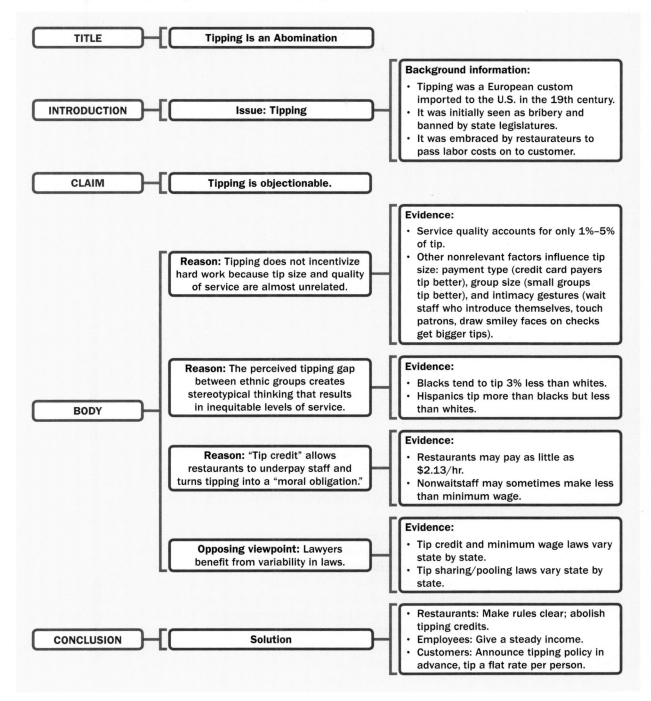

For more on evaluating evidence, see Chapter 6.

ANALYZING THE BASIC COMPONENTS OF AN ARGUMENT

As you read an argument, consider the following aspects of all persuasive writing.

- **The writer's purpose.** Ask yourself: Why does the writer want to convince me of this? What does he or she stand to gain, if anything? Be particularly skeptical if a writer stands to profit personally from your acceptance of an argument.
- **The intended audience.** Use the tone and the formality or informality of the language to figure out the type of audience—receptive, hostile, interested but skeptical—the author is expecting to address. How receptive the intended audience is expected to be might help you understand and evaluate the writer's argument. For example, writers addressing a receptive audience may not argue as carefully for their claims as would writers addressing a skeptical or hostile audience.
- **The writer's credibility.** Consider the writer's knowledge and trustworthiness. Ask yourself whether the writer has a thorough understanding of the issue, acknowledges opposing views and represents them fairly, and establishes common ground with readers by acknowledging their needs and values.
- **Support: reasons and evidence.** To assess the reasons and evidence, ask yourself questions like these: Does the writer offer enough reasons, do those reasons make sense, and are they relevant? Does the author supply enough evidence, and is that evidence accurate, complete, representative, up-to-date, and taken from reputable sources? Are the authorities cited experts in their field? Are sources cited formally or informally?
- **Definitions of key terms.** Underline any terms that can have more than one meaning. Then read through the essay to see if the author defines these terms clearly and uses them consistently. Pay particular attention to words that **appeal to values,** because not everyone considers the same principles or qualities important or agrees on the definition of a value.

IDENTIFYING EMOTIONAL APPEALS

Emotional appeals are a legitimate part of an argument. However, writers should not attempt to manipulate readers' emotions to distract them from the issue and the evidence. Table 20.1 presents some common unfair emotional appeals.

EVALUATING OPPOSING VIEWPOINTS

If an argument essay takes into account opposing viewpoints, you must evaluate how the writer presents them. Ask yourself the following questions.

- **Does the author state the opposing viewpoint clearly?**
- **Does the author present the opposing viewpoint fairly and completely?** That is, does the author treat the opposing viewpoint with respect or attempt to discredit or demean those holding the opposing view? Does the author present all the major parts of the opposing viewpoint or only those parts that he or she is able to refute?

- **Does the author clearly show why he or she considers the opposing viewpoint wrong or inappropriate?** Does the author apply sound logic? Does the author provide reasons and evidence?
- **Does the author acknowledge or accommodate points that cannot be refuted?**

TABLE 20.1 Common Unfair Emotional Appeals

Unfair Emotional Appeal	Example
Name-calling: Using an emotionally loaded term to create a negative response	"That reporter is an *egotistical bully*."
Ad hominem: Attacking the opponent rather than his or her position on the issue	"How could anyone who didn't fight in a war criticize the president's foreign policy?"
False authority: Quoting the opinions of celebrities or public figures about topics on which they are not experts	"According to singer Jennifer Hope, entitlement reform is America's most urgent economic problem."
Plain folks: Urging readers to accept an idea or take an action because it is suggested by someone who is just like they are	"Vote for me. I'm just a regular guy."
Appeal to pity: Arousing sympathy by telling hard-luck or excessively sentimental stories	"Latchkey children come home to an empty house or apartment, a can of soup, and a note on the refrigerator."
Bandwagon: Appealing to readers' desire to conform ("Everyone's doing it, so it must be right")	"It must be okay to exceed the speed limit, since so many people speed."

DETECTING FAULTY REASONING

In some arguments, a writer may commit **fallacies,** errors in reasoning or thinking. Fallacies can weaken an argument, undermine a writer's claim, and call into question the relevancy, believability, or consistency of supporting evidence. Table 20.2 provides a brief review of the most common types of faulty reasoning.

For more on reasoning, see Chapter 21, pp. 529–31.

EXERCISE 20.6 **Evaluating an Argument**

Locate at least one brief argument essay or article and bring it to class. Working in a group of two or three students, analyze each argument using the preceding guidelines.

TABLE 20.2 Common Fallacies

Fallacy	Example
Circular reasoning (begging the question): Using the claim (or part of it) as evidence by simply repeating the claim in different words	*"Cruel* and unusual experimentation on helpless animals is *inhumane."*
Hasty generalization: Drawing a conclusion based on insufficient evidence or isolated examples.	"Based on the three chocolate cakes I just tasted, I can tell you that all chocolate cakes are overly sweet."
Sweeping generalization: Claiming that something applies to all situations or instances without exception	"All computers are easy to use."
False analogy: Comparing two situations that are not sufficiently similar; just because two items or events are alike in some ways does not mean they are alike in all ways.	"A human body needs rest after strenuous work, and a car needs rest after a long trip."
Non sequitur ("It does not follow" in Latin): Joining two or more ideas when no logical relationship exists between them	"Because my sister is financially independent, she will make a good parent."
Red herring: Distracting readers from the main issue by raising an irrelevant point.	In an argument about banning advertisements for alcohol on T.V., mentioning that some parents give their children sips of alcohol could distract readers from the main issue.
Post hoc fallacy ("after this, therefore because of this" in Latin): Assuming that event A caused event B simply because B followed A.	"Student enrollment fell dramatically this semester because of the recent appointment of the new college president." (Other factors may have contributed to the decline in enrollment.)
Either-or fallacy (false dilemma): Arguing that there are only two sides to an issue and that only one of them is correct.	"Marijuana must be *either* legalized *or* banned." (A third alternative is to legalize marijuana for medical use, such as to reduce nausea for those undergoing chemotherapy.)

READINGS: ARGUMENT IN ACTION

READING

How (and Why) to Stop Multitasking

PETER BREGMAN

Peter Bregman is a leadership consultant and CEO of Bregman Partners, Inc., a global management consulting firm. He is the author of *Point A: A Short Guide to Leading a Big Change*

(2007). He blogs for *Harvard Business Review*, where this essay appeared in 2010. As you read, highlight Bregman's claim and the reasons he gives to support it.

During a conference call with the executive committee of a nonprofit board on which I sit, I decided to send an email to a client. I know, I know. You'd think I'd have learned. Last week I wrote about the dangers of using a cell phone while driving. Multitasking is dangerous. And so I proposed a way to stop. But when I sent that email, I wasn't in a car. I was safe at my desk. What could go wrong?

Well, I sent the client the message. Then I had to send him another one, this time with the attachment I had forgotten to append. Finally, my third email to him explained why that attachment wasn't what he was expecting. When I eventually refocused on the call, I realized I hadn't heard a question the Chair of the Board had asked me.

I swear I wasn't smoking anything. But I might as well have been. A study showed that people distracted by incoming email and phone calls saw a 10-point fall in their IQs. What's the impact of a 10-point drop? The same as losing a night of sleep. More than twice the effect of smoking marijuana.

Doing several things at once is a trick we play on ourselves, thinking we're getting more done. In reality, our productivity goes down by as much as 40%. We don't actually multitask. We switch-task, rapidly shifting from one thing to another, interrupting ourselves unproductively, and losing time in the process.

You might think you're different, that you've done it so much you've become good at it. Practice makes perfect and all that. But you'd be wrong. Research shows that heavy multitaskers are *less competent* at doing several things at once than light multitaskers. In other words, in contrast to almost everything else in your life, the more you multitask, the worse you are at it. Practice, in this case, works against you.

I decided to do an experiment. For one week I would do no multitasking and see what happened. What techniques would help? Could I sustain a focus on one thing at a time for that long? For the most part, I succeeded. If I was on the phone, all I did was talk or listen on the phone. In a meeting I did nothing but focus on the meeting. Any interruptions — email, a knock on the door — I held off until I finished what I was working on.

During the week I discovered six things:

- **First, it was delightful.** I noticed this most dramatically when I was with my children. I shut my cell phone off and found myself much more deeply engaged and present with them. I never realized how significantly a short moment of checking my email disengaged me from the people and things right there in front of me. Don't laugh, but I actually — for the first time in a while — noticed the beauty of leaves blowing in the wind.
- **Second, I made significant progress on challenging projects,** the kind that — like writing or strategizing — require thought and persistence. The kind I usually

try to distract myself from. I stayed with each project when it got hard, and experienced a number of breakthroughs.

- **Third, my stress dropped dramatically.** Research shows that multitasking isn't just inefficient, it's stressful. And I found that to be true. It was a relief to do only one thing at a time. I felt liberated from the strain of keeping so many balls in the air at each moment. It felt reassuring to finish one thing before going to the next.
- **Fourth, I lost all patience for things I felt were not a good use of my time.** An hour-long meeting seemed interminably long. A meandering pointless conversation was excruciating. I became laser-focused on getting things done. Since I wasn't doing anything else, I got bored much more quickly. I had no tolerance for wasted time.
- **Fifth, I had tremendous patience for things I felt were useful and enjoyable.** When I listened to my wife Eleanor, I was in no rush. When I was brainstorming about a difficult problem, I stuck with it. Nothing else was competing for my attention so I was able to settle into the one thing I was doing.
- **Sixth, there was no downside.** I lost nothing by not multitasking. No projects were left unfinished. No one became frustrated with me for not answering a call or failing to return an email the second I received it.

That's why it's so surprising that multitasking is so hard to resist. If there's no downside to stopping, why don't we all just stop? I think it's because our minds move considerably faster than the outside world. You can hear far more words a minute than someone else can speak. We have so much to do, why waste any time? So, while you're on the phone listening to someone, why not use that *extra* brain power to book a trip to Florence? What we neglect to realize is that we're already using that brain power to pick up nuance, think about what we're hearing, access our creativity, and stay connected to what's happening around us. It's not really extra brain power, and diverting it has negative consequences. 8

So how do we resist the temptation? First, the obvious: the best way to avoid interruptions is to turn them off. Often I write at 6 a.m. when there's nothing to distract me, I disconnect my computer from its wireless connection and turn my phone off. In my car, I leave my phone in the trunk. Drastic? Maybe. But most of us shouldn't trust ourselves. Second, the less obvious: Use your loss of patience to your advantage. Create unrealistically short deadlines. Cut all meetings in half. Give yourself a third of the time you think you need to accomplish something. There's nothing like a deadline to keep things moving. And when things are moving fast, we can't help but focus on them. How many people run a race while texting? If you really only have 30 minutes to finish a presentation you thought would take an hour, are you really going to answer an interrupting call? Interestingly, because multitasking is so stressful, single-tasking to meet a tight deadline will actually reduce your stress. In other words, giving yourself less time to do things could make you more productive and relaxed. 9

Finally, it's good to remember that we're not perfect. Every once in a while it 10 might be OK to allow for a little multitasking. As I was writing this, Daniel, my two-year-old son, walked into my office, climbed on my lap, and said "*Monsters, Inc.* movie please." So, here we are, I'm finishing this piece on the left side of my computer screen while Daniel is on my lap watching a movie on the right side of my computer screen. Sometimes, it is simply impossible to resist a little multitasking.

EXAMINING THE READING

1. **Reasons** Why does Bregman believe we should stop most of our multitasking?
2. **Summary** Summarize the opposing views favoring multitasking that Bregman refutes.
3. **Details** What did Bregman discover after he stopped multitasking?
4. **Vocabulary** Explain the meaning of each of the following words as it is used in the reading: *refocused* (para. 2), *competent* (5), *disengaged* (7), *persistence* (7), and *meandering* (7).

ANALYZING THE WRITER'S TECHNIQUE

1. **Claim** What is Bregman's claim? Is it a claim of fact, value, or policy? Explain how you know.
2. **Appeals** What types of emotional appeals does Bregman make? Identify the needs and values to which he appeals.
3. **Evidence** What types of evidence does Bregman use to support his claim?
4. **Reasoning** Are there any errors in reasoning? If so, explain.

VISUALIZING THE READING

Create a graphic organizer for the argument in this essay.

THINKING CRITICALLY ABOUT ARGUMENT

1. **Tone** Describe Bregman's tone. Highlight several words or phrases that reveal this tone.
2. **Evidence** Bregman mentions research but fails to cite his sources. How does that affect the effectiveness of his argument?
3. **Connotation** What is the connotation of the word *delightful* (para. 7)?
4. **Euphemism** What is "smoking anything" (3) a euphemism for?

RESPONDING TO THE READING

1. **Reaction** What do you think of Bregman's tips for how to stop multitasking? Are these things you could apply to your life? Why or why not?
2. **Discussion** Evaluate Bregman's description of his discoveries when he stopped multitasking. Are they persuasive? Could he have added anything that would make them more persuasive?

3. **Journal** Keep a journal for a day, and record all the times you multitask and how doing so affects you.
4. **Essay** Write an essay arguing for or against multitasking. Use examples of why it has or has not been useful for you as evidence.

READING

In Defense of Multitasking

DAVID SILVERMAN

David Silverman has worked in business and taught business writing. He is the author of *Typo: The Last American Typesetter or How I Made and Lost Four Million Dollars* (2007). He blogs for *Harvard Business Review*, where this essay appeared in 2010, ten days after the previous one by Peter Bregman. As you read, notice how Silverman attempts to refute Bregman's position.

HBR.org blogger Peter Bregman recently made some excellent points about the downside of multitasking. I will not deny that single-minded devotion often produces high quality. Nor will I attempt to join the misguided (and scientifically discredited) many who say, "Yeah, other people can't do it, but I'm super awesome at doing 10 things at once." 1

But let's remember, unitasking has a downside too — namely, what works for one person slows down others. Multitasking isn't just an addiction for the short-attention-spanned among us; it's crucial to survival in today's workplace. To see why, take a look at computing, where the concept of multitasking came from. 2

Long ago, in the days of vacuum tubes and relays, computers worked in "batch" mode. Jobs were loaded from punched cards, and each job waited until the one before it was completed. This created serious problems. You didn't know if your job had an error until it ran, which could be hours after you submitted it. You didn't know if it would cause an infinite loop and block all the other jobs from starting. And any changes in external information that occurred during processing couldn't be accounted for. 3

The invention of time-sharing resolved these issues: Multiple tasks can now be done concurrently, and you can interrupt a task in an emergency. Incoming missile? Stop the backup tape and send an alert to HQ. So, how does all that apply to the way people work? In several ways: 4

1. **Multitasking helps us get and give critical information faster.** You can get responses to questions quickly, even if the person you're asking is on another task. For example: I was at an all-day off-site (no BlackBerrys allowed) when one of my direct reports received a request from an internal customer to make a slide. Since I was unreachable by phone when he started on it, my employee worked the entire afternoon on something that, after I finally read my e-mail and called him, took us only 30 minutes to do together because I had information he didn't have.

Electronic Multitasking Is on the Rise

The percentage of youngsters who multitask while using electronic media— such as checking their Facebook page on their laptops while watching TV— has increased in recent years, but the percentage who multitask while reading has changed very little.

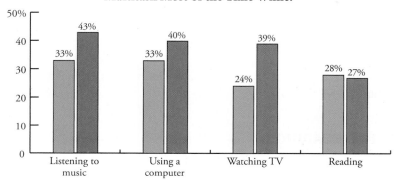

Percentage of 7th- to 12th-graders Who Multitask Most of the Time While:

Source: "Generation M2: Media in the Lives of 8-to-18-Year-Olds" (#8010), Henry J. Kaiser Family Foundation, January 2010.

2004
2009

2. **It keeps others from being held up.** If I don't allow for distractions in an attempt to be more efficient, other people may be held up waiting for me. This is the classic batch job problem. Going back to my slide example: The next day, the person who had requested the slide said he only needed a couple of bullet points. Had he been reachable earlier, and not devoted to a single task and blocking all interruptions, we wouldn't have wasted what ended up being nearly six hours of work time (my employee's and mine).

3. **It gives you something to turn to when you're stuck.** Sometimes it's good to butt your head against a task that is challenging. And sometimes it's good to walk away, do something else, and let your subconscious ponder the ponderable. When you return 25 minutes later, maybe you'll reach a better solution than you would have if you'd just stuck it out. And in the meantime, you've finished some other task, such as writing a blog post. (By the way, my 10.6 minute attempt to uncover how many minutes it takes to get back to a task after an interruption yielded a variety of answers — 11, 25, 30 — and links to a lot of dubious research, such as this University of California study of 36 workers and this study that tracked "eleven experienced Microsoft Windows users [3 female].")

4. **The higher up you are in the organization, the more important multitasking is.** The fewer things you have to do, the more you should concentrate on them. If I'm painting my house, and I'm on a ladder, I've got to keep on that one task. But if I'm the general contractor, I need to stay on top of the house painter, the carpenter, the electrician, and the guy swinging that big ball on the end of a giant chain, lest

the wrong wall or an unsuspecting worker get demolished. To take this to the logical extreme: Does Barack Obama get to unitask? Can he say, "I'm not available for the rest of the day, because I'll be working on that spreadsheet I've been trying to get done on the number of my Facebook friends who aren't updating their pages with posts about their pet cats?" Or does he have to keep doing his job while handling whatever spilled milk (or, say, zillions of gallons of oil) comes his way?

What do you think? Are we comfortable pretending we really can live our lives not multitasking? Or are we like my father and others who say smoking is bad but can be found on the front porch in the dead of night, a small red glow at their lips, puffing away while texting their BFFs and playing Words with Friends?   5

Before you answer, think about the eight *Washington Post* reporters who tried to go a week without the Internet and failed miserably. The truth is, we need multitasking as much as we need air.   6

EXAMINING THE READING

1. **Summary** Summarize Silverman's reasons for defending multitasking.
2. **Analogy** Explain Silverman's analogy about computers. What is he trying to show with it?
3. **Comparison** What message does Silverman convey by discussing his father in the next-to-last paragraph?
4. **Vocabulary** Explain the meaning of each of the following words as it is used in the reading: *discredited* (para. 1), *unitasking* (2), *concurrently* (4), *ponderable* (4), and *lest* (4).

ANALYZING THE WRITER'S TECHNIQUE

1. **Claim** What type of claim does Silverman make?
2. **Analogy** Is Silverman's analogy about computers effective? Why or why not?
3. **Support** What additional information, evidence, or explanation would make this essay more convincing?
4. **Example** The end of the essay talks about multitasking and the presidency. Is this an effective example? How useful is it in applying the issues in this essay to regular people?
5. **Audience** Who is Silverman's intended audience?

VISUALIZING THE READING

Create a graphic organizer for the argument in this essay.

THINKING CRITICALLY ABOUT TEXT AND VISUALS

1. **Appeals** To what needs and values does Silverman appeal?
2. **Reasoning** What fallacies, if any, can you find in Silverman's essay?

must also be true. The most common deductive argument is a **syllogism**, which consists of two premises and a conclusion.

Syllogism	Definition	Example
Major premise	A general statement about a group	Food containing dairy products makes you ill.
Minor premise	A statement about an individual belonging to that group	Frozen yogurt contains dairy products.
Conclusion	Logically necessary result	Frozen yogurt will make you ill.

When you use deductive reasoning, putting your argument in the form of a syllogism will help you write your claim, then organize and evaluate your reasons and evidence. Suppose you want to support the claim that state funding for Kids First, an early childhood program, should remain intact. You might use the following syllogism to build your argument.

MAJOR PREMISE	State-funded early childhood programs have increased the readiness of at-risk children to attend school.
MINOR PREMISE	Kids First is a popular early childhood program in our state, where it has had many positive effects.
CONCLUSION	Kids First is likely to increase the readiness of at-risk children to attend school.

Your thesis statement would be, "Because early childhood programs are likely to increase the readiness of at-risk children to attend school, state funding for Kids First should be continued." Your evidence would be information demonstrating the effectiveness of Kids First, such as the school performance of at-risk students who attended Kids First versus the school performance of at-risk students who did not and the cost of remedial education in later years versus the cost of Kids First.

EFFECTIVE ARGUMENTS DEPEND ON CAREFUL AUDIENCE ANALYSIS

To build a convincing argument, you need to know your audience. Analyze your audience to determine their education, background, and experience. Then also consider the following.

For more on audience analysis, see Chapter 5, pp. 103–05.

1. How familiar your audience is with the issue
2. Whether your audience is likely to agree, be neutral or wavering, or disagree with your claim

This knowledge will help you select reasons and evidence and choose appeals that your readers will find compelling.

Agreeing audiences. Agreeing audiences are the easiest to write for because they already accept your claim. When you write for an audience that is likely to agree with your claim, the focus is usually on urging readers to take a specific action. Instead of having to offer large amounts of facts and statistics as evidence, you can concentrate on reinforcing your shared viewpoint and building emotional ties with your audience. By doing so, you encourage readers to act on their beliefs.

Neutral or wavering audiences. Although they may be somewhat familiar with the issue, neutral or wavering audiences may have questions about, misunderstandings about, or no interest in the issue. When writing for this type of audience, emphasize the importance of the issue or shared values, and clear up misunderstandings readers may have. Your goals are to make readers care about the issue, establish yourself as a knowledgeable and trustworthy writer, and present solid evidence in support of your claim.

Disagreeing audiences. The most challenging audience is one that holds viewpoints in opposition to yours. The people in such an audience may have strong feelings about the issue and may distrust you because you don't share their views. In writing for a disagreeing audience, your goal is not necessarily to persuade readers to adopt your position but rather to convince them to consider your views. To be persuasive, you must follow a logical line of reasoning. Rather than stating your claim early in the essay, it may be more effective to build slowly to your thesis, first establishing **common ground**, a basis of trust and goodwill, by mentioning shared values, interests, concerns, and experiences.

> **EXERCISE 21.3**   **Developing an Argument for a Specific Audience**

Choose one of the following claims and discuss how you would argue in support of it for (a) an agreeing audience, (b) a neutral or wavering audience, and (c) a disagreeing audience.

1. Public school sex education classes should be mandatory because they help students make important decisions about their lives.
2. Portraying the effects of violent crime realistically on television may help reduce the crime rate.
3. Children who spend too much time interacting with a computer may fail to learn how to interact with people.

EFFECTIVE ARGUMENTS PRESENT REASONS AND EVIDENCE READERS WILL FIND COMPELLING

In developing an argument, you need to provide reasons for making a claim. A **reason** is a general statement that backs up a claim; it answers the question, "Why do I have this opinion about this issue?" You also need to support each reason with evidence.

Suppose you want to argue that high school uniforms should be mandatory. You might give three reasons.

1. Uniforms reduce clothing costs for parents.
2. They help eliminate distractions in the classroom.
3. They reduce peer pressure.

You would need to support each of your reasons with some combination of evidence, facts, statistics, examples, personal experience, or expert testimony. Carefully linking your evidence to reasons helps your readers see how the evidence supports your claim.

Choose reasons and evidence that will appeal to your audience. In the argument about mandatory school uniforms, high school students would probably not be impressed by your first reason, but they might be persuaded by your second and third reasons if you cite evidence that appeals to them, such as personal anecdotes from other students. For an audience of parents, facts and statistics about reduced clothing costs and improved academic performance would be appealing types of evidence.

EFFECTIVE ARGUMENTS APPEAL TO READERS' NEEDS AND VALUES

Although an effective argument relies mainly on credible evidence and logical reasoning, **emotional appeals** to readers' needs and values can help support and strengthen a sound argument. **Needs** can be biological or psychological (food and drink, sex, a sense of belonging, self-esteem). **Values** are principles or qualities that readers consider important, worthwhile, or desirable. Examples include honesty, loyalty, privacy, and patriotism.

For more on emotional appeals, see Chapter 20, pp. 505–06, 516–17.

EFFECTIVE ARGUMENTS RECOGNIZE ALTERNATIVE VIEWS

Recognizing and countering alternative perspectives on an issue forces you to think hard about your claims. When you anticipate readers' objections, you may find reasons to adjust your reasoning and develop a stronger argument. Readers will also be more willing to consider your claim if you take their point of view into account.

You can recognize alternative views in an argument essay by acknowledging, accommodating, or refuting them.

1. **Acknowledge** an alternative viewpoint by admitting that it exists and showing that you have considered it.

    EXAMPLE   Readers opposed to mandatory high school uniforms may argue that a uniform requirement will not eliminate peer pressure because students will use other objects to gain status, such as backpacks, iPads, and smartphones. You could acknowledge this viewpoint by admitting that there is no way to stop teenagers from finding ways to compete for status.

2. **Accommodate** an alternative viewpoint by acknowledging readers' concerns, accepting some of them, and incorporating them into your argument.

    EXAMPLE   In arguing for mandatory high school uniforms, you might accommodate readers' view that uniforms will not eliminate peer pressure by arguing only that uniforms will eliminate one major and expensive means of competing for status.

3. **Refute** an opposing viewpoint by demonstrating the weakness of the opponent's argument.

EXAMPLE   To refute the viewpoint that uniforms force students to give up their personal style, you can argue that the majority of students' lives are spent outside school, where uniforms are not necessary and where each student is free to express his or her individuality.

EXERCISE 21.4 | **Identifying Opposing Viewpoints**

For the three claims listed in Exercise 21.3, identify opposing viewpoints and consider how you could acknowledge, accommodate, or refute them.

The following readings demonstrate the techniques for writing effective argument essays discussed above. The first reading is annotated to point out how Amitai Etzioni and Radhika Bhat make an arguable claim, provide reasons and evidence in support of their claim, and respond to alternative views. As you read the second essay, pay particular attention to the logic of the argument and the strategies William Safire uses to appeal to his audience.

READING

Second Chances, Social Forgiveness, and the Internet

AMITAI ETZIONI AND RADHIKA BHAT

Amitai Etzioni is University Professor and director of the Institute for Communitarian Policy Studies at George Washington University. He is the author of twenty-four books, including *Law in a New Key* (2010), *Security First: For a Muscular, Moral Foreign Policy* (2007), and *The Limits of Privacy* (2004), as well as numerous popular and scholarly articles published in journals and magazines such as *The Diplomat, The Atlantic,* and *The Huffington Post.* Radhika Bhat is a research assistant at the George Washington University's Institute for Communitarian Policy Studies. This article was first published in 2009 in *American Scholar,* a publication of the Phi Beta Kappa Society that addresses issues in literature, science, history, and public affairs.

A young man in upstate New York drinks too much and gets a little rowdy, picks   1
a fight, smashes up the bar, and is arrested. When he gets into trouble again a short time later, the judge sends him to jail for a week. After his release, he gets fired and cannot find a new job because he has a record. The local newspaper carries a story about his misconduct. The merchants on Main Street refuse to sell him anything on credit. The young women gossip about him and refuse to date him. One day he has

had enough. He packs his meager belongings, leaves without a good-bye, and moves to a small town in Oregon. Here, he gains a new start. Nobody knows about his rowdy past, and he has learned his lesson. He drinks less, avoids fights, works in a lumber-yard, and soon marries a nice local woman, has three kids, and lives happily ever after. Cue the choir of angels singing in the background.

The idea that people deserve a second chance is an important American value. Perhaps it grows out of our history, in which those who got into trouble in Europe (whether it was their fault or not) moved to the United States to start a new life. And as the American West was settled, many easterners and midwesterners found a place there for a second beginning. Under the right conditions, criminals can pay their debt to society and be rehabilitated, sex offenders can be reformed, and others who have flunked out can pass another test. Just give them a second chance.

2   **Emotional appeal:** Appeals to shared values

The latest chapter of this deeply entrenched narrative introduces a big bad wolf, the Internet. It stands charged with killing the opportunity for people to have that much-deserved second chance. By computerizing local public records, the Internet casts the shadow of people's past far and fast; like a curse they cannot undo, their records now follow them wherever they go. True, even in the good old days, arrest records, criminal sentences, bankruptcy filings, and even divorce records were public. Some were listed in blotters kept in police stations, others in courthouses; anyone who wished to take the trouble could go there and read them. But most people did not. Above all, there was no way for people in distant communities to find these damning facts without going to inordinate lengths.

3

Issue: Identifies controversy

In recent decades, online databases have dramatically increased the size of the audience that has access to public information and the ease with which it can be examined. Several companies have started compiling criminal records, making them available to everyone in the country and indeed the world. For instance, PeopleFinders, a company based in Sacramento, recently introduced CriminalSearches.com, a free service to access public criminal records, which draws data from local courthouses. A similar thing is happening to many other types of public records, ranging from birth records to divorces.

4

These developments disturb privacy advocates and anyone who is keen on ensuring that people have the opportunity for a new start. Beth Givens, director of the Privacy Rights Clearinghouse, says that Internet databases cause a "loss of 'social forgiveness.'" For instance, a person's "conviction of graffiti vandalism at age 19 will still be there at age 29 when [he's] a solid citizen trying to get a job and raise a family" — and the conviction will be there for anyone to see. Furthermore, as companies "rely on background checks to screen workers, [they] risk imposing unfair barriers to rehabilitated criminals," wrote reporters Ann Zimmerman and Kortney Stringer in *The Wall Street Journal*. In short, as journalist Brad Stone wrote in *The New York Times,* by allowing the producers of databases to remove "the obstacles to getting criminal information," we are losing "a valuable, ignorance-fueled civil peace."

5   **Alternative views:** Identifies those who hold alternative viewpoint

Transition: Transitional sentence highlights upcoming rebuttal.

But hold on for just a minute. Is the Internet age really destroying second chances, making us less forgiving and hindering the possibility for rehabilitation and even redemption? The sad fact is that most convicted criminals in the pre-digital age did not use the second chance that their obscurity gave them, nor did they use their third or fourth chances. Convincing data show that most criminal offenders — especially those involved in violent crimes — are not rehabilitated; they commit new crimes. And many commit numerous crimes before they are caught again. Thus, while obscurity may well help a small percentage of criminals get a second chance, it helps a large percentage of them strike again.   6

Reason 1: Offers protection against criminals

Supporting evidence: Example 1

Take the case of James Webb (not the U.S. Senator from Virginia of the same name). He had served 20 years in prison for raping six women when, on August 16, 1995, he was released on parole. But rather than look for a new start, he raped another woman the day after he was released. Then he raped three more women in the next few months. He was rearrested in December 1995, after he committed the fourth rape. Or consider the case of James Richardson, a New York resident who served 20 years of a life term for raping and murdering a 10-year-old girl. After he was paroled in 1992, he committed three bank robberies before being re-incarcerated. Both cases happened before the advent of databanks of criminal convictions.   7

Supporting evidence: Example 2

Supporting evidence: Statistics

These two are typical cases. In its most recent study on recidivism in the United States, the Justice Department's Bureau of Justice Statistics tracked two-thirds of the prisoners released in 15 states in 1994. It found that within three years of their release, 67.5 percent of them were re-arrested for a new offense. In short, most people who commit crimes are more likely to commit crimes in the future than to make good use of a second chance. This was true long before the digitization of criminal data and the loss of obscurity.   8

In short, the image of a young person who goes astray, and who would return to the straight and narrow life if just given a second chance, does not fit most offenders. Indeed, prisons are considered colleges for crime; they harden those sentenced to spend time in them, making them *more* disposed to future criminal behavior upon release. Social scientists differ about whom to blame for the limited success of rehabilitation. Some fault "the system," or poor social conditions, or lack of job training. Others place more blame on the character of those involved. In any case, obscurity hardly serves to overcome strong factors that agitate against rehabilitation.   9

Reason 2: Offers protection against bad doctors

Online databases also display the records of physicians who do not live up to the Hippocratic oath; these doctors do harm, and plenty of it. The National Practitioner Data Bank allows state licensing boards, hospitals, and other health-care entities to find out whether the license of a doctor has been revoked recently in another state or if the doctor has been disciplined. Doctors' licenses are generally revoked only if they commit very serious offenses, such as repeated gross negligence, criminal felonies, or practicing while under the influence of drugs or alcohol.   10

If these databases had been used as intended in the late 1990s and early 2000s, they could have tracked Pamela L. Johnson, a physician who was forced to leave Duke University Medical Center after many of her patients suffered from unusual complications. In response, Johnson moved to New Mexico and lied about her professional history in order to obtain a medical license there and continue practicing. After three patients in New Mexico filed lawsuits alleging that she was negligent or had botched surgical procedures, she moved again and set up shop in Michigan.

Similarly, Joseph S. Hayes, a medical doctor licensed in Tennessee, was convicted of drug abuse and assault, including choking a patient, actions which resulted in the revocation of his Tennessee license in 1991. But his license was reinstated in 1993. When he was charged with fondling a female patient in 1999, he simply moved to South Carolina to continue practicing medicine. Similar stories could be told about scores of other doctors. (The exploits of one of the most notorious of these doctors are laid out in a new book, *Charlatan,* by Pope Brock.)

Beyond assuming that Internet databases do little harm to those who are not likely to reform themselves, we can show real benefits from the widespread dissemination of information about wrongdoers—for their potential victims. Few doctors are hired by hospitals these days without first being checked through the digitized data sources. Before you hire an accountant, such data makes it possible to discover whether he or she has a record of embezzlement. A community can find out if a new school nurse is a sex offender. Employers may direct ex-offenders to other jobs, or they may still hire them but provide extra oversight, or just decide that they are willing to take the risk. But they do so well informed—and thus warned—rather than ignorant of the sad facts.

Registration and notification laws for sex offenders provide a good case in point. The Washington State Institute for Public Policy conducted a study in 2005 that evaluated the effectiveness of the state's community notification laws. In 1990, Washington passed the Community Protection Act, a law that requires sex offenders to register with their county sheriff and authorizes law enforcement to release information to the public. The study found that by 1999 the recidivism rate among felony sex offenders in the state had dropped 70 percent from the pre-1990 level, in part due to communities' awareness of the sex offenders in their neighborhoods. In addition, offenders subject to community notification were arrested for new crimes much more quickly than offenders who were released without notification.

True, online databases increase the size of the community that has access to information, but these technological developments merely help communities catch up with other social developments. People do business over greater distances and move around much more, and much farther, than they did in earlier eras. Our travel and transactions are no longer limited to the county store and local diner. Our access to data needs to expand to match the new scope of our lives.

11 **Supporting evidence:** Example 1

12 **Supporting evidence:** Example 2

13 **Reason 3:** Benefits possible victims

Supporting evidence: Examples

14 **Supporting evidence:** Study, statistics

15 **Alternative views:** Acknowledges alternative viewpoint

Alternative views: Offers rebuttal evidence; reason

Alternative views: Acknowledges alternative viewpoint

All of this is not to deny that we face a moral dilemma. Although most offenders
are not rehabilitated, some are. It is incorrect to assume that "once a criminal, always
a criminal." Take the case of Mike Kolomichuk, who in 1979 pleaded guilty to two
counts of battery after having an altercation with an undercover police officer in a
bar in Florida. As punishment, he received unsupervised probation, during which he
conducted himself well. Kolomichuk eventually moved to Ohio, where almost 30 years
later he ran as a write-in candidate for mayor of the village of Lakemore and won.
His criminal past was not an issue in the election because his record was unknown in
the village of 2,500 people. When his criminal history came out a few months later,
there was talk of the need for a new election, but it soon subsided. Today, Kolomichuk
remains mayor and is continuing his efforts to revitalize the community. In this case,
obscurity may well have helped.

The argument can be made, then, that just as we believe it is better to let a
hundred guilty people walk free than to condemn one innocent person, we should let a
hundred criminals benefit from obscurity in order to provide a chance at rehabilitation
for the few who put obscurity to good use. But there are ways, although imperfect, for
allowing second chances.

Claim: Thesis makes a claim of policy

Supporting evidence: Transitions emphasize example, contrasts between pre-Internet era and today

What is needed is a mixture of technological and legal means to replace the
measures that were once naturally woven into the fabric of communities with measures
that can satisfy the needs of a large, complex, and mobile society. For example,
where the inefficiency of paper records once ensured that information would not
travel far, we now must introduce into the digitized world barriers for information that
should not be spread. Formerly, in smaller communities, if a person was arrested, his
neighbors would learn whether he had been exonerated or convicted. The community might even have had a sense of whether a person who was released had in fact
committed the crime, or whether the arrest was unjustified. These days, an arrest
record may travel across the globe in nanoseconds, but it is difficult to find out if it
was justified. Either arrest records should not be made public (although they might be
available to police in other jurisdictions) or they must be accompanied with information about the outcome of the case.

Specific action 1: Transition introduces recommended action

Specific action 2: Transition highlights recommended action

In addition, a criminal record could be sealed both locally and in online databases,
say after seven years, if the person has not committed a new crime. There is considerable precedent for such a move. For instance, information about juvenile offenders and
presentations to grand juries are often sealed.

Specific action 3: Transitions highlight recommended action and example of a measure that has been taken

Another measure could limit access to certain databanks to those who are trained
to understand the limitations of these databanks. For instance, several states allow
only police authorities and educational institutions to access databases on sex
offenders.

Alternative view: Transition highlights alternative view

One other major concern is that lawbreakers who have paid their debt to society
will face discrimination in hiring and housing. Protections against such discrimination

16

17

18

19

20

21

are already in place, but others might be added. For instance, employers cannot, as a general rule, legally maintain a policy of refusing to hire people merely because they are ex-cons, whether the employer gets this information from a police blotter or a computer.

Internet databases should be held accountable for the information they provide. 22 If they rely on public records, then they should be required to keep up with the changes in these records. They should also provide mechanisms for filing complaints if the online data are erroneous, and they should make proper corrections in a timely fashion, the way those who keep tabs on credit records are expected to do.

These are a few examples of measures that provide obscurity equivalents in the 23 digital age. Still, let's remember the importance of gossip fueled by public records. As a rule, we care deeply about the approval of others. In most communities, being arrested is a source of major humiliation, and people will go to great pains to avoid ending up in jail. In such cases, the social system does not work if the information is not publicly available. This holds true for the digitized world, where the need for a much wider-ranging "informal social communication," as sociologists call gossip, applies not merely to criminals, sexual predators, and disgraced physicians. It holds for people who trade on eBay, sell used books on Amazon, or distribute loans from e-banks. These people are also eager to maintain their reputation — not just locally but globally. If we cannot find ways to deal in cyberspace with those who deceive and cheat, then our ability to use the Internet for travel, trade, investment, and much else will be severely set back.

This need is served in part by user-generated feedback and ratings, which inform 24 others who may do business via the Internet — much like traditional community gossip would. The ability of people to obscure their past in pre-Internet days made it all too easy for charlatans, quacks, and criminal offenders to hurt more people by simply switching locations. The new, digitized transparency is one major means of facilitating deals between people who do not know each other. With enough effort, its undesirable side effects can be curbed, and people can still gain a second chance.

Alternative view: Transition highlights example of precaution taken to address concerns

Conclusion: Transitional sentences summarize main idea of preceding section and introduce conclusion

VISUALIZING AN ARGUMENT ESSAY: A GRAPHIC ORGANIZER

The graphic organizer in Figure 21.2 will help you analyze arguments as well as plan those that you write. Unlike the graphic organizers in Part 3, this organizer does not necessarily show the order in which an argument is presented. Some arguments, for example, may begin with a claim, whereas others may start with evidence or opposing viewpoints. In addition, not every element will appear in every argument. Thus you will likely need to adapt this organizer to fit the essays you analyze and write.

For more on creating a graphic organizer, see pp. 52–55.

FIGURE 21.2 **Graphic Organizer for an Argument Essay**

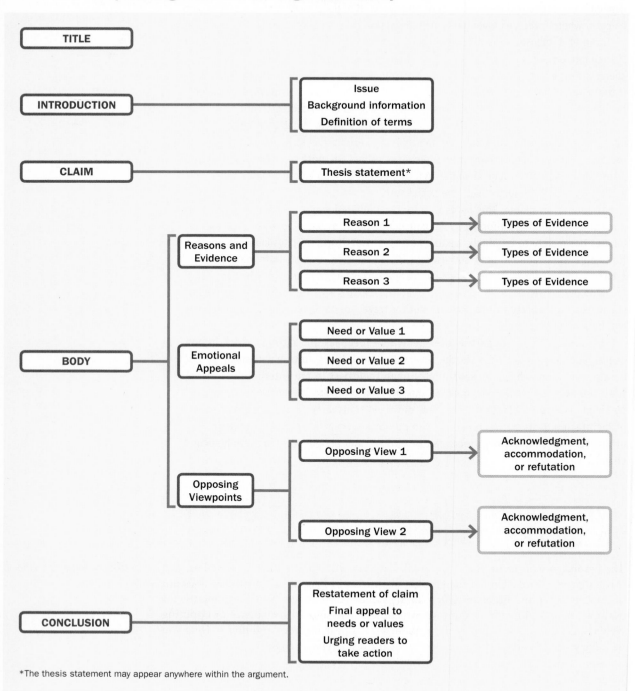

*The thesis statement may appear anywhere within the argument.

Abolish the Penny

WILLIAM SAFIRE

William Safire (1929–2009), a former speechwriter for President Richard Nixon and Vice President Spiro Agnew, was a longtime political columnist for *The New York Times*. He was also well known for "On Language," his column on grammar, usage, and etymology in the weekly *New York Times Magazine*, and he published many books, including novels, collections of his columns, and *Before the Fall: An Inside View of the Pre-Watergate White House* (2005). He won the Pulitzer Prize for commentary in 1978. As you read the following essay, published in 2004, notice how Safire gives his own reasons for abolishing the penny and anticipates possible counterarguments.

Because my staunch support of the war in Iraq has generated such overwhelming reader enthusiasm, it's time to reestablish my contrarian credentials. (Besides, I need a break.) Here's a crusade sure to infuriate the vast majority of penny-pinching traditionalists: The time has come to abolish the outdated, almost worthless, bothersome, and wasteful penny. Even President Lincoln, who distrusted the notion of paper money because he thought he would have to sign each greenback, would be ashamed to have his face on this specious specie.

That's because you can't buy anything with a penny any more. Penny candy? Not for sale at the five-and-dime (which is now a "dollar store"). Penny-ante poker? Pass the buck. Any vending machine? Put a penny in and it will sound an alarm. There is no escaping economic history: it takes nearly a dime today to buy what a penny bought back in 1950. Despite this, the U.S. Mint keeps churning out a billion pennies a month.

Where do they go? Two-thirds of them immediately drop out of circulation, into piggy banks or—as the *Times*'s John Tierney noted five years ago—behind chair cushions or at the back of sock drawers next to your old tin-foil ball. Quarters and dimes circulate; pennies disappear because they are literally more trouble than they are worth. The remaining 300 million or so—that's 10 million shiny new useless items punched out every day by government workers who could be more usefully employed tracking counterfeiters—go toward driving retailers crazy. They cost more in employee-hours—to wait for buyers to fish them out, then to count, pack up, and take them to the bank—than it would cost to toss them out. That's why you see "penny cups" next to every cash register; they save the seller time and the buyer the inconvenience of lugging around loose change that tears holes in pockets and now sets off alarms at every frisking place.

Why is the U.S. among the last of the industrialized nations to abolish the peskiest little bits of coinage? At the G-8 summit next week, the Brits and the French—even the French!—who dumped their low-denomination coins thirty years ago, will be laughing at our senseless jingling. The penny-pinching horde argues: those $9.98 price tags save the consumer 2 cents because if the penny was abolished, merchants would "round up" to the nearest dollar. That's pound-foolish: the idea behind the 98-cent (and I can't even find a cent symbol on my keyboard any more) price is to fool you into thinking that "it's less than 10 bucks." In truth, merchants would round down to $9.95, saving the consumer billions of paper dollars over the next century.

What's really behind America's clinging to the pesky penny? Nostalgia cannot be the answer; if we can give up the barbershop shave with its steam towels, we can give up anything. The answer, I think, has to do with zinc, which is what pennies are mostly made of; light copper plating turns them into red cents. The powerful, outsourcing zinc lobby—financed by Canadian mines as well as Alaskan—entices front groups to whip up a frenzy of save-the-penny mail to Congress when coin reform is proposed.   5

But when the penny is abolished, the nickel will boom. And what is a nickel made of? No, not the metallic element nickel; our 5-cent coin is mainly composed of copper. And where is most of America's copper mined? Arizona. If Senator John McCain would get off President Bush's back long enough to serve the economic interests of his Arizona constituents, we'd get some long-overdue coin reform.   6

What about Lincoln, who has had a century-long run on the penny? He's still honored on the $5 bill, and will be as long as the dollar sign remains above the 4 on keyboards. If this threatens coin reformers with the loss of Illinois votes, put Abe on the dime and bump F.D.R.[1]   7

What frazzled pollsters, surly op-ed[2] pages, snarling cable talkfests, and issue-starved candidates for office need is a fresh source of hot-eyed national polarization. Coin reform can close the controversy gap and fill the vitriol void. Get out those bumper stickers: Abolish the penny!   8

---

[1] *F.D.R.:* Franklin Delano Roosevelt, U.S. president from 1933 to 1945.

[2] *op-ed:* the opinion section of the newspaper that is opposite the editorial page.

EXERCISE 21.5 Creating a Graphic Organizer

Using Figure 21.2 or 21.3 as a basis, draw a graphic organizer for "Second Chances, Social Forgiveness, and the Internet" (pp. 534–39).

to frequently enough, naturally implants negative thoughts in the minds of its listeners.

Furthermore, consider the unique influence of music as opposed to other forms of media. Unlike movies, video games, and magazines, music has a way of saturating one's mind. Everyone knows the feeling of having a song "stuck" in their head, repeating itself throughout the day. Unlike a movie, which is seen once, discussed among friends, and then forgotten, a song can remain lodged in one's mind for weeks on end. And if the songs are steeped in content such as violence against women, happiness found in harmful drugs, and hatred of the police, these themes will continue reverberating in the minds of the listener, slowly desensitizing them to otherwise repulsive ideas. Becoming numb to such ideas is the first step toward passively agreeing with them or even personally acting upon them.

Whereas adults can usually listen to such music with no behavioral ramifications, children are far more susceptible to its subtle influence. With less experience of life, a lower level of maturity, and a lack of long-term thinking, young people are prone to make impulsive decisions. Providing them with access to music that fuels negative and harmful thoughts is a dangerous decision. We live in an age where violent tragedies such as school shootings are increasingly commonplace. Although various factors contribute to such acts of violence, hatred-themed music is likely a part of the equation. Therefore, given the influential power of music and the heightened effect it can have on those still in the developmental stage of their lives, young people should have limited access to music with explicit lyrics.

I propose sixteen years of age as a reasonable cut-off. Until children reach that age, they should not be allowed to purchase music with a Parental Advisory label. At sixteen, they are becoming young adults and making more and more of their own decisions. Before sixteen, they are weathering the turbulent transition from middle school to high school. This transition should not be accompanied by music that promotes rebellion as a means of coping with stress and difficulty. After reaching age sixteen, however, most young people will have obtained a driver's license, and the freedom that it allows eliminates the possibility of protecting youth from certain music. That is, those with a driver's license can seek out their own venues to hear explicit content, whether concerts or elsewhere.

4   **Reason 2:** Sturm presents his second reason and supports it by establishing common ground with his audience. Here and in the next paragraph, he includes transitions between his reasons.

5   **Reason 3:** Sturm presents his third reason and accommodates two opposing viewpoints; he refers back to the previous paragraph to create coherence.

6   Sturm offers an explanation for choosing sixteen as an age cutoff.

Opposing viewpoints: In this paragraph and the next two, Sturm recognizes three opposing viewpoints and accommodates each of them. Notice that he cites a source for the first viewpoint and includes transitions between them.

The main critique of my position is not new. Many say that it's pointless to censor music's explicit content because, as the RIAA's Web site contends, "music is a reflection, not a cause; it doesn't create the problems our society faces, it forces us to confront them" ("Freedom of Speech"). It is true that music reflects our culture. But it is also true that music fuels the perpetuation of that culture, for better or for worse. Guarding youth from explicit music does not equate to ignoring the issues raised in the music. It merely delegates that task to adults rather than to children.

7

Another critique says that limiting youth access to explicit music would take a financial toll on the music industry. This is true, but it would also force the music industry to adapt. We can either allow the youth of our nation to adapt to the music industry, or we can force the industry to adapt to an impressionable generation of kids.

8

A third critique is that even if explicit music were restricted to those of a certain age, younger kids would find access to it anyway. This is a legitimate concern, especially given the explosion of music-downloading software. But if not only music outlet stores but also online companies such as Amazon.com and iTunes were included in the regulations, progress would surely come.

9

Conclusion: Sturm quotes a hip-hop artist (and cites the source) to offer final support for his claim.

Hip-hop artist Ja Rule has spoken in favor of the current Parental Advisory system, saying, "That's what we can do as musicians to try to deter the kids from getting that lyrical content." But he added, "I don't think it deters the kids—it's just another sticker on the tape right now" (Bowes). Even hip-hop artists agree that protecting the minds of our youth is a necessity. But until laws are passed to restrict access to this music, the "Parental Advisory" label will just be another logo on the CD cover.

10

Works Cited

Bowes, Peter. "Spotlight on Explicit Lyrics Warning." *BBC News World Edition*, 27 May 2002, news.bbc.co.uk/2/hi/entertainment/2010641.stm.

"Freedom of Speech." Recording Industry Association of America, riaasalestool.shoshkey.com/aboutus.php?content_selector=Freedom-Of-Speech. Accessed 12 Apr. 2016.

"Parental Advisory Label." Recording Industry Association of America, www.riaa.com/resources-learning/parental-advisory-label/. Accessed 12 Apr. 2016.

ANALYZING THE WRITER'S TECHNIQUE

1. **Thesis** Analyze Sturm's thesis statement. What does it suggest about the organization of the essay? What aspect of the essay does it give no hint about?
2. **Evidence** What additional types of evidence could Sturm have used to support his reasons?
3. **Definition** How precisely does Sturm define the term *explicit lyrics*? Does his definition need to be more precise? Why or why not?

THINKING CRITICALLY ABOUT ARGUMENT

1. **Author's Attitude** What is Sturm's attitude toward explicit lyrics? Highlight words and phrases that reveal it.
2. **Fact or Opinion** Is Sturm relying on fact, opinion, or both to support his argument? Identify passages that support your answer.
3. **Audience** Who is Sturm's main audience? How do you know?
4. **Euphemism** What is "explicit music" a euphemism for?
5. **Needs and Values** To what needs and values does Sturm appeal?

RESPONDING TO THE READING

1. **Discussion** Discuss Sturm's proposal to ban the sale of "explicit music" to children. How are other media, such as books, movies, magazines, and TV shows, treated similarly or differently when it comes to children?
2. **Journal** What is the benefit, if any, of having explicit lyrics in music? Why are they needed, or why should they be allowed at all?
3. **Essay** Write an essay discussing the following dilemma: A middle school student wants to listen to explicit music, but it is not legally available to her age group. Her parents do not want her to have access to such music. Is there a compromise position? What advice would you offer to each side?

APPLYING YOUR SKILLS: ADDITIONAL ESSAY ASSIGNMENTS

TO PERSUADE YOUR READER

Write an argument essay on one of the following issues.

1. Professional sports
2. E-waste (electronic waste)
3. Alternative energy options
4. Genetic testing
5. Presidential campaigns

e macmillanhighered.com/successfulwriting
E-reading > *Should College Football Be Banned?* (video), Intelligence Squared U. S.

Narrow the issue to one that is arguable, such as a problem that could be solved by reforms or legislation. Narrow the issue to one that can be addressed in a brief paper (3–5 pages). Depending on the issue you choose, you may need to conduct research. Your audience is your classmates and instructor.

CASES USING ARGUMENT

1. Write an essay for a sociology course, arguing your position on the following statement: The race of a child and that of the prospective parents should be taken into consideration in making adoption decisions.
2. You have a job as a copyeditor at a city newspaper. Write a proposal that explains and justifies your request to work at home one day per week. Incorporate into your argument the fact that you could use your home computer, which is connected to the newspaper's computer network.

statistics showing how much less federal assistance is provided now than was provided in earlier decades, or you could quote education experts to support your position.

- **Provide historical information or context.** If you are writing about space stations, for example, find out when the first one was established, what country launched it, and what it has been used for. These details add useful background information to your research project.
- **Compare information about similar events or ideas with those you are discussing.** For example, if you are writing about a president's intervention in a labor strike, find out if other presidents have intervened in similar strikes. You can then point out similarities and differences.

Instructors will also expect you to **synthesize**, or make connections, among sources. When you synthesize information and ideas, you engage in a kind of conversation with your sources, making connections among ideas and information that reinforce or challenge each other to create new meaning of your own. Synthesis allows you to:

For more on synthesizing, see pp. 592–95.

- **Explore different points of view.** For example, in a paper about the consequences of divorce on children, you might use some sources that discuss the negative consequences and others that discuss the benefits.
- **Review key ideas on a topic.** For example, in a paper for an economics class explaining the reasons for increased income disparity in the past ten years, you might begin by reviewing the main reasons others have offered and respond to ideas you agree or disagree with.
- **Understand your topic in depth.** For example, synthesizing information and ideas from a variety of sources on global warming will help you see the issue from a variety of perspectives, leading you to think more deeply about the issue.

PLANNING YOUR RESEARCH PROJECT

The best place to start a research project is at your desk. There you can think about the assignment and devise a plan for completing it. This section describes several tasks that you should accomplish *before* you begin your research. (See Figure 22.1, p. 559).

DEFINING THE ASSIGNMENT

Before you begin researching an assigned topic, be sure you understand your instructor's expectations. Often the assignment will be written on the syllabus. Read the assignment carefully, noting all the requirements, which may include the following:

- the length of the final paper (number of pages, exclusive of the works-cited page)
- the number and types of sources you must use (for example, an assignment may specify that your works cited list must include at least three books and at least ten articles)
- the purpose of the assignment—**informative** projects ask you to *explain* a topic (for example, "Explain the treatment options for breast cancer") or

explore an issue (for example, "Examine the pros and cons of legalizing casino gambling"); **persuasive** projects ask you to *defend* or *argue for* a position (for example, "Defend or argue against your college's proposal to eliminate athletic scholarships")

- the genre of the assignment and the format you must follow (for example, are you writing a case study? a lab report? an evaluation?)
- any limitations placed on the research (for example, "No citations from Wikipedia," "No sources published before 2007," "No citations from for-profit organizations")
- the due date and any penalties for lateness
- the documentation style you are required to follow (see Chapter 24)

If your instructor announces the assignment in class, write down what he or she says, including as many details as possible. Sometimes instructors make "model papers" available for students to consult. Don't miss any opportunity to learn from, and be inspired by, these models.

Often major research projects are announced the first week of class. Because a large research project is a major undertaking, your professor is trying to give you as much time as possible to think about, plan, write, and revise your paper. As you proceed through the course, create a schedule for deciding on a topic, conducting the research, writing your first draft, revising your paper, ensuring your citations follow the required format exactly, and polishing your paper. You might build time into your schedule to discuss your ideas or share your drafts with friends or classmates or to get feedback from a writing center tutor.

Do not wait until the last minute to begin a research project! Writing a research project is a multistep process; it is likely to be a large part of your final grade, so put your best foot forward and devote the time necessary to making it the best it can be.

CHOOSING AN INTERESTING AND WORKABLE TOPIC

Most instructors allow you to choose your own topic for a research project. You will save time in the long run if you spend enough time at the outset choosing a topic that is both interesting and workable. Too many students waste hours researching a topic that they finally realize is too difficult, broad, or ordinary. The following tips will help you avoid such pitfalls.

1. **Choose a topic that interests you.** You will be able to write more enthusiastically if you work with a topic that captures your interest. If you have trouble choosing a topic, brainstorm with a classmate or friend.
2. **Choose a manageable topic.** Make sure you can adequately cover the topic within the assigned length of your paper. For example, don't try to write about all kinds of family counseling programs in a five- to ten-page paper. Instead, limit your topic to one type, such as programs for troubled adolescents.
3. **Avoid ordinary topics.** Familiar subjects that have been thoroughly explained in many sources seldom make good topics. For example, the subjects of "childhood obesity" and "reality TV" have been thoroughly discussed in many

newspapers and magazines and *ad nauseam* on Web sites. If you choose such a topic, be sure to come up with a different slant on it. A conversation will often help you discover new angles on ordinary topics.

4. **Choose a practical topic.** Topics that are in the news or for which a new breakthrough has just been reported do not typically make good choices because often little reliable information is available. Topics that require extensive technical knowledge that you lack do not typically make good choices because they may require more research than you can do in the time allowed.

NARROWING AND DISCOVERING IDEAS ABOUT YOUR TOPIC

To write effectively, you must narrow your topic enough that you can explore it thoroughly in the space allowed. The following techniques will help you narrow your topic as well as discover ideas about it.

For more on narrowing a topic and discovering ideas, see Chapter 5.

Do some preliminary reading. To get a sense of the scope, depth, and breadth of your topic, as well as to identify more manageable subtopics, you might skim an article on your topic in a general encyclopedia, such as *Encyclopaedia Britannica*, or in a specialized encyclopedia, such as *The McGraw-Hill Encyclopedia of Science and Technology*. Searching for your topic in your library's holdings, in a specialized database such as the weekly *CQ Researcher* (which contains thousands of articles on current topics) or even Google can also help you identify the subtopics into which a topic can be broken. You can also ask a reference librarian for assistance.

Try prewriting. To uncover an interesting angle on your topic or to narrow a broad topic, use one or more prewriting techniques. A branching diagram may be particularly helpful in narrowing a topic. The questioning technique, which challenges you to see your topic from different perspectives—psychological, sociological, scientific or technical, historical, political, and economic—can help you find an interesting subtopic or get an interesting angle. Here is how one student used questioning to analyze different perspectives on television advertising.

TOPIC: TELEVISION ADVERTISING

Perspective	*Questions*
Psychological	• How does advertising affect people?
	• Does it affect everyone the same way?
	• What emotional appeals are used, and how do they work?
Sociological	• Do different age groups respond differently to ads?
	• Is advertising targeted toward specific racial and ethnic groups?
Scientific or technical	• How are ads produced?
	• Who writes them?
	• Are the ads tested before they are broadcast?
Historical	• What is the history of advertising?
	• When and where did it begin?

Perspective	*Questions*
Political	• What legislation affects the content of advertising?
	• Why are negative political advertisements effective?
Economic	• How much does a television ad cost?
	• Is the cost of advertising added to the price of the product?

This list of questions yielded a wide range of interesting subtopics about advertising, including emotional appeals, targeting ads to specific racial or ethnic groups, and negative political advertising. You might work with a friend or classmate to devise and answer questions.

EXERCISE 22.1   **Narrowing a Topic for a Research Project**

Working with one or two classmates, narrow each of the following topics until you reach a topic that would be manageable for a five- to ten-page research project.

1. Taxes
2. U.S. prison system
3. Health care reform
4. Drones
5. Alternative energy sources

Research Project in Progress 1

Choose a broad topic for your research project. Come up with one on your own, or choose one of the broad topics below. Your audience consists of your classmates. Begin by using one or more prewriting techniques to generate ideas and narrow your focus. Then reread your work and highlight useful ideas.

1. Extreme sports
2. Adopting children from foreign countries
3. Employer-employee relations
4. Internet or identity fraud
5. Piracy of intellectual property (books, music, etc.)

Feel free to consult with your instructor about your topic. Your instructor may suggest a way to narrow your topic, recommend a useful source, or offer to review your outline.

WRITING A WORKING THESIS AND LISTING RESEARCH QUESTIONS

For more on drafting and revising a thesis statement, see Chapter 6, pp. 122–24.

Once you have chosen and narrowed a topic, try to determine, as specifically as possible, the kinds of information you need to know about it. Begin by writing a working thesis for your paper and listing the research questions you need to answer.

For example, one student working on the general topic of child abuse used prewriting and preliminary reading to narrow his focus to physical abuse and its causes. Since he already had a few ideas about possible causes, he used those ideas to write a working thesis. He then used his thesis to generate a list of research questions. Notice how the student's questions follow from his working thesis.

WORKING THESIS	The physical abuse of children often stems from parents' emotional instability and a family history of child abuse.
RESEARCH QUESTIONS	If a person was physically abused as a child, how likely is that person to become an abusive parent?
	What kinds of emotional problems seem to trigger the physical abuse of children?
	Which cause is more significant—a family history of abuse or emotional problems?
	Is there more physical abuse of children now than there was in the past, or is more abuse being reported?

A working thesis and a list of research questions will help you approach your research in a focused way. Instead of running helter-skelter from one aspect of your topic to another, you will be able to identify the specific information you need from sources.

EXERCISE 22.2 **Writing a Working Thesis and Research Questions**

For one of the following topics, write a working thesis and four or more research questions.

1. Methods of controlling pornography on the Internet
2. The possibility that some form of life has existed (or currently exists) on other planets
3. The rise of celebrity worship in the United States (or in any other country)
4. Benefits of tracing your family's genealogy (family tree)
5. Ways that elderly family members affect family life

Research Project in Progress 2

Review the list of ideas you generated in Research Project in Progress 1. Underline the ideas for which you need further details or supporting evidence, and list the information you need. Then, using the preceding guidelines, write a working thesis and a list of research questions.

CONSIDERING SOURCE TYPES

Once you have a working thesis and a list of research questions, stop for a moment. Think about which kinds of sources will be most useful, appropriate, relevant, and reliable. Keep in mind that you are unlikely to find all the sources you need online. Researchers must be equally skilled at locating sources in print and in electronic formats.

The types of sources that you will be expected to use will vary from discipline to discipline and assignment to assignment. The sources that are most appropriate will depend on your writing situation:

To learn more about the writing situation, see Chapter 5, pp. 103–07.

- the assignment,
- your purpose for writing,
- your audience, and
- the genre (or type).

For example, if you were writing an article for a local PTA newsletter (genre) to inform (purpose) parents (audience) about the school board's decision to provide more nutritious lunches for children, you might interview the school's nutritionist and gather data comparing the nutritional value of the typical new lunch (mini carrots, pita, hummus, and roasted chicken) to the nutritional value of the typical previous lunch (pizza, french fries, and Jell-o). You might also talk with the parents in the school district who were instrumental in getting the lunch menu improved and perhaps even ask some of the children their opinions regarding the new menu.

In contrast, if you were writing a research project (genre) for a history class (audience: your instructor) in which you argued (purpose) that skilled military commanders enabled the South to prolong the American Civil War, you might consult diaries written by Union soldiers, scholarly books and journal articles on Civil War battles and strategy, and maps showing troop movements.

PRIMARY AND SECONDARY SOURCES

The examples above mention primary (or firsthand) sources, such as interviews and diary entries, as well as secondary sources, such as books and articles. **Primary sources** include the following:

- historical documents (letters, diaries, speeches),
- literary works, autobiographies,
- original research reports,
- eyewitness accounts, and
- your own interviews, observations, or correspondence.

For example, a report on a study of heart disease written by the researcher who conducted the study is a primary source, as is a novel by William Faulkner. In addition, what *you* say or write can be a primary source. Your own interview with a heart attack survivor for a paper on heart disease is a primary source.

Secondary sources, in contrast, report or comment on primary sources. A journal article that reviews several previously published research reports on heart disease is a secondary source. A book written about William Faulkner by a literary critic or biographer is a secondary source.

Depending on your topic, you may use primary sources, secondary sources, or both. For a research project comparing the speeches of Abraham Lincoln with those of Franklin D. Roosevelt, you would probably read and analyze the speeches and listen to recordings of Roosevelt delivering his speeches (primary sources). But to learn about Lincoln's and Roosevelt's domestic policies, you would probably rely on several histories or biographies (secondary sources).

SCHOLARLY, POPULAR, AND REFERENCE SOURCES

For more on using a database to narrow sources by type, see Chapter 23, pp. 579–81.

In addition to primary and secondary, sources can also be classified as scholarly, popular, or reference sources. **Scholarly sources** are written by professional academics and scientific researchers and include both books by university presses or professional publishing companies and articles in discipline-specific academic journals that are edited by experts in the field. University presses include Oxford University Press, Princeton University Press, and the University of Nebraska Press (among many others).

There are thousands of highly regarded academic journals, ranging from *Nature* (a key journal in biology and the life sciences) to *The Lancet* (an important medical journal) to *American Economic Review* (a key journal for economists). Articles in academic journals often fall into two main categories.

1. Reports on original research conducted by the writer.
2. Surveys of previous research on a topic to identify key areas of agreement, which then become part of the accepted body of knowledge in the discipline.

Many scholarly sources are **peer reviewed**, which means the articles and books undergo a rigorous process of review by other scholars in the same discipline before they are accepted for publication. For these reasons, scholarly resources are accepted as accurate and reliable, and they usually form the basis of most research in academic papers.

Reference works are well-organized compendiums of facts, data, and information. They are intended to be consulted to answer specific questions rather than to be read from beginning to end. Dictionaries, encyclopedias, and thesauruses are common reference works.

Students and researchers frequently use discipline-specific reference works. For example, students of literature might consult *Benet's Reader's Encyclopedia* or *The Oxford Companion to English Literature*. Like scholarly resources, reference works are checked closely for accuracy, which makes them reliable sources of information. Many reference works also include suggestions for further reading, which can help researchers in their quest for additional resources. While reference works are a handy place to look up background information, they are not appropriate sources on which to base a research project.

Popular sources (newspapers, magazines, and general-interest nonfiction books) typically discuss what is going on in the "real world." For example, they publish stories about what happened and to whom—effects of a piece of legislation on a community, one woman's story of overcoming adversity to become successful in college or business. The subject matter is treated in a way that makes it accessible to most readers. Difficult topics are explained simply. One type of popular source, known as a **trade journal**, is aimed at people in specific professions. Trade journals provide the latest information on new ideas, products, personnel, events, and trends in an industry.

"Popular" does not necessarily mean unreliable. For example, a newspaper like the *Wall Street Journal* and a magazine like *Time* are good sources of information. The articles they publish are written by journalists who are trained in methods of research. Some popular magazines such as *Scientific American* and the *Economist* are quite serious indeed. At the other end of the spectrum are mass-circulation magazines, like *People* and *Sports Illustrated*, that are concerned primarily with celebrities and showmanship. Sources at the "celebrity" end of the spectrum may be useful for finding examples, but these publications often have little or no academic credibility.

Table 22.1 summarizes some of the differences between scholarly and popular sources. For most college research projects, consulting and citing popular sources is acceptable, but no academic paper should rely solely on popular sources. Distinguishing among scholarly, popular, and reference sources when they are accessed through a database can be tricky, since visual cues, like the glossy paper and splashy photographs, that distinguish

For more on choosing and evaluating sources, see pp. 569–73.

TABLE 22.1 A Comparison of Scholarly Journals and Popular Sources

	Scholarly Journals	Popular Sources
Who reads it?	Researchers, professionals, students	General public
Who writes it?	Researchers, professionals	Reporters, journalists, free-lance writers
Who decides what to publish in it?	Other researchers (peer reviewers)	Editors, publishers
What kind of information does it contain?	Results of research studies and experiments, statistics and analysis, in-depth evaluations of specialized topics, overviews of all the research on a subject (literature review), technical vocabulary, bibliographies and references	Articles of general interest, easy-to-understand language, news items, interviews, opinion pieces, no bibliographies (sources cited informally within the article)
How often is it published?	Mostly quarterly (every three months)	Daily (newspapers), weekly or monthly (magazines)
What are some examples?	*Journal of Bioethics, American Journal of Family Law, Film Quarterly*	*Popular Science, Psychology Today, The Week*

popular sources from scholarly ones are missing. Instead, you can use database tools or consult a reference librarian to help you determine source type.

BOOKS, ARTICLES, AND MEDIA SOURCES

A useful way to choose appropriate source types is to consider your needs in terms of the depth and type of content the source provides. **Books** often take years of study to produce and are often written by authorities on the subject, so they are likely to offer the most in-depth, comprehensive discussions of topics. Most scholarly books also provide pages and pages of research citations to help you dig further into any topic you find interesting or useful. Printed books provide an index to help you locate specific topics; e-books allow you to conduct keyword searches.

Articles are much briefer than books. In fact, most articles are under twenty pages, and some are as short as two or three pages. They tend to be more focused than books, exploring just one or two key points. They may also be more up-to-date, since they can be written and produced more rapidly than books can.

Most of the articles you access through your library's databases begin with an **abstract**, or brief summary. Reading the abstract can help you determine whether the article will be useful to your research. Keyword searches in electronic articles can help you locate the topics you are researching, and many academic databases use keywords to link you to other articles that may be useful in your research.

Media sources, such as photographs and information graphics, documentaries, audio podcasts, or works of fine art, can be useful for ideas and information. While in

For more on keyword searching, see Chapter 23, pp. 578–79.

popular sources, media items may be used to illustrate a text simply to attract readers, in academic texts, media must play a more substantial role. Use images in printed texts, or video and sound files in online texts, to illustrate a concept or to provide an example, but do not include illustrations merely for window dressing. Finally, keep in mind that documentaries may include fictional elements. Evaluate media sources carefully before including them as sources (see pp. 570–71).

As you seek answers to your research questions, you will likely need to consult various types of sources. Let's suppose you are writing a research project about narcissistic personality disorder (NPD), a recognized psychological disorder in which a person is obsessively concerned with ideas of his or her own personal superiority, power, and prestige. Through the process of narrowing your topic, you have decided to focus your paper on the behaviors associated with the disorder. What types of sources might you use?

- To help your readers understand exactly what NPD is, you might look to a reference book, such as the DSM-V (*Diagnostic and Statistical Manual of Mental Disorders,* 5th edition), a key reference work in psychology. The DSM is published by the American Psychological Association, which makes it a reliable resource.
- To research the real-world behaviors of people with NPD, you might consult several types of books. Scholarly books written by psychologists and published by university presses might offer case studies of people with NPD. You will likely also find books written by people who have NPD, in which they talk about their experiences and feelings. By using both types of sources, you can explore two sides of the issue: not only the clinical, diagnostic side of NPD but also the human side of it.
- To get your audience interested in your topic, you might begin by talking about celebrity behaviors that may reveal NPD. If you can find videos of celebrity interviews in which the celebrity exhibits behaviors associated with NPD, you will have found a good, reliable source to cite.

EVALUATING SOURCES

Evaluating sources is an essential part of writing a paper using sources. Unless you locate solid, relevant, and reliable sources and think critically about the ideas presented in each, your essay will lack academic rigor and credibility.

CHOOSING RELEVANT SOURCES

A *relevant* source contains information that helps you answer one or more of your research questions. Ask yourself the following questions to determine whether a source is relevant.

1. **Is the source appropriate for your intended audience, or is it too general or too specialized?**
2. **Is the source up-to-date or recent enough for your purposes?** In rapidly changing fields of study, outdated sources are not useful unless you need to give a historical perspective.

CHOOSING RELIABLE SOURCES

A *reliable* source is honest, accurate, and credible. Ask the following questions to help you determine whether a source is reliable, regardless of whether you accessed it in print or online.

1. **Is the source scholarly?** Although scholars often disagree with one another, they make a serious attempt to present accurate information.

2. **Does the source have a solid reputation?** Some news sources — magazines such as *Time* or the *Economist* and newspapers such as the *Washington Post* and the *New York Times* — are known for responsible reporting, whereas other newspapers and magazines have a reputation for sensationalism or bias. Such sources may be useful when you are exploring multiple perspectives on an issue, but be careful about interpreting articles in these publications as "the truth."

3. **What is the publication's purpose?** Why was the source published? In the case of general-interest magazines like *The Week*, which summarizes many articles from magazines and newspapers around the world, the purpose is clear: to provide readers with a wide variety of perspectives on issues of local and global importance. The purpose of a flyer left in your mailbox may be to introduce a new business in your neighborhood or to get you to convert to a new religion. To determine purpose, look for a link on the publication's Web site labeled "About Us" or "Mission Statement."

4. **Is the source professionally edited and presented?** Professionally published, reliable sources are generally free of typographical errors. Materials with obvious mistakes, as well as amateur typesetting or design, are often unreliable. Blogs may be good sources of viewpoint pieces, but a blog is really just one person's online diary. This means that blogs are subject to heavy bias as well as possible factual errors.

5. **Is the author an expert in the field?** Check the author's credentials. Information about authors may be given in a headnote, in a link to the author's biography, in the preface, or elsewhere. You might also check a reference work such as *Contemporary Authors* or Google the author to verify credentials.

6. **Does the author approach the topic fairly and objectively?** A writer who states a strong opinion is not necessarily biased. However, a writer who ignores opposing views, distorts facts, or ignores information that does not fit his or her opinion is presenting a biased and incomplete view of a topic.

7. **Can the content be verified?** The content in reliable sources can be verified in other reliable sources. Be cautious about using a piece of information you can find in only one source. Also be skeptical of any source that purports to summarize research or cite facts but does not provide a list of works cited (or, in the case of popular sources, attribution within the article or in footnotes).

For more on evaluating sources, see Chapter 4, pp. 82–97.

EXERCISE 22.3 **Evaluating the Relevance and Reliability of Sources**

Working in a small group, discuss the context in which the sources listed for each topic below would or would not be considered appropriate sources.

1. Topic: Caring for family members with Alzheimer's disease
   a. Introductory health and nutrition textbook
   b. Article in *Woman's Day* titled "Mother, Where Are You?"
   c. Article from a gerontology journal on caring for aging family members
2. Topic: Analyzing the effects of heroin use on teenagers
   a. Newspaper article written by a former heroin user
   b. Article from the *Journal of Neurology* on the biochemical effects of heroin on the brain
   c. Pamphlet on teenage drug use published by the National Institutes of Health
3. Topic: Implementing training programs to reduce sexual harassment in the workplace
   a. Article from the *Christian Science Monitor* titled "Removing Barriers for Working Women"
   b. Personal Web site or blog relating an incident of harassment on the job
   c. Training manual for employees of General Motors

EVALUATING RESOURCES IN THE DIGITAL LANDSCAPE

Use special care in evaluating the quality of the electronic materials you consult. In addition to the guidelines listed above, also consider the following.

- If you accessed the source through a library database or found the source through your college library's catalog, it is most likely reliable.
- If the source is an electronic version of a respected print publication (such as the *New York Times* or *Boston Globe*), the source is likely reliable. Be careful, however, about distinguishing between content that is edited and checked by the publication (and is therefore reliable) and links to other sources or any comments posted by readers.
- If the source does not specify its authorship or does not provide any information about the author's qualifications, proceed with caution.
- If the source contains factual errors, poor layout or design, too many photos and not enough words, or highly charged or emotional language, these are all signs that the source may be biased and lack credibility.

THINKING CRITICALLY ABOUT SOURCES

As you select sources for possible use in your paper, it is important to think critically about each. The following list of questions will help you analyze and evaluate sources.

- **Analyze the author's ideas.** Does the author make reasonable inferences, use reliable evidence, and make it clear when he or she is expressing an opinion?
- **Analyze the author's language.** Does the author's use of connotation and figurative language reveal bias? What does the author's tone indicate about his or her attitude? Does the author use euphemisms to hide something or to spare feelings?
- **Analyze the author's assumptions, generalizations, and omissions.** Are the author's assumptions and generalizations fair and reasonable? Are they supported by evidence? Do they reinforce or challenge social standards? Does any information seem to be omitted or treated in a less than thorough or complete way (pp. 82–85)?

For more on identifying bias by examining the writer's use of language, see Chapter 4, pp. 78–82.

The way an author presents ideas, the language an author uses, and the assumptions, generalizations, and omissions that he or she makes may all help you detect bias. **Bias** refers to a publisher's or writer's own views or particular interest in a topic. A biased source is not necessarily unreliable, but you need to recognize bias when you see it and find additional sources that present other points of view. Pay particular attention to the writer's tone.

Many relevant and reliable sources demonstrate bias. Some provide only a portion of the information you need for your paper. For example, if you are writing an essay on problems in the nursing profession, *The American Journal of Nursing* might be a reliable source, but it would probably not contain articles that are critical of nurses.

Other sources may have a strong opinion and present information from that point of view. For example, suppose you are writing an essay on home schooling for an introductory education class, and you find a book titled *The Home Schooling Movement: What Children Are Missing*. The author taught at a public high school for thirty years. This book may offer valuable information, but you need to recognize that its author supports classroom instruction and so may emphasize the shortcomings of home schooling or downplay its advantages. To use a biased source effectively, take the author's point of view into consideration as you evaluate the evidence the source provides.

EXERCISE 22.4 **Examining Sources for Bias**

Examine each of the following sources and their annotations. Discuss whether the source is likely to be objective (O), somewhat biased (SB), or heavily biased (HB).

1. Roleff, Tamara L., editor. *Gun Control: Opposing Viewpoints*. Greenhaven Press, 2007.

   This book contains several articles that present the pros and cons of different issues relating to gun control. The articles are written by experts and give bibliographic references.

2. Malcolm X. *The Autobiography of Malcolm X*. Ballantine Books, 1965.

   Malcolm X tells his life story in this autobiography, which was published just before his death.

3. Green, Amy. "Missions Boot Camp." *Christianity Today*, vol. 52, no. 2, Feb. 2008, www.christianitytoday.com/ct/2008/march/.

   This article describes a summer camp for young people heading off on mission trips.

4. Fink, George, editor. *Encyclopedia of Stress*. Academic Press, 2007.

   Four volumes of in-depth coverage related to the psychology and physiology of stress.

The following worksheet can help you evaluate the relevance and reliability of sources.

WORKSHEET: EVALUATING SOURCES

Title:

Author:

Author's qualifications or experience:

Publication information (journal, volume, issue; publisher, URL):

Month, date, and year of publication:

Is this source up-to-date? ☐ yes ☐ no

Type of source: ☐ primary ☐ secondary ☐ multimedia
  ☐ book ☐ article (specify: _____)
  ☐ scholarly work ☐ reference work ☐ popular source

Is the source appropriate for your audience? ☐ yes ☐ no

Does the source have a good reputation? ☐ yes ☐ no

   Does the source exhibit bias? ☐ yes ☐ no

What evidence do you have that the source is biased?

_____

_____

   Are opinions clearly stated as such? ☐ yes ☐ no

What is the purpose of the source?

   Who publishes the source?

   What are the publisher's goals?

Are the visual aids included with the source useful and credible? ☐ yes ☐ no

Is the source professionally presented and edited? ☐ yes ☐ no

Does the source contain any factual errors? ☐ yes ☐ no

Does the source provide documentation for all of its cited sources, either within the text or in a Works Cited/References section (or both)? ☐ yes ☐ no

Are there any hints that information has been omitted? ☐ yes ☐ no

   If yes, describe: _____

SCENES FROM COLLEGE AND THE WORKPLACE

- For an *anthropology course*, you are asked to write a research project in which you analyze the differences between the religious practices of two cultures.
- For an *art history course*, you must write a biography of a famous Renaissance artist as a final research project.
- As *supervisor* of a health care facility, you decide to conduct a survey of the staff to determine employees' interest in flexible working hours.

AN OVERVIEW OF LIBRARY SOURCES

Your college library is an immense collection of print, media, and online sources. Learning your way around the library is the first step in locating sources effectively.

LEARNING YOUR WAY AROUND THE LIBRARY

It is a good idea to become familiar with your college library *before* you need to use it. Following are a few ways to do so.

1. **Take a tour of the library.** Many colleges offer formal library tours during the first few weeks of the term, or your instructor may arrange one. On a tour, you'll learn where everything is located and discover how to use important services, such as interlibrary loan (borrowing materials from other libraries), and how to find reliable sources using your library's search tools. Check the library, too, for places to study, such as a library carrel or cubicle or a room where you can collaborate with classmates.

2. **Take a tour of your library's Web site.** Most college libraries provide access to rich resources through the library's Web site (see Figure 23.2). Often students can search for books, articles, multimedia sources, and more; access citation (or reference) managers (to help you manage sources and create lists of works cited or references); request sources through interlibrary loan; find a list of library hours or extended hours during midterms and finals; or ask a reference librarian for help. Visit your library's Web site to find out what services are available online as well as face-to-face.

MAKING USE OF REFERENCE LIBRARIANS

Reference librarians can help you at any stage in the research process, advising you about what sources to use and where to locate them. For example, reference librarians can help you do all of the following.

- Use library resources to make a topic broader, narrower, or more relevant.
- Get you started by steering you toward reference resources or basic books and articles that provide background information on your topic.

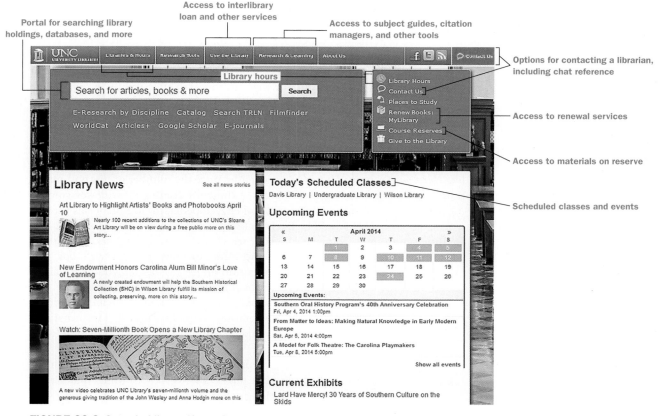

Portal for searching library holdings, databases, and more

Access to interlibrary loan and other services

Access to subject guides, citation managers, and other tools

Options for contacting a librarian, including chat reference

Access to renewal services

Access to materials on reserve

Scheduled classes and events

FIGURE 23.2 Sample Library Home Page
The University of North Carolina Library home page allows students to search for books, articles, and other resources all through a single portal. The home page also provides access to a wealth of other useful information. Courtesy of University of North Carolina at Chapel Hill Libraries

- Identify other libraries or special collections that might be relevant to your research, then help you request those materials through interlibrary loan.
- Help you decide which search terms to use, identify appropriate specialized databases, and learn how to search those databases most efficiently.
- Obtain the full text of articles for which you have only summary information (abstracts).
- Show you how to use various citation management systems such as EndNote or RefWorks. (Citation management systems are discussed in more detail on p. 606.)

In short, reference librarians can often save you time, so don't hesitate to ask them for help.

USING KEYWORDS EFFECTIVELY

Whether you use your library's search options or Google, you will use **keywords**, words or phrases that describe your topic, to search for information. You type your keywords into a search box, hit "Enter," and the search engine scans all the items in its index for those that include your keywords. In other words, to search effectively, you must figure out which words your sources are likely to use and use those as your keywords. The tips below can help improve your search results.

- **More specific terms yield more relevant results.** For example, if you were writing about alternative political parties in the United States, using keywords like *politics* or even *political parties* would be too broad. Searching on phrases like *third parties in the United States* would reduce the number of hits and make those hits more relevant. If you are having difficulty coming up with keywords, use a reference resource, like a specialized encyclopedia, to find the terms those writing about a topic would be likely to use.
- **Include synonyms.** To make sure your search yields the best results, brainstorm a list of synonyms for your keywords and search for those terms as well. For example, if you are searching for information on *welfare reform*, you might also search for *entitlement programs*, *government benefits*, and *welfare spending*.
- **Use full names and titles.** Search for people using full names, including middle initials when available. If the name is common, add other pieces of information, such as the college or university where the person teaches. When searching for books or articles, use complete titles.
- **Use the advanced search functions.** For example, Google's advanced search feature allows you to search for an exact phrase and to exclude words that should not appear in your search results (among other options). Google also allows you to filter your results by language, reading level, date, region, and several other criteria. Library search options also allow you to narrow your results, for example, to scholarly articles or to books published within a specific timeframe, in a specific language, or on a specific subject.
- **Use subject headings.** Most libraries and database vendors (such as EBSCO or LexisNexis) use standard subject headings to index their contents. To generate more relevant search results, make sure your keywords match the Library of Congress subject headings, or use the Thesaurus or Subject Terms link on the search page to check and refine your list of keywords. For instance, checking the thesaurus for a medical database may reveal that the ideal search term is not *heart attack* but *myocardial infarction*.

If your keyword searches are returning too many results or too many irrelevant results, try the following.

- Combine keywords to make your search terms more specific, or remove search terms to broaden your results.
- Once you find a relevant source, look at the subject terms associated with it, and use those for subsequent searches.

- Conduct a new search using a specialized database.
- Read the tool's search tips or FAQs for specific advice on how to improve your results.

Keep in mind that effective research requires ingenuity and persistence, so don't give up too easily.

USING APPROPRIATE SEARCH TOOLS

As you analyze your writing assignment, you will likely find yourself wondering where to begin. The key entry portal for research is your library's homepage. Student researchers may also benefit from using **research**, or **subject**, **guides**, discipline- and course-specific lists of useful resources. Each research guide has been created by a librarian and is tailored to the kinds of assignments that college students get regularly.

SEARCHING FOR BOOKS AND OTHER LIBRARY HOLDINGS

Libraries own a variety of source types: books and e-books, magazines and newspapers (in print), some printed government documents, special collections, and multimedia items such as video and audio recordings. Researchers identify relevant items in the library's collection by accessing a computerized catalog, which allows users to search online for sources by keyword, title, author, or subject from terminals in the library as well as from computers at home or in a campus computer lab. Some systems, like the one shown in Figure 23.3, allow users to narrow a search by subject, author, and publication date. Often the catalog will indicate not only where an item is shelved, but also whether it has been checked out and when it is due back.

Once you have a specific call number, use a library floor plan and the call number guides posted on shelves to locate the appropriate section of the library and the book you need. While looking for your book, be sure to scan the surrounding books, which are usually on related topics. You may discover other useful sources that you overlooked in the catalog.

SEARCHING FOR ARTICLES IN YOUR LIBRARY'S DATABASES

College libraries subscribe to databases that list articles in **periodicals**, publications that are issued at regular intervals (daily, weekly, monthly, or quarterly), such as scholarly journals, magazines, and newspapers. Database entries usually include an **abstract**, or brief summary of the article, as well as information about the article itself (title, author, publishing information, and keywords used in the article). As with library catalogs, databases allow users to refine their searches by limiting results by date or publication type, for example. They also may allow you to email, print, or save relevant articles.

Many articles will be available through the database in full text. They may appear in PDF format, which usually shows the article just as it appeared in the periodical, or in

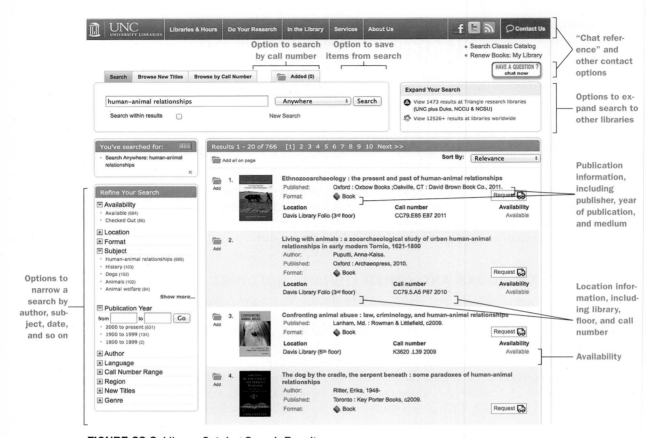

FIGURE 23.3 Library Catalog Search Results
Search results for the University of North Carolina Library holdings using the keywords *human-animal relationships* Courtesy of University of North Carolina at Chapel Hill Libraries

HTML format, which is usually text only. For articles that are not available in full text, a librarian can help you request them via interlibrary loan.

Your library probably subscribes to a wide array of databases. Two general categories are general and specialized. **General databases** list articles on a wide range of subjects in both popular magazines and scholarly journals. Academic Search Complete, for example, provides access to the full text of all the articles published in more than 8,600 journals, magazines, and newspapers, as well as abstracts for another 12,500 periodicals (see Figure 23.4).

Specialized databases index either articles within specific academic disciplines, or fields, or particular types of articles, such as book reviews, abstracts of doctoral dissertations, and articles and essays published in books. Some examples of specialized databases are *Book Review Digest Plus, Dissertation Abstracts, PsycArticles, Science Citation Index (Web of Science),* and *Sociological Abstracts.*

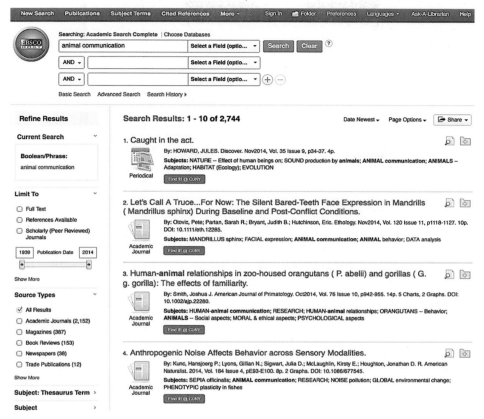

FIGURE 23.4 Academic Search Complete: Sample Search Results
Search results on the keywords *animal communication* EBSCO Information Services

Note: Names of databases may change, the number of sources a database indexes or includes full text for may change, and database vendors may make different packages of databases available at different times, so consult a reference librarian if you are not sure which database to use.

USING THE INTERNET FOR RESEARCH

The Internet provides access to millions of Web sites, but you need to use a search engine to find them. **Search engines** allow you to find information by typing a keyword or phrase into a search box. Google is such a popular search engine that you might never have used anything else, but other excellent search engines exist, and some of them are listed below.

Search engine	Why try it?
Ask.com	Ask (formerly called "Ask Jeeves") groups answers so you more readily find relevant results.
Bing.com	Bing provides a list of results in the main column but also includes a list of "Related searches," which may help you refine your search strategy.
Dogpile.com	Dogpile is a metasearch engine; in other words, it draws its results from a variety of other search engines.
DuckDuckGo.com	DuckDuckGo allows users to search anonymously and lists all results on a single page, making less clicking necessary.
Mahalo.com	Editors manually vet the content, so a search may yield fewer results, but they tend to be more relevant.
Yahoo.com	In addition to being a search engine, Yahoo also aggregates news sources, and it offers categories (or *subject directories*) that you can browse.

Because different search engines usually generate different results, it is a good idea to try your search on more than one search engine.

Note: If your keywords are too general, a search will return thousands (sometimes hundreds of thousands) of results, most of which will not be helpful to you. So use the strategies for keyword searching discussed on pages 578–579 to fine-tune your search.

For more on evaluating sources, see Chapter 4, pp. 78–87, and Chapter 22, pp. 569–73.

While the Internet is an amazing resource for researchers, the quality of the content you will find varies wildly. As a result, researchers must evaluate content very carefully before relying on it.

News sites. Newspapers, television and radio networks, and magazines have companion Web sites that provide current information and late-breaking news stories. Some of the most useful are listed below.

BBC	www.bbc.co.uk
CNN Interactive	www.cnn.com
MSNBC	www.msnbc.com
New York Times	www.nytimes.com
National Public Radio	NPR.org
Washington Post	www.washingtonpost.com

General reference sites. Reference works are available online, through the Web or through the databases your library subscribes to. Some of the most useful general reference sites are listed on the next page.

Britannica Online	www.eb.com
Columbia Encyclopedia	education.yahoo.com/reference/encyclopedia
Encyclopedia.com	www.encyclopedia.com
Encyclopedia Smithsonian	www.si.edu/encyclopedia_si
Merriam-Webster Online	www.merriam-webster.com
PLoL: Public Library of Law	www.plol.org/Pages/Search.aspx

Some of these sites may not be available for free through Google; check to find out if your college library provides access to these or other general reference sources.

Government documents. The federal government makes hundreds of thousands of documents freely available online every year on a vast range of subjects. Some government sites that students find particularly useful are listed below.

U.S. Bureau of Labor Statistics	www.bls.gov
U.S. Census Bureau	www.census.gov
The Central Intelligence Agency's World Fact Book	www.cia.gov/library/publications/the-world-factbook
FedStats	fedstats.gov
Library of Congress	www.loc.gov
National Institutes of Health	www.nih.gov

In addition, you can access many useful government documents through library databases such as *CQ Electronic Library*.

USING LISTSERVS AND NEWSGROUPS

The Internet's listservs and newsgroups are discussion forums where people interested in a particular topic or field of research can communicate and share information. A **listserv** is an email discussion group; messages are sent automatically to subscribers' email accounts. Some listservs allow anyone to subscribe, whereas others require a moderator's permission. In contrast, a **newsgroup** does not require membership, and messages are posted to a news server for anyone to read and respond to. A central network called *Usenet* provides access to thousands of newsgroups.

Consult the frequently asked questions (FAQs) for a listserv or newsgroup to determine if it suits your needs and, for a listserv, to see how to subscribe. Keep in mind that messages posted to listservs and newsgroups are not usually checked for accuracy and are not always reliable sources of information (though, in general, listserv discussions tend to be more serious and focused than newsgroup discussions). You can use electronic discussion forums to become familiar with a topic; obtain background information; discover new issues, facets, or approaches; and identify print sources of information.

To locate discussion groups, use a Web search engine to search for the term *discussion groups* or *Usenet* plus your topic.

CONDUCTING FIELD RESEARCH

Depending on your research topic, you may need—or want—to conduct field research to collect original information. This section discusses three common types of field research.

1. Interviews
2. Surveys
3. Observation

All of these methods generate primary source material.

INTERVIEWING

An **interview** allows you to obtain firsthand information from a person who is knowledgeable about your topic. For example, if the topic of your research project is *treatment of teenage alcoholism,* it might be a good idea to interview an experienced substance abuse counselor who works with teenagers. Use the following suggestions to conduct effective interviews.

1. **Choose interviewees carefully.** Be sure your interviewees work in the field you are researching or are experts on your topic. Also try to choose interviewees who may offer different or unexpected points of view. If you are researching a corporation, for example, try to interview someone from upper management as well as white- and blue-collar workers.

2. **Arrange your interview by phone, email, or letter well in advance.** Describe your project and purpose, explaining that you are a student working on an assignment. Indicate the amount of time you think you'll need, but don't be disappointed if the person offers you less time or denies your request altogether. Be flexible about whom you interview. For example, a busy vice president may refer you to an assistant or to another manager.

3. **Plan the interview.** Do some research to make sure the information you need is not already available through more traditional sources. Then devise a list of questions you want to ask. Try to ask *open questions,* which generate discussion, rather than *closed questions,* which can be answered in a word or two. For example, "Do you think your company has a promising future?" could be answered yes or no, whereas, "How do you account for your company's turnaround last year?" might spark a detailed response. Open questions usually encourage people to open up and reveal attitudes as well as facts.

4. **Take notes during the interview.** Write the interviewee's responses in note form and ask whether you may quote him or her directly. If you want to record the interview, be sure to ask the interviewee's permission.

5. **Evaluate the interview.** As soon as possible after the interview, reread your notes and fill in information you did not have time to record. Also write down your reactions while they are still fresh in your mind. Try to write down your overall impression and an answer to this question: What did I learn from this interview?

Many authors, researchers, and corporations are also willing to respond to email requests for specific information. When you send an email message to someone you don't know, be sure to introduce yourself and briefly describe the purpose of your inquiry. Include a specific subject line so that your email is not deleted as spam. Provide complete information about yourself, including the name of your school and how to contact you, and politely request the information you need.

CONDUCTING A SURVEY

A **survey** is a set of questions designed to elicit information quickly from a large number of people. Surveys are often used to assess people's attitudes or intentions. They can be conducted face-to-face, by phone, by email, by regular mail, or online.

Use the following suggestions to prepare effective surveys.

1. **Clarify the purpose of the survey.** Prepare a detailed list of what you want to learn from the survey.
2. **Design your questions.** A survey can include closed or open questions or both, but most surveys use mostly closed questions (either a multiple-choice or a ranking-scale format), so responses can be tabulated easily.
3. **Test your survey questions.** Try out your questions on a few classmates, family members, or friends to be sure they are clear, unambiguous, and easily understood. Ask yourself: Will the answers to these questions provide the information I need? Are the questions phrased in an unbiased and nonleading way?
4. **Select your respondents.** Your respondents—the people who provide answers to your survey—must be *representative* of the group you are studying and must be *chosen at random*. For example, if you are planning a survey to learn what students on your campus think about mandatory drug testing for athletes, you should choose a group of respondents (a *sample*) that accurately represents your school's student population. For most campuses, then, your group of respondents would contain both men and women, be racially and ethnically diverse, and represent students' various ages and socioeconomic groups. Your sample should also be random; respondents should be unknown to you and not chosen for a specific reason. One way to draw a random sample is to give the survey to every fifth or tenth name on a list or to every fifteenth person who walks by.
5. **Summarize and report your results.** Tally the results and look for patterns in the data. If the sample is fairly large, use a computer spreadsheet to tabulate results. In your paper, discuss your overall findings, not individual respondents' answers (though you may choose to quote representative answers from open-ended questions). Explain the purpose of the survey as well as how you designed it, selected the sample, and administered the survey to respondents. You may also want to include a copy of the survey and tabulations in an appendix.

CONDUCTING OBSERVATIONS

An **observation**—the inspection of an event, a scene, or an activity—can be an important primary source in a research project. For instance, you might observe children at play to analyze differences in play between boys and girls. Firsthand observation can yield valuable insights on the job as well. You might, for example, need to observe and report on the condition of hospital patients or the job performance of your employees.

Use the following tips to conduct observations effectively.

1. **Arrange your visit in advance.** Unless you are conducting an observation in a public place, obtain permission from the company or organization in advance. Make the purpose of your visit clear when arranging your appointment.

2. **Take detailed notes on what you observe.** Write down the details you will need to describe the scene vividly in your paper. For instance, if you visit a mental health clinic, note details about patient care, security, hygiene, and the like. You might sketch the scene, especially if you are a spatial learner, or record a video if you have permission to do so.

For more on creating a dominant impression, see Chapter 13, pp. 267–68.

3. **Create a dominant impression.** As soon as possible after your visit, evaluate your observations. Think about what you saw and heard. Then describe your dominant impression of what you observed and the details that support it.

WORKING WITH SOURCES: TAKING NOTES, SUMMARIZING, AND PARAPHRASING

For more on previewing, see Chapter 3, pp. 45–47.

Reading sources involves some special skills. Unlike textbook reading, in which your purpose is to learn and recall the material, you usually read sources to extract the information you need about a topic. Therefore, you can often read sources selectively, previewing the source to identify relevant sections and reading just those sections.

TAKING NOTES

Your purpose in conducting research is to explore your topic, consider multiple perspectives, and gradually arrive at your own main point—your thesis. As you conduct research, your ideas will develop, and you will generate topic sentences based on a synthesis of sources that you've read. In fact, the development of these integrated or synthesized ideas is a key goal of writing a research project.

For more on creating entries in a works-cited or references list, see Chapter 24, pp. 620–31, 642–49.

Because you must give credit to those who informed your thinking, record all the source information that you will need when creating your list of works cited. Be particularly cautious when cutting and pasting source materials into your notes. Always place quotation marks around anything you have cut and pasted. Be sure to clearly separate your ideas from the ideas you found in sources. If you copy an author's exact words, place the information in quotation marks, and write the term *direct quotation* as well as the page number(s) in parentheses after the quotation. If you write a summary note (see pp. 588–89) or paraphrase (see pp. 589–91), write *paraphrase* or *summary* and the page number(s) of the source. Be sure to include page numbers; you'll need them to double-check your notes against the source and to create a works-cited entry.

Note-taking tools. Many students use a series of computer folders or a notebook for their research. In a notebook, you might use section dividers for different components of your research; in a computer folder, you might use various subfolders. A notebook or computer file is a good place to store copies of research materials that you have copied or downloaded.

While many students prefer to take notes in computer files or notebooks, some researchers still like to use index cards for note-taking. (There are also programs available that allow you to create computerized note cards.) Note cards allow you to arrange and rearrange the material to experiment with different ways of organizing your project. If you decide to use note cards, put information from only one source or about only one subtopic on each card. At the top of the card, indicate the author of the source and the page numbers on which the information appears, and note the subtopic that the note covers. Figure 23.5 below shows a sample note card. Use a separate set of note cards to list the bibliographic information you will need to cite the source. (See Figure 23.6 on p. 592.)

Citation (or reference) managers, programs like Mendeley, RefWorks, and Zotero, can be useful tools throughout the research process because they allow you to save sources, take notes, and incorporate those notes into your research project as you write. They may also help you format your works cited or reference list entries.

Annotating and highlighting source materials. Annotating and highlighting (or underlining) can be a useful system of engaging closely with source materials. You may annotate and highlight using a pencil and a highlighting marker or using the annotation and highlighting features available with some electronic documents. You can then store these annotated documents in a notebook pocket, a computer file, or a citation manager. Remember to be selective about what you mark or comment on as you annotate, keeping the purpose of your research in mind.

For more on annotating and highlighting, see Chapter 3, pp. 50–51.

FIGURE 23.5 Sample Note Card

Schmoke & Roques, 17-25
Medicalization
Medicalization is a system in which the government would control the release of narcotics to drug addicts.
— would work like a prescription does now — only gov't official would write prescription
— addicts would be required to get counseling and health services
— would take drug control out of hands of drug traffickers (paraphrase, 18)

TAKING NOTES THAT SUMMARIZE, PARAPHRASE, OR QUOTE

Much of your note-taking should summarize, or condense, information from sources, since you will mostly not need the exact wording or the kinds of details you would include in a paraphrase.

After summarizing, paraphrasing is probably the second-most common form your notes should take. Paraphrase when recording the supporting details is important, but paraphrase only the ideas or details you intend to use. Both summarizing and paraphrasing force you to understand the source.

Including **direct quotations**—writers' exact words—is probably the least common form your notes should take, but including quotations in your notes can still be advisable, even necessary. Use quotations to record wording that is unusual or striking, capture technical details you might get wrong, or report the exact words of an expert on your topic.

SUMMARIZING

As you write summary notes, keep the following in mind.

- Everything you put in summary notes must be *in your own words and sentences*.
- Your summary notes should accurately reflect the relevant main points of the source.

For more on writing summaries, see Chapter 3, pp. 53, 56.

Use the guidelines below to write effective summary notes.

1. **Record only information that relates to your topic and purpose.**
2. **Write notes that condense the author's ideas into your own words.** Include key terms and concepts or principles, but omit specific examples, quotations, or anything else that is not essential to the main point and your own opinion. You can write comments in a separate note.
3. **Record the ideas in the order in which they appear in the original source.** Reordering ideas might affect the meaning.
4. **Reread your summary to determine whether it contains enough information.** Consider whether it would it be understandable to someone who has not read the original source.
5. **Record the complete publication information for the sources you summarize.** Unless you summarize an entire book or poem, you will need to include page references when you write your paper and prepare a works-cited list.

A sample summary of the first four paragraphs of the essay "Dude, Do You Know What You Just Said?" (pp. 438–40) appears below. Read or reread paragraphs 1–4, and then study the summary.

SAMPLE SUMMARY

"Dude, Do You Know What You Just Said?" reports on the findings of Scott Kiesling, a linguist who has studied the uses and meanings of the popularly used word *dude*. Historically, *dude* was first used to refer to a dandy and then became a slang term used by various social groups. For his study, Kiesling listened to tapes of fraternity members and asked undergraduate students to record uses of the term. He determined that it is used for a variety of purposes, including to show enthusiasm or excitement, one-up someone, avoid confrontation, and demonstrate agreement.

PARAPHRASING

When you paraphrase, you restate the author's ideas *in your own words and sentences*. You do not condense ideas or eliminate details as you do in a summary; instead, you keep the author's intended meaning but express that meaning in different sentence patterns and vocabulary. In most cases, a paraphrase is approximately the same length as the original material.

When paraphrasing, be careful not to *plagiarize*—that is, do not use an author's words or sentences as if they were your own. Merely replacing some words with synonyms is not enough; you must also use your own sentence structures and may want to reorganize the presentation of ideas. Reading the excerpt from a source below and comparing it, first, with the acceptable paraphrase that follows and then with the example that includes plagiarism will help you see what an acceptable paraphrase looks like.

For more on avoiding plagiarism, see Chapter 24, pp. 601–03.

EXCERPT FROM ORIGINAL

Learning some items may interfere with retrieving others, especially when the items are similar. If someone gives you a phone number to remember, you may be able to recall it later. But if two more people give you their numbers, each successive number will be more difficult to recall. Such proactive interference occurs when something you learned earlier disrupts recall of something you experienced later. As you collect more and more information, your mental attic never fills, but it certainly gets cluttered.

David G. Myers, Psychology

ACCEPTABLE PARAPHRASE

According to David Myers, when proactive interference happens, things you have already learned prevent you from remembering things you learn later. In other words, details you learn first may make it harder to recall closely related details you learn subsequently. You can think of your memory as an attic. You can always add more junk to it. However, it will become messy and disorganized. For example, you can remember one new phone number, but if you have two or more new numbers to remember, the task becomes harder.

UNACCEPTABLE PARAPHRASE — INCLUDES PLAGIARISM

When you learn some things, it may interfere with your ability to remember others. This happens when the things are similar. Suppose a person gives you a phone number to remember. You probably will be able to remember it later. Now, suppose two persons give you their numbers. Each successive number will be harder to remember. Proactive interference happens when something you already learned prevents you from recalling something you experience later. As you learn more and more information, your mental attic never gets full, but it will get cluttered.

Replaces terms with synonyms

Copied terms and phrases

The unacceptable paraphrase does substitute some synonyms—*remember* for *retrieving,* for example—but it is still an example of plagiarism. Not only are some words copied directly from the original, but also the structure of the sentences is nearly identical to the original.

Paraphrasing can be tricky, because letting an author's language creep in is easy. These guidelines will help you paraphrase without plagiarizing.

1. **Read first; then write.** Read material more than once before you try paraphrasing. To avoid copying an author's words, cover up the passage you are paraphrasing (or switch to a new window on your computer), and then write.

2. **Use synonyms that do not change the author's meaning or intent, and if you must use distinctive wording of the author's, enclose it in quotation marks.** Consult a dictionary or thesaurus if necessary. Note that for some specialized terms and even for some commonplace ones, substitutes may not be easy to come by. In the acceptable paraphrase above, the writer uses the key term *proactive interference,* as well as the everyday word *attic,* without quotation marks. However, if the writer paraphrasing the original were to borrow a distinctive turn of phrase, this would need to be in quotation marks. Of course, deciding when quotation marks are or are not needed requires judgment, and if you are not sure, using quotation marks is never wrong.

For more on varying sentence structure, see Chapter 10, pp. 197–203.

3. **Use your own sentence structure.** Using an author's sentence structure can be considered plagiarism. If the original uses lengthy sentences, for example, your paraphrase may use shorter sentences. If the original phrases something in a compound sentence, try recasting the information in a complex one.

4. **Rearrange the ideas if possible.** If you can do so without changing the sense of the passage, rearrange the ideas. In addition to using your own words and sentences, rearranging the ideas can make the paraphrase more your own. Notice that in the acceptable paraphrase above, the writer starts by introducing the term *proactive interference,* whereas in the original source, this term is not used until the fourth sentence.

Be sure to record the publication information (including page numbers) for the sources you paraphrase. You will need this information to document the sources in your paper.

> **EXERCISE 23.1** **Writing a Paraphrase**

Write a paraphrase of the following excerpt from a source on animal communication.

> Another vigorously debated issue is whether language is uniquely human. Animals obviously communicate. Bees, for example, communicate the location of food through an intricate dance. And several teams of psychologists have taught various species of apes, including a number of chimpanzees, to communicate with humans by signing or by pushing buttons wired to a computer. Apes have developed considerable vocabularies. They string words together to express meaning and to make and follow requests. Skeptics point out important differences between apes' and humans' facilities with language, especially in their respective abilities to order words using proper syntax. Nevertheless, these studies reveal that apes have considerable cognitive ability.
>
> David G. Myers, *Psychology*

EXERCISE 23.2 **Evaluating a Paraphrase for Plagiarism**

The piece of student writing below is a paraphrase of a source on the history of advertising. Working with another student, evaluate the paraphrase and discuss whether it would be considered an example of plagiarism. If you decide the paraphrase is plagiarized, rewrite it so that it is not.

ORIGINAL SOURCE

Everyone knows that advertising lies. That has been an article of faith since the Middle Ages—and a legal doctrine, too. Sixteenth-century English courts began the Age of Caveat Emptor by ruling that commercial claims—fraudulent or not—should be sorted out by the buyer, not the legal system. ("If he be tame and have ben rydden upon, then caveat emptor.") In a 1615 case, a certain Baily agreed to transport Merrell's load of wood, which Merrell claimed weighed 800 pounds. When Baily's two horses collapsed and died, he discovered that Merrell's wood actually weighed 2,000 pounds. The court ruled the problem was Baily's for not checking the weight himself; Merrell bore no blame.

Cynthia Crossen, *Tainted Truth*

PARAPHRASE

It is a well-known fact that advertising lies. This has been known ever since the Middle Ages. It is an article of faith as well as a legal doctrine. English courts in the sixteenth century started the Age of Caveat Emptor by finding that claims by businesses, whether legitimate or not, were the responsibility of the consumer, not the courts. For example, there was a case in which one person (Baily) used his horses to haul wood for a person named Merrell. Merrell told Baily that the wood weighed 800 pounds, but it actually weighed 2,000 pounds. Baily discovered this after his horses died. The court did not hold Merrell responsible; it stated that Baily should have weighed the wood himself instead of accepting Merrell's word.

RECORDING QUOTATIONS

Enclose quotations within quotation marks. When writing your paper, you may adjust a quotation to fit your sentence, so long as you do not change the meaning of the quotation, but when taking notes, be sure to record the quotation precisely as it appears in the source. Also provide the page number(s) on which the material being quoted appears in the original source. In your notes, be sure to indicate that you are copying a direct quotation by including quotation marks, the term *direct quotation,* and the page number(s) in parentheses.

For more on how to adjust a quotation to fit your sentence, see Chapter 24, pp. 611–12.

KEEPING TRACK OF SOURCES

In addition to gathering information from sources, you must carefully record the information you will need to cite each source. Using a form like the one shown in Figure 23.6 can help you make sure you record all the information you will need. Using a citation manager (p. 606) can also help.

For more on citing sources, see Chapter 24.

FIGURE 23.6 Bibliographic Information Worksheet

Author(s) _____

Title and subtitle of source _____

Title of work source appears in (if any): Journal/anthology/Web site _____

Other contributors: Editor/translator/director _____

Version: Edition/director's cut _____

Volume/issue _____

Publisher/sponsor _____

Publication date _____

Location: Pages/URL/DOI (Digital Object Identifier) _____

WORKING WITH SOURCES: EVALUATING YOUR NOTES AND SYNTHESIZING

Before you begin drafting, you'll need to make sense of the information you've gathered by synthesizing information and ideas. *Synthesis* means "a pulling together of information to form a new idea or point." You synthesize information every day. For example, after you watch a preview of a movie, talk with friends who have seen the film, and read a review of it, you then pull together the information you have acquired and come up with your own idea — that the movie is your cup of tea, or that you will probably not like it.

You often synthesize information for your college courses. In a biology course, for instance, you might evaluate your own lab results, those of your classmates, and the data in your textbook or another reference source to reach a conclusion about a particular experiment.

Synthesis involves putting ideas together to see how they agree, disagree, or otherwise relate to one another. When working with sources, ask yourself the following questions.

- Do my sources reinforce or contradict one another?
- How do their claims and lines of reasoning compare?
- Do they make similar or dissimilar assumptions and generalizations?
- Is their evidence alike in any way?

Before you begin the synthesis process, however, you must evaluate the sources you've consulted in terms of how well they suit your purposes and audience.

EVALUATING YOUR RESEARCH

Before you began researching your topic, you most likely wrote a *working thesis*—a preliminary statement of your main point about the topic—and a list of research questions you hoped to answer. Then, as you researched your topic, you may have discovered facts, statistics, or experts' ideas about the topic that surprised you.

For more on evaluating the reliability of sources, see Chapter 22, p. 570.

As you evaluate your research notes, keep the following questions in mind.

1. What research questions did I begin with?
2. What answers did I find to those questions?
3. What other information did I discover about my topic?
4. What conclusions can I draw from what I've learned?
5. How does my research affect my working thesis?

In many cases, the answers to these questions will influence your thinking on the topic, requiring you to modify your working thesis. If you can't answer these questions in a way that you find satisfactory, you will need to conduct more research to clarify or refine your thinking. In some cases, you may even need to rethink the direction of your paper.

The process of evaluating your research will often result in decisions not to use specific sources in your final paper. Perhaps the source does not provide any new or relevant information; perhaps it comes from a source that you decide is unreliable; perhaps you have too much information to fit in the length of your assignment, and you need to narrow your focus. View this research as information that has contributed to your understanding of the topic, and then set aside the note cards or move the information to a separate notebook section or file where it will not get in your way.

USING CATEGORIES TO SYNTHESIZE INFORMATION FROM SOURCES

In order to make sense of what you've learned, you will need to find patterns in the information you have gathered. One way to find patterns is to categorize information according to your research questions. For example, one student found numerous sources on and answers to his research question "What causes some parents to abuse their children physically?" After rereading his research notes, he realized the information could be divided into three categories:

Category	*Sources*
1. Lack of parenting skills	Lopez, Wexler, Thomas
2. Emotional instability	Wexler, Harris, Thompson, Wong
3. Family history of child abuse	Thompson, Harris, Lopez, Strickler, Thomas

Evaluating his research in this way made him see that he needed to revise both his working thesis and the scope of his paper to include lack of parenting skills as a major cause of child abuse. Notice how he modified his working thesis accordingly:

Some
~~The main reasons that~~ children are physically abused ~~are~~ *because of* their parents' emotional instability ~~and~~ family history of child abuse *, and lack of parenting skills*.

For controversial topics, you may want to categorize the information you've gathered in terms of each position on the issue (pro, con, or somewhere in between). Alternatively, you could categorize information in terms of the reasons sources offer to support their positions. On the issue of gun control legislation, for example, some sources may favor it for national security reasons: Gun control makes it harder for terrorists to acquire guns. Others may favor it for statistical reason: Statistics prove that owning a gun does not prevent crime. Still others may favor it for emotional reasons: A loved one was injured or killed by a firearm.

If your research project focuses on comparing or contrasting two things (for example, communism and capitalism), you could categorize the information you found on each subtopic separately, and then use that organized information to prepare an outline or graphic organizer of your paper.

DRAWING A GRAPHIC ORGANIZER TO SYNTHESIZE SOURCES

Using a graphic organizer is another way to make sense of the information you gather from sources. Simply the process of creating a graphic organizer may reveal patterns, as well as show you how main ideas and supporting details connect.

Suppose, for example, that you are arguing in favor of adopting voluntary simplicity — the minimizing of personal possessions and commitments to create a happier, more manageable life. You have located three reliable and relevant sources on voluntary simplicity, but each develops the idea somewhat differently.

1. Source 1 (Walker) is a practical how-to article that includes some personal examples.
2. Source 2 (Parachin) offers a theoretical look at statistics about workloads and complicated lifestyles and the reasons that voluntary simplicity is appealing.
3. Source 3 (Remy) presents some strategies for simplifying but emphasizes the values of a simplified life.

Figure 23.7 presents a sample organizer that synthesizes information from these three sources.

Depending on the types of information you uncover, you can use a variety of organizer formats: If all your sources compare and contrast the same things, such as the policies and effectiveness of two U.S. presidents, you could adapt one of the graphic organizers for comparison and contrast shown in Chapter 16. If most of your sources focus on effects, such as the effects of a recession on retail sales and employment, you could adapt one of the cause-and-effect graphic organizers shown in Chapter 19. Whatever style of organizer you use, be sure to keep track of the sources for each idea and to include them in your organizer.

FIGURE 23.7 Graphic Organizer for Synthesizing Sources

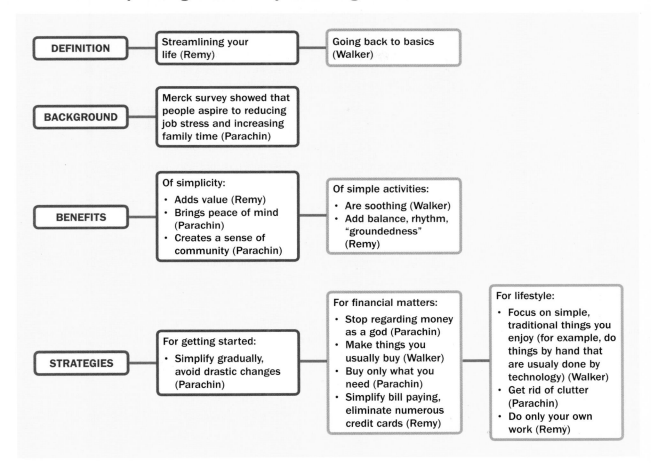

CREATING AN ANNOTATED BIBLIOGRAPHY

As part of the process of writing a research project, some instructors may require you to create an **annotated bibliography,** a list of sources that includes both publication information and a brief summary for each source. Annotated bibliographies are useful ways to document your research process, so they include all the sources you consulted in researching your topic.

Your writing situation will influence the information you include in your annotations, but for most college research projects, the annotations should summarize the main point of the source. They may also evaluate the source in terms of how it relates to your thesis. For example, does it provide useful background information or supporting examples, or does it represent a popular alternative viewpoint? A sample annotated bibliography for researching the use of digital textbooks and e-learning in college classrooms appears on the next page.

SAMPLE ANNOTATED BIBLIOGRAPHY

Bajarin, Ben. "Reinventing the Book for the Digital Age." *Time*, 12 Nov. 2013, techland.time
.com/2013/11/12/reinventing-the-book-for-the-digital-age/.

> This article from a general-interest magazine describes the features that
> e-books provide while suggesting even more ideas for future e-books.

Falc, Emilie O. "An Assessment of College Students' Attitudes towards Using an Online
E-Textbook." *Interdisciplinary Journal of E-Learning and Learning Objects*, vol. 9,
2013, pp. 1-12, www.ijello.org/Volume9/IJELLOv9p001-012Falc831.pdf.

> This article from a scholarly journal reports on research studying student expe-
> riences with e-textbooks. Recommendations are given for faculty to guide their
> students on effective use of e-textbooks.

Giacomini, Cara, et al. "The Current State and Potential Future of E-Textbooks." *EDU-
CAUSE Library*, 5 Nov. 2013, library.educause.edu/~/media/files/library/2013/11/
elib1304-pdf.

> This reports on a pilot study looking at how students interact with particular
> e-textbook platforms and includes results and recommendations.

Keengwe, Jared. *Research Perspectives and Best Practices in Educational Technology Inte-
gration*. Information Science Reference, 2013.

> This book provides research-based information on how e-learning can be inte-
> grated into the college classroom in ways that make technological, practical,
> and educational sense.

Young, Jeffrey R. "The Object Formerly Known as the Textbook." *The Chronicle of Higher
Education*, vol. 59, no. 21, 27 Jan. 2013, pp. A16-A17, chronicle.com/article/
Dont-Call-Them-Textbooks/136835/.

> This article from a periodical aimed at college faculty discusses the rise of
> online textbooks on college campuses. It also explains all the extra features
> these resources include and suggests that universities should begin producing
> them as well as traditional publishers.

If you used . . .	then . . .
note cards	sort them into piles by subtopic or category.
a research notebook	pull out pages and keep the notes on each subtopic in a separate manila folder.
photocopies of sources	attach sticky notes to indicate the subtopic and place copies in separate manila folders for each subtopic.
computer files	copy and paste notes into folders by subtopic.
a citation (or reference) manager	save notes and sources in separate subfolders for each subtopic.

Regardless of the medium in which you worked, be careful to keep track of which material belongs to which source as you rearrange your notes. Once your notes are organized by subtopic, you are ready to develop your outline or graphic organizer.

DEVELOPING AN OUTLINE OR GRAPHIC ORGANIZER

Use an outline or a graphic organizer to show how you plan to arrange the divisions and subdivisions you intend to use. Preparing such a plan is especially important for a research project because you are working with a substantial amount of information. Without something to follow, it is easy to get lost and write an unfocused paper.

For more on creating outlines and graphic organizers, see Chapter 7, pp. 144–46.

Pragmatic learners tend to prefer organizing in detail before they begin to write. If this is your tendency, make sure that you are open to change and new ideas as you write your draft. Creative learners, in contrast, may prefer to start writing and try to structure the paper as they work. Most students should not take this approach, however; those who do should allow extra time for reorganizing and making extensive revisions.

Learning Style Options

Whatever your learning style, writing an outline or sketching a graphic organizer can help you test several different organizations. Be sure to save your original outline or graphic organizer and any revised versions as separate files in case you need to return to earlier versions.

> **Research Paper in Progress 6**
> Using the synthesis categories or graphic organizer that you developed for Research Project in Progress 5 (p. 597), sort your notes into categories and evaluate your working thesis. Then prepare an outline or a graphic organizer for your research project.

AVOIDING PLAGIARISM

After you have decided what source information to use, you will need to build that information into your essay. Three common methods for extracting information — summarizing, paraphrasing, and quoting — are discussed in Chapter 23 (pp. 588–91). In general, it is best to paraphrase or summarize information rather than quote it directly unless the wording is unusual, beautiful, or unique or if you want to provide the exact statement of an expert on the topic. Quotations are also appropriate when discussing works of literature and historical (primary) sources. (More information on integrating quotations into your paper appears on pp. 608–12.)

Regardless of how you integrate sources, be sure to acknowledge and document all ideas or information you have borrowed from sources that is not common knowledge (p. 603). Remember that you must cite your sources regardless of whether you are using direct quotations, paraphrases, or summaries and regardless of whether the information or ideas came to you from a book, an article, a Web site, or even a conversation. Failing to cite a source, even by mistake, may be considered plagiarism.

WHAT IS PLAGIARISM?

Plagiarism is the use of someone else's ideas, wording, organization, or sentence structure without acknowledging the source. At most schools, both intentional (deliberate) plagiarism and unintentional (done by accident) plagiarism are considered serious forms of cheating and carry the same academic penalties, generally a failing grade or even permanent expulsion.

- **Accidental plagiarism:** Taking information from a journal article on the uses of eye contact in communication and not indicating where you got the information.
- **Deliberate plagiarism:** Copying the six-word phrase "Eye contact, particularly essential in negotiations" from a source without enclosing it in quotation marks.

Buying a paper and submitting it as your own work is plagiarism, but so is cutting and pasting text directly from an electronic source into your notes and then into your essay without giving credit.

Instructors may use Internet tracking resources like Turnitin.com, or they may paste a student's paper into a Google search box to check for plagiarism, so managing the information you have borrowed from sources is crucial. The quick reference guide below can help you determine if you have plagiarized.

QUICK REFERENCE GUIDE TO PLAGIARISM

You have plagiarized if you:

- copied information word for word without using quotation marks, whether or not you acknowledge the source,
- paraphrased information (put it in your own words and sentences) without acknowledging the source,
- borrowed someone else's organization, sentence structure, or sequence of ideas without acknowledging the source,
- reused someone else's visual material (graphs, tables, charts, maps, diagrams, and so on) without acknowledging the source, and
- submitted another writer's paper as your own.

HOW TO AVOID PLAGIARISM

Plagiarism is a serious matter, but it can be avoided if you follow these tips.

- **Take careful notes.** Place anything you copy directly in quotation marks and record the source. Record the source for any information you quote, paraphrase, summarize, or even comment on.
- **Be sure to separate your own ideas from ideas expressed in the sources you are using.** Use different colors, different font sizes, different sections of a notebook, or different computer files to distinguish your ideas from those of others. Or take notes in two columns, with ideas and information from sources in one column and your own comments in another.
- **Never copy and paste directly from an online source into your paper.** Instead, cut and paste information you want to save into a separate file. Enclose the material you pasted in quotation marks to remind yourself that it is someone else's wording, and record the source information.
- **Paraphrase information from sources carefully.** Paraphrasing is a great way to test your understanding of sources and to avoid overquoting, but be careful that when you paraphrase, you restate the author's ideas in your own words and sentences.
- **Record all the information you will need to access and cite the source.** Include the name of the site, the URL, your date of access, and so on.

For detailed instructions on how to paraphrase without plagiarizing, see Chapter 23, pp. 589–91.

For a bibliographic information worksheet, see Chapter 23, p. 592.

DECIDING WHAT TO DOCUMENT

You must document all information and ideas you get from a source unless that information is common knowledge. But what is common knowledge, and how can you tell? **Common knowledge** is information that is widely available and undisputed. The fact that George Washington was the United States' first president is common knowledge; so is the fact that the earth revolves around the sun. A good rule of thumb is that if a piece of information is available in a minimum of three reliable sources, then it is considered common knowledge. Of course, you will never be wrong if you cite the source, and you can always ask your instructor or a reference librarian if you are unsure about whether to document something. Table 24.1 also summarizes the types of material that *do* and *do not* require documentation.

DRAFTING YOUR RESEARCH PROJECT

When drafting your research project, keep the following guidelines in mind:

1. **Remember your audience.** Academic audiences will expect you to take a serious, academic tone, and may expect you to use the third person (*he, she, it*). The third person is more impersonal, sounds less biased, and may lend credibility to your ideas. Although your instructor may know a great deal about your topic, he or she may want you to demonstrate that you understand key terms and concepts, so definitions and explanations may be required.

For more on tone, see Chapter 4, p. 81; for more on audience, see Chapter 5, pp. 103–05.

e macmillanhighered.com/successfulwriting
Tutorials > Documentation and Working with Sources > Do I Need to Cite That?

TABLE 24.1 What Does and Does Not Require Documentation

Documentation Required	Documentation Not Required
• Summaries, paraphrases, and quotations • Obscure or recently discovered facts (such as a little-known fact about Mark Twain or a recent discovery about Mars) • Others' opinions • Others' field research (results of opinion polls, case studies, statistics) • Quotations or paraphrases from interviews you conduct • Others' visuals (photographs, charts, maps, Web images) • Information from others that you use to create visuals (statistics or other data that you use to construct a table, graph, or other visual)	• Common knowledge (George Washington was the first U.S. president, the earth revolves around the sun) • Facts that can be found in numerous sources (winners of Olympic competitions, names of Supreme Court justices) • Standard definitions of academic terms • Your own ideas or conclusions • Your own field research (surveys or observations) • Your own visuals (such as photographs you take)

2. **Follow the introduction, body, and conclusion format, and for most research papers, place your thesis in the introduction.** A straightforward organization, with your thesis in the introduction, is usually the best choice for a research paper, since it allows readers to see from the outset how your supporting reasons relate to your main point. However, for papers analyzing a problem or proposing a solution, placing your thesis near the end may be more effective. For example, if you were writing an essay proposing stricter traffic laws on campus, you might begin by documenting the problem — describing accidents that have occurred and detailing their frequency. You might conclude your essay by suggesting that your college lower the speed limit on campus and install two new stop signs.

3. **Follow your outline or graphic organizer, but feel free to make changes as you work.** You may discover a better organization, think of new ideas about your topic, or realize that a subtopic belongs in a different section. Don't feel compelled to follow your outline or organizer to the letter, but be sure to address the topics you list.

4. **Refer to your source notes frequently as you write.** If you do so, you will be less likely to overlook an important piece of evidence. If you suspect that a note is inaccurate in some way, check the original source.

For more on writing and placing topic sentences, see Chapter 8, pp. 161–64; for more on supporting your ideas with evidence, see Chapter 6, pp. 125–30.

5. **State and support the main point of each paragraph.** Use your sources to substantiate, explain, or provide detail to support your main points. Make clear for your readers how your paragraph's main point supports your thesis as well as how the evidence you supply supports your paragraph's main point. Support your major points with evidence from a variety of sources. Doing so will strengthen your position. Relying on only one or two sources may make readers think you did insufficient research. But remember that your paper should not

be just a series of facts, quotations, and statistics taken from sources. The basis of the paper should be *your* ideas and thesis, not merely a summary of what others have written about the topic. (For more on writing effective supporting paragraphs for a research project, see below.)

6. **Use strong transitions.** Because a research paper may be lengthy or complex, readers need strong transitions to guide them from paragraph to paragraph and section to section. Make sure your transitions help readers understand how you have divided the topic and how one point relates to another.

For more on using transitions, see Chapter 8, p. 169.

7. **Use source information in a way that does not mislead your readers.** Although you are presenting only a portion of someone else's ideas, make sure you are not using information in a way that is contrary to the writer's original intentions.

8. **Include source material only for a specific purpose.** Just because you discovered an interesting statistic or a fascinating quote, don't feel that you must use it. Information that doesn't support your thesis will distract your reader and weaken your paper. Images may add visual interest, but in most academic disciplines, illustrations should be used only when they serve a useful purpose (such as when they provide evidence or are the subject of your analysis, as for an art history project).

9. **Incorporate in-text citations for your sources as you draft.** Whenever you paraphrase, summarize, or quote a source, be sure to include an in-text citation. (See pp. 608–12, 617–20, 639–42.)

USING RESEARCH TO SUPPORT YOUR IDEAS

Supporting paragraphs in research projects have three parts, as shown in Figure 24.2.

FIGURE 24.2 **The Structure of a Paragraph in a Research Project**

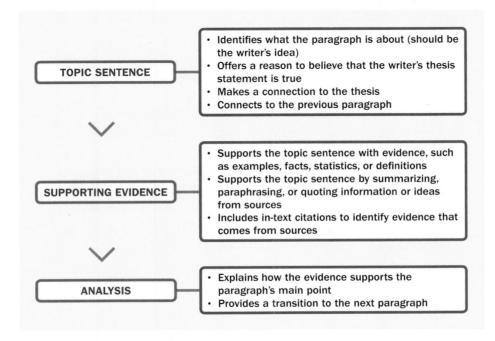

TOPIC SENTENCE
- Identifies what the paragraph is about (should be the writer's idea)
- Offers a reason to believe that the writer's thesis statement is true
- Makes a connection to the thesis
- Connects to the previous paragraph

SUPPORTING EVIDENCE
- Supports the topic sentence with evidence, such as examples, facts, statistics, or definitions
- Supports the topic sentence by summarizing, paraphrasing, or quoting information or ideas from sources
- Includes in-text citations to identify evidence that comes from sources

ANALYSIS
- Explains how the evidence supports the paragraph's main point
- Provides a transition to the next paragraph

For more on using transitions and repetition to make connections, see Chapter 8, pp. 169–70.

Each of these three parts is crucial: Without a topic sentence, readers are left to wonder what the main point is. Without the evidence, readers are left to wonder whether the main point is supported. Without the analysis, readers are left to make sense of the evidence and figure out how the evidence supports the topic on their own. Of course, writers must also connect the parts within the paragraph and connect the paragraph to the rest of the essay. The paragraph in Figure 24.3 shows this three-part structure at work. (The essay from which it was taken appears on pp. 632–38.)

USING IN-TEXT CITATIONS TO INTEGRATE SOURCE INFORMATION

When writing a research project, the goal is to support your own ideas with information from sources, integrating that information so that you achieve an easy-to-read flow. Along with transitions and strategic repetition, **in-text citations** (brief references in the body of your paper) make this seamless flow possible. These in-text citations direct readers to the list of works cited (or references) at the end of the research project, where they can find all the information they need to locate the sources for themselves. When used effectively, in-text citations also mark where the writer's ideas end and information from sources begins.

Many academic disciplines have a preferred format, or style, for in-text citations and lists of works cited (or references). In English and the humanities, the preferred documentation format is usually that of the Modern Language Association (MLA) and is known as **MLA style**. In the social sciences, the guidelines of the American Psychological Association (APA) are often used; these guidelines are called **APA style**. These are the two most widely used formats and are discussed in detail later in this chapter. A third popular style, which many scientists follow, was created by the Council of Science Editors (CSE); you can find a book detailing CSE style in your college library; citation managers, like RefWorks or EndNote, can also help you format citations in CSE style.

FIGURE 24.3 Sample Paragraphs from a Research Project

Transitions

Topic sentence

Supporting evidence: summary

In-text citation

Writer's analysis

There is another popular explanation for why a bird of one species might help a bird of another species, however. Scientists who favor a related scientific theory called *mutual altruism* believe that animals will help each other because some day they themselves may need help, and then they will be able to count on reciprocal help (Hemelrijk 479–81). This theory is a plausible, nonanthropomorphic explanation for why animals show sympathy, regardless of whether they actually feel sympathy. This point is crucial because after all, humans can't actually observe how an animal feels; we can only observe how it behaves. It is then up to the observer to draw some logical conclusion about why animals behave in the ways they do.

In MLA style, an in-text citation usually includes the author's last name and the page number(s) on which the information appeared in the source. (Use just the author's name for one-page sources and online sources, like Web pages, that do not have page numbers.) This information can be incorporated in two ways:

1. In a signal, or attribution, phrase
2. In a parenthetical citation

Using a signal phrase. When using a **signal phrase**, include the author's name with an appropriate verb before the borrowed material, and put the page number(s) in parentheses at the end of the sentence:

signal phrase
As Jo-Ellan Dimitrius observes, big spenders often suffer from low

page number
self-esteem (143).

Using a signal phrase before and a page number after borrowed material also helps readers clearly distinguish *your* ideas from those of your sources. Notice how the writer in Figure 24.3 uses in-text citations to make this clear.

Often, providing some background information about the author the first time you mention a source is useful to readers, especially if the author is not widely known:

relevant background information
Jo-Ellan Dimitrius, a jury-selection consultant whose book *Reading People*
discusses methods of predicting behavior, observes that big spenders often suffer from
low self-esteem (143).

Such information helps readers understand that the source is relevant and credible.

Using a signal phrase will help you integrate information from sources smoothly into your paper. Most summaries and paraphrases and *all* quotations need such an introduction. Compare the paragraphs below.

QUOTATION NOT INTEGRATED

Anecdotes indicate that animals experience emotions, but anecdotes are not considered scientifically valid. "Experimental evidence is given almost exclusive credibility over personal experience to a degree that seems almost religious" (Masson and McCarthy 3).

QUOTATION INTEGRATED

Anecdotes indicate that animals experience emotions, but anecdotes are not considered scientifically valid. Masson and McCarthy, who have done extensive field observation, comment, "Experimental evidence is given almost exclusive credibility over personal experience to a degree that seems almost religious" (3).

In the first example paragraph, the quotation is merely dropped in. In the second, the signal phrase, including background of the source authors, smooths the connection.

When writing signal phrases, vary the verbs you use and where you place the signal phrase. The following verbs are useful for introducing many kinds of source material:

advocates	contends	insists	proposes
argues	demonstrates	maintains	shows
asserts	denies	mentions	speculates
believes	emphasizes	notes	states
claims	explains	points out	suggests

In most cases, a neutral verb such as *states, explains,* or *maintains* will be most appropriate. Sometimes, however, a verb such as *denies* or *speculates* may more accurately reflect the source author's attitude.

Using a parenthetical citation. When you are merely citing facts or have already identified a source author, a **parenthetical citation** that includes the author's last name and the page number may be sufficient:

Some behavioral experts claim that big spenders often suffer from low self-

       parenthetical citation

esteem (Dimitrius 143).

INTEGRATING QUOTATIONS INTO YOUR RESEARCH PROJECT

Although quotations can lend interest to your paper and provide support for your ideas, they must be used appropriately. The following sections answer some common questions about the use of quotations. The in-text citations follow MLA style. (See p. 639 for creating in-text citations in APA style.)

Using quotations. Do not use quotations to reveal ordinary facts and opinions. Look carefully at what you intend to quote. Quote only when

- The author's wording is unusual, noteworthy, or striking. The quotation "Injustice anywhere is a threat to justice everywhere" from Martin Luther King Jr.'s "Letter from Birmingham Jail" is probably more effective than any paraphrase.
- The original words express the exact point you want to make and a paraphrase might alter or distort the statement's meaning.
- The statement is a strong, opinionated, exaggerated, or disputed idea that you want to make clear is not your own.

Formatting long quotations. In MLA style, lengthy quotations (more than three lines of poetry or more than four typed lines of prose) are indented in a block, one-half inch from the left margin. In APA style, quotations of more than forty words are indented as a block half an inch from the left margin. In both styles, quotation marks are omitted, and quotations are double spaced.

Like a shorter quotation in the main text, a block quotation should always be introduced by a signal phrase. Use a colon at the end of the signal phrase if it is a complete sentence, as in the following example:

In her book *Through a Window,* which elaborates on her thirty years of experience studying and living among the chimps in Gombe, Tanzania, Jane Goodall gives the following account of Flint's experience with grief:

> Flint became increasingly lethargic, refused most food and, with his immune system thus weakened, fell sick. The last time I saw him alive, he was hollow-eyed, gaunt and utterly depressed, huddled in the vegetation close to where Flo had died. . . . The last short journey he made, pausing to rest every few feet, was to the very place where Flo's body had lain. There he stayed for several hours, sometimes staring and staring into the water. He struggled on a little further, then curled up — and never moved again. (196–97)

Unlike a shorter quotation in the main text, the page numbers in parentheses appear *after* the final sentence period. (For a short quotation within the text, the page numbers within parentheses *precede* the period.)

Punctuating quotations. There are specific rules and conventions for punctuating quotations. The most important rules are listed below.

1. **Use single quotation marks to enclose a quotation within a quotation.**

   Coleman and Cressey argue that "concern for the 'decaying family' is nothing new" (147).

2. **Use a comma after a verb that introduces a quotation.** Begin the first word of the quotation with a capital letter (enclosed in brackets if it is not capitalized in the source).

   As Thompson and Hickey report, "There are three major kinds of 'taste cultures' in complex industrial societies: high culture, folk culture, and popular culture" (76).

3. **When a quotation is not introduced by a verb, it is not necessary to use a comma or capitalize the first word.**

   Buck reports that "pets play a significant part in both physical and psychological therapy" (4).

4. **Use a colon to introduce a quotation preceded by a complete sentence.**

   The definition is clear: "Countercultures reject the conventional wisdom and standards of the dominant culture and provide alternatives to mainstream culture" (Thompson and Hickey 76).

:e: **macmillanhighered.com/successfulwriting**
LearningCurve > Working with Sources (MLA); Working with Sources (APA)

5. **For a paraphrase or quotation integrated into the text, punctuation *follows* the parenthetical citation; for a block quotation, the punctuation *precedes* the parenthetical citation.**

   Scientists who favor a related scientific theory called *mutual altruism* believe that animals help each other because when they themselves need help, they would like to be able to count on reciprocal assistance (Hemelrijk 479–81).

   Franklin observed the following scene:

   Her unhappy spouse moved around her incessantly, his attention and tender cares redoubled. . . . At length his companion breathed her last; from that moment he pined away, and died in the course of a few weeks. (qtd. in Barber 116)

6. **Place periods and commas inside quotation marks.**

   "The most valuable old cars," notes antique car collector Michael Patterson, "are the rarest ones."

7. **Place colons and semicolons outside quotation marks.**

   "Petting a dog increases mobility of a limb or hand"; petting a dog, then, can be a form of physical therapy (Buck 4).

8. **Place question marks and exclamation points inside quotation marks when they are part of the original quotation. No period is needed if the quotation ends the sentence.**

   The instructor asked, "Does the text's description of alternative lifestyles agree with your experience?"

9. **Place question marks and exclamation points that belong to your own sentence outside quotation marks.**

   Is the following definition accurate: "Sociolinguistics is the study of the relationship between language and society"?

Adapting quotations. Use the following guidelines when adapting quotations to fit in your own sentences.

1. **You must copy the spelling, punctuation, and capitalization exactly as they appear in the original source, even if they are in error.** (See item 5 on p. 612 for the only exception.) If a source contains an error, copy it with the error and add the word *sic* (Latin for "thus") in brackets immediately following the error.

   According to Bernstein, "The family has undergone rapid decentralization since Word
   [sic] War II" (39).

2. **You can emphasize words in a quotation by underlining or italicizing them.** However, you must add the notation *emphasis added* in parentheses at the end of the sentence to indicate the change.

   "In *unprecedented* and *increasing* numbers, patients are consulting practitioners
   of every type of complementary medicine" (emphasis added) (Buckman and
   Sabbagh 73).

3. **You can omit part of a quotation, but you must add an ellipsis — three spaced periods (. . .) — to indicate that material has been deleted.** You may delete words, sentences, paragraphs, or entire pages as long as you do not distort the author's meaning by doing so.

   According to Buckman and Sabbagh, "Acupuncture . . . has been rigorously tested
   and proven to be effective and valid" (188).

   When an omission falls at the end of a quoted sentence, use the three spaced periods after the sentence period.

   Thompson maintains that "marketers need to establish ethical standards for personal
   selling. . . . They must stress fairness and honesty in dealing with customers" (298).

   If you are quoting only a word or phrase from a source, do not use an ellipsis before or after it because it will be obvious that you have omitted part of the original sentence. If you omit the beginning of a quoted sentence, you need not use an ellipsis unless what you are quoting begins with a capitalized word and appears to be a complete sentence.

4. **You can add words or phrases in brackets to make a quotation clearer or to make it fit grammatically into your sentence.** Be sure that in doing so you do not change the original sense.

> Masson and McCarthy note that the well-known animal researcher Jane Goodall finds that "the scientific reluctance to accept anecdotal evidence [of emotional experience is] a serious problem, one that colors all of science" (3).

5. **You can change the first word of a quotation to a capital or lowercase letter to fit into your sentence.** If you change it, enclose it in brackets.

> As Aaron Smith said, "The . . ." (32).
>
> Aaron Smith said that "[t]he . . ." (32).

> **Research Paper in Progress 7**
> Using your research notes, your revised thesis, and the organizational plan you developed for your research paper, write a first draft. Be sure to integrate sources carefully and to include in-text citations. (See pp. 617–20 for MLA style guidelines for in-text citations; see pp. 639–42 for APA style.)

REVISING YOUR RESEARCH PROJECT

For more on revision, see Chapter 10.

Revise a research paper in two stages. First, focus on the paper as a whole; then consider individual paragraphs and sentences for effectiveness and correctness. If time allows, wait at least a day before rereading your research paper.

ANALYZING AND REVISING YOUR PAPER AS A WHOLE

Begin by evaluating your paper as a unified piece of writing. Focus on general issues, overall organization, and the key points that support your thesis. Use the flowchart in Figure 24.4 to help you discover the strengths and weaknesses of your research paper as a whole. You might also ask a classmate to review your draft paper by using the questions in the flowchart.

ANALYZING AND REVISING PARAGRAPHS AND SENTENCES

After evaluating your paper as a whole, check each paragraph to be sure that it supports your thesis and integrates sources appropriately. Then check your sentences for correct structure, transitions, and in-text citation format. Use your earlier work with Figure 24.3 to guide your analysis.

> **Research Paper in Progress 8**
> Using the questions in Figure 24.4, revise the first draft of your research paper.

FIGURE 24.4 **Flowchart for Revising a Research Project**

QUESTIONS	REVISION STRATEGIES

1. Highlight your thesis statement. Is it clear and specific? Is the assertion based on some of your own (and not just the sources') ideas about the subject?

 NO

- Delete your thesis statement. Then have a peer read the paper and tell you what he or she believes the thesis to be.
- Brainstorm about the main point you wish to make.
- Review the guidelines for writing a thesis in Chapter 6, pp. 122–24.

YES

2. Underline the topic sentence of each paragraph. Does each topic sentence make a point that supports your thesis?

 NO

- Ask yourself, Would my paper be stronger if this point were eliminated? If so, eliminate the point.
- Revise any remaining topic sentence that does not support the thesis.

YES

3. [Bracket] the ideas that support each topic sentence. Are some of these your own ideas? Do you avoid strings of quotations, paraphrases, and summaries from sources?

 NO

- Rewrite to focus more on your own ideas, using source material to support them.
- Delete source material where there is too much.

YES

4. Draw a ⟨circle⟩ around terms that are essential to your thesis or that your audience might not know. Is each defined?

 NO

- Add definitions where necessary.
- Read the circled terms and definitions to a classmate and ask if he or she understands them.
- Ask the classmate to read your paper and circle any terms he or she doesn't understand.

YES

(continued on next page)

(Figure 24.4 continued)

QUESTIONS		REVISION STRATEGIES

5. Place a checkmark ✔ next to each idea that came from an outside source. Do you give credit to each source in an in-text citation?

 NO

- Add in-text citations wherever you need them. Paraphrases, summaries, and quotations, whether from printed or online sources, all need in-text citations.

YES

6. Is it clear where information from each source (✔) begins and ends?

 NO

- Add introductory attributions (p. 607).
- Vary the verbs you use and the placement of attributions to avoid ineffective repetition (p. 608).

YES

7. Draw a box around your introduction and conclusion. Does the introduction provide a context for your research? Is the conclusion satisfying and relevant to your research?

 NO

- Revise your introduction and conclusion to meet the guidelines in Chapter 7, pp. 147–50 and pp. 150–51.
- Review what the research suggests and then revise your conclusion, proposing an action or way of thinking that is appropriate in light of the research.

PREPARING YOUR FINAL DRAFT

After you have revised your paper and compiled a list of references or works cited, you are ready to prepare the final draft. Following are some guidelines to help you format, edit, and proofread your final paper. For an example of an essay in MLA style, see "Do Animals Have Emotions?" by Nicholas Destino on pages 632–38. For an example of an essay in APA style, see "Schizophrenia: Definition and Treatment" by Sonia Gomez on pages 650-56.

FORMATTING YOUR PAPER

Academic papers should follow a standard format that meets the expectations of the genre in which you are writing. For example, if you are writing a research report for a psychology class, you will probably be expected to include a title page, an abstract, and headings for each of your main sections. If you are writing a research paper for a literature class, in contrast, no title page or abstract is typically required, and headings are considered necessary only in lengthy essays.

For college papers, the following guidelines are common for writing projects in the humanities. If your instructor suggests or requires a different format, be sure to follow it. If your instructor does not recommend a format, these guidelines would likely be acceptable.

1. **Paper.** Use 8½- by 11-inch white paper. Use a paper clip; do not staple or use a binder.

2. **Your name and course information.** Do not use a title page unless your instructor requests one. Instead, position your name at the left margin one inch from the top of the page. Underneath it, on separate lines, list your instructor's name, your course name and number, and the date.

3. **Title.** Place the title two lines below the date, and center it. Capitalize the first word and all other important words (all except articles, coordinating conjunctions, and prepositions). Do not underline or italicize your title or put quotation marks around it. Start your paper one line space below the title.

4. **Margins, spacing, and indentation.** Use one-inch margins. Double-space your paper (including your name and course information, your title, block quotations, and works-cited entries). Indent block quotations and the first line of each paragraph half an inch, and use a **hanging indent** (first line flush left, subsequent lines indented half an inch) in the list of works cited.

5. **Numbering of pages.** Number all pages using arabic numerals (1, 2, 3) in the upper-right corner. Place the numbers one-half inch below the top of the paper. (If your instructor requests a title page, do not number it and do not count it in your numbering.) Precede each page number with your last name, leaving a space between your name and the number.

6. **Headings.** The MLA does not provide any guidelines for using headings. However, the system recommended by the American Psychological Association (APA) should work for most papers. Main headings should be centered, and the first letter of key words should be capitalized. Subheadings should begin at the left margin, with important words capitalized.

7. **Visuals.** If you include tables and figures (graphs, charts, maps, photographs, and drawings) in your paper, label each table or figure with an arabic numeral (*Table 1, Table 2; Fig. 1, Fig. 2*) and give it a title. Place the table number and title on separate lines above the table. Give each figure a number and title and place the figure number and title below the figure.

EDITING AND PROOFREADING YOUR PAPER

As a final step, edit and proofread your revised paper for errors in grammar, spelling, punctuation, mechanics, and documentation style. As you edit and proofread, check for the types of errors you commonly make, and watch for these ten common problems.

For more on editing and proofreading, see Chapter 10.

1. **Long, cumbersome sentences:** Try splitting them into separate sentences.

2. **Incomplete sentences:** Correct sentence fragments (a group of words that cannot stand alone as a sentence because it is missing a subject, a complete verb, or both), comma splices (two or more independent clauses linked by a

comma but without a coordinating conjunction), and run-on (or fused) sentences (two or more independent clauses joined without a punctuation mark or coordinating conjunction).

3. **Verb problems:** Avoid tense shifts (shifting from present to past or future tense) throughout your paper unless there is a good reason to do so. Also, make sure the subjects and verbs in all your sentences agree in person (*first*: I, we; *second*: you; *third*: he/she/it/they) and number (singular/plural). Be particularly careful when words come between the subject and verb.

4. **Wordiness:** Avoid wordy expressions (*at this particular point in time* rather than simply *now*), redundancy (*dashing quickly*), intensifiers (such as *very* or *really*), and weak verb-noun combinations (*wrote a draft* rather than *drafted*).

5. **Inappropriate tone/level of diction:** Avoid slang, abbreviations, and emoticons (☺). Aim for a clear and direct tone, and use words with appropriate connotations.

6. **Incorrect in-text citations:** Make sure you punctuate and format them to conform to MLA style or that of another system of documentation.

7. **Inaccurate direct quotations:** Check quotations carefully against the original source for accuracy, and double-check your use of quotation marks, capital letters, commas, and ellipses.

8. **Plagiarism:** Avoid plagiarism by carefully quoting, paraphrasing, and summarizing the ideas of others, and citing your sources for all ideas and opinions and all facts except those that are common knowledge.

9. **Incorrect formatting:** Check that you have formatted your paper consistently, following these or your instructor's formatting instructions. Check the citations in your list of works cited carefully using the models provided later in the chapter (pp. 621-31).

10. **Incomplete list of works cited/references:** Make sure all sources cited in your paper are included in the list in alphabetical order.

> **Research Paper in Progress 9**
> Edit and proofread your paper, paying particular attention to the questions in the preceding list.

DOCUMENTING YOUR SOURCES: MLA STYLE

The system described in this section is recommended by the Modern Language Association (MLA). MLA style is commonly used in English and the humanities. If you are unsure whether to use MLA style, check with your instructor.

MLA style uses in-text citations to identify sources within the text of a research paper and a list of works cited at the end of the paper to document them. For additional examples of in-text citations or works-cited entries, consult the following source:

MLA Handbook. 8th ed., The Modern Language Association of America, 2016.

The first student paper that appears later in this chapter (see pp. 632–38) uses MLA style.

MLA STYLE FOR IN-TEXT CITATIONS

Your paper must include in-text citations — either signal phrases (attributions) or parenthetical citations — for all material you paraphrase, summarize, or quote from sources. Many instructors prefer that you use signal phrases rather than only parenthetical citations in most places because signal phrases allow you to put sources in context. (For more on using signal phrases and parenthetical citations, see pp. 607–08.)

For either type of citation, use the following rules.

- Omit the word *page* or the abbreviation *p.* or *pp.*
- Place the sentence period after the closing parenthesis unless the citation follows a block quotation. (See p. 609.)
- If a quotation ends the sentence, insert the closing quotation marks before the parentheses enclosing the page reference.

Examples showing in-text citations in MLA style follow.

One author

According to Vance Packard . . . (58).

. . . (Packard 58).

Two authors.
Include all authors' names, in either a signal phrase or a parenthetical citation.

Marquez and Allison assert . . . (74).

. . . (Marquez and Allison 74).

Three or more authors. Include the first author's last name followed by either a phrase referring to the other authors (in a signal phrase) or *et al.,* Latin for "and others" (in a parenthetical citation).

> Hong and colleagues maintain . . . (198).

> . . . (Hong et al. 198).

Two or more works by the same author. When citing two or more sources by the same author or group of authors in your paper, include the full or abbreviated title in the citation to indicate the proper work.

FIRST WORK

In *For God, Country, and Coca-Cola,* Pendergrast describes . . . (96).

Pendergrast describes . . . (*For God* 96).

. . . (Pendergrast, *For God* 96).

SECOND WORK

In *Uncommon Grounds,* Pendergrast maintains . . . (42).

Pendergrast maintains . . . (*Uncommon Grounds* 42).

. . . (Pendergrast, *Uncommon Grounds* 42).

Corporate or organizational author. When the author is given as a corporation, an organization, or a government office, reference the organization's name as the author name.

> According to the National Institute of Mental Health . . . (2).

> . . . (National Institute of Mental Health 2).

Unknown author. If the author is unknown, use the full title in a signal phrase or a shortened form in parentheses.

> According to the article "Medical Mysteries and Surgical Surprises," . . . (79).

> . . . ("Medical Mysteries" 79).

Authors with the same last name. Include the first initial of these authors in all parenthetical citations. Use the complete first name if both authors have the same first initial.

> John Dillon proposes . . . (974).

> . . . (J. Dillon 974).

Two or more sources in the same citation. When citing two or more sources of one idea in parentheses, separate the citations with a semicolon.

> . . . (Breakwater 33; Holden 198).

Entire work. To refer to an entire work, such as a Web page, a film, or a book, it is generally preferable to cite the source within the text rather than in a parenthetical reference; do not include page numbers.

> In *For God, Country, and Coca-Cola,* Pendergrast presents an unauthorized history of Coca-Cola, the soft drink and the company that produces it.

Chapter in an edited book or work in an anthology. An *anthology* is a collection of writings (articles, stories, poems) by different authors. In the in-text citation, name the author who wrote the work (not the editor of the anthology) and include the page number(s) from the anthology. The corresponding entry in the list of works cited begins with the author's last name; it also names the editor of the anthology.

IN-TEXT CITATION

According to Ina Ferris . . . (239).

. . . (Ferris 239).

WORKS-CITED ENTRY

Ferris, Ina. "The Irish Novel 1800–1829." *Cambridge Companion to Fiction in the Romantic Period*, edited by Richard Maxwell and Katie Trumpener, Cambridge UP, 2008, pp. 235–49.

Multivolume work. When citing two or more volumes of a multivolume work, indicate the volume number, followed by a colon and the page number.

Terman indicates . . . (2: 261).

. . . (Terman 2: 261).

Indirect source. When quoting an indirect source (someone whose ideas came to you through another source, such as a magazine article or book), make this clear by adding, in parentheses, the last name and page number of the source in which the quote or information appeared, preceded by the abbreviation *qtd. in.*

According to Ephron (qtd. in Thomas 33), . . .

Personal interview, letter, email, conversation. The *MLA Handbook* does not provide advice for citing a personal interview or correspondence, but it would make sense to name the person in your text.

In an interview with Professor Emilio Lopez, . . .

Literature and poetry. Include information that will help readers locate the material in any edition of the literary work. Include page numbers from the edition you use.

- *For novels:* Cite page and chapter numbers.

    (109; ch. 5)

- *For poems:* Cite line numbers instead of page numbers; use the word *line* or *lines* in the first reference only.

    FIRST REFERENCE   (lines 12–15)
    LATER REFERENCES   (16–18)

- *For plays:* Give the act, scene, and line numbers in arabic numerals, separated by periods.

    (*Mac.* 2.1.32–37)

Include complete publication information for the edition you use in the list of works cited.

Internet sources. In general, Internet sources are cited like their printed counterparts. Give enough information in the citation so that readers can locate the source in your list of works cited. If the electronic source provides page numbers, you should provide them too. If the source uses another ordering system, such as paragraphs (*par.* or *pars.*), sections (*sec.*), or screens (*screen*), provide the abbreviation with the appropriate number.

> Brian Beckman argues that "centrifugal force is a fiction" (par. 6).
>
> . . . (Beckman, par. 6).

If the source does not have paragraphs or page numbers, which is often the case, cite the work by author, title of the document or site, or sponsor of the site, whichever begins your entry in the list of works cited.

Author

> Teresa Schmidt discusses . . .
>
> . . . (Schmidt).

Title

> The "Band of Brothers" section of the History Channel site . . .
>
> . . . ("Band").

Sponsor

> According to a Web page posted by the Council for Indigenous Arts and Culture, . . .
>
> . . . (Council).

MLA STYLE FOR THE LIST OF WORKS CITED

Follow these general guidelines for preparing the list.

1. **List only the sources you cite in your paper.** If you consulted a source but did not cite it in your paper, do not include it in the list of works cited.
2. **Put the list on a separate page at the end of your paper.** The heading *Works Cited* should be centered an inch below the top of the page. Do not use quotation marks, underlining, or bold type for the heading.
3. **Alphabetize the list by authors' last names.** For works with multiple authors, invert only the first author's name. If no author is listed, begin the entry with the title.

   > Trask, R. L., and Robert M. C. Millar. *Why Do Languages Change?* Cambridge UP, 2010.

4. **Capitalize the first word and all other words in a title except *a, an, the, to,* coordinating conjunctions, and prepositions.**
5. **Italicize or underline titles of books, Web sites, and names of periodicals.**
6. **Give inclusive page numbers of articles in periodicals.** Use the abbreviation *p.* or *pp.*
7. **Indent the second and all subsequent lines half an inch or five spaces.** This is known as the *hanging indent* style.
8. **Double-space the entire list.**

The following sections describe how to format works-cited entries for books, periodicals, Internet sources, and other sources.

LIST OF MLA WORKS-CITED ENTRIES

Books

General guidelines and sample entries for books follow. Include the elements listed below, which you will find on the book's title page and copyright page. See Figure 24.5 on page 622 for an example.

1. *Author.* Begin with the author's last name, followed by the first name.

2. *Title.* Provide the full title of the book, including the subtitle. It should be capitalized and italicized.

---

3. *Publisher.* Use the full name of the publisher (*W. W. Norton* or *Basic Books*). Do not use words or abbreviations such as *Company, Ltd.,* or *Inc.* Standardize the punctuation, using the word *and* in place of *&* (ampersand). For university presses, use the abbreviations *U* for *University* and *P* for *Press* with no periods.

4. *Date.* Use the most recent publication date listed on the book's copyright page.

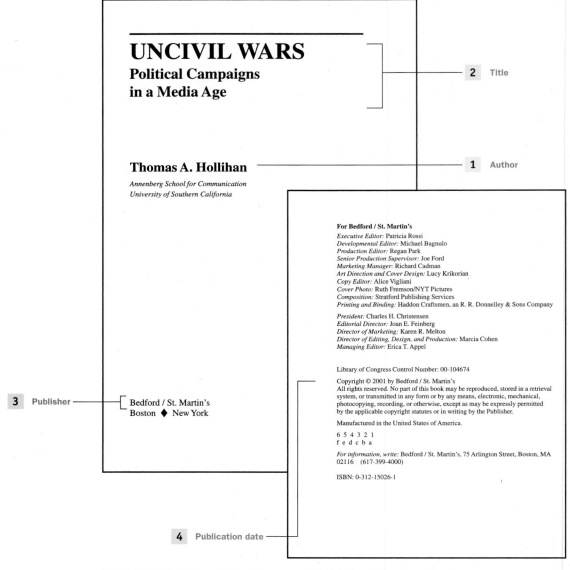

FIGURE 24.5 Where to Find Documentation Information for a Book

MLA FORMAT FOR CITING A BOOK

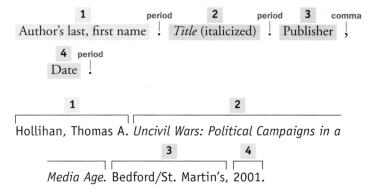

If applicable, also include the original publication date, editor, translator, edition, and volumes used; these should be placed immediately after the title of the work.

Book with one author

Rybczynski, Witold. *Makeshift Metropolis: Ideas about Cities*. Scribner, 2010.

Book with two or more authors.

List the names in the order they appear on the title page of the book, and separate the names with commas. The second author's name is *not* reversed. For books with three or more authors, include only the first author's name followed by *et al.*

TWO AUTHORS

Botkin, Daniel B., and Diana Pérez. *Powering the Future: A Scientist's Guide to Energy Independence*. FT Press, 2010.

THREE OR MORE AUTHORS

Lewin, Benjamin, et al. *Lewin's Genes X*. Jones and Bartlett Publishers, 2011.

Book with no named author.

Put the title first and alphabetize the entry by title. (Do not consider the words *A, An,* or *The* when alphabetizing.)

The New Interpreter's Dictionary of the Bible. Abingdon Press, 2006.

Book by a corporation or organization.

List the organization or corporation as the author, omitting any initial article (*A, An, The*). If author and publisher are the same, omit the author and include the publisher following the title.

American Red Cross. *First Aid and Safety for Babies and Children*. StayWell, 2009.

Government publication.

If there is no author, list the government first, followed by the department and agency. With an author, list government, department, and agency as the publisher.

United States, Office of Management and Budget. *A New Era of Responsibility: Renewing America's Promise*. Government Printing Office, 2009.

Edited book or anthology. List the editor's name followed by a comma and the word "editor" (or "editors" as shown.)

> Szeman, Imre, and Timothy Kaposy, editors. *Cultural Theory: An Anthology*. Wiley-Blackwell,
>
> 2011.

Chapter in an edited book or work in an anthology. List the author and title of the work, followed by the title and editor of the anthology. (Include the words "edited by" before the editor's name.) Publisher, date, and the pages where the work appears follow.

> Riss, Jacob. "How the Other Half Lives." *The Affordable Housing Reader*, edited by J. R.
>
> Tighe, Routledge, 2013, pp. 6-13.

Introduction, preface, foreword, or afterword

> Aaron, Hank. Foreword. *We Are the Ship: The Story of Negro League Baseball*, by Kadir
>
> Nelson, Disney Publishing, 2008, p. vi.

Translated book. After the title, include the phrase "Translated by" followed by the first and last names of the translator.

> Kawakami, Hiromi. *Manazuru*. Translated by Michael Emmerich, Counterpoint Press,
>
> 2010.

Two or more works by the same author(s). Use the author's name for only the first entry. For subsequent entries, use three hyphens followed by a period. List the entries in alphabetical order by title. List works for which the person is the only author before those for which he or she is the first coauthor.

> Adams, Ryan. *Hellosunshine*, Akashic Books, 2009.
>
> ---. *Infinity Blues*. Akashic Books, 2009.
>
> Myers, Walter D. *Lockdown*, Amistad Press, 2010.
>
> Myers, Walter D., and Christopher Myers. *Jazz*, Holiday House, 2006.

Edition other than the first. Indicate the number of the edition following the title.

> Barker, Ellen M. *Neuroscience Nursing*. 3rd ed., Mosby-Elsevier, 2008.

Multivolume work. If the reference is to all the volumes in a multivolume work, give the number of volumes at the end of the citation.

> Price, Emmett G. *Encyclopedia of African American Music*. ABC-CLIO, 2011. 3 vols.

One volume of a multivolume work. If the reference is to one volume in a multivolume work, give the volume number before the publisher.

> Price, Emmett G. *Encyclopedia of African American Music*. Vol. 1, ABC-CLIO, 2011. 3 vols.

Encyclopedia or dictionary entry. Note that when citing well-known reference books, you do not need to give the full publication information, just the edition and year.

> Robinson, Lisa Clayton. "Harlem Writers Guild." *Africana: The Encyclopedia of the African*
>
> *and African American Experience*, 2nd ed., Oxford UP, 2005.

If more than one of these rules applies to a source, cite the necessary information in the order given in the preceding examples. For instance, to cite a reading from this textbook, treat it as a work in an anthology (p. 624) in an edition other than the first (p. 624):

> Zaitchik, Alexander. "Alien World: How Treacherous Border Crossing Became a Theme
> Park." *Successful College Writing: Skills, Strategies, Learning Styles*, edited by Kathleen T.
> McWhorter, 5th ed., Bedford/St. Martin's, 2012, pp. 258-63.

Articles in Periodicals

A periodical is a publication that appears at regular intervals: newspapers generally appear daily, magazines weekly or monthly, and scholarly journals quarterly. General guidelines and sample entries for various types of periodical articles follow. Include the elements listed below, most of which you should find on the first page of the article. See Figure 24.6 for an example.

1. *Author.* Use the same format for listing authors' names as for books (see p. 623). If no author is listed, begin the entry with the article title and alphabetize the entry by its title (ignore *The, An,* or *A*).

2. *Article title.* The title should appear in double quotation marks; a period falls inside the ending quotation mark.

3. *Periodical title.* Italicize the title of the periodical, including the word *A, An,* or *The* at the beginning: *The Journal of the American Medical Association, The New York Times.*

4. *Volume/issue and date.* For scholarly journals, give the volume and issue numbers and date of publication (often a season and year or just a year): *vol. 54, no. 1, Autumn 2012.* List the date in the following order: day, month, year; abbreviate the names of months except for *May, June,* and *July.*

5. *Location.* In a print article, the location of the source is indicated by page numbers. When citing an online article, include the DOI (digital object identifier, a permanent code) or URL (permalink preferred). If you obtained an article from a subscription database, include just the URL for the database (for example, *go.galegroup.com/*), not the specific URL for the article, since readers may not have access to the article through the subscription service. If an article begins in one place, such as on pages 19 to 21, and is continued elsewhere, such as on pages 79 to 80, write *pp. 19+* for the page numbers (*not* pp. 19-80). Otherwise, include the first and last page number separated by a hyphen, for instance, *p. 40* or *pp. 39-43.*

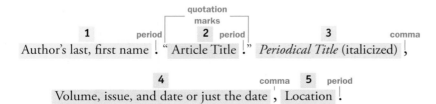

1 period **2** period **3** comma
Author's last, first name . " Article Title ." *Periodical Title* (italicized) ,

4 comma **5** period
Volume, issue, and date or just the date , Location .

Article in a magazine

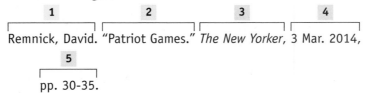

1 **2** **3** **4**

Remnick, David. "Patriot Games." *The New Yorker*, 3 Mar. 2014,

5

pp. 30-35.

LETTER FROM *SOCHI*

PATRIOT GAMES

Vladimir Putin lives his Olympic dream.

BY DAVID REMNICK

2 Article title

1 Author

A quarter century ago, as jubilant citizens took sledgehammers to the Berlin Wall, Vladimir Vladimirovich Putin, an officer in the Dresden station of the K.G.B., fed a raging furnace with the documentary evidence of Soviet espionage activities in East Germany. Putin was grateful for his Dresden posting. He had grown up in a pretty wife and two young daughters, and enough leisure to play Ping-Pong, fish in the rivers outside town, and drink beer in the city's pubs and breweries. He drank so much beer that he gained twenty-five pounds. Now the happy days were ending. The Wall had been breached, and Putin was shovelling top-secret files into the fire so few months, Putin slipped back home to Leningrad and took a position as "vice-rector"—the residential spy—at the local university.

As the Soviet Union began to unravel, there was a pervasive mood of desperation in its most repressive offices. Occasionally, that desperation took on comic dimensions. One fall morning in 1990, when I was working as a Moscow correspondent, I was reading a stack of newspapers—a requirement of the job—and came across an article of tangy interest in *Komsomolskaya Pravda*. The headline read "MISS K.G.B."; below was a photograph of a woman in her twenties, named Katya Mayorova, provocatively adjusting the strap of her bulletproof vest. She had, it seemed, won a beauty

Putin's aim was to put on a display of renewed national confidence and modernity. "Russia is back," officials kept insisting.

Leningrad, an uneven student with early dreams of serving the state. One of his grandfathers was a cook for Lenin and Stalin. His father was an undercover operative during the war. Putin's parents barely survived the Nazi siege; an older brother did not. After a rough upbringing, Putin had enjoyed a halcyon four years in Dresden. He had quickly, he recalled in a book-length interview, that "the furnace burst." This was early in November, 1989. Later, angry Germans threatened to break into the K.G.B. compound. Putin's superiors called Moscow for reinforcements, but, he says, "Moscow was silent." The state was failing even its most resolute foot soldiers. Within a contest at Lubyanka, the K.G.B. headquarters. This was new. I took a sip of coffee. The article described how Comrade Mayorova wore her vest with "exquisite softness, like a Pierre Cardin model." Beyond "mere beauty," her talents included the ability to deliver a karate kick "to her enemies' head." I called Lubyanka, which, by now, had a press

30 THE NEW YORKER, MARCH 3, 2014

5 **3** Periodical title **4** Date

Page

FIGURE 24.6 Where to Find Documentation Information for an Article
© The New Yorker Magazine/Condé Nast. *Photo:* © Pascal Le Segretain/Getty

Other Sources

Film, video, or DVD. Begin with the title, followed by the director and key performer(s), unless you are focusing on the work of the director or another contributor in which case, list that person in the author position. Include the name of the production company and the release date. For supplementary material on a DVD, include the title of that information, along with the information for the movie; at the end of the citation include the disc number if there was more than one disc. If you watched the video online, include the URL.

> *Birdman or (The Unexpected Virtue of Ignorance)*. Directed by Alejandro González Iñárritu, performances by Michael Keaton, Emma Stone, Zach Galifianakis, Edward Norton, and Naomi Watts, Fox Searchlight, 2014.
>
> Scott, Ridley, director. *The Martian*. Performances by Matt Damon, Jessica Chastain, Kristen Wiig, and Kate Mara, Twentieth Century Fox, 2015.
>
> "Sweeney's London." Produced by Eric Young. *Sweeney Todd: The Demon Barber of Fleet Street*, directed by Tim Burton, DreamWorks, 2007, disc 2.
>
> Lewis, Paul. "Citizen Journalism." *YouTube*, 14 May 2011, www.youtube.com/watch?v=9AP09_yNbcg.

Television or radio program. Unless you are focusing on the work of a contributor (the director, screenwriter, or actor), list the title of the episode, if any (in quotation marks), and the title of the program (italicized) first. Then give key names (narrator, producer, director, actors) as necessary. Identify the network and include the broadcast date. If you watched or listened to the program online, include the URL.

> "Free Speech on College Campuses." *Washington Journal*, narrated by Peter Slen, C-SPAN, 27 Nov. 2015.
>
> "The Cathedral." *Reply All*, narrated by Sruthi Pinnamaneni, episode 50, Gimlet Media, 7 Jan. 2016, gimletmedia.com/episode/50-the-cathedral/.

Music recording. Begin with a contributor or title of the work, depending on the focus of your research project. Include the composer or performer and the title of the recording or composition as well as the production company, and the date. Titles of recordings should be italicized, but titles of compositions identified by form (for example, Symphony No. 5) should not.

> Blige, Mary J. "Don't Mind." *Life II: The Journey Continues (Act 1)*, Geffen, 2011.
>
> Bizet, Georges. *Carmen*. Performances by Jennifer Larmore, Thomas Moser, Angela Gheorghiu, and Samuel Ramey, Bavarian State Orchestra and Chorus, conducted by Giuseppe Sinopoli, Warner, 1996.

Research Paper in Progress 10

For the final paper you prepared in Research Paper in Progress 9, prepare a list of works cited in MLA style.

STUDENTS WRITE

The following research paper was written by Nicholas Destino for his first-year writing course while he was a student at Niagara County Community College. Destino used MLA style for documenting his sources and formatted his research project using the instructions in this chapter (pp. 615, 620). Notice how he uses in-text citations and quotations to provide evidence that supports his thesis.

Header: Student's name and page number

Double-spaced identification: Writer's name, instructor's name, course title, and date

Title: Centered and double-spaced

½ inch

Destino 1   1 inch

1 inch

1 inch

Nicholas Destino

Professor Thomas

English 101

22 Nov. 2013

Do Animals Have Emotions?

½ inch

Somewhere in the savannas of Africa a mother elephant is dying in the company of many others of her kind. Some of them are part of her family; some are fellow members of her herd. The dying elephant tips from side to side and seems to be balancing on a thin thread in order to sustain her life. Many of the other elephants surround her as she struggles to regain her balance. They also try to help her by feeding and caressing her. After many attempts by the herd to save her life, they seem to realize that there is simply nothing more that can be done. She finally collapses to the ground in the presence of her companions. Most of the other elephants move away from the scene. There are, however, two elephants who remain behind with the dead elephant--another mother and her calf. The mother turns her back to the body and taps it with one foot. Soon the other elephants call for them to follow and eventually they do (Masson and McCarthy 95). These movements, which are slow and ritualistic, suggest that elephants may be capable of interpreting and responding to the notion of death.

Citation: Parenthetical in-text citation of a work with 2 authors

The topic of animal emotions is one that, until recently, has rarely been discussed or studied by scientists. However, since the now-famous comprehensive field studies of chimpanzees by the internationally renowned primatologist Jane Goodall, those who study animal behavior have begun to look more closely at whether animals feel emotions. As a result of their observations of various species of animals, a number of these researchers have come to the conclusion that animals do exhibit a wide range of emotions, such as grief, sympathy, and joy.

Destino 2

One of the major reasons that research into animal emotions was traditionally avoided is that scientists fear being accused of *anthropomorphism* -- the act of attributing human qualities to animals. To do so is perceived as unscientific and has been cause for much debate in the scientific community (Bekoff, *Emotional Lives* 124-25). However, Frans de Waal, of the Yerkes Regional Primate Research Center in Atlanta, argues that if people are not open to the possibility of animals having emotions, they may be overlooking important information about both animals and humans. He defends his position in his book, *Primates and Philosophers*. The term *anthropodenial*, which he coined, "denotes willful blindness to the human-like characteristics of animals, or the animal-like characteristics of ourselves" (65). De Waal proposes that because humans and animals are so closely related, it would be impossible for one not to have some characteristics of the other. He contends, "While it is true that animals are not humans, it is equally true that humans are animals. Resistance to this simple yet undeniable truth is what underlies the resistance to anthropomorphism" (65). If de Waal is correct, then we should see animal emotions as on a continuum with humans' and can infer the existence of animal emotions through their behavior, just as we infer the emotions of fellow humans.

In many instances, their behaviors (and presumably, therefore, their emotions) are uncannily similar to the behaviors of humans. Consider grief: In "Animal Emotions: Exploring Passionate Natures," Marc Bekoff provides several examples of animals who exhibit behaviors that can only reflect their grief. He notes that sea lions wail at the loss of their young, dolphins struggle to save their babies, and orphaned elephants who have witnessed their mothers' deaths have been observed to wake up screaming (866). In his book *The Emotional Lives of Animals*, he includes a description from Cynthia Moss's *Elephant Memories* about elephants suffering the loss of one of their group:

½ inch

←—They stood around Tina's carcass, touching it gently. . . . Because it was rocky and the ground was wet, there was no loose dirt; but they tried to dig into it . . . and when they managed to get a little earth up they sprinkled it over the body. Trista, Tia, and some of the others went off and broke branches from the surrounding low brushes and brought them back

---

Sources: Abbreviated title included because another work by this author cited earlier

Sources: Signal phrase, with author background, establishes author credentials and introduces paraphrase and quotation

Sources: Page number follows quotation

Sources: Titles included because 2 works by this author are cited

Quotation: Quote longer than four lines indented one-half inch and not enclosed in quotations marks; period precedes citation

Destino 3

and placed them on the carcass. . . . By nightfall they had nearly buried her with branches and earth. Then they stood vigil over her for most of the night and only as dawn was approaching did they reluctantly begin to walk away. (qtd. in Bekoff, *Emotional Lives* 66-67)

Diane Ackerman, a columnist for *The New York Times* who writes regularly about the intersection of human and animal worlds, notes that "[b]iologists tell of sea lions wailing when their babies have been mutilated by killer whales, of grief-stricken monkey mothers carrying dead infants around for days, of geese singing both halves of a duet when their partners have died."

Perhaps the most extreme case of grief experienced by an animal is exemplified by the story of Flint, a chimp, when Flo, his mother, died. In her book, *Through a Window*, which elaborates on her thirty years of experience studying and living among the chimps in Gombe, Tanzania, Jane Goodall gives the following account of Flint's experience with grief.

Flint became increasingly lethargic, refused most food and, with his immune system thus weakened, fell sick. The last time I saw him alive, he was hollow-eyed, gaunt and utterly depressed, huddled in the vegetation close to where Flo had died. . . . The last short journey he made, pausing to rest every few feet, was to the very place where Flo's body had lain. There he stayed for several hours, sometimes staring and staring into the water. He struggled on a little further, then curled up--and never moved again. (196-97)

Of course, animal emotions are not limited to sadness and grief. Indeed, evidence indicates that animals also experience happier emotions, such as sympathy and joy.

Many scientists who study animal behavior have found that several species demonstrate sympathy for one another. In other words, they act as if they care about one another. It is probably safe to assume that no animal displays behaviors more closely associated with sympathy than chimpanzees. Those who have studied apes in the wild, including de Waal, have observed that animals who had been fighting make up with one another by kissing and hugging. Chimps have also been found to console the loser of a fight or try to restore peace (Wilford).

Sources: Citation for indirect source

Quotation: First letter of a quotation changed to lower-case to fit into sentence

Sources: Author's credentials included within the text

Sources: Page number follows quotation

Sources: Information at beginning of this paragraph can be found in many sources, so does not need to be documented

Sources: Information from a source paraphrased, no page number because source is an online newspaper

Destino 4

Sympathy and caring have been noted in non-primate species as well. Researchers have found that young barn owls are "impressively generous" towards each other, saving portions of their food for smaller and hungrier owls (Angier). Likewise, the *Nature* episode "Animal Odd Couples" documents a number of instances in which animals of one species have cared for animals of another. In one example (00:25:26-00:31:41), Jack, a goat, led Charlie, a blind horse, around the ranch where they lived *every day for sixteen years,* until Jack's death (fig. 1). The animals' caretaker even compared Jack to the television character Lassie, describing how Jack got human help to rescue Charlie after he became trapped in a grove of trees following a microburst of wind.

Fig. 1.   Seeing is believing: Jack leading Charlie (a blind horse). Film still from "Animal Odd Couples" (00:27:23).

What makes this example particularly noteworthy is that the animals were of different species. Had the goat been helping another goat, it would be easy to assume that the act of caring was the result of what scientists call *genetic altruism,* animals helping others of their own species because there is something in it for them--namely, the assurance that their kin (and, therefore, their genes) will continue. This theory certainly provides an adequate, unbiased scientific explanation for why animals might care for others. However, if

Destino 5

animals really help each other out only when doing so will perpetuate their species, then Jack would have had no genetic reason to help Charlie.

There is another popular explanation for why an animal would help another from a different species. Scientists who favor a related scientific theory called *mutual altruism* believe that animals will help each other because someday, they themselves may need help, and then their generous behavior will be reciprocated (Hemelrijk 479-81). This theory is a plausible, nonanthropomorphic explanation for why animals show sympathy, regardless of whether they actually feel sympathy. This point is crucial because, after all, humans can't actually observe how an animal feels; we can only observe how it behaves. It is then up to the observer to draw some logical conclusions about why animals behave in the ways they do.

The mutual altruism theory, however, can also be disputed. In many cases, animals have helped others even when the receiver of the help would probably never be in a position to return the favor. For example, there are many accounts of dolphins helping drowning or otherwise endangered swimmers. Phil Mercer, on the BBC Web site, reported that dolphins stopped a shark from attacking swimmers off the coast of New Zealand. The animals surrounded the swimmers for about forty minutes while the great white shark circled. When the swimmers reached the shore, they remarked that they were sure that the dolphins acted deliberately to save them. Marathon swimmer Matril Strel also believes that he was deliberately helped by pink dolphins during his 2007 swim of the entire Amazon River, even believing that he heard them communicating (Butler).

Not only do animals show sympathy, but they are also clearly able to express joy. For example, Takahisa Matsusaka, a primatologist, has found that when chimpanzees demonstrate "panting" while tickling or chasing each other, the chance of such play becoming aggressive is reduced (222). Dog laughter has been observed to soothe other dogs, even when not playing (Bekoff, *Emotional Lives* 56). According to Jaak Panksepp, an author at

Citation of a Web page includes only author's name and site's sponsor; no page numbers available

Destino 6

J. P. Scott Center for Neuroscience, Mind, and Behavior, "Research on rough-housing play in mammals, both sapient and otherwise, clearly indicates that the sources of play and laughter in the brain are both instinctual and subcortical," meaning that many animals, and not just humans, are evolutionarily hardwired to laugh. Panksepp reports that rats who are tickled emit high-frequency chirps, and the process socially bonds them so that they want to spend time with other rats who chirp (62).

The actions of animals who are not able to laugh uproariously also indicate that they feel joy. John Webster, a professor of animal husbandry at the University of Bristol, said the following about joy:

> Sentient animals have the capacity to experience pleasure and are
> motivated to seek it. . . . You only have to watch how cows and lambs
> both seek and enjoy pleasure when they lie with their heads raised to the
> sun on a perfect English summer's day. Just like humans. (qtd. in Bekoff,
> *Emotional Lives* 55)

The body language of geese, from the way they move to the kinds of honks they emit, tell experts whether they feel curious, apprehensive, terrified, or ready to attack. For example, a blogger who keeps geese has indicated that they make "a low throaty sound" when pleased to find something they like to eat (Goose Girl).

In short, animals exhibit a large number of behaviors that indicate that they possess not only the capacity to feel but the capacity to express their feelings in some overt way, sometimes through vocalizations, but most often through body language. If these are not proof enough that animals have emotions, people need look no further than their own beloved cat or dog. Pets are so frequently the cause of joy, humor, love, sympathy, empathy, and even grief that it is difficult to imagine that animals could elicit such emotions in humans without actually having these emotions themselves. The question, then, is not, *do* animals have emotions? but *which* emotions do animals have and *to what degree* do they feel them?

Works-cited list appears on a new page; heading is centered; entries are double spaced

Entries alphabetized by author's last name

First line of each entry is flush left with margin; subsequent lines indented half an inch

Destino 7

Works Cited

Ackerman, Diane. "The Lonely Polar Bear." *The New York Times*, 2 July 2011, www.nytimes.com/2011/07/03/opinion/sunday/03gus.html?_r=0.

Angier, Natalie. "The Owl Comes into Its Own." *The New York Times*, 25 Feb. 2013, www.nytimes.com/2013/02/26/science/long-cloaked-in-mystery -owls-start-coming-into-full-view.html?.

"Animal Odd Couples." *Nature*, PBS, 7 Nov. 2012, www.pbs.org/wnet/nature/ animal-odd-couples-full-episode/8009/.

Bekoff, Marc. "Animal Emotions: Exploring Passionate Natures." *Bioscience*, vol. 50, no. 10, Oct. 2000, pp. 861-70, bioscience.oxfordjournals.org/ content/50/10/861.full.

---. *The Emotional Lives of Animals.* New World Library, 2007.

Butler, Rhett A. "Marathon Swimmer: An Interview with the First Man to Swim the Length of the Amazon." *Mongabay.com*, 23 Jan. 2011, news .mongabay.com/2011/01/marathon-swimmer-an-interview-with-the-first -man-to-swim-the-length-of-the-amazon/.

de Waal, Frans. *Primates and Philosophers.* Princeton UP, 2006.

Goodall, Jane. *Through a Window: My Thirty Years with the Chimpanzees of Gombe.* Houghton Mifflin, 1990.

Goose Girl, The. "Intro to Goose Body Language, Please – Page 2." *Backyard Chickens*, 22 May 2011, www.backyardchickens.com/t/509237/intro-to -goose-body-language-please/10.

Hemelrijk, Charlotte K. "Support for Being Groomed in Long-Tailed Macaques, *Macaca Fasciularis.*" *Animal Behaviour*, vol. 48, no. 2, Aug. 1994, pp. 479-81.

Masson, Jeffrey Moussaieff, and Susan McCarthy. *When Elephants Weep: The Emotional Lives of Animals.* Dell Publishing, 1995.

Matsusaka, Takahisa. "When Does Play Panting Occur during Social Play in Wild Chimpanzees?" *Primates*, vol. 45, no. 4, Oct. 2004, pp. 221-29. *SpringerLink*, doi:10.1007/s10329-004-0090-z.

Mercer, Phil. "Dolphins Prevent NZ Shark Attack." *BBC News,* 23 Nov. 2004, news.bbc.co.uk/2/hi/asia-pacific/4034383.stm.

Panksepp, Jaak. "Beyond a Joke: From Animal Laughter to Human Joy?" *Science*, vol. 308, no. 5718, 1 Apr. 2005, pp. 62-63. *JSTOR*, doi:10.1126/science.1112066.

Wilford, John Noble. "Almost Human, and Sometimes Smarter." *The New York Times,* 17 Apr. 2007, www.nytimes.com/2007/04/17/science/17chimp.html?_r=0.

DOCUMENTING YOUR SOURCES: APA STYLE

APA style, recommended by the American Psychological Association, is commonly used in the social sciences. Both in-text citations and a list of references are used to document sources, as the models below show. For more information on citing sources in APA style, consult the following reference work.

American Psychological Association. (2010). *Publication Manual of the American Psychological Association* (6th ed.). Washington, DC: Author.

The student paper that appears at the end of this chapter uses APA style.

APA STYLE FOR IN-TEXT CITATIONS

Your paper must include in-text citations for all material you summarize, paraphrase, or quote from sources. There are two basic ways to write an in-text citation.
1. **Use a signal phrase (attribution) and a parenthetical citation.** Mention the author's name in a phrase or sentence introducing the material, and include the year of publication in parentheses immediately following the author's name.
2. **Use a parenthetical citation.** Include the author's last name, each year of publication, and page number in parentheses (separated by commas).

APA style requires only that you include page numbers for quotations, but your instructor may want you to include a page number for paraphrases and summaries as well, so make sure you ask. Signal phrases allow you to put your sources in context, so use a signal phrase for most citations. For either type of citation, follow these rules.
- Place the sentence period after the closing parenthesis. When a quotation ends the sentence, insert the closing quotation mark before the opening parenthesis. Block quotations are an exception to these rules; see pages 608–09.
- For direct quotations and paraphrases, include the page number after the year, separating it from the year with a comma. Use the abbreviation *p.* or *pp.* followed by a space and the page number.

SIGNAL PHRASE
Avery and Ehrlich (2008) said "nasal sounds are made with air passing through the nose" (p. 21).

PARENTHETICAL CITATION
Snorts, snores, and other such sounds are created "with air passing through the nose" (Avery & Ehrlich, 2008, p. 21).

The following section provides guidelines for formatting in-text citations in APA style.

One author

According to Adams (2009), . . .

. . . (Adams, 2009).

Two authors. Include both authors' last names and the year in a signal phrase or parenthetical citation. In the latter case, use an ampersand (&) in place of the word *and.*

Avery and Ehrlich (2008) have asserted . . .

. . . (Avery & Ehrlich, 2008).

Three to five authors. Include all authors' last names the first time the source is mentioned. In subsequent references to the same source, use the first author's last name followed by *et al.* (Latin for "and others").

First Reference

Lewin, Krebs, Kilpatrick, and Goldstein (2011) have found . . .

. . . (Lewin, Krebs, Kilpatrick, & Goldstein, 2011).

Later References

Lewin et al. (2011) discovered . . .

. . . (Lewin et al., 2011).

Six or more authors. Use the first author's last name followed by *et al.* in all in-text citations.

Two or more works by the same author(s). Cite the works chronologically, in order of publication.

Gaerlan (2001, 2011) believed that . . .

. . . (Gaerlan, 2001, 2011).

Two or more works by the same author in the same year. Add the lowercase letter *a* after the publication year for the first source as it appears alphabetically by title in your reference list. Add the letter *b* to the publication year for the source that appears next, and so forth. Include the years with the corresponding lowercase letters in your in-text citations. (See p. 645 for the corresponding reference entries.)

Adams (2009a) believed that . . .

. . . (Adams, 2009a).

Authors with the same last name. Use the first author's initials with his or her name.

Research by V. M. Hoselton (2001) exemplified . . .

. . . (V. M. Hoselton, 2001).

Unknown author. Use the first few words of the title and the year in the signal phrase or parenthetical citation. Italicize a book title; put the title of a journal article in quotation marks. Unlike the entry in the list of references, use standard capitalization in the in-text citation. (See p. 647.)

As noted in "Gluten Free Recipes" (2009), . . .

. . . ("Gluten Free Recipes," 2009).

Two or more sources in the same citation. When citing two or more sources in parentheses, put a semicolon between them and list them in alphabetical order.

. . . (Hoffman, 2011; Murphy, 2009)

Specific part of a work. When quoting, paraphrasing, or summarizing a passage, include the page number on which the passage appears. If the work does not have page numbers, use paragraph numbers, if available (with the abbreviation *para.*), or the heading of the section in which the material appears.

Pinker (2007) offered an explanation for why swearing occurs across cultures: Obsceni-

ties "may tap into deep and ancient parts of the emotional brain" (p. 331).

If obscenities "tap into deep and ancient parts of the emotional brain" (Pinker, 2007, p.

331), then it makes sense that swearing occurs across cultures.

Chapter in an edited book or work in an anthology. An *anthology* is a collection of writings by different authors. In the in-text citation, name the author who wrote the work (*not* the editor of the anthology) and give the year. The corresponding entry in the list of references begins with the author's last name; it also names the editor of the anthology.

IN-TEXT CITATION

As Pedelty (2010) noted . . .

. . . (Pedelty, 2010).

REFERENCES ENTRY

Pedelty, M. (2010). Musical news: Popular music in political movements. In S. E. Bird

(Ed.), *The anthropology of news and journalism: Global perspectives* (pp. 215–240).

Bloomington: Indiana University Press.

Multivolume work. When you cite one volume of a multivolume work, include the year of publication for that volume.

> Terman (2008) indicated . . .

> . . . (Terman, 2008).

When you cite two or more volumes of a multivolume work, give inclusive years for the volumes.

> Terman (2008–2011) indicated . . .

Indirect sources. When you quote a source indirectly (rather than from the original source), include the words *cited in* along with the information for the source in which you found the quote.

> According to Ephron, . . . (as cited in Thomas, 2009, p. 33).

Personal interviews, letters, emails, and conversations. Give the last name and initial of the person, the source of the communication, and the exact date. Do not include these sources in the list of references.

> . . . (J. Lopez, personal communication, October 30, 2011).

Internet sources. For direct quotations, give the author, year, and page (if available) in the signal phrase or parenthetical citation. If paragraph numbers are available, cite them with the abbreviation *para.*

> Stevens (2011) has maintained . . .

> . . . (Stevens, 2011).

APA STYLE FOR THE LIST OF REFERENCES

Follow these general guidelines for preparing the list of references.

1. **List only the sources you cite in your paper.** If you consulted a source but did not cite it in your paper, do not include it in the list of references.

2. **Put the list on a separate page at the end of your paper.** The heading *References* should be centered an inch below the top of the page. Do not use quotation marks, underlining, or bold type for the heading.

3. **Alphabetize the list by authors' last names.** Give the last name first, followed by a comma and an initial or initials. Do not spell out authors' first names; use a space between initials: *Myers, D. G.* For works with multiple authors, list all authors' names in inverted order.

> Avery, P., & Ehrlich, S. (2008). *Teaching American English pronunciation.*
>
> New York, NY: Oxford University Press.

4. **Put the publication date in parentheses after the author's name.**

5. **For titles of books and articles capitalize the first word, the first word following a colon, and any proper nouns. For titles of periodicals, capitalize all important words.**

6. **Include the word *A, An,* or *The* at the beginning of titles.**

7. **Italicize titles of books and names of journals, newspapers, and magazines.** Do not italicize, underline, or use quotation marks with article titles.

8. **For magazine and journal articles, italicize the volume number.**

9. **Indent the second and all subsequent lines half an inch — hanging indent style.**

10. **Double-space the entire list.**

The following sections describe how to format reference list entries for books, articles in periodicals, Internet sources, and other sources.

LIST OF APA REFERENCE ENTRIES

Book with one author 644

Book with more than one author 644

Book with no named author 644

Book by an agency or a corporation 644

Government publication 644

Edited book or anthology 645

Chapter in an edited book or work in an anthology 644

Translated book 645

Two or more works by the same author(s) 645

Two or more works by the same author in the same year 645

Edition other than the first 645

Multivolume work 645

Article in a multivolume work 645

Article in a scholarly journal 646

Article in a magazine (weekly) 647

Article in a magazine (monthly) 647

Article in a newspaper 647

Editorial or letter to the editor 647

Book or film review 647

Article with no author 647

Document posted on an organization's Web site 648

Article from an online journal 649

Article from an online encyclopedia 649

Article from an online newspaper 649

Online government document 649

Film, video, or DVD 649

Television program 649

Computer software 649

Books

The basic format for a book is as follows.

1. *Author.* Give the author's last name and initial(s). Do not spell out authors' first names; include a space between initials: *Myers, D. G.*

2. *Year.* Include the year of publication in parentheses following the author's name. Use the most recent copyright year if more than one is given.

3. *Title.* Italicize the title of the book. Capitalize only the first word of the title and subtitle (if any) and any proper nouns or adjectives, such as *Juan* or *French.*

4. *Place of publication.* Give the city of publication followed by the postal abbreviation for the state and a colon (*Hillsdale, NJ:*). For cities outside the United States, add the country after the city.

5. *Publisher.* Include the name of the publisher followed by a period. Use a shortened form of the name: *Alfred A. Knopf* would be listed as *Knopf.* Omit words such as *Publishers* and abbreviations such as *Inc.*, but do not omit the word *Books* or *Press* if it is part of the publisher's name: *Academic Press, Basic Books.*

APA FORMAT FOR CITING A BOOK

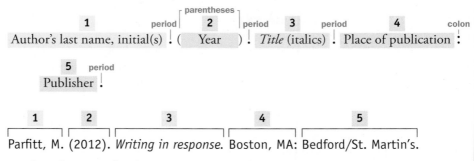

Book with one author

> Olson, Z. (2010). *The constant giraffe: Stretchmarks of a lost generation.* Charleston, SC:
>
> CreateSpace.

Book with more than one author. Use inverted order (*last name, initial*) for all authors' names. Separate the names with commas and use an ampersand (&) in place of the word *and.*

> Myers, W. D., & Myers, C. (2006). *Jazz.* New York, NY: Holiday House.

For citations with more than seven authors, list the first six (in the order they appear on the title page), an ellipsis (. . .), and then the last author's name.

Book with no named author. Give the full title first, and alphabetize the entry by title. (Do not consider the words *A, An,* or *The* when alphabetizing.)

> *The new interpreter's dictionary of the Bible.* (2006). Nashville, TN: Abingdon Press.

Book by an agency or a corporation. List the agency as the author. If the publisher is the same as the author, write *Author* for the name of the publisher.

> Bill and Melinda Gates Foundation. (2013). *Feedback for better teaching: Nine principles*
>
> *for using measures of effective teaching.* Seattle, WA: Author.

Government publication. List the agency as the author, followed by the date. Include the document or publication number if available.

> U.S. Office of Management and Budget. (2009). *A new era of responsibility: Renewing*
>
> *America's promise.* Washington, DC: Government Printing Office.

Edited book or anthology. List the editor's or editors' names, followed by the abbreviation *Ed.* or *Eds.* in parentheses and a period.

> Bradley, B., Feldman, F., & Johansson, J. (Eds.). (2013). *The Oxford handbook of the philosophy of death*. New York: Oxford University Press.

Chapter in an edited book or work in an anthology. List the author of the work first and then the date the work was published in the anthology. The title of the work follows. Then name the editor of the anthology (not in inverted order), give the title of the anthology (italicized), and insert the inclusive page numbers in parentheses for the work (preceded by *pp.*). The publication information follows in normal order.

> Dachyshyn, D. (2006). Refugee families with preschool children: Adjustment to life in Canada. In L. Adams (Ed.), *Global migration and education: Schools, children and families* (pp. 251–262). London, England: Erlbaum.

Translated book. After the title, include the initial(s) and last name of the translator followed by a comma and *Trans.*

> Kawakami, H. (2010). *Manazuru* (M. Emmerich, Trans.). Berkeley, CA: Counterpoint.

Two or more works by the same author(s). Begin each entry with the author's name. Arrange the entries in chronological order of publication.

> Pollan, M. (2006). *The omnivore's dilemma: A natural history of four meals*. New York, NY: Penguin.
>
> Pollan, M. (2008). *In defense of food: An eater's manifesto*. New York, NY: Penguin.

Two or more works by the same author in the same year. Arrange the works alphabetically by title; then assign a lowercase letter (*a*, *b*, *c*) to the year of publication for each source. (See p. 641 for the corresponding in-text citation.)

> Adams, R. (2009a). *Hellosunshine*. New York, NY: Akashic Books.
>
> Adams, R. (2009b). *Infinity blues*. New York, NY: Akashic Books.

Edition other than the first

> Myers, D. G. (2014). *Exploring psychology* (9th ed.). New York, NY: Worth.

Multivolume work. Give the volume numbers in parentheses after the title. If all volumes were not published in the same year, the publication date should include the range of years.

> McAuliffe, J. D. (Ed.). (2001–2006). *Encyclopedia of the Qur'an* (Vols. 1–5). Leiden, The Netherlands: Brill.

Article in a multivolume work. Include the author and title of the article, as well as the title, volume number, and publication information for the work.

> Meerdink, J. E. (2006). Sleep. In *Encyclopedia of human development* (Vol. 3, pp. 1180–1181). Thousand Oaks, CA: Sage.

If more than one of these rules applies to a source, cite the necessary information in the order given in the preceding examples. For instance, to cite a reading from this textbook, treat it as a work in an anthology (p. 644) in an edition other than the first. To do this, list the author of the reading, the date the reading was published in the anthology, the title of the reading, the editor and the title of this book, the edition number, the pages where the reading appears, and all other publication information.

Le Mieux, R. (2009). The lady in red. In K. T. McWhorter (Ed.), *Successful college writing: Skills, strategies, learning styles* (6th ed., pp. 253–255). Boston, MA: Bedford/St. Martin's.

Articles in Periodicals

General guidelines and sample entries for various types of periodical articles follow.

1. *Author.* Follow the basic format for listing authors' names (see p. 643). If no author is listed, begin with the article title and alphabetize the entry by its title (ignoring the words *A, An,* and *The*).

2. *Date.* For articles in journals, the year of publication appears in parentheses following the author's name. For articles in newspapers and magazines, the issue, month and day, if relevant, follow the year.

3. *Article title.* Do not enclose article titles in quotation marks. Capitalize only the first word of the article title, along with any proper nouns or proper adjectives (*American*) and the first word following a colon.

4. *Periodical title.* Italicize the name of the periodical. Use standard capitalization.

5. *Volume/issue.* For scholarly journals and magazines, give the volume number in italics; if each issue is paginated separately, starting with page 1, give the issue number in parentheses and roman type.

6. *Pages.* The abbreviation *p.* or *pp.* is used only in entries for newspaper articles.

7. *DOI.* Include the digital object identifier (DOI), a code assigned to articles in scholarly journals, when it is available.

APA FORMAT FOR CITING A PERIODICAL ARTICLE

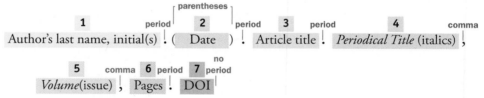

Article in a scholarly journal. If issues in each volume are numbered continuously (issue 1 ends on page 159 and issue 2 begins on page 160, for example), omit the issue number. If the journal article has been assigned a DOI (digital object identifier), add it at the end of the citation.

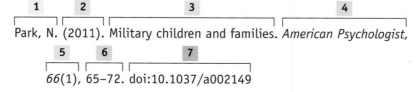

Article in a magazine (weekly)

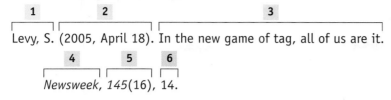

Article in a magazine (monthly). Include the month of publication after the year.

> Purple, M. (2013, October). Road ragin'. *American Spectator, 46*(8), 64–65.

Article in a newspaper. Include the year, month, and day in parentheses following the author's name. Page numbers for newspaper articles should be preceded by a *p.* or *pp.*

> Gugliotta, G. (2012, November 27). Looking to cities, in search of global warming's sil-
>
> ver lining. *The New York Times,* p. D3.

Editorial or letter to the editor. Cite the editorial or letter beginning with the author's name (if available). Include *Editorial* or *Letter to the editor* in brackets following the title (if any). If the author's name is not available, begin with the title.

> Exposing the pay gap [Editorial]. (2013, September 25). *The New York Times,*
>
> p. A28.
>
> Ginn, L. (2008, December). [Letter to the editor]. *Wired, 16*(12), 19.

Book or film review. List the reviewer's name, the date, and the title of the review. In brackets, give a description of the work reviewed, including the medium (*book* or *motion picture*), title, and the author for a book or the year for a film.

> Peters, J. (2013, September–October). Original sin. [Review of the book *Spam: A shadow*
>
> *history of the Internet,* by F. Brunton]. *Columbia Journalism Review, 52*(3), 58–59.

Article with no author. Use the full title as the author.

> The *Business Week* fifty. (2006, April 3). *Business Week,* 82.

Internet Sources

For Internet sources, include enough information to allow readers to locate the sources online. Guidelines for documenting Internet sources are listed below. For more help with formatting entries for Internet and other electronic sources in APA style, consult the American Psychological Association's Web site at http://apastyle.org/index.aspx, the APA Style Blog at http://blog.apastyle.org, and APA Style on Twitter at http://twitter.com/APA_Style.

1. *Author.* Give the author's name, if available. If not, begin the entry with the name of the sponsor of the site or with the title of the document.

2. *Date.* Include in parentheses the year of Internet publication or the year of the most recent update, if available. If there is no date, use the abbreviation *n.d.*

3. *Document title.* Capitalize only the first word of the title of the Web page or document or the subject line of the message, the first word following a colon, and any proper nouns or proper adjectives. The other words are lowercase.

4. *Web site.* Include "Retrieved from" and publisher's name; omit if publisher is listed as author and insert "Retrieved from" before URL. (Note: APA spells *website* all lowercase.)

5. *DOI/URL.* End with the digital object identifier (DOI), a permanent code associated with specific online articles or books, or, if there is no DOI, insert the URL of the homepage for the journal or publishing company that published the source or give the URL for the source, preceded by the words *Retrieved from,* if the source will be difficult to find from the homepage. If necessary, break URLs before punctuation marks, such as dots (.) and question marks (?). DOIs and URLs are not followed by periods.

APA FORMAT FOR CITING INTERNET SOURCES

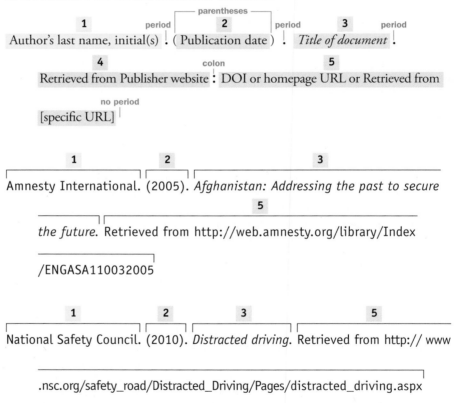

Document posted on an organization's Web site. If the document is not dated or the content could change, include a retrieval date.

The American Society for the Prevention of Cruelty to Animals. (2009). *ASPCA Milestones.* Retrieved February 15, 2011, from http://www.aspca.org/pressroom /~/media/files /pressroom/press-kit/aspca-milestones-2009.pdf

:e: **macmillanhighered.com/successfulwriting**
Tutorials > Documentation and Working with Sources > How to Cite a Web Site in APA Style

Article from an online journal Provide page numbers if available. Include the digital object identifier (DOI), if one has been assigned. Look for the DOI in the database where you get the name and author of the article.

> Schubert, C. (2008). The need to consider the impact of previous stressors on current
>
> stress parameter measurements. *Stress: The International Journal on the Biology of*
>
> *Stress, 11*(2), 85–87. doi:10.1080/10253890801895811

For articles with no DOI, give the URL for the journal's homepage. Use the article's URL if your source will be difficult to locate from the journal's homepage.

> Carter, M. (2013, April 6). The moral identity and group affiliation. *Current Research in*
>
> *Social Psychology, 21*(1). Retrieved from http://www.uiowa.edu/~grpproc/crisp
>
> /crisp21_1.pdf

Article from an online encyclopedia

> Calef, S. (2008). Dualism and mind. In J. Fieser & B. Dowden (Eds.), *The Internet ency-*
>
> *clopedia of philosophy*. Retrieved from http://www.iep.utm.edu/

Article from an online newspaper

> Sullivan, P. (2008, May 6). Quiet Va. wife ended interracial marriage ban. *The Washing-*
>
> *ton Post*. Retrieved from http://www.washingtonpost.com

Online government document

> U.S. Justice Department, Federal Bureau of Investigation. (2011, August 2). *Byte out of*
>
> *history: Communist agent tells all*. Retrieved from http://www.fbi.gov/news/stories
>
> /august/communist_080211/communist_080211

Other Sources

Film, video, or DVD

> Greenfield, L. (Director). (2006). *Thin* [Motion picture]. New York, NY: Home Box Office.

Television program

> Murphy, R. (Writer), & Buecker, B. (Director). (2011). Comeback [Television series epi-
>
> sode]. In I. Brennan, R. Murphy, & B. Falchuk (Creators), *Glee*. New York, NY: Fox
>
> Broadcasting.

Computer software

> Rosenbloom, C., & American Dietetic Association. (2006). Sports nutrition: Client educa-
>
> tion [Computer software]. Chicago, IL: American Dietetic Association.

Research Paper in Progress 11

For the final paper you prepared in Research Paper in Progress 10, prepare a list of references in APA style.

macmillanhighered.com/successfulwriting

Tutorials > Documentation and Working with Sources > How to Cite a Database in APA Style

The following research paper was written by Sonia Gomez for her introductory psychology course. She used APA style for formatting her paper and documenting her sources. Notice her use of in-text citations and paraphrases and summaries of sources to provide evidence in support of her thesis.

Header: Title at top left, page number at top right

SCHIZOPHRENIA: DEFINITION AND TREATMENT   1

Schizophrenia: Definition and Treatment

Sonia Gomez

Psychology 101

Professor McCombs

Identification: Double-space and include on title page: Writer's name, instructor's name, and course title.

Information on title page should be centered vertically and horizontally. (Vertical centering not shown here.)

SCHIZOPHRENIA: DEFINITION AND TREATMENT   2

Abstract

Schizophrenia is a mental/brain disorder that affects about 1% of the population. The five types of schizophrenia include paranoid, disorganized, catatonic, undifferentiated, and residual. There are three categories of symptoms—positive, disorganized or cognitive, and negative. The causes of schizophrenia are not well known, but there is likely a genetic component and an environmental component. The structure of the brain of schizophrenics is also unusual. Treatments include drug therapy with typical and atypical anti-psychotics and psychosocial and cognitive-behavioral therapies.

Abstract: Include an abstract, a brief summary of the report; heading centered, not bold

Formatting: Double-space essay, leave one-inch margins on all sides

SCHIZOPHRENIA: DEFINITION AND TREATMENT   3

Schizophrenia: Definition and Treatment

The disorder schizophrenia comes with an ugly cultural stigma. There is a common belief that all schizophrenics are violent. In fact, they are more a danger to themselves than to others because they often commit suicide. Many of the movies, books, and TV shows in our culture do not help to diminish this stigma. The movie *A Beautiful Mind*, for example, features a paranoid schizophrenic who comes close to harming his family and others around him because of his hallucinations and delusions. He believes that the government is out to get him (Grazer & Howard, 2001). Many people are afraid of schizophrenics and believe their permanent home should be in a mental hospital or psychiatric ward. This paper helps to dispel misperceptions of the disorder by providing facts about and treatments of the disorder.

What Is Schizophrenia?

Schizophrenia is a mental/brain disorder that affects about 1% of the population or 2.2 million Americans (National Institutes of Mental Health, 2010). This disease can be very disruptive in people's lives. It causes problems with communication and maintaining jobs. It is a widely misunderstood disease; many people believe schizophrenics to be dangerous. There is no cure for schizophrenia, but it can often be successfully treated (National Institutes of Mental Health, 2010). Schizophrenia does not seem to favor a specific gender or ethnic group. The disease rarely occurs in children. Hallucinations and delusions usually begin between ages sixteen and thirty (National Alliance on Mental Illness, 2007).

Types of Schizophrenia

There are five types of schizophrenia—paranoid, disorganized, catatonic, undifferentiated, and residual. People with paranoid schizophrenia are illogically paranoid about the world around them. They often hold false beliefs about being persecuted. People with disorganized schizophrenia are confused and incoherent and jumble their speech. People with disorganized schizophrenia often show symptoms of schizophasia—creating their own words and using them in a word salad, a jumbling of coherent and noncoherent words. People with catatonic schizophrenia are usually immobile and unresponsive to everything around them.

Title: Repeat full title just before text of paper begins; title centered, not bold

Introduction: Presentation of the topic researched by Gomez

Sources: Authors named in parenthetical citation; ampersand (&), not the word *and*, between names

Heading: First-level heading is centered, bold

Sources: No individual author named, so Web site sponsor listed as author

Heading: Second-level heading at left margin, bold

SCHIZOPHRENIA: DEFINITION AND TREATMENT 4

Undifferentiated schizophrenia is diagnosed when the patient does not fit into the other three categories. Residual schizophrenia occurs when schizophrenic symptoms have decreased but still exist (WebMD, 2010).

Symptoms of Schizophrenia

The symptoms of schizophrenia are separated into three categories—positive, disorganized or cognitive, and negative. Positive symptoms include hallucinations and delusions (WebMD, 2010). According to Barch (2003), disorganized or cognitive symptoms cause the person to be unable to think clearly. Disorganized or cognitive symptoms include difficulty communicating, use of nonsense words, inability to focus on one thought, slow movement, inability to make decisions, forgetfulness and losing of things, repetitive movements, inability to make sense of everyday senses, and problems with memory. Negative symptoms are an absence of normal behavior (WebMD, 2010). They include a lack of emotion or inappropriate emotions, isolation, lack of energy and motivation, loss of interest or pleasure in life, problems functioning in everyday life (such as bad hygiene), rapid mood changes, and catatonia (remaining in the same position for a long time) (WebMD, 2010).

The diagnosis of schizophrenia is often difficult because it can be confused with a number of other mental disorders including bipolar disorder. The process of diagnosis begins with an interview by a psychiatrist. The patient is usually tested for other physical illnesses using various blood tests. If the symptoms last for at least six months and there is seemingly no other cause of the problem, the person is considered to have schizophrenia (National Alliance on Mental Illness, 2007).

Causes of Schizophrenia

No one is completely sure of the causes of schizophrenia. Most scientists believe that genetics are involved, and it seems that there is either a genetic mutation in DNA or a gene that can be activated by a number of situations. Scientists are coming very close to determining the exact chromosome where the gene for schizophrenia might be located (Conklin & Iacono, 2002). The circumstances surrounding birth may have a great effect on whether the child's schizophrenic gene becomes activated or not. For example, if a fetus is exposed to viruses or

Sources: Author named in text; date follows in parentheses

SCHIZOPHRENIA: DEFINITION AND TREATMENT 5

malnourished before birth or if there are complications during birth, the gene may be activated. Conklin and Iacono (2002) reported a link between schizophrenia and complications during birth that result in lack of oxygen (hypoxia). Also, Bower (2008) observed that poor children or children who deal with highly stressful situations may be more likely to develop the disorder.

Besides all of these factors, the brains of schizophrenics seem to be different from other people's. People with schizophrenia have an imbalance of dopamine and glutamate in their brains. The ventricles at the center of the brain seem to be larger, and there appears to be a loss of brain tissue in comparison with a normal brain (Figure 1).

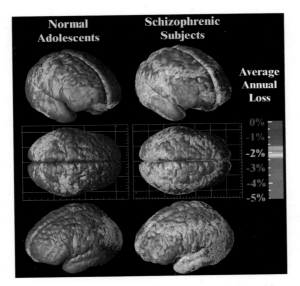

Figure 1. Brain-tissue loss. The image shows a loss of brain tissue (the areas in red) for the teens with schizophrenia. (Internet Mental Health Initiative, 2001, image by Thompson, Vidal, Rapoport, & Toga, *UCLA Laboratory of Neuro Imaging*).

Courtesy Dr. Paul Thompson, Laboratory of Neuro Imaging at UCLA, published in the Atlantic. Thompson et al. (2001). Mapping adolescent brain change reveals dynamic wave of accelerated gray matter loss in very early-onset schizophrenia. Proc Natl Acad Sci USA 98(20): 11650-11655. Copyright © (2001) National Academy of Science, USA.

Sources: Authors named in text, so *and*, not ampersand (&), used between names

Illustration: The figure is referred to in the text; the word *Figure* and a figure number appears in the caption. Professional publications in psychology require authors to place figures on a separate page at the end of the paper, but your instructor may prefer that you integrate your figures.

Also, some areas of the brain seem to have more or less activity than normal brains do. According to Conklin and Iacono (2002), these abnormalities in the brain appear to be preexisting rather than caused by the disease. Schizophrenia tends to appear during puberty because of hormonal interactions occurring in the brain (WebMD, 2010).

Treatment

There is a wide variety of treatments for schizophrenia. Typical antipsychotic drugs, such as chlorpromazine and perphenazine, are an obvious choice, especially for people with hallucinations and delusions. They can help to clear up thinking problems. However, many of these drugs cause unpleasant side effects such as nausea and anxiety. Because of this, schizophrenics may stop taking or refuse to take their medication. Many of these antipsychotic drugs have not changed since the 1950s. In the 1990s, a new set of drugs—atypical antipsychotics—was developed. Clozapine was one of these drugs, and it was deemed very effective. However, it can cause agranulocytosis, a loss of white blood cells. Between the constant testing for agranulocytosis and the cost of clozapine, many schizophrenics did not particularly like the drug (National Institutes of Mental Health, 2010).

Other treatments do not rely on medication. Psychosocial and cognitive-behavioral therapies are often used. People with schizophrenia can learn illness-management skills. They can go to rehabilitation, and their families can be educated about how to care for them. Self-help groups are also common. However, if the disease becomes unmanageable, the person with schizophrenia may end up in the hospital. Electroconvulsive therapy, in which seizures are induced, is one of the more extreme treatments for schizophrenia. It is often used to treat catatonia. If the schizophrenia is still unmanageable, a lobotomy may be performed. A lobotomy is surgery in which the connections to and from the prefrontal cortex are cut. Lobotomies cause severe personality changes; they were used much more often in the 1950s than they are today (National Alliance on Mental Illness, 2007).

SCHIZOPHRENIA: DEFINITION AND TREATMENT   7

People with schizophrenia are very susceptible to substance abuse. Many schizophrenics have severe drinking problems, and tobacco addiction is also common. It is harder for them than most people to break this addiction. If they combine substance abuse treatment with the other treatments for their disease, they get much more beneficial results (WebMD, 2010).

Conclusion

As scientists begin to understand schizophrenia, better treatments are becoming available. There is starting to be a better outlook for schizophrenics, and because of this, the public might develop a more sympathetic view of schizophrenics.

Conclusion: Conclusion is indicated by heading (bold and centered). Gomez references her introduction in her conclusion.

SCHIZOPHRENIA: DEFINITION AND TREATMENT   8

References: Heading centered, not bold; list appears on a new page.

DOI: The DOI is provided when available for printed and online works.

Formatting: Double-spaced throughout

Entries: Alphabetize entries by author's last name or name of sponsor. Only the first word and proper nouns/adjectives are capitalized in titles of shorter works (such as articles in a periodical, or Web pages on a Web site). First, last, and all key words are capitalized in titles of longer, stand-alone works (such as books, periodicals, films, Web sites).

URLs: The URL is provided for Web sites and Web pages.

References

Barch, D. (2003). Cognition in schizophrenia: Does working memory
    work? *Current Directions in Psychological Science, 12*(4), 146–150.
    doi:10.1111/1467-8721.01251

Bower, B. (2008). Rare mutations tied to schizophrenia. *Science News, 173*(14),
    222.

Conklin, H., & Iacono, W. (2002). Schizophrenia: A neurodevelopmental
    perspective. *Current Directions in Psychological Science, 11*(1), 33–37.

Grazer, B. (Producer), & Howard, R. (Director). (2001). *A beautiful mind*
    [Motion Picture]. Los Angeles, CA: Universal Pictures.

Internet Mental Health Initiative. (2001). UCLA maps how schizophrenia
    engulfs teen brains. Retrieved from http://www.schizophrenia.com/
    research/schiz.brain.htm

National Alliance on Mental Illness. (2007). Schizophrenia. In *Mental
    illnesses.*
    Retrieved from http://www.nami.org/Template.cfm? Section=By_Illness
    &Template=/TaggedPage/TaggedPageDisplay.
    cfm&TPLID=54&ContentID
    =23036

National Institutes of Mental Health. (2010). Schizophrenia. In *Health topics.*
    Retrieved from http://www.nimh.nih.gov/health/topics/schizophrenia/
    index
    .shtml

WebMD. (2010). Schizophrenia guide. In *Mental health center.* Retrieved from
    http://www.webmd.com/schizophrenia/guide/default.htm

4. **Reread once again to identify themes and patterns and piece together your interpretation.** Study your annotations to discover how the ideas in the work link together to suggest a theme. **Themes** are large or universal topics that are important to nearly everyone. For example, the theme of a poem or short story might be that death is inescapable or that growing up involves a loss of innocence. Think of the theme as the main point a poem or short story makes. To understand the work's theme, consider why the writer wrote the work and what message, view, or lesson about human experience the writer is trying to communicate. (For more about themes, see page 670.)

5. **Write one or more paragraphs identifying the conflict and how it gets resolved, and stating what you think is the main theme.** Concluding your study of a work of literature with your own statement will help you move from interpretation of the work to your own analysis of its significance.

Literary works are complex; you should not expect to understand a poem or short story immediately. You will need to reread parts or the entire work several times. As you reread and think about the work, its meanings will often come clear gradually.

UNDERSTANDING THE LANGUAGE OF LITERATURE

Many writers, especially writers of literary works, use figures of speech to describe people, places, or objects and to communicate ideas. Figurative language is language used in a nonliteral way; it makes sense imaginatively or creatively but not literally. Three common figures of speech—*similes, metaphors,* and *personification*—make comparisons. Writers often use another literary device, *symbols,* to suggest larger themes. In addition, some writers use *irony* to convey the incongruities of life.

For more on figures of speech, see Chapter 10 (pp. 210-11) and Chapter 13 (p. 268).

SIMILES, METAPHORS, AND PERSONIFICATION

Similes and metaphors are comparisons between two unlike things that have at least one common trait. A **simile** uses the word *like* or *as* to make a comparison, whereas a **metaphor** states or implies that one thing is another thing. If you say, "My father's mustache is a house painter's brush," your metaphor compares two dissimilar things—a mustache and a paintbrush—that share a common trait: straight bristles. If you say, "Martha's hair looks like she just walked through a wind tunnel," your simile creates a more vivid image of Martha's hair than if you simply stated, "Martha's hair is messy." Here are some additional examples from literary works.

SIMILE

My soul has grown deep like the rivers.

Langston Hughes, "The Negro Speaks of Rivers"

METAPHOR

Time is but the stream I go a-fishing in.

Henry David Thoreau, *Walden*

When writers use **personification**, they attribute human characteristics to objects or ideas. A well-known example of personification is found in an Emily Dickinson poem in which the poet likens death and immortality to passengers in a carriage: "Because I could not stop for Death—/ He kindly stopped for me—/ The carriage held but just Ourselves—/ and Immortality." Like similes and metaphors, personification often creates a strong visual image.

SYMBOLS

A **symbol** suggests more than its literal meaning. The sun breaking through the clouds, for instance, might suggest hope; the color white often suggests innocence and purity. Because the writer does not directly state the abstract idea that a symbol represents, a symbol may suggest more than one meaning. A white handkerchief, for example, might symbolize retreat in one context but good manners in another. Some literary critics believe the white whale in Herman Melville's novel *Moby Dick* symbolizes evil, whereas others see the whale as representing the forces of nature.

To recognize symbols in a literary work, look for objects that are given a particular or unusual emphasis. The object may be mentioned often, may be suggested in the title, or may appear at the beginning or end of the work. Also be on the lookout for familiar symbols, such as flowers, doves, and colors.

IRONY

Irony is literary language or a literary style in which actions, events, or words are contrary to what readers expect. For example, a prizefighter cowering at the sight of a spider is ironic because you expect prizefighters to be brave, a fire station burning down is ironic because you expect that a firehouse would be protected against fires, and a student saying that she is glad she failed an important exam is ironic because you expect the student to be upset that she failed the exam.

> **EXERCISE 25.1** **Figures of Speech in Everyday Language**
>
> Working with another student, make a list of common metaphors and similes; examples of personification; and symbols you have heard or seen in everyday life, in films or television programs, or in works of literature.

ANALYZING SHORT STORIES

A **short story** is a brief fictional narrative. Short stories are shorter than novels, and their scope is much more limited. For example, a short story may focus on one event in a person's life, whereas a novel may chronicle the events in the lives of an entire family. Like a novel, a short story makes a point about some aspect of the human experience.

When analyzing short stories, pay particular attention to five key elements.

1. Setting
2. Characters
3. Point of View
4. Plot
5. Theme

Read the following short story, "The Secret Lion," before continuing with this section of the chapter. The sections that follow will explain these five key elements and how each of them works in "The Secret Lion."

The Secret Lion

ALBERTO RÍOS

Alberto Ríos (b. 1952), the son of a Guatemalan father and an English mother, was raised in Nogales, Arizona, near the Mexican border. His work has appeared in numerous national and international literature anthologies. In addition to fellowships from the Guggenheim Foundation and the National Endowment for the Arts, Ríos has won several awards: the Walt Whitman Award from the Academy of American Poets, the Arizona Governor's Arts Award, the PEN Beyond Margins Award, and the Western States Book Award for *The Iguana Killer: Twelve Stories of the Heart*—a collection of stories (originally published in 1984) that includes the one reprinted here. Ríos is currently a Regents Professor of English at Arizona State University.

I was twelve and in junior high school and something happened that we didn't   1
have a name for, but it was there nonetheless like a lion, and roaring, roaring that way the biggest things do. Everything changed. Just that. Like the rug, the one that gets pulled—or better, like the tablecloth those magicians pull where the stuff on the table stays the same but the gasp! from the audience makes the staying-the-same part not matter. Like that.

What happened was there were teachers now, not just one teacher, teach-erz, and   2
we felt personally abandoned somehow. When a person had all these teachers now, he didn't get taken care of the same way, even though six was more than one. Arithmetic went out the door when we walked in. And we saw girls now, but they weren't the same girls we used to know because we couldn't talk to them anymore, not the same way we used to, certainly not to Sandy, even though she was my neighbor, too. Not even to her. She just played the piano all the time. And there were words, oh there were words in junior high school, and we wanted to know what they were, and how a person did them—that's what school was supposed to be for. Only, in junior high school, school wasn't school, everything was backward-like. If you went up to a teacher and said the word to try and find out what it meant you got in trouble for saying it. So we didn't. And we figured it must have been that way about other stuff, too, so we never said anything about anything—we weren't stupid.

But my friend Sergio and I, we solved junior high school. We would come home   3
from school on the bus, put our books away, change shoes, and go across the highway to the arroyo.[1] It was the one place we were not supposed to go. So we did. This was, after all, what junior high had at least shown us. It was our river, though, our

_____

[1] *arroyo:* A creek or stream in a dry part of the country.

personal Mississippi, our friend from long back, and it was full of stories and all the branch forts we had built in it when we were still the Vikings of America, with our own symbol, which we had carved everywhere, even in the sand, which let the water take it. That was good, we had decided; whoever was at the end of this river would know about us.

At the very very top of our growing lungs, what we would do down there was shout every dirty word we could think of, in every combination we could come up with, and we would yell about girls, and all the things we wanted to do with them, as loud as we could—we didn't know what we wanted to do with them, just things—and we would yell about teachers, and how we loved some of them, like Miss Crevelone, and how we wanted to dissect some of them, making signs of the cross, like priests, and we would yell this stuff over and over because it felt good, we couldn't explain why, it just felt good and for the first time in our lives there was nobody to tell us we couldn't. So we did.

One Thursday we were walking along shouting this way, and the railroad, the Southern Pacific, which ran above and along the far side of the arroyo, had dropped a grinding ball down there, which was, we found out later, a cannonball thing used in mining. A bunch of them were put in a big vat which turned around and crushed the ore. One had been dropped, or thrown—what do caboose men do when they get bored—but it got down there regardless and as we were walking along yelling about one girl or another, a particular Claudia, we found it, one of these things, looked at it, picked it up, and got very very excited, and held it and passed it back and forth, and we were saying "Guythisis, this is, geeGuythis . . .": we had this perception about nature then, that nature is imperfect and that round things are perfect: we said "GuyGodthis is perfect, thisisthis is perfect, it's round, round and heavy, it'sit's the best thing we'veeverseen. Whatisit?" We didn't know. We just knew it was great. We just, whatever, we played with it, held it some more.

And then we had to decide what to do with it. We knew, because of a lot of things, that if we were going to take this and show it to anybody, this discovery, this best thing, was going to be taken away from us. That's the way it works with little kids, like all the polished quartz, the tons of it we had collected piece by piece over the years. Junior high kids too. If we took it home, my mother, we knew, was going to look at it and say "throw that dirty thing in the, get rid of it." Simple like, like that. "But ma it's the best thing I" "Getridofit." Simple.

So we didn't. Take it home. Instead, we came up with the answer. We dug a hole and buried it. And we marked it secretly. Lots of secret signs. And came back the next week to dig it up and, we didn't know, pass it around some more or something, but we didn't find it. We dug up that whole bank, and we never found it again. We tried.

Sergio and I talked about that ball or whatever it was when we couldn't find it. All we used were small words, neat, good. Kid words. What we were really saying, but

4

5

6

7

8

didn't know the words, was how much that ball was like that place, that whole arroyo: couldn't tell anybody about it, didn't understand what it was, didn't have a name for it. It just felt good. It was just perfect in the way it was that place, that whole going to that place, that whole junior high school lion. It was just iron-heavy, it had no name, it felt good or not, we couldn't take it home to show our mothers, and once we buried it, it was gone forever.

The ball was gone, like the first reasons we had come to that arroyo years earlier,   9
like the first time we had seen the arroyo, it was gone like everything else that had been taken away. This was not our first lesson. We stopped going to the arroyo after not finding the thing, the same way we had stopped going there years earlier and headed for the mountains. Nature seemed to keep pushing us around one way or another, teaching us the same thing every place we ended up. Nature's gang was tough that way, teaching us stuff.

When we were young we moved away from town, me and my family. Sergio's was   10
already out there. Out in the wilds. Or at least the new place seemed like the wilds since everything looks bigger the smaller a man is. I was five, I guess, and we had moved three miles north of Nogales where we had lived, three miles north of the Mexican border. We looked across the highway in one direction and there was the arroyo; hills stood up in the other direction. Mountains, for a small man.

When the first summer came the very first place we went to was of course the   11
one place we weren't supposed to go, the arroyo. We went down in there and found water running, summer rain water mostly, and we went swimming. But every third or fourth or fifth day, the sewage treatment plant that was, we found out, upstream, would release whatever it was that it released, and we would never know exactly what day that was, and a person really couldn't tell right off by looking at the water, not every time, not so a person could get out in time. So, we went swimming that summer and some days we had a lot of fun. Some days we didn't. We found a thousand ways to explain what happened on those other days, constructing elaborate stories about the neighborhood dogs, and hadn't she, my mother, miscalculated her step before, too? But she knew something was up because we'd come running into the house those days, wanting to take a shower, even—if this can be imagined—in the middle of the day.

That was the first time we stopped going to the arroyo. It taught us to look the   12
other way. We decided, as the second side of summer came, we wanted to go into the mountains. They were still mountains then. We went running in one summer Thursday morning, my friend Sergio and I, into my mother's kitchen, and said, well, what'zin, what'zin those hills over there—we used her word so she'd understand us—and she said nothingdon'tworryaboutit. So we went out, and we weren't dumb, we thought with our eyes to each other, ohhoshe'stryingtokeepsomethingfromus. We knew adults.

We had read the books, after all; we knew about bridges and castles and wild-treacherousraging alligatormouth rivers. We wanted them. So we were going to go out and get them. We went back that morning into that kitchen and we said, "We're going out there, we're going into the hills, we're going away for three days, don't worry." She said, "All right." 13

"You know," I said to Sergio, "if we're going to go away for three days, well, we ought to at least pack a lunch." 14

But we were two young boys with no patience for what we thought at the time was mom-stuff: making sa-and-wiches. My mother didn't offer. So we got out little kid knapsacks that my mother had sewn for us, and into them we put the jar of mustard. A loaf of bread. Knivesforksplates, bottles of Coke, a can opener. This was lunch for the two of us. And we were weighed down, humped over to be strong enough to carry this stuff. But we started walking anyway, into the hills. We were going to eat berries and stuff otherwise. "Goodbye." My mom said that. 15

After the first hill we were dead. But we walked. My mother could still see us. And we kept walking. We walked until we got to where the sun is straight overhead, noon. That place. Where that is doesn't matter; it's time to eat. The truth is we weren't anywhere close to that place. We just agreed that the sun was overhead and that it was time to eat, and by tilting our heads a little we could make that the truth. 16

"We really ought to start looking for a place to eat." 17

"Yeah. Let's look for a good place to eat." We went back and forth saying that for fifteen minutes, making it lunchtime because that's what we always said back and forth before lunchtimes at home. "Yeah, I'm hungry all right." I nodded my head. "Yeah, I'm hungry all right too. I'm hungry." He nodded his head. I nodded my head back. After a good deal more nodding, we were ready, just as we came over a little hill. We hadn't found the mountains yet. This was a little hill. 18

And on the other side of this hill we found heaven. 19

It was just what we thought it would be. 20

Perfect. Heaven was green, like nothing else in Arizona. And it wasn't a cemetery or like that because we had seen cemeteries and they had gravestones and stuff and this didn't. This was perfect, had trees, lots of trees, had birds, like we had never seen before. It was like *The Wizard of Oz*, like when they got to Oz and everything was so green, so emerald, they had to wear those glasses, and we ran just like them, laughing, laughing that way we did that moment, and we went running down to this clearing in it all, hitting each other that good way we did. 21

We got down there, we kept laughing, we kept hitting each other, we unpacked our stuff, and we started acting "rich." We knew all about how to do that, like blowing on our nails, then rubbing them on our chests for the shine. We made our sandwiches, opened our Cokes, got out the rest of the stuff, the salt and pepper shakers. I found this particular hole and I put my Coke right into it, a perfect fit, and I called it my Coke-holder. I got down next to it on my back, because everyone knows that rich people eat lying down, and I got my sandwich in one hand and put my other arm 22 around the Coke in its holder. When I wanted a drink, I lifted my neck a little, put out my lips, and tipped my Coke a little with the crook of my elbow. Ah.

We were there, lying down, eating our sandwiches, laughing, throwing bread at 23
each other and out for the birds. This was heaven. We were laughing and we couldn't believe it. My mother was keeping something from us, ah ha, but we had found her out. We even found water over at the side of the clearing to wash our plates with—we had brought plates. Sergio started washing his plates when he was done, and I was being rich with my Coke, and this day in summer was right.

When suddenly these two men came, from around a corner of trees and the tallest 24
grass we had ever seen. They had bags on their backs, leather bags, bags and sticks.

We didn't know what clubs were, but I learned later, like I learned about the 25
grinding balls. The two men yelled at us. Most specifically, one wanted me to take my Coke out of my Coke-holder so he could sink his golf ball into it.

Something got taken away from us that moment. Heaven. We grew up a little bit, 26
and couldn't go backward. We learned. No one had ever told us about golf. They had told us about heaven. And it went away. We got golf in exchange.

We went back to the arroyo for the rest of that summer, and tried to have fun the 27
best we could. We learned to be ready for finding the grinding ball. We loved it, and when we buried it we knew what would happen. The truth is, we didn't look so hard for it. We were two boys and twelve summers then, and not stupid. Things get taken away.

We buried it because it was perfect. We didn't tell my mother, but together it was 28
all we talked about, till we forgot. It was the lion.

SETTING

The **setting** of a short story is the time, place, and circumstance in which the story occurs. The setting provides the framework and atmosphere in which the plot develops and characters interact. For example, Charles Dickens's "A Christmas Carol" is set in nineteenth-century London in December. The setting of "The Secret Lion" is between the arroyo and the mountains just outside Nogales, Arizona. The action occurs near the arroyo and on the golf course.

CHARACTERS

The **characters** are the actors in the story. They reveal themselves through dialogue, actions, appearance, thoughts, and feelings. Drawing a character map (Figure 25.1, p. 668) can help you understand the relationships among characters. In the center of a blank piece of paper, write the main character's name inside a circle. Then add other characters' names, connecting them with lines to the main character. On the connecting lines, briefly describe the relationships between characters and the events or other factors (such as emotions) that affect their relationship.

FIGURE 25.1 Sample Character Map for "The Secret Lion"

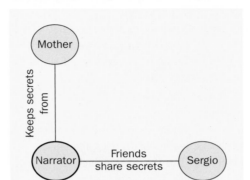

The **narrator**, the person who tells the story, may also comment on or reveal information about the characters. The narrator is not necessarily the author of the story. The narrator can be one of the characters in the story or an onlooker who observes but does not participate in the action. Think critically about what the narrator reveals about the personalities, needs, and motives of the characters and whether the narrator's opinions may be colored by his or her perceptions and biases.

"The Secret Lion" involves two principal characters: the narrator and his childhood friend, Sergio. Both twelve-year-old boys are playful, spirited, and inquisitive. They explore, disobey, and test ideas. The narrator's mother is a secondary character in the story.

POINT OF VIEW

The **point of view** is the perspective from which the story is told. There are two common points of view: first person and third person.

- In the **first-person** (*I, we*) point of view, the narrator tells the story as he or she sees or experiences it ("*I* saw the crowd gather at the cemetery"). A first-person narrator may be one of the characters or someone observing but not participating in the story.
- In the **third-person** (*he, she, they*) point of view, the narrator tells the story as if someone else is experiencing it ("*Laura* saw the crowd gather at the cemetery"). Third-person narrators fall into three categories.
    1. The third-person narrator reports only the actions that can be observed from the outside; the narrator does not know or report the characters' thoughts.
    2. The *omniscient*, or all-knowing, third-person narrator is aware of and reports on the thoughts and actions of all characters in the story.
    3. The third-person narrator enters the minds of one or more (but not all) characters and writes about their thoughts and motives.

To identify the point of view, consider who is narrating the story and what the narrator knows about the characters' actions, thoughts, and motives. "The Secret Lion" is narrated by a first-person narrator who both participates in the action and looks back on the events to interpret them. For example, he says of the preparations for the trip to the mountains, "But we were two young boys with no patience for what we thought at the time was mom-stuff" (para. 15). He also uses a fast-talking narrative style characteristic of twelve-year-old boys, intentionally bending rules of spelling and grammar to achieve this effect. For example, he uses sentence fragments — "Lots of secret signs" (7), "Out in the wilds" (10) — and runs words together or emphasizes syllables to show how they are pronounced — "wild-treacherousraging alligatormouth rivers" (13), "sa-and-wiches" (15). He also uses slang words — "neat" (8) — and contractions to create an informal tone.

PLOT

The **plot** is the basic story line — that is, the sequence of events and actions through which the story's meaning is expressed. The plot often centers on a **conflict** — a problem or clash between opposing forces — and the resolution of the conflict. Once the scene is set and the characters are introduced, a problem or conflict arises. Suspense and tension build as the conflict unfolds and the characters wrestle with the problem. Near the end of the story, the events come to a **climax** — the point at which the conflict is resolved. The story ends with a conclusion.

For stories with complicated plots that flash backward and forward in time, creating a time line (Figure 25.2), a chronological listing of events, may be helpful.

FIGURE 25.2 Sample Time Line for "The Secret Lion"

Sample Time Line: "The Secret Lion"

Age 5 ——————————	Main character moves three miles north of Nogales.
First half of summer ———	He visits the arroyo with Sergio; goes swimming, mother suspects.
Second half of summer	Boys visit mountains; think they have found heaven but learn it is a golf course.
	They return to the arroyo; try to have fun.
Age 12 (junior high school)	They visit the arroyo.
	They shout dirty words and yell about girls.
One Thursday	They find grinding ball.
	They bury grinding ball.
	They can't find the buried ball; stop going to the arroyo.

In "The Secret Lion," two childhood friends, while playing near an arroyo, discover a grinding ball. They bury the ball but are unable to find it when they return. The narrator recollects an earlier time, when the two boys had planned a trip to the mountains and stopped to have lunch on what they soon discovered was a golf course. The conflict, illustrated by several events, is between the boys' imaginations and adult realities.

THEME

The **theme** of a story is its central or dominant idea — the main point the author makes about the human experience. (Recall that themes are large or universal topics that are important to nearly everyone.) Readers do not always agree about a story's theme. Therefore, in analyzing a short story, you must give evidence to support your interpretation of the theme. The following suggestions will help you uncover clues.

1. **Study the title.** What meanings does it suggest?
2. **Analyze the main characters.** Do the characters change? If so, how, and in response to what?
3. **Look for broad statements about the conflict.** What do the characters and narrator say about the conflict or their lives?
4. **Look for symbols, figures of speech, and meaningful names** (Young *Goodman* Brown, for example).

Once you uncover a theme, try expressing it in a sentence rather than as a single word or brief phrase. For example, saying that a story's theme is "dishonesty" or "parent-child relationships" does not reveal the story's full meaning. When expressed as a sentence, however, a story's theme becomes clear: "Dishonesty sometimes pays" or "Parent-child relationships are often struggles for power and control."

One possible theme of "The Secret Lion" is that change is inevitable, that nothing remains the same, and this change brings on a loss of innocence. After the boys discover that they can't find the buried grinding ball, the narrator hints at this theme: "The ball was gone . . . like everything else that had been taken away" (para. 9). When the boys encounter the two men on the golf course, the narrator again comments on the theme of change: "Something got taken away from us that moment. Heaven. We grew up a little bit, and couldn't go backward" (26).

Another possible theme of Ríos's story is that perfection is unattainable. The boys are attracted to the ball because it is perfect: "GuyGodthis is perfect, thisisthis is perfect . . . it'sit's the best thing we'veeverseen" (5). But once the "perfect" ball is buried, it can never be found again. In much the same way, the boys cannot return to the "heaven" they once knew at the golf course.

> **EXERCISE 25.2** **Identifying the Elements of a TV Program**
>
> Working in groups of two or three, choose a television situation comedy and watch one episode, either together or separately. After viewing the program, identify each of the following elements: setting, characters, point of view, and plot. Then consider whether you think the episode has a theme.

Use the worksheet below to guide your analysis of short stories.

WORKSHEET FOR ANALYZING SHORT STORIES

Author:

Title:

Publisher:

Year of Publication:

Setting: Time
1. In what general time period (century or decade) does the story take place?
2. What major events (wars, revolutions, famines, political or cultural movements) occurred during that time, and what bearing might they have on the story?

Setting: Place
1. In what geographic area does the story take place? (Try to identify the country and the city or town, as well as whether the area is an urban or rural one.)
2. Where does the action occur? (For example, does it occur on a battlefield, in a living room, or on a city street?)
3. Why is the place important? (Why couldn't the story occur elsewhere?)

Characters
1. Who are the main characters in the story?
2. What are the distinguishing qualities and characteristics of each character?
3. Why do you like or dislike each character?
4. How and why do characters change (or not change) as the story progresses?

Point of View
1. Is the narrator a character in the story or strictly an observer?
2. Is the narrator knowledgeable about the motives, feelings, and behavior of any or all of the characters?
3. Does the narrator affect what happens in the story? If so, how? What role does the narrator play?

Plot
1. What series of events occurs? Summarize the action.
2. What is the conflict? Why does it occur? How does it build to a climax?
3. How is the conflict resolved?
4. Is the outcome satisfying? Why or why not?

Theme
1. What is the theme? What broad statement about life or the human experience does the story suggest?
2. What evidence from the story supports your interpretation of the theme?

The Story of an Hour

KATE CHOPIN

Kate Chopin (1851–1904), a nineteenth-century American writer, is best known for her novel *The Awakening* (1899), which outraged early literary critics with its portrayal of a woman in search of sexual and professional independence. As you read the following short story, originally published in *Vogue* magazine in 1894, look for, highlight, and annotate the five primary elements of short stories discussed in this chapter.

Knowing that Mrs. Mallard was afflicted with a heart trouble, great care was taken to break to her as gently as possible the news of her husband's death. 1

It was her sister Josephine who told her, in broken sentences, veiled hints that revealed in half concealing. Her husband's friend Richards was there, too, near her. It was he who had been in the newspaper office when intelligence of the railroad disaster was received, with Brently Mallard's name leading the list of "killed." He had only taken the time to assure himself of its truth by a second telegram, and had hastened to forestall any less careful, less tender friend in bearing the sad message. 2

She did not hear the story as many women have heard the same, with a paralyzed inability to accept its significance. She wept at once, with sudden, wild abandonment, in her sister's arms. When the storm of grief had spent itself she went away to her room alone. She would have no one follow her. 3

There stood, facing the open window, a comfortable, roomy armchair. Into this she sank, pressed down by a physical exhaustion that haunted her body and seemed to reach into her soul. 4

She could see in the open square before her house the tops of trees that were all aquiver with the new spring life. The delicious breath of rain was in the air. In the street below a peddler was crying his wares. The notes of a distant song which someone was singing reached her faintly, and countless sparrows were twittering in the eaves. 5

There were patches of blue sky showing here and there through the clouds that had met and piled one above the other in the west facing her window. 6

She sat with her head thrown back upon the cushion of the chair, quite motionless, except when a sob came up into her throat and shook her, as a child who has cried itself to sleep continues to sob in its dreams. 7

She was young, with a fair, calm face, whose lines bespoke repression and even a certain strength. But now there was a dull stare in her eyes, whose gaze was fixed away off yonder on one of those patches of blue sky. It was not a glance of reflection, but rather indicated a suspension of intelligent thought. 8

There was something coming to her and she was waiting for it, fearfully. What was it? She did not know, it was too subtle and elusive to name. But she felt it, creeping out of the sky, reaching toward her through the sounds, the scents, the color that filled the air. 9

Now her bosom rose and fell tumultuously. She was beginning to recognize this   10
thing that was approaching to possess her, and she was striving to beat it back with
her will—as powerless as her two white slender hands would have been.

When she abandoned herself a little whispered word escaped her slightly parted lips.   11
She said it over and over under her breath: "Free, free, free!" The vacant stare and the
look of terror that had followed it went from her eyes. They stayed keen and bright. Her
pulses beat fast, and the coursing blood warmed and relaxed every inch of her body.

She did not stop to ask if it were not a monstrous joy that held her. A clear and   12
exalted perception enabled her to dismiss the suggestion as trivial.

She knew that she would weep again when she saw the kind, tender hands folded in   13
death; the face that had never looked save with love upon her, fixed and gray and dead.
But she saw beyond that bitter moment a long procession of years to come that would
belong to her absolutely. And she opened and spread her arms out to them in welcome.

There would be no one to live for during those coming years; she would live for   14
herself. There would be no powerful will bending her in that blind persistence with
which men and women believe they have a right to impose a private will upon a fellow
creature. A kind intention or a cruel intention made the act seem no less a crime as
she looked upon it in that brief moment of illumination.

And yet she had loved him—sometimes. Often she had not. What did it matter!   15
What could love, the unsolved mystery, count for in face of this possession of self-
assertion which she suddenly recognized as the strongest impulse of her being.

"Free! Body and soul free!" she kept whispering.   16

Josephine was kneeling before the closed door with her lips to the keyhole,   17
imploring for admission. "Louise, open the door! I beg; open the door—you will make
yourself ill. What are you doing, Louise? For heaven's sake open the door."

"Go away. I am not making myself ill." No; she was drinking in a very elixir of life   18
through that open window.

Her fancy was running riot along those days ahead of her. Spring days, and summer   19
days, and all sorts of days that would be her own. She breathed a quick prayer that life
might be long. It was only yesterday she had thought with a shudder that life might be
long.

She arose at length and opened the door to her sister's importunities. There was   20
a feverish triumph in her eyes, and she carried herself unwittingly like a goddess
of Victory. She clasped her sister's waist, and together they descended the stairs.
Richards stood waiting for them at the bottom.

Some one was opening the front door with a latchkey. It was Brently Mallard who   21
entered, a little travel-stained, composedly carrying his gripsack and umbrella. He had been
far from the scene of accident, and did not even know there had been one. He stood amazed
at Josephine's piercing cry; at Richards' quick motion to screen him from the view of his
wife.

But Richards was too late.   22

When the doctors came they said she had died of heart disease—of joy that kills.   23

ANALYZING POETRY

Poetry is written in lines and stanzas instead of in sentences and paragraphs. Because of the genre's unique format, poets often express ideas in compact and concise language, and reading and analyzing a short poem may take as much time and effort as analyzing an essay or a short story. To grasp the meaning of a poem, pay attention to the sound and meaning of individual words and consider how the words work together to convey meaning. Use the following general guidelines to read and analyze poetry effectively.

1. **Read the poem through once, using the poem's punctuation as a guide.** Try to get a general sense of what the poem is about. If you come across an unfamiliar word or a confusing reference, keep reading. Although poetry is written in lines, each line may not make sense by itself. Meaning often flows from line to line, and a single sentence can be composed of several lines. Use the poem's punctuation to guide you. If there is no punctuation at the end of a line, read the line with a slight pause at the end and with an emphasis on the last word. Think about how the poet breaks lines to achieve a certain effect.

2. **Read the poem several more times, annotating as you read.** The meaning of the poem will become clearer with each successive reading. At first you may understand some parts but not others. If you are a spatial or an abstract learner, try to visualize, or see, what the poem is about. If you are a pragmatic or rational learner, you will probably want to work through the poem line by line, from beginning to end. With poetry, however, this approach does not always work. Instead, you may need to use later stanzas to help you understand earlier ones. If you find certain sections of the poem difficult or confusing, read these sections aloud several times. You might try copying them, word for word. Look up the meanings of any unfamiliar words in a dictionary.

Learning Style Options

As you read, annotate the poem, highlighting striking elements (figures of speech, symbols, revealing character descriptions, striking dialogue, and the like) and recording your reactions (A sample annotated passage appears in Figure 25.3, p. 678). Pay particular attention to the following.

- **The speaker and tone.** Try to understand the speaker's viewpoint or feelings to figure out who he or she is. Also consider the speaker's tone: Is it serious, challenging, sad, frustrated, joyful? To determine the tone, read the poem aloud. Your emphasis on certain words or the rise and fall of your voice may provide clues to the tone; you may "hear" the poet's anger, despondency, or elation.

- **To whom the poem is addressed.** Is it written to a person, the reader, an object? Consider the possibility that the poet may be writing to work out a personal problem or express strong emotions.

- **Allusions.** Look up unfamiliar **allusions**, or references, to people, objects, or events outside the poem. If you see Oedipus mentioned in a poem, for example, you may need to use a dictionary or encyclopedia to learn that he was a figure in Greek mythology who unwittingly killed his father and married his mother. Your knowledge of Oedipus would then help you interpret the poem.

- **The language of the poem.** Consider the *connotations,* or shades of meaning, of words in the poem. Study the poem's use of descriptive language, similes, metaphors, personification, and symbols.
- **The poem's theme.** Does its overall meaning involve a feeling, a person, a memory, or an argument? Paraphrase the poem; express it in your own words and connect it to your own experience. Then link your ideas together to discover the poem's overall meaning. Ask yourself: What is the poet trying to tell me? What is the theme?

For more on connotations, see Chapters 4 and 10, pp. 79 and 209; for more on descriptive language, see Chapter 13, pp. 265–66.

3. **Write a response. Copying passages from the poem and responding to those passages in writing can help you explore your reaction to the poem and grasp its meaning.** Choose quotations from the poem that convey a main point or opinion, reveal a character's motives, or say something important about the plot or theme. Describe your reaction to each quotation, interpreting, disagreeing with, or questioning it. Comment on the language of the quotation and relate it to other quotations or elements in the work. Here is a sample response to Frost's "Two Look at Two."

"With thoughts of the path back, how rough it was" (line 5)	The couple's past has been difficult; returning to daily life may be difficult, too. Nature is rough and challenging.
. . . "This is all," they sighed, "Good-night to woods.". . . (lines 13–14)	The couple will soon come to the end — of their relationship or their lives.

WORKSHEET FOR ANALYZING POETRY

Poet:

Poem:

Source:

Publisher:

Year of Publication:

1. How does the poem make you feel—shocked, saddened, angered, annoyed, happy? Write a sentence or two describing your reaction.
2. Who is the speaker? What do you know about him or her? What tone does the speaker use? To whom is he or she speaking?
3. What is the poem's setting? If it is unclear, why does the poet not provide a setting?

> ## WORKSHEET FOR ANALYZING POETRY — CONT'D
>
> 4. What emotional atmosphere or mood does the poet create? Do you sense, for example, a mood of foreboding, excitement, or contentment?
> 5. How does the poet use language to create an effect? Does the poet use similes, metaphors, personification, or symbols?
> 6. Does the poem tell a story? If so, what is its point?
> 7. Does the poem express emotion? If so, for what purpose?
> 8. Does the poem rhyme? If so, does the rhyme affect the meaning? (For example, does the poet use rhyme to emphasize key words or phrases?)
> 9. What is the meaning of the poem's title?
> 10. What is the theme of the poem?

READING: POEM

Two Look at Two

ROBERT FROST

Robert Frost (1874–1963) is a major American poet whose work often focuses on familiar objects, natural scenes, and the character of New England. In his early life Frost was a farmer and teacher; later he became a poet in residence at Amherst College and taught at Dartmouth, Yale, and Harvard. Frost was awarded Pulitzer Prizes for four collections of poems: *New Hampshire* (1923), from which "Two Look at Two" is taken; *Collected Poems* (1930); *A Further Range* (1936); and *A Witness Tree* (1942). As you read the selection, use the questions in the preceding worksheet to think critically about the poem.

Love and forgetting might have carried them
A little further up the mountain side
With night so near, but not much further up.
They must have halted soon in any case
With thoughts of the path back, how rough it was   5
With rock and washout, and unsafe in darkness;
When they were halted by a tumbled wall
With barbed-wire binding. They stood facing this,
Spending what onward impulse they still had
In one last look the way they must not go,   10
On up the failing path, where, if a stone
Or earthslide moved at night, it moved itself;
No footstep moved it. "This is all," they sighed,
"Good-night to woods." But not so; there was more.
A doe from round a spruce stood looking at them   15
Across the wall, as near the wall as they.

She saw them in their field, they her in hers.
The difficulty of seeing what stood still,
Like some up-ended boulder split in two,
Was in her clouded eyes: they saw no fear there.   20
She seemed to think that two thus they were safe.
Then, as if they were something that, though strange,
She could not trouble her mind with too long,
She sighed and passed unscared along the wall.
"*This,* then, is all. What more is there to ask?"   25
But no, not yet. A snort to bid them wait.
A buck from round the spruce stood looking at them
Across the wall, as near the wall as they.
This was an antlered buck of lusty nostril,
Not the same doe come back into her place.   30
He viewed them quizzically with jerks of head,
As if to ask, "Why don't you make some motion?
Or give some sign of life? Because you can't.
I doubt if you're as living as you look."
Thus till he had them almost feeling dared   35
To stretch a proffering hand—and a spell-breaking.
Then he too passed unscared along the wall.
Two had seen two, whichever side you spoke from.
"This *must* be all." It was all. Still they stood,
A great wave from it going over them,   40
As if the earth in one unlooked-for favor
Had made them certain earth returned their love.

The poem takes place on a mountainside path, near dusk. A couple walking along the path finds a tumbled wall. Looking beyond the wall, the couple encounters first a doe and then a buck. The doe and buck stare at the human couple and vice versa; hence the title "Two Look at Two." Neither the animals nor the humans are frightened; both couples observe each other and continue with their lives. The action is described by a third-person narrator who can read the thoughts of the humans. The speaker creates an objective tone by reporting events as they occur.

In "Two Look at Two," Frost considers the relationship between humans and nature. The wall is symbolic of the separation between them. Beyond the wall the couple looks at "the way they must not go" (line 10). Although humans and nature are separate, they are also equal and in balance. These qualities are suggested by the title as well as by the actions of both couples as they observe each other in a nonthreatening way. The third-person point of view contributes to this balance in that the poem's narrator is an outside observer rather than a participant. One possible theme of the poem, therefore, is the balance and equality between humans and nature.

As you read the following poem, "How I Discovered Poetry," by Marilyn Nelson, use the guidelines for reading a poem (pp. 674–75) and the worksheet (p. 676) to help you analyze its elements and discover its meaning.

FIGURE 25.3 A Sample Annotated Passage from "Two Look at Two"

Love and forgetting might have carried them

A little further up the mountain side

With night so near, but not much further up. ←——— *limitations of humans*

They must have halted soon in any case

With thoughts of the path back, how rough it was ←——— *road of life?*
difficulty of life

With rock and washout, and unsafe in darkness;

When they were halted by a tumbled wall ←——— *separates man and nature*—
Why is it tumbled?

With barbed-wire binding. They stood facing this, ←——— *sharp, penetrating*

Spending what onward impulse they still had

In one last look the way they must not go, ←——— *prohibited from crossing*

READING: POEM

How I Discovered Poetry

MARILYN NELSON

Marilyn Nelson (b. 1946) is an American poet and translator and the author of books for young adults. She is the author of numerous collections of poetry, including *The Homeplace* (1990), *The Fields of Praise: New and Selected Poems* (1997), in which this poem appeared, and *The Cachoiera Tales and Other Poems* (2005), which won the L. E. Phillabaum Award and was a finalist for the Los Angeles Book Award for poetry. Her most recent work is *How I Discovered Poetry* (2014), a memoir in verse form. In 2012 Nelson was awarded the Frost Medal by the Poetry Society of America, and in 2013 she was elected to the board of chancellors of the Academy of American Poets. Respond to the poem as you read it by making notes in the margin.

It was like soul-kissing, the way the words
filled my mouth as Mrs. Purdy read from her desk.
All the other kids zoned an hour ahead to 3:15,
but Mrs. Purdy and I wandered lonely as clouds borne
by a breeze off Mount Parnassus. She must have seen   5
the darkest eyes in the room brim: The next day
she gave me a poem she'd chosen especially for me
to read to the all except for me white class.
She smiled when she told me to read it, smiled harder,
said oh yes I could. She smiled harder and harder   10
until I stood and opened my mouth to banjo playing
darkies, pickaninnies, disses and dats. When I finished
my classmates stared at the floor. We walked silent
to the buses, awed by the power of words.

Pay particular attention to the following:

1. **Use the literary present tense.** Even though the poem or short story was written in the past, as a general rule write about the events in it and the author's writing of it as if they were happening in the present. An exception to this rule occurs when you are referring to a time earlier than that in which the narrator speaks, in which case a switch to the past tense is appropriate.

   Example: Keats in "Ode on a Grecian Urn" ~~referred~~ *refers* to the urn as a "silent form" (line 44).

   Example: In "Two Look at Two," it is not clear why the couple *decided* to walk up the mountain-side path.

   The couple made the decision before the action in the poem began.

2. **Punctuate quotations correctly.** Direct quotations from a literary work, whether spoken or written, must be placed in quotation marks. Omitted material should be marked by an ellipsis (...). The lines of a poem when they are run together in an essay are separated by a slash (/).

   Example: In "Two Look at Two," Frost concludes "that the earth in one unlooked-for favor / Had made them certain earth returned their love" (lines 41–42).

   Periods and commas appear within quotation marks. Question marks and exclamation points go within or outside quotation marks, depending on the meaning of the sentence. In the following excerpt, the question mark goes inside the closing quotation marks because it is part of Frost's poem (line 32). Notice, too, that double and single quotation marks are required for a quotation within a quotation. (See Chapter 24, pp. 608–12 for more on incorporating quotations into your writing.)

   Example: The buck seems "to ask, 'Why don't you make some motion' ?" (line 32).

FIGURE 25.4 **Flowchart for Revising a Literary Analysis Essay**

QUESTIONS	REVISION STRATEGIES

1. Highlight your thesis statement. Does it identify the work, the one aspect of it you are analyzing, and the main point of your analysis?

 NO

- Revise your thesis so that all of these items are included.
- Ask a classmate to read your thesis and convey his or her understanding of your main point.

 YES

2. Place a ✔ by the evidence from the literary work that supports your thesis. Is all of your evidence relevant to your thesis? Is there enough evidence?

 NO

- Delete examples that do not support your thesis or that might be confusing to readers.
- Add relevant quotations, paraphrases, and summaries.
- Explain how the examples support your point.

 YES

3. [Bracket] each quotation from the work. Do you include a paragraph, page, or line numbers for each and a works-cited entry for the edition of the work you used?

 NO

- Add paragraph, page, or line numbers where they are required and a list of works cited.

 YES

4. *Write* a sentence describing your instructor's goals for the assignment. Does the essay include enough information (about the author, plot, characters, and so on) to achieve these goals?

 NO

- Add any information that your instructor requires or that readers will need to understand your analysis.

 YES

(Figure 25.4 continued)

QUESTIONS		REVISION STRATEGIES

5. each verb. Have you used the present tense consistently when writing about events in the work?

 NO

· Maintain the present tense unless you are writing about an event that preceded another event in the story.

YES

6. Place an ✘ next to words that reveal your feelings or judgments about the work. Does your tone suggest a serious, objective view of the work?

 NO

· Tone down or eliminate any overly critical or enthusiastic statements.

YES

7. Underline the topic sentence of each body paragraph. Does each paragraph have a clear topic sentence and focus on one main point or idea?

 NO

· Be sure each paragraph has a clear topic sentence (see Chapter 7) and supporting evidence from the work.
· Consider combining closely related paragraphs or splitting paragraphs that cover two or more main points or ideas.

YES

8. Reread your introduction and conclusion. Does the introduction suggest the importance of your thesis and engage your readers' interest? Is your conclusion satisfying?

 NO

· Ask yourself, Why would my audience be interested in my thesis? Incorporate the answer into your introduction.
· Revise your introduction and conclusion using the guidelines in Chapter 7 (pp. 147–51). Try including a meaningful quotation or brief statement about your response to the work. Be sure your essay satisfies your assignment.

The Keeping of "The Secret Lion"

ANDREW DECKER

Andrew Decker was a student at Niagara County Community College when he wrote the following literary analysis of Ríos's "The Secret Lion" in response to an assignment in his first-year writing class. As you read the essay, notice the one aspect of the literary work that Decker focuses on, his thesis, and the evidence he uses to support it.

Introduction: Decker gives a one-sentence synopsis, assuming his audience is familiar with the work. In his thesis statement, he indicates that he will focus on a specific aspect of it.

Organization: Clear topic sentences identify main point of each body paragraph.

Support: Decker gives background for the essay, quoting the "secret lion" passage and associating it with adolescence. He identifies quotations with paragraph numbers.

Tense: Decker uses present tense when discussing events in the story.

Support: Quotations are used as supporting evidence.

Alberto Ríos's "The Secret Lion" charts the initiation of a young boy into adolescence. During this climactic period of growth, the narrator experiences several shifts in perception that change him from a child to an adolescent by teaching him the value of secrets. [1]

Within the first paragraph, the author introduces the reader to the new and perplexing feelings of the main character during his junior high years. His impression of what happened during those years remains nameless, "but it was there nonetheless like a lion, and roaring, roaring that way the biggest things do. Everything changed. Just that" (paragraph 1). It is as if the boy is being swept away by a great swell, the wave of anticipation traditionally associated with the child's entry into adolescence. [2]

He finds that these changes are confusing and yet enticing. Evident within the context of the first page is the boy's newfound curiosity about and fascination with the opposite sex. He is also bewildered by the use of profanity and delights in the opportunity to verbally (and very loudly) explore his own feelings with respect to the use of such words. [3]

Although adults scold him when he questions them about the meaning of these words, their dismay does not discourage him from saying the words privately. He and his friend Sergio like to hide away from such authoritarian voices, and so they cross the highway to the arroyo where they are not supposed to play. In the arroyo, they "shout every dirty word we could think of, in every combination we could come up with, and we would yell about girls, and all the things we wanted to do with them, as loud as we could" (4). Of course, they take great pleasure in this youthful audacity for "it just felt good and for the first time in our lives there was nobody to tell us we couldn't" (4). All is new. All is fresh. [4]

Opportunity abounds, and possibilities remain infinite, for time has not yet become an enemy.

One day when the two boys are playing and cussing in the arroyo, they find a perfectly round iron ball. It is heavy and smooth, and to them it is the perfect object. In the eyes of the two children, the world is form-less and pure, as is the ball. Similarly, they consider the arroyo to be the perfect place--their perfect place. When faced with deciding what to do with the ball, they choose to bury it so that nobody can take it away--if only in a less literal sense.

Their minds are still free of the narrow vision of an adult. They are free to roam and roar and echo the spirit of the lion, which is for Sergio and the narrator the spirit of that time. In their own words, when they talk of that ball, they speak of "how much that ball was like that place, that whole arroyo: couldn't tell anybody about it, didn't understand what it was, didn't have a name for it. It just felt good. It was just perfect in the way it was that place, that whole going to that place, that whole junior high school lion" (8). They know that once they bury the grinding ball (they only learn later what it is), it will be gone forever and yet thereby preserved.

The two boys are applying a lesson they have already learned. They understand that an experience can be stolen or changed by a shift in perception so that the original feeling, the original reality, ceases to exist in its more pure and innocent form. The boys had experienced disillusion before; when they were very young, they had also played in the arroyo and gone swimming in the stream. It was a time of naiveté, but their naiveté had been challenged when they learned that the water was at times filled with the waste flushed downstream by a local sewage plant.

Another shift in perception happened later that same summer, when the boys think they have found a new haven beyond some small hills near their houses. On the other side of a hill they find a green clearing, and they declare its lush beauty their "heaven." They learn, however, that this heaven is merely a product of their unworldly imagination; the boys have youthfully glorified a simple golf course, in which they were unwelcome visitors.

These events and others teach the boys to protect a new experience, to keep new feelings safe and virginal so as not to lose them to the ravages

---

5 **Symbolism:** Decker discusses the iron ball as a symbol of the purity of childhood.

6 **Organization:** Decker organizes his essay by presenting events from the work in chronological order, since his thesis focuses on changes in perception over time.

7

8 **Transitions:** Decker uses transitional words and phrases to connect ideas, to move to the final events in the story and to move to the conclusion of his essay.

Conclusion: Decker offers a final interpretation of the work by making reference to its title and reflecting the introduction of the essay.

9

of time and change. When they return to the arroyo several years later, when they are twelve and experiencing the exuberance and excitement of adolescence, they know enough not to share or expose their experiences. The grinding ball is a symbol of that age, that sense of newness, and as they say, "when we buried it we knew what would happen" (27). Burying the ball is an attempt on their part to crystallize a certain time, a certain perception, "because it was perfect" (28). "It was the lion" (28), and the lion was the "roaring" of both that time and that place, and they bury it so that it might never truly be lost.

Sources: Cites edition of "The Secret Lion" that Decker used

Work Cited

Ríos, Alberto. "The Secret Lion." *The Iguana Killer: Twelve Stories of the Heart*, Blue Moon, 1984.

ANALYZING THE WRITER'S TECHNIQUE

1. **Thesis** Does Decker provide sufficient evidence to support his thesis? Choose one example Decker offers and evaluate its effectiveness.
2. **Introduction and Conclusion** Evaluate Decker's introduction and conclusion. In what ways could they be improved?
3. **Development** Which paragraphs are particularly well developed? Which, if any, need further development?

RESPONDING TO THE ESSAY

1. **Discussion** How does Decker's interpretation of "The Secret Lion" compare with yours?
2. **Journal** Evaluate Decker's perception of childhood and adolescence. Write a journal entry comparing his perception with your own.

26

Essay Examinations and Portfolios

The cartoon on this page humorously comments on the process of taking tests. No doubt you've taken tests throughout your school years, and they are an important part of college classes as well. Assume you are taking a short, timed writing test. You have been asked to write about your experiences with taking tests. You might write about how you prepare for exams or share test-taking tips, for example. You have fifteen minutes to complete the writing test.

Oogy flunks his cave drawing final—

© www.Cartoonstock.com

- prepare for and take essay examinations, and
- create a writing portfolio.

In completing the timed writing test in the Writing Quick Start, did you feel pressured by the fifteen-minute limit? How did you decide what to write about? Did you have as much time as you would have liked to organize, plan, develop, and revise your ideas? Probably not.

You may wonder why instructors give essay exams and other kinds of timed writing assignments. In many college courses, essay exams allow instructors to determine how well students have grasped important concepts and whether they can organize and integrate key concepts with other material. In addition, essay exams require students to use different and more advanced thinking skills than they use when taking a more objective type of exam, such as a multiple-choice test. For instance, an essay exam for a history course might require you to pull ideas together and focus on larger issues, perhaps analyzing historical trends or comparing two political figures.

This chapter will help you prepare for the timed essay exams you will encounter in college. Although the chapter focuses on essay exams, you can also apply the skills you learn here to other kinds of writing assignments you need to complete under time pressure. This chapter will also help you prepare a portfolio of your writing.

TIMED WRITING AND PORTFOLIOS IN COLLEGE AND THE WORKPLACE

- For the midterm exam in your *philosophy of religion course*, you have one hour to answer the following essay question: "Contrast the beliefs of Islam with those of either Judaism or Christianity."

- For a *business communication class*, you are asked to assemble a portfolio that illustrates your mastery of the six course objectives.

- As a *freelance artist*, you need to prepare a portfolio of your illustration styles to help art directors evaluate your work.

ESSAY EXAMINATIONS

Doing well on essay examinations involves not only preparing for the exam, but also analyzing the questions and answering the questions clearly and fully.

PREPARING FOR ESSAY EXAMS

Because essay exams require you to produce a written response, the best way to prepare for them is by organizing and writing.

Create study sheets to synthesize information. Most essay exams require you to *synthesize*, or pull together, information. To prepare for this task, try to identify the key topics in a course, and then create a **study sheet** for each main topic. Study sheets help you organize, consolidate, and study complex or detailed information.

For more on synthesizing sources, see Chapter 23, pp. 592–95.

To prepare a study sheet, draw on information from your textbook as well as from class notes, handouts, previous exams (look for emphasized topics), and assigned readings. You can organize a study sheet in a variety of ways. For example, you might:

- draw a graphic organizer to create a visual study sheet,
- create a time line to connect historical events,
- write an outline to organize information,
- construct a comparison-and-contrast chart to see relationships among topics, or
- develop a list of categories and use them to organize information.

Whatever method of organization you use for your study sheet, be sure to include key information about each topic: definitions, facts, principles, theories, events, research studies, and the like.

Here is part of one student's study sheet for a speech communication course on the topic *audience analysis*.

SAMPLE STUDY SHEET

Topic: Audience Analysis
1. Demographic characteristics
   —Age and gender
   —Educational background (type and level of education)
   —Group membership (people who share similar interests or goals)
   —Social and religious activities
   —Hobbies and sports
2. Psychological characteristics
   —Beliefs (about what is true or false, right or wrong)
   —Attitudes (positive or negative)
   —Values (standards for judging worth of thoughts and actions)

EXERCISE 26.1 **Preparing a Study Sheet**

Use the preceding guidelines to prepare a study sheet on a general topic that you expect will be covered on an upcoming exam in one of your courses.

Predict essay exam questions. Once you prepare study sheets for a particular course, the next step is to predict questions that might be asked on an essay exam. Although essay exam questions usually focus on general topics, themes, or patterns, these questions generally also require you to supply details in your response. For example, an essay question on a psychology exam might ask you to compare and contrast the James-Lange and Cannon-Bard theories of motivation. Your answer would focus on the similarities and differences between these key theories, incorporating relevant details where necessary.

Use the following strategies to help you predict the types of questions you might be asked on an essay exam.

1. **Group topics into categories.** Review your textbook, class notes, and study sheets to devise categories. For example, if you find a chapter on kinship in your anthropology textbook and several entries in your class notes on this topic, a question on kinship is likely to appear on an essay exam for the course.

2. **Study your syllabus and objectives.** These documents contain important clues about what your instructor expects you to learn during the course.

3. **Study previous exams.** Notice which key ideas are emphasized in previous exams. If you had to explain the historical significance of the Boston Tea Party on your first American history exam, you can predict that future exams will ask you to explain the historical significance of other events.

4. **Listen to your instructor's comments.** When your instructor announces or reviews material for an upcoming essay exam, pay close attention to the key topics he or she reveals or to the areas he or she suggests that you study.

5. **Draft possible essay questions.** Use Table 26.1 (p. 695) to draft possible essay questions using key verbs that hint at how you must answer effectively.

> **EXERCISE 26.2**   **Predicting Essay Questions for a College Course**

For an upcoming essay exam in one of your courses, predict and write at least three possible questions your instructor might ask about the course material.

Draft answers in outline form. After you predict several possible essay exam questions, the next step is to write a brief, rough outline of the information that answers each question. Be sure each outline responds to the *wording* of the question; that is, it should *explain*, *compare*, *describe*, or do whatever else the question asks (see Table 26.1, p. 695). Writing a rough outline will strengthen your recall of the material. It will also save you time during the actual exam because you will have already spent some time thinking about, organizing, and writing about the material.

Here is a sample essay question and an informal outline written in response to it.

> **ESSAY QUESTION**
>
> Explain how material passes in and out of cells by crossing plasma membranes.
>
> **Informal Outline**
> *Types of Transport*
>
> 1. Passive—no use of cellular energy; random movement of molecules
>   a. Diffusion—molecules move from areas of high to areas of low concentration (example: open bottle of perfume, aroma spreads)
>   b. Facilitated diffusion—similar to simple diffusion; differs in that some kinds of molecules are moved more easily than others (helped by carrier proteins in cell membrane)
>   c. Osmosis—diffusion of water across membranes from area of lower to area of higher solute concentration

2. Active—requires cellular energy; usually movement against the concentration gradient
   a. Facilitated active transport—carrier molecules move ions across a membrane
   b. Endocytosis—material is surrounded by a plasma membrane and pinched off into a vacuole
   c. Exocytosis—cells expel materials

EXERCISE 26.3 **Preparing an Informal Outline**

For one of the questions you predicted in Exercise 26.2, prepare a brief informal outline in response to the question.

Reduce informal outlines to key-word outlines. To help you recall your outlined answer during the exam, reduce it to a brief key-word outline or list of key topics. Here is a sample key-word outline for the essay question about cells:

KEY-WORD OUTLINE

Types of Transport

1. Passive
   —Diffusion
   —Facilitated diffusion
   —Osmosis
2. Active
   —Facilitated active transport
   —Endocytosis
   —Exocytosis

EXERCISE 26.4 **Preparing a Key-word Outline**

Reduce the outline answer you wrote in Exercise 26.3 to a key-word outline.

TAKING ESSAY EXAMS

Once you have done some preparation, you should be more confident about taking an essay exam. The general guidelines below will help you when you confront the exam itself.

1. **Arrive at the room where the exam is to be given a few minutes early.** You can use this time to collect your thoughts and get organized.

2. **Sit in the front of the room.** You will be less distracted and better able to see and hear the instructor as last-minute directions or corrections are announced.

3. **Read the directions carefully.** Some exams may direct you to answer only one of three questions, whereas other exams may ask you to answer all questions.

4. **Consider your audience and purpose.** For most essay exams, your instructor is your audience. Since your instructor is already knowledgeable about the topic, your purpose is to demonstrate what you know about the topic. Therefore, you should write thorough and complete answers, pretending that your instructor knows only what you tell him or her.

5. **Preview the exam and plan your time carefully.** Read through the whole exam to get a complete picture of the task at hand and then plan how you will complete the exam within the allotted time. If you have fifty minutes, spend roughly ten minutes planning; thirty minutes writing; and ten minutes editing, proofreading, and making last-minute changes. Begin by writing a brief thesis statement. Then jot down the key supporting points and number them in the order you will present them. Leave space under each supporting point for your details. If the question is one you had predicted, write down your keyword outline. If an idea for an interesting introduction or an effective conclusion comes to mind, jot it down as well. At the end of your allotted time for writing, reread your essay and correct surface errors.

6. **Notice the point value of each question.** If your instructor assigns points to each question, use the point values to plan your time. For example, spend more time answering a 30-point question than a 10-point question.

7. **Choose topics or questions carefully.** Often you will have little or no choice of topic or question. If you do have a choice, choose the topics or answer the questions that you know the most about. If the question asks you to write about a broad topic, such as a current social issue, narrow the topic to one you can write about in the specified amount of time.

8. **Answer the easiest question first.** Answering the easiest question first will boost your confidence and allow you to spend the remaining time working on the more difficult questions. Generally if an exam contains both objective and essay questions, get the objective questions out of the way first.

9. **Remember that your first draft is your final draft.** Plan on writing your first draft carefully and correctly so that it can serve as your final copy. However, you can always make minor changes and additions as you write or edit and proofread.

ANALYZING ESSAY EXAM QUESTIONS

Essay exam questions are often concise, but if you read them closely, you will find that they *do* specifically tell you what to write about. Consider the following sample essay question from a sociology exam.

Choose a particular institution, define it, and identify its primary characteristics.

The question tells you exactly what to write about—*a particular institution.* In addition, the key verbs *define* and *identify* tell you how to approach the subject. To get full credit for this essay question, then, you would have to give an accurate definition of an institution and discuss its primary characteristics.

Table 26.1 lists key verbs commonly used in essay exam questions along with sample questions and tips for answering them. As you study the list, notice that many of the verbs suggest a particular pattern of development. For example, *trace* suggests using a narrative sequence, and *justify* suggests using argumentation. For key verbs such as *explain* or *discuss,* you might use a combination of patterns.

TABLE 26.1 Responding to Key Verbs in Essay Exam Questions

Key Verbs	Sample Essay Questions	Tips for Answering Questions
Compare	Compare the poetry of Judith Ortiz Cofer with that of Julia Alvarez.	Show how the poems are similar as well as different; use details and examples.
Contrast	Contrast classical and operant conditioning.	Show how the two types of conditioning are different; use details and examples.
Define	Define *biofeedback* and describe its uses.	Give an accurate explanation of the term with enough detail to demonstrate that you understand it.
Discuss	Discuss the halo effect, and give examples of its use.	Consider important characteristics and main points; include examples.
Evaluate	Evaluate the accomplishments of the feminist movement over the past fifty years.	Assess merits, strengths, weaknesses, advantages, or limitations.
Explain	Explain the functions of amino acids.	Use facts and details to make the topic or concept clear and understandable.
Illustrate	Illustrate with examples from your experience how culture shapes human behavior.	Use examples that demonstrate a point or clarify the idea.
Justify	Justify laws outlawing smoking in federal buildings.	Give reasons and evidence that support the action, decision, or policy.
List	List the advantages and disadvantages of sales promotions.	List or discuss one by one; use most-to-least or least-to-most organization.
Summarize	Summarize Maslow's hierarchy of needs.	Briefly review all the major points.
Trace	Trace the life cycle of a typical household product.	Describe its development or progress in chronological order.

WRITING ESSAY ANSWERS

Use the following guidelines to write the answers to essay questions.

1. **Since your first-draft essay exam is also your final draft, write in complete and grammatically correct sentences.** Supply sufficient detail and follow a logical organization. It is acceptable to cross out words or sentences neatly and indicate corrections in spelling or grammar.

2. **Add ideas neatly.** If you think of an idea you would like to add to your answer, write the sentence at the top of the paper and draw an arrow to indicate where it should be inserted.

3. **Provide a brief introduction and, in some cases, a conclusion.** Depending on how much time you have, the introduction may consist of only your thesis statement, or it may also include necessary background information on the topic. Write a conclusion only if the question seems to require a final evaluative statement.

4. **If you run out of time, jot the unfinished portion of your outline at the end of the essay.** Your instructor may give you partial credit.

For more on writing a thesis, see Chapter 6, pp. 119–24.

Write your thesis statement. Your thesis statement should be clear and direct. Identify your subject and suggest your approach to the topic. Often the thesis statement rephrases or answers the essay exam question. Consider the following examples.

Essay Exam Question	*Thesis Statement*
Explain how tides are produced in the Earth's oceans. Account for seasonal variations.	The Earth's gravitational forces are responsible for producing tides in the Earth's oceans.
Distinguish between bureaucratic agencies and other government decision-making bodies.	Bureaucratic agencies are distinct from other government decision-making bodies because of their hierarchical organization, character, culture, and professionalism.

Your thesis may also suggest the organization of your essay. For example, if the question asks you to explain the differences between primary and secondary groups, you might state your thesis as follows: "Primary groups differ from secondary groups in their membership, purpose, level of interaction, and level of intimacy." Your essay would then discuss membership first, purpose second, and so on.

(**EXERCISE 26.5**) **Writing Thesis Statements for Essay Exam Questions**

Write thesis statements for two of the following essay exam questions.

1. Define and illustrate the meaning of the term *freedom of the press.*
2. Distinguish between the medical care provided by private physicians and that provided by medical clinics.
3. Choose a recent television advertisement and describe its rational and emotional appeals.
4. Evaluate a current news program in terms of its breadth and depth of coverage, objectivity, and political and social viewpoints.

Develop supporting details. Write a separate paragraph for each of your key points. For example, in an essay answer distinguishing primary from secondary groups, devote one paragraph to each distinguishing feature: membership, purpose, level of interaction, and level of intimacy. The topic sentence for each paragraph should identify and briefly explain the key point. For example, a topic sentence for the first main point about groups might be: "Membership, or who belongs, is one factor that distinguishes primary from secondary groups." The rest of the paragraph would explain membership: what constitutes membership, what criteria are used to decide who belongs, and who decides.

For more on topic sentences, see Chapter 8, pp. 161–64.

Whenever possible, supply examples to make it clear that you can apply the information you have learned. Keep in mind that your goal is to demonstrate your knowledge and understanding of the material.

Reread and proofread your answer. Leave enough time to reread and proofread your essay answer. First, reread to make sure you have answered all parts of the question. Then reread your answer, checking it for content. Add missing information, correct vague or unclear sentences, and add facts or details. Next, proofread for errors in spelling, punctuation, and grammar. A clear, nearly error-free essay makes a positive impression on your instructor and identifies you as a serious, conscientious student. An error-free essay may also improve your grade.

For more on editing and proofreading, see Chapter 10.

> **EXERCISE 26.6** **Writing a Complete Essay Exam Answer**

For one of the essay questions you worked on in Exercise 26.5, use the preceding guidelines to write a complete essay answer.

STUDENTS WRITE

Essay Exam Response

RONALD ROBINSON

The model essay exam response on the next page was written by Ronald Robinson for his sociology course. First read the exam question below and then read Robinson's essay exam. As you read, consider how effectively and fully Robinson has answered the exam question. The essay has been annotated to point out the essay's key features.

Essay Exam Question

Distinguish between fads and fashions, explaining the characteristics of each type of group behavior and describing the phases each usually goes through.

Introduction: Includes only the thesis statement

Body paragraph 1: Definition and characteristics of *fashion*

Body paragraph 2: Definition and characteristics of *fad*

Body paragraph 3: Description of 5-phase process

Essay Exam Answer

Fashions and fads, types of collective group behavior, are distinct from one another in terms of their duration, their predictability, and the number of people involved. Each type follows a five-stage process of development.

A fashion is a temporary trend in behavior or appearance that is followed by a relatively large number of people. Although the word *fashion* often refers to a style of dress, there are fashions in music, art, and literature as well. Trends in clothing fashions are often engineered by clothing designers, advertisers, and the media to create a particular "look." The hip-hop look is an example of a heavily promoted fashion. Fashions are more universally subscribed to than fads. Wearing athletic shoes as casual attire is a good example of a universal fashion.

A fad is a more temporary adoption of a particular behavior or look. Fads are in-group behaviors that often serve as identity markers for a group. Fads also tend to be adopted by smaller groups, often made up of people who want to appear different or unconventional. Unlike fashions, fads tend to be shorter-lived, less predictable, and less influenced by people outside the group. Examples of recent fads are bald heads, tattoos, and tongue piercings. Fads are usually harmless and have no long-range effects.

Fashions and fads each follow a five-phase process of development. In the first phase, latency, the trend exists in the minds of a few people but shows little evidence of spreading. In the second phase, the trend spreads rapidly and reaches its peak. After that, the trend begins a slow decline (phase three). In the fourth phase, its newness is over and many users drop or abandon the trend. In its final phase, quiescence, nearly everyone has dropped the trend, and it is followed by only a few people.

PORTFOLIOS

A **portfolio** is a collection of materials that represents a person's work. It often demonstrates or exemplifies skill, talent, or proficiency. Architects create portfolios that contain drawings and photographs of buildings they have designed. Sculptors' portfolios may include photographs of their sculptures, as well as copies of reviews, awards, or articles about their work. Similarly, your writing instructor may ask you to create a portfolio that represents your skill and proficiency as a writer. Think of your portfolio as a summary of your development as a writer over time.

PURPOSES OF A WRITING PORTFOLIO

Instructors assign writing portfolios for two main reasons.

- **Grading and assessment.** Your instructor may use your collection of writing to evaluate your mastery of the objectives outlined in the course syllabus. That evaluation will become part of your final grade in the course.
- **Learning and self-assessment.** Building a portfolio makes you think about yourself as a learner and as a writer. By building a writing portfolio, you learn a great deal about the writing process, assess your strengths and weaknesses as a writer, and observe your own progress as you build writing proficiency.

Think of your writing portfolio as an opportunity to present yourself in the best possible way—highlighting the work you are proud of and demonstrating the skills you have mastered. It is also an opportunity, as you track your progress, to realize that your hard work in the course has paid off.

DECIDING WHAT TO INCLUDE IN YOUR PORTFOLIO

Instructors often specify what their students' portfolios should include. If you are uncertain about what to include, ask your instructor. You might ask to see a sample of a portfolio that meets your instructor's expectations.

To get the best grade on your portfolio, be sure you can answer each of the following questions about the portfolio and its contents.

- How many pieces of writing should I include? Are there limits to what I can include?
- Should the portfolio include only writing done in the course, or can I include materials I wrote for other courses or materials I wrote outside school (work-related email or service-learning projects, for example)?
- What version(s) should be included—drafts, outlines, and revisions or just the final drafts?
- Should essays be based on personal experience, research, or some combination of these?
- Is the portfolio limited to essays, or can research notes, downloaded Web pages, or completed class exercises also be included?
- How should the portfolio be organized?
- What type of introductory letter or essay is required? What length and format are appropriate?
- How much does the portfolio count in my grade?
- What is the due date, or is the portfolio to be submitted at various intervals throughout the term?
- How will it be graded? That is, is the grade based on improvement or only on the quality of the work included?

USING YOUR COURSE SYLLABUS AS A GUIDE

Your course syllabus is an important guide to deciding what to include in your portfolio. If it contains objectives, which outline what your instructor expects you to learn in the course, you can use several or all of these objectives to structure your portfolio.

Suppose one objective states, "Students will develop prewriting strategies that accommodate their learning style." Then in your portfolio, you might include a copy of the results of the Learning Style Inventory (pp. 32–36) and then show examples of your use of two or more prewriting strategies. If another objective states, "Students will demonstrate control over errors in sentence structure, spelling, and punctuation," you would want to include examples of essays in which you identified and corrected these types of errors. You might also include a list of exercises you completed to develop mastery.

ORGANIZING AND PREPARING TO PRESENT YOUR PORTFOLIO

Begin collecting materials for your portfolio as soon as your instructor assigns it. If you wait until the due date to assemble what you need, you may have already discarded or misplaced important prewriting, revision materials, or drafts.

Use a file folder or accordion folder divided into sections to hold any prewriting, outlines, or graphic organizers you completed by hand. If you are including research materials, include your notes and annotated photocopies or printouts of sources. Also keep peer-review comments as well as papers with your instructor's comments. (Alternatively, you could scan these materials and save them with your other electronic files.) Online, create a system of folders that will make it easy for you to locate all of your work. Save backup copies of your files on a thumb drive or to the cloud.

Use the following suggestions to present a well-organized portfolio.

- **Cover page.** Include a cover or title page that provides your name, course number, instructor's name, and date.
- **Table of contents.** Include a table of contents that identifies the elements in the portfolio and the page number on which each piece begins. Number the portfolio consecutively from beginning to end. Since your essays may already have page numbers, put the new page numbers in a different position or use a different color ink. If your instructor has not indicated how the contents should be sequenced, choose a method of organization that presents your work and skill development in the best possible way. For example, if you are including two essays to demonstrate your effective use of narration, you might present the better one first, thereby making the strongest possible first impression. If you are trying to show growth in your ability to use narration, you might present the weaker essay first. Use Table 26.2 to guide your selection and sequence.
- **Reflective letter or essay.** Most instructors will expect you to include an essay or a letter that reflects on your development as a writer. This essay is the key to the portfolio, since it reflects on and explains the portfolio's contents. It should explain how your portfolio is organized and give an overview of its contents and why you chose them. It should also include an appraisal of what you learned in the course and discuss your strengths, weaknesses, and development as a writer. Point out specific examples in the portfolio to support your claims.
- **Drafts.** Attach earlier drafts behind the final draft, clearly labeling each draft. Date and label each piece so that your instructor can identify its place within your growth process and so that he or she knows what it demonstrates. For example, if an essay demonstrates your ability to use narration, label it as such.

Your portfolio represents you. Be sure it is neat, complete, and carefully assembled.

TABLE 26.2 Guidelines for Building a Writing Portfolio

If you are asked to . . .	Include . . .
demonstrate your growth as a writer	• weak papers from early in the semester and your best papers written toward the end of the semester. • an essay that demonstrates major changes from first to final draft.
demonstrate your ability to approach writing as a process	• work you did for topic selection, generating ideas, drafting, revising, and proofreading. • first and final drafts that show your essay gradually developing and evolving as you worked.
feature your best work of the semester	• essays that solidly exemplify the method of organization you are using. • essays that demonstrate your ability to develop and support ideas. • essays that demonstrate thoughtfulness and creativity.
demonstrate your ability to write for a variety of audiences and purposes	• essays for courses in different areas of study. • pieces that use widely different tones or levels of diction. • non-course-related and nonacademic pieces, if allowed.
demonstrate your ability to use library and Internet sources	• essays that cite sources accurately in a list of works cited or references. • essays that use both library and Internet sources rather than one or the other.

WHAT TO AVOID

Here are a few things to avoid when building your portfolio.

- **Avoid writing about writing in general.** Instead, write about what you learned about *your* writing. That is, do not repeat points from the textbook about the writing process. Instead, explain how you used that information to become a better writer.
- **Do not exaggerate your progress or say what you think the instructor wants to hear.** Instead, be honest and forthright in assessing your progress.
- **Avoid flattery or praise of the instructor or the course.** Most instructors will give you a separate opportunity to evaluate the course and their teaching methods.

Portfolio Contents and Reflective Letter

BRYAN SCOTT

The portfolio assignment below was given to Bryan Scott, a nursing student and former Marine, for his first-year writing course.

Portfolio Assignment

For your final assignment you will submit a portfolio containing the following:

- A table of contents listing the titles and page numbers of all included writing pieces

- A reflective letter that introduces your portfolio
- One series of writing pieces (prewriting, outlines, drafts) that demonstrates your ability to move successfully through the steps in the writing process
- At least two pieces of writing that demonstrate your growth as a writer
- One piece of writing done this term for another class
- Essays that demonstrate your ability to use various methods of organization
- A limited number of materials of your own choice

In your reflective letter, include answers to the following questions:

1. What are your current strengths and weaknesses as a writer?
2. What specific writing skills have you developed?
3. How have you changed as a writer?
4. How has your awareness of learning style improved your ability to write?
5. What critical reading and thinking skills have you learned, *or* in what ways have you strengthened your critical reading and thinking skills?

Scott organizes his reflective letter using the principles of good writing he learned in the course: Within this organization, he is able to identify his strengths and weaknesses as a writer throughout the letter, discuss learning styles, and analyze his essays. Compare the assignment Scott received with his table of contents and reflective letter.

CONTENTS

Scott 1

Bryan Scott
May 16, 2014
Final Portfolio
English 109

From the Marines to the Writing Classroom

I enrolled in this course because it was a required course in my nursing
curriculum, but I can now say that I am glad that it was required. As a
former Marine, I had little experience with writing, other than writing
letters home to my wife and parents. Now, as I prepare for a career as a
nurse, I realize that writing is an important communication skill. Writing
reports about patients, such as "Nursing Care Plan: Patient 4," requires
me to present clear, precise, and accurate information about patients
and their care. Through this course I have learned to do so. Although I
improved in almost every area of writing, my greatest improvements were
in approaching writing as a process, moving from personal to informative
writing, and developing an awareness of audience.

Through this course I have learned to view writing as a process rather
than a "write-it-once-and-I-am-done" activity. As shown in the packet of
writing for "The Wall at Sunset," I have discovered the value of prewriting
as a way of coming up with ideas. Before I started writing this essay, I knew
that visiting the Vietnam Veterans Memorial had been an emotional experience for me, but I found that mapping helped me define and organize my
feelings. Since I am a spatial learner, I could visualize the wall and map
my responses to seeing the names of other soldiers. My first draft in the
packet demonstrates my ability to begin with a thesis statement and build
ideas around it. My second draft shows how I added detail and arranged
my impressions into an organized essay. My final draft shows my ability to
catch most errors in spelling, grammar, and punctuation.

Moving from personal writing to informative writing was a valuable
learning experience that is essential for my career. My first essay, "The
Wall at Sunset," was a very personal account of my visit to the Vietnam

Scott 2

Veterans Memorial, as was the essay "How the Marines Changed My Life," a personal account of life in the U.S. Marine Corps. While I had a lot to say about my own experiences, I found it difficult to write about topics that did not directly involve me. I found that learning to use sources, especially Internet sources, helped me get started with informative writing. By visiting news Web sites, doing Internet research, and reading blogs, I learned to move outside of myself and begin to think about and become interested in what other people were saying and thinking. My essay "Miracle in the Operating Room" demonstrates my ability to use sources, both print and Internet, to learn how kidney transplants are done.

As I moved from personal to informative writing, I found that the patterns of development provided a framework for developing and organizing informative writing. Process seemed to be an effective way to present information for the essay "Miracle in the Operating Room." My essay "Emotional Styles of Athletes" initially contained a lot of my own personal impressions (see the first draft that I have included), but by using classification, I was able to focus on characteristics of athletes rather than on my opinions of them. 4

Before I took this course, I had no idea that I should write differently for different audiences. My essay "How the Marines Changed My Life" was written for my classmates, many of whom had no military experience. I found I had to explain things about chain of command, regimentation, and living conditions--all things that I and other Marines are familiar with. In my case report for my nursing class, "Nursing Care Plan: Patient 4," my audience was other nurses and medical staff, even doctors. Because I was writing for a specialized audience, I could mention medical terms, procedures, and medications freely without defining them. However, in "Miracle in the Operating Room," I was writing for a general, nonspecialized audience, so I realized it was necessary to explain terms such as *dialysis*, *laparoscopy*, and *nephrectomy*. This essay and my nursing case report demonstrate my ability to write in a clear, direct, and concise manner in my chosen field for different audiences. 5

Scott 3

While I developed many strengths as a writer, I am still aware of many   6
weaknesses. I have difficulty with descriptive writing; I just cannot come up
with words to paint a visual picture as effectively as I would like. Fortunately,
nursing will not require much creative description. I also have difficulty
choosing a topic. Although I found the suggestions in our textbook helpful, I
still feel as if I am overlooking important or useful topics. Finally, I have not
benefited from peer review as much as others have. I still find myself uncomfortable when accepting criticism and revision ideas from other students.
Perhaps my military training to look to authority for direction is still getting in
the way.

As I developed strengths as a writer, I also became a more critical reader   7
and thinker. I am enclosing my annotations for the professional essay "Bad
Conduct, by the Numbers." These annotations demonstrate my ability to ask
questions and challenge the author. I also found enlightening discussions in
the text on connotative language, bias, and fact and opinion. These are things
I had never thought much about, and now I find myself being aware of these
things as I read.

Overall, by taking this course, I have become a more serious and aware   8
writer and have come to regard writing as a rewarding challenge.

- **Use presentation software to aid understanding.** Project key words or concepts you want to emphasize or provide an outline so your audience can follow your main points.
- **Use a design template that suits your audience and purpose.** A simple color scheme with a sharp contrast between text and background will be easiest to read. Avoid using reds and greens if differences between the two colors are significant, because color-blind members of the audience will not be able to differentiate between them. Use subdued color schemes and easily readable fonts (such as Arial or Verdana) for business or academic presentations. For PowerPoint slides, use just a few animation schemes (how text enters and leaves a slide) consistently.
- **Format your slides so they are easily readable.** Use a large point size (usually 24 points or greater) so everyone in the audience can read the text easily. Keep the number of words per slide low: slides crammed with text are difficult to read, and if audience members are busy reading lengthy slides, they are not listening to what you are saying. A good rule of thumb is to use no more than six bullet points per slide, with no more than six words per bullet point. (If you can do so clearly, use just words and phrases rather than complete sentences.)
- **Use presentation software to display visuals and graphics.** Photos, cartoons, graphics, and embedded videos can convey your message in a memorable way. They also keep your audience interested and alert. But keep graphics simple, so the audience can take them in at a glance, and use visuals and graphics only when they are relevant to your point, not just as decoration.
- **Edit your slides carefully.** Check for errors in spelling, grammar, and formatting as well as other kinds of typos. Run the entire slide show for yourself several times before presenting it to correct any errors you find.

Below are two sample PowerPoint slides prepared by a sales representative for a Web design company to accompany his oral presentations to clients. He shows the slide on the left when he discusses how to design a Web site that search engines can find easily. He uses the slide on the right to explain the basis for site ranking.

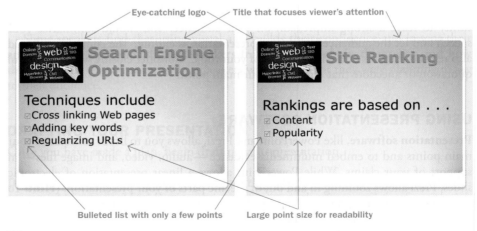

macmillanhighered.com/successfulwriting
Tutorials > Digital Writing > Audio Editing with Audacity
Tutorials > Digital Writing > Presentations

REHEARSING YOUR PRESENTATION

Practice is the key to comfortable and effective delivery. The following tips can help you rehearse effectively.

- **Practice giving the entire presentation, not just parts of it.** Rehearse at least three or four times, using your visual aids. Try to improve your presentation each rehearsal.
- **Time yourself.** If you are over or seriously under the time limit, make necessary cuts or additions, and edit your presentation slides accordingly.
- **If possible, rehearse the presentation in the room in which you will give it.** This will make you more comfortable on the day of the presentation and gives you an opportunity to find out in advance if the room can support the technology you plan to use.
- **Rehearse in front of an audience of a few friends or classmates.** Ask them for constructive criticism. Some students videotape their presentations to build their confidence and identify areas that need improvement.

OVERCOMING APPREHENSION

Many students are nervous about making presentations. Often called "stage fright," this apprehension is normal. The first step to overcoming stage fright is to understand its causes.

Some speakers are apprehensive because they feel conspicuous—at the center of attention. Others feel they are competing with other, better speakers in the class. Still others are apprehensive because the task is new and they have never done it before. You can often overcome these feelings by following these suggestions.

- **Prepare thoroughly.** Knowing you have put together a solid, interesting presentation can build your self-confidence and lessen your sense of competition.
- **Practice, practice, practice.** To reduce the newness of the task, practice your presentation several times. (See the previous section on rehearsal.)
- **Use desensitization.** If someone is afraid of snakes, a desensitization therapist might begin by showing the person a photograph, then a video, then a small snake at a distance, and so forth, gradually building up the person's exposure time and tolerance. You can use the same technique to overcome your fear of oral presentations by gradually building up to making presentations. Begin by asking a question in class. Next, move on to answering questions in class. Then try speaking in front of small groups (practicing your speech on a group of friends, for example). Eventually you will become more comfortable with public speaking and ready to make a presentation to the class.
- **Use visualization.** Visualization involves imagining yourself successfully completing a task. For a presentation, create a mental recording that begins with your arrival at the classroom and takes you through each step: confidently walking to the front of the room, beginning your presentation, engaging your audience, handling your notes, and so on. Visualize the presentation positively, and avoid negative thoughts, to create the image of yourself as a successful

speaker. Review your visualized performance often, especially on the day of your presentation. As you give your presentation, try to model the look and feel of your visualization.

- **Imagine a friend in the audience.** If you feel conspicuous, try to imagine that you are talking to one friend or one friendly and supportive classmate. Looking directly at one member of the audience at the beginning of your presentation can help.

DELIVERING AN EFFECTIVE PRESENTATION

The delivery of your presentation ultimately determines its effectiveness. Use the suggestions below, as well as Table 27.1, to improve the delivery of your presentation.

- **Avoid using too many notes or a detailed outline.** Instead, construct a key word outline that will remind you of major points in the order you wish to present them.
- **Make eye contact with your audience.** Make the audience part of your presentation.
- **Move around a little rather than standing stiffly.** Use gestures to add an expressive quality to your presentation.
- **Speak slowly.** Speaking too fast is a common mistake, but try not to overcompensate by speaking too slowly or your audience may lose interest.

TABLE 27.1 Frequently Asked Questions for Making Presentations

Question	Suggested Solutions
What should I do if I go blank?	Refer to your notes or presentation slides.
	Ask if there are any questions. Even if no one asks any, the pause will give you time to regroup.
What should I do if classmates are restless, uninterested, or even rude?	Make eye contact with as many members of the class as possible as you speak.
	For a particularly troublesome person, you might lengthen your eye contact.
	Change the tone or pitch of your voice.
	Try to make your speech more engaging by asking questions or using personal examples.
What should I do if I accidentally omit an important part of the presentation?	Go back and add it in. Say something like, "I neglected to mention . . ." and present the portion you skipped.
What if I realize that my speech will be too short or too long?	If you realize it will be too short, try to add examples, anecdotes, or more detailed information.
	If you realize it will be too long, cut out examples or summarize instead of fully explaining sections that are less important.

PREPARING A WEB-BASED PRESENTATION

At some point in your education or career, you may be asked to use an online meeting application, such as GoToMeeting or Glance, which allows you to conduct virtual meetings with instructors, colleagues, clients, and vendors. These applications allow others to view what you have on your computer screen, so you can pull up Word documents, spreadsheets, presentation slides, and anything else for everyone to look at together in real time. You may communicate by phone, by Skype, or via an online instant messenger system through the application. The following tips will help you give an effective Web-based presentation.

- **Become familiar with the technology before your presentation.** Your audience may become restless if you cannot resolve technical difficulties.
- **Review all documents and materials prior to the meeting.** Be sure you know where to find the documents you need to display.
- **Prepare thoroughly, but be ready to adjust your presentation in response to questions from the audience.** You should know the content well enough to respond to a question or comment that draws you away from your prepared remarks.
- **Turn off all notifications and programs that are running on your computer.** You do not want an email from a friend popping up on your screen while you are delivering a presentation.

BUSINESS WRITING

Business writing will be an important part of your life after college. Good business writing is concise and correct. It is often more direct than some forms of academic or personal writing. Because you are judged on the business documents that you write, prepare materials that will present you and your accomplishments in the best light possible.

PREPARING A RÉSUMÉ AND JOB APPLICATION LETTER

A **résumé** (Figure 27.1, p. 714) is a complete listing of all of your education, training, and work experience in an easy-to-read format. A **job application (or cover) letter** (Figure 27.2, p. 716) highlights the qualifications that make you right for the job and convinces the employer that you are an excellent candidate for the opening. Because your application packet will determine whether a potential employer will interview you, tailor each one to the job for which you are applying.

Most employers invite applicants to upload résumés and job application (or cover) letters to their Web sites or to send the application letter as an e-mail message with the résumé attached. If you are sending a hard copy résumé and job application letter, print both documents on good-quality white paper.

e **macmillanhighered.com/successfulwriting**
Tutorials > Digital Writing > Job Search/Personal Branding

FIGURE 27.1 Sample Résumé

Contact information: Displayed at the top of the page

Headings: Boldfaced type used to make résumé easy to read

Organization: Reverse chronological order used for information under Education and Experience headings, so most recent items listed first

Key words: Nouns used so skills and experience match words in employer's electronic job database

Proofreading: Résumé proofread carefully to correct spelling, punctuation, and capitalization errors

---

Micah Jackson

3912 Elm Street

Des Moines, IA 42156

555-666-7777

mjackson@burroughscc.edu

Position Desired

Full-time legal assistant

Education

2012–2014: Burroughs Community College, Legal Assistant A.A.S. degree, May 2014. Coursework: legal research, legal writing, business communication, word processing, legal office billing, transcription.

2009–2012: Regents diploma, Kennedy Central High School

Employment History

2013–present: Photographer's Assistant, Jane G. Matthews Photography Responsibilities include billing, customer service, selling packages, answering phones, packaging orders, and assisting with shoots.

2010–2013: Associate, Walmart Responsibilities included cashing and stocking shelves.

Special Skills

Fluent in Spanish

Excellent customer service skills

References

Available on request

Follow these tips when preparing your résumé.

- **Simple is best.** Prepare your résumé as a document with an unlined, white background, as if you were going to print it on 8½ x 11-inch paper. Leave 1-inch margins on all sides. Do not include graphics, colors, or elaborate underlining and formatting. If possible, save your résumé in PDF format. Be sure to check it before sending.

- **Display your name, address, and contact information at the top of the page.** Check that your contact information is correct. (A computer's spell-check function will not identify such mistakes.)
- **Fit your résumé onto a single page whenever possible.** If providing a printed copy, use only one side of an 8½- x 11-inch sheet of paper. Write clearly and concisely, and use categories (such as "Education," "Experience," and "Skills") so that potential employers can scan your résumé quickly.
- **Use key words.** Software may scan résumés electronically for key words, so use nouns ("supervisor" instead of "supervised other employees") to help employers match your skills and experience with their job database.
- **List education, work experience, and any awards or special skills in reverse chronological order.** Include dates you attended school or received a degree, listing your most recent education and experience first.
- **Specify how the employer can obtain your references.** This is usually done by stating, "References are available on request," but be prepared to supply references by asking instructors or previous employers whether they are willing to give you a good recommendation and whether you can share their contact information with prospective employers.
- **Proofread carefully.** Résumés must be clear, concise, and free of errors in grammar, punctuation, mechanics, and spelling.

For more about proofreading, see Chapter 10, p. 211–13.

Follow these tips when writing a job application letter or email.
- **Use standard business formats.** Block-style business letters have one-inch margins on all sides and are single-spaced, with an extra line space between paragraphs. All type is aligned at the left edge of the page. (The sample job application letter in Figure 27.2 is in block style.) Use letterhead or list your address at the top of the page. The date should appear below your address, and the address of the person to whom you are writing should appear below the date. Job applications, like résumés, should be prepared with a white, unlined background.
- **Include a formal salutation and closing.** Begin with "Dear Ms._____:" or "Dear Mr. _____:" and call the company for a name if you are unsure to whom you should address your letter. Close with "Sincerely," or "Yours truly," followed by your signature. Formal salutations and closings are appropriate, even when sending a job application by email.
- **Include key information in the body.** If submitting your job application letter by email, use the subject line to identify the job you are applying for. In both job application emails and letters, identify the job you are applying for in the opening paragraph. You may also indicate where you learned about the position or where it was posted or listed. The second paragraph should briefly state the qualifications that make you especially qualified. (Do not repeat everything you have listed in your résumé.) In a final paragraph, indicate that you are available for an interview at the employer's convenience or specify when you are available.
- **Proofread carefully.** If job application letters or emails are not clear, concise, and free of errors in grammar, punctuation, mechanics, and spelling, they are likely to wind up in the "reject" pile.

Block style: Standard block style used (double line space between paragraphs, type aligned at left edge)

Formatting: Return address appears at top of page

Formatting: Inside address follows the date

Salutation: Letter begins with salutation ("Dear Ms. Alvarez:")

Content: Opening paragraph identifies desired position; second, third, and fourth paragraphs mention specific aspects of Blake's education and experience, not everything in résumé

Content: Last paragraph provides contact information and indicates available references

Closing: The letter ends with standard closing: "Sincerely"; signature follows closing, and name typed below

FIGURE 27.2 Sample Job Application Letter

31 Maple Drive
Ankeny, IA 50021

June 19, 2014

Juanita Alvarez
Northtown Animal Hospital
5513 Main St.
San Diego, CA 34561

Dear Ms. Alvarez:

In response to your ad on Monster.com, I am applying for the position of full-time veterinary assistant at Northtown Animal Hospital.

I recently completed my Veterinary Technician A.A.S. degree at Burroughs Community College and obtained my state certification. My coursework included animal anatomy, animal nutrition, veterinary office management, medical mathematics, animal reproduction, animal grooming, and diagnostic imaging.

In addition, I have been a volunteer at the Copper Mountain SPCA for three years, where I assist with feeding, grooming, cleaning, and visitor management. I also work part-time at Jonelle's Dog Salon as a shampoo specialist.

My coursework in animal grooming and experience at the SPCA and at a dog salon would allow me to perform normal veterinary technician work and also to perform grooming services for your clients.

As my enclosed résumé indicates, my education and experience working with animals have prepared me well for the opening you have.

I am available for an interview at your convenience and will gladly supply additional references as needed. Please call me at 555-121-1212 or email me at BHuan715@burroughscc.edu.

Sincerely,

Blake Huan

Blake Huan

- **Follow instructions for uploading your documents.** If you are applying by email, be sure to double-check that you have attached your résumé before hitting "send."

USING ELECTRONIC MEDIA FOR BUSINESS WRITING

In your career, you will likely use electronic media—email (Figure 27.3, p. 718) but perhaps also Facebook, Twitter, text messages, and interoffice information management systems—as your main means of communication. Follow the tips below to communicate effectively with supervisors, colleagues, clients, and other business contacts.

- **Keep it brief and get right to the point.** Typically the most important information is in the first paragraph. Paragraphs are usually only one to three sentences long, and wordiness is frowned upon. Messages overall are usually brief (just a few paragraphs), so they can be scanned quickly for important information. If more detail is required, supporting documents may be attached.

For more about writing concisely, see Chapter 10, pp. 196–97.

- **Do not say anything you do not want shared.** Online communications can easily be forwarded to others. Remember at all times that you are representing your employer and serving as the voice of your company. Do not say anything in an email that you would not say to your entire company and all your clients.
- **Use a specific and relevant subject line.** Using a specific and relevant subject line is crucial, not only so recipients can know how to prioritize the communications they receive, but also to locate important messages later. Without a subject line that clearly references a client, case number, file name, or other specific identifier, a message can be impossible to retrieve. Be particularly careful when replying that you adjust the subject line as needed.
- **Write in complete words and sentences and with a formal tone.** Avoid online slang (such as *LOL* and *OMG*) and emoticons (such as the smiley face), avoid writing in all capital or all lowercase letters, and always reread email messages to be sure the tone is cordial and professional. Abbreviations are acceptable, but only if your recipient will understand them.

For more about tone and level of diction, see Chapter 10, pp. 206–08.

- **Copy only people who need to be informed about the topic.** Do not automatically carbon copy (cc) your boss or everyone else in your company on every message. Avoid "Reply all" unless the content of your reply is truly relevant to "all."
- **Remember to attach relevant files.** It makes more work for everyone if you forget to include the attachment.
- **Use an automatic signature file.** An automatic signature should include your name, title, company address, and telephone and fax numbers so that people can contact you easily.
- **Proofread carefully.** You are a representative of your business, so take the time to communicate concisely and professionally, and proofread your messages carefully before sending.

FIGURE 27.3 Sample Business Email

Subject line: Accurately reflects memo's main point

Attachment: File mentioned in email message is attached

Proofreading: Writer uses correct grammar, spelling, and punctuation; writes formally, as is appropriate in business correspondence

Automatic signature: Includes sender's complete name, title, company, address, and telephone and fax numbers

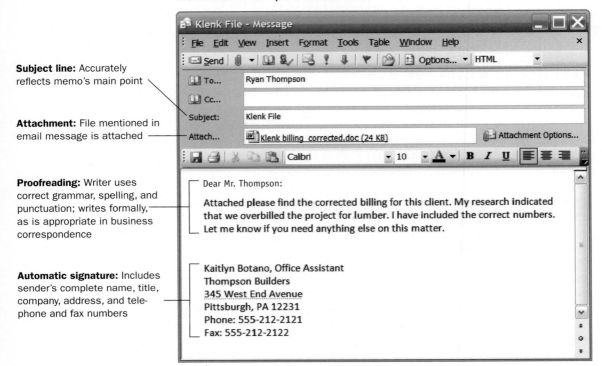

part seven

Handbook: *Writing Problems and How to Correct Them*

REVIEW OF BASIC GRAMMAR

1   Parts of Speech

Each word in a sentence acts as one of eight parts of speech: *nouns, pronouns, verbs, adjectives, adverbs, conjunctions, prepositions,* and *interjections*. These are the building blocks of our language. Often, to revise your writing or to correct sentence errors, you need to understand how a word or phrase functions in a particular sentence.

1a Nouns

A **noun** names a person (*waiter, girlfriend*), a place (*classroom, beach*), a thing (*textbook, computer*), or an idea (*excitement, beauty*). **Proper nouns** name specific people (*Professor Wainwright*), places (*Texas*), things (*Xbox*), or ideas (*Marxism*) and are always capitalized.

- *James* drove to *Williamsville* in a *Toyota* in *March*.

Common nouns name one or more of a general class or type of person, place, thing, or idea and are not capitalized.

- A *holiday* is a *celebration* of an *event*.

Collective nouns name groups: *class, jury, team*. **Concrete nouns** name tangible things that can be tasted, seen, touched, smelled, or heard: *instructor, exam, desk*. **Abstract nouns** name ideas, qualities, beliefs, and conditions: *love, faith, trust*.

Most nouns express **number** and can be singular or plural: *one test, two tests; one pen, five pens*. **Count nouns** name items that can be counted. Count nouns can be made plural, usually by adding *-s* or *-es: one telephone, three telephones; one speech, ten speeches*. Some count nouns form their plurals in an irregular way: *mouse, mice; goose, geese*. **Noncount nouns**—such as *water, anger, courage,* and *knowledge*—name ideas or entities that cannot be counted. Most noncount nouns do not have a plural form. (See Section 26 of this Handbook for more on count and noncount nouns.)

1b Pronouns

Pronouns are words that take the place of nouns. The noun or pronoun to which a pronoun refers is called the pronoun's **antecedent**.

- Because the *researcher* developed a new drug, *she* became famous.

  The noun *researcher* is the antecedent of the pronoun *she*.

Personal pronouns name specific people, places, or things. Personal pronouns come in three cases that describe a pronoun's function in a sentence. The **subjective case** indicates that a pronoun is a subject—a doer of an action (*I, you, he, she, it, we, they*).

- *She* asked questions about the job.

The **objective case** indicates that a pronoun is an object—a receiver of an action (*me, you, him, her, it, us, them*).

- The career counselor has been advising *her*.

The **possessive case** indicates ownership or belonging (*my, mine, your, yours, his, her, hers, its, our, ours, your, yours, their, theirs*).

- *His* enthusiasm for the company does not match *theirs*.

Personal pronouns also indicate **person**, to distinguish among the speaker (first person: *I, we*), the person spoken to (second person: *you*), and the person or thing spoken about (third person: *he, she, it, they*). The **gender** of personal pronouns identifies them as masculine (*he, him*), feminine (*she, her*), or neuter (*it*). Personal pronouns also show **number**: singular (one person or thing: *I, you, he, she, it*) or plural (more than one person or thing: *we, you, they*).

Demonstrative pronouns point out a particular person or thing: *this, that, these,* and *those*. A demonstrative pronoun can be used as an adjective to describe a noun.

- *These* research procedures are questionable.

Reflexive pronouns indicate that a subject performs actions to, for, or on itself. Reflexive pronouns end in *-self* or *-selves*.

	Singular	*Plural*
First person	myself	ourselves
Second person	yourself	yourselves
Third person	himself	themselves
	herself	
	itself	

- We allowed *ourselves* two hours to complete the experiment.

Intensive pronouns have the same forms as reflexive pronouns and are used to emphasize their antecedents.

- Not even the computer programmer *herself* could correct the error.

Reflexive and intensive pronouns cannot be used as the subject of a sentence, and their antecedents must appear in the same sentence as the pronoun.

INCORRECT   *Myself* disagreed with the speaker's proposal, despite my sympathy with the movement.

CORRECT   *I myself* disagreed with the speaker's proposal, despite my sympathy with the movement.

Interrogative pronouns introduce or ask a question.

REFER TO PEOPLE   who, whoever, whom, whomever, whose
REFER TO THINGS   what, which

- *Who* will pay the bill?

Relative pronouns introduce **dependent clauses** that function as adjectives. Relative pronouns refer back to a noun or pronoun that the clause modifies.

> A **dependent clause** contains a subject and a verb but does not express a complete thought.

REFER TO PEOPLE   who, whoever, whom, whomever, whose
REFER TO THINGS   that, what, whatever, which, whose

- The research *that* caused the literacy-test controversy was outdated.

- Sylvia Plath was married to Ted Hughes, *who* later became poet laureate of England.

Indefinite pronouns do not refer to specific nouns; they refer to people, places, or things in general (*everyone, anywhere, everything*). Commonly used indefinite pronouns include the following:

Singular

another	either	nobody	somebody
anybody	enough	none	someone
anyone	everybody	no one	something
anything	everyone	nothing	
anywhere	everything	one	
each	neither	other	

Plural

both	many	several
few	others	

- Hardly *anyone* had heard of the Sapir-Wharf hypothesis.
- Although a number of psychologists have researched brain dominance, *few* have related it to learning style.

Several indefinite pronouns, such as *all*, *any*, *more*, *most*, *some*, and *none*, can be either singular or plural, depending on their antecedent (see 5e).

The **reciprocal pronouns** *each other* and *one another* indicate an interchange of information or physical objects between two or more parties.

- The debate semifinalists congratulated each other on their scores.

See Section 7 of the Handbook for more on pronoun usage.

1c Verbs

Verbs show action (*read*, *study*), occurrence (*become*, *happen*), or a state of being (*be*, *feel*). There are three types of verbs: action verbs, linking verbs, and helping verbs (also called auxiliary verbs).

Action verbs express physical or mental activities.

- My hair *grew* longer and longer.
- Amelia *thought* her answer was correct.

Action verbs may be either transitive or intransitive. A **transitive verb** (TV) has a **direct object** (DO) that receives the action and completes the meaning of the sentence. (In the examples, S stands for *subject*.)

- $\overset{\text{S}}{\text{Juan}} \overset{\text{TV}}{\textit{wrote}} \overset{\text{DO}}{\text{lyrics}}$ for songs.

An **intransitive verb** (IV) does not need a direct object to complete the meaning of the sentence.

- $\overset{\text{S}}{\text{The lights}} \overset{\text{IV}}{\textit{flickered}}$.

Some verbs can be either transitive or intransitive, depending on how they are used in a sentence.

INTRANSITIVE   The student *wrote* quickly.

TRANSITIVE   The student *wrote* a paper on hypnotism.

Linking verbs show existence, explaining what something is, was, or will become. A linking verb connects a word to words that describe it.

- Dr. Lopez *is* the new college president.
- Their answers *were* evasive.

The forms of the verb *be* (*am*, *is*, *are*, *was*, *were*, *be*, *being*, *been*) are linking verbs. Some action verbs can also function as linking verbs. These include *appear*, *become*, *feel*, *grow*, *look*, *prove*, *remain*, *seem*, *smell*, *sound*, *stay*, and *taste*.

- The sky *grew* dark.
- Something in the kitchen *smells* delicious.

Helping verbs, also called **auxiliary verbs**, are used along with action or linking verbs to indicate tense, mood, or voice or to add further information. A **verb phrase** is a combination of one or more helping verbs and a main verb.

SIMPLE VERB	The newspaper *reports* the incident.
SIMPLE VERB + **HELPING VERB**	The newspaper *should report* the incident.

Helping verbs include the different forms of *do*, *be*, and *have* (which can also serve as main verbs in a sentence) along with *can*, *could*, *may*, *might*, *must*, *shall*, *should*, *will*, and *would*.

Verb Forms

All verbs except *be* have five forms: the base form, the past tense, the past participle, the present participle, and the *-s* form for the present tense when the subject is singular and in the third person.

The first three forms are called the verb's principal parts. The base form is the form of the verb as it appears in the *dictionary*: *review*, *study*, *prepare*. For regular verbs, the past tense and past participle are formed by adding *-d* or *-ed* to the base form. For regular verbs ending in *y*, the *y* is changed to *i*: *rely*, *relied*. For one-syllable regular verbs ending in a vowel plus a consonant, the consonant is doubled: *plan*, *planned* (see 25c).

	Regular	*Irregular*
Base form	walk	run
Past tense	walked	ran
Past participle	walked	run
Present participle	walking	running
-s form	walks	runs

Irregular verbs follow no set pattern to form their past tense and past participle.

Forms of Common Irregular Verbs

Base Form	Past Tense	Past Participle
be	was/were	been
become	became	become
begin	began	begun
bite	bit	bitten, bit
blow	blew	blown
build	built	built
burst	burst	burst
catch	caught	caught
choose	chose	chosen
come	came	come
dive	dived, dove	dived
do	did	done
draw	drew	drawn
drive	drove	driven
eat	ate	eaten
fall	fell	fallen
feel	felt	felt
fight	fought	fought
find	found	found
fling	flung	flung
fly	flew	flown
get	got	gotten, got
give	gave	given
go	went	gone
grow	grew	grown
have	had	had
know	knew	known
lay	laid	laid
lead	led	led
leave	left	left
lie	lay	lain
lose	lost	lost
make	made	made
prove	proved	proved, proven
ride	rode	ridden
ring	rang	rung
rise	rose	risen
run	ran	run

Forms of Common Irregular Verbs *(continued)*

Base Form	Past Tense	Past Participle
say	said	said
set	set	set
sit	sat	sat
speak	spoke	spoken
swear	swore	sworn
swim	swam	swum
take	took	taken
tear	tore	torn
tell	told	told
think	thought	thought
throw	threw	thrown
wear	wore	worn
win	won	won
write	wrote	written

If you are unsure of a verb's principal parts, check your dictionary. See Section 6 of the Handbook for more about verb forms.

Verb Tense

The **tenses** of a verb express time. They convey whether an action, a state of being, or an occurrence takes place in the present, past, or future. There are six basic tenses: present, past, future, present perfect, past perfect, and future perfect. There are also three groups of tenses: simple, perfect, and progressive.

Simple tenses indicate whether an action occurs in the present, past, or future.

- He *loves* Kabuki theater.
- I *downloaded* their new release immediately.
- Oprah's reputation *will grow*.

Perfect tenses indicate that the action was or will be finished by the time of some other action.

- By now, Rosa *has taken* the exam.
- Dave Matthews *had* already *performed* when they arrived.
- The centennial celebration *will have begun* before he completes the sculpture.

Progressive tenses indicate that the action does, did, or will continue.

- She *is going* to kindergarten.
- When the ambulance arrived, he *was sweating* profusely.
- During spring break, we *will be basking* on a sunny beach.

A SUMMARY OF VERB TENSES

Present Tense

Simple present: happening now or occurring regularly

· He *performs* his own stunts.

Present progressive: happening now; going on (in progress) now

· The governor *is considering* a Senate campaign.

Present perfect: began in the past and was completed in the past or is continuing now

· The children's benefactor *has followed* their progress closely.

Present perfect progressive: began in the past and is continuing now

· She *has been singing* in nightclubs for thirty years.

Past Tense

Simple past: began and ended in the past

· The doctor *treated* him with experimental drugs.

Past progressive: began and continued in the past

· They *were* not *expecting* any visitors.

Past perfect: occurred before a certain time in the past or was completed before another action was begun

· The birds *had eaten* all the berries before we knew they were ripe.

Past perfect progressive: was taking place until a second action occurred

· He *had been seeing* a psychiatrist before his collapse.

Future Tense

Simple future: will take place in the future

· The play *will begin* on time.

Future progressive: will both begin and end in the future

· After we get on the plane, we *will be sitting* for hours.

Future perfect: will be completed by a certain time in the future or before another action will begin

· By next month, the new apprentice *will have become* an expert.

Future perfect progressive: will continue until a certain time in the future

· By the time she earns her Ph.D., she *will have been studying* history for twelve years.

Most of the time you will not need to think about verb tense; you will use the correct tense automatically. There are, however, a few situations in which you need to pay special attention to verb tense.

- Use the present tense to make a generalization or to state a principle or fact.

  - Thanksgiving *falls* on the fourth Thursday of November each year.
  - Walking *is* excellent exercise.

- Use the present tense to indicate an action that occurs regularly or habitually.

  - My sister *takes* frequent trips to Dallas.

- Use the present tense when referring to literary works and artwork, even though the work was written or created in the past.

  - *Hamlet is* set in Denmark.

- Use the present tense to refer to authors no longer living when you are discussing their works.

  - Borges frequently *employs* magical realism in his fiction.

Voice

A verb is in the **active voice** when the subject of the clause or sentence performs the action of the verb.

- The diplomats *have arrived.*
- He *plays* soccer professionally.

A verb is in the **passive voice** when the subject of a clause or sentence is the receiver of the action that the verb describes. Passive verbs are formed using a form of *be* and the past participle of a verb.

- The child *was* badly *bitten* by mosquitoes.
- Her car *was stolen.*

Since the passive voice may make it difficult for your readers to understand who is performing the action of a sentence, in most writing situations, use the active voice. If you do not know who performed an action, however, or if you want to emphasize the receiver of the action, consider using the passive voice.

PASSIVE VOICE   The evidence had been carefully removed by the defendant.

ACTIVE VOICE   The defendant had carefully removed the evidence.

Mood

The **mood** of a verb indicates whether it states a fact or asks a question (**indicative**); gives a command or direction (**imperative**); or expresses a condition, wish, or suggestion (**subjunctive**). The subjunctive mood is also used for hypothetical situations or impossible or unlikely events.

INDICATIVE	Redwood trees can pull moisture from the air.
IMPERATIVE	Read the play and write an analysis of it.
SUBJUNCTIVE	It would be nice to win the lottery.

The subjunctive mood, often used in clauses that begin with *if* or *that*, expresses a wish, suggestion, or condition contrary to fact. Use the base form of the verb for the present subjunctive. For the verb *be*, the past tense subjunctive is *were*, not *was*.

- I suggested that she *walk* to the station.
- The new student in class wished that he *were* more outgoing.

1d Adjectives

Adjectives modify a noun or pronoun by describing it, limiting it, or giving more information about it. They answer the following questions.

WHICH ONE?	The *cutest* puppy belongs to the neighbors.
WHAT KIND?	Use only *academic* sources for the paper.
HOW MANY?	*Several hundred* protesters gathered at City Hall.

There are three types of adjectives: descriptive, limiting, and proper. **Descriptive adjectives** name a quality of the person, place, thing, or idea that they describe.

yellow backpack	*pretty* face	*disturbing* event

Limiting adjectives narrow the scope of the person, place, or thing they describe.

my laptop	*second* building	*that* notebook

Proper adjectives are derived from proper nouns. They are always capitalized.

Japanese culture	*Elizabethan* England	*Scandinavian* mythology

The articles *a*, *an*, and *the* appear immediately before nouns and are considered adjectives. *The* refers to a specific item, while *a* and *an* do not. *A* is used before words that begin with consonant sounds. *An* is used before words that begin with vowel sounds.

- **The person behind us laughed.**

  The refers to a specific person.

- **An answer will be forthcoming.**

  Some answer will be provided.

The can also be used to refer to a group or class of items.

- **The cat is a playful animal.**

For more on the use of adjectives, see Section 9 of the Handbook. For more on articles, see Section 26 of the Handbook.

1e Adverbs

Adverbs modify verbs, adjectives, other adverbs, entire sentences, or clauses by describing, qualifying, or limiting the meaning of the words they modify. They answer the following questions.

HOW?	Andrea Bocelli performed *brilliantly*.
WHEN?	*Later*, they met to discuss the proposal.
WHERE?	The taxi driver headed *downtown*.
HOW OFTEN?	The bobcat is *rarely* seen in the wild.
TO WHAT EXTENT?	He agreed to cooperate *fully* with the investigation.

Most adverbs end in *-ly:*

particular*ly*   beautiful*ly*   secret*ly*

Note that not all words ending in *-ly* are adverbs; some are adjectives (*scholarly*, *unfriendly*). Common adverbs that do not end in *-ly* include *almost, never, quite, soon, then, there, too,* and *very.* Some words can function as either adjectives or adverbs depending on their use in the sentence.

ADJECTIVE	The flu victims were finally *well*.
ADVERB	His paper was *well* written.

Adverbs that modify adjectives or other adverbs appear next to the word they modify.

- Tired sloths move *especially* slowly.

- A pregnant woman may feel *extremely* tired.

Adverbs that modify verbs can appear in several different positions, however.

- He *carefully* put the toys together.
- He put the toys together *carefully*.

For more on the use of adverbs, see Section 9 of the Handbook.

1f Conjunctions

Conjunctions connect words, phrases, or clauses. **Coordinating conjunctions** connect words or word groups of equal importance. There are seven coordinating conjunctions: *and, but, for, nor, or, so,* and *yet.*

- He attended the inauguration *but* looked unhappy.

Coordinating conjunctions must connect words, phrases, or clauses of the same kind. For example, *and* may connect two nouns, but it cannot connect a noun and a clause.

NOUNS	Books by *Russell Simmons* and *Glenn Beck* were on the recommended reading list.
PHRASES	We searched *in the closets* and *under the beds.*
CLAUSES	*Custer graduated last in his West Point class,* but *he distinguished himself in the Civil War.*

Conjunctions that are used in pairs are called **correlative conjunctions**: *as . . . as, both . . . and, either . . . or, just as . . . so, neither . . . nor, not . . . but, not only . . . but also,* and *whether . . . or.*

- *Neither* the strikers *nor* the management was satisfied with the compromise.

A **dependent clause** contains a subject and a verb but does not express a complete thought.

An **independent clause** contains a subject and a verb and can stand alone as a sentence.

Subordinating conjunctions connect **dependent clauses** to **independent clauses**. They connect ideas of unequal importance. Often used at the beginning of a dependent clause, subordinating conjunctions indicate how a less important idea (expressed in a dependent clause) relates to a more important idea (expressed in an independent clause). Here is a list of common subordinating conjunctions and the relationships they express.

Subordinating Conjunctions

Time	after, before, until, when, while
	■ *While* **the sky was still dark, the army prepared for battle.**
Cause or effect	because, since, so that
	■ *Since* **he doesn't like math, he should avoid calculus.**
Condition	even if, if, unless, whether
	■ **We don't do volunteer work** *unless* **it is for a good cause.**
Circumstance	as, as far as, as if, as soon as, as though, even if, even though, in order to
	■ **In-line skating is a popular sport,** *even though* **it is somewhat dangerous.**

Conjunctive adverbs link sentence parts that are of equal importance; they also serve as modifiers. Conjunctive adverbs show the following relationships between the elements they connect.

Conjunctive Adverbs

Time	afterward, finally, later, meanwhile, next, subsequently, then
	■ **The candidates campaigned for months;** *finally,* **a primary election was held.**
Example	for example, for instance, to illustrate
	■ **Some members of the party—***for example,* **the governor—supported another candidate.**
Continuation or addition	also, furthermore, in addition, in the first place, moreover
	■ **He is poorly organized;** *in addition,* **his arguments are not logical.**
Cause or effect	accordingly, as a result, consequently, hence, therefore, thus, unfortunately
	■ *As a result,* **he may convince few voters.**
Differences or contrast	however, nevertheless, on the contrary, on the other hand, otherwise
	■ *Nevertheless,* **he has support from some groups.**
Emphasis	in fact, in other words, that is, undoubtedly
	■ *In fact,* **some politicians are tired of constantly needing to raise money for campaigns.**
Similarities or comparison	conversely, in contrast, likewise, similarly
	■ *In contrast,* **their opponents have received many large donations.**

1g Prepositions

A **preposition** is a word or phrase that links and relates a noun or a pronoun (the object of the preposition) to the rest of the sentence. A **prepositional phrase** includes the preposition along with its object and modifiers. Prepositions often show relationships of time, place, direction, or manner.

- Steve Prefontaine could run *despite* excruciating pain.
- The continental shelf lies *beneath* the ocean.

Common Prepositions

about	below	except	outside	under
against	beneath	for	over	underneath
along	beside	from	past	unlike
among	between	in	since	until
around	beyond	near	through	up
as	by	off	throughout	upon
at	despite	on	till	with
before	down	onto	to	within
behind	during	out	toward	without

Compound prepositions consist of more than one word.

- *According to* historical records, the town is three hundred years old.
- The department gained its reputation *by means of* its diversity.

Common Compound Prepositions

according to	because of	in place of	out of
along with	by means of	in regard to	up to
aside from	except for	in spite of	with regard to
as of	in addition to	instead of	with respect to
as well as	in front of	on account of	

1h Interjections

Interjections are words that express surprise or some other strong feeling. An exclamation point or a period often follows an interjection; a comma may precede or follow an interjection if it is a mild one.

- *Oh*, it wasn't important.
- *Ouch!*
- There were no fires reported last month, *by the way*.

2 Sentence Structure

2a Sentence parts

A **sentence** is a group of words that expresses a complete thought about something or someone. Every sentence must contain two basic parts: a subject and a predicate.

Subjects

The **subject** of a sentence names a person, place, or thing and tells whom or what the sentence is about. It identifies the performer or receiver of the action expressed in the predicate.

- *Lady Gaga*, the flamboyant performer, has made savvy decisions about her career.
- The *clock* on the mantel was given to her by her grandmother.

The noun or pronoun that names what the sentence is about is called the **simple subject**.

- *Mozart* began composing at the age of four.
- The postal *worker* was bitten by a dog.

The simple subject of an imperative sentence is understood as *you*, but *you* is not stated directly.

- Be quiet.

  The sentence is understood as *[You] be quiet.*

The **complete subject** is the simple subject plus its modifiers—words that describe, identify, qualify, or limit the meaning of a noun or pronoun.

  ┌──── complete subject ────┐
- A series of very bad *decisions* doomed the project.
  ┌──────── complete subject ────────┐
- There are too many *books* to fit on the shelves.

A sentence with a **compound subject** contains two or more simple subjects joined by a coordinating conjunction (*and, but, for, nor, or, so,* or *yet*).

- *Joel <u>and</u> Ethan Coen* produce and direct their films.
- *A doctor <u>or</u> a physician's assistant* will explain the results.

Predicates

The **predicate** of a sentence indicates what the subject does, what happens to the subject, or what is said about the subject. The predicate, then, can indicate an action or a state of being.

ACTION	Plant respiration *produces* oxygen.
STATE OF BEING	Stonehenge *has existed* for many centuries.

A **helping verb** (also called an **auxiliary verb**) combines with a main verb to indicate tense, mood, or voice or to add further information.

A **complement** is a word or group of words that describes or renames a subject or an object.

The **simple predicate** is the main verb along with its helping verbs.

- Reporters *should call* the subjects of their stories for comment.
- A snow bicycle for Antarctic workers *has been developed*.

The **complete predicate** consists of the simple predicate plus its modifiers and any objects or complements. (See below for more about complements.)

———— complete predicate ————
- The growth of Los Angeles *depended* to a large extent on finding a way to get water to the desert.

———— complete predicate ————
- Watching fishing boats *is* a relaxing and pleasant way to spend an afternoon.

A **compound predicate** contains two or more predicates that have the same subject and that are joined by *and, but, or, nor,* or another conjunction (see 1f).

- AIDS drugs *can save many lives <u>but</u> are seldom available in poor countries that need them desperately.*
- President Johnson *<u>neither</u> wanted to run for a second term <u>nor</u> planned to serve if elected.*

Objects

A **direct object** is a noun or pronoun that receives the action of a verb. A direct object answers the question, What? or Whom?

- The Scottish fiddler played a lively *reel*.

  The noun *reel* answers the question, What did he play?

- The crowd in the stadium jeered the *quarterback*.

  The noun *quarterback* answers the question, Whom did they jeer?

An **indirect object** is a noun or pronoun that names the person or thing to whom or for whom something is done.

- Habitat for Humanity gave *him* an award for his work.
- A woman on a bench tossed the *pigeons* some crumbs.

Complements

A **complement** is a word or group of words that describes a subject or object and completes the meaning of the sentence. There are two kinds of complements: subject complements and object complements.

A **linking verb** (such as *be, become, feel, seem,* or *taste*) connects the subject of a sentence to a **subject complement**, a noun, a noun phrase, or an adjective that renames or describes the subject.

- Michael Jackson was a *much-loved performer*.
- She was *too disorganized to finish her science project*.

An **object complement** is a noun, a noun phrase, or an adjective that modifies or renames the **direct object**. Object complements appear with transitive verbs (such as *name*, *find*, *make*, *think*, *elect*, *appoint*, *choose*, and *consider*), which express action directed toward something or someone.

A **direct object** receives the action of the verb: *He drove me home.*

- The council appointed him *its new vice president.*
- The undercooked meat made several children *sick.*

2b Phrases

A **phrase** is a group of related words that lacks a subject, a predicate, or both. A phrase cannot stand alone as a sentence. Phrases can appear at the beginning, middle, or end of a sentence and can help make your writing more detailed and interesting.

WITHOUT PHRASES	The burglars escaped. Bus travel is an inexpensive choice.
WITH PHRASES	Startled by the alarm, the burglars escaped without getting any money. For adventurers on a budget, bus travel, while not luxurious, is an inexpensive choice.

There are four common types of phrases: prepositional phrases, verbal phrases, appositive phrases, and absolute phrases.

Prepositional Phrases

A **prepositional phrase** consists of a preposition (*in*, *above*, *with*, *at*, *behind*), the object of the preposition (a noun or pronoun), and any modifiers of the object. Prepositional phrases usually function as adjectives or adverbs to tell more about people, places, objects, or actions. They can also function as nouns. A prepositional phrase generally adds information about time, place, direction, or manner.

ADJECTIVE PHRASE	The plants *on the edge of the field* are weeds.
	On the edge and *of the field* tell *where.*
ADVERB PHRASE	New Orleans is very crowded *during Mardi Gras.*
	During Mardi Gras tells *when.*
NOUN PHRASE	*Down the hill* is the shortest way to town.
	Down the hill acts as the subject of the sentence.

Each of the following sentences has been edited to include a prepositional phrase or phrases that expand the meaning of the sentence by adding detail.

- He fell ^*on the icy sidewalk.*

- The ship suddenly appeared ^*through the mist near the shore.*

Verbal Phrases

A **verbal** is a verb form used as a noun (the *barking* of the dog), an adjective (a *barking* dog), or an adverb (continued *to bark*). It cannot be used alone as the verb of a sentence, however. The three kinds of verbals are participles, gerunds, and infinitives. A **verbal phrase** consists of a verbal and its modifiers.

Participles and participial phrases. All verbs have two participles: present and past. The **present participle** is the *-ing* form of a verb (*being, hoping, studying*). The **past participle** of most verbs ends in *-d* or *-ed* (*hoped, consisted*). The past participle of irregular verbs has no set pattern (*been, ridden*). Both the present participle and the past participle can function as adjectives modifying nouns and pronouns.

- The planes flew over the foggy airport in a *holding* pattern.

- The pot was made of *molded* clay.

A **participial phrase**, which consists of a participle and its modifiers, can also function as an adjective in a sentence.

- The suspect, *wanted for questioning* on robbery charges, had vanished.

Gerunds and gerund phrases. A **gerund** is the present participle, or *-ing* form, of a verb that functions as a noun in a sentence.

- *Driving* can be a frustrating activity.
- The government has not done enough to build *housing*.

A **gerund phrase** consists of a gerund and its modifiers. Like a gerund, a gerund phrase is used as a noun and can therefore function in a sentence as a subject, a direct object, an indirect object, an object of a preposition, or a subject complement.

SUBJECT	*Catching the flu* is unpleasant.
DIRECT OBJECT	All the new recruits practiced *marching*.
INDIRECT OBJECT	One director gave his *acting* a chance.
OBJECT OF A PREPOSITION	An ambitious employee may rise by *impressing* her boss.
SUBJECT COMPLEMENT	The biggest thrill was the *skydiving*.

Infinitives and infinitive phrases. An **infinitive** is the base form of a verb preceded by *to*: *to study, to sleep*. An **infinitive phrase** consists of the infinitive plus any modifiers or objects. An infinitive phrase can function as a noun, an adjective, or an adverb.

SUBJECT	*To become* an actor is my greatest ambition.
ADJECTIVE	She had a job *to do*.
ADVERB	The weary travelers were eager *to sleep*.

Sometimes the *to* in an infinitive phrase is understood but not written.

- **Her demonstration helped me learn the software.**

Note: Be sure to distinguish between infinitive phrases and prepositional phrases beginning with the preposition *to*. In an infinitive phrase, *to* is followed by a verb (*to paint*); in a prepositional phrase, *to* is followed by a noun or pronoun (*to a movie*).

Appositive Phrases

An **appositive** is a word that explains, restates, or adds new information about a noun. An **appositive phrase** consists of an appositive and its modifiers.

- **Ben Affleck,** *a famous actor,* **is very active in trying to improve conditions in the Congo.**

    The appositive phrase adds information about the noun *Ben Affleck*.

Absolute Phrases

An **absolute phrase** consists of a noun or pronoun and any modifiers, usually followed by a participle. An absolute phrase modifies an entire sentence, not any particular word or words within the sentence. It can appear anywhere in a sentence and is set off from the rest of the sentence with commas.

- *Their shift completed,* **the night workers walked out at sunrise.**
- *An unsuspecting insect clamped in its mandible,* **the praying mantis,** *its legs folded piously,* **appears serenely uninvolved.**

2c Clauses

A **clause** is a group of words that contains a subject and a predicate. A clause is either independent (also called *main*) or dependent (also called *subordinate*). An **independent clause** can stand alone as a grammatically complete sentence.

- **Einstein was a clerk at the Swiss Patent Office.**
- **Ethnic disputes followed the disintegration of Yugoslavia.**

A **dependent clause** has a subject and a predicate, but it cannot stand alone as a grammatically complete sentence because it does not express a complete thought. A dependent clause usually begins with either a subordinating conjunction or a relative pronoun that connects it to an independent clause.

Common Subordinating Conjunctions

after	in as much as	that
although	in case that	though
as	in order that	unless
as far as	in so far as	until
as if	in that	when
as soon as	now that	whenever
as though	once	where
because	provided that	wherever
before	rather than	whether
even if	since	while
even though	so that	why
how	supposing that	
if	than	

Relative Pronouns

that	whatever	who (whose, whom)
what	which	whoever (whomever)

- *When the puppies were born*, the breeder examined them carefully.

   — dependent clause —

- Van Gogh's paintings began to command high prices *after he died*.

   — dependent clause —

- Isadora Duncan, *who personified modern dance*, died in a bizarre accident.

   — dependent clause —

When joined to independent clauses, dependent clauses can function as adjectives, adverbs, or nouns and are known as **adjective clauses** (also called **relative clauses**), **adverb clauses**, or **noun clauses**. A noun clause can function as a subject, an object, or a complement.

- Graphic novels, *which were once considered "kid stuff,"* are now taken seriously.

   — adjective clause —

- The whistle blew *as the train approached the crossing*.

   — adverb clause —

- The starving artist ate *whatever he could get*.

   — noun clause —

Relative pronouns are generally the subject or object in their clauses. *Who* and *whoever* change to *whom* and *whomever* when they function as objects. Sometimes the relative pronoun or subordinating conjunction is implied or understood rather than stated.

- **African rituals are among the subjects [that] the essay discusses.**

  That is the understood relative pronoun in the subordinate clause.

A dependent clause may contain an implied predicate. When a dependent clause is missing an element that can be inferred from the context of the sentence, it is called an **elliptical clause**.

- **The shooting of former Congresswoman Gabrielle Giffords disturbed**

  ┌─── elliptical clause ───┐
  Americans *more than gang shootings.*

  The predicate *disturbed them* is implied.

2d Types of Sentences

A sentence can be classified as one of four basic types: simple, compound, complex, or compound-complex.

Simple Sentences

A **simple sentence** has one main or **independent clause** and no subordinate or **dependent clauses**. A simple sentence contains at least one subject and one predicate. It may have a compound subject, a compound predicate, and various phrases, but it has only one clause.

- **She sprints.**
- **She and her teammates sprint.**
- **She and her teammates sprint and run laps.**
- **She and her teammates in the track-and-field events sprint and run laps to achieve their goal of winning medals.**

Compound Sentences

A **compound sentence** consists of two or more independent clauses and no dependent clauses. The two independent clauses are usually joined with a comma and a coordinating conjunction (*and*, *but*, *for*, *nor*, *or*, *so*, or *yet*).

- **She runs laps, but her teammates practice throwing the javelin.**

Sometimes two clauses are joined with a semicolon and no coordinating conjunction.

- **She runs laps; her teammates practice throwing the javelin.**

An **independent clause** contains a subject and a verb and can stand alone as a sentence.

A **dependent clause** contains a subject and a verb but does not express a complete thought.

Or they may be joined with a semicolon and a conjunctive adverb (such as *nonetheless* or *still*), followed by a comma.

- She runs laps; however, her teammates practice throwing the javelin.

Complex Sentences

A **complex sentence** has one independent clause and one or more dependent clauses. The dependent clauses usually begin with a subordinating conjunction or a relative pronoun (see 2c for a list).

- They are training *while he recovers from a sprained ankle.*
- Runners *who win their event at more than one local track meet* will be eligible for the district trials.

Compound-Complex Sentences

A **compound-complex sentence** contains two or more independent clauses and one or more dependent clauses.

- She and her teammates won the meet, and as they were celebrating, a reporter approached them for an interview.
- A reporter approached them while they were celebrating their victory, and after they doused him with champagne, they answered his questions.

WRITING CORRECT SENTENCES

3   Sentence Fragments

A **sentence** is a group of words that must include at least one independent clause (a subject and a verb that express a complete thought).

A **sentence fragment** is a group of words that cannot stand alone as a complete **sentence**. A fragment is often missing a subject, a complete verb, or both.

FRAGMENT	Are hatched in sand.
	This group of words does not tell *who* or *what* are hatched in sand. It lacks a subject.
FRAGMENT	Especially his rebounding ability.
	This group of words has a subject, *his rebounding ability,* but lacks a verb.
FRAGMENT	To notice a friendly smile.
	This group of words lacks both a subject and a verb. *To notice* is not a complete verb. It is an infinitive.

e macmillanhighered.com/successfulwriting
LearningCurve > Fragments

How to Identify a Fragment

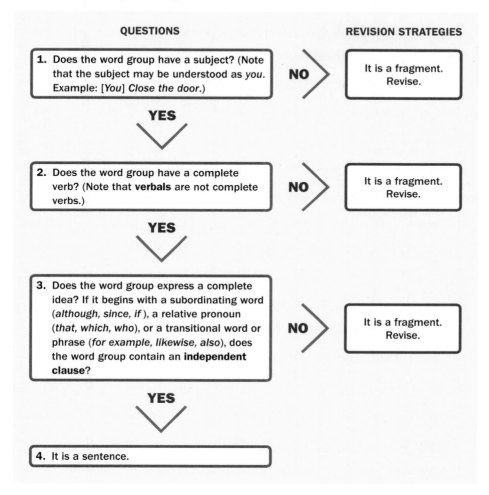

QUESTIONS

REVISION STRATEGIES

1. Does the word group have a subject? (Note that the subject may be understood as *you*. Example: [*You*] *Close the door.*)

NO ⟩ It is a fragment. Revise.

YES

2. Does the word group have a complete verb? (Note that **verbals** are not complete verbs.)

NO ⟩ It is a fragment. Revise.

YES

3. Does the word group express a complete idea? If it begins with a subordinating word (*although, since, if*), a relative pronoun (*that, which, who*), or a transitional word or phrase (*for example, likewise, also*), does the word group contain an **independent clause**?

NO ⟩ It is a fragment. Revise.

YES

4. It is a sentence.

A group of words can have both a subject and a verb but still be a fragment because it does not express a complete thought.

subject verb

FRAGMENT   Because the *number* of voters *has* declined.

> This group of words does not tell what happened as a result of the voter decline. Its meaning is incomplete.

Notice that the preceding fragment begins with the subordinating conjunction *because*. A clause that begins with a subordinating conjunction cannot stand alone as a complete sentence. (For a list of common subordinating conjunctions, see 2c.)

Word groups that begin with a relative pronoun (*that, which, who*) are also not complete sentences.

> ⌜ **subject** ⌝ ⌜ **verb** ⌝
>
> **FRAGMENT**   Which *scientists studied* for many years.
>
> The group of words does not tell *what* the scientists studied.

Finally, when a word group begins with a transitional word or phrase (*for example, also*), make sure that it includes both a subject and a verb.

> ⌜——— **subject** ———⌝
>
> **FRAGMENT**   For example, *the Gulf Coast of Florida*.

Use the flowchart on page 743 to help you decide whether a particular word group is a complete sentence or a sentence fragment. Also try reading your essays backward from the end to the beginning, sentence by sentence, to check for fragments. This method allows you to evaluate each sentence in isolation, without being distracted by the flow of ideas throughout the essay. You might also try turning each sentence into a *yes* or *no* question by adding a helping verb, such as *do, does,* or *did.* A complete sentence can be turned into a *yes* or *no* question, but a fragment cannot.

> **SENTENCE**   Sociology has wide applications.
>
> **YES/NO QUESTION**   Does sociology have wide applications?
>
> **FRAGMENT**   While sociology has wide applications.
>
> **YES/NO QUESTION**   [Cannot be formed]

A sentence fragment can be revised in two general ways: (1) by attaching it to a nearby sentence or (2) by rewriting the fragment as a complete sentence. The method you choose depends on the element the fragment lacks as well as your intended meaning.

- *Certain turtle eggs are*
  ~~Are~~ hatched in sand.

- Jamal is a basketball player of many talents. ^e^ ~~E~~specially his rebounding ability.

- *Sam was too busy to*
  ~~To~~ notice a friendly smile.

- *The*
  ~~Because the~~ number of voters has declined.

3a Join a fragment lacking a subject to another sentence or rewrite it as a complete sentence.

Attach a fragment lacking a subject to a neighboring sentence if the two are about the same person, place, or thing.

- Jessica speaks Spanish fluently. *and* ~~And~~ reads French well.

As an alternative, you can add a subject to turn the fragment into a complete sentence.

- Jessica speaks Spanish fluently. *She also* ~~And~~ reads French well.

3b Add a helping verb to a fragment lacking a complete verb.

Make sure that every sentence you write contains a *complete* verb. For example, verb forms ending in *-ing* need helping verbs to make them complete. Helping verbs include forms of *do, be,* and *have* as well as such words as *will, can, could, shall, should, may, might,* and *must.* When you use an *-ing* verb form in a sentence without a helping verb, you create a fragment. To correct the fragment, add the helping verb.

- The college *is* installing a furnace to heat the library.

3c Join a fragment that lacks both a subject and a verb to another sentence, or add the missing subject and verb.

Often, fragments lacking a subject and verb begin with an **infinitive** such as *to hope, to walk,* and *to play,* which are not complete verbs, or they begin with an *-ed* or *-ing* form of a verb. Revise a fragment that begins with an infinitive or an *-ed* or *-ing* verb form by combining it with a previous sentence.

An **infinitive** is a verb form made up of *to* plus the base form (*to run, to see*).

- I plan to transfer next semester. *to* ~~To~~ live closer to home.

- Robert E. Lee and Ulysses S. Grant met on April 9, 1865. *bringing* ~~Bringing~~ an end to the Civil War.

You can also revise a fragment beginning with an infinitive or an *-ed* or *-ing* verb form by adding both a subject and a verb to make it a complete sentence.

- Linda was reluctant to go out alone at night. *She was unwilling to* ~~To~~ walk across campus from the library.

- Kyle was determined to do well on his math exam. *He studied* ~~Studied~~ during every available hour.

Watch out for fragments that begin with a transitional word or phrase. They can usually be corrected by joining them to a previous sentence.

- Annie has always wanted to become an orthopedist. *— that* ~~That~~ is, a bone specialist.

3d Join a fragment beginning with a subordinating word to another sentence, or drop the subordinating word.

You can correct a fragment beginning with a subordinating word by joining it to the sentence before or after it.

- The students stared spellbound. *while* ~~While~~ the professor lectured.

- Until Dr. Jonas Salk invented a vaccine. *polio* ~~Polio~~ was a serious threat to public health.

As an alternative, you can revise this type of fragment by dropping the subordinating word.

- *The*
  ~~Because the~~ 800 area code for toll-free dialing is overused. New codes—888
  ^and 877—have been added.

3e Join a fragment beginning with a relative pronoun such as *who* or *whom* to another sentence, or rewrite it as a complete sentence.

Another common type of sentence fragment begins with a relative pronoun. **Relative pronouns** include *who, whom, whose, whoever, whomever, what, whatever, which,* and *that.*

- My contemporary fiction instructor assigned a novel by Stephen King. ^*whose*^ ~~Whose~~
  work I admire.
- The dodo is an extinct bird. ^*It*^ ~~That~~ disappeared in the seventeenth century.

Professional writers sometimes use sentence fragments intentionally to achieve special effects, particularly in works of fiction or articles written for popular magazines. An *intentional* fragment may be used to emphasize a point, answer a question, recreate a conversation, or make an exclamation. However, you should avoid using intentional fragments in academic writing. Instructors and other readers may find the fragments distracting or too informal, or they may assume you used a fragment in error.

EXERCISE 3.1

Correct any fragments in the following sentences. Some groups of sentences may be correct as written.

- More people are going to college every year. ^*, especially*^ ~~Especially~~ young women.

1. In the past, higher education was only accessible to a small number of people. However, access to higher education has expanded over the last 200 years.
2. In the United States, for example. Colleges and universities provide education to Americans of all classes and backgrounds.
3. At first, state universities were publicly funded schools. That trained students in fields such as engineering, education, and agriculture.
4. During the nineteenth and early twentieth centuries. Graduates of state universities played a key role in America's development as an industrial and economic power.
5. The number of students in college. Increased greatly in the years after World War II.
6. Because federal funding from the 1944 GI Bill made it possible. Millions of returning veterans attended colleges.
7. Many people credit this program with helping to create a strong middle class. In the United States during the 1950s and 1960s.
8. Now, about two-thirds of high school graduates will attend college. Because those with bachelor's degrees earn $20,000 more a year on average than do people with only high school diplomas.
9. Most people agree that America needs an educated workforce to compete globally.
10. However, as education costs continue to rise. Some wonder whether a traditional four-year college is always worth the expense.

EXERCISE 3.2

Rewrite the following passage as needed to eliminate sentence fragments.

> ■ How much and what kind of intervention should be undertaken/~~On~~ behalf of endangered
> species?

    Gila trout are endangered in some stretches of water. That are managed as designated wilderness. A hands-off policy would be their doom. Because exotic trout species now swim in the same streams. Gila trout can survive the competition and the temptation to interbreed only if they swim in isolated tributaries. In which a waterfall blocks the upstream movement of other fish. Two decades ago, one such tributary was fortified. With a small concrete dam. In other words, a dam deliberately built in the wilderness. It is often difficult to choose the right way. To manage a wilderness area. A scientific grasp of the way the ecosystem works is essential. Yet not always available.

4   Run-on Sentences and Comma Splices

A **run-on sentence** occurs when two or more independent clauses are joined without a punctuation mark or a coordinating conjunction. Run-on sentences are also known as **fused sentences**.

> **RUN-ON SENTENCE**
>
>   ————— independent clause ——————┐ ┌—— independent
> A television addict is dependent on television I have suffered this
> clause ——————┐
> addiction for years.

A **comma splice** occurs when two or more independent clauses are joined with a comma but without a coordinating conjunction (such as *and, or,* or *but*).

> **COMMA SPLICE**
>
>   ————— independent clause ——————┐ ┌—— independent
> A typical magic act includes tricks and illusions, both depend on
> clause ——┐
> deception.

Notice that only a comma separates the two independent clauses, causing the comma splice.

Another type of comma splice occurs when a word other than a coordinating conjunction is used with a comma to join two or more independent clauses.

> **COMMA SPLICE**
>
>   ————— independent clause ——————┐ ┌—
> A typical magic act includes tricks and illusions, however, both
> independent clause ——————┐
> depend on deception.

    In the preceding sentence, *however* is a conjunctive adverb, not a coordinating conjunction. There are only seven coordinating conjunctions: *and, but, for, nor, or, so,* and *yet.*

Recognizing Run-on Sentences and Comma Splices

Many students have difficulty spotting run-on sentences and comma splices in their own writing. Use the accompanying flowchart to help you identify these types of errors in your sentences.

How to Identify Run-on Sentences and Comma Splices

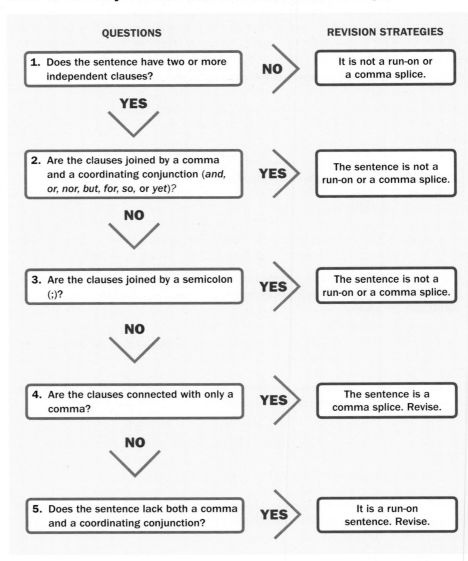

Correcting Run-on Sentences and Comma Splices

There are four basic ways to correct a run-on sentence or comma splice. Choose the method that best fits your sentence or intended meaning.

4a Revise by creating two separate sentences.

Correct a run-on sentence or comma splice by creating two separate sentences. Make sure each independent clause has the appropriate end punctuation mark—a period, a question mark, or (on rare occasions) an exclamation mark.

period   period

Independent clause **.** *Independent clause* **.**

RUN-ON SENTENCE	A résumé should be directed to a specific audience $\overset{It}{\underset{\wedge}{\text{it}}}$ should emphasize the applicant's potential value to the company.
COMMA SPLICE	To evaluate a charity, you should start by examining its goals$\underset{\wedge}{\overset{.}{,}}$ $\underset{\wedge}{\overset{T}{\text{then}}}$ you should investigate its management practices.

4b Revise by joining the clauses with a semicolon (;).

When the independent clauses are closely connected in meaning, consider joining them with a semicolon. Note that a coordinating conjunction (such as *and, or,* or *but*) is *not* included when you revise with a semicolon (see 4c).

semicolon

Independent clause **;** *Independent clause* **.**

RUN-ON SENTENCE	Specialty products are unique items that consumers take time purchasing$\underset{\wedge}{;}$ these items include cars, parachutes, and skis.
COMMA SPLICE	Studies have shown that male and female managers have different leadership styles$\underset{\wedge}{\overset{.}{,}}$ as a result, workers may respond differently to each.

In the second example, the semicolon joins the two clauses connected by the conjunctive adverb *as a result.* When two independent clauses are joined by a conjunctive adverb, a semicolon is needed.

4c Revise by joining the clauses with a comma and a coordinating conjunction.

Two independent clauses can be joined by using *both* a comma and a coordinating conjunction (*and, but, for, nor, or, so,* or *yet*). The coordinating conjunction indicates how the two clauses are related.

comma + coordinating conjunction

| Independent clause | , | and | independent clause | . |

RUN-ON SENTENCE Closed-minded people often refuse to recognize opposing views, *and* they reject ideas without evaluating them.

COMMA SPLICE Some educators support home schooling, *but* others oppose it vehemently.

4d Revise by making one clause dependent or by turning one clause into a phrase.

A **dependent clause** contains a subject and a verb but does not express a complete thought. It must always be linked to an independent clause. You can correct a run-on sentence or a comma splice by adding a **subordinating conjunction** (such as *because* or *although*) to one of the independent clauses, thereby making it a dependent clause. The subordinating conjunction makes the thought incomplete and dependent on the independent clause.

subordinating conjunction

| *Because* | dependent clause | , | independent clause | . |

or

subordinating conjunction

| Independent clause | because | dependent clause | . |

RUN-ON SENTENCE	Facial expressions are very revealing they are an important communication tool.
INDEPENDENT CLAUSE	Facial expressions are very revealing.
DEPENDENT CLAUSE	*Because* facial expressions are very revealing
JOINED TO INDEPENDENT CLAUSE	Because facial expressions are very revealing, they are an important communication tool.

You can also correct a run-on sentence or a comma splice by changing one of the independent clauses to a phrase.

Phrase , *independent clause .*

or

Independent clause , *phrase .*

or

Beginning of independent clause , *phrase ,* *end of independent clause .*

COMMA SPLICE	Medieval peasants in Europe ate a simple, hearty diet, they relied almost totally on agriculture.
INDEPENDENT CLAUSE	Medieval peasants in Europe ate a simple, hearty diet.
CLAUSE REDUCED TO PHRASE	having a simple, hearty diet
EMBEDDED IN INDEPENDENT CLAUSE	Medieval peasants in Europe—having a simple, hearty diet—relied almost totally on agriculture.

Note: A comma or commas may or may not be needed to separate a phrase from the rest of the sentence, depending on how the phrase affects the meaning of the sentence (see 12e). Here are two more examples that show how to revise run-on sentences and comma splices using subordination.

| **RUN-ON SENTENCE** | Distributors open big-budget movies late in the week, ~~they hope~~ *hoping* movie goers will flock to theaters over the weekend. |
| **COMMA SPLICE** | *Although the* ~~The~~ remote fishing lodge has no heat or electricity, ~~nevertheless~~ it is a popular vacation spot. |

EXERCISE 4.1

Correct any run-ons or comma splices in the following sentences.

■ A deadly nerve poison is found on the skin of some Amazon tree frogs, native tribes use the poison on the tips of their arrows when they hunt.

1. Nearly every American child dreams of going to Disney World, it has become one of the most popular family vacation destinations.
2. Shopping through online bookstores is convenient, some people miss the atmosphere of a traditional bookstore.

3. Openness is one way to build trust in a relationship another is to demonstrate tolerance and patience.
4. In the 1960s some Americans treated Vietnam veterans disrespectfully this situation has changed dramatically since that time.
5. William Faulkner wrote classic novels about life in the U.S. South, Eudora Welty has also written vividly about southern life.
6. With large bodies and tiny wings, bumblebees have long been a puzzle, how do they fly?
7. The Taj Mahal is aptly called the Pearl Mosque it glows in the moonlight with unearthly beauty.
8. The Supreme Court often makes controversial decisions, the justices must decide how to interpret the Constitution.
9. Although the clouds were threatening, the storm had not yet struck, however, most boats turned toward shore.
10. Restoring a painting is, indeed, delicate work too much enthusiasm can be dangerous.

EXERCISE 4.2

Correct any run-on sentences and comma splices in the following paragraph. Some sentences may be correct as written.

■ Some people believe dreams are revealing, *but* others think the brain is simply unloading excess information.

   Throughout recorded history, people have been fascinated by dreams, they have wondered what meaning dreams hold. Whether the dreams are ominous or beautiful, people have always wanted to understand them. There are many ancient stories about dream interpretation one of these is the biblical story of Daniel. Daniel is able to interpret a ruler's dream, this power to interpret convinces the ruler that Daniel is a prophet. Other early writers considered the topic of dream interpretation, to Latin writers, some dreams were meaningful and some were not. Meaningful dreams could reveal the future, these writers argued, but other dreams were simply the result of eating or drinking too much. Sigmund Freud, the founder of psychoanalysis, dramatically changed the field of dream interpretation he believed that dreams come from the subconscious. According to Freud, ideas too frightening for the waking mind often appear in dreams, patients in Freudian therapy often discuss dream images. Today, not everyone agrees with Freud, scientists trying to understand the brain still pay attention to dreams. They are certain that dreams reflect modern life more and more people today dream about computers.

5   Subject-Verb Agreement

Subjects and verbs must agree in person and number. **Person** refers to the forms *I* or *we* (first person), *you* (second person), and *he, she, it,* and *they* (third person). **Number** shows whether a word refers to one thing (singular) or more than one thing (plural). In a sentence, subjects and verbs need to be consistent in person and number: *I drive, you drive, she drives.*

e **macmillanhighered.com/successfulwriting**
LearningCurve > Subject-Verb Agreement

Subject-verb agreement errors often occur in complicated sentences, in sentences with compound subjects, or in sentences where the subject and verb are separated by other words or phrases. The following sections will help you look for and revise common errors in subject-verb agreement.

5a Make sure the verb agrees with the subject, not with words that come between the subject and verb.

- The *number* of farm workers *has* remained constant over several decades.

  The subject *number* is singular and requires a singular verb, even though the words *of farm workers* appear between the subject and verb.

5b Use a plural verb when two or more subjects are joined by *and*.

- A dot and a dash represents the letter *A* in Morse code.

- Basketball star Shaquille O'Neal, comedian D. L. Hughley, and actor Tom Arnold was all born on March 6.
  were

5c Revise to make the verb agree with the subject closest to it when two or more subjects are joined by *or, either . . . or*, or *neither . . . nor*.

When two or more singular subjects are joined by *or, either . . . or,* or *neither . . . nor,* use a singular verb.

- *Math* or *accounting appears* to be a suitable major for you.
- Either the *waiter* or the *customer has* misplaced the bill.
- Neither the *doctor* nor the *patient is* pessimistic about the prognosis.

When one singular and one plural subject are joined by *or, either . . . or,* or *neither . . . nor,* the verb should agree in number with the subject nearest to it.

- Neither the *sailors* nor the *boat was* harmed by the storm.

- Neither the *boat* nor the *sailors were* harmed by the storm.

- Either my daughters or my wife water that plant daily.
  s

5d Use a singular verb with most collective nouns, such as *family, couple*, and *class*.

When a **collective noun** refers to a group as one unit acting together, use a singular verb. When the members of the group are acting as individuals, use a plural verb.

To make their meaning clearer and avoid awkwardness, writers often add *members* or a similar noun.

- The school *committee has* voted to increase teachers' salaries.

  The committee is acting as a unit.

- The family ~~are~~ living in a cramped apartment.

  is

- The *team members are* traveling by train, bus, and bike.

  The team members are acting individually.

- The members of the jury ~~is~~ divided and unable to reach consensus.

  are

5e Use a singular verb with most indefinite pronouns, such as *anyone*, *everyone*, *each*, *every*, *no one*, and *something*.

Indefinite pronouns do not refer to a specific person, place, or object. They refer to people, places, or things in general. Singular indefinite pronouns include the following: *each, either, neither, anyone, anybody, anything, everyone, everybody, everything, one, no one, nobody, nothing, someone, somebody, something.*

- *Everyone* in this room *is* welcome to express an opinion.
- Neither of the candidates ~~have~~ run for office before.

  has

Other indefinite pronouns, such as *several, both, many,* and *few,* take a plural verb.

- Every year *many succeed* in starting new small businesses.
- Several of you jogs at least three miles a day.

Some indefinite pronouns, such as *all, any, more, most, some,* and *none,* take either a singular or a plural verb depending on the noun they refer to. To decide which verb to use, follow this rule: Treat the indefinite pronoun as singular if it refers to something that cannot be counted and as plural if it refers to more than one of something that can be counted.

- Most of the water go into this kettle.

  es

  You cannot count water.

- Some of the children in the study chooses immediate rather than delayed rewards.

  You can count children.

5f Revise to make verbs agree with the antecedents of *who, which,* and *that*.

When a **relative pronoun** (*who, which, that*) refers to a singular noun, use a singular verb. When it refers to a plural noun, use a plural verb.

- *Toni Morrison, who enjoys* unique success as both a popular and a literary author, won the Nobel Prize in literature in 1993.

    Who refers to Toni Morrison, and because *Toni Morrison* is singular, the verb *enjoys* is singular.

- Look for *stores that display* this sign.

    That refers to *stores,* a plural noun.

Using *one of the* often leads to errors in subject-verb agreement. The phrase *one of the* plus a noun is plural.

- A pigeon is *one of the two birds that drink* by suction.

    That refers to *birds,* and since *birds* is plural, the verb *drink* is plural.

However, *only one of the* plus a noun is singular: *The cheetah is the only one of the big cats that has nonretractable claws.*

5g Revise to make the verb agree with a subject that follows it.

When a sentence begins with either *here* or *there* (which cannot function as a subject) or with a **prepositional phrase**, the subject often follows the verb. Look for the subject after the verb and make sure the subject and verb agree.

- There *is* a false *panel* somewhere in this room.

- Under the stairs *lurks* a solitary *spider.*

5h Make sure a linking verb agrees with its subject, not a word or phrase that renames the subject.

Linking verbs, such as forms of *be* and *feel, look,* and *taste,* connect a subject with a word or phrase that renames or describes it. In sentences with linking verbs, the verb should agree with the subject.

- The *bluebell is* any of several plants in the lily family.

- The *issue* discussed at the meeting *was* the low wages earned by factory workers.

An **antecedent** is the noun or pronoun to which a pronoun refers.

A **relative pronoun** introduces a dependent clause that functions as an adjective: *the patient who injured her leg.*

5i   Use a singular verb when the subject is a title.

- *Gulliver's Travels* ~~are~~ ^{is} a satire by the eighteenth-century British writer Jonathan Swift.

5j   Use singular verbs with singular nouns that end in -s, such as *physics* and *news*.

- *Linguistics deals* with the study of human speech.

EXERCISE 5.1

Correct any subject-verb agreement errors in the following sentences. Some sentences may be correct as written.

- Most of the people in the world believes that learning a second language is important.

1. Many members of the international business community communicates by speaking English, the international language of business.
2. A student in most non-English-speaking industrialized nations expect to spend six or more years studying English.
3. The United States are different.
4. Working for laws that requires all Americans to speak English is a fairly common U.S. political tactic.
5. In American schools, often neither a teaching staff nor enough money have been available for good foreign-language programs.
6. Some linguists joke that a person who speaks two languages are called bilingual, while a person who speaks one language is called American.
7. Some states around the country has begun to change this situation.
8. If a class is given lessons in a foreign language, the students feel that they will be better prepared for the new global economy.
9. In a Spanish or French class, children of immigrants for whom English was a second language learns a new language and perhaps gains a new appreciation of their parents' accomplishments.
10. Everyone who study a foreign language are likely to benefit.

EXERCISE 5.2

Correct any sentences with subject-verb agreement errors in the following paragraph. Some sentences may be correct as written.

Everyone in the colder climates want to know whether the next winter will be severe. The National Weather Service, however, usually predict the weather only a short time in advance. Another method of making weather predictions are popular with many Americans. According to folklore, there is a number of signs to alert people to a hard winter ahead. Among these signs are the brown stripe on a woolly bear caterpillar. If the brown stripe between the caterpillar's two black stripes are wide, some people believe the winter will be a short one. Another of the signs that indicate a hard winter is a large apple harvest. And, of course, almost everyone in the United States have seen news stories on February 2 about groundhogs predicting the end of winter. Folk beliefs, which are not based on science, seems silly to many people. Neither the National Weather Service nor folklore are always able to forecast the weather accurately, however.

6 Verb Forms

Except for *be,* all English verbs have five forms.

Base Form	*Past Tense*	*Past Participle*	*Present Participle*	*-s Form*
move	moved	moved	moving	moves

- Many designers *visit* Milan for fashion shows each year.
- Sarah *visited* her best friend in Thailand.
- Students have *visited* the state capital every spring for decades.
- His cousin from Iowa is *visiting* this week.
- Maria *visits* her grandmother in Puerto Rico as often as possible.

6a Use -s or -es endings for present tense verbs that have third-person singular subjects.

The *-s* form is made up of the verb's base form plus *-s* or *-es.*

- Mr. King *teaches* English.

A third-person singular subject can consist of a singular noun, a singular pronoun (*he, she,* and *it*), or a singular indefinite pronoun (such as *everyone*).

SINGULAR NOUN	The flower opens.
SINGULAR PRONOUN	He opens the door.
SINGULAR INDEFINITE PRONOUN	Everybody knows the truth.

- She ~~want~~ to be a veterinarian.
  _{wants}
- None of the townspeople ~~understand~~ him.
  _{understands}

6b Do not omit -*ed* endings on verbs.

For regular verbs, both the past tense and the past participle are formed by adding *-ed* or *-d* to the base form of the verb. (For more on verb tense, see 1c and 27a.)

- She *claimed* to be the czar's daughter, Anastasia.
- The defendant *faced* his accusers.

Some speakers do not fully pronounce the *-ed* endings of verbs (*asked, fixed, supposed to, used to*). As a result, they may unintentionally omit these endings in their writing.

- He ~~talk~~ to the safety inspectors about plant security.
  _{*talked*}

- They ~~use~~ to order lattes every morning.
  _{*used*}

6c Use the correct form of irregular verbs such as *lay* and *lie*.

The verb pairs *lay* and *lie* and *sit* and *set* have similar forms and are often confused. Each verb has its own meaning: *lie* means to recline or rest on a surface, and *lay* means to put or place something; *sit* means to be seated, as in a chair, and *set* means to place something on a surface.

- Our dog likes to ~~lay~~ on the couch all afternoon.
  _{*lie*}

- Let me ~~set~~ in this chair for a while.
  _{*sit*}

For more on irregular verbs, see 1c.

6d Use the active and passive voice appropriately.

When a verb is in the **active voice**, the subject performs the action.

ACTIVE VOICE   The Mississippi River flows into the Gulf of Mexico.

When a verb is in the **passive voice**, the subject receives the action.

PASSIVE VOICE   The computer file was deleted.

Notice that the sentence in the passive voice does not tell *who* deleted the file.

The active voice expresses ideas more vividly and emphatically than does the passive voice. Whenever possible, use the active voice in your sentences.

- ~~Tea was thrown~~ into Boston Harbor ~~by the colonists.~~
  _{*The colonists threw tea*}

- ~~Illegal drugs are not allowed to be sold.~~
  _{*No one is allowed to sell illegal*}

Sentences in the passive voice may seem indirect, as if the writer is purposely withholding information. In general, use the passive voice sparingly. There are two situations in which it is the better choice, however.

e macmillanhighered.com/successfulwriting
LearningCurve > Active and Passive Voice

1. When you do not know or do not want to reveal who performed the action of the verb:

   PASSIVE   Several historic buildings had been torn down.

2. When you want to emphasize the object of the action rather than the person who causes the action:

   PASSIVE   The poem "My Last Duchess" by Robert Browning was discussed in class.

   In this sentence, the title of the poem is more important than the people who discussed it.

6e Use the present tense when writing about literary works, even though they were written in the past.

■ Chaucer's *Canterbury Tales* depicts ~~depicted~~ a tremendously varied group of travelers.

6f Be sure to distinguish between the immediate past and the less immediate past.

Use the past perfect form of the verb, formed by adding *had* to the past participle, to indicate an action that was completed before another action or a specified time.

   UNCLEAR   Roberto finished three research papers when the semester ended.

   Roberto did not finish all three right at the end of the semester.

   REVISED   Roberto had finished three research papers when the semester ended.

For more on verb tense, see 1c and 27a.

EXERCISE 6.1

Correct the errors in verb form in the following sentences. Some sentences may be correct as written.

■ The Spanish-American War ~~was entered by the~~ United States entered the ~~United States~~ in 1898.

1. When the nineteenth century change into the twentieth, many people in the United States became eager to expel Spain from the Americas.
2. Cuba, an island that lays ninety miles off the Florida coast, provided them with an excuse to do so.
3. Cuban rebels were trying to free themselves from Spain, and many Americans wanted to help them.
4. In addition, many people in the United States wanted to take over Spain's territories for a long time.
5. The United States won the war very quickly and assume control of Cuba, the Philippines, Guam, and Puerto Rico.
6. Cuba was allow to take control of its own affairs right away.

7. Puerto Rico became a commonwealth in 1952, a position that place it between state-hood and independence.
8. In a 1998 election, the people of Puerto Rico were offered the option of full statehood.
9. It was rejected by them.
10. Many Puerto Ricans are worried that statehood would destroy the native culture of their island, and none of them want that to happen.

EXERCISE 6.2

Correct the errors in verb form in the following paragraph. Some sentences may be correct as written.

contains
■ **Walt Whitman's *Leaves of Grass* ~~contain~~ long, informally structured poems.**
              ^

Walt Whitman was usually considered one of the greatest American poets. He spent almost his whole life in Brooklyn, New York, but he like to write about all of America. He was fired from several jobs for laziness and admitted that he liked to lay in bed until noon. But he had a vision: He wanted to create an entirely new kind of poetry. Rhyme was considered unimportant by him, and he did not think new American poetry needed formal structure. Unfortunately for Whitman, his great masterpiece, *Leaves of Grass,* was not an overnight success. Ralph Waldo Emerson admire it, but Whitman sold very few copies. He revise it continuously until his death. Today, people admires *Leaves of Grass* for its optimism, its beautiful language, its very modern appreciation of the diversity of America, and its astonishing openness about sexuality. Whitman's body of work still move and surprise readers.

7 Pronoun Problems

Pronouns are words used in place of nouns. They provide a quick, convenient way to refer to a word that has already been named. Common problems in using pronouns include problems with pronoun reference, agreement, and case.

Pronoun Reference

A pronoun should refer clearly to its **antecedent**, the noun or pronoun for which it substitutes.

If an antecedent is missing or unclear, the meaning of the sentence is also unclear. Use the following guidelines to make certain your pronoun references are clear and correct.

7a Make sure each pronoun refers clearly to one antecedent.

■ **The hip-hop radio station battled the alternative rock station for the highest ratings.**

the alternative rock station
Eventually, ~~it~~ won.
              ^

The revised sentence makes it clear which station won: the alternative rock station.

7b Be sure to check for vague uses of *they, it,* **and** *you.*

They, it, and *you* often refer vaguely to antecedents in preceding sentences or to no antecedent at all.

OMITTED ANTECEDENT	On the Internet, they claimed that an asteroid would collide with the earth.
	On the Internet does not explain what *they* refers to.
CLEAR	On the Internet, a blog claimed that an asteroid would collide with the earth.
	Adding the noun *a blog* clears up the mystery.

- When political scientists study early political cartoons, <s>it provides</s> ^they gain^ insight into historical events.
- In Florida, ^people often talk^ <s>you often hear</s> about hurricane threats of previous years.

7c Make sure pronouns do not refer to adjectives or possessives.

Pronouns must refer to nouns or other pronouns. Adjectives and possessives cannot serve as antecedents, although they may seem to suggest a noun the pronoun *could* refer to.

- He became so depressed that ^he was^ <s>it made him</s> unable to get out of bed.

  The pronoun *it* seems to refer to the adjective *depressed,* which suggests the noun *depression.* This noun is not in the sentence, however.

- The stock market's rapid rise made ^stocks^ it appear to be an attractive investment.

  The pronoun *it* seems to refer to *stock market's,* which is a possessive, not a noun.

7d Make sure the pronouns *who, whom, which,* **and** *that* **refer to clear, specific nouns.**

- Lake-effect storms hit cities along the Great Lakes. ^These storms make^ <s>That makes</s> winter travel treacherous.

EXERCISE 7.1

Correct any errors in pronoun reference in the following sentences.

- Innovative codes are important because <s>it means that</s> they ^are^ <s>will be</s> hard to break.

1. A country at war must be able to convey information to military personnel. That is always a challenge.
2. The information's importance often requires it to be transmitted secretly.
3. Military strategists use codes for these transmissions because they baffle the enemy.
4. They say that "invisible ink," which cannot be seen until the paper is heated, was once a popular way to communicate secretly.
5. Lemon juice and vinegar are good choices for invisible ink because you can't see them unless they are burned.

6. During World War II, U.S. government code specialists hired Navajo Indians because it is a difficult and little-studied language.
7. In early code writing, it involved substituting letters throughout the message.
8. These cryptograms are no longer used to transmit messages because they are too simple.
9. The Nazis' Enigma code was extremely difficult to crack. This was an enormous problem for the Allied forces.
10. Alan Turing's mathematical genius saved the day. He was a British civil servant who finally solved the Enigma code.

Pronoun-Antecedent Agreement

An **antecedent** is the noun or pronoun to which a pronoun refers.

Person indicates whether the subject is speaking (first person: *I, we*), is being spoken to (second person: *you*), or is being spoken about (third person: *he, she, it, they*).

Number is a term that classifies pronouns as singular (*I, you, he, she, it*) or plural (*we, you, they*).

Gender is a way of classifying pronouns as masculine (*he, him*), feminine (*she, her*), or neuter (*it, its*).

An **indefinite pronoun** does not refer to a specific person, place, or object. It refers to people, places, or things in general (*anywhere, everyone, everything*).

Pronouns and **antecedents** must agree in **person**, **number**, and **gender**. The most common agreement error occurs when pronouns and antecedents do not agree in number. If the antecedent is singular, use a singular pronoun. If the antecedent is plural, use a plural pronoun.

In most situations you will instinctively choose the correct pronoun and antecedent. Here are a few guidelines to follow for those times when you are unsure of which pronoun or antecedent to use.

7e Use singular pronouns to refer to indefinite pronouns that are singular in meaning.

Singular indefinite pronouns include the following:

another	anywhere	everyone	none	other
anybody	each	everything	no one	somebody
anyone	either	neither	nothing	someone
anything	everybody	nobody	one	something

- *Each* of the experiments produced *its* desired result.

- If *anyone* wants me, give *him or her* my email address.

- *Everyone* in America should exercise *his or her* right to vote so *his or her* voice can be heard.

If the pronoun and antecedent do not agree, change either the pronoun or the indefinite pronoun to which it refers. If you need to use a singular pronoun, use *he or she* or *him or her* to avoid sexism.

- People
  ~~Everyone~~ should check their credit card statements monthly.

- Everyone should check ~~their~~ credit card statement monthly.
  his or her

An alternative is to eliminate the pronoun or pronouns entirely.

- **No one should lose** ~~**their**~~ ^a^ **job because of family responsibilities.**

Note: Overuse of *him or her* and *his or her* can create awkward sentences. To avoid this problem, you can revise your sentences in one of two ways: by using a plural antecedent and a plural pronoun or by omitting the pronouns altogether.

The indefinite pronouns *all, any, more, most,* and *some* can be either singular or plural, depending on how they are used in sentences. When an indefinite pronoun refers to something that can be counted, use a plural pronoun to refer to it. When an indefinite pronoun refers to something that cannot be counted, use a singular pronoun to refer to it.

- **Of the tropical plants studied,** *some* **have proven** *their* **usefulness in fighting disease.**

  Because the word *plant*s is a plural, countable noun, the pronoun *some* is plural in this sentence.

- **The water was warm, and** *most* **of** *it* **was murky.**

  Water is not countable, so *most* is singular.

7f Use a plural pronoun to refer to a compound antecedent joined by *and*.

- **The** *walrus <u>and</u> the carpenter* **ate** *their* **oysters greedily.**

Exception: When the singular antecedents joined by *and* refer to the same person, place, or thing, use a singular pronoun.

- **As** *a father and a husband, he* **is a success.**

Exception: When *each* or *every* comes before the antecedent, use a singular pronoun.

- *<u>Every</u> nut and bolt* **was in** *its* **place for the inspection.**

When a compound antecedent is joined by *or* or *nor,* the pronoun should agree with the noun closer to the verb.

- **Either the panda or the sea otters should have** ~~**its**~~ ^their^ **new habitat soon.**

7g Use a singular or plural pronoun to refer to a collective noun, depending on the meaning.

A **collective noun** names a group of people or things acting together or individually (*herd, class, team*) and may be referred to by a singular or plural pronoun depending on your intended meaning. When you refer to a group acting together as a unit, use a singular pronoun.

- The *wolf pack* surrounds *its* quarry.

  The pack is acting as a unit.

When you refer to the members of the group as acting individually, use a plural pronoun.

- After the false alarm, *members* of the bomb squad returned to *their* homes.

  The members of the squad acted individually.

EXERCISE 7.2

Correct any errors in pronoun-antecedent agreement in the following sentences. Some sentences may be correct as written.

- Every scientist has ~~their~~ own idea about the state of the environment.

  his or her

  1. Neither the many species of dinosaurs nor the flightless dodo bird could prevent their own extinction.
  2. A team of researchers might disagree on its conclusions about the disappearance of the dinosaur.
  3. However, most believe that their findings indicate the dodo died out because of competition from other species.
  4. In one way, animals resemble plants: Some are "weeds" because it has the ability to thrive under many conditions.
  5. Any species that cannot withstand their competitors may be doomed to extinction.
  6. When a "weed" and a delicate native species compete for its survival, the native species usually loses.
  7. If the snail darter and the spotted owl lose their fight to survive, should humans care?
  8. Everyone should be more concerned about the extinction of plants and animals than they seem to be.
  9. Every extinction has their effect on other species.
  10. The earth has experienced several mass extinctions in its history, but another would take their toll on the quality of human life.

Pronoun Case

Most of the time you will automatically know which form, or *case*, of a pronoun to use: the **subjective**, **objective**, or **possessive** case. A pronoun's case indicates its function in a sentence. When a pronoun functions as a subject in a sentence, the subjective case (*I*) is used. When a pronoun functions as a **direct object**, an **indirect object**, or an **object of a preposition**, the objective case (*me*) is used. When a pronoun indicates ownership, the possessive case (*mine*) is used.

Subjective Case	*Objective Case*	*Possessive Case*
I	me	my, mine
we	us	our, ours
you	you	your, yours
he, she, it	him, her, it	his, her, hers, its
they	them	their, theirs
who	whom	whose

A **direct object** receives the action of the verb: *He drove me home.*

An **indirect object** indicates to or for whom an action is performed: *I gave her the keys.*

An **object of a preposition** is a word or phrase that follows a preposition: *with him, above the table.*

Use the following guidelines to correct errors in pronoun case.

7h Read the sentence aloud without the noun and the word *and* to decide which pronoun to use in a compound construction (*Yolanda and I, Yolanda and me*).

INCORRECT   Yolanda and me graduated from high school last year.

If you mentally delete *Yolanda and,* the sentence sounds wrong: *Me graduated from high school last year.*

REVISED   Yolanda and I graduated from high school last year.

If you mentally delete *Yolanda and,* the sentence sounds correct: *I graduated from high school last year.*

INCORRECT   The mayor presented the citizenship award to Mrs. Alvarez and I.

If you delete *Mrs. Alvarez and,* the sentence sounds wrong: *The mayor presented the citizenship award to I.*

REVISED   The mayor presented the citizenship award to Mrs. Alvarez and me.

If you delete *Mrs. Alvarez and,* the sentence sounds correct: *The mayor presented the citizenship award to me.*

7i Read the sentence aloud with the pronoun as the subject when a pronoun follows a form of the verb *be* (*is, are, was, were*).

INCORRECT   The leader is him.

If you substitute *him* for *the leader,* the sentence sounds wrong: *Him is the leader.*

REVISED   The leader is he.

If you substitute *he* for *the leader,* the sentence sounds correct: *He is the leader.*

- The best singer in the group is ~~her~~. *she.*

7j Read the sentence aloud without the noun to determine whether *we* or *us* should come before a noun.

- **If we hikers frighten them, the bears may attack.**

  If you mentally delete *hikers*, the sentence sounds correct: *If we frighten them, the bears may attack.*

- **The older children never paid attention to us kindergartners.**

  If you mentally delete *kindergartners*, the sentence sounds correct: *The older children never paid attention to us.*

7k Choose the correct pronoun form for a comparison using *than* or *as* by mentally adding the verb that is implied.

- **Diedre is a better athlete than I [am].**
- **The coach likes her better than [he likes] me.**

7l Use *who* or *whoever* when the pronoun functions as the subject of a sentence. Use *whom* or *whomever* when the pronoun functions as the object of a verb or preposition.

An **object** is the target or recipient of the action described by the verb: *I gave her the keys.*

To decide whether to use *who* or *whom* in a question, answer the question yourself by using the words *he* or *him* or *she* or *her*. If you use *he* or *she* in the answer, you should use *who* in the question. If you use *him* or *her* in the answer, use *whom* in the question.

An **object of a preposition** is a word or phrase that follows a preposition: *with him, above the table.*

QUESTION	(*Who, Whom*) photocopied the article?
ANSWER	*She* photocopied the article.
CORRECT PRONOUN	*Who* photocopied the article?

QUESTION	To (*who, whom*) is that question addressed?
ANSWER	It is addressed to *him*.
CORRECT PRONOUN	To *whom* is that question addressed?

A **dependent clause** contains a subject and a verb but does not express a complete thought.

Similarly, to decide whether to use *who* or *whom* in a **dependent clause**, turn the dependent clause into a question. The pronoun you use to answer that question will tell you whether *who* or *whom* should appear in the clause.

- **Aphra Behn's *Oronooko* dramatizes the life of a slave ~~whom~~ who came from African royalty.**

  If you ask the question (*Who, whom*) *came from African royalty?*, the answer, *He came from African royalty*, indicates that the correct pronoun is *who*.

- **The leader ~~who~~ whom we seek must unite the community.**

  If you ask the question (*Who, whom*) *do we seek?*, the answer, *We seek him*, indicates that the correct pronoun is *whom*.

7m Use a possessive pronoun to modify a gerund.

- *His moralizing* has never been welcome.

  The possessive pronoun *his* modifies the gerund *moralizing*.

Gerunds are often confused with **participles** because both end in *-ing*.

PARTICIPLE	Teenagers across the United States watched *her singing* on *American Idol*.
	The teenagers watched her, not the singing.
GERUND	The professor discovered *their cheating* on the final exam.
	The cheating was discovered, not the students doing the cheating.

A **gerund** is an *-ing* form of a verb that functions as a noun (*complaining, jogging*).

A **participle** is an *-ing* or *-ed* form of a verb that is used as an adjective (*the terrifying monster*) or with a helping verb to indicate tense (*he was running away*). Pronouns used with participles should be in the objective case; pronouns used with gerunds should be in the possessive case.

EXERCISE 7.3

Correct any errors in pronoun case in the following sentences. Some sentences may be correct as written.

- Cave explorers, ~~whom~~ who are called spelunkers, sometimes find underground rooms no one has seen before.

1. Whomever discovers a large cave is usually able to attract tourists.
2. Much of Kentucky's Mammoth Cave was explored in the 1830s by Stephen Bishop, a slave who worked as a cave guide.
3. Few spelunkers today are better known than he.
4. Following the success of Mammoth Cave, many Kentucky cavers hoped to make a fortune from them spelunking.
5. Floyd Collins was one Kentucky native whom searched his property for caves.
6. In January 1925, a falling rock trapped Collins, whom was spelunking in a narrow passage in Sand Cave.
7. When his brothers found him, Collins and them worked unsuccessfully to free his trapped leg.
8. For several days, the most famous man in Kentucky was him.
9. The plea to rescue Floyd Collins was answered by whoever could travel to rural Kentucky.
10. Them failing to save Collins was a terrible tragedy for his family and the rescuers.

EXERCISE 7.4

Correct any errors in pronoun reference, agreement, and case in the following paragraph. Some sentences may be correct as written.

- *She*
  ~~Her~~ and her husband married for love, which was unusual at the time.

Lady Mary Wortley Montagu, whom was a wealthy aristocrat, was one of the eighteenth century's most interesting characters. Few women then were as well educated as her. Every parent wanted their daughter to be charming, not intellectual, so Lady Mary secretly taught herself Latin. When her husband was appointed ambassador to Turkey, she and he traveled there together. Her letters to friends in London, which were later published, were filled with detail. She described a

Turkish bath's atmosphere so vividly that it became a popular setting for paintings and literature. She also learned that smallpox was rare in Turkey. Of the Turkish people she met, most had gotten his or her immunity to smallpox from a kind of inoculation. This had an effect on Lady Mary herself. Lady Mary's children were among the first British citizens who were inoculated against it.

8   Shifts and Mixed Constructions

A **shift** is a sudden, unexpected change in point of view, verb tense, voice, mood, or level of diction that may confuse your readers. Shifting from a direct to an indirect question or quotation can also confuse readers. A **mixed construction** is a sentence containing parts that do not sensibly fit together. This chapter will help you identify and correct shifts and mixed constructions in your sentences.

Shifts

8a Refer to yourself, your audience, and the people you are writing about in a consistent way.

Person shows the writer's point of view. Personal pronouns indicate whether the subject is the speaker (first person: *I, we*), the person spoken to (second person: *you*), or the person or thing spoken about (third person: *he, she, it, they, one*). (For more on person, see 1b and Chapter 5, p. 106.)

INCONSISTENT	*I* discovered that *you* could touch some of the museum exhibits.
	Notice that the writer shifts from first-person *I* to the second-person *you*.
CONSISTENT	*I* discovered that *I* could touch some of the museum exhibits.
	The writer uses the first-person *I* consistently within the sentence.

- When people study a foreign language, ~~you~~ _{they} also learn about another culture.

8b Maintain consistency in verb tense throughout a paragraph or an essay unless the meaning requires you to change tenses.

INCONSISTENT	The virus *mutated* so quickly that it *develops* a resistance to most vaccines.
	The sentence shifts from past to present.
REVISED	The virus *mutates* so quickly that it *develops* a resistance to most vaccines.

Shifts between the present and past tense are among the most common shifts writers make.

- The city's crime rate continues to drop, but experts disagreed on the reasons.

8c Change verb tense when you want to indicate an actual time change.

Use the present tense for events that occur in the present; use the past tense for events that occurred in the past. When the time changes, be sure to change the tense. Notice the intentional shifts in the following passage (the verbs are in italics).

> Every spring migratory birds *return* to cooler climates to raise their young. This year a pair of bluejays *is occupying* a nest in my yard, and I *spy* on them. The hatchlings *are growing* larger and *developing* feathers. Last spring, robins *built* the nest that the jays now *call* home, and I *watched* them every morning until the young birds *left* home for the last time.

As the events switch from this year (present) to the previous year (past), the writer changes from the present tense (*is occupying*) to the past tense (*built*). (For more on verb tense, see 1c and 27a.)

8d Use a consistent voice.

Needless shifts between the **active voice** and the **passive voice** can disorient readers and create wordy sentences.

In the **active voice**, the subject of the sentence performs the action.

- One group of volunteers ~~was given~~ a placebo, and ~~the researchers~~ treated
  The researchers gave one ~~they~~
  another group with the new drug.

In the **passive voice**, the subject receives the action.

- Drought and windstorms made farming impossible, and many families ~~were~~
  the specter of starvation forced
  ~~forced~~ to leave Oklahoma ~~by the specter of starvation.~~

To change a sentence from the passive voice to the active voice, make the performer of the action the subject of the sentence. The original subject of the sentence becomes the direct object. Delete the form of the verb *be*.

PASSIVE   The restraining order was signed by the judge.

ACTIVE   The judge signed the restraining order.

For more on voice, see 1c and 6d.

8e Avoid sudden shifts from indirect to direct questions or quotations.

An indirect question tells what a question is or was.

INDIRECT QUESTION   The defense attorney asked where I was on the evening of May 10.

DIRECT QUESTION   "Where were you on the evening of May 10?"

Avoid shifting from direct to indirect questions.

■ Sal asked what ^he^ could ~~I~~ do to solve the problem.

8f Use a consistent mood throughout a paragraph or an essay.

Mood indicates whether the sentence states a fact or asks a question (**indicative mood**); gives a command or direction (**imperative mood**); or expresses a condition contrary to fact, a wish, or a suggestion (**subjunctive mood**). The subjunctive mood is also used for hypothetical situations or impossible or unlikely events. (For more on mood, see 1c.)

INCONSISTENT

You shouldn't expect to learn ballroom dancing immediately, and remember that even Fred Astaire had to start somewhere. First, find a qualified instructor. Then, you should not be embarrassed even if everyone else seems more graceful than you are. Finally, keep your goal in mind, and you need to practice, practice, practice.

This paragraph contains shifts between the indicative and imperative moods.

CONSISTENT

Don't expect to learn ballroom dancing immediately, and remember that even Fred Astaire had to start somewhere. First, find a qualified instructor. Then, don't be embarrassed if everyone else seems more graceful than you are. Finally, keep your goal in mind, and practice, practice, practice.

This revised paragraph uses the imperative mood consistently.

8g Use a consistent level of diction.

Your level of diction can range from formal to informal. The level you choose should be appropriate for your audience, your subject matter, and your purpose for writing. As you revise your essays, look for inappropriate shifts in diction, such as from a formal to an informal tone or vice versa.

William H. Whyte's studies of human behavior in public space yielded a number of surprises. Perhaps most unexpected was the revelation that people seem to be drawn toward, rather than driven from, crowded spaces. They tend to congregate near the entrances of stores or on street corners. Plazas and shopping districts crowded with pedestrians attract more pedestrians. For some reason, people seem to *enjoy gathering together in public spaces.* ~~get a charge out of hanging out where lots of other folks are hanging out, too.~~

For academic writing, including class assignments and research papers, use formal language. (For more on levels of diction, see Chapter 10, pp. 206–08.)

EXERCISE 8.1

Correct the shifts in person, verb tense, voice, mood, and level of diction in the following sentences.

■ Experts continue to break new ground in child psychology, and their research. <u>has been studied by many parents.</u>
many parents have studied

1. A new idea about the development of children's personalities had surprised many American psychologists because it challenges widely accepted theories.
2. We wondered whether our professor knew of the new theory and did she agree with it.
3. Personality is believed by some experts to be the result of parental care, but other specialists feel that biology influences personality more strongly.
4. Most parents think you have a major influence on your child's behavior.
5. The new theory suggests that children's peers are a heck of a lot more influential than parents.
6. Peer acceptance is strongly desired by children, and they want to be different from adults.
7. If adults were to think about their childhood experiences, they realize that this idea has merit.
8. Most adults recall that in childhood, your friends' opinions were extremely important to you.
9. The way people behave with family members is often different from the way we act with our friends.
10. Jittery moms and dads would be really, really relieved if this hypothesis were proven.

EXERCISE 8.2

Correct the shifts in person, verb tense, voice, mood, and level of diction in the following paragraph.

■ Some artists long ago used techniques that still ~~surprised~~ modern students of their work.
surprise

   Museum visitors can see paintings by the seventeenth-century Dutch artist Jan Vermeer, but you cannot see how he achieved his remarkable effects. Most of his paintings showed simply furnished household rooms. The people and objects in these rooms seem so real that the paintings resembled photographs. Vermeer's use of perspective and light would also contribute to the paintings' realism. Some art historians believe he used a gizmo called a *camera obscura*. This machine projected an image onto a flat surface so you could draw it. For most experts, Vermeer's possible use of technological aids does not make his totally fabulous results less impressive. It is agreed by art historians that the paintings are masterpieces. Vermeer's paintings are admired even more now than they are in his own lifetime.

Mixed Constructions

8h Make sure clauses and phrases fit together logically.

A **mixed construction** contains phrases or clauses that do not work together logically and that cause confusion in meaning.

> **MIXED**   The fact that the marathon is twenty-six miles, a length that explains why I have never finished it.

> The sentence starts with a subject (*The fact*) followed by a dependent clause (*that the marathon is twenty-six miles*). The sentence needs a predicate to complete the independent clause; instead it includes a noun (*a length*) and another dependent clause (*that explains why I have never finished it*). The independent clause that begins with *The fact* is never completed.

> **REVISED**   The marathon is twenty-six miles long, which is why I have never finished it.
>
> > In the revision, the parts of the sentence work together.

To avoid mixed constructions in your writing, it often helps to check the words that connect clauses and phrases, especially prepositions and conjunctions.

8i Make subjects and predicates consistent.

Faulty predication occurs when a subject does not work grammatically with its predicate.

> **FAULTY**   The most valued trait in an employee is a person who is loyal.
>
> > A person is not a trait.
>
> **REVISED**   The most valued trait in an employee is loyalty.

- Rising health-care costs decrease health insurance ^*the number of people who can afford* for many people.

  Costs do not decrease health insurance.

8j Avoid the constructions *is when* or *is where* or *reason . . . is because.*

> **FAULTY**   Indigestion is when you cannot digest food.
>
> **REVISED**   Indigestion is the inability to digest food.

- Gravitation is ^*the attraction of* ~~where~~ one body ~~is being attracted by~~ ^*for* another.

- ~~The reason~~ I enjoy jogging ~~is~~ because it provides outdoor exercise.

Correct the mixed constructions in the following sentences.

- ~~The reason~~ internships are valuable ~~is~~ because they give students real-world experience.

1. Many interns earn college credit for their work, but they also gain practical experience and important contacts.
2. Surveys showing that college graduates who intern receive higher salary offers than their classmates who do not.
3. The fact that students must be careful, as all internships are not created equal.
4. The most important qualities are an intern with curiosity and a good work ethic.
5. A good internship is when the intern gains knowledge and skills in a professional environment.
6. Some companies provide little guidance that interns do not learn much from the experience.
7. Other companies may use unpaid interns that is free labor instead of hiring full-time employees.
8. The U.S. Department of Labor has strict guidelines that apply to unpaid internships.
9. Companies do not meet these federal requirements, because they must pay minimum wage or face lawsuits.
10. By having these strict federal standards, some worry that companies will eliminate internship programs rather than risk any legal problems.

9   Adjectives and Adverbs

Adjectives and adverbs are powerful. Used appropriately, they can add precision and force to your writing, as the following excerpt demonstrates.

> Seated cross-legged on a brocade pillow, wrapped in burgundy robes, was a short, rotund man with a shiny pate. He looked very old and very tired. Chhongba bowed reverently, spoke briefly to him in the Sherpa tongue, and indicated for us to come forward.
>
> Jon Krakauer, *Into Thin Air*

Adjectives modify nouns or pronouns and indicate which one, what kind, or how many. **Adverbs** modify verbs, adjectives, other adverbs, clauses, or entire sentences and indicate how, when, where, how often, or to what extent. (See also 1d and 1e.)

The two most common errors involving adjectives and adverbs occur when writers use (1) an adjective instead of an adverb (or vice versa) and (2) the wrong form of an adjective or adverb in a comparison. Use the following guidelines to identify and correct these and other common errors in your writing.

9a Use adverbs, not adjectives, to modify verbs, adjectives, or other adverbs.

Although in conversation you may often use adjectives in place of adverbs, you should be careful in your writing to use adverbs to modify verbs, adjectives, or other adverbs.

- Those pants are ~~awful~~ *awfully* expensive.

- The headlights shone ~~bright.~~ *brightly.*

9b Use adjectives, not adverbs, after linking verbs.

Linking verbs, often forms of *be* and other verbs such as *feel, look, make,* and *seem,* express a state of being. A linking verb takes a **subject complement**—a word group that completes or renames the subject of the sentence. Verbs such as *feel* and *look* can also be action verbs. When they function as action verbs in a sentence, they may be modified by an adverb.

If you are not sure whether a word should be an adjective or adverb, determine how it is used in the sentence. If the word modifies a noun, it should be an adjective.

ADJECTIVE   Our *waiter* looked *slow.*

> *Slow* modifies the word *waiter,* a noun. In this sentence, *looked* is a linking verb.

ADVERB   Our waiter *looked slowly* for some menus.

> In this sentence, *looked* is expressing an action and is not a linking verb; *slowly* modifies *looked.*

9c Use *good* and *bad* as adjectives; use *well* and *badly* as adverbs.

- Einstein was not a *good student.*

  The adjective *good* modifies the noun *student.*

- Einstein did not *perform well* in school.

  The adverb *well* modifies the verb *perform.*

- He did ~~bad~~ *badly* in the leading role.

  The adverb *badly* modifies the verb *did.*

When you are describing someone's health, *well* can also function as an adjective.

- The disease was in remission, but the *patients* were not yet *well.*

9d Be careful not to use adjectives such as *real* and *sure* to modify adverbs or other adjectives.

- The produce was crisp and ~~real~~ *really* fresh.

  The adverb *really* modifies the adjective *fresh.*

9e Avoid double negatives.

A sentence with two negative words or phrases contains a **double negative**, which conveys a positive meaning. Do not use two negatives in a sentence unless you want to express a positive meaning (for example, *not uncommon* means "common").

- The company is not doing ~~nothing~~ ^anything^ to promote its incentive plan.

- No one under eighteen ~~can't~~ ^can^ vote in the presidential election.

  POSITIVE MEANING INTENDED

  Athletic sportswear is not uncommon as casual attire.

9f Use the comparative form of adjectives and adverbs to compare two things; use the superlative form to compare three or more things.

Adjectives and adverbs can be used to compare two or more persons, objects, actions, or ideas. The **comparative** form of an adjective or adverb compares two items. The **superlative** form compares three or more items. Use the list below to check the comparative and superlative forms of most regular adjectives and adverbs in your sentences.

	Comparatives	*Superlatives*
One-syllable adjectives and adverbs	Add *-er: colder, faster*	Add *-est: coldest, fastest*
Two-syllable adjectives	Add *-er: greasier**	Add *-est: greasiest**
Adjectives with three or more syllables or adverbs ending in *-ly*	Add *more* in front of the word: *more beautiful, more quickly*	Add *most* in front of the word: *most beautiful, most quickly*

Irregular adjectives and adverbs form their comparative and superlative forms in unpredictable ways, as the following list illustrates.

	Comparative	*Superlative*
Adjectives		
good	better	best
bad	worse	worst
little	less	least
Adverbs		
well	better	best
badly	worse	worst
Words That Function as Adjectives and Adverbs		
many	more	most
some	more	most
much	more	most

---

*To form the comparative and superlative forms of adjectives ending in *-y*, change the *y* to *i* and add *-er* or *-est*.

Do not use comparative or superlative forms with absolute concepts, such as *unique* and *perfect*. Something cannot be more or less unique, for example; it is either unique or not unique.

- This is ~~the most~~ ^a unique solution to the pollution problem.

9g Check your comparisons to be sure they are complete when using comparative and superlative forms.

An incomplete comparison can leave your reader confused about what is being compared.

INCOMPLETE	The Internet works more efficiently.
REVISED	For sending correspondence and documents, the Internet works more efficiently than the postal service.
INCOMPLETE	The catcher sustained the most crippling knee injury.
REVISED	The catcher sustained the most crippling knee injury of his career.

9h Do not use *more* or *most* with the *-er* or *-est* form of an adjective or adverb.

- The hypothesis must be ~~more~~ clearer.

> **EXERCISE 9.1**

Correct any errors involving adjectives and adverbs in the following sentences.

- *Wikipedia* is probably ~~a more~~ ^{the most} popular reference source in the world.

1. The site is an open source, online encyclopedia where anyone can contribute, even if he or she writes bad or inaccurate.
2. *Wikipedia* has many advantages that reflect good upon it as a source.
3. There is not nothing more convenient for getting information real quick.
4. In a way, encyclopedias are more unique because Web sites can grow to include any subject that anyone finds interesting.
5. *Wikipedia* relies heavy on the knowledge and interests of millions of people, rather than on the choices of a small group of experts.
6. The site has some really downsides too.
7. Some of the information on *Wikipedia* can be awful inaccurate.
8. Many teachers and professors don't allow no students to use *Wikipedia* for research.
9. When students rely entire on the site, their papers usually don't get good grades.
10. If they choose to use the site, students should make it more clearer to their professors that they have researched their subjects thorough.

EXERCISE 9.2

Correct any errors involving adjectives and adverbs in the following paragraph. Some sentences may be correct as written.

- Originating in China, *feng shui* is a traditionally art of balancing elements to achieve harmony.

   Feng shui is taken very serious in many Asian societies. Some Hong Kong business executives, for example, will not feel comfortably working in an office until it has been approved by a *feng shui* master. Other people are more interested in *feng shui* for its elegance. A room designed with this idea in mind looks tranquilly. The name *feng shui* means "wind and water," and balancing elements is the more important aspect of the art. Some people believe that this balance brings good luck. Others will admit only that surroundings can have a psychologically effect. It is easier to feel comfortable in a room designed according to *feng shui* principles. The placement of doors, windows, and furnishings contributes to the peaceful effect. Whether *feng shui* is magic or simple great interior design, something about it seems to work.

10 Misplaced and Dangling Modifiers

A **modifier** is a word or group of words that describes, changes, qualifies, or limits the meaning of another word or group of words in a sentence.

- The contestant *smiled delightedly.*

   The adverb *delightedly* modifies the verb *smiled*.

- *Pretending to be surprised, he* greeted the guests.

   The adjective phrase *Pretending to be surprised* modifies the pronoun *he*.

Modifiers that are carefully placed in sentences give your readers a clear picture of the details you want to convey. However, when a sentence contains a **misplaced modifier**, it is hard for the reader to tell which word or group of words the modifier is supposed to be describing.

10a Place modifiers close to the words they describe.

MISPLACED	The mayor *chided* the pedestrians for jaywalking *angrily.*
	The adverb *angrily* should be closer to the verb it modifies, *chided*. Here, the adverb appears to be modifying *jaywalking,* so the sentence is confusing.
REVISED	The mayor *angrily chided* the pedestrians for jaywalking.
MISPLACED	The press *reacted* to the story leaked from the Pentagon *with horror.*
	The adverb phrase *with horror* should explain how the press reacted, not how the story was leaked, so the modifier should be closer to the verb *reacted*.
REVISED	The press *reacted with horror* to the story leaked from the Pentagon.

10b Make sure each modifier clearly modifies only one word or phrase in a sentence.

When a modifier is placed near or next to the word or phrase it modifies, it may also be near another word it could conceivably modify. When a modifier's placement may cause such ambiguity, rewrite the sentence, placing the modifier so that it clearly refers to the word or phrase it is supposed to modify.

UNCLEAR The film's attempt to portray war accurately depicts a survivor's anguish.

Does the film attempt to portray war accurately, or does it accurately depict a survivor's anguish? The following revisions eliminate the uncertainty.

REVISED *In its* ~~The film's~~ attempt to portray war accurately *, the film* depicts a survivor's anguish.

REVISED The *film* ~~film's attempt to portray war~~ accurately depicts a survivor's anguish *in its attempt to portray war realistically.*

10c Revise a dangling modifier by rewriting the sentence.

A **dangling modifier** is a word or phrase that does not modify or refer to anything in a sentence. Instead, it seems to modify something that has been left out of the sentence. A dangling modifier can make the meaning of a sentence unclear, inaccurate, or even comical. Most dangling modifiers appear at the beginning or end of sentences.

DANGLING After singing a thrilling ballad, the crowd surged toward the stage.

This sentence suggests that the crowd sang the ballad.

DANGLING Laying an average of ten eggs a day, the neighboring farmer is proud of his henhouse.

This sentence suggests that the farmer lays eggs.

To revise a sentence with a dangling modifier, follow these steps.
1. Identify the word or words that the modifier is supposed to modify.
2. Revise the sentence to correct the confusion either by changing the modifier into a clause with its own subject and verb or by rewriting the sentence so that the word being modified becomes the subject.

- After *Kelly sang* ~~singing~~ a thrilling ballad, the crowd surged toward the stage.
- Laying an average of ten eggs a day, *his prize chickens give* the neighboring farmer *reason to be* ~~is~~ proud of his henhouse.

EXERCISE 10.1

Correct any misplaced or dangling modifiers in the following sentences.

■ Hoping to get a message from outer space, a huge telescope. ~~has been built.~~
scientists have built

1. Solar systems exist throughout the galaxy like our own.
2. So far, no proof on other planets of the existence of life forms has been found.
3. A tremendously powerful telescope searches distant stars for signs of life in the Caribbean.
4. Astronomers monitor signals coming from other parts of the solar system carefully.
5. Wondering whether humans are alone in the universe, the telescope may provide answers.
6. Most of the signals have been caused by cell phone and satellite interference received so far.
7. While trying to intercept signals from other planets, a signal has also been sent from earth.
8. The message is on its way to other parts of our galaxy, containing information about earth.
9. The message will take twenty thousand years to reach its destination or more.
10. A signal sent to earth similarly would take a long time to reach us.

EXERCISE 10.2

Correct any misplaced or dangling modifiers in the following paragraph. Some sentences may be correct as written.

■ The measurement is now based on atomic vibrations. ~~of one second.~~
of one second

Making sure standard weights and measures are the same all over the world is an important task. To trade internationally, a kilogram in Mexico must weigh the same as a kilogram in Japan. In the past, countries set standards for weighing and measuring individually. One English king declared a yard to be the distance from his nose to his thumb egotistically. Weight was once measured in barleycorns, so unethical merchants soaked barleycorns to make them heavier in water. Today, the metric system is the worldwide standard, and the weight of the U.S. pound is based even on the standard kilogram. In France, a cylinder is the world standard kilogram made of platinum. Securely, this official kilogram is kept in an airtight container. Nevertheless, losing a few billionths of a gram of weight each year, world standards might eventually be affected. Hoping to find a permanent solution, scientists want to base the kilogram measurement on an unchanging natural phenomenon.

USING PUNCTUATION CORRECTLY

11 End Punctuation

The end of a sentence can be marked with a period (.), a question mark (?), or an exclamation point (!).

11a Use a period to mark the end of a sentence that makes a statement, gives an instruction, or includes an indirect question; use periods with most abbreviations.

An **indirect question** is a statement that reports what was asked or is being asked: *He asked where the classroom was.*

Writers seldom omit the period at the end of a sentence that makes a statement or gives directions.

STATEMENT	Amnesty International investigates human-rights violations.
INSTRUCTION	Use as little water as possible during the drought.

Writers sometimes mistake an indirect question for a direct one, however.

- **Most visitors want to know where the dinosaur bones were found?**
    This sentence states what question was asked; it does not ask the question directly.

Many abbreviations use periods (*Mass., Co., St.,*). If you are not sure whether an abbreviation should include periods, check a dictionary.

When an abbreviation that uses periods ends a sentence, an additional period is not needed.

- **My brother works for Apple Computer, Inc./**

Note, however, that the Modern Language Association (MLA) recommends omitting periods in abbreviations that consist of capital letters (*IBM, USA, BC*) but including periods in abbreviations that consist of lowercase letters (*a.m.*).

11b Use a question mark to end a sentence that asks a direct question.

DIRECT QUESTION	Why was the flight delayed?

When a question is also a quotation, the question mark is placed within the quotation marks (see also 15d).

- **"What did she want?"? Marcia asked.**

11c Use an exclamation point to end a sentence that expresses a strong emotion or a forceful command.

- Altering experimental results to make them conform to a hypothesis is never ethical!

Use exclamation points sparingly; they lose their impact when used too frequently.

- Government officials immediately suspected terrorism!

EXERCISE 11.1

Correct any errors in the use of end punctuation marks in the following sentences. Some sentences may be correct as written.

- Is it possible that hemophilia in the Russian czar's family contributed to the Russian Revolution.?

1. When the daughters of Queen Victoria of England, who carried the gene for hemophilia, married royalty in Germany and Russia, those royal families inherited hemophilia as well?
2. The Russian czar's only son and heir to the throne suffered from hemophilia.
3. You might ask if internal bleeding can occur when a hemophiliac receives a bruise?
4. Czar Nicholas and his wife Alexandra often saw their little boy in terrible pain!
5. A phony monk named Rasputin eased the child's pain, but was he a gifted healer or just a con man.

12 Commas

A **comma** (,) is used to separate parts of a sentence from one another. Commas, when used correctly, make your sentences clear and help readers understand your meaning.

12a Use a comma before a coordinating word (*and, but, for, nor, or, so, yet*) that joins two independent clauses.

- The ball flew past the goalie but the score did not count.

- Her dog was enormous so many people found it threatening.

An **independent clause** contains a subject and verb and can stand alone as a sentence.

12b Use a comma to separate three or more items in a series.

A **series** is a list of three or more items—words, phrases, or clauses.

- Dancing, singing, and acting are just a few of her talents.
- Sunflowers grew on the hillsides, along the roads, and in the middle of every pasture.

e macmillanhighered.com/successfulwriting
LearningCurve > Commas

Some writers omit the comma before the coordinating conjunction (such as *and, or*) in a brief series when using a casual or journalistic style. Occasionally this omission can create confusion, so it is better to include the final comma.

CONFUSING	She insured her valuable heirlooms, watches and jewelry.
	Do her heirlooms consist entirely of watches and jewelry, or did she insure three kinds of items?
CLEAR	She insured her valuable heirlooms, watches, and jewelry.

A comma is not used after the last item in a series.

- Aphids, slugs, and beetles can severely damage a crop.

(See also 13c on when to use semicolons to separate items in a series.)

12c Use a comma to separate two or more adjectives that modify the same noun when they are not joined by a coordinating word.

- Rescue workers found the frightened, hungry child.

To be sure a comma is needed, try reversing the two adjectives. If the phrase still sounds correct when the adjectives are reversed, a comma is needed. If the phrase sounds wrong, a comma is not needed.

- The airy, open atrium makes visitors feel at home.

  The phrase *open, airy atrium* sounds right, so a comma is needed.

- Local businesses donated the bright red uniforms.

  The phrase *red, bright uniforms* sounds wrong because *bright* modifies *red uniforms* in the original sentence. A comma is not needed.

12d Use a comma to separate introductory words, phrases, and clauses from the rest of a sentence.

INTRODUCTORY WORD	Above, the sky was a mass of clouds.
	Without the comma, this sentence would be confusing.
INTRODUCTORY PHRASE	At the start of the project, the researchers were optimistic.
INTRODUCTORY CLAUSE	When alcohol was outlawed, many solid citizens broke the law.

Exception: A comma is not needed after a single word or short phrase or clause when there is no possibility of confusion.

- Then a rainbow appeared.

12e Use a comma to set off a nonrestrictive word group from the rest of the sentence.

A **nonrestrictive word group** describes or modifies a word or phrase in a sentence, but it does not change the meaning of the word or phrase. To decide whether a comma is needed, read the sentence without the word group. If the basic meaning is unchanged, a comma is needed.

- Most people either love or hate fruitcake, *which is a traditional holiday dessert.*

  The meaning of *fruitcake* is not changed by the relative clause *which is a traditional holiday dessert,* so the word group is **nonrestrictive** and a comma is needed.

- The child *wearing a tutu* delights in ballet lessons.

  The phrase *wearing a tutu* identifies which child delights in ballet lessons, so the word group is **restrictive**—necessary to explain what the word it modifies means—and a comma is not needed.

12f Use a comma to set off parenthetical expressions.

A **parenthetical expression** provides extra information. It can also be a transitional word or phrase (*however, for example, at the beginning*) that is not essential to the meaning of the sentence.

- *Furthermore*, his essay had not been proofread.
- Islamic countries were, *in fact*, responsible for preserving much classical scientific knowledge.

12g Use commas with dates, addresses, titles, and numbers.

- She graduated on June 8, 2014.

When you give only a month and year, a comma is not needed.

- She graduated in June 2014.

Place a comma after the date when it appears before the end of the sentence.

- The 2014 winter Olympics began on February 7, 2014, in Socci, Russia.

When you give an address within a sentence, do not place a comma between the state and the ZIP code.

- Send the package to PO Box 100, McPherson, Kansas 67460.

Separate a name from a title with a comma.

- The featured speaker was Kate Silverstein, Ph.D.

Use commas in numbers that have more than four digits.

- **Estimates of the number of protesters ranged from 250,000 to 700,000.**

In a number with four digits, the comma is optional: *1500* or *1,500.*

A **direct quotation** gives a person's *exact* words, either spoken or written, set off by quotation marks.

12h Use a comma to separate a direct quotation from the words that explain it.

- **She asked, "What's the score?"**

Place the comma before the closing quotation mark.

- **"Wait and see"∧/ was his infuriating response.**

(See also 15b and 15e.)

12i Use commas to set off the name of someone directly addressed, to set off an echo question, and with a "not" phrase.

DIRECT ADDRESS	"James, answer the question concisely." "Bail has not been granted, your honor."
ECHO QUESTION	More development will require a more expensive infrastructure, won't it?
"NOT" PHRASE	Labor Day, not the autumnal equinox, marks the end of summer for most Americans.

12j Omit unnecessary commas.

As you edit and proofread your papers, watch out for the following common errors in comma usage.

OMIT A COMMA BETWEEN A SUBJECT AND VERB.

┌─── subject ───┐ ┌─ verb ─┐
- **The poet Wilfred Owen / was killed a week before World War I ended.**

A **complement** is a word or group of words that describes or renames a subject or object.

OMIT A COMMA BETWEEN A VERB AND COMPLEMENT.

┌─ verb ─┐ ┌─ complement ─┐
- **The school referendum is considered / very likely to pass.**

OMIT A COMMA BETWEEN AN ADJECTIVE AND THE WORD IT MODIFIES.

adjective   noun modified
- **A growing family needs a large / house.**

OMIT A COMMA BETWEEN TWO VERBS IN A COMPOUND PREDICATE.

compound predicate
- **We sat / and waited for our punishment.**

OMIT A COMMA BETWEEN TWO NOUNS OR PRONOUNS IN A COMPOUND SUBJECT.

 ┌─────── compound subject ───────┐
- Harold Johnson, and Margaret Simpson led the expedition.

OMIT A COMMA BEFORE A COORDINATING WORD JOINING TWO DEPENDENT CLAUSES.

 ┌─ dependent clause ─┐ ┌─ dependent clause ─┐
- The band began to play before we arrived, but after the rain stopped.

OMIT A COMMA AFTER *THAN* IN A COMPARISON.

- The Homestead Act made the cost of land to pioneers less than, the price the government had paid.

OMIT A COMMA AFTER *LIKE* OR *SUCH AS*.

- Direct marketing techniques such as, mass mailings and telephone solicitations can be effective.

OMIT COMMAS APPEARING NEXT TO A QUESTION MARK, AN EXCLAMATION POINT, OR A DASH, OR BEFORE AN OPENING PARENTHESIS.

- "Where have you been?," she would always ask.
- "Stop!," the guard shouted.
- Keep spending to a minimum,—our resources are limited—and throw nothing away.
- Fast food, (which is usually high in fat), is growing in popularity all over the world.

OMIT COMMAS AROUND WORDS THAT RENAME AND RESTRICT ANOTHER WORD BEFORE THEM.

If the words are **restrictive**—necessary to explain what the word they modify means—do not enclose them with commas.

- The man, who brought his car in for transmission work, is a lawyer.

EXERCISE 12.1

Correct any errors in the use of commas in the following sentences. Some sentences may be correct as written.

- After slavery was abolished in New York in 1827, several black settlements were established in what is now New York City.

1. Seneca Village a crowded shantytown on the Upper West Side was the home of many poorer black New Yorkers.
2. The city of New York, bought the land where the Seneca villagers lived.
3. The land became part of Central Park and everyone, who lived there, had to leave in the 1850s.

4. Household items from Seneca Village still turn up in Central Park today and a museum exhibit was recently devoted to life in the long-gone settlement.
5. In present-day Brooklyn, there was once a middle-class black settlement, called Weeksville.
6. James Weeks, an early resident owned much of the land.
7. Another, early, landholder, Sylvanus Smith, was a trustee of the African Free Schools of Brooklyn.
8. His daughter, Susan Smith McKinney-Steward, was born in Weeksville, and was the valedictorian of New York Medical College in 1870.
9. McKinney-Steward became the first, female, African American physician in New York, and the third in the United States.
10. Weeksville was a success story, for some of the houses survived into the twentieth century and have been preserved as historical monuments.

> **EXERCISE 12.2**

Correct any errors in the use of commas in the following paragraph. Some sentences may be correct as written.

■ **In June, 1998, fifty years after Korczak Ziolkowski began sculpting the Crazy Horse monument, the face of Crazy Horse was unveiled.**

A monument to the Lakota Sioux warrior, Crazy Horse, is under construction in the Black Hills of South Dakota. Korczak Ziolkowski a sculptor, who also worked on Mount Rushmore, began the project in 1948. Ziolkowski was born on September 6, 1908,—thirty-one years to the day after Crazy Horse died. A Sioux chief asked Ziolkowski, if he would create a monument to honor Crazy Horse, and other Indian heroes. Ziolkowski designed a sculpture of Crazy Horse on horseback that, when it is completed, will be the largest statue in the world. The sculpture is being shaped from Thunderhead Mountain a six-hundred-foot granite rock. Tons of rock have been blasted, from the mountain. The sculptor died in 1982 but his widow, children, and grandchildren have carried on the work. There has been no government funding so, they have paid for the work entirely with donations and admission fees. By the middle of the twenty-first century the statue should be finished, and will depict the great Sioux hero pointing at the hills he loved.

13   Semicolons

A **semicolon** (;) indicates a stronger pause than a comma but not as strong a pause as a period.

13a Use a semicolon to join two closely related independent clauses.

An **independent clause** contains a subject and a verb and can stand alone as a sentence.

Use a semicolon to join two closely related independent clauses not connected by a coordinating word (*and, but, for, nor, or, so,* or *yet*).

■ **In January and February, sunny days are rare and very short in northern countries; winter depression is common in the north.**

For advice on other ways to join two independent clauses, see Section 4 of the Handbook.

13b Use a semicolon to join two independent clauses linked by a conjunctive adverb or transitional expression.

- The stunt pilot had to eject from the cockpit; nevertheless, he was not injured.

- Mass transit is good for the environment; for example, as many people can fit in a bus as in fifteen cars.

A **conjunctive adverb** is a word (such as *also*, *however*, or *still*) that links two independent clauses.

13c Use semicolons to separate items in a series if commas are used within the items.

Semicolons help prevent confusion in a sentence that contains a series of items with one or more commas within the items.

- Fairy tales inspire children by depicting magical events, which appeal to their imaginations; clever boys and girls, who encourage young readers' problem-solving skills; evil creatures, who provide thrills; and good, heroic adults, who make the childhood world seem safer.

Also use a semicolon to separate a series of independent clauses that contain commas.

- He is stubborn, selfish, and conservative; she is stubborn, combative, and liberal; and no one is surprised that they do not get along.

(See also 12b on when to use commas to separate items in a series.)

13d Do not use a semicolon to introduce a list or to separate a phrase or dependent clause from the rest of the sentence.

- A growing number of companies employ prison inmates for certain jobs; selling magazines, conducting surveys, reserving airplane tickets, and taking telephone orders.

(For more on introducing lists, see 14a.)

- On the other hand; taking risks can bring impressive results.
- I'll always wonder; if things could have been different.

EXERCISE 13.1

Correct any errors in the use of semicolons in the following sentences. Some sentences may be correct as written.

- Myths and stories about vampires have been around for centuries; however, Bram Stoker's 1897 novel *Dracula* is probably the most famous fictional account of these monsters.

  1. In the years since Stoker's novel, vampires have become a movie fixture; in America and throughout the world.

2. Silent versions of the vampire tale include *Les Vampires* (1915), a French film, *Nosferatu* (1921), a German film, and *London After Midnight* (1927), an American film.

3. Actor Bela Lugosi played Count Dracula as more of a romantic figure than a monster in the 1931 film *Dracula*; this depiction provided the standard image of the vampire as a sexy fiend.

4. The vampire tale has several standard traits; yet it remains remarkably versatile.

5. The vampire tale was adapted to the American movie western; for example, in *Billy the Kid vs. Dracula* in 1966.

6. The popular *Blacula* (1972); which recast the vampire as an African prince in 1970s Los Angeles; inspired a series of black-themed "blaxploitation" horror movies.

7. In the 1980s and 1990s, filmmakers used the vampire theme in teen films like *Fright Night* (1985); *The Lost Boys* (1987); and *Buffy the Vampire Slayer* (1992).

8. In the late 1990s, *Buffy the Vampire Slayer* was revived as a popular TV series; starring Sarah Michelle Gellar.

9. Now, the *Twilight* books and films have introduced vampires to a whole new generation of readers and movie goers; who remain fascinated by this ancient character.

10. Perhaps vampires do live forever; if only in books and on screen.

EXERCISE 13.2

Correct any errors in the use of semicolons in the following paragraph. Some sentences may be correct as written.

■ The word *placebo* is Latin for "I will please,"; placebos have long been used in medical experiments.

In medicine, a placebo is a substance; often a sugar pill, that has no medicinal use. Placebos alone cannot cure any medical problem, nevertheless, many patients improve when taking them. Because patients who receive placebos do not know that the pills are useless, they think they are getting help for their condition; and they get better. This strange but true fact—recognized by doctors; pharmacists; and other professionals—is called the placebo effect. Chemically, a placebo does nothing, theoretically, the patient should not respond, but somehow this trick works on many people. The placebo effect is often seen in patients; but it is not widely understood. Since the Middle Ages, people have considered the mind and the body as separate; the placebo effect indicates that this separation may not really exist. The mind can play tricks on the body, for example, the brain produces phantom-limb pain in amputees. Doctors wonder; if the mind can also help to heal the body. If the answer is "yes," then the advances in medical knowledge could be enormous.

14 Colons

You can use a **colon** (:) to introduce a list, an explanation, an example, or a further thought within a sentence. The information following the colon should clarify or offer specifics about the information that comes before it.

14a Use a colon to introduce a list or a series.

When you use a **colon** to introduce a list, make sure the list is preceded by a complete sentence.

- The archaeologists uncovered several items: pieces of pottery, seeds, animal bones, and household tools.
- All students must be immunized against: measles, mumps, and rubella.

common childhood illnesses
^

14b Use a colon to introduce an explanation, an example, or a summary.

- In many ways Hollywood is very predictable: Action movies arrive in the summer, dramas in the fall.
- One tree is particularly famous for its spectacular autumn colors: the sugar maple.
- Disaster relief efforts began all over the country: Volunteers raised forty million dollars.

Note: If the group of words following a colon is a complete sentence, the first word can begin with either a capital or a lowercase letter. Whichever option you choose, be consistent throughout your paper.

14c Use a colon to introduce a word or phrase that renames another noun.

- A hushed group of tourists stared at the most famous statue in Florence: Michelangelo's *David*.

14d Use a colon to introduce a lengthy or heavily punctuated quotation.

A quotation that is more than one or two lines long or that contains two or more commas can be introduced by a colon.

- Without pausing for breath, his campaign manager intoned the introduction: "Ladies and gentlemen, today it is my very great privilege to introduce to you the person on whose behalf you have all worked so tirelessly and with such impressive results, the man who is the reason we are all here today—the next president of the United States."
- The instructions were confusing: "After adjusting toggles A, B, and C, connect bracket A to post A, bracket B to post B, and bracket C to post C, securing with clamps A, B, and C, as illustrated in figure 1."

14e Use a colon to separate hours and minutes, in salutations for business letters, between titles and subtitles, and in ratios.

HOURS AND MINUTES	9:15 a.m.
SALUTATIONS	Dear Professor Sung:
TITLES AND SUBTITLES	*American Sphinx: The Character of Thomas Jefferson*
RATIOS	7:1

14f Use a colon only at the end of an independent clause.

An **independent clause** contains a subject and a verb and can stand alone as a sentence.

A colon should always follow an independent clause, which could stand on its own as a complete sentence. Do not use a colon between a verb and its object; between a preposition and its object; or before a list introduced by such words as *for example, including, is,* and *such as.*

- **A medieval map is hard to read: The top of the map points to the east, not the north.**

  A medieval map is hard to read is an independent clause.
- **Even a small garden can produce: beans, squash, tomatoes, and corn.**
- **My cat had hidden a ball of twine under: the sofa.**
- **Bird-watchers are thrilled to spy birds of prey such as: peregrine falcons, red-tailed hawks, and owls.**

> ### EXERCISE 14.1

Correct any errors in the use of colons in the following sentences. Some sentences may be correct as written.

- **Young, impeccably dressed couples participated in the latest craze: swing dancing.**
  ^

1. The shuttle launch is scheduled for precisely 10.00 a.m.
2. The proposed zoning change was defeated by a margin of 2/1.
3. On early rap records, listeners heard percussion from unusual sources such as: turntables, microphones, and synthesizers.
4. To find out whether a film is historically accurate, consult *Past Imperfect: History According to the Movies.*
5. He believes that the most American of all sports is: baseball.
6. As the entourage rushed past, the star's press agent snapped her orders: "No questions, no photos, no comment, no kidding!"
7. Travel advisories are in effect for the following areas, the northern Rocky Mountains and the upper Great Plains.
8. The neon lights gleamed: above stores and in diner windows.
9. We were not hungry, we had just eaten lunch an hour earlier.
10. Some music historians claim that the American songwriting tradition reached its peak in: the 1930s.

15 Quotation Marks

Quotation marks (" ") are used to indicate **direct quotations** or to mark words used as words in your sentences. Quotation marks are always used in pairs. The opening quotation mark (") appears at the beginning of a word or quoted passage, and the closing mark (") appears at the end.

A **direct quotation** gives a person's *exact* words, either spoken or written, set off by quotation marks.

15a Place quotation marks around direct statements from other speakers or writers.

Be careful to include the *exact* words of the speaker or writer within the quotation marks.

- Lincoln recalled that the United States was "dedicated to the proposition that
  all men are created equal. "

  Because *dedicated to the proposition that all men are created equal* repeats Lincoln's exact words, quotation marks are required.

- Lincoln recalled that the United States was "dedicated to the idea that all men
  are created equal."

  proposition

  Words in quotation marks must be quoted *exactly* as they appear in the original source.

In dialogue, place quotation marks around each speaker's words. Every time a different person speaks, begin a new paragraph.

> He said, "Sit down."
> "No, thank you," I replied.

With longer passages, indent prose quotations of more than four lines and verse quotations of more than three lines if you are following MLA style; do not use quotation marks. Indent the quotation ten spaces or one inch from the left margin. When you quote a poem, follow the line breaks exactly.

> In "A Letter to Her Husband, Absent upon Public Employment," Ann Bradstreet poignantly longs for him to return:
>
> > My chilled limbs now numbed lie forlorn;
> >
> > Return, return, sweet Sol, from Capricorn;
> >
> > In this dead time, alas, what can I more
> >
> > Than view those fruits which through thy heat I bore?
> >
> > Which sweet contentment yield me for a space,
> >
> > True living pictures of their father's face. (11–16)

Note: If you are following APA style, indent quotations of forty or more words five spaces from the left margin. For more on the MLA and APA styles of documentation, see Chapter 23 (pages 616–49).

792   QUOTATION MARKS
PUNCTUATION   " "
15F

15b **Place a comma or period that follows a direct quotation _within_ the quotation marks.**

- "Play it, Sam," Rick tells the piano player in _Casablanca_.
- Willie Sutton robbed banks because "that's where the money is."

15c **Place colons and semicolons _outside_ of quotation marks.**

- The marching band played "Seventy-Six Trombones"; the drum major's favorite song.
- A new national anthem should replace "The Star-Spangled Banner"; no one can sing that song.

15d **Place question marks and exclamation points according to the meaning of the sentence.**

If the quotation is a question or exclamation, place the question mark or exclamation point _within_ the closing quotation mark. If the punctuation mark comes at the end of a sentence, no other end punctuation is needed.

- "How does the bridge stand up?" the child wondered.

- Poe's insane narrator confesses, "It is the beating of his hideous heart"!

If the entire sentence, of which the quotation is part, is a question or exclamation, the question mark or exclamation point goes _outside_ the closing quotation marks at the end of the sentence.

- Was Scarlett O'Hara serious when she said, "Tomorrow is another day"?

15e **Use a comma to separate a short quotation from an introductory or identifying phrase such as _he replied_ or _she said_.**

- "Video games improve eye-hand coordination," he replied.

- "The homeless population," she reported, "grew steadily throughout the 1980s."

15f **Use single quotation marks (' ') to indicate a quotation or a title within a quotation.**

- The mysterious caller repeatedly insists, "Play 'Misty' for me."

15g Place quotation marks around the titles of short works.

SECTION OF A BOOK	Chapter 1, "Ozzie and Harriet in Spanish Harlem"
POEM	"Ode on a Grecian Urn"
SHORT STORY	"The Yellow Wallpaper"
ESSAY OR ARTICLE	"Their Malcolm, My Problem"
SONG	"Bad Romana"
EPISODE OF A TELEVISION PROGRAM	"Larry's Last Goodbye"

15h Do not use quotation marks to call unnecessary attention to words or phrases.

- **The manager who was originally in charge of the project "jumped ship" before the deadline.**

Quotation marks can be used to mark words used as words (as an alternative to italics).

- **The word "receive" is often misspelled.**

EXERCISE 15.1

Correct any errors in the use of quotation marks in the following sentences. Some sentences may be correct as written.

- **The hotel has an excellent restaurant specializing in "fresh" fish.**

1. Her essay was entitled, " "To Be or Not to Be": Shakespeare and Existentialism."
2. Why did the professor assign "To an Athlete Dying Young?"
3. A movie line many teenagers imitated was "Hasta la vista, baby".
4. After September 11, 2001, President Bush said he was going to "fight terror".
5. "I have a dream," Martin Luther King Jr. told the civil rights marchers.
6. Come live with me and be my love, pleads the speaker in Marlowe's poem.
7. The grand jury was not "completely" convinced of the need for a trial.
8. It turned out that the pianist could play only Chopsticks.
9. O'Brien originally published the chapter called "Speaking of Courage" as a short story.
10. Our waitress announced, "The special is prime rib;" unfortunately, we are vegetarians.

16 Ellipsis Marks

An ellipsis mark (. . .) is written as three equally spaced periods. It is used within a direct quotation to indicate where you have left out part of the original quotation. You use an **ellipsis mark** to shorten a quotation so that it includes just the parts you want or need to quote.

ORIGINAL QUOTATION	"The prison, a high percentage of whose inmates are serving life sentences, looked surprisingly ordinary."
SHORTENED	"The prison . . . looked surprisingly ordinary."
	Notice that the two commas were also omitted when the quotation was shortened.

However, when you shorten a quotation, be careful not to change the meaning of the original passage. Do not omit any parts that will alter or misrepresent the writer's intended meaning.

ORIGINAL	"Magicians create illusions, but sometimes audience members want to believe that magic is real."
MEANING ALTERED	"Magicians . . . want to believe that magic is real."

When you omit the last part of a quoted sentence, add a sentence period, for a total of four periods (a period plus the ellipsis mark).

ORIGINAL QUOTATION	"In the sphere of psychology, details are also the thing. God preserve us from commonplaces. Best of all is to avoid depicting the hero's state of mind; you ought to try to make it clear from the hero's actions. It is not necessary to portray many characters. The center of gravity should be in two persons: him and her."
	Anton Chekhov, Letter to Alexander P. Chekhov
SHORTENED	"God preserve us from commonplaces. Best of all is to avoid depicting the hero's state of mind. . . . It is not necessary to portray many characters. The center of gravity should be in two persons: him and her."

An ellipsis mark is not needed to indicate that the quoted passage continues after the sentence ends.

- He is modest about his contributions to the abolitionist cause: "I could do but little; but what I could, I did with a joyful heart⌢." (Douglass 54).

Do not use an ellipsis mark at the beginning of a quotation, even though there is material in the original that comes before it.

ORIGINAL QUOTATION	"As was the case after the recent cleaning of the Sistine Chapel, the makeover of the starry ceiling in Grand Central Station has revealed surprisingly brilliant color."
SHORTENED	"[T]he makeover of the starry ceiling in Grand Central Station has revealed surprisingly brilliant color."

Note: The first word of a quoted sentence should be capitalized. If you change from a lowercase to a capital letter, enclose the letter in brackets (see 18d). (For more on MLA style for ellipsis marks, see Chapter 24, p. 611.)

EXERCISE 16.1

Shorten each of the following quotations by omitting the underlined portion and adding an ellipsis mark where appropriate.

■ "Some people who call themselves vegetarians still eat ~~less cuddly creatures such as~~ chicken and fish."

1. "The structure of DNA, <u>as Watson and Crick discovered</u>, is a double helix."
2. "<u>Although African Americans had won Academy Awards before</u>, Halle Berry was the first African American woman to win the Academy Award for Best Actress."
3. Hamlet muses, "To be or not to be, <u>that is the question</u>."
4. "<u>Many Americans do not realize that</u> people of all classes receive financial help from the government."
5. "Cole Porter cultivated a suave, sophisticated urban persona <u>even though he came from a small town in Indiana</u>."
6. "<u>From an anthropological perspective</u>, Zora Neale Hurston's collections of folklore proved to be valuable."
7. "<u>We take modern conveniences for granted today</u>, <u>but</u> two hundred years ago households <u>even</u> had to make their own soap."
8. "Folic acid, <u>doctors now believe</u>, can help prevent certain birth defects."
9. "<u>Although</u> saltwater aquariums <u>are beautiful</u>, <u>they</u> are difficult and expensive to maintain."
10. "She wrote rather doubtful grammar sometimes, and in her verses took <u>all sorts of</u> liberties with the metre" (Thackeray 136–37).

17 Apostrophes

An **apostrophe** (') has three functions: to show ownership or possession, to indicate omitted letters in contractions, and to form some plurals.

17a Use an apostrophe to indicate possession or ownership.

Add -'s to make a singular noun possessive, including nouns that end with s or the sound of s and **indefinite pronouns** (*anyone, nobody*).

- The *fox's* prey led it across the field.
- Whether she can win the nomination is *anybody's* guess.

Note that the possessive forms of personal pronouns do not take apostrophes: *mine, yours, his, hers, ours, theirs, its.*

- Each bee has it's function in the hive.

The possessive form of *who* is *whose* (not *who's*).

- Marie Curie, *whose* work in chemistry made history, discovered radium.

Add an apostrophe to a plural noun to make it possessive, or add -'s if the plural noun does not end in s.

- Both *farms'* crops were lost in the flood.
- Our *children's* children will reap the benefits of our efforts to preserve the environment today.

To show individual possession by two or more people or groups, add an apostrophe or -'s to each noun.

- Sam is equipment manager for both the *boys'* and the *girls'* basketball teams.
  Sam works for two different teams.

To show joint possession by two people or groups, add an apostrophe or -'s to the last noun.

- The *coaches and players'* dream came true at the end of the season.

Add -'s to the last word of a compound noun to show possession.

- My *father-in-law's* boat needs a new engine.
- We were ushered into the *chairman of the department's* office.

An **indefinite pronoun** does not refer to a specific person, place, or object. It refers to people, places, or things in general (*anywhere, everyone, everything*).

17b   Use an apostrophe to indicate the omitted letter or letters in a contraction.

- *I've* [I have] seen the answers.
- Jason *didn't* [did not] arrive last night.

17c   Use an apostrophe to form the plural of a number, letter, symbol, abbreviation, or word treated as a word.

- There are three *5*'s on the license plate.
- She spells her name with two *C*'s.
- The *?*'s stand for unknown quantities.
- Using two *etc.*'s is unnecessary.
- Replace all *can*'s in the contract with *cannot*'s.

In the sentences above, note that numbers, letters, and words used as themselves are in italics. The *-s* ending should not be italicized, however. (For more on italics and underlining, see Section 23.)

When referring to the years in a decade, no apostrophe is used.

- The fashions of the 1970s returned in the 1990s.

Apostrophes are used to signal the omission of the numerals that indicate the century.

     the class of '03   music of the '90s

17d   Avoid using apostrophes to form plurals and to form possessives for personal pronouns.

- The trapper̶'̶s came to town to trade.
- She paid for my lunch as well as her̶'̶s.

EXERCISE 17.1

Correct the errors in the use of apostrophes in the following sentences. Some sentences may be correct as written.

- As newer forms of communication like Twitter, Facebook, and text messaging take over our lives, we should ask whether we're becoming more connected or less connected with other people.

1. Our's is a society almost too willing to share.
2. We probably know more about the day-to-day lives of other's than ever before, as the details of our many friend's days are recorded in online status report's.
3. Its unclear, however, whether anyone is truly benefiting from all this sharing of private information, even as the various social networking sites privacy settings reveal more and more about user's.
4. Todays parents' can find out about their sons and daughters personal live's online, but they have less face-to face contact with their children.
5. Of course, theyll have to figure out the meaning of all the LOLs', BTWs, and other shorthand slang in their kids online and text messages.

18 Parentheses and Brackets

Parentheses

Parentheses—( )—are used to separate nonessential information from the rest of a sentence or paragraph.

18a Use parentheses to add words, phrases, or sentences that expand on, clarify, or explain material that precedes or follows.

- The EPA (Environmental Protection Agency) is responsible for developing water-pollution standards.
- The application fee for the four-day workshop (a total of $500, including the registration fee) is due Friday.

Be sure to use parentheses sparingly; they can clutter your writing.

18b Use parentheses to insert dates or abbreviations.

- Elizabeth Cady Stanton (1815–1902) helped organize the first American women's rights convention.
- Guidelines for documenting research papers in the humanities are published by the Modern Language Association (MLA).

18c Check the placement of other punctuation used with parentheses.

Parenthetical information that appears at the end of a sentence should be inserted before the period that ends the sentence.

- Ballroom dancing has become popular in the United States (probably because of the success of *Dancing with the Stars*).

When parenthetical information appears after a word that would be followed by a comma, the comma is always placed after the closing parenthesis.

- He called when his plane landed (or so he said), but no one answered.

When a complete sentence appears within parentheses, punctuate the sentence as you would normally.

- Timber companies propose various uses for national forests. (Public land can be leased for commercial purposes.)

Exception: If the material within the parentheses is a question, it should end with a question mark.

- A few innocent-looking plants (have you heard of the Venus flytrap?) capture and eat insects and animals.

Brackets

Brackets ([ ]) are used within quotations and within parentheses.

18d Use brackets to add information or indicate changes you have made to a quotation.

- Whitman's preface argued, "Here [the United States] is not merely a nation but a teeming nation of nations."

  The explanation tells where *here* is.

- "Along came a spider and sat down beside [Miss Muffett]," who apparently suffered from a phobia.

  The bracketed name replaces *her* in the original.

Use brackets to enclose the word *sic* when signaling an error in original quoted material.

- The incumbent's letter to the editor announced, "My opponant's [sic] claims regarding my record are simply not true."

The Latin word *sic* lets your readers know that the misspelled word or other error in the quoted material is the original author's error, not yours.

18e Use brackets to enclose parenthetical material in a group of words already enclosed in parentheses.

- The demonstrators (including members of the National Rifle Association [NRA]) crowded around the candidate.

EXERCISE 18.1

Correct the errors in the use of parentheses or brackets in the following sentences. Some sentences may be correct as written.

- Typhoid Mary would probably not have infected so many victims if she had stopped working (she was a cook.).

1. Nathan Hale regretted that he had "but one life to give for (his) country."
2. The Committee for Scientific Investigation of Claims of the Paranormal (CSICOP) tests claims of supernatural abilities.
3. Malcolm X [1925–1965] was an American political figure assassinated in the 1960s.
4. The invention of anesthesia made possible many advances in medicine (including lengthy surgery.)
5. Children believe what they see on television, (at least most of it) and therefore parents should monitor their children's viewing.

19 Dashes

Use a **dash** (—) to separate parts of a sentence. A dash suggests a stronger separation than a comma, colon, or semicolon does. To type a dash, hit the hyphen key twice (--), with no spaces before, between, or after the hyphens. Some word-processing programs automatically convert the two hyphens to a dash (—).

19a Use a dash or dashes to emphasize a sudden shift or break in thought or mood.

- Computers have given the world instant communication—and electronic junk mail.

19b Use a dash or dashes to introduce an explanation, an example, or items in a series.

- The tattoo artist had completed a large body of work—Fred's!
- The tattoo artist had seen everything—a full-size bear claw on a back, bleeding heart on a bicep, even an Irish cross on the tip of a nose.

When the added thought appears in the middle of a sentence, use two dashes to set it off.

- The tattoo artist—who would prefer to remain nameless—thinks tattoos are a waste of money.

19c Use dashes sparingly.

Dashes are emphatic. Do not overuse them, or they will lose their effectiveness. Also be careful not to use a dash as a substitute for a **conjunction** or transition.

A **conjunction** is a word or words used to connect clauses, phrases, or individual words.

- Einstein's job in Switzerland was dull $\overset{but}{\diagup}$ it offered him plenty of time to think $\overset{while\ working\ there}{\diagup}$ he came up with the theory of relativity.

> **EXERCISE 19.1**

Add a dash or pair of dashes where they might be effective, and correct any errors in the use of dashes in the following sentences.

- Food $\diagup$ who eats what and why? $\diagup$ is now a subject studied by academics.

1. One issue particularly concerns scholars of food; why are certain foods acceptable in some cultures but not in others?
2. Some foods were once popular, but today—hardly anyone has heard of them.
3. In the 1990s, people in Great Britain were alerted to a new danger, mad cow disease.
4. In the 1960s, frozen foods—icy blocks of corn, peas, and string beans—were popular—and convenient—alternatives to fresh produce.
5. Today fresh fruits and vegetables are valued once again, unless a busy cook has no time for peeling and chopping.

MANAGING MECHANICS AND SPELLING

20 Capitalization

Capitalize the first word of a sentence, **proper nouns**, and the pronoun *I*.

A **proper noun** names a particular person, place, thing, or group.

20a Capitalize the first word in a sentence and in a direct quotation.

- ~~r~~evision is important.
  R

Capitalize the first word in a direct quotation unless it is incorporated into your own sentence or it continues an earlier quotation.

- The union representative said, "~~t~~hat meeting did not take place."
  T

- Sam Verdon complained that "~~N~~o one takes college athletes seriously."
  n

- "I prefer not to interpret my paintings," replied the famous watercolorist, "~~B~~ecause they should speak for themselves."
  b

20b Capitalize proper nouns, including the names of specific people, places, things, and groups.

PEOPLE AND ANIMALS	Franklin Roosevelt, his dog Fala
CITIES, STATWES, NATIONS	St. Paul, Minnesota, the United States
GEOGRAPHIC REGIONS	the Gulf Coast, the U.S. Southwest
GOVERNMENT OFFICES, DEPARTMENTS, BUILDINGS	the Pentagon, the Supreme Court, the Puck Building
ORGANIZATIONS (CULTURAL, POLITICAL, ETC.)	League of Women Voters, National Basketball Association
MONTHS, DAYS, HOLIDAYS	February, Thursday, Labor Day
CHAPTER OR SECTION TITLES IN BOOKS	"Why America Has Changed"
NATIONALITIES AND LANGUAGES	Ethiopian, Dutch
RELIGIONS AND SACRED BOOKS	Judaism, the Koran
TRADE NAMES	Coca-Cola, Brillo
HISTORIC EVENTS	the Treaty of Versailles, Reconstruction
SPECIFIC COURSE TITLES	Organic Chemistry 101

20c Do not capitalize common nouns.

FAMILY MEMBERS	my uncle, his father
GENERAL AREAS OF THE COUNTRY	southwestern United States
SUBJECTS	my chemistry class
CENTURIES	seventeenth-century England
GEOGRAPHICAL AREAS	the lake in the park

20d Capitalize the titles of literary and other works, such as books, articles, poems, plays, songs, films, and paintings.

Capitalize the first and last words of the title, the first word following a colon, and all other words except **articles**, **coordinating conjunctions**, and **prepositions**.

BOOK	*The Fault in Our Stars*
ARTICLE	"Making History at Madison Park"
POEM	"Aunt Jennifer's Tigers"
PLAY	*A Raisin in the Sun*
SONG	"Rolling in the Deep"
FILM	*Gone Girl*
PAINTING	*The Starry Night*

Articles are the words *a, an,* and *the.*

Coordinating conjunctions (*and, but, for, nor, or, so, yet*) connect sentence elements that are of equal importance.

Prepositions (such as *before, on,* and *to*) are used before a noun or pronoun to indicate time, place, space, direction, position, or some other relationship.

20e Capitalize a personal title only when it directly precedes a person's name.

- Vice President Maria Washington briefed the stockholders.
- Maria Washington was hired from a rival company to be the new vice president.

It is acceptable to capitalize the titles of certain high government officials regardless of whether they precede a name: *the President of the United States.*

> **EXERCISE 20.1**

Correct the capitalization errors in the following paragraph.

- The united nations meets at its headquarters in New York City.

During world war II, the governments of twenty-six countries pledged their willingness to continue fighting on behalf of the Allies. United States president Franklin Roosevelt came up with a name for the group: the united nations. The "Declaration By United Nations" promised the support of those twenty-six governments for the war effort. The Nations signed this document on New Year's day of 1942. By 1945, the number of countries involved in the united nations had grown to fifty-one. From April through June of that year, fifty Representatives attended the united nations Conference on International Organization in San Francisco. There, the Nations debated the contents of a charter. Although the War was nearing an end, the governments foresaw a need to continue international cooperation. The charter was ratified on October 24, 1945, by China, France, The Soviet Union, The United Kingdom, The United States, and a majority of the other Nations. Every year since then, October 24 has been known as united nations day.

21 Abbreviations

Abbreviations are shortened forms of words and phrases. It is acceptable to use abbreviations for some personal titles, names of organizations, time references, and Latin expressions. Most abbreviations use periods, but those composed of all capital letters often do not.

21a Abbreviate titles before and after a person's name.

Ms. Susan Orlean	Arthur Rodriguez, M.D.
St. Mary	Bill Cosby, Ph.D.
Dr. Gregory House	Martin Luther King Jr.

21b Abbreviate names of familiar organizations, corporations, and countries.

Use common abbreviations such as *PBS, CIA,* and *HIV* when you are certain that your readers will recognize them.

ABC	FBI	NATO
UNICEF	USA	DVD

21c Abbreviate time references that precede or follow a number.

- The meeting will begin at 10:15 a.m. and end at 12 p.m.
- The statues were carved in about 300 BCE.

    The letters *BCE* stand for "before the common era." An alternative is *BC* ("before Christ").

- Alfred became king in AD 871.

    The letters *AD* stand for the Latin term *anno Domini* and precede the date. The alternative *CE* ("common era") follows the date.

21d Use common abbreviations for Latin terms in parentheses, footnotes, or references.

It is acceptable to use abbreviations for Latin terms in parenthetical comments as well as in source notes or citations. Avoid using these abbreviations outside of parentheses in the text of your essay; use the English equivalent instead.

e.g.	for example
et al.	and others
etc.	and so forth
i.e.	that is
vs. *or* v.	versus

- Edison invented the lightbulb, the motion picture camera, ^such items as^ sound recording devices, ^and^ etc.

21e Do not abbreviate certain words and phrases when they are used in sentences.

Some abbreviations that are acceptable in scientific or technical writing should be spelled out in most other kinds of writing.

UNITS OF MEASUREMENT	ten inches [*not* ten in.]
PARTS OF WRITTEN WORKS	chapter 6 [*not* ch. 6]
DAYS, MONTHS, AND HOLIDAYS	Thursday [*not* Thurs.]
NAMES OF SUBJECT AREAS	biology [*not* bio]
PERSONAL TITLES USED WITHOUT A PROPER NAME	doctor [*not* Dr.]
GEOGRAPHICAL OR PLACE NAMES	I live in New York City [*not* N.Y.C.]. (*Exceptions: Washington, D.C.; U.S.* when it is used as an adjective, as in *U.S. Senate*)

EXERCISE 21.1

Correct the misused abbreviations in the following sentences.

■ Students of ~~poli sci~~ *political science* know that public opinion often moves in cycles.

1. According to Washington Irving's story, Rip van Winkle fell asleep in the Catskill Mts. for twenty years.
2. The average American woman is five ft. four in. tall.
3. Since it is only ninety pp. long, the text is really a novella, not a novel.
4. The Great Depression began with the stock-market crash on Black Mon.
5. The Coen brothers have a reputation for creating unorthodox films: e.g., *Fargo* and *Inside Llewyn Davis.*

22   Numbers

As a general rule, use numbers according to the rules of your field of study. Be sure to represent numbers as numerals or as words consistently.

22a Spell out numbers that begin sentences.

■ *Two hundred ten* ~~210~~ students attended the lecture.

22b Spell out numbers that can be written in one or two words.

twenty-six checks   two hundred women
sixty students   one thousand pretzels

Use numerals for numbers that cannot be spelled out in one or two words.

- There are ~~three hundred seventy-five~~ ^375^ students enrolled this fall.

Use numerals for all numbers in a sentence if one of the numbers needs to be written in numerals.

- Of the 420 students in my school, only ~~twenty-eight~~ ^28^ have a driver's license.

When two numbers appear in succession, spell out one and use numerals for the other.

- Each counselor is in charge of nine ~~three~~ ^3^-year-olds.

22c Use numerals according to convention.

DATES	August 10, 2008; the 1990s
DECIMALS, PERCENTAGES, FRACTIONS	56.7, 50% *or* 50 percent, 1¾ cups
EXACT TIMES	9:27 a.m.
PAGES, CHAPTERS, VOLUMES	page 27, chapter 12, volume 4
ADDRESSES	122 Peach Street
EXACT AMOUNTS OF MONEY	$5.60, $1.3 million
SCORES AND STATISTICS	23–6 victory, a factor of 12

EXERCISE 22.1

Correct the errors in the use of numbers in the following sentences. Some sentences may be correct as written.

- The quotation you're looking for is on page ~~seventy-seven~~ ^77^.

1. 77% of those responding to the poll favored increased taxes on cigarettes.
2. The estimated cost was too low by eighty-seven dollars and fourteen cents.
3. Each window is composed of 100s of small pieces of colored glass.
4. All traffic stopped as a 90-car train went slowly past.
5. February twenty-two is George Washington's birthday, but Presidents' Day is always celebrated on a Monday.

23 Italics and Underlining

Italic or *slanted type* is used for emphasizing particular words or phrases. It is also used to set off titles of longer works, names of vehicles, non-English words, and words deserving special emphasis.

When writing by hand or using a typewriter, use <u>underlining</u> to indicate italics. Most word-processing programs provide italic type, and most style guides used for college writing, such as the *MLA Handbook for Writers of Research Papers* and the *Publication Manual of the American Psychological Association* (APA), require it.

23a Italicize or underline titles of works published separately.

BOOKS	*Great Expectations*
PLAYS AND MUSICALS	*Rent*
LONG POEMS	*The Iliad*
MAGAZINES AND JOURNALS	*Entertainment Weekly;* the *New York Review of Books*
NEWSPAPERS	the *Columbus Dispatch*
MOVIES AND DVDS	*The Twilight Saga: Eclipse*
LONG MUSICAL WORKS, RECORDINGS	*Exile on Main St.*
TELEVISION AND RADIO SERIES	*Jersey Shore*
VISUAL WORKS OF ART (PAINTINGS, SCULPTURES)	*Birth of Venus*

The titles of shorter works, such as the titles of articles, short stories, and songs, should be enclosed in quotation marks (see 15g).

23b Italicize or underline the names of ships, trains, aircraft, and spacecraft.

Titanic   *Spirit of St. Louis*
Orient Express   space shuttle *Challenger*

23c Italicize or underline non-English words not in everyday use.

Words from other languages should be italicized unless they have become a part of the English language, such as "chic" or "burrito." If you are unsure, check an English dictionary. If the word is not listed, it should be italicized.

- Our instructor lectured on the technique of *Verstehen.*
- Tacos are now as much a part of American cuisine as pizza.

23d Italicize or underline numbers, letters, words, or phrases called out for special emphasis.

Use italics for numbers, letters, or words used as terms.

- Every bottle has *33* on the label.
- Hester Prynne is forced to wear a scarlet *A.*
- Today, *ain't* is listed in most dictionaries.

Italicize a word or phrase that is being defined or emphasized.

- *Alliteration*—the same sounds repeated at the beginning of each word in a group—can be an effective literary device.

Use italics for emphasis sparingly. When you italicize too many words in a sentence or paragraph, the emphasis is lost.

- The U.S. National Park system is *extremely important* (no italics) because it protects some of the most *beautiful* (no italics) and *unusual* (no italics) parts of this country.

EXERCISE 23.1

Correct the errors in the use of italics in the following sentences. Some sentences may be correct as written.

- Oedipus, written by Sophocles in the fifth century BC, is possibly the most famous play of the classical period.

1. The exchange student greeted everyone with a hearty *"Bonjour!"*
2. His professor insisted that Soap Opera Digest was not an acceptable research source.
3. Cartoons like The Simpsons have become surprisingly popular with adult audiences.
4. The first European settlers at Plymouth arrived on the Mayflower.
5. His book is discussed in depth in the article *Africa: The Hidden History*.

24 Hyphens

A **hyphen** (-) is used to join compound words, to connect parts of words, and to split words at the end of typewritten lines of text.

24a Use a hyphen to join words that function as a unit.

Some compound nouns and verbs are spelled as one word (*download*), some are spelled as two words (*washing machine*), and some are spelled using hyphens (*foul-up*). Check a dictionary when you are unsure; if you do not find the compound listed in your dictionary, spell it as two words.

Use a hyphen to join words that together modify a noun.

- An *icy-fingered* hand tapped her shoulder.

However, when the first word of the compound ends in *-ly* or when the compound adjective follows the noun it modifies, no hyphen is used.

- The guard found a *clumsily hidden* duplicate key.
- Her voice was *well trained*.

24b Use a hyphen with some prefixes (*all-*, *ex-*, *great-*, *self-*) and suffixes (*-elect*).

- Most Americans' parents, grandparents, or *great-grandparents* came from another country.
- The *governor-elect* made a stirring victory speech.

Use a hyphen for clarity to prevent confusion with certain combinations of prefixes and base words.

- She wants the taxpayers to approve the funding for her ~~recreation~~ of the demolished town hall. ^re-creation^

    Recreation has a different meaning from *re-creation*.

24c Use a hyphen when spelling out fractions and the numbers *twenty-one* to *ninety-nine*, in word-number combinations, and to indicate inclusive numbers.

two-thirds finished   *twenty-two* sources

- The *675-yard* path winds through a landscaped garden.
- Pages *99-102* cover the military campaigns.

24d Use a hyphen between syllables to split a word at the end of a typewritten or handwritten line.

Although most word-processing programs automatically break the line before a long word and move the word to the next line, in typewritten or handwritten text, you should use a hyphen to divide any words that fall at the end of a line. Divide words between syllables; never break a one-syllable word. Divide a compound word between its parts. Words can also be divided between a prefix and root or between a root and suffix. Check your dictionary if you are uncertain about where to break a word.

    Viking invaders failed to conquer Ireland because the country was governed by a number of petty kings rather than by a central authority that could be effectively overthrown; however, by the tenth century this situation began to change.

EXERCISE 24.1

Correct the errors in the use of hyphens in the following sentences. If you are not sure about a word, check your dictionary. Some sentences may be correct as written.

- Does any ~~teen-ager~~ really need liposuction? ^teenager^

1. Adolescents today who are unhappy with their looks can turn to the increasingly-popular option of plastic surgery.
2. For many selfconscious teens and young adults, surgery seems to be the perfect solution.
3. Until recently, very few sixteen year olds considered making permanent surgical changes.

4. But as more adults pay for nose-jobs and tummy tucks, more teens are expressing interest.
5. Are images of people with apparently perfect bodies and faces unduly influencing less-than-perfect young Americans?

25 Spelling

Misspelled words are among the most common errors for many student writers. Be sure to pay attention to spelling as you edit and proofread your papers, and keep a dictionary close at hand. Misspellings can make your paper appear carelessly written. Use the tips in the accompanying box and the basic spelling rules that follow to help improve your spelling.

25a Remember to put *i* before *e* except after *c* or when pronounced as an *a*, as in *neighbor* and *weigh*.

> *i* before *e:* ach*ie*ve, th*ie*f
> except after *c:* conc*ei*ve, rec*ei*ve
> or when pronounced as an *a:* fr*ei*ght, th*ei*r

Memorize the exceptions, such as *either, foreign, height, leisure, neither, seize,* and *weird.*

TIPS FOR IMPROVING YOUR SPELLING

- **Purchase a collegiate dictionary and take the time to look up the correct spellings of unfamiliar words.**

- **Use your word processor's spell-checker function.** Be sure to take advantage of the spell-checker as you edit and proofread your drafts. However, keep in mind that this function will not catch all spelling errors; for example, it cannot detect the incorrect use of *it's* versus *its* or of homonyms such as *there* versus *their* and *weather* versus *whether.* (See 25d for a list of homonyms.)

- **Proofread your drafts for spelling errors.** To avoid being distracted by the flow of ideas in your essays, proofread them backward, from the last word to the first, looking only for misspellings. For words that sound alike but have different spellings (*to/too/two, their/there*), stop to check their use in the sentence and determine whether you have used the correct word.

- **Keep a list of words you commonly misspell.** Whenever you catch spelling errors in a draft or see misspellings marked by your instructor in papers returned to you, add the words to your list. Use your dictionary to locate the correct spelling and pronunciation of each word in the list. Review your list of words periodically, and practice pronouncing and writing the words until you master their correct spellings and usage.

- **Develop a spelling awareness.** As you read and write, pay attention to words and how they are spelled. When you encounter a new word, pronounce it slowly and carefully while taking note of its spelling. Try to create a mental image of each word, especially words with silent letters or unusual spellings.

25b Add -s or -es to form the plural of most nouns.

Singular common nouns ending in *-s, -ch, -sh,* or *-x* form the plural by adding *-es.* Nouns ending in *-o* usually form the plural by adding *-s* when the *-o* follows a vowel or *-es* when the *-o* follows a consonant.

Add -s:	professor, professor*s*	zoo, zoo*s*
Add -es:	sandwich, sandwich*es*	hero, hero*es*

To form the plural of common nouns ending in *-y,* change the *y* to *i* and add *-es* when the *y* is preceded by a consonant. Add only *-s* when the *y* is preceded by a vowel.

story	stor*ies*	day	day*s*
baby	bab*ies*	key	key*s*

Compound nouns form the plural by adding *-s* or *-es* to the most important word or, when all the words are equally important, to the last word of the compound.

mother-in-law	mother*s*-in-law
passerby	passer*s*by
stand-in	stand-in*s*

A **proper noun** names a particular person, place, thing, or group.

Proper nouns form the plural by adding *-s* or *-es* without changing the noun's ending.

Thursday	Thursday*s*
Mr. and Mrs. Jones	the Jones*es*

- The Gunderson's met us for dinner last night.

25c Drop, keep, change, or double the final letter when adding endings to some words.

Drop the silent *e* when adding an ending that begins with a vowel (*a, e, i, o, u*). Keep the silent *e* when adding an ending that begins with a consonant.

hope	hop*ing*	care	care*ful*
force	forc*ing*	encourage	encourage*ment*
advise	advis*able*	love	love*ly*

For words that end in *y,* change the final *y* to *i* before adding an ending when the *y* follows a consonant. Keep the final *y* when the *y* follows a vowel, when the ending is *-ing,* or when *y* ends a proper name.

study	stud*ies*	buy	buy*er*
marry	marr*ied*	marry	marry*ing*
		Fahey	Fahey*s*

Exception: Drop the final *y* whenever you add *-ize.*

| memory | memor*ize* |
| category | categor*ize* |

When adding an ending to one-syllable words, double the final consonant if the ending starts with a vowel and the final consonant follows a single vowel. Do *not* double the consonant when two vowels or a vowel and another consonant precede it.

| hop | hop*ped* | pair | pair*ed* |
| trek | trek*ked* | rent | rent*ed* |

When adding an ending to words with two or more syllables, double the final consonant if a single vowel precedes it and the stress falls on the last syllable.

| transmit | transmit*ted* |
| refer | refer*ral* |

Do *not* double the final consonant when two vowels or a vowel and another consonant precede it.

| react | react*ed* |
| redeem | redeem*ing* |

Do *not* double the final consonant if the ending starts with a consonant.

| commit | commit*ment* |
| regret | regret*fully* |

25d Watch out for homonyms, groups of words that sound the same but are spelled differently.

The following list includes some commonly confused groups of words.

Homonyms	*Examples of Usage*
accept (to take or receive)	Most stores *accept* credit cards.
except (other than)	Everyone has arrived *except* Harry.
affect (to influence)	The new law will *affect* us.
effect (the result, outcome)	The *effect* of the storm was frightening.
allusion (a reference to)	The poem contained an *allusion* to Greek mythology.
illusion (a fantasy)	Josette is under the *illusion* that she is famous.
already (by now)	Marguerite is *already* in class.
all ready (fully prepared)	Geoffrey is *all ready.*

(continued on next page)

Homonyms	Examples of Usage
cite (to refer to)	Be sure to *cite* your sources.
sight (vision, or a tourist attraction)	Her *sight* is failing.
site (a place)	We visited the *site* of the accident.
complement (to complete, a counterpart)	The side dishes *complement* the main course.
compliment (praise)	Allison received numerous *compliments*.
elicit (to bring out)	The film *elicits* an emotional response.
illicit (illegal)	The sale of *illicit* drugs is prohibited on campus.
its (possessive of *it*)	The show has found *its* audience.
it's (contraction of *it is*)	*It's* too late to go back.
lead (verb: to guide or direct)	Professor Hong will *lead* the discussion group.
led (past tense of verb *lead*)	Professor Hong *led* the discussion group.
lead (noun: a heavy metal)	*Lead* poisoning is dangerous.
loose (not securely attached)	The button was *loose*.
lose (to fail to keep)	I often *lose* my keys.
principal (most important, or a head of a school)	The citizens' *principal* concern is educational costs.
principle (a basic rule or truth)	This *principle* should govern all of your actions.
their (possessive of *they*)	The students brought *their* books to class.
there (in that place, opposite of *here*)	*There* is the bus.
they're (contraction of *they are*)	*They're* early.
to (toward)	Please move *to* the front of the class.
too (also, or excessively)	Sal is coming *too*.
two (following *one*)	The *two* speeches were similar.
who's (contraction of *who is*)	*Who's* taking a cab?
whose (possessive of *who*)	*Whose* book is this?
your (possessive of *you*)	*Your* experiment is well designed.
you're (contraction of *you are*)	*You're* passing the course.

25e Watch out for commonly misspelled words.

absence	accuracy	analysis	argument
accept	achievement	analyze	ascend
accessible	acquaintance	apologize	athlete
accidentally	acquire	apparent	attendance
accommodate	amateur	appearance	beginning

believe	excellence	marriage	reference
benefited	exercise	mathematics	referred
boundary	existence	miniature	relieve
Britain	experience	mischievous	repetition
bureaucracy	explanation	necessary	restaurant
business	familiar	niece	rhythm
calendar	fascinate	ninety	ridiculous
cemetery	February	noticeable	roommate
changeable	foreign	occasionally	sacrifice
characteristic	forty	occurrence	schedule
column	fulfill *or* fulfil	omission	secretary
committee	government	originally	seize
conceive	grammar	parallel	separate
conscience	guarantee	particularly	sergeant
conscious	harass	permissible	several
convenience	height	physical	similar
criticism	humorous	picnicking	sincerely
criticize	hypocrisy	pleasant	sophomore
curiosity	imagination	possible	succeed
deceive	immediately	practically	successful
decision	incredible	precede	summary
definitely	inevitable	preference	surprise
descendant	intelligence	prejudice	tendency
disappearance	interest	preparation	thorough
disappoint	irresistible	prevalent	through
disastrous	judgment	privilege	tragedy
discipline	knowledge	probably	truly
efficiency	laboratory	proceed	unanimous
efficient	leisure	professor	usually
eighth	length	pronunciation	vacuum
eligible	library	psychology	vengeance
embarrass	license	quantity	villain
emphasize	lightning	quiet	weird
environment	loneliness	receive	writing
especially	maintenance	recognize	
exaggerate	maneuver	recommend	

25f Be alert for words that are formed from the same root (they may
have different spellings) and for words with silent letters.

heir/heredity
aisle
pneumonia

EXERCISE 25.1

Correct the spelling errors in the following paragraph. If you are not sure about a word, check the list of commonly misspelled words on pages 812–13 or your dictionary. Some sentences may be correct as written.

■ After two ~~centurys~~ of isolation, Japan modernized very quickly.
centuries

In 1542, the first European visitors arrived in Japan. Traders and missionarys from the West brought firarms, tobacco, and Christianity to the island nation, which was suffring from internal strife. Japanese rulers welcomed Christianity at first, seing it as a way to reunify the country. However, after large numbers of Japanese converted, some official intolerence toward Christianity appeared. Finally, the rebellion of a Catholic Japanese community ensured that the government would act to prevent Western missionaries and merchants from joining forces with Japanese dissidents. In 1640, a policy of isolation took affect. No foreiners were aloud to enter Japan, and no Japanese were permitted to travel abroad. This policy was finaly relaxed in 1853, and a new era began in 1868, with the arrival of a new imperial government. The new leaders were youthful and visionary, and they wanted to bring their country up to date. Although some Japanese who had enjoied privileges in the old society lost them during modernization, most people where delighted with the country's new direction.

ESL TROUBLESPOTS

26 Nouns and Articles

The two primary types of nouns in English are proper nouns and common nouns. A **proper noun** names a specific, unique person, place, thing, calendar item, or idea and is always capitalized.

Sarah Palin	Lake Erie	Toyota	Tuesday	Marxism

A **common noun** refers to a person, place, thing, or idea in general and is not capitalized.

writer	lake	car	day	ideology

Common nouns are classified as either count nouns or noncount nouns. A **count noun** names items that can be counted.

artists	books	towns

Count nouns have both singular and plural forms.

Singular Form	*Plural Form*
one artist	three artist*s*
every book	most book*s*
each town	all town*s*

A **noncount noun** names items that cannot be easily counted.

rain   traffic   mail

Most noncount nouns do not have a plural form.

Incorrect	*Correct*
advices	advice
informations	information
vocabularies	vocabulary

This chapter will help you use these categories—proper noun versus common noun, count noun versus noncount noun—to avoid errors in your writing, especially in your use of articles (*a*, *an*, and *the*).

26a Keep the following guidelines in mind for recognizing and using noncount nouns.

Nouns in the following categories are likely to be noncount nouns.

ABSTRACTIONS	advice, courage, grief, information, knowledge, love, satisfaction, wealth
FIELDS OF STUDY OR RESEARCH	chemistry, law, medicine, pollution, sociology, weather
SPORTS AND GAMES	chess, football, soccer, tennis
LIQUIDS	milk, water
THINGS THAT CANNOT BE EASILY COUNTED	rice, sand, snow

- He offered some good advices.

Do not use numbers or plural quantity words before noncount nouns.

- Many rains hit the windowpane.

Do not use the article *a* or *an* with noncount nouns.

- The horses were covered with ~~a~~ mud.

Noncount nouns are used with singular verbs.

- The milk ~~were~~ *was* sour.

Some nouns can be noncount or count, depending on whether they refer to something considered as a whole.

NONCOUNT   *Bread* is a staple in almost every cuisine. [*Bread* considered as a kind of food]

COUNT   Some *breads* are made without yeast. [Particular types of bread, such as rye or whole wheat]

26b Use an article or a demonstrative pronoun (*this*, *that*, *these*, *those*) with a count noun.

- Her client sent her *a* fax.
- I found *this* fax on my chair.

26c Use *a* or *an* before a singular count noun that does not refer to a specific person, place, object, or concept.

- *A* laptop is *a* useful tool.
- She was excited to order *an* electric car.

When using the articles *a* and *an,* remember that *a* is used before words beginning with a consonant sound and *an* is used before words beginning with a vowel sound.

a baby	an eagle
a city	an hour
a fish	an island
a hope	an orange
a unicycle	an outrage

26d Use *the* before a noun that refers to something specific.

- Mohammad pointed out *the* planets in *the* evening sky.
- *The* lamp on my desk is an antique.

Be sure not to omit the article.

- He was awake before *the* alarm rang.

26e Use *a*, *an*, or *the* with most singular count nouns considered as general examples; no article is necessary for plural count nouns considered as general examples.

- *A* bird feeder is an entertaining addition to any yard.
- *The* cat is among the most agile creatures on earth.
- *Plants* add a cheery note to any room.

26f Use *the* with plural proper nouns (*the United States*, *the Joneses*, *the Koreans*) and certain types of singular proper nouns.

Some singular proper nouns use *the*.

COMMON NOUN PLUS *OF*	*the* Arch of Triumph, *the* state of Vermont, *the* University of Florida
BUILDINGS	*the* Eiffel Tower, *the* White House
COUNTRIES NAMED WITH A PHRASE	*the* Dominican Republic, *the* United Kingdom
HIGHWAYS	*the* Kensington Expressway
HOTELS, MUSEUMS	*the* Hilton Hotel, *the* Guggenheim Museum
PARTS OF THE GLOBE	*the* Equator, *the* Northwest, *the* South Pole
HISTORICAL PERIODS, EVENTS	*the* Renaissance, *the* Industrial Revolution
SEAS, OCEANS, GULFS, RIVERS, DESERTS	*the* Red Sea, *the* Atlantic Ocean, *the* Gulf of Mexico, *the* Missouri River, *the* Sahara
GROUPS OF ISLANDS	*the* Hawaiian Islands
MOUNTAIN RANGES	*the* Alps

26g Do not use an article with most other singular proper nouns.

- The houses are beautiful on ~~the~~ Maple Street.

EXERCISE 26.1

For each of the following sentences, choose the correct article. Note that X = no article.

- For many Americans, (a/the) civil rights movement began when (X/the) Rosa Parks refused to give up her seat on a bus to a white man.

1. Rosa Parks, (an/the) African American woman living in Montgomery, Alabama, was riding (a/the) bus with sections reserved for white passengers.
2. (X/The) back of the bus, where African Americans were supposed to sit, was crowded.
3. Parks sat in (X/the) front of the bus, which took tremendous courage.

4. (A/The) bus driver forced her to get off (a/the) bus, but (X/the) incident set off the Montgomery bus boycott.

5. (X/The) people all over the United States heard (a/the) story of Rosa Parks, and the civil rights movement had its first hero.

27 Verbs

A **verb** shows an action, an occurrence, or a state of being. ESL writers need to pay special attention to their use of verb tenses, helping or modal verbs (also called *auxiliary verbs*), and verbs followed by an infinitive or a gerund.

27a Use the appropriate verb tense to express time accurately.

Verb tenses express time. They indicate when an action occurs, occurred, or will occur. The following sections will help you understand and form the simple, perfect, and progressive tenses.

The Simple Tenses

The simple tenses are used to show clear and simple time relationships. The accompanying box summarizes how each of the simple tenses is formed and used.

The Perfect Tenses

The **base form** is the form of a verb as it appears in the dictionary.

The Simple Tenses		
Tense	**How It Is Formed**	**Examples**
Simple present		
Expresses an action or condition occurring at the time of speaking or writing, a statement of fact, or a habitual action	First- and second-person singular and plural, third-person plural: base form Third-person singular: base form + -s or -es	I *cook* for five people. They *cook* many unusual dishes. He *cooks* for a family of five.
Simple past		
Indicates that an action occurred in the past and was completed in the past	Regular verbs: base form + -d or -ed Irregular verbs: Forms vary; check the list on pages 726–27 or a dictionary.	We *played* roller hockey yesterday. He *became* agitated when the doctor approached.
Simple future		
Indicates that an action will take place in the future	*will* or form of *be* + *going to* + base form	His doctor *will try* a new approach. Ron *is going to find* a way out.

The Perfect Tenses

Tense	How It Is Formed	Examples
Present perfect		
Indicates that a past action took place at an unspecified time or is continuing to the present	*has* or *have* + past participle	The landlord *has offered* to repair the damage.
		I *have worked* in this office for two years.
Past perfect		
Indicates that an action was completed in the past before some other past action	*had* + past participle	Rafika *had offered* to babysit, but she got sick.
Future perfect		
Indicates that an action will take place before some specified time in the future	*will* + *have* + past participle	By Monday, the team *will have offered* him a new contract.

The perfect tenses are also used to show time relationships. A verb in one of the perfect tenses indicates an action that was or will be completed by or before some specified time. The perfect tenses are constructed by using a form of *have* along with the verb's **past participle**. The box above summarizes how each of the perfect tenses is formed and used.

The Progressive Tenses

The simple progressive tenses describe actions in progress, indicating that an action did, does, or will continue. They are formed by using a form of *be* along with the **present participle**.

The perfect progressive tenses are used to describe actions that continue to the present or until another action takes place. They are often used to emphasize the length of time involved. The box on the next page summarizes how the progressive and perfect progressive tenses are formed and used.

The **past participle** of regular verbs is formed by adding -d, -ed, or -en to the verb's base form. It can be used as an adjective.

The **present participle** is the -ing form of a verb; it shows an action that is in progress or ongoing. It can be used as an adjective.

The Progressive and Perfect Progressive Tenses

Tense	How It Is Formed	Examples
Present progressive		
Indicates that an action began in the past, is happening now, and will end sometime in the future	form of *be* + present participle	Consultants *are changing* the workforce.
Past progressive		
Indicates that an action was in progress at a specified time in the past	*was* or *were* + present participle	He *was changing* a lightbulb when the ladder collapsed.
		They *were driving* to the beach when their car stalled.
Future progressive		
Indicates that an action will begin and continue in the future. The time is often specified.	*will be* + present participle, or present tense of *be* + *going to be* + present participle	New parents *will be changing* diapers for at least two years.
		Exams *are going to be changing* under the new principal.
Present perfect progressive		
Emphasizes the ongoing nature of an action that began in the past and continues into the present	*has* or *have been* +present participle	Her secretary *has been running* errands all morning.
		They *have been planning* this party for several weeks.
Past perfect progressive		
Emphasizes the duration of an action that began and continued in the past and was completed before some other past action	*had been* + present participle	He *had been running* two miles a day until he broke his toe.
Future perfect progressive		
Emphasizes the duration of an action that will continue in the future for a specified amount of time before another future action	*will have been* + present participle	When she takes over, her family *will have been running* the company for four generations.

EXERCISE 27.1

Choose the correct verb tense in the sentences below.

■ Throughout most of American history, women (have had/will have) relatively few career opportunities.

1. Over the last several decades, however, women (had been/have been) making great strides in education and the workplace.
2. Now, for every two men who (were receiving/receive) a college degree, three women (earn/have been earning) the same academic credential.
3. Many manufacturing jobs that (have been relying/relied) on the physical strength of men have disappeared over the last several years.
4. As of 2010, women (become/have become) a majority of the United States work force for the first time in history.
5. These gains have led some to predict that soon women (will surpass/will be surpassing) men in economic and social power.

27b Use helping verbs to form tenses and express your meaning precisely.

Helping verbs are used before main verbs to form certain tenses. Some helping verbs—*have, do,* and *be*—change form to indicate tense (see 27a). The helping verb *do* indicates tense in questions, inverted phrases, and negative sentences. *Do you know her? Little did I realize what would happen. She does not like him.* It is also used for emphasis: *The sentence does need a comma.* The forms of these helping verbs are as follows.

have, has, had

be, am, is, are, was, were, being, been

do, does, did

Other helping verbs, called *modals,* do not change form. Modals include *can, could, may, might, must, shall, should, will,* and *would.* They are used to express ability, necessity, permission, intention, and so forth. The box on page 822 summarizes the common uses of modals.

How to Use Modals

Meaning	Present or Future Time	Past Time
Ability	*can*	*could + have +* past participle
	Most five-year-olds *can* tie their own shoes.	Jim *could have registered* early if he wanted to.
Necessity	*must* or *have to*	*had to*
	International travelers *must* carry passports.	The governor *had to* work with other officials.
	must or *have to*	*had to*
	Students *have to* read critically.	
Permission	*may, can*	*might + have +* past participle
	Anyone with a ticket *may* see the film.	*could + have +* past participle
	You *can* come in now.	You *might have waited* inside, out of the rain.
		We *could have gone* to the movies.
Intention	*will*	*would + have +* past participle
	He *will* encourage real estate development.	I *would have hiked* last weekend, but it rained.
Advisability	*should, had better*	*should + have +* past participle
	Everyone *should* get an education.	The trainee *should have read* the manual.
	She *had better* buy a ticket.	
Possibility	*may, might*	*may* or *might + have +* past participle
	An accountant *may* work long hours during tax season.	*could + have +* past participle
		The burglar *might have entered* through the window.
		They *could have lost* their keys.
Speculation	*would*	*would + have +* past participle
	He *would* like her.	No one *would have recognized* him without his moustache.

EXERCISE 27.2

In each sentence, fill in the blank with a modal from the list. In most cases, more than one modal will work in the sentence. Use each modal only once.

can	may	should	would
could have	might	will	would have

■ Busy professionals who are looking for a husband or wife __can__ try online dating.

1. Other people feel that they _____ meet their potential mate in person.
2. Speed dating _____ be another way to find romance.
3. In the past, few _____ imagined such uses for technology.
4. Now people fear that technology _____ soon make many human activities obsolete, including matchmaking.
5. Human matchmakers _____ become obsolete if online dating remains popular.

27c Use gerunds or infinitives following verbs according to convention.

Often, you will need to use an **infinitive** or a **gerund** as the object of a verb in a sentence, as in the following examples.

> An **infinitive** is a verb form made up of *to* plus the base form (*to run, to see*).

> ■ Mustafa needs *to find* his lecture notes.
> ■ Lara avoids *studying* in her dormitory.

> A **gerund** is an *-ing* form of a verb that functions as a noun (*complaining, jogging*).

When you use an infinitive or a gerund as an object, you need to remember that some verbs are followed by infinitives, some verbs are followed by gerunds, and some can be followed by either form without a change in meaning. The following guidelines will help you determine which form to use.

Verbs Followed by Infinitives

Some verbs, including the verbs listed here, are usually followed by an infinitive in English.

agree	claim	manage	promise
ask	decide	need	refuse
beg	expect	offer	venture
bother	fail	plan	want
choose	hope	pretend	wish

In general, use these verbs with an infinitive, not a gerund.

> ■ Kristen managed ~~finishing~~ the project.
>   to finish

Some verbs are followed by a noun or a pronoun and then by an infinitive. These verbs include *allow, cause, convince, hire, instruct, order, remind, tell,* and *warn.*

■ The bank *reminded your office to send* proof of employment.

When using a negative word (such as *no* or *not*) in a sentence containing a verb followed by an infinitive, place the word carefully; its position in the sentence often affects meaning.

■ Bella did *not* claim to know.

She never mentioned it.

■ Bella claimed *not* to know.

She said she did not know.

The causative verbs *have, let,* and *make* are followed by a noun or a pronoun and the base form of the verb (without the word *to*).

■ The noise made her *lose* her concentration.
■ The hotel lets visitors *bring* pets.
■ Have your assistant *type* those letters.

Verbs Followed by Gerunds
The following verbs are often followed by a gerund.

admit	dislike	postpone
appreciate	enjoy	practice
avoid	finish	recall
consider	imagine	resist
delay	keep	risk
deny	mention	suggest
discuss	miss	tolerate

Use these verbs with a gerund, not an infinitive.

■ The zoning committee considered ~~to approve~~ the proposal.
   approving

In a sentence containing a gerund, place a negative word (such as *no* or *not*) between the verb and the *-ing* form.

■ Some vacationers consider *not* returning to work.

Verbs Followed by Infinitives or Gerunds

Some verbs (such as *begin*, *continue*, *like*, and *prefer*) can be followed by an infinitive or a gerund with little or no change in meaning.

    INFINITIVE   Anita likes to jog.

    GERUND   Anita likes jogging.

Other verbs (such as *forget, remember, stop,* and *try*) can be followed by either an infinitive or a gerund, but the meaning of the sentence changes.

    INFINITIVE   Dien remembered to answer the letter.

                  He remembered that he had an obligation to do something.

    GERUND   Dien remembered answering the letter.

                  He remembered (the action of) doing something.

EXERCISE 27.3

Correct the errors in the use of gerunds and infinitives in the following sentences. Some sentences may be correct as written.

to discover
■ Archaeologists hope ~~discovering~~ when the first Americans arrived.

1. Many archaeologists have considered to change the date they estimate that humans arrived in the Americas.
2. Until recently, scientists didn't expect finding evidence of human inhabitants older than 11,000 years, the age of stone tools found in Clovis, New Mexico, in the 1930s.
3. Recently, however, after discovering older evidence in Monte Verde, Chile, and other sites, some scientists have suggested to change this date.
4. Archaeologists began to reexamine their assumptions after it was established that Monte Verde was older than the Clovis site.
5. One site in Virginia may be over 15,000 years old, and archaeologists who keep to dig deeper may find even older evidence.

28   The Prepositions *in*, *on*, and *at*

These three common prepositions are used before nouns or pronouns to indicate time or location.

    Time

        Use *in* with

            Months: *in* April

            Years: *in* 2011

            Seasons: *in* the winter

            Certain parts of the day: *in* the morning, *in* the afternoon

Use *on* with
    Days of the week: *on* Tuesday
    Dates: *on* June 20, 2011
Use *at* with
    Specific times: *at* 8 p.m., *at* noon
    Other parts of the day: *at* night, *at* dawn, *at* dusk

Location
Use *in* with
    Geographic places: *in* San Francisco, *in* rural areas
    Enclosed areas: *in* the stadium
Use *on* with
    A surface: *on* a shelf
    Forms of public transportation: *on* the bus
    Street names: *on* Main Street
    Floors of buildings: *on* the fourth floor
    Some areas of the country: *on* the Gulf Coast
Use *at* with
    Specific addresses (number and street): *at* 130 Washington Street
    Named locations: *at* Juanita's house
    General locations: *at* the college
    Locations with specific functions: *at* the library

For more on prepositions, see 1g.

EXERCISE 28.1

In the following sentences, fill in the blank with *in*, *on*, or *at*:

■ Every year ___*in*___ the spring, filmmakers gather in Hollywood for the Academy Awards ceremony.

1. The Academy Awards ceremony was first televised _____ 1953.
2. The participants gathered in the RKO Pantages Theater _____ Hollywood, California.
3. In 2002, the ceremony moved from its previous location _____ the Dorothy Chandler Pavilion _____ Los Angeles to its new location _____ the Kodak Theatre _____ Hollywood.
4. The participants have to arrive _____ the middle of the afternoon because the show is timed for evening _____ the East Coast.
5. The ceremony appears on television around the world, and many members of the audience watch it very late _____ night or early _____ the morning.

29   Adjectives

An **adjective** modifies a noun or pronoun.

When using **adjectives**, ESL writers need to pay special attention to how adjectives are arranged when they modify the same noun and how adjectives are combined with prepositions. (For more on adjectives, see 1d and Section 9 of the Handbook.)

29a Follow the conventional order when two or more adjectives modify the same noun.

Possessives come before numbers.

- *Anita's three* papers were accepted.

Ordinal numbers (*first, second*) come before cardinal numbers (*one, two*).

- James's *first three* requests were denied.

Descriptive adjectives should appear in the following order.
1. Article or possessive noun: *an, Dr. Green's, these*
2. Opinion: *favorite, hideous, lovely*
3. Size: *big, enormous, tiny*
4. Shape: *circular, rectangular, round*
5. Age: *elderly, teenaged, three-year-old*
6. Color: *black, blue, maroon*
7. National origin: *English, Nigerian, Vietnamese*
8. Religion: *Christian, Jewish, Muslim*
9. Matter or substance: *crystal, onyx, tweed*
10. Noun used as an adjective: *book* (as in *book jacket*), *picture* (as in *picture frame*), *record* (as in *record producer*)
    - *beautiful large white* horse
    - *Juan's old* coat
    - *a valuable new red British* car
    - *small oval* table

29b Combine adjectives with specific prepositions to express your meaning precisely.

Keep a list of adjective-**preposition** combinations that you hear in conversation or notice in your reading. Consult an ESL dictionary when you are not sure whether a particular combination expresses the meaning you intend. Here are some common adjective-preposition combinations.

Prepositions (such as *before, on,* and *to*) are used before a noun or pronoun to indicate time, place, space, direction, position, or some other relationship.

afraid of	responsible for (thing or action)
ashamed of	responsible to (person)
full of	satisfied with
grateful for (thing)	sorry for
grateful to (person)	suspicious of
interested in	tired of
proud of	

EXERCISE 29.1

Correct the errors in the order of adjectives and in adjective-preposition combinations in the following sentences.

> *insane Roman emperor*
> ■ The ~~emperor Roman insane~~ Caligula succeeded his uncle, the emperor Tiberius.

1. Caligula made favorite his horse a Roman senator.
2. He was also responsible to declaring war on the sea god Neptune.
3. Brief Caligula's violent reign made many Roman citizens afraid for their emperor.
4. The emperor's notorious temper led to the deaths of unfortunate those Romans who angered him.
5. Upstanding many citizens were relieved when assassins left Caligula dead.

30 Common Sentence Problems

As you edit and proofread your writing, watch out for the following problems involving word order, relative pronouns, and negatives.

30a Place sentence elements in the correct order.

Place words and phrases that indicate time or place at the beginning or at the end of a clause. Do not place them between the verb and its direct object (DO).

INCORRECT   We did this afternoon our homework.

CORRECT   We did our homework this afternoon.

Place the indirect object (IO) after the verb and before the direct object (DO).

- Ramon bought his sister a videotape.
- Ramon bought her a videotape.

Exception: When a prepositional phrase takes the place of an indirect object, the phrase should follow the direct object.

- Ramon bought a videotape for his sister.

Some verbs (such as *describe, explain, illustrate, mention, open,* and *say*) cannot be followed by an indirect object.

INCORRECT   Lu described us the figurine.

CORRECT   Lu described the figurine to us.

> ## EXERCISE 30.1

Correct the errors involving the placement of sentence elements in the following sentences. Some sentences may be correct as written.

- A park ranger explained ~~the visitors~~ the habits of the cave's bats. *to the visitors.*

1. Every evening at sunset, thousands of bats hunt from the entrance of Carlsbad Caverns in New Mexico mosquitoes.
2. Bat experts tell people that bats are actually helpful to humans.
3. One bat can eat in a single night a huge number of insect pests.
4. At the cave entrance at dusk, the bats provide to curious onlookers a spectacular show.
5. They give the crowds who come to see them when they fly out of the cave a thrilling experience.

30b Do not omit a relative pronoun when it is the subject of a relative clause or the object of a verb or preposition within a relative clause.

A **relative clause** is a **dependent clause** that begins with a **relative pronoun** (such as *that, which, who, whom,* or *whose*) and modifies a noun or pronoun. Sometimes a relative clause begins with a preposition followed by a relative pronoun (the reason *for which* I am writing).

A **relative pronoun** is a noun substitute that relates groups of words to nouns or other pronouns: *the patient who injured her leg.*

A **dependent clause** contains a subject and a verb but does not express a complete thought.

INCORRECT	The firefighter rescued the child was given a hero's welcome.
REVISED	The firefighter *who* rescued the child was given a hero's welcome.
INCORRECT	Juanita found the book for she had been searching all morning.
REVISED	Juanita found the book for *which* she had been searching all morning.

Exception: The relative pronoun and the verb *be* are often omitted in relative clauses when the clause is restrictive (essential to the meaning of the word or phrase it modifies); they should usually be included in a nonrestrictive clause (not essential to the meaning of the word or phrase it modifies). For more on nonrestrictive word groups, see 12e.

RESTRICTIVE	Michael grabbed the newspapers [that were] on the table.
	That were is optional because the clause is restrictive; it tells which newspapers are meant.
NONRESTRICTIVE	Michael tripped over the stack of day-old newspapers, which were ready to be recycled.
	The clause supplies additional but nonessential information about the newspapers. It is nonrestrictive, so *which were* should be included.

Use the relative pronoun *whose* to show possession with a relative clause.

INCORRECT	The committee sat at a table that its surface was scratched.
REVISED	The committee sat at a table *whose* surface was scratched.

Use relative pronouns, not personal pronouns, to introduce relative clauses.

INCORRECT	Computer terminals, they are scarce at certain times of the day, are an obsession for many students.
REVISED	Computer terminals, *which* are scarce at certain times of the day, are an obsession for many students.

EXERCISE 30.2

Correct the errors in the use of relative pronouns in the following sentences. Some sentences may be correct as written.

- The United States is a nation _^ was founded by settlers from other lands. *(that)*

  1. Immigration in the United States is a controversial subject that its implications have been debated for years.
  2. Early laws, they were sometimes discriminatory, restricted immigrants from certain countries.
  3. Both legal and undocumented immigrants who come to the United States often seek employment.
  4. Some Americans want to limit immigration fear that new arrivals will compete for scarce jobs.
  5. New immigrants, their dreams and wishes resemble those of many previous generations of Americans, continue to arrive.

30c Make a sentence negative by adding *not* or a negative adverb such as *never* or *seldom*.

Place *not* after the first helping verb.

- The speech will *not* begin on time.

In questions, the helping verb should be followed by *not* or the contraction for *not* (-*n't*). Place the helping verb and *not* before the subject and the main verb.

- *Didn't* I read that story in the newspaper yesterday?

Place negative adverbs before the main verb. In a sentence with a helping verb, place the negative adverb after the first helping verb.

- Arthur *seldom forgets* an assignment.
- Eva *may never play* the violin again.

If a negative adverb is used at the beginning of a clause, the helping verb *do* is needed.

- *Rarely* does one see a bald eagle.

EXERCISE 30.3

Correct the errors in the use of negatives in the following sentences. Some sentences may be correct as written.

- Most reports of UFO sightings and aliens ~~not~~ are believed. [*not* inserted before *are*]

1. Reputable scientists have confirmed never a UFO sighting.
2. A simple explanation for a sighting is difficult seldom to find.
3. People who believe aliens have contacted them offer convincing proof almost never.
4. Isn't it possible that many people simply want to convince themselves that humans are not alone?
5. Aliens may exist, but they not have arrived on earth yet.

SUMMARY EXERCISE FOR SECTIONS 26–30

Review Sections 26–30, and then correct the errors in standard English usage in the following paragraph.

- Many people ~~am~~ *are* worried about obesity in America.

Between the 1980 and the 2008, the obesity rate among Americans to increase from 15 percent to 34 percent. According to studies recent, over 30 percent of childrens in United States are now either overweight or obese. These studies also suggest that most overweight teenagers will overweight adults become. All these excess weight will cause harms to their healths, including a increased risk of cancer and heart disease. While most people agree that obesity am a real problem, they are disagreeing about its causes. Some claiming that Americans make food choices bad, eat too much, and exercise too little Those with point of view want overweight people take more responsibility for their own healths. On the same time, others see obesity as an economic, social, and cultural problem. They point to popularity of fast-food restaurants, junk food, and sugary soft drinks, especially among younger people. In fact, companies that sell unhealthy products appeal to that children in their advertisings. People with this view also argue that healthy foods are often more expensive than unhealthy foods. Whatever its causes, widespread obesity having enormous social and financial effects. According to a study by Cornell University, the annual cost of treating obesity and obesity-related illnesses is $168 billion. Clearly, Americans not should ignore this problem.

SECTION 3
EXERCISE 3.1, p. 746
Possible Revisions

2. In the United States, for example, colleges and universities provide education to Americans of all classes and backgrounds.
4. During the nineteenth and early twentieth centuries, graduates of state universities played a key role in America's development as an industrial and economic power.
6. Federal funding from the 1944 GI Bill made it possible for millions of returning veterans to attend college.
8. Now, about two-thirds of high school graduates will attend college because those with bachelor's degrees earn $20,000 more a year on average than do people with only high school diplomas.
10. However, as education costs continue to rise, some wonder whether a traditional four-year college is always worth the expense.

SECTION 4
EXERCISE 4.1, p. 751
Possible Revisions

2. Shopping through online bookstores is convenient, but some people miss the atmosphere of a traditional bookstore.
4. In the 1960s some Americans treated Vietnam veterans disrespectfully, a situation that has changed dramatically since that time.
6. With large bodies and tiny wings, bumblebees have long been a puzzle. How do they fly?
8. The Supreme Court often makes controversial decisions because the justices must decide how to interpret the Constitution.
10. Restoring a painting is, indeed, delicate work, and too much enthusiasm can be dangerous.

SECTION 5
EXERCISE 5.1, p. 756
Answers

2. A student in most non-English-speaking industrialized nations expects to spend six or more years studying English.
4. Working for laws that require all Americans to speak English is a fairly common U.S. political tactic.
6. Some linguists joke that a person who speaks two languages is called "bilingual," while a person who speaks one language is called "American."
8. Correct
10. Everyone who studies a foreign language is likely to benefit.

SECTION 6
EXERCISE 6.1, p. 759
Answers

2. Cuba, an island that lies ninety miles off the Florida coast, provided them with an excuse to do so.
4. In addition, many people in the United States had wanted to take over Spain's territories for a long time.
6. Cuba was allowed to take control of its own affairs right away.
8. Correct
10. Many Puerto Ricans are worried that statehood would destroy the native culture of their island, and none of them wants that to happen.

SECTION 7
EXERCISE 7.1, p. 761
Possible Revisions

2. Because of the importance of the information, it often must be transmitted secretly.

4. "Invisible ink," which cannot be seen until the paper is heated, was once a popular way to communicate secretly.

6. During World War II, U.S. government code specialists hired Navajo Indians because Navajo is a difficult and little-studied language.

8. Because these cryptograms are so simple, they are no longer used to transmit messages.

10. Alan Turing, a British civil servant and mathematical genius, finally solved the Enigma code.

EXERCISE 7.2, p. 764
Answers

2. A team of researchers might disagree on their conclusions about the disappearance of the dinosaur.

4. In one way, animals resemble plants: Some are "weeds" because they have the ability to thrive under many conditions.

6. When a "weed" and a delicate native species compete for their survival, the native species usually loses.

8. People should be more concerned about the extinction of plants and animals than they seem to be.

10. The earth has experienced several mass extinctions in its history, but another would take its toll on the quality of human life.

EXERCISE 7.3, p. 767
Answers

2. Correct

4. Following the success of Mammoth Cave, many Kentucky cavers hoped to make a fortune from their spelunking.

6. In January 1925, a falling rock trapped Collins, who was spelunking in a narrow passage in Sand Cave.

8. For several days, the most famous man in Kentucky was he. [*Or*: For several days, he was the most famous man in Kentucky.]

10. Their failing to save Collins was a terrible tragedy for his family and the rescuers.

SECTION 8
EXERCISE 8.1, p. 771
Possible Revisions

2. We wondered whether our professor knew of the new theory and whether she agreed with it.

4. Most parents think they have a major influence on their children's behavior.

6. Children strongly desire peer acceptance, and they want to be different from adults.

8. Most adults recall that, in childhood, their friends' opinions were extremely important to them.

10. Anxious parents would be greatly relieved if this hypothesis were proven.

EXERCISE 8.3, p. 773
Possible Revisions

2. Surveys show that college graduates who intern receive higher salary offers than their classmates who do not.

4. The most important qualities are curiosity and a good work ethic.

6. Some companies provide little guidance so interns do not learn much from the experience.

8. Correct

10. Some worry that strict federal guidelines will cause companies to eliminate internship programs rather than risk any legal problems.

SECTION 9
EXERCISE 9.1, p. 776
Answers

2. *Wikipedia* has many advantages that reflect well on it as a source.

4. In a way, encyclopedias are unique because Web sites can grow to include any subject that anyone finds interesting.

6. The site has some real downsides too.

8. Many teachers and professors don't allow students to use *Wikipedia* for research.

10. If they choose to use the site, students should make it clear to their professors that they have researched their subjects thoroughly.

SECTION 10
EXERCISE 10.1, p. 779

Possible Revisions

2. So far, no proof of the existence of life forms on other planets has been found.

4. Astronomers carefully monitor signals coming from other parts of the solar system.

6. Most of the signals received so far have been caused by cell phone and satellite interference.

8. The message, containing information about earth, is on its way to other parts of our galaxy.

10. A signal sent to earth would take a similarly long time to reach us.

SECTION 11
EXERCISE 11.1, p. 781

Answers

2. Correct

4. Czar Nicholas and his wife Alexandra often saw their little boy in terrible pain.

SECTION 12
EXERCISE 12.1, p. 785

Answers

2. The city of New York bought the land where the Seneca villagers lived.

4. Household items from Seneca Village still turn up in Central Park today, and a museum exhibit was recently devoted to life in the long-gone settlement.

6. James Weeks, an early resident, owned much of the land.

8. His daughter, Susan Smith McKinney-Steward, was born in Weeksville and was the valedictorian of New York Medical College in 1870.

10. Correct

SECTION 13
EXERCISE 13.1, p. 787

Answers

2. Silent versions of the vampire tale include *Les Vampires* (1915), a French film; *Nosferatu* (1921), a German film; and *London After Midnight* (1927), an American film.

4. The vampire tale has several standard traits, yet it remains remarkably versatile.

6. The popular *Blacula* (1972), which recast the vampire as an African prince in 1970s Los Angeles, inspired a series of black-themed "blaxploitation" horror movies.

8. In the late 1990s, *Buffy the Vampire Slayer* was revived as a popular TV series starring Sarah Michelle Gellar.

10. Perhaps vampires do live forever if only in books and on screen.

SECTION 14
EXERCISE 14.1, p. 790

Answers

2. The proposed zoning change was defeated by a margin of 2:1.

4. Correct

6. Correct

8. The neon lights gleamed above stores and in diner windows.

10. Some music historians claim that the American songwriting tradition reached its peak in the 1930s.

SECTION 15
EXERCISE 15.1, p. 793

Answers

2. Why did the professor assign "To an Athlete Dying Young"?

4. After September 11, 2001, President Bush said he was going to "fight terror."

6. "Come live with me and be my love," pleads the speaker in Marlowe's poem.

8. It turned out that the pianist could play only "Chopsticks."

10. Our waitress announced, "The special is prime rib"; unfortunately, we are vegetarians.

SECTION 16
EXERCISE 16.1, p. 795

Answers

2. "Halle Berry was the first African American woman to win the Academy Award for Best Actress."

4. "[P]eople of all classes receive financial help from the government."

6. "Zora Neale Hurston's collections of folklore proved to be very valuable."

8. "Folic acid . . . can help prevent certain birth defects."

10. "She wrote rather doubtful grammar sometimes, and in her verses took . . . liberties with the metre" (Thackeray 136–37).

SECTION 17
EXERCISE 17.1,   p. 797
Answers

2. We probably know more about the day-to-day lives of others than ever before, as the details of our many friends' days are recorded in online status reports.

4. Today's parents can find out about their sons and daughters' personal lives online, but they have less face-to-face contact with their children.

SECTION 18
EXERCISE 18.1,   p. 799
Answers

2. Correct

4. The invention of anesthesia made possible many advances in medicine (including lengthy surgery).

SECTION 19
EXERCISE 19.1,   p. 800
Answers

2. Some foods were once popular, but today hardly anyone has heard of them.

4. In the 1960s, frozen foods — icy blocks of corn, peas, and string beans — were popular and convenient alternatives to fresh produce.

SECTION 21
EXERCISE 21.1,   p. 804
Answers

2. The average American woman is five feet four inches tall.

4. The Great Depression began with the stock-market crash on Black Monday.

SECTION 22
EXERCISE 22.1,   p. 805
Answers

2. The estimated cost was too low by $87.14.

4. All traffic stopped as a ninety-car train went slowly past.

SECTION 23
EXERCISE 23.1,   p. 807
Answers

2. His professor insisted that *TV Guide* was not an acceptable research source.

4. The first European settlers at Plymouth arrived on the *Mayflower*.

SECTION 24
EXERCISE 24.1,   p. 808
Answers

2. For many self-conscious teens and young adults, surgery seems to be the perfect solution.

4. But as more adults pay for nose jobs and tummy tucks, more teens are expressing interest.

SECTION 26
EXERCISE 26.1,   p. 817
Answers

2. The

4. The; the; the

SECTION 27
EXERCISE 27.1,   p. 821
Answers

2. Now, for every two men who receive a college degree, three women earn the same academic credential.

4. As of 2010, women have become a majority of the U.S. work force for the first time in history.

EXERCISE 27.2,   p. 823
Answers

2. may *or* might

4. will, may, *or* might

EXERCISE 27.3, p. 825

Answers

2. Until recently, scientists didn't expect to find evidence of human inhabitants older than 11,000 years, the age of stone tools found in Clovis, New Mexico, in the 1930s.

4. Correct

SECTION 28

EXERCISE 28.1, p. 826

Answers

2. in

4. in; on

SECTION 29

EXERCISE 29.1, p. 828

Answers

2. He was also responsible for declaring war on the sea god Neptune.

4. The emperor's notorious temper led to the deaths of those unfortunate Romans who angered him.

SECTION 30

EXERCISE 30.1, p. 829

Answers

2. Correct

4. At the cave entrance at dusk, the bats provide a spectacular show to curious onlookers. [*Or:* At the cave entrance at dusk, the bats provide curious onlookers with a spectacular show.]

EXERCISE 30.2, p. 830

Answers

2. Early laws, which were sometimes discriminatory, restricted immigrants from certain countries.

4. Some Americans who want to limit immigration fear that new arrivals will compete for scarce jobs.

EXERCISE 30.3, p. 831

Answers

2. A simple explanation for a sighting is seldom difficult to find.

4. Correct

Alter, Adam. "How Labels Like 'Black' and 'Working Class' Shape Your Identity - The Week 5/4/2013," from *Drunk Tank Pink: And Other Unexpected Forces that Shape How We Think, Feel, and Behave* by Adam Alter, © 2013 by Adam Alter. Used by permission of The Penguin Press, a division of Penguin Group (USA) LLC.

Beato, Greg. "Amusing Ourselves to Death: Is The Onion Our Most Intelligent Newspaper?" from *Reason* (November 2007). Copyright © 2007 by Greg Beato. Reprinted by permission from Reason magazine and Reason.com.

Beato, Greg. "Internet Addiction." Greg Beato is a columnist for *Reason* magazine and Reason.com, where this column first appeared in the July 2010 issue. Reprinted by permission from Reason magazine and Reason.com.

Brooks, Gwendolyn. "The Bean Eaters" from *Blacks*. Copyright © 1991 by Gwendolyn Brooks. Reprinted by consent of Brooks Permissions.

Bryson, Bill. "Snoopers at Work," excerpt(s) from *I'm a Stranger Here Myself: Notes on Returning to America after Twenty Years Away* by Bill Bryson, copyright © 1999 by Bill Bryson. Used by permission of Broadway Books, an imprint of the Crown Publishing Group, a division of Random House LLC and Doubleday Canada. All rights reserved.

Callahan, Nicole Soojung. "What to Expect When You're … Adopted: My Search for My Birth Parents Began When I Got Pregnant." *Slate*, April 23, 2013.

Chupack, Cindy. "Dater's Remorse" from *The Between Boyfriends Book*. Copyright © 2003. By Cindy Chupack. Reprinted by permission of St. Martin's Press, LLC.

Crissey, Mike. "Linguist Deciphers Uses of Word 'Dude.'" *Associated Press* (December 8, 2004). Copyright © 2004 by Associated Press. All rights reserved.

de Waal, Frans. "The Brains of the Animal Kingdom." *Wall Street Journal*, March 22, 2013.

Etzioni, Amitai and Radhika Bhat. "Second Chances, Social Forgiveness, and the Internet." *The American Scholar*, April 2009. Copyright © 2009 by the authors.

Fassler, Joe and Michael Moss. "The Language of Junk Food Addiction." The *Atlantic*, April 30, 2013.

Frazier, Ian. "Dearly Disconnected" from *Mother Jones Wire* (January/February 2000). Copyright © 2000 by the Foundation for National Progress. Reprinted with permission.

Frost, Robert. "Two Look at Two" from *The Poetry of Robert Frost*, edited by Edward Connery Lathem. Copyright © 1951 by Robert Frost. Copyright ©1923, © 1969 by Henry Holt and Company, LLC. Reprinted with the permission of Henry Holt and Company, LLC.

Goleman, Daniel. Excerpt(s) from *Emotional Intelligence* by Daniel Goleman, copyright © 1995 by Daniel Goleman. Used by permission of Bantam Books, an imprint of Random House, a division of Random House LLC. All rights reserved.

Goodwin, Jan. "She Lives Off What We Throw Away." From *Marie Claire*, March 11, 2009. Reprinted by permission of the author.

Gottfried, Martin. "Rambos of the Road" from *Newsweek* (September 8, 1986). Copyright © 1986 by Martin Gottfried. Reprinted with the permission of the author.

Jarrett, Christian. "The Psychology of Stuff and Things." *The Psychologist*, 2013; 26 (8): 560-565.

Jensen, Derrick. "Against Forgetting." *Orion*, July/August 2013. Reprinted by permission.

Kamp, Jurriaan. "Can Diet Help Stop Depression and Violence?" from *Ode Magazine* (September 2007). Reprinted with the permission of the author and Ode Magazine.

Konnikova, Maria. "Why Summer Makes Us Lazy." *New Yorker*, July 22, 2013. Copyright © New Yorker Magazine/Maria Konnikova/Condé Nast.

Lamott, Anne. "Shitty First Drafts," from *Bird by Bird: Some Instructions on Writing and Life* by Anne Lamott, copyright © 1994 by Anne Lamott. Used by permission of Pantheon Books, an imprint of the Knopf Doubleday Publishing Group, a division of Random House LLC. All rights reserved.

LeMieux, Richard. "The Lady in Red." Reprinted from *Breakfast at Sally's* by special arrangement with Skyhorse Publishing.

MacClancy, Jeremy. "Eating Chili Peppers," from *Consuming Culture: Why You Eat*, by Jeremy MacClancy (Copyright © Jeremy MacClancy, 1983). Reprinted by permission of A.M. Heath & Co. Ltd. Author's Agents.

Maizes, Rachel. "Bad Dog." *New York Times*, September 10, 2013.

Nelson, Marilyn. "How I Discovered Poetry," from *The Fields of Praise: New and Selected Poems*. Copyright © 1997 Louisiana State University Press.

Newman, Jerry. Excerpt from "My Secret Life on the McJob: Lessons from Behind the Counter Guaranteed to Supersize Any Management Style." Copyright © 2007 by Jerry Newman. Reprinted with the permission of McGraw-Hill, Inc.

Oremus, Will. "Superhero or Supervillain? If Science Gives Us Superpowers, Will We Use Them for Good or Evil?" *Slate*, May 3, 2013.

Orner, Peter. "Writing About What Haunts Us." *New York Times* Opinion Pages, January 12, 2013.

Palmer, Brian. "Tipping Is an Abomination." *Slate*, July 9, 2013.

Ríos, Alberto Alvaro. "The Secret Lion," from *The Iguana Killer: Twelve Stories of the Heart*. Copyright © 1984 by Alberto Alvaro Ríos. Reprinted with the permission the author and Confluence Press, Lewiston, Idaho.

Roach, Mary. Excerpt from *The Best of Bicycling: The Very Best Stories from the First Fifty Years of Bicycling* Magazine, ed. Peter Flax (New York: Rodale, 2011), pp. 41-42.

Safire, William. "Abolish the Penny." *New York Times* Op-Ed, June 2, 2004.

Schwartz, Todd. "American Jerk: Be Civil, or I'll Beat You to a Pulp," excerpted from *Oregon Humanities* (Fall-Winter 2008), www.oregonhumanities.org.

Segal, Carolyn Foster. "The Dog Ate My Disk, and Other Tales of Woe," from *The Chronicle of Higher Education* (August 11, 2000). Copyright © 2000 by Carolyn Foster Segal. Reprinted with the permission of the author.

Shire, Emily. "Dating on Autism Spectrum." *The Atlantic*, August 2013.

Silk, Susan and Barry Goldman. "How Not to Say the Wrong Thing." *LA Times* Op-Ed, April 07, 2013. Reprinted by permission of the authors.

Spence, Charles and Betina Piqueras-Fiszman. "Dining in the Dark." *The Psychologist*, vol. 25, no. 12. December 2012.

Staples, Brent. "Black Men and Public Space" from *Harpers* (1987). Copyright © 1987 by Brent Staples. Reprinted with the permission of the author.

Thompson, Gabriel. "Speaking Quiché in the Heart of Dixie," from *Working in the Shadows: A Year of Doing the Jobs (Most) Americans Won't Do* (2010). Reprinted by permission of the author.

Turkle, Sherry. Excerpt from "Alone Together: Why We Expect More from Technology and Less from Each Other." Copyright © Oct 2, 2012 Sherry Turkle. Reprinted by permission of Basic Books, a member of the Perseus Books Group.

White, Alton Fitzgerald. "Right Place, Wrong Face," from *The Nation* (October 11, 1999). Originally titled "Ragtime, My Time." Reprinted with permission. For subscription information, call 1-800-333-8536. Portions of each week's Nation magazine can be accessed at http://www.thenation.com.

Zuger, Abigail. "Defining a Doctor, with a Tear, a Shrug, and a Schedule," from *The New York Times*, November 2, 2004.

Original cartoon caption (page 137): "Class of 2008, never let the excuse 'I can't find my pants' stand in the way of your dreams."

REVISION SYMBOLS

The numbers and letters refer to chapters and sections in the Handbook. Page numbers are provided for references to sections outside of the Handbook.

abbr	Faulty abbreviation **21**		no ⌣	No comma **12j**
ad	Misuse of adjective or adverb **1d, 1e, 9, 29**		;	Semicolon **13**
agr	Faulty agreement **5, 7e, 7f, 7g**		:	Colon **14**
appr	Inappropriate language *p. 199*		⸝ᵛ	Apostrophe **17**
art	Article **26**		" "	Quotation mark **15**
awk	Awkward **7, 8, 10**		. ? !	End punctuation **11**
cap	Capital letter **20**		—	Dash **19**
case	Error in pronoun case **7h–7m**		( )	Parentheses **18a, 18b, 18c**
cliché	Cliché *pp. 210–11*		[ ]	Brackets **18d, 18e**
coh	Coherence *pp. 169–70*		. . .	Ellipsis mark **16**
cs	Comma splice **4**		ref	Reference, pronoun **7a–7d**
coord	Coordination *p. 199,* **1f**		run-on	Run-on sentence **4**
dm	Dangling modifier **10c**		sexist	Sexist language **7e**
ESL	ESL problem **26–30**		shift	Shift **8a–g**
exact	Inexact word *pp. 206–10*		sl	Slang *pp. 206–08*
frag	Fragment **3**		sp	Spelling **25**
fs	Fused sentence **4**		sub	Subordination *pp. 197–201,* **1f, 2c, 2d**
hyph	Error in use of hyphen **24**		t	Error in verb tense **1c, 6e, 6f, 27a**
irreg	Error in irregular verb **1c**		trans	Transition *pp. 169–70*
ital	Italics **23**		v	Voice **1c, 6d**
lc	Lowercase letter **20**		var	Sentence variety *pp. 197–203*
mix	Mixed construction **8h, 8i, 8j**		vb	Verb error **6, 27**
mm	Misplaced modifier **10a, 10b**		wrdy	Wordiness *pp. 196–97*
num	Number **22**		//	Faulty parallelism *p. 204*
para, ¶	New paragraph *pp. 160–61*		⌣	Close up
pass	Ineffective passive *pp. 205–06,* **6d**		^	Insert
p	Punctuation **11–19**		X	Obvious error
,	Comma **12**			

HANDBOOK CONTENTS